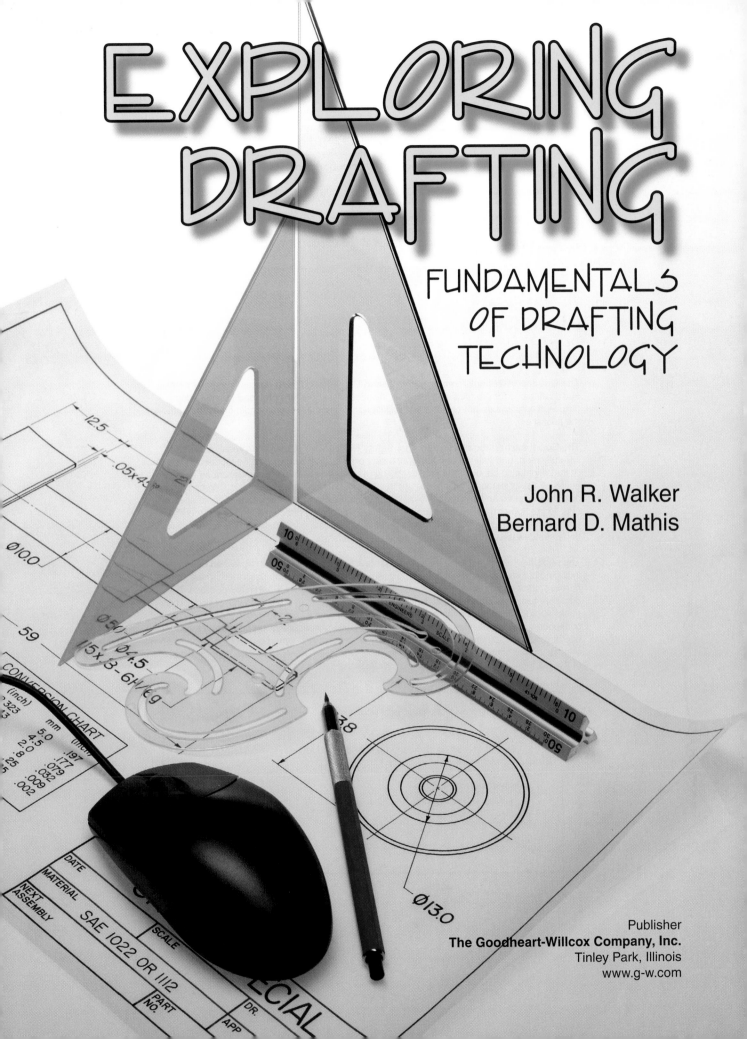

EXPLORING DRAFTING

FUNDAMENTALS OF DRAFTING TECHNOLOGY

John R. Walker
Bernard D. Mathis

Publisher
The Goodheart-Willcox Company, Inc.
Tinley Park, Illinois
www.g-w.com

Manufactured in the United States of America.

Library of Congress Catalog Card Number 2005040336

ISBN-13: 978-1-59070-575-9
ISBN-10: 1-59070-575-0

3 4 5 6 7 8 9 – 07 – 11 10 09 08

The Goodheart-Willcox Company, Inc. Brand Disclaimer: Brand names, company names, and illustrations for products and services included in this text are provided for educational purposes only and do not represent or imply endorsement or recommendation by the author or the publisher.

The Goodheart-Willcox Company, Inc. Safety Notice: The reader is expressly advised to carefully read, understand, and apply all safety precautions and warnings described in this book or that might also be indicated in undertaking the activities and exercises described herein to minimize risk of personal injury or injury to others. Common sense and good judgment should also be exercised and applied to help avoid all potential hazards. The reader should always refer to the appropriate manufacturer's technical information, directions, and recommendations; then proceed with care to follow specific equipment operating instructions. The reader should understand these notices and cautions are not exhaustive.

The publisher makes no warranty or representation whatsoever, either expressed or implied, including but not limited to, equipment, procedures, and applications described or referred to herein or their quality, performance, merchantability, or fitness for a particular purpose. The publisher assumes no responsibility for any changes, errors, or omissions in this book. The publisher specifically disclaims any liability whatsoever, including any direct, indirect, incidental, consequential, special, or exemplary damages resulting, in whole or in part, from the reader's use or reliance upon the information, instructions, procedures, warnings, cautions, applications, or other matter contained in this book. The publisher assumes no responsibility for the activities of the reader.

Library of Congress Cataloging-in-Publication Data

Walker, John R., 1924-
    Exploring drafting : fundamentals of drafting technology/ by John R. Walker, Bernard D. Mathis.
      p. cm.
    ISBN 1-59070-575-0
    1. Mechanical drawing. I. Mathis, Bernard D. II. Title.

T353.W22 2005
604.2--dc22

                    2005040336

Introduction

A course in drafting should be a part of your education. It will help you develop the capacity to plan and solve problems in an organized fashion, to interpret the ideas of others, and to express yourself in a manner that can be easily understood by anyone.

Exploring Drafting provides information about drafting fundamentals and concepts. It also provides opportunities to learn about basic geometric constructions. These are the mathematical tools used to solve practical problems and create the various types of drawings that communicate information about products. As you read and work through the book, you will learn the drafting methods and processes used by industry. You will also develop and practice drafting skills and techniques.

Exploring Drafting is current with the latest ANSI/ASME (American National Standards Institute/American Society of Mechanical Engineers) practices. You will learn how to use standard symbols to communicate in the international language—drafting.

Exploring Drafting provides you with the basic understanding necessary to allow you to progress from manual drafting into CAD (computer-aided drafting and design). The information and activities in this text will supply you with the solid foundation of drafting skills and techniques you will need to efficiently draw and design using most CAD systems. It is important to note that CAD is a tool that incorporates the concepts of manual drafting. *The principles of drafting are common to both traditional (manual) drafting and CAD.*

Exploring Drafting provides information and activities that are consistent with and satisfy the basic *Engineering Principles* and *Engineering Graphics* standards that have been adopted by many states and/or school districts. The content and activities in the book also are consistent with the International Technology Education Association (ITEA) standards for technological literacy.

Drafting, the "language of industry," offers many career opportunities. Some of these exciting and rewarding futures are described in the chapter *Careers in Drafting* (Chapter 2).

You will find that the ability to draw and to understand drafting will be of benefit throughout your lifetime as a consumer, as well as in the career you pursue. The ability to draft and understand drawings is an ability that most anyone will find useful.

Using the Text

A number of elements in this text help reinforce the material as it is presented. You will encounter the following features as you progress through the text. They are intended to guide you through the material and help you evaluate your progress.

Objectives

Chapter objectives are presented at the beginning of each chapter. They outline important concepts and skills that are discussed. After completing a chapter, you should be able to meet the objectives.

Drafting Vocabulary

Important terms are presented at the beginning of each chapter in the *Drafting Vocabulary*. In most cases, these terms will appear in **bold italic** typeface within the chapter. Before starting each chapter, look over the list of terms. This will help you familiarize yourself with the content. You may want to review the terms after you finish the chapter to verify your understanding of the material.

Careers in Drafting

Throughout the text, *Careers in Drafting* profiles are presented in appropriate locations to discuss the types of careers that are available in the related area of drafting. These provide you with pertinent, real-world examples that will keep you focused on where drafting instruction can lead you. The profiles should prove especially useful in drafting programs that are specifically designated "vocational" or "career and technical" in nature.

Academic Links

Many of the concepts and skills that you will learn while studying drafting relate to other areas of study. For example, you will often use mathematical skills when making measurements and preparing drawings. Academic links appear in this text to provide you references to different study areas. These areas include communications, mathematics, science, and social studies. Each academic link discusses topics that pertain to material in the related chapter.

Test Your Knowledge

Questions are provided at the end of each chapter to help you check your comprehension of the material. They are intended to reinforce instruction and measure your knowledge of the chapter content.

Drawing Problems

Throughout this text, conventional drawings are constructed in a step-by-step fashion to demonstrate drawing principles. In chapters with drawing instruction, the *Drawing Problems* section at the end of the chapter gives you an opportunity to practice your drafting skills and improve your techniques. These problems progress in difficulty from basic to advanced. More challenging design problems are also provided to help you develop your originality and creativity.

Outside Activities

Student activities are presented at the end of most chapters in this text. They will help you apply the material and build your skills. They are designed for individual or group participation.

Useful Information

This text includes a reference section with tables and charts containing helpful resources for various types of drafting. This section provides standard symbols and abbreviations, conversion tables, and screw thread data. The information provided expands on material covered in the book.

Glossary

A glossary of terms is included at the end of the book. This section provides definitions for many of the terms that appear in the *Drafting Vocabulary* listings.

About the Authors

John R. Walker is the author of 13 textbooks and has written many magazine articles. Mr. Walker did his undergraduate studies at Millersville University and has an MS in Industrial Education from the University of Maryland. He taught industrial arts and vocational education for 32 years and was Supervisor of Industrial Education for 5 years. Mr. Walker also worked as a machinist for the US Air Force and as a drafter at the US Army Aberdeen Proving Grounds.

Bernard D. "Bernie" Mathis has bachelor's and master's degrees in Industrial Arts Education from the University of Northern Colorado. He has taught mechanical engineering drawing and architectural engineering drawing for 28 years and computer-aided drafting for 20 years. Prior to teaching drafting classes, Mr. Mathis taught other industrial arts courses, including woodworking, metalworking, general crafts, leather crafts, lapidary, and jewelry. Mr. Mathis has been sole proprietor of his own drafting and design business for 25 years.

Acknowledgments

The authors wish to thank those in industry who helped gather the necessary material, information, and illustrations for this text. The individuals, companies, and organizations that provided helpful input are listed below.

Allied Signal Aerospace
Alvin & Co.
American Die Casting Institute
American Foundrymen's Society, Inc.
Amp, Inc.
Autodesk, Inc.
Avtek Corp.
basysPrint
Bell Helicopter Textron
Bill Hannan, *Peanuts & Pistachios*
Boeing
Bombardier Inc., Canadair of Canada
Buick
CalComp
Champion Spark Plug Co.
Chartpak, Inc.
Walter Cheever
Chief Architect
Clem Cizewski
Clausing Industrial, Inc.
Cybernation Cutting Systems, Inc.
DaimlerChrysler
Delcam International
Discreet
Tony Dudek
Emerson Electronics
Engineering Geometry Systems
Epson America, Inc.
Frank Fanelli, *Flying Models*
Fanuc Robotics North America, Inc.
Ford Motor Company

Formatt
French National Railroad
General Electric
General Motors Corp.
Graphtec
Graymark International, Inc.
Harley-Davidson
Jet Equipment & Tools
Jones & Shipman, Inc.
Jack Klasey
KMA Design & Construction
Koh-I-Noor Rapidograph, Inc.
Landis Division of Western Atlas
Laserdyne Div., Lumonics Corp.
Light Machines Corp.
Lockheed-Martin Corp.
Miller Electric Mfg. Co.
Nachi Robotics
NASA
NAVSEA/Naval Sea Systems Command
Nederman, Inc.
Don Nelson
Northrop-Grumman Aerospace Corp.
Okuma America Corporation
Steve Olewinski
Pontiac
Pratt & Whitney
Regional Development Institute at
    Northern Illinois University
Republic-Lagun Machine Tool Co.
Re-1 Valley School District

RL Design, Inc.

ROBO Systems

Sandvik Coromant Co.

Saturn

Scale Reproductions, LLC

Sears-Roebuck

Sharp Industries, Inc.

Tom Short

SkillsUSA

SoftPlan Architectural Design Software

Solid Edge (www.solidedge.com)

Surfware, Inc.

T & W Systems, Inc.

US Army

Robert Walker

WAM!NET, Inc.

Westinghouse

Xerox

The authors and publisher wish to extend special thanks to Walter Cheever for his efforts in reviewing the text and coordinating the use of architectural drawings from KMA Design & Construction.

Contacting Goodheart-Willcox

Your feedback is important. If you have any suggestions or comments about the text, please direct your findings to:
Managing Editor—Technology
Goodheart-Willcox Publisher
18604 West Creek Dr.
Tinley Park, IL 60477

BRIEF CONTENTS

CONTENTS

Features and Applications

Careers in Drafting

Computer-Aided Drafting Applications

Academic Links

1 Why Study Drafting?

OBJECTIVES

After studying this chapter, you should be able to:

◆ Identify the many fields of drafting.

◆ Explain why drafting is called a universal language.

◆ Explain why drawings are often the best way to describe or show ideas.

◆ Describe, in a limited way, the technological changes that have occurred in how drawings are made and stored.

DRAFTING VOCABULARY

Computer-aided
 drafting and
 design (CAD)
Drafting

Drafting is a form of graphic communication that is concerned with the preparation of the drawings needed to develop and manufacture products, **Figure 1-1**. It is a very important part of modern industry because drawings are often the only way to explain or show our ideas, **Figure 1-2**.

Figure 1-1 Mechanical engineers are responsible for the design and development of new machines, devices, and ideas. (Nachi Robotics)

Drafting is frequently called a "universal language." Like other languages, symbols (lines and figures) that have specific meaning are used. The symbols accurately describe the shape, size, material, finish, and fabrication or assembly of a product. These symbols have been standardized over most of the world. This makes it possible to interpret or understand drawings made in other countries, **Figure 1-3**.

Drafting is also the "language of industry." Industry uses this precise language because the drawing must communicate the information the designer had in mind to those who produce the product. The more accurate and precise the use of this drafting language, the more efficient the communication of the designer's idea.

Drawings can be made manually (by hand) on paper or film using drafting tools such as a drawing board, pencil or pen, triangle, and compass, **Figure 1-4**. Drawings are also produced using *computer-aided drafting and design (CAD)* systems, **Figure 1-5**. When the design is completed, high-speed plotters or printers turn out hard (paper) copy showing the part or design, **Figure 1-6**. (Computer graphics and CAD is explained in more detail in Chapter 7.)

It would be difficult in today's world to name an occupation that does not require the ability to read and understand graphic information such as drawings, charts, or diagrams. You use drawings when you construct a model or electronic kit, **Figure 1-7**. You also use drawings when assembling products such as bicycles, grills, and computer desks, **Figure 1-8**.

Many specialized fields of drafting have developed. These fields include aerospace, architectural, automotive, electrical and electronic,

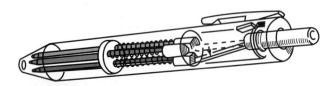
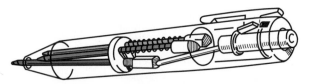

Figure 1-2 Drawings are often the best way to explain or show ideas. Think how difficult it would be to explain how this simple three-color pen operates using only the written word.

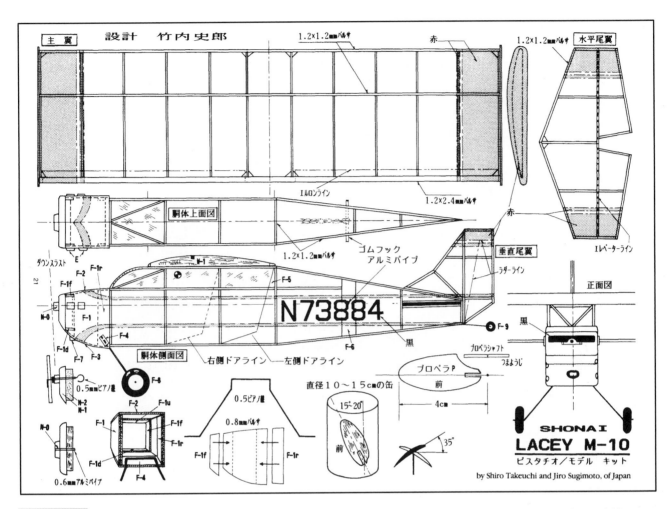

Figure 1-3 Although the instructions are in Japanese and the dimensions in the metric system, it would be possible for you to construct this model airplane. (Bill Hannan, *Peanuts & Pistachios*)

Figure 1-4 A drafter working at a manual drafting station. Manual skills remain important despite the growing use of CAD in industry.

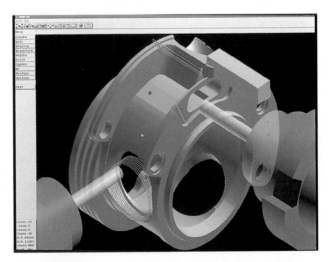

Figure 1-5 Computer-generated graphics use the computer to aid in designing and engineering a product. (Courtesy of SURFCAM by Surfware)

Figure 1-6 CAD drawings are converted to hard copy using laser printers and pen plotters. (Emerson Electronics)

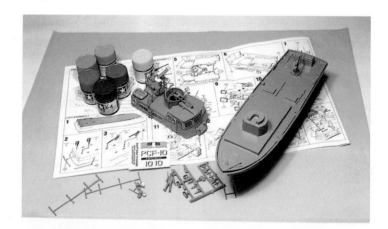

Figure 1-7 You use drawings when you construct models. The instructions for building this boat are in pictorial form.

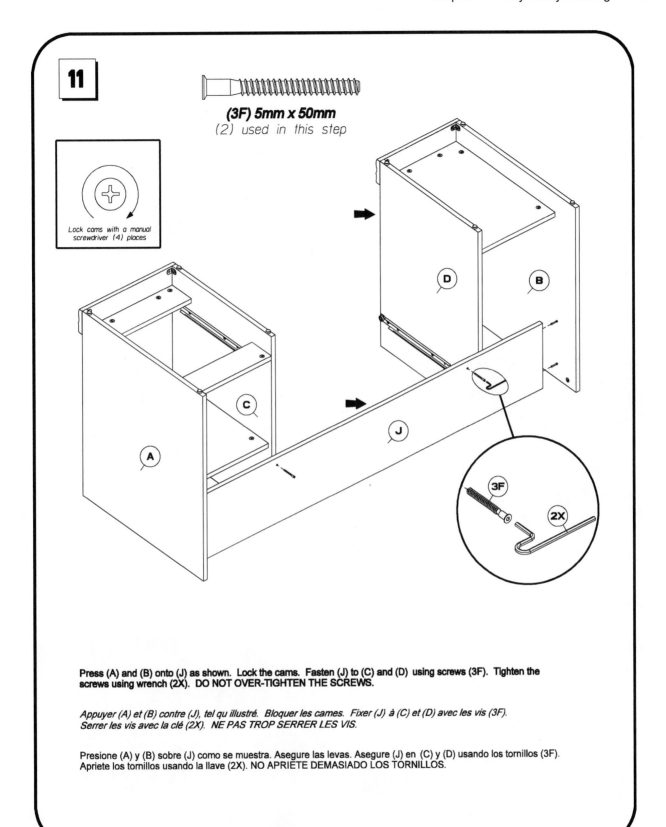

(3F) 5mm x 50mm
(2) used in this step

Lock cams with a manual
screwdriver (4) places

Press (A) and (B) onto (J) as shown. Lock the cams. Fasten (J) to (C) and (D) using screws (3F). Tighten the
screws using wrench (2X). DO NOT OVER-TIGHTEN THE SCREWS.

*Appuyer (A) et (B) contre (J), tel qu illustré. Bloquer les cames. Fixer (J) à (C) et (D) avec les vis (3F).
Serrer les vis avec la clé (2X). NE PAS TROP SERRER LES VIS.*

Presione (A) y (B) sobre (J) como se muestra. Asegure las levas. Asegure (J) en (C) y (D) usando los tornillos (3F).
Apriete los tornillos usando la llave (2X). NO APRIETE DEMASIADO LOS TORNILLOS.

Figure 1-8 Drawings are used to illustrate assembly procedures for consumers.

printed circuitry design, and topographical. Basically, all drafting fields use the same drafting equipment and use similar drafting techniques. Also, they all use both manual and computer graphics. However, the finished product of each field varies greatly, **Figure 1-9**, **Figure 1-10**, and **Figure 1-11**. You will learn the skills and techniques of the drafter as you study this book.

Figure 1-9   An aerospace drafter must have the technical knowledge to carry out the ideas of the aerospace engineer. (Bombardier Inc., Canadair of Canada)

Figure 1-10   The drafter conveys or communicates with drawings all the information required to construct this motel.

Figure 1-11   An electronics drafter detailed this circuit board prior to manufacturing.

CAREERS IN DRAFTING

Drafter

What would I do if I were to become a drafter? I would create technical drawings that are used to manufacture or construct products. I would make drawings for products such as cars, aircraft, houses, bridges, highways, toys, appliances, furniture, and electronic equipment.

What would I need to know? I would have to know how to use various resources to find the information necessary to create the technical drawings. I would have to know how to create the drawings using the knowledge, skills, techniques, and procedures relating to both manual drafting and CAD (computer-aided drafting). Also, I would need to know how to create accurate freehand sketches.

Where would I work? I would work in an office furnished with the tools necessary to allow me to do my work efficiently. I would either sit at a manual drafting table or at a computer workstation to create my drawings.

For whom would I work? I would probably work for an engineer, surveyor, architect, or other comparable professional.

What sort of education would I need? At the high school level, I would need to take courses in math, science, computer technology, design, and computer graphics, as well as any drafting courses that are available. In addition to high school training, most employers prefer prospective drafters to have completed postsecondary training in drafting from a community college, technical institute, or four-year college or university.

What are the special fields relating to this career? There are many special fields of drafting that require special skills and knowledge. These fields include aeronautical, architectural, civil, electrical, electronics, and mechanical drafting, as well as other types of drafting.

What are my chances of finding a job? Most job openings for drafters in the next several years are expected to arise from the need to replace drafters who transfer to another occupation, leave the labor force, or retire. Opportunities will be best for individuals who have at least two years of postsecondary training in the field of drafting and as much CAD training as possible. The demand for drafting specialists will vary across the country by locale based on the needs of local industry.

How much money could I expect to make? I can expect earnings to vary by specialty and level of responsibility. Median annual incomes in recent years were as follows—architectural/civil drafting, $37,330; mechanical drafting, $40,730; and electrical/ electronics drafting, $41,090. The lowest salaries ranged from $24,570 to $25,710 and the highest ranged from $56,260 to $68,000.

Where else could I look for more information about becoming a drafter? See the US Department of Labor's Bureau of Labor Statistics Occupational Outlook Handbook (at www.bls.gov), visit the American Design Drafting Association Web site (www.adda.org), or request information from the Accrediting Commission of Career Schools and Colleges of Technology (at www.accsct.org).

If I decide to pursue a different career, what other fields are related to drafting? Professionals closely related to the field of drafting include architects, landscape architects, designers, engineers, surveyors, cartographers (map drafters), science technicians, photogrammetrists, and surveying technicians.

Test Your Knowledge

Please do not write in this book. Place your answers on another sheet of paper.

1. Define the term *drafting*.

2. Drawings are often used because _____.
   A. they are easy to make
   B. they are the best means available to explain or show many ideas
   C. people who cannot read can understand drawings

3. Name five occupations that require the ability to read and understand graphic information.

4. What does the term CAD mean?

5. When a CAD-designed problem is completed, it is converted into hard copy on a high-speed _____ or _____.

6. List five specialized fields of drafting.

Outside Activities

1. Prepare a list with two columns. In the first column, write the names of as many occupations as you can that require the ability to read and understand graphic information. In the second column, record the names of occupations that do not require this skill.

2. Obtain samples of drawings used by the following industries:
   A. Aerospace.
   B. Building construction.
   C. Structural.
   D. Manufacturing.
   E. Mapmaking.
   F. Electrical and electronic.

3. Make a collection of pictures (magazine clippings, photographs, drawings, etc.) that show products made by the industries listed in Activity 2.

4. Visit a local architect who designs residences. After discussing a project in progress, prepare a report on the steps normally followed when designing a home for a client. Prepare your questions carefully before you make your visit.

5. Visit a local surveyor and make a report on the work he or she does. Borrow samples of completed work for a bulletin board display.

6. Obtain and display copies of drawings made in a foreign country. Discuss and compare them with drawings made in the United States.

Clear, concise drawings are required to manufacture a product, regardless of its complexity. Many drafting and design tasks were involved in creating the drawings for this F-15 fighter aircraft model. (NASA)

2 Careers in Drafting

OBJECTIVES

After studying this chapter, you should be able to:

- Identify many career possibilities related to the fields of drafting and design.
- Cite many of the skills needed to prepare for the various fields that use drafting.
- Identify the traits of leadership.
- Summarize the role of leadership in society and how it relates to drafting technology.
- Describe what to expect when entering the world of work.
- Identify sources of information about careers in drafting technology.

DRAFTING VOCABULARY

Architect
Assistant drafter
Career information centers
Chief drafter
Color boards
Detail drafter
Detailer
Dictionary of Occupational Titles
Discrimination
Drafter
Drafting trainee
Engineer
Harassment
Industrial designer
Interior designer
Junior drafter
Lead drafter
Leader
Leadership
Modelmakers
Occupational Outlook Handbook
Senior drafter
SkillsUSA
Technical illustrator
Technology Student Association (TSA)
Tool designer

It would be difficult to name an industry that does not use drawings. The many different types include conventional production drawings, instructional booklets, charts, graphs, and maps. It typically takes more than 27,000 drawings to manufacture an automobile. The field of drafting provides employment for over 1 million men and women. The work of other millions requires them to be able to read and interpret drawings. See **Figure 2-1**.

Figure 2-1 Quality control specialists must be able to read and understand drawings. Here, a laser measuring system is being set up and calibrated. It will be used to inspect the fit of car doors. (Ford Motor Company)

Drafting Occupations

Job titles and duties will vary from one company to another. However, the following drafting occupations are typical of those found in industry.

Drafters make working drawings and detail drawings. Drafters prepare these drawings from specifications and information received verbally, from sketches, and from notes. Drafters on all levels must have a solid understanding of manual drawing and CAD techniques, **Figure 2-2**.

The drafter usually starts out as a *drafting trainee* where he or she redraws or repairs damaged drawings. The trainee may revise engineering drawings or make simple detail

Figure 2-2 Today's drafter must be familiar with conventional drafting techniques before he or she can work with computer-aided design and drafting equipment. (Delcam International)

drawings under the direct supervision of a senior drafter.

During the training period, trainees are often enrolled in formal classes teaching CAD, mathematics, electronics, or manufacturing processes. These classes may be held within the company or at a local technical school or community college.

Upon completion of the training period, the drafting trainee usually advances to *junior drafter*. Similar positions are known as: *detailer*, *detail drafter*, and *assistant drafter*.

A junior drafter prepares detail and working drawings from rough design drawings. The junior drafter may develop drawings for

CAREERS IN DRAFTING

Construction Manager

What would I do if I were to become a construction manager? I would plan and coordinate construction projects. I might plan and direct an entire project or only a specialized part. I would oversee construction supervisors and workers. I would also schedule and coordinate all design and construction processes, including the selection, hiring, and overseeing of all specialty trade contractors.

What would I need to know? I would need to understand contracts, plans, and specifications. I would need to be knowledgeable about construction methods, materials, and regulations. I would need to be familiar with computers and software for job costing, online collaboration, scheduling, and estimating. Knowledge of drafting and computer-aided drafting (CAD) skills would also be useful in communicating with both workers and subcontractors.

Where would I work? I would divide my time between working in my main (or field) office and the job site. I would divide my time between creating plans of action for coordinating construction projects and managing supervisors and workers. These duties may require considerable travel if I am managing more than one project at a time (some travel may not be in the same state).

For whom would I work? I may work for myself since more than half of all construction managers are self-employed. However, I could also work for a general building contractor, an architectural or engineering firm, any one of a number of specialty trade subcontractors, or a government agency.

What sort of education would I need? Traditionally, I could advance to a construction management position after acquiring considerable experience as a skilled construction worker. However, many larger construction firms now prefer that I not only have the practical experience but also a bachelor's degree in construction science, construction management, or civil engineering.

What are the special fields relating to this career? Specialization in construction management is directly related to the type of business I would work for. I could be an electrical construction manager, plumbing construction manager, heating and air conditioning construction manager, and so on.

What are my chances of finding a job? The outlook for employment as a construction manager is very good over the next several years. As mentioned previously, the best ways to enter the field and work for a large construction company are to earn a bachelor's degree (or a more advanced degree) and acquire a solid background in building technology. It is also necessary to prove the ability to supervise or manage people, materials, and equipment. This ability can be gained by working in the industry as much as possible.

How much money could I expect to make? The median salary for construction managers in recent years was $63,500. Salaries ranged from $38,130 to $112,810 and up. Prospects for higher salaries can be enhanced by working in commercial construction rather than residential construction.

Where else could I look for more information about becoming a construction manager? See the US Department of Labor's Bureau of Labor Statistics Occupational Outlook Handbook (at www.bls.gov) or request information from the American Institute of Constructors (www.constructorcertification.org or www.aicnet.org), the Construction Management Association of America (www.cmaanet.org), or the American Council for Construction Education (www.acce-hq.org).

If I decide to pursue a different career, what other fields are related to construction management? Architecture, civil engineering, cost estimating, landscape architecture, and natural science management.

machine parts, electrical/electronic devices, or structures. In addition, junior drafters may also prepare simple assembly drawings, charts, and graphs. The junior drafter must be able to make simple calculations and apply established drafting room procedures.

From junior drafter, the next step forward is *drafter*. The drafter applies independent judgment in the preparation of original layouts with intricate details. He or she must understand machine shop practices, must use materials properly, and must be able to make extensive use of reference books and handbooks.

With experience, the drafter will become a *senior drafter* and be expected to do complex original work.

In time, the senior drafter can become a *lead drafter* or *chief drafter*. Such a person is responsible for all work done by the department.

Most drafters specialize in a particular field of technical drawing, such as aerospace, architectural, or structural. Regardless of the field of specialization, drafters should be able to draw rapidly, accurately, and neatly.

All drafters must have a thorough understanding of CAD software, mathematics, science, materials, and manufacturing processes in their areas of specialization. Manufacturing industries, **Figure 2-3**, employ large numbers of drafters. Others are employed by architectural firms and various types of engineering firms as well as local, state, and federal government agencies. There are many other businesses that employ drafters or contract them to provide consulting or special services.

Industrial Designers

The work of the *industrial designer* influences most every item used in our daily living, whether it is the design of a small CD player or a giant commercial jet airplane. Many industrial designers are on the staffs of major automobile manufacturers, **Figure 2-4**.

In general, the chief function of the industrial designer is to simplify and improve the operation and appearance of industrial products. Design simplification usually means fewer parts to wear or malfunction. Appearance plays an important role in the sale of a product. The industrial designer must be aware of changing customs and tastes. He or she must know why people buy and use different products.

It is recommended that prospective industrial designers have an engineering degree and a working knowledge of engineering

Figure 2-3 Many drafters are required to prepare drawings for models of aircraft such as this F-22 Raptor. The aircraft has flying control systems designed and developed by mechanical and electronic engineers. (Lockheed-Martin Corp.)

Figure 2-4 A thorough knowledge of advanced technical practices is required to place a present-day automobile into production. (Ford Motor Company)

and manufacturing techniques and materials. Artistic ability is essential to become an efficient and capable industrial designer.

Tool Designers

Tools and devices needed to manufacture industrial products are designed by the *tool designer*. The tool designer originates the designs for cutting tools, special holding devices (fixtures), jigs, dies, and machine attachments that are necessary to manufacture the product. He or she must be familiar with machine shop practices, be an accomplished drafter, and have a working knowledge of algebra, geometry, and trigonometry. It is also important to be familiar with computer-aided design, computer-aided manufacturing (CAD/CAM), and robotics, **Figure 2-5**.

Figure 2-5 Design engineers develop the tools and devices needed to manufacture industrial and commercial products. Here engineers are determining the special tooling that must be designed to machine these castings. (American Foundrymen's Society, Inc.)

As industrial technology expands and more automated machinery is utilized, there will be a constantly increasing demand for competent tool designers.

Interior Designers

A common misconception by many people is that interior designers are only responsible for selecting the paint, carpet, and window coverings for the interior of buildings. This would be a somewhat accurate description of what an interior decorator does. However, this greatly oversimplifies what an interior designer actually does.

An *interior designer* is responsible for the physical design and decoration of interior spaces of buildings. It is not uncommon for an interior designer to spend many hours drafting various designs, either manually or with CAD software, **Figure 2-6**. Interior designers apply some of the same skills practiced by architects. They must have much of the working knowledge required in architecture. Many times, interior designers work side-by-side with architects to determine the appearance and arrangement of the interior space of a structure. Interior designers are space-planning specialists.

Interior designers must have artistic skill. They must be well-versed in model construction and in the development of color boards. *Color boards* are tools interior designers use to describe the interior decoration of the structure.

Figure 2-6 An interior designer is responsible for the physical design and decoration of interior spaces of buildings. (RL Design, Inc.)

One can become an interior designer in several different ways. Various trade schools and art institutes offer programs in interior design. The types of degrees or certifications offered by these schools vary by the school and should be researched individually by the prospective student. Many colleges and universities offer interior design programs leading to a bachelor's degree. Various types of advanced degrees may be earned as well. Some schools have accreditation from the Foundation for Interior Design Education Research (FIDER). Graduation from a FIDER accredited program is desirable but not required to work in the field.

Teachers

Teaching is a satisfying and challenging profession. Teachers of industrial technology, technology education, and career and technical education are in demand nearly everywhere. Drafting and CAD teachers are needed in schools such as yours, **Figure 2-7**. Many industries employ professional teachers on their staffs to keep their employees well-educated about new processes and technological changes, **Figure 2-8**.

Figure 2-8 Teaching is a challenging and rewarding profession. (Amp, Inc.)

Figure 2-7 Teachers of industrial technology, technology education, and career and technical education are in demand nearly everywhere. (Re-1 Valley School District)

A minimum of four years of college training is needed to become a licensed teacher. It is very highly recommended that a student who desires to become a teacher in a technical program (such as a drafting or CAD program) gain industrial experience along with his or her teacher training. Industrial experience helps an aspiring teacher acquire his or her vocational credential, which is required by many states for teachers instructing technical courses. The vocational credential is required in addition to the regular licensing or certification necessary for all teachers.

Engineers

An *engineer* usually specializes in one of the recognized engineering specialties—aeronautical, industrial, marine, structural, civil, electrical/electronic, or metallurgical, to name but a few. See **Figure 2-9**. Engineers provide technical and, in many instances, managerial leadership in industry and government. Depending upon the area of specialization, engineers may be responsible for the design and development of new products and processes, the planning of structures and highways, or the introduction of new ways to transform raw materials into salable products.

Figure 2-9   A virtual reality computer-controlled simulator is used by this engineer to judge the ergonomics of a proposed car. Ergonomics is the science concerned with matching a design to the human body. In this example, ergonomics is concerned with matching the car's design, seating comfort, and location of controls to the human body. The simulator realistically portrays vehicle operation. This information is important in helping designers and engineers design car interiors for driver and passenger comfort and safety. (Ford Motor Company)

Laws provide for licensing engineers whose work may affect life, health, and property. A professional engineering license usually requires graduation from an approved engineering college, four years of experience, and passing an examination. Some states accept experience in place of a college degree provided the required tests are passed.

Architects

In general, an *architect* plans and designs all kinds of structures, **Figure 2-10**. However, architects may specialize in specific fields of architecture, such as private homes, industrial buildings, schools, or commercial buildings.

When planning a structure, an architect first consults the client on the purpose of the building, size, location, cost range, and other requirements. Upon completion and approval

Figure 2-10   Architects plan and design all kinds of structures.

of preliminary design drawings, detailed working drawings and specification sheets are prepared. As construction progresses, the architect usually makes periodic inspections to determine whether the plans are being followed and construction details are to specifications.

Most architects are licensed. This requires a bachelor's degree from an approved college program, several years of experience working for an architectural firm (similar to the internship of a physician), and passing a special examination. In many cases, a master's degree for advanced or specialized study is obtained.

Modelmakers

Industry makes extensive use of models, mockups, and prototypes for engineering and planning purposes. Their preparation is often the responsibility of the engineering drafting group, although professional *modelmakers* are frequently used. See **Figure 2-11**. Modelmakers must be able to read and understand drawings. They must also have skills in working with a variety of modelmaking materials, including metal, wood, and plastics.

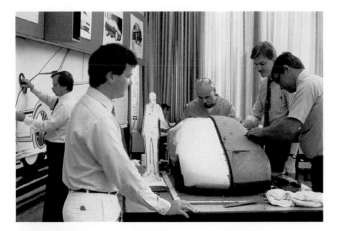

Figure 2-11 In order to interpret the designer's or engineer's plans accurately, modelmakers must be able to read and understand drawings.

Technical Illustrators

Technical illustration is a process of preparing artwork for industry. The *technical illustrator* prepares pictorial matter for engineering, marketing, or educational purposes. See **Figure 2-12**. Technical illustrators must have both technical and artistic abilities. The technical ability is necessary to understand the mechanical aspects of the job. The artistic ability allows the illustrator to show the building or product in three dimensions, whether it be manually or with 3D CAD software. A technical illustrator must be able to make accurate sketches and finished drawings according to industry standards.

Leadership in Drafting Technology

So far in your study of this chapter, you have learned that drafting technology requires highly skilled people. However, the nature of industry is that strong and dynamic leadership is required at all levels of an organization if it is to be competitive with other organizations in the same field.

Leadership is the ability to be a leader. A *leader* is a person who is in charge or in command. The quality of leadership usually

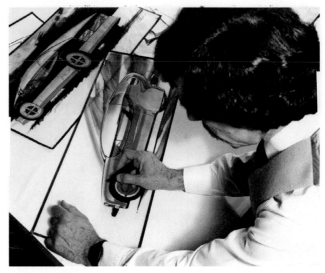

Figure 2-12 It takes many years to progress from the original concept for an automobile to production and sale of the first model. Technical illustrators help contribute to the design, development, and production of such a product. (General Motors Corp.)

determines whether an organization will be successful or be a failure, **Figure 2-13**.

What Makes a Good Leader?

Most good leaders usually have the following traits in common:
- **Vision**. Knows what must be done and continually looks for positive ways to reach these goals.
- **Ability to communicate**. Can communicate in a way that encourages the assistance and cooperation of others.
- **Persistence**. Willing to work long hours to achieve success.
- **Organizational ability**. Knows how to organize and direct the activities of the group.
- **Responsibility**. Accepts responsibility for actions but readily gives credit to others when they deserve or warrant it.
- **Willingness to delegate authority**. Confidently makes assignments that will help others within the group to take on leadership roles.

Figure 2-13 Good leadership brings about the development of efficient manufacturing devices, such as this welding robot used to fabricate automotive components. (Fanuc Robotics North America, Inc.)

Getting Leadership Experience

How can you get leadership experience? The Industrial Technology program as well as other programs and clubs in your school offer leadership training to students willing to take advantage of the opportunities. Many programs provide leadership experience through student technology education organizations such as the *Technology Student Association (TSA)* and *SkillsUSA*. These organizations develop leadership and personal abilities as they relate to the industrial-technical world. Contact the national offices for information, **Figure 2-14**. (See the *Outside Activities* section at the end of this chapter for the Web site addresses of these organizations.)

What to Expect as a Leader

As a leader, you will be expected to set a good example. The responsibility of leadership also means that you must get all members of the group involved in activities. This requires encouragement and tact. A good leader is not expected to have answers for every problem the group encounters. Members should be encouraged to recommend possible solutions. It is up to the leader to decide which to use.

Figure 2-14 Student organizations such as the Technology Student Association (TSA) and SkillsUSA-VICA offer many opportunities for students to develop leadership skills. These organizations sponsor skills competitions, where students showcase their technical skills. (SkillsUSA/Craig E. Moore photo)

ACADEMIC LINK

Drafting is a form of communication. It is commonly described as the "language of industry." Just as verbal communication is needed to convey instructions and information from employee to employee in the workplace, drawings are made to provide manufacturing information to many different areas and work sites. Often, drawings are needed to communicate information about parts that could be in existence for many years.

Using standards that dictate how drawings are drawn and dimensioned, drafters must illustrate the manufacture of parts and assemblies in the simplest terms. Drawing views must logically communicate the necessary information to a variety of users, from shop workers and machinists to construction workers, electricians, and technicians.

Drawings are communication devices that are delivered in printed or electronic form. They are viewed and interpreted on drawing sheets and computer monitor screens. In order to convey the correct information, drawings must be accurate and understandable, regardless of the drawing tools and methods used.

Leadership is not easy or without difficulties. Decisions must be made that some group members may not like. People and even friends may have to be reprimanded or dismissed (fired) for being incompetent (doing poor work) or for trying to take advantage of the group.

A team is made up of team members and one or more leaders. The leaders guide the direction and set goals for the team. The leaders also make sure that all members of the team contribute to the team's success. Problems are solved using teamwork by involving all team members' ideas and abilities.

What to Expect When You Enter the World of Work

You will be very disappointed if you think that graduation means the end of training and study. Advancing technology, **Figure 2-15**, means constantly developing new ideas,

Figure 2-15 This advanced concept aircraft required new materials in its manufacture. The Bell 609 is a cross between a fixed wing aircraft and a helicopter. After taking off vertically, the propellers are lowered to the line of flight. The sequence is reversed for a vertical landing. New metals and composites had to be developed to handle stresses imposed by these transitions in flight. (Bell Helicopter Textron)

materials, processes, and manufacturing techniques that in turn are creating occupations and jobs that did not previously exist. It has been said that new graduates will be employed on the average in five different jobs during their lifetime, and three of them do not now exist! There is only one constant and that is change.

To hold your job and advance in it, you will have to study to keep up-to-date with the knowledge and new skills needed by modern technology.

Industry expects a fair day's work for a fair day's pay. You will be expected to start work on time and be on the job each workday. You must manage your time well and meet deadlines. Discrimination and harassment, whether by an employer or an employee, is unacceptable and illegal. Employers promote and expect equality.

Do your assigned work and never knowingly turn out a piece of substandard or faulty work. Take pride in everything you do. *You* must assume the responsibility for your actions. Industry is always on the lookout for bright young people who are not afraid to work and assume responsibility.

Where to Get Information about Careers in Drafting Technology

Information on careers can be found in many sources. The guidance office and industrial technology department in your school are the two good starting places. Almost all community colleges have *career information centers*. They can furnish any needed occupational and career information.

Look in the *Occupational Outlook Handbook* published by the United States Department of Labor and available through the Government Printing Office. You can also find the handbook online at www.bls.gov/oco. The Department of Labor also publishes the *Dictionary of Occupational Titles*, which has

job descriptions of most occupations. Both books can usually be found in the school library or guidance office.

The local State Employment Service (it may have a different name in your state) is another excellent source of occupational and career information. The employment service will also be able to tell you about local and statewide employment opportunities.

Time Management

In order to be an efficient drafter, you must develop a work schedule. This requires an assessment of your assigned tasks and an estimate of the time required to complete each task. Efficient use of time also requires that you prioritize your tasks. You may choose to create a written schedule of all of your time commitments and their order of priority. It also may be beneficial to set a routine for yourself in which you work on similar tasks at the same time every day.

Learning how to manage your time is essential in order to meet deadlines. Most activities need to be completed within a certain time limit. Companies often have contracts that state the deadlines for completion. Developing and maintaining your work schedule will help you meet these deadlines.

Depending on the task, you may need to work with others to meet your deadline. This requires additional planning and cooperation. When working with a group, it is often best to divide the work and delegate specific tasks to each group member. Using these time management techniques, you should be able to complete your tasks successfully and meet your deadlines.

Employer Expectations

Many general qualities are needed to be successful in the workplace. Behavior required for professional success and advancement includes the following:

- **Cooperative**. An employee must cooperate with supervisors, other employees, and customers.
- **Dependable**. A dependable employee is timely, completes all assignments, and sets realistic goals for completing projects. A dependable employee is trusted by others.
- **Committed**. Good employees put an honest effort into their work and have a good work ethic.
- **Respectful**. In order to be respected, employees must show respect for others, the company, and themselves.

Today's workplace emphasizes *equality*— that is, the idea that all employees are to be treated alike. ***Harassment*** (an offensive and unwelcome action against another person) and ***discrimination*** (treating someone differently due to a personal characteristic such as age, sex, or race) are not tolerated. These negative behaviors often result in termination of employment.

Test Your Knowledge

Please do not write in this book. Place your answers on another sheet of paper.

1. Name two basic types of drawings developed by drafters.
2. The drafter usually starts as a(n) _____, advances to a(n) _____, and then to a(n) _____.
3. The industrial designer's main job is to _____.
4. What is the function of an interior designer?
5. What are the basic requirements for becoming a teacher of industrial technology?
6. Describe the credentials required to become a licensed architect.
7. The engineer usually specializes in one of the many branches of the profession. List four types of engineering.
8. The modelmaker makes models, mockups, or _____ to show the engineer's or designer's plans.
9. What is the main function of a technical illustrator?
10. Name six common traits that good leaders have in common.
11. What two technology education organizations provide ways for students to gain leadership experience?
12. Name four behavioral qualities expected of employees in the workplace.

Outside Activities

1. Invite a representative from the local State Employment Service Office to visit your class and discuss employment opportunities in the field of drafting.

2. Make a study of the Help Wanted columns in your daily newspaper for a period of two weeks. Prepare a list of drafting and related jobs available, salaries offered, and the minimum requirements for securing the jobs. How often are additional benefits (such as insurance) mentioned in the ads? Note the length of time (number of days) each ad is run in the column. Calculate the average number of days jobs are listed.

3. Summarize the information on drafting occupations given in the Occupational Outlook Handbook and make it available to the class. Research the Web sites for the Technology Student Association (www.tsawww.org) and SkillsUSA (www.skillsusa.org) for information on how to organize a technology or vocational club in your school. Conduct a student survey to see if there is interest in forming such a club.

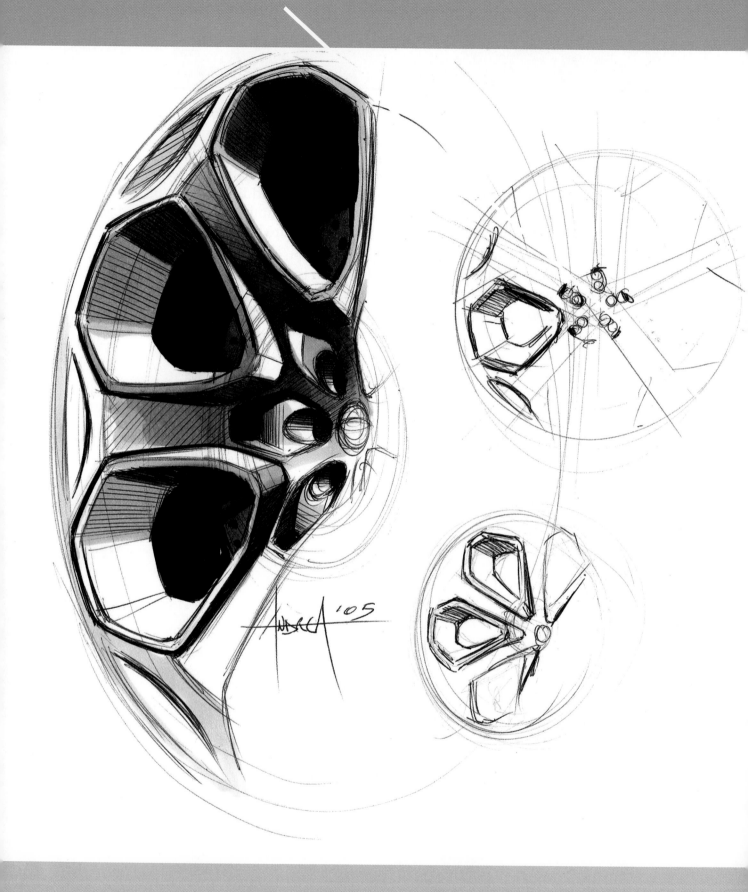

3 Sketching

OBJECTIVES

After studying this chapter,
you should be able to:

- Demonstrate sketching skills and techniques.
- Apply the Alphabet of Lines to a freehand drawing.
- Sketch basic geometric shapes.
- Enlarge or reduce the size of an object using the graph method.

DRAFTING VOCABULARY

Alphabet of Lines
Border lines
Centerlines
Construction lines
Cutting-plane lines
Dimension lines
Equidistant
Extension lines
Graph method
Guidelines

Hidden lines
Linear
Object lines
Phantom lines
Primary centerline
Right angle
Secondary centerline
Section lines
Sketching
Symmetry centerline

Sketching is one of many drafting techniques. It is a quick way to show an idea that would be difficult to describe with words alone. Industry uses many sketching techniques to develop engineering concepts (ideas). See **Figure 3-1**.

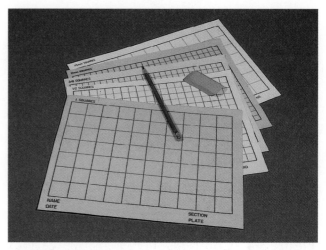

Figure 3-2 Preprinted graph paper is useful in sketching. A good eraser is also a necessity. The colors indicate different size grids.

Figure 3-1 Sketching is a quick way to show ideas that would be difficult to describe with words alone. A—Sketch used in a sports car study, which was one of the many used. While the car will never be produced, the front end of the sketch (slightly modified) has already found its way into production. B—The "Mighty Mouse" is an ultra-light, single-person, high-mileage vehicle for use within the city. It was used in a study to reduce air pollution in urban areas.

A good sketch shows the shape of the object. It also provides dimensions and may include special instructions on how the object is to be made or finished.

Sketching does not require a great deal of equipment. Properly sharpened F, 2H, or HB grade pencils and sheets of standard-size paper (8 1/2″ × 11″) are well-suited for this purpose. See **Figure 3-2**. The paper can be plain or cross-sectioned (graph or grid paper). A good eraser is also needed.

In sketching, a line is drawn by making a series of short, overlapping strokes, **Figure 3-3**. (Please realize that it is impossible in a textbook to illustrate "overlapping" strokes. The breaks in the lines in **Figure 3-3** should not be part of the final sketched line. They are only present because overlapping strokes cannot be shown in the text without visible breaks.) The short stroke technique allows the sketcher to make small corrections in direction as the line is being drawn. This should increase the accuracy of the sketched line.

It is recommended that light (thin) construction lines be drawn first. Corrections will then be easier to make. For right-handed people, horizontal lines are drawn from left to right. In addition, vertical lines are drawn from the top down. For left-handed people, the direction of drawing is opposite.

The sections that follow instruct you on how to sketch lines and basic geometric shapes. You will find that even the most complex drawings are made using a combination of basic geometric shapes.

Alphabet of Lines

A drafter uses lines of various weights (thicknesses) to make a drawing. Each line in

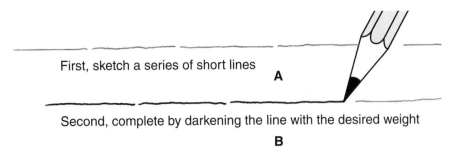

First, sketch a series of short lines

A

Second, complete by darkening the line with the desired weight

B

Figure 3-3   When sketching, a line is drawn by first making a series of short pencil strokes. It is then darkened to the desired thickness.

the *Alphabet of Lines* has a special meaning, **Figure 3-4**. Contrasts between the various line weights help to make a drawing easier to read. It is essential that you learn the different lines in the Alphabet of Lines. Throughout this text, a color coding system is used to identify different types of lines. This system is used in **Figure 3-4** and illustrated in **Figure 3-5**.

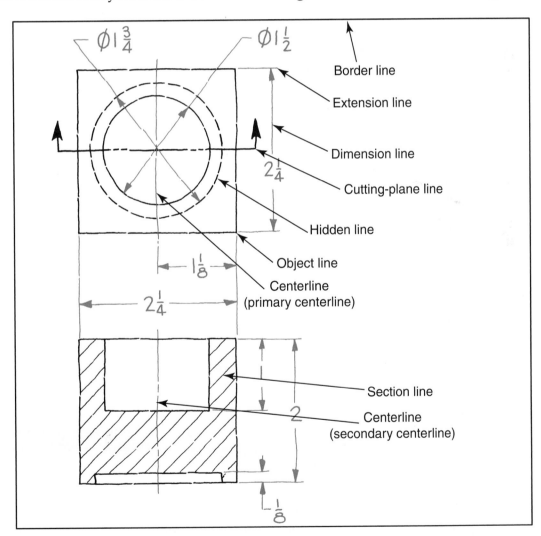

Figure 3-4   The Alphabet of Lines employs different thicknesses for the various lines identified here. Notice the primary centerline is shown in the top view, where the round hole is in its true shape. The secondary centerline is in the front view. Also, note that the cutting-plane line takes priority over the horizontal portion of the primary centerline.

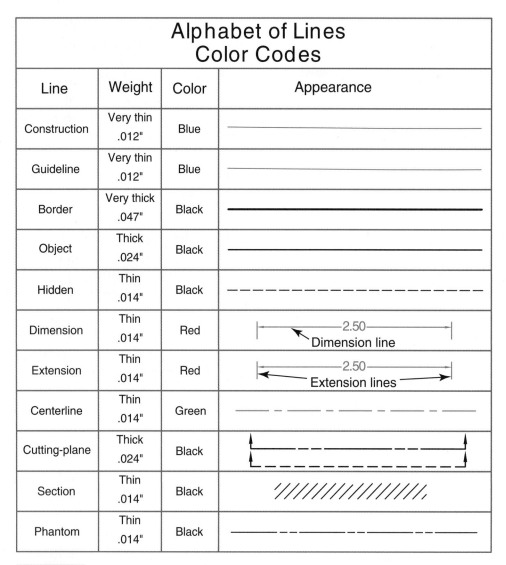

Alphabet of Lines Color Codes			
Line	Weight	Color	Appearance
Construction	Very thin .012"	Blue	
Guideline	Very thin .012"	Blue	
Border	Very thick .047"	Black	
Object	Thick .024"	Black	
Hidden	Thin .014"	Black	
Dimension	Thin .014"	Red	2.50 — Dimension line
Extension	Thin .014"	Red	2.50 — Extension lines
Centerline	Thin .014"	Green	
Cutting-plane	Thick .024"	Black	
Section	Thin .014"	Black	
Phantom	Thin .014"	Black	

Figure 3-5 This table introduces the colors used in the text to identify different types of lines in drawings. Refer to **Figure 3-4** as you study these conventions.

In the Alphabet of Lines, discussed in the following sections, certain lines are composed of specific lengths of dashes and breaks, while others are continuous, solid lines. They vary in thickness by line style (ranging from very thin to very thick). Continuous lines should not be sketched with breaks when using the short stroke technique. As discussed earlier, the strokes should overlap and the line should maintain its continuity from end to end.

Construction Lines and Guidelines

Construction lines are used to lay out drawings. *Guidelines* are used when lettering to help keep the lettering uniform in height. These lines are drawn very lightly using a pencil with the lead sharpened to a long, conical point. They are drawn very thin (approximately .012" thick). These lines, if drawn correctly, will be more gray in color instead of black.

Border Lines

Border lines are the heaviest (thickest) lines used in sketching. They are drawn approximately .047″ thick. First, draw very light construction lines as a guide. Then, go over them using a pencil with a heavy rounded point to provide the thick, black border lines.

Object Lines

Object lines are drawn as heavy, black lines but about half as thick as border lines (approximately .024″ thick). An object line indicates visible edges and intersections of an object. For this reason, it is also called a *visible object line.* In sketching object lines, use a pencil with a medium lead and a rounded point. The final product should be a sharp, black line.

Hidden Lines

Hidden lines are used to indicate or show the hidden features of a part. In other words, a hidden line indicates edges and intersections that are not visible from the viewer's point of view. For this reason, it is also called an *invisible object line.* A hidden line is drawn thin (approximately .014″ thick). Instead of being a continuous line, it is made up of a series of dashes (.125″) with spaces (.06″) between the dashes.

Dimension Lines

Dimension lines generally terminate (end) with arrowheads at the ends. They are usually placed between two extension lines with the tips of the arrows touching the extension lines. A break is made, usually in the center of the dimension line, to place the

actual distance being indicated. A dimension line is a thin line (approximately .014″ thick) and is drawn using a pencil sharpened to a long, conical point. It should be just as black as an object line but approximately half as thick. The thickness of the line provides the necessary contrast to the appearance of the other lines.

Extension Lines

Extension lines are the same weight as dimension lines. They are drawn as continuous (solid) lines. Extension lines indicate the beginning and ending points of a *linear* (straight-line) distance. An extension line begins .06″ away from the edge, intersection, or feature of the object being dimensioned and extends .125″ past the last dimension line it is used for.

Centerlines

Centerlines are used to indicate the centers of round objects. There are three types: primary centerlines, secondary centerlines, and symmetry centerlines.

A *primary centerline* is used to indicate the center of a round object in the primary (true-shape) view of the round feature or object. It is composed of a small crosshair (.125″) with .06″ breaks around the crosshair and long lines that extend through the perimeter of the largest circle or arc for which the center point is valid. See **Figure 3-6A**.

A *secondary centerline* is made up of alternating long (.75″ to 1.50″) and short (.125″) dashes with .06″ spaces between. It is drawn on the secondary (not true-shape) views of round objects. It should extend through the limits of the round object. See **Figure 3-6B**.

A *symmetry centerline* is made up of the same dashes as a secondary centerline. It is used to locate the center of a symmetric object. See **Figure 3-7**.

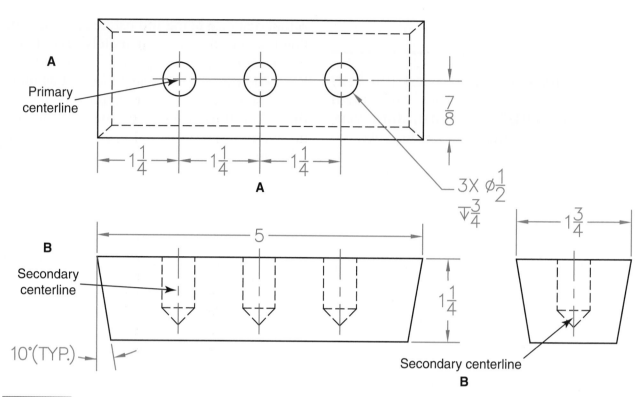

Figure 3-6 Primary centerlines are placed on the primary (true shape) view of the round feature or object, while secondary centerlines are placed on all secondary (adjacent) views.

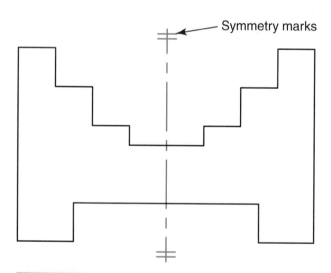

Figure 3-7 A symmetry centerline indicates the midpoint of a symmetrical object.

All types of centerlines are drawn to the same weight as dimension lines and extension lines (approximately .014″ thick). No centerline should ever start or stop at an object line.

Cutting-Plane Lines

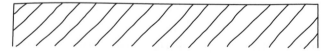

Cutting-plane lines indicate where an object has been cut to show interior features. There are two ways to draw cutting-plane lines. One type consists of a long dash (.75″ to 1.50″) followed by two short dashes (.125″) with .06″ breaks. The second type consists of a series of .25″ dashes with .06″ breaks. The cutting-plane line, regardless of the type used, should be drawn to the same weight as an object line (approximately .024″ thick), using a pencil with a rounded point.

Section Lines

Section lines are used when drawing inside features of an object to indicate the surfaces exposed by a cutting plane. Section lines are also used to indicate general classifications of materials. These lines are parallel, inclined (45°) lines spaced approximately .125″ apart. They are drawn to the same weight as centerlines (approximately .014″ thick) with a pencil sharpened to a long, conical point.

Phantom Lines

Phantom lines are used to show alternate positions of a moving part, repeated details, or the path of motion of an object. A phantom line consists of dashes .75″ to 1.50″ long with alternating sets of two short (.125″) dashes spaced .06″ apart. They are drawn to the same weight as centerlines (approximately .014″ thick).

Sketching Guidelines

All sketched lines should be done freehand. No straight edges should be used in sketching an object. It should be assumed that the sketch can be made using only a piece of paper, a pencil, and an eraser.

All sketched lines, regardless of their style, should have good continuity from end to end. In other words, they should have the same weight and width throughout their entire length. Also, just because they are drawn freehand does not mean they should not consist of a smooth, continuous line. Sketched lines should not be "hairy" in appearance. They should not look like they need a "shave."

Guidelines for Overlapping Lines

Determining which line should be displayed when two lines overlap on a drawing is relatively easy. Cutting-plane lines always take priority over any other line. However, in many cases, object lines are most often shown when lines overlap. (Cutting-

plane lines only apply to drawings with sectional views. Sectional views are discussed in Chapter 11).

In cases where lines depicting object features overlap, the following order of priority can be used: 1. Cutting-plane lines; 2. Object lines; 3. Hidden lines; 4. Centerlines.

Sketching Geometric Shapes

As previously discussed, many types of drawings are created from basic geometric shapes. Shapes such as lines, arcs, circles, and ellipses can be used in sketches to develop complex objects. The following sections discuss basic sketching techniques for common geometric shapes.

How to Sketch a Horizontal Line

1. Mark off two points spaced a distance apart equal to the length of the line to be drawn. The points should be equal in distance (*equidistant*) from the top or bottom edge of your paper.

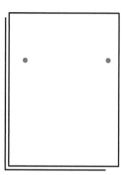

2. Move your pencil back and forth and connect these points with a very light construction line.

3. Start from the left point and sketch an object line to the right point (reverse this if left-handed). Use short, overlapping strokes. This line is sketched over the construction line.

How to Sketch a Vertical Line

1. Mark off two points spaced a distance equal to the length of the line to be drawn. The two points should be equidistant from the right or left edge of the sheet. Move your pencil up and down and connect these points with a construction line.

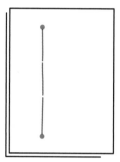

2. Start from the top point and sketch an object line down and over the construction line. Again, use short, overlapping strokes.

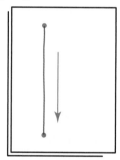

3. Vertical lines can also be sketched by rotating the paper into a horizontal position and proceeding as explained in the previous section *How to Sketch a Horizontal Line*.

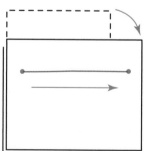

How to Sketch an Inclined Line

1. Mark off two points at the desired angle. Connect these points with a construction line.

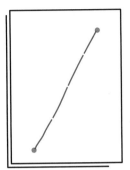

2. Sketch the desired weight line over the construction line. Sketch in the directions illustrated. Sketch up when the line inclines to the right. Sketch down when the line inclines to the left.

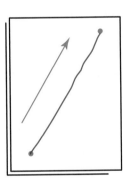

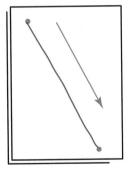

3. Inclined lines can also be sketched by rotating the sheet so the points are in a horizontal position. Sketch the line as previously described.

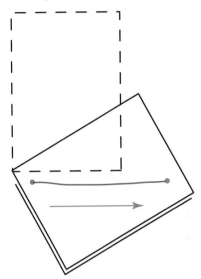

4. For some sketching problems, it may be easier to rotate the paper so the points are in a vertical position. Proceed as explained in the section *How to Sketch a Vertical Line*.

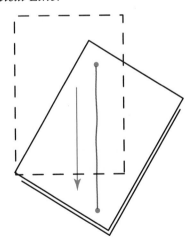

How to Sketch Squares and Rectangles

1. Sketch a horizontal line and a vertical line. These lines represent the axes for layout.

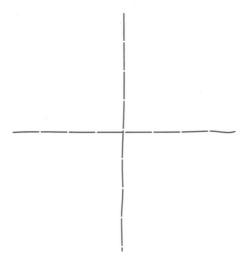

2. Begin at the intersection of these lines and lay out equal units on both lines in each direction. For example, to draw a 2-1/2″ square, estimate a unit of 1/4″ and mark off five of these units on the vertical axis above and below the horizontal axis. Lay out the horizontal axis in the same manner.

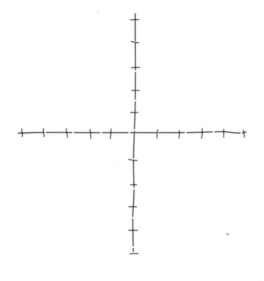

3. Sketch vertical and horizontal construction lines through the desired points.

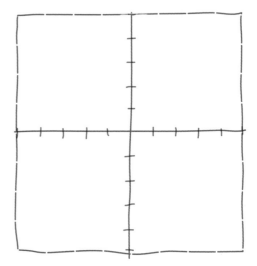

4. Go over the construction lines forming the square to produce the desired weight line.

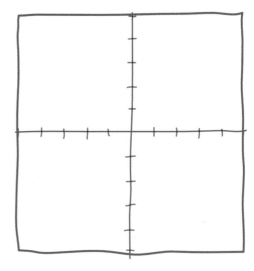

5. Rectangles are sketched in the same way except that there will be more units on one layout axis than the other axis.
6. Take special care to keep the opposing lines parallel.

How to Sketch Angles

1. Sketch vertical and horizontal construction lines. These lines will form a 90° angle (a *right angle*).

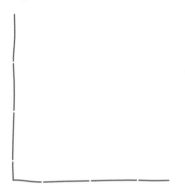

2. A 45° angle is sketched by marking off an equal number of units on both lines. Connect the last unit of each line. This will form a 45° angle with the vertical and horizontal lines.

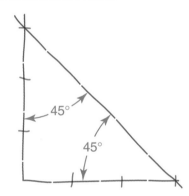

3. To sketch 30° and 60° angles, mark off three units on one line and five units on the other line. Connecting the last unit on each line will establish the required angles.

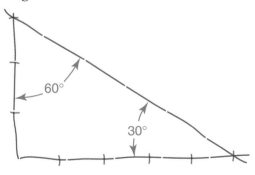

4. Other angles may be drawn by sketching an angle and subdividing it by the approximate number of degrees required. For example, dividing a 30° angle into thirds will create 10° angles.

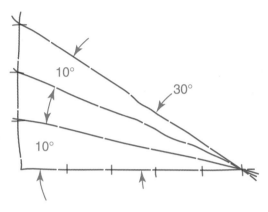

5. Another method used to develop angles in sketching is to sketch a quarter circle and divide the resulting arc into the desired divisions. For example, dividing the arc into three parts will create 30° and 60° angles.

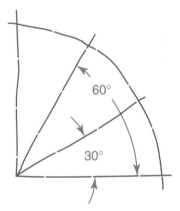

How to Sketch Circles

1. Sketch vertical, horizontal, and inclined axes.

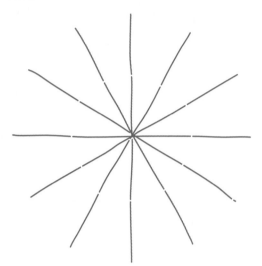

2. Mark off units equal to the radius of the required circle on each axis.

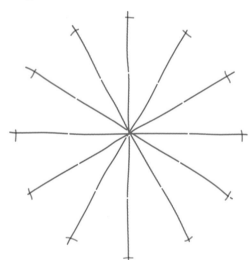

3. The radius units can be quickly and accurately located by marking off the desired radius on a piece of paper and using the paper as a measuring tool.

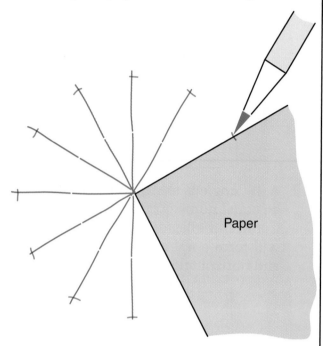

Paper

4. Connect the radius points created with a construction line. When satisfied with the shape of the resulting circle, fill in with a line of the desired weight.

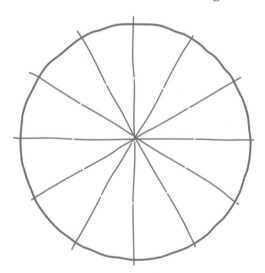

How to Sketch an Arc

1. Sketch a right (90°) angle. Use construction lines.

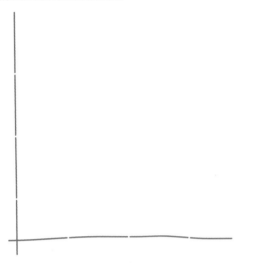

2. Mark units equal to the length of the desired radius on each leg of the angle. Connect these points with an inclined, straight construction line.

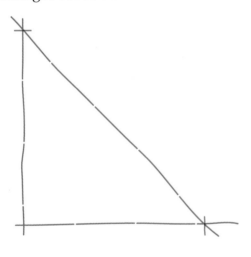

3. Divide this line into two equal parts. Starting from the point where the legs of the angle intersect, sketch a line through the dividing point of the inclined line.

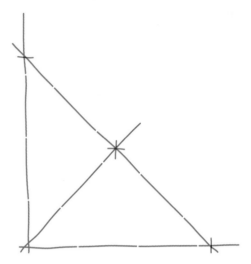

4. Mark off a point halfway between the diagonal line and the intersection of the legs of the angle. Sketch an arc through the three points as shown.

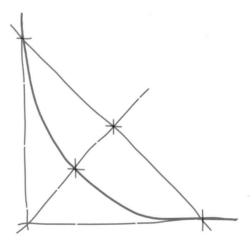

How to Sketch an Ellipse

1. Sketch horizontal and vertical axis lines as shown. Mark off equal size units on the centerline axes to construct a rectangle with the dimensions equal to the major axis (the long axis) and the minor axis (the small axis) of the desired ellipse.

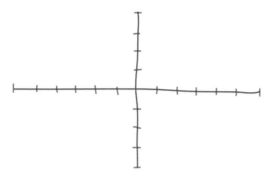

2. Construct the rectangle by sketching construction lines through the outer points.

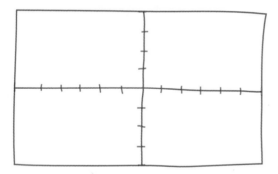

3. Lightly sketch arcs tangent to the lines that form the rectangle.

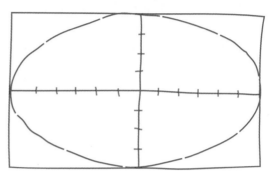

4. When you are satisfied with the shape of the ellipse, complete it by going over the construction lines with lines of the desired weight.

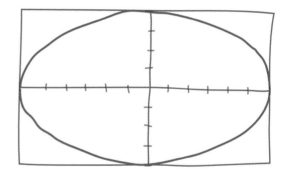

How to Sketch a Hexagon

1. Sketch vertical and horizontal axis centerlines, and inclined lines at 30° and 60°. Construct a circle with a diameter equal to the distance across the flats (flat sides) of the required hexagon. Use construction lines.

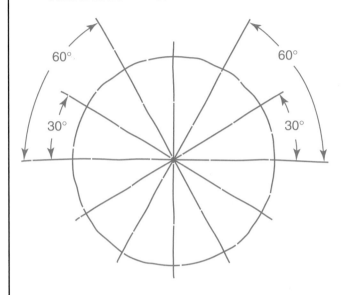

2. Sketch horizontal parallel lines at right angles (90°) to the vertical centerline. The lines are tangent to the circle at these points.

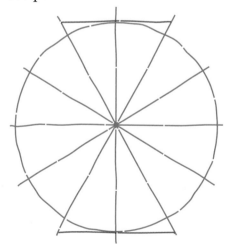

3. Sketch inclined parallel lines at 60° to the circle. Sketch the lines tangent to the circle at the points where the 30° inclined lines intersect the circle.

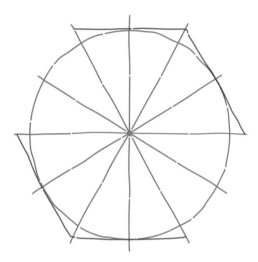

4. Complete the hexagon and go over the construction lines to produce the proper weight line.

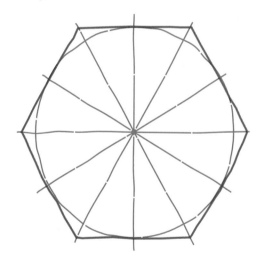

How to Sketch an Octagon

1. Sketch vertical and horizontal axis centerlines and inclined lines at 45°. Construct a circle with a diameter equal to the distance across the flats of the required octagon. Use construction lines.

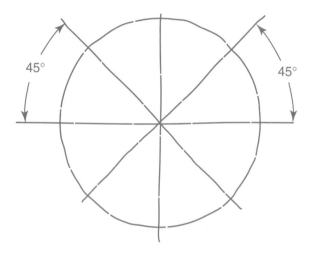

2. Sketch parallel lines tangent to the circle where the horizontal and vertical centerlines intersect the circle.

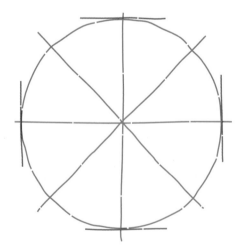

3. Sketch inclined parallel lines at 45° and tangent to the circle at the points where the 45° inclined lines intersect the circle.

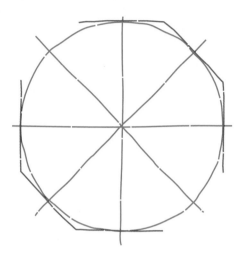

4. Complete the octagon and go over the construction lines to produce the desired weight line.

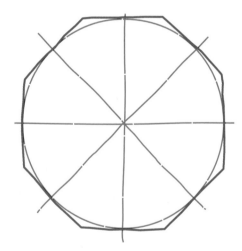

Sheet Layout for Sketching

Drawing sheets should be prepared with a border and information about the drawing, such as the drawing name or number, prior to sketching. The following procedure can be used to lay out an 8-1/2″ × 11″ sheet of plain or graph paper.

1. Sketch a construction line for a 1/2″ border around the edges of the paper. Sketch in guidelines as shown in **Figure 3-8**.
2. The edge of your drawing board or desk may be used as a guide in sketching the border lines and guidelines, **Figure 3-9**. Place the pencil in a fixed position and move your fingers along the edge of the drawing board or desk.
3. Sketch a border line over the construction lines. Letter in information as shown in **Figure 3-10**, or as specified by your instructor.

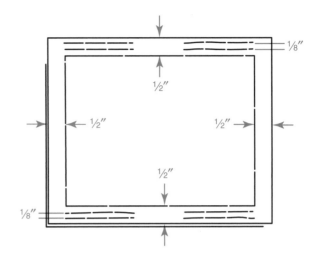

Figure 3-8 Sketching border lines and lettering guidelines. Since no rule is used, these dimensions are only approximate.

4. Take your time and sketch in the border and information carefully and neatly.

Figure 3-9 The edge of your drawing board can be used as a guide when sketching border lines. Note how the pencil is held.

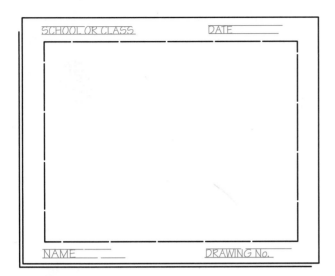

Figure 3-10 Lettering in the required information.

Enlarging and Reducing Drawings

Drawings can be reduced or enlarged easily and quickly using the *graph method* with predrawn grids or graph paper. In this method, sketched drawings can be "blocked off" at one scale and then drawn at a different scale. First, the original drawing is blocked off into grid squares, **Figure 3-11**. The grid is numbered as shown. The horizontal divisions are referred to as X coordinates, and the vertical divisions are referred to as Y coordinates. After deciding how much larger or smaller the new drawing is to be made, draw grid squares of the new size on a blank sheet of paper. Add coordinates to the new grid. Using the design in the original drawing as a guide, sketch the design into the larger or smaller blank grid squares.

For example, a drawing of the design shown in **Figure 3-11** is to be enlarged to twice its original size. The original drawing is marked off into 1/4" grid squares. The square size will vary depending on the size of the original design. Number the grid squares as shown in **Figure 3-11**. Another sheet is made up with grid squares that are twice the size of the 1/4" squares, or 1/2" squares. Identify the large squares in the same manner as the smaller squares with coordinates. Then, sketch in the details freehand, **Figure 3-12**.

Computer-aided design and drafting software provides a similar system of coordinates and grid spacing to create, enlarge, reduce, or duplicate original drawings. You will learn more about computer graphics in Chapter 7.

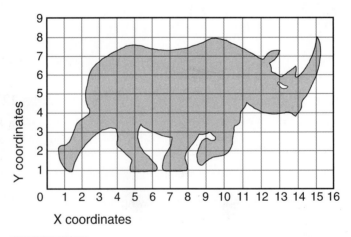

Figure 3-11 The drawing to be enlarged has been blocked in.

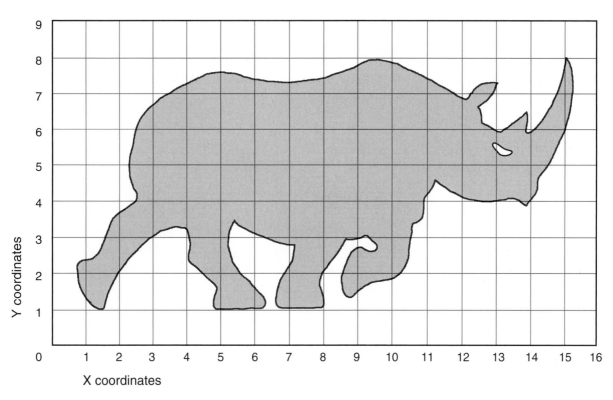

Figure 3-12 The enlarged drawing sketched into larger squares.

Test Your Knowledge

Please do not write in this book. Place your answers on another sheet of paper.

1. In sketching, a line is drawn by making a series of short, overlapping _____.

2. The heaviest line used in sketching is the _____ line.

3. What is the purpose of an *object line*?

4. What type of line is made up of a series of dashes and is used to show features that are not visible from the viewer's point of view?

5. _____ lines are parallel, inclined (45°) lines spaced approximately .125″ apart.

6. _____ centerlines are used to indicate the centers of round objects in true-shape views.

7. Dimension lines generally terminate in _____ at the ends.

8. _____ lines indicate where an object has been cut to show interior features.

9. When sketching an inclined line, sketch up when a line inclines to the _____ and down when a line inclines to the _____.

10. Sketches can be enlarged or reduced easily by using coordinates and grids in what method?

Drawing Problems

Practice your sketching techniques using the objects shown on the problem sheets on the following pages. The sketches shown have 1/2" grid spacing. You may enlarge or reduce each drawing by using the graph method.

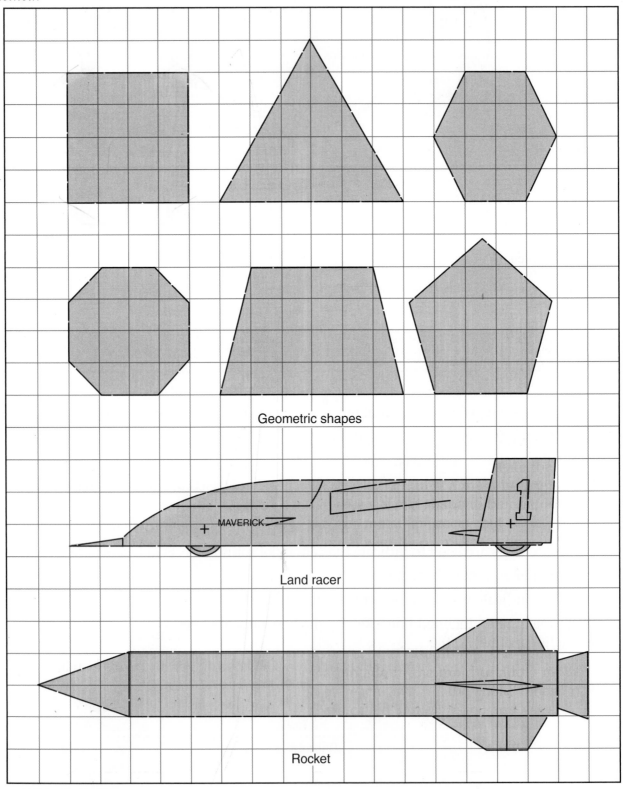

Geometric shapes

Land racer

Rocket

Problem Sheet 3-1 Sketching Problems.

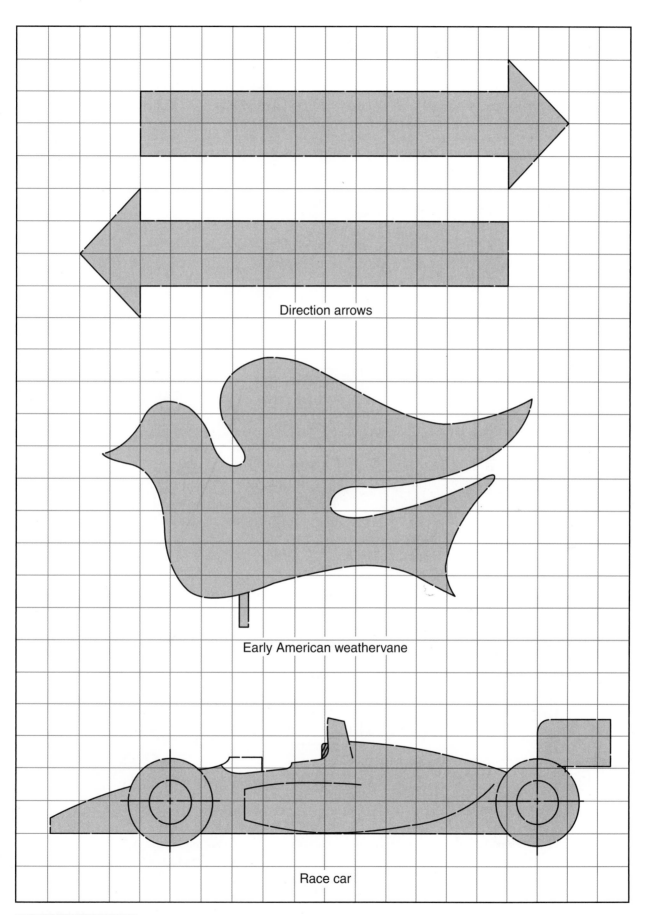

Direction arrows

Early American weathervane

Race car

Problem Sheet 3-2 Sketching Problems.

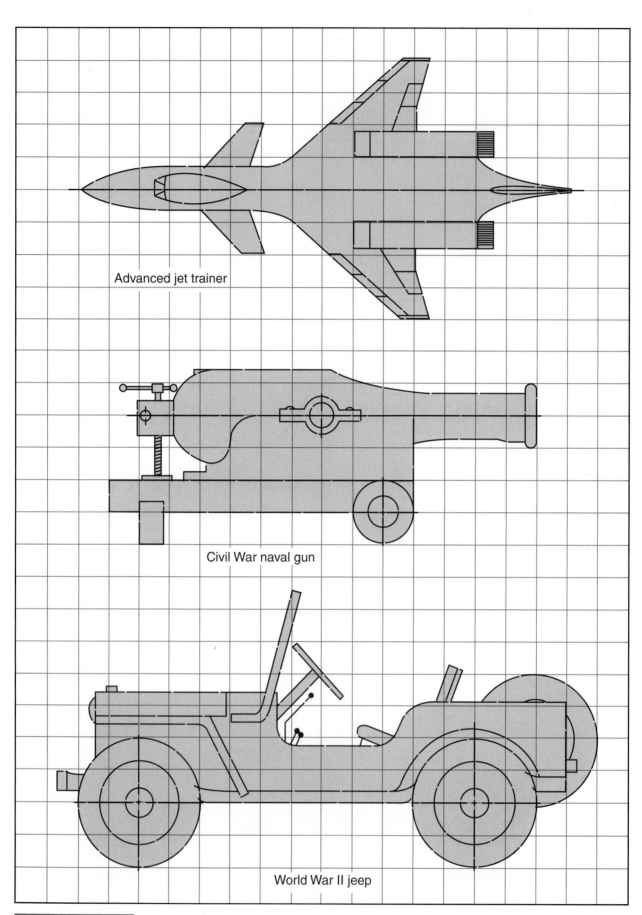

Advanced jet trainer

Civil War naval gun

World War II jeep

Problem Sheet 3-3 Sketching Problems.

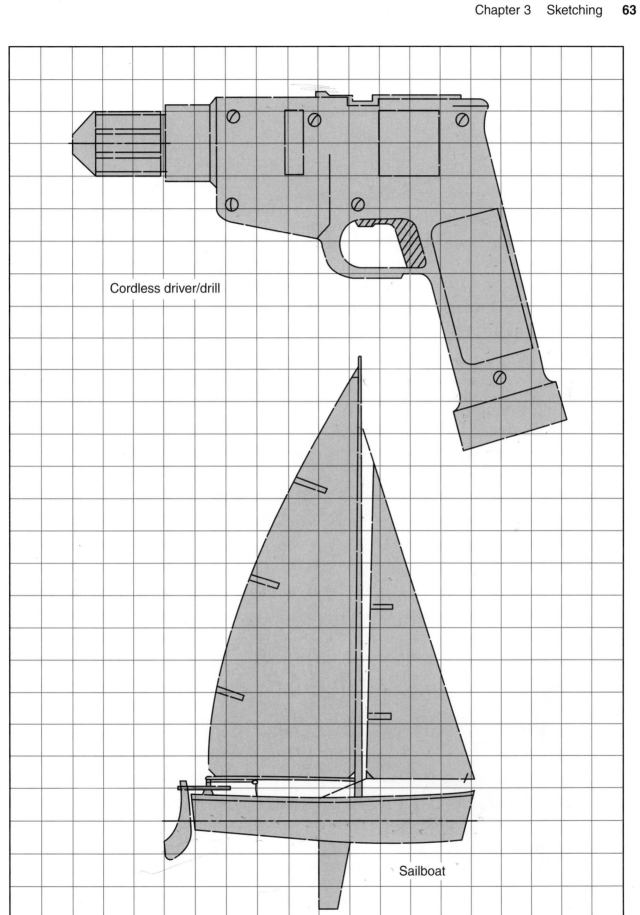

Cordless driver/drill

Sailboat

Problem Sheet 3-4 Sketching Problems.

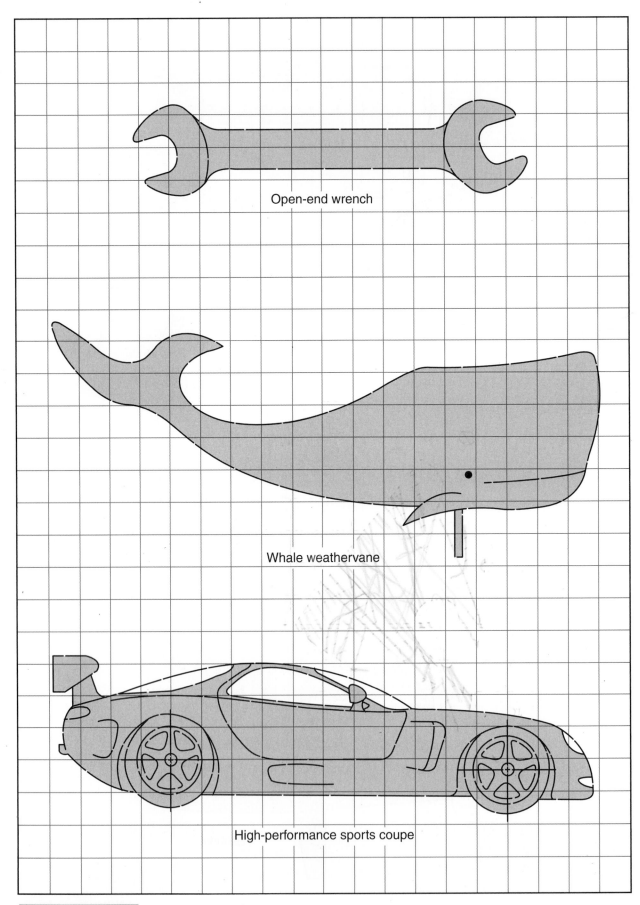

Open-end wrench

Whale weathervane

High-performance sports coupe

Problem Sheet 3-5 Sketching Problems.

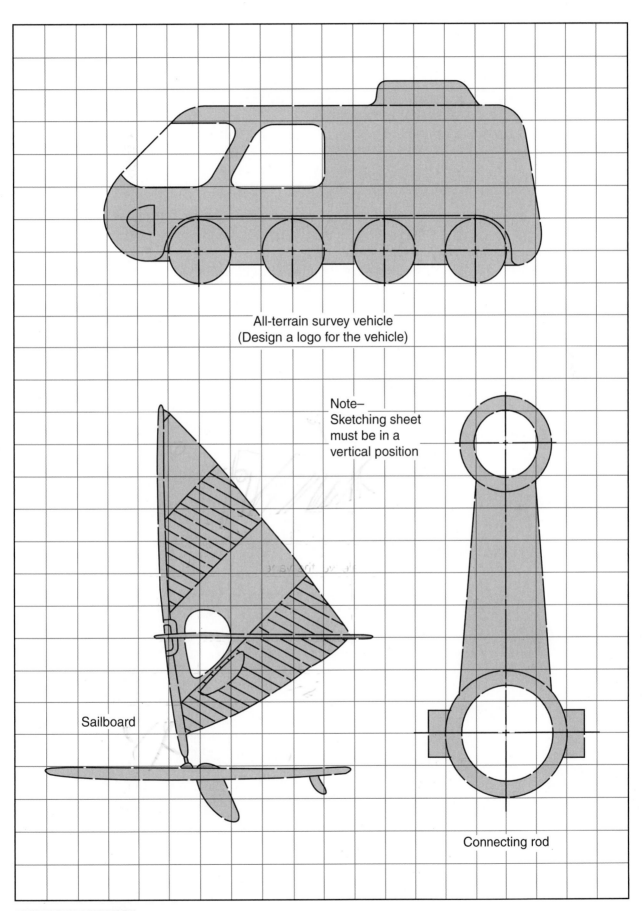

All-terrain survey vehicle
(Design a logo for the vehicle)

Note–
Sketching sheet
must be in a
vertical position

Sailboard

Connecting rod

Problem Sheet 3-6   Sketching Problems.

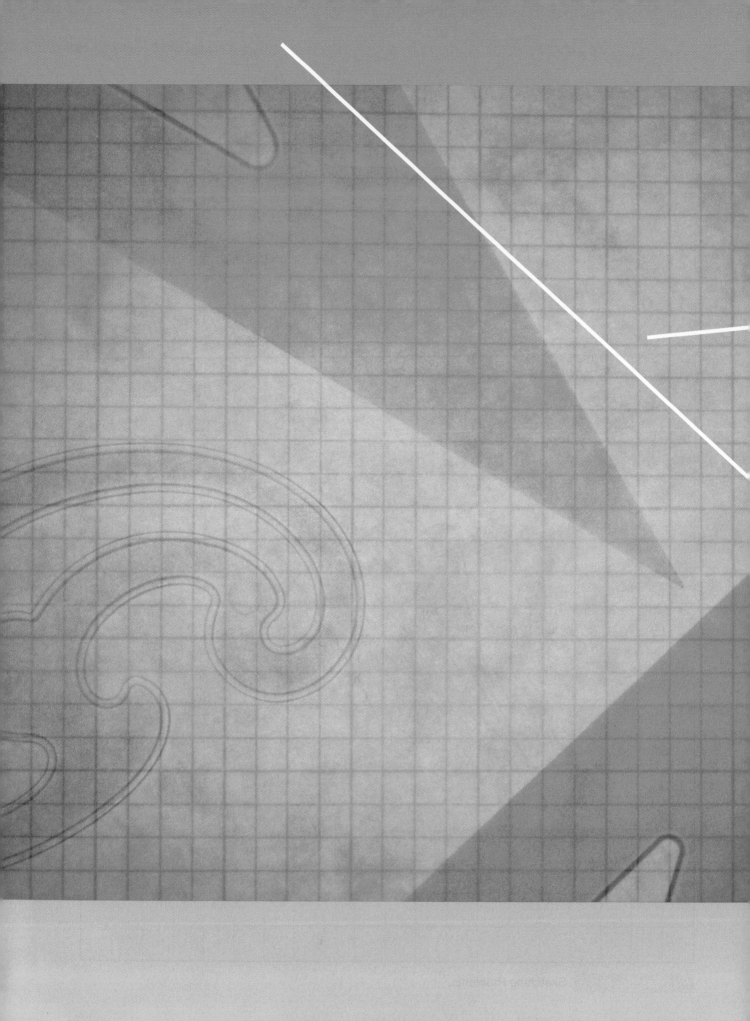

4 Drafting Equipment

OBJECTIVES

After studying this chapter, you should be able to:

- Identify basic drafting equipment.
- Use drafting equipment in a safe and efficient manner.
- Describe the tools used by a CAD drafter.
- Explain why the principles of drafting are common to both traditional drafting and CAD.

DRAFTING VOCABULARY

- Architect's scale
- Beam compass
- CAD software
- Cathode ray tube (CRT)
- CD-RW drive
- Central processing unit (CPU)
- Compass
- Computer
- Digitizing tablet
- Dividers
- Drafting machine
- Drafting media
- Drafting powder
- Drawing board
- Dry cleaning pad
- Dusting brush
- Engineer's scale
- Erasers
- Erasing shield
- Ergonomics
- French curve
- Hard drive
- Irregular curve
- Keyboard
- Lead holders
- Liquid crystal display (LCD)
- Mechanical drafter's scale
- Mechanical pencils
- Metric scale
- Monitor
- Mouse
- Open-divided scale
- Pencil pointer
- Pointing device
- Protractor
- Puck
- Random access memory (RAM)
- Scale
- SI Metric System
- Stylus
- Templates
- Triangles
- T-square
- US Customary System

Drafting tools must be in good condition to make high-quality, accurate drawings. Typical equipment found in many schools is shown in **Figure 4-1**. It is always a good idea to check the condition of your drafting tools before you use them.

Certain procedures should be followed when working with drafting instruments and equipment. It is also important to maintain a safe environment when using drafting tools. This chapter discusses the various tools used in manual and CAD drafting and guidelines for proper usage.

Drawing Board

The *drawing board* provides the smooth, flat surface needed for drafting. The tops of many drafting tables are designed for this purpose. Drawing boards are manufactured in a variety of sizes. The highest-quality drawing boards are made from selected, seasoned basswood. Basswood is selected for its smooth, even grain and its stability. In other words, it does not warp easily.

A right-handed drafter uses the left edge of the board as a working edge. A left-handed drafter uses the right edge. The working edge should be checked periodically for straightness.

Drafters often tape a piece of heavy paper or special vinyl board cover to the working face of the drawing board to protect its surface. The vinyl cover is easily cleaned and provides an excellent surface on which to draw. A compass point can easily seat into the vinyl cover without slipping and the vinyl will somewhat self-heal (the contact will not leave a hole).

T-Square

A *T-square* consists of two parts, the head and the blade (or straightedge). See **Figure 4-2**. The head is usually fixed solidly to the blade. However, a T-square with a protractor head and adjustable blade is available.

The T-square serves two basic purposes. First, when held against the working edge of the drawing board or table, its blade provides a horizontal baseline. This baseline is the

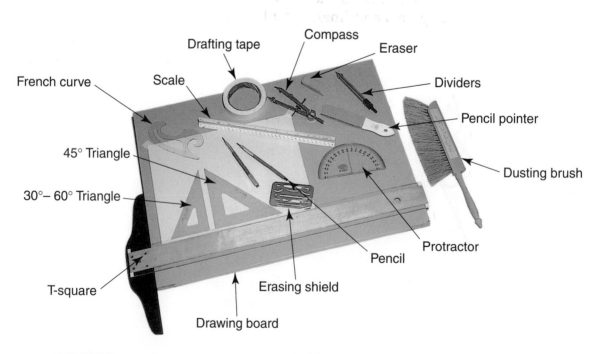

Figure 4-1 Common drafting equipment found in school drafting rooms.

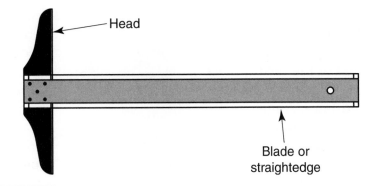

Figure 4-2 The T-square consists of a head and a blade (straightedge).

origin for the entire drawing. All lines are created with respect to the baseline. Second, the T-square is used to draw all horizontal lines by drawing along the top edge of the blade. The head of the T-square should never be placed against any other edge of the board, especially not the top or bottom edges. The T-square is not intended for drawing vertical lines. When vertical or inclined lines are to be drawn, the T-square is used in combination with a triangle by placing the triangle along the top edge of the blade. Triangles are discussed in the next section.

Clear plastic strips are commonly inserted in the blade edge of a T-square. These make it easier to locate reference points and lines.

The blade must never be used as a guide for a knife or other cutting tool since this may affect the "trueness" of the edge.

In order to create accurate line work, it is essential that the T-square be held firmly against the working edge of the board. Also, it is recommended that the blade be left flat on the board or stored suspended from the hole in its end. This will keep warping or bowing of the blade to a minimum.

Triangles

When supported on a T-square blade, 30°-60° and 45° *triangles* are used to draw vertical and inclined lines, **Figure 4-3**. They

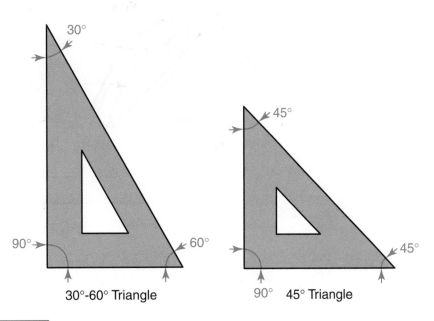

Figure 4-3 Triangles are used with a T-square to draw vertical and inclined lines.

are made of transparent plastic and are available in a number of different sizes.

While holding the T-square head firmly against the working edge of the board, place the triangle along the top edge of the blade to draw vertical or inclined lines. Angles of 15° and 75° can be drawn by combining different triangles. See **Figure 4-4**.

To prevent warping, a triangle should be left flat on the drawing board when not being used.

Drafting Machine

A *drafting machine* combines the functions of the T-square and triangles, **Figure 4-5**. This device provides a consistent and accurate baseline for creating drawings. The straightedges can be adjusted to any angle using the built-in protractor blade. The angle of adjustment stays consistent regardless of where the straightedge is moved about the drawing. Drafting machines are often used in place of T-squares and triangles in school drafting rooms.

Figure 4-5 Typical drafting machine. Note the adjustable protractor blade.

Compass

In drafting, circles and arcs are drawn with a *compass*, **Figure 4-6**. For best results, the lead should be adjusted so that it is about 1/32″ (0.5 mm) shorter than the needle. Both legs will be the same length when the needle penetrates the paper. Fit the compass with lead that is one grade softer than the pencil used to make the drawing. The lead must be kept sharp. Proper adjustment and sharpening of the compass lead is discussed and illustrated in Chapter 5.

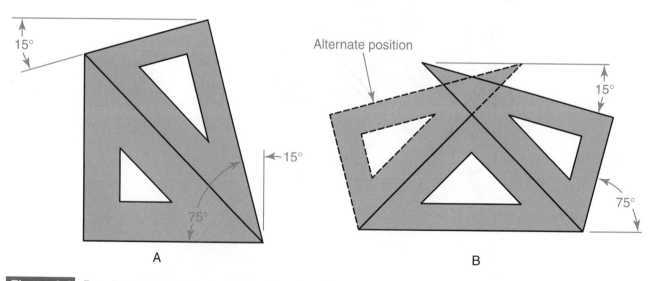

Figure 4-4 Drawing 75° and 15° angles. A—Note how the two triangles are combined. B—An alternate combination. This method requires a bit less vertical height and works well when drawing board space is limited.

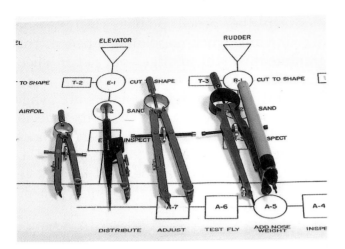

Figure 4-6 Compasses are used to draw circles and arcs. Shown from left to right are a small bow compass, drop bow compass, big bow compass, and big bow compass with inking attachment and pen.

Several compass attachments are available. A ruling pen is substituted for the pencil "leg," **Figure 4-7**. The technical pen, shown in **Figure 4-6**, is now commonly used for inking

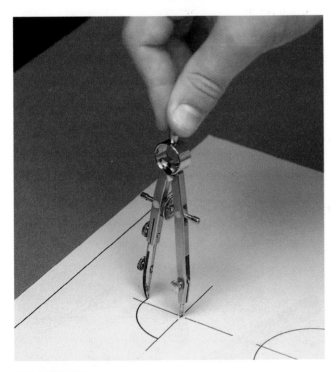

Figure 4-7 Inking a circle using a compass. Some compass models replace the inking "leg" with a technical pen.

tasks. An extension is used to draw large circles. The *beam compass* is better suited for the job, **Figure 4-8**.

To set a compass to the size of the circle radius, first draw a straight line on a piece of scrap paper and then measure off the required distance equal to the radius. Set the compass on this line. Avoid setting a compass on a scale. "Sticking" the compass needle into the scale will eventually destroy the scale's accuracy.

Dividers

Distances are subdivided and measurements are transferred with *dividers*, **Figure 4-9**. Careful adjustment of the divider points is necessary for accuracy. The points should extend equally on both legs of the dividers.

Safety Note

Be careful where and how you place dividers or a compass after use. It is very painful to accidentally run the point into your hand when reaching for the tool.

Figure 4-8 When drawing large circles, it is easier to use a beam compass rather than a compass with an extension.

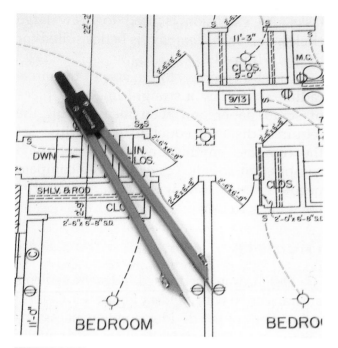

Figure 4-9 Dividers are used to divide and transfer measurements.

Pencil Pointer

It is not necessary to re-sharpen a drawing pencil every time it starts to dull. It can be re-pointed quickly with a *pencil pointer*, **Figure 4-10**. Use the wooden pencil sharpener only when the point becomes very blunt, or when it breaks.

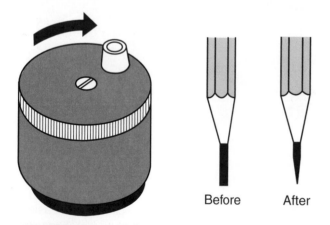

Figure 4-10 Mechanical pencil pointers sharpen the lead, but do not remove any wood. Always rotate the pointer in a clockwise direction.

Keep the pencil pointer clear of the drawing area when re-pointing a pencil. The graphite dust will smudge your paper when you attempt to remove eraser crumbs.

Many types of pencil pointers are available. A sandpaper pad, such as the one in **Figure 4-11**, may be found in the school drafting room. A piece of foam cemented to the back of the pad can be used to remove graphite dust from the newly pointed pencil.

Erasers

Many shapes and kinds of *erasers* are manufactured for use in the drafting room, **Figure 4-12**. The type of media being drawn

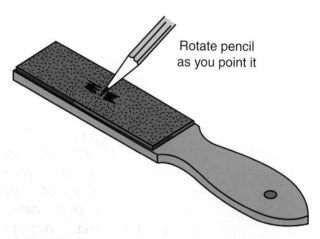

Rotate pencil as you point it

Figure 4-11 Using a sandpaper pad to point a drafting pencil. Do not hold the pencil over the drawing board when pointing the lead.

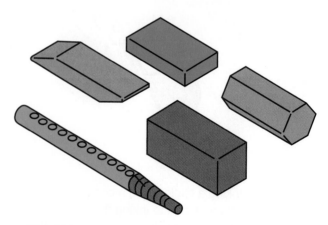

Figure 4-12 Examples of typical erasers used in the drafting room.

upon—paper, film, or vellum—will help determine the type of eraser to be used. Also, a drafter's body chemistry can help determine which eraser to use. Because some natural oils in the skin do not mix well with certain types of erasers, smudging can occur. If you find that the eraser you are using is smearing or smudging your work, try a different kind. It may be that your body chemistry does not mix with that particular type of eraser.

Note

Always brush away eraser crumbs with a dusting brush, not the side of your hand, before starting to draw again.

Erasing Shield

Small errors can be removed without erasing a large section of the drawing if an *erasing shield* is employed, **Figure 4-13**. The erasing shield is used to mask items and lines you wish to keep. Simply orient an appropriate hole or slot in the erasing shield over the area to be changed while masking items you wish to keep and then erase through the opening. The erasure is made without touching other parts of the drawing.

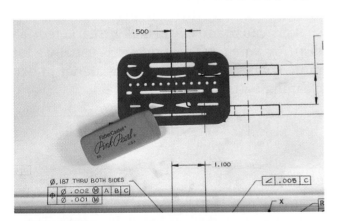

Figure 4-13 An erasing shield is used to protect a portion of the drawing while you are erasing another area.

The most popular type of shield is made from stainless steel. It is very thin, wear-resistant, and does not stain or "smudge" drawings.

Media Fasteners

Two preferred methods of attaching drafting media to a drawing board are shown in **Figure 4-14**. Drafting tape is recommended as the most desirable because of the type of adhesive it uses. Also, it does not puncture the paper or affect the surface of the drawing board. Other types of tape may leave an adhesive residue, which is hard to remove. Unwanted adhesive also collects graphite dust from pencils, thereby soiling the working surface.

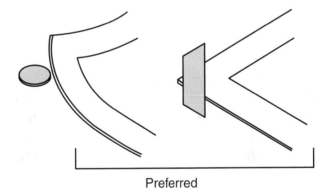

Preferred

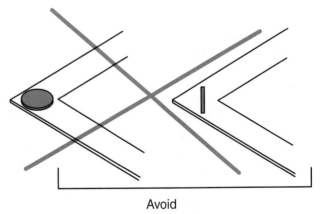

Avoid

Figure 4-14 Two-sided drafting tape dots and drafting tape are preferred methods of attaching paper to the drawing board. Staples and tacks should not be used.

Adhesive tape is sometimes used to attach large drawing sheets. However, continued use may affect the working surface of the drawing board.

Thumbtacks and staples are to be avoided. These quickly destroy the smooth surface of a drawing board.

Dusting Brush

No matter how careful you are, some erasing crumbs and dirt particles will collect on the drawing area. They should be removed with a *dusting brush*, **Figure 4-15**. *Do not remove unwanted debris with your hand*. Using your hand will cause smudges and streaks.

Dry Cleaning Pads and Drafting Powder

Some drafters have a very difficult time keeping their drawings clean. Most of the time, the best way to help this problem is to wash all equipment frequently. However, sometimes even that is not enough. One solution that works well for some drafters is to use a dry cleaning pad, **Figure 4-16**. A *dry cleaning pad* is a small mesh pouch filled with very fine eraser particles. To use, the drafter pounces the pad around the surface of the drawing. The fine particles are fed through

Figure 4-15 Removing erasure particles from the drawing surface with a dusting brush.

Figure 4-16 A dry cleaning pad may be used to assist in keeping smudges from appearing on a drawing. (Alvin & Co.)

the mesh and onto the drawing surface. As the drafter creates the drawing, the particles roll back and forth under the instruments and collect the excess graphite. The particles must remain on the drawing surface the entire time the drawing is being created.

As previously mentioned, this method works well for some drafters, but some find it irritating. Those who do are the ones who frequently use a dusting brush to remove graphite and eraser particles.

Fine eraser dust is also available in shaker cans and is usually marketed as *drafting powder*. This powder is usually a bit more coarse than the erasing material in dry cleaning pads.

Note

If you wish to use a dry cleaning pad or drafting powder, you must train yourself to not use your dusting brush frequently. The particles must remain on the surface of the drawing for this method to be effective.

Protractor

A *protractor* is used to measure and lay out angles other than angles best created with triangles (angles other than 15°, 30°, 45°, 60°, and 75°). See **Figure 4-17**. Protractors are usually made from clear plastic and may be either circular or semicircular in shape. The degree graduations are scribed or engraved around the perimeter of the tool.

When measuring or laying out an angle, place the crosshairs of the protractor at the point of the apex or vertex of the angle as shown in **Figure 4-17**. The apex or vertex is where the two sides of the angle intersect. Read and mark the angle using the graduations of the protractor.

French Curves

Irregular curved lines are drawn with a *French curve*, **Figure 4-18**. This tool is also called an *irregular curve*. After the irregular curved line is carefully plotted, it is drawn with a French curve as shown in **Figure 4-19**. These types of curved lines cannot be drawn with a compass. In general, no part of an irregular curve is a circle or an arc, making a compass unsuitable for the design.

French curves are made of transparent acrylic plastic. They range in size from a few inches to several feet in length and may be purchased individually or as a set.

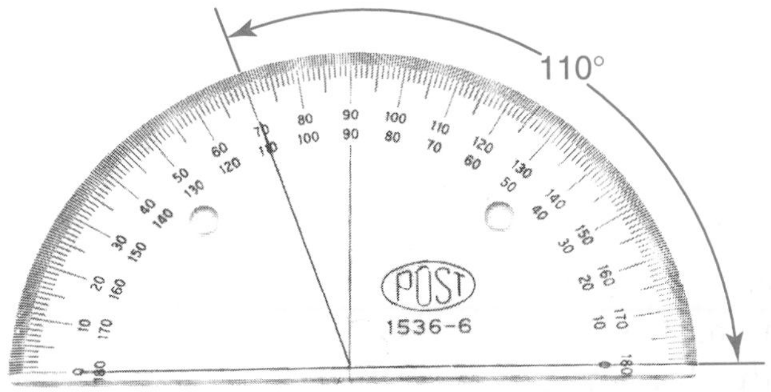

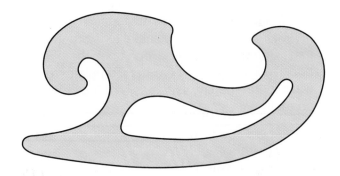

Figure 4-17 Measuring angles with a protractor.

Figure 4-18 A French curve, also known as an *irregular curve*. It is available in many sizes and configurations.

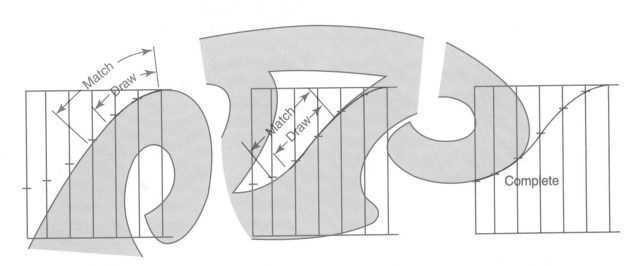

Figure 4-19 Using a French curve to draw an irregular curve.

Templates

Templates are available in an almost unlimited range of shapes and sizes, **Figure 4-20**. Made of thin, transparent plastic, they contain openings of different sizes and shapes. The openings in most templates allow for the thickness of the pencil lead or pen tip. In other words, the actual openings are slightly larger than the size indicated on the template. This is done to preserve the accuracy of the drawn shape.

Templates enable a drafter to perform normally time-consuming tasks with ease and accuracy, **Figure 4-21**.

> ## Note
>
> Because templates are made of thin plastic, it is highly advisable to store them flat. Some students even use them as bookmarks to keep them flat. Templates can warp permanently very easily if not stored correctly.

Drafting Media

Drawings are made on many different types of material—paper, tracing vellum, drafting film, etc. These various types of

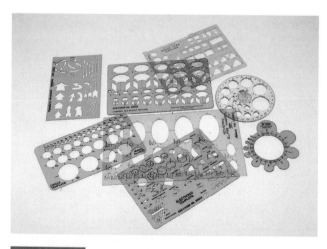

Figure 4-20 A few of the many types of templates used in a drafting room.

Figure 4-21 Templates enable the drafter to reduce drawing time for more complex shapes.

materials are generally referred to in a drafting environment as *drafting media*. Heavyweight opaque paper that is buff (light yellow), pale green, or white in color is used in many school drafting rooms.

While most types of paper take pencil lines well, they are often difficult to erase because the pencil point makes a depression in the paper when a line is drawn. Plan your work carefully to minimize the number of mistakes you make. Most drafting media is not very forgiving. Lines that have been darkened properly are often very difficult to erase.

Industry makes much use of tracing vellum and film because reproductions or prints must be made of most drawings. These are chosen for their translucent qualities, which is necessary for printmaking.

The bulk of the drawings used by industry are put on standard size drawing sheets. This makes them easier to file and identify. A listing of standard sheet sizes is shown in **Figure 4-22** and **Figure 4-23**.

Designers, drafters, surveyors, engineers, and architects make considerable use of commercially prepared graph paper to make preliminary design studies, **Figure 4-24**. Preprinted graph paper speeds up sketching.

Isometric grid paper makes it very easy to convert an orthographic drawing into an

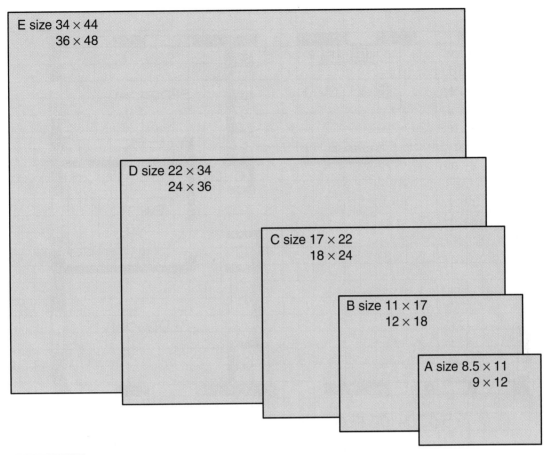

Figure 4-22   Standard inch-size drawing sheets.

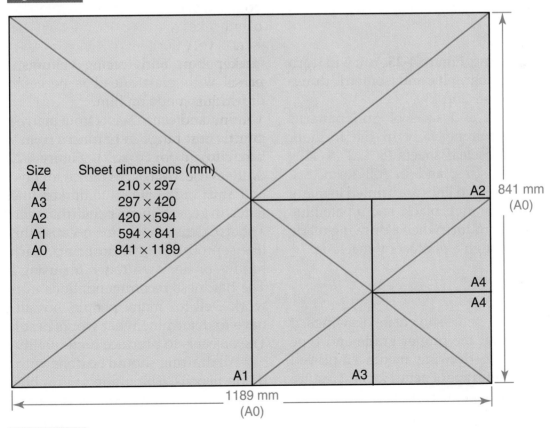

Figure 4-23   Standard metric-size drawing sheets.

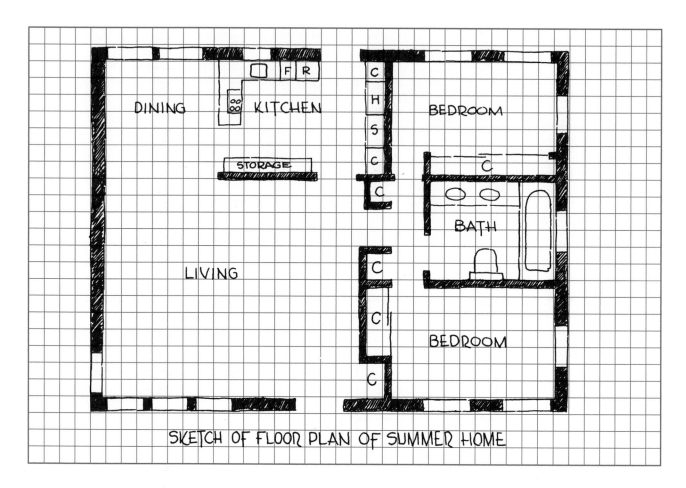

Figure 4-24 A floor plan sketched on graph paper. Each square equals 1′-0″.

isometric drawing, **Figure 4-25**. You will learn more about orthographic and isometric drawings in Chapters 9 and 13.

Many types and sizes of grid patterns are available commercially in the form of prepunched looseleaf sheets (8 1/2″ × 11″), in other sheet sizes, and in roll form. See **Figure 4-26**. The grid lines are printed in many colors—green, orange, black, and a pale blue that will not reproduce when a drawing made on it is run through a photocopy machine.

Pencils

When using pencils to create drawings, it is important that the proper grade and type be selected. The drawing media employed will determine the type of pencil for best results. A conventional lead pencil is satisfactory with most papers and tracing vellums, while a pencil with plastic lead is necessary if the drawing is made on film.

The drafter can select from many grades of pencils that range in hardness from 9H (very hard) to 6B (very soft), **Figure 4-27**. Many drafters use a 4H or 5H pencil for layout work and an H or 2H pencil to darken lines and to letter. In general, use a pencil that will produce a sharp, dense black line because this type of line reproduces best on prints. Each drafter has his or her own touch for using a pencil. The hardness recommendations in this book work well for many people, but all drafters have to determine what works best for them. The object is to produce high-quality results.

All drafting should be done with drafting grade pencils. The grade of graphite present in standard writing pencils is much too soft.

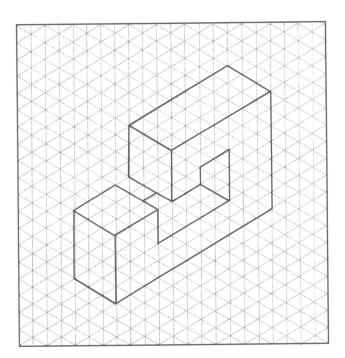

Figure 4-25   An isometric drawing made on graph paper designed for that purpose.

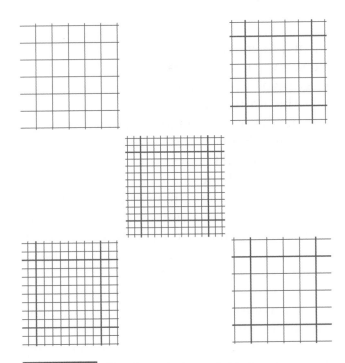

Figure 4-26   Graph paper is available in many different grid (square) sizes.

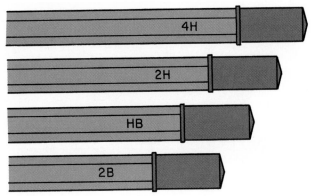

Figure 4-27   Common pencil grades used in drafting. Pencils are available in a wide range of hardness.

Avoid using a pencil that is too soft. It will wear rapidly, smear easily, and soil your drawing. Also, the line will be "fuzzy" and will not produce usable prints. You do not want to use pencils that create fuzzy, gray lines. You want to use pencils that produce sharp, black lines.

A conical-shaped pencil point is preferred for most general-purpose drafting when using woodcase pencils. To sharpen the pencil, cut the wood away from the unlettered end. Sharpen with a knife or mechanical sharpener and point the lead with a pencil pointer, **Figure 4-28**.

There are several other types of pencils that may be used for drafting, including *lead holders*. See **Figure 4-29**. Lead holders grip a

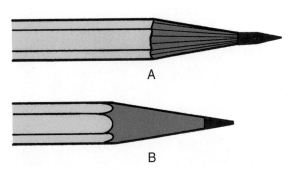

Figure 4-28   Pencil points. A—Sharpened with a knife and pointed on a sandpaper pad. B—Sharpened with a regular pencil sharpener.

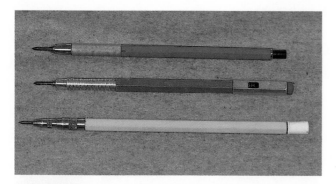

Figure 4-29 A variety of lead holders. Only the lead needs to be replaced. The lead is available in the same hardness range available with wooden pencils.

length of 2 mm lead much like the lead found in a woodcase pencil. They require a special lead pointer to sharpen the lead, **Figure 4-30**.

Mechanical pencils are available in different lead diameters. They produce accurate results and are very popular. See **Figure 4-31**. The four basic lead diameters available are 0.3 mm, 0.5 mm, 0.7 mm, and 0.9 mm. Mechanical pencils may be purchased individually or in sets. Sets usually include 0.3 mm, 0.5 mm, and 0.7 mm pencils, or 0.5 mm, 0.7 mm, and 0.9 mm pencils. The

Figure 4-30 A lead holder with a sharpened lead point.

Figure 4-31 Mechanical pencils require no sharpening. The line width is determined by the diameter of the lead. (Alvin & Co.)

advantage to this type of pencil is that the diameter of the lead determines the line thickness. No sharpening is necessary.

Many drafting instructors prefer the young drafter to begin using woodcase pencils so that they may learn various drawing techniques that are not required with lead holders or mechanical pencils. After becoming capable with the wooden pencil, the drafter may then move on to using other types of pencils.

Scales

The term *scale* has a dual meaning in drafting. A scale is a measuring device, **Figure 4-32**. However, the term "scale" also refers to the size to which an object is drawn. The actual, real-life size of the object and the size of the drawing sheet to be used will determine the scale or size to which an object is to be drawn.

A **scale** (measuring instrument) can be used to make measurements that are full size, larger than full size, or smaller than full size. Scales are in constant use on the drawing board because almost every line on a mechanical drawing (a drawing made with instruments) must be a measured length. Accurate drawings require accurate measurements. Accuracy is the most important attribute that all drawings must have.

Due to the diversity of work that must be drawn, scales used by drafters are made in many shapes, lengths, and measurement graduations. They may be made of wood, plastic, or a combination of both materials. Graduations are printed on inexpensive scales, and are machine engraved (with much more accuracy) on the more costly scales of greater quality.

Measurements made on drawings are based on one of two systems of measurement. These are the US Customary and SI Metric systems. The basic unit of measurement in the **US Customary system** is the inch. This is the standard form of measure used in the United

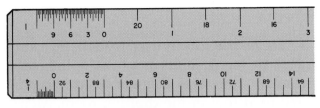

Architect's scale

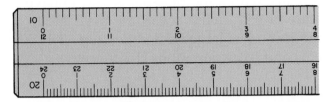

Engineer's scale

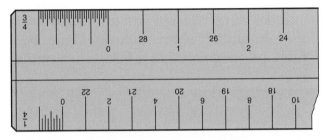

Mechanical drafter's scale

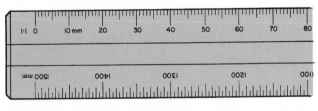

Metric scale

Figure 4-32 The common types of scales used in drafting.

States. The basic unit of measurement in the *SI Metric system* is the meter. The SI Metric system is the international standard.

There are three common types of scales used to make drawings in inches and feet. These are the architect's scale, engineer's scale, and mechanical drafter's scale. Metric scales are used for drawings made in metric units. The different types of scales are discussed in the following sections.

Architect's Scale

An *architect's scale* is normally used to make drawings of buildings and building details. These types of drawings represent a large reduction in size in order to fit measurements on the drafting media used. For this reason, architect's scales are designed to make measurements in feet. For instance, a drawing made using a 1/4″ = 1′-0″ scale means that 1/4″ on the drawing represents 1′ on the object.

Architect's scales commonly provide multiple scales, such as 1/8″ = 1′-0″, 1/4″ = 1′-0″, 1/2″ = 1′-0″, and 1″ = 1′-0″ scales. Each scale is identified on one end, and two of the scales are normally grouped together. For example, the 1/8″ = 1′-0″ and 1/4″ = 1′-0″ scales are grouped together along the same edge because the measurements on a 1/4″ = 1′-0″ drawing are twice as large as those on a 1/8″ = 1′-0″ drawing. One of these scales is read from one end of the instrument, and the other is read from the opposite end.

Each scale on an architect's scale is an *open-divided scale*. This refers to the way in which divisions are read on the scale. The whole number divisions on the scale represent feet. These divisions are not subdivided (this makes the scale easier to read). The smaller divisions at the end of the scale represent subdivisions of a foot (inches). The number of subdivisions vary depending on the scale. For example, there are 12 subdivisions on a 1/4″ = 1′-0″ scale, each representing 1″. There are 48 subdivisions on a 1″ = 1′-0″ scale, each representing 1/4″. To read the scale, the number of foot divisions is first determined (beginning at zero). Then, the number of inches is determined by reading the number of inch subdivisions at the end.

Other scales available on architect's scales include the 3/32″, 3/16″, 3/8″, 3/4″, 1-1/2″, and 3″ scales. The 16 scale is also available. This is the only scale that is not open-divided. This scale is a fully divided, 1′-0″ scale divided into 1/16″ increments. The scale is labeled "16" to reflect the 1/16″ increments.

Engineer's Scale

An *engineer's scale* is a fully divided scale used for drawings where large reductions are required, such as site plans for architectural drawings. An engineer's scale has six scales along its edges. The scales have inch divisions that are multiples of 10. The scales are labeled 10, 20, 30, 40, 50, and 60. The labels identify the number of divisions of an inch. For example, the 40 scale has 40 units to the inch and the 20 scale has 20 units to the inch.

Typical drawing scales created with an engineer's scale are 1″ = 10′-0″ (where 1″ on the drawing equals 10′ on the actual object) and 1″ = 40′-0″ (where 1″ on the drawing equals 40′ on the object). An engineer's scale can also be used to scale to 1″ = 100′ or 1″ = 1000′ (to reduce the size of very large objects) or to 1″ = 0.1′ or 1″ = .01′ (to enlarge very small objects).

The 50 scale may also be used to measure decimal inches full size for decimal inch drawings. When using the engineer's scale in this manner, each of the smallest increments equals .02″. (There are 50 units to the inch, and 50 × .02″ = 1″.)

Mechanical Drafter's Scale

The *mechanical drafter's scale* is an open-divided scale used to create drawings in inches at scales such as full size, 3/4 size, 1/2 size, 1/4 size, and 1/8 size. For example, an object drawn with a 1/4 size scale (where 1/4″ = 1″) is one-fourth as large as the actual object. The main increments on these scales are equal to 1″ on a full size scale, 3/4″ on a 3/4 size scale, and so on. On one end of the scale, the primary division is subdivided into standard fractional units—sixteenths, eighths, fourths, and halves.

Metric Scale

The *metric scale* is used to make measurements in metric units (such as millimeters) for metric drawings. The metric scale is now a required tool in the drafting room. Metric scaling is expressed in ratios. An object drawn full size with a metric scale is said to have a scale of 1:1. Metric scales are available in a number of enlargement ratios (2:1, 3-1/3:1, etc.) and reduction ratios (1:2, 1:3, etc.).

Computer-Aided Drafting Equipment

Today, much design and drafting work is done electronically with computers, **Figure 4-33**. Drawings are created at a CAD workstation

Figure 4-33 Many drafting firms use computers to develop the drawings needed to manufacture the many products we use. (Amp, Inc.)

and then printed or distributed electronically as needed. Many drafting firms utilize CAD in producing drawings. There are many types of CAD software programs available, including 2D-based programs and advanced 3D modeling systems. The software used depends on the needs of the company. Many consumers purchase CAD software for use on their home computers. The software may be useful for designing personal items used in the home, such as a new picnic table or storage shed.

The basic CAD system is made up of several hardware devices, including a computer, monitor, keyboard, pointing device, and output device. See **Figure 4-34**. The system also includes a specific type of CAD software.

The *computer* is the primary component of the CAD workstation. It includes the *central processing unit (CPU)*, where opera-

tions are performed and data is processed. When information is entered into a computer, it is stored temporarily in memory so that it can be later retrieved. This type of memory is known as *random access memory (RAM)*. As you work on a file, data is placed in RAM and processed. When data is saved, it is placed in storage. In many cases, files are saved onto the computer's *hard drive*. Data may also be written to a *CD-RW drive* for storage. A *CD-RW* is a rewritable compact disc. The use of CDs permits large-capacity storage in a portable format and allows files to be used on different computers.

A *monitor* displays the image of the drawing being created. Two common types of monitors are the *cathode ray tube (CRT)* monitor and the *liquid crystal display (LCD)* monitor. A CRT monitor is a standard monitor used with most desktop computers. LCD monitors are typically used with laptop

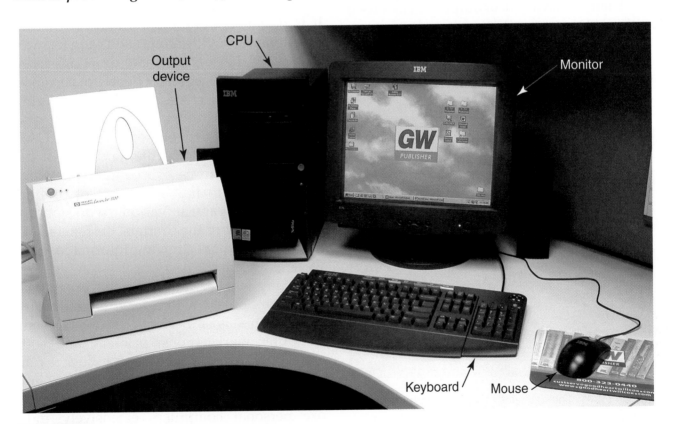

Figure 4-34 A typical computer workstation.

computers. LCD panels are much lighter in weight and require less electricity to operate in comparison to CRT monitors. However, LCD systems are much more expensive.

A *keyboard* is used for inputting text and other operations. A *pointing device* is also used for input. In most cases, the pointing device of a computer is a mouse. A *mouse* is an input device with a trackball that allows the user to move the on-screen cursor quickly and easily. Some CAD workstations use a digitizing tablet. See **Figure 4-35**. A *digitizing tablet* is an input device on which a *puck* or *stylus* is maneuvered to select commands and position the on-screen cursor. Digitizing tablets are not often found in school environments because of their cost. However, professional drafting departments in industrial settings use them often because they offer more input and customization options than a typical mouse.

There are a variety of output devices used with CAD systems to produce hard copy. The most common are printers and plotters, **Figure 4-36**. Many CAD drawings are printed with inkjet plotters. These devices are capable

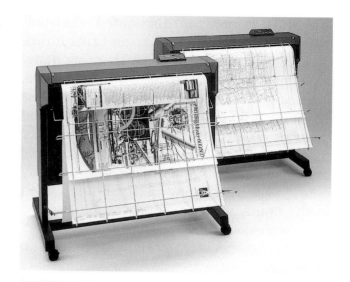

Figure 4-36 Prints of CAD drawings are most typically made on high-speed plotters. (CalComp)

Figure 4-35 The digitizing tablet is an input device connected to a computer. It is especially useful for transferring conventional drawings into CAD files. The puck or stylus is used to "digitize" drawings. (CalComp)

of generating high-quality output on large-format media. Laser and inkjet printers are also used to output CAD drawings.

CAD software is the core of the system. It is designed to automate manual drafting functions. It provides commands and features that allow drafters to create drawings more rapidly and with a greater degree of accuracy. Using basic object creation and modifying commands, operators design, draw, and edit throughout the course of a project. CAD software is installed to the hard disk of the computer. In many cases, a computer network is established to link a number of drafters with the software at various workstations. This allows all of the drafters, designers, and engineers to share drawing information and work as a team.

Many smaller businesses have personal computers linked with a *local area network (LAN)*. This is a network of file servers, computer workstations, printers, and software linking users in a setting such as an office building. School districts operate in a similar manner. Because many school districts use personal computers extensively, individual buildings within the district are typically connected with a LAN and the buildings are connected to a larger network called a *wide area network (WAN).* A WAN is made up of many different computers linking users over an entire geographical area. Local and wide area networks may use fiber optic or wireless technology. Regardless of the connectivity, these types of systems allow greater communication between all users through various methods of data sharing.

The selection of software and computer equipment is a major consideration in the operation of a CAD system. There are many types and kinds of CAD software, from very simple consumer programs to specialized programs tailored to very application-specific tasks. CAD programs range in price from approximately $50 to thousands of dollars. As CAD software gets more sophisticated, so does the hardware to operate it. More RAM and disk space, special graphics cards, and other high-end needs are typical of industrial-level CAD systems.

The principles of drafting are common to both traditional (manual or board) drafting and CAD. Drafting technicians must have a working knowledge of the same drafting practices, standards, and procedures you are now learning before being able to use CAD to its fullest potential. CAD is an amazingly powerful tool designed to execute the same tasks performed with T-squares and triangles in a faster and more accurate manner. However, industry wants problem-solvers, not button-pushers. There is no demand for CAD technicians who can use the software but have little idea of why they are doing what they are doing. The study of manual drafting provides the essential foundation for success in the efficient use of a CAD system.

CAD tools and other computer graphics functions are discussed in more detail in Chapter 7.

ACADEMIC LINK

When measuring linear distances, it is sometimes necessary to convert values from one unit of measure to another. For example, you may need to convert inches into feet or vice versa. This type of calculation and other mathematic skills are often used in drafting.

When converting linear measurements in the US Customary system, you can determine the number of feet in a given distance by dividing the measurement by 12. This is because 1′-0″ is equal to 12″.

When using the metric system, measurements are converted based on values of 10. The standard unit of measure in this system is the meter. There are 10 millimeters in one centimeter, 10 centimeters in one decimeter, 10 decimeters in one meter, and so on. Metric prefixes such as *milli* and *centi* are used to designate values in relation to the meter. Each prefix represents a division or multiple of 10 in comparison to the meter. For example, 1 m is equal to 1/1000 mm (0.001 mm). To convert 150 meters into millimeters, you would divide 150 by 1000 (150/1000 = 0.15 mm).

Metric drawings are most commonly dimensioned in millimeters. If you need to convert a distance in inches to millimeters, you must use a formula based on the conversion 1″ = 25.4 mm. For example, to convert 3″ to millimeters, you would multiply 3 by 25.4 (3 × 25.4 = 76.2 mm). To convert a distance in millimeters to inches, you would use a formula based on the same conversion, except you would divide rather than multiply. For example, to convert 152.4 mm to inches, you would divide 152.4 by 25.4 (152.4 ÷ 25.4 = 6″).

Inspecting, Maintaining, and Servicing Drafting Tools

The equipment used in drafting requires periodic inspection and regular maintenance to remain reliable and safe. The owner's manuals for all office and drafting equipment should be kept in an organized library. These manuals provide detailed inspection, maintenance, and service information. Additional information may be found at the manufacturers' Web sites.

Plotters, printers, and other equipment should be cleaned and serviced according to the instructions and schedules established by the manufacturers. An inventory of replacement toner and ink cartridges, plotter pens, paper, and other consumables should be kept on hand to prevent work stoppage when these items need to be replaced.

In addition to maintaining equipment, standards must be incorporated and adhered to when using a CAD system. File management and layer management policies must be established and strictly followed. (*Layers* are common tools in CAD software and are discussed in more detail in Chapter 7.) If changes are made to the file management or layer management policies, all macros, scripts, subroutines, and templates affected by the change should be updated. Important files should be backed up at scheduled intervals.

Manual drafting equipment, such as triangles, T-squares, French curves, and protractors, should be inspected periodically for warping, chips, or other physical defects. An inventory of manual drafting equipment and consumables, such as paper, erasers, and pencils, should be maintained to prevent work stoppage.

Working Safely

As you work, you should always keep safety in mind. Before using or servicing equipment, you should familiarize yourself with the proper operating procedures and safety considerations. Review your company's safety policies, as well as all applicable safety manuals, safety instructions, and safety requirements from governmental agencies and equipment and material manufacturers. Also, exercise caution around electrical or electronic devices.

In addition to protecting your personal safety, you should also protect your work. For example, keep beverages and food away from your work area, save your work often, and properly store all media. All critical electronic equipment should be protected by surge protectors and uninterruptible power supplies.

Creating an Ergonomic Environment

Like other workers who spend long periods of time doing detailed work with a computer, drafters may be susceptible to eyestrain, back discomfort, and hand and wrist problems. *Ergonomics* is the science of adapting the workstation to fit the needs of the drafter. Applying ergonomic principles results in a comfortable and efficient environment. There are many types of ergonomic accessories that may improve a computer workstation, including wrist rests, ergonomically designed chairs, and back supports. The following chart identifies a few things that can be done to create a comfortable environment and help prevent injury or strain to the operator's body. Finally, cleanliness is an important part of the drafting environment. Keep papers, computer discs, pens, rules, reference books, and other materials organized. The work area should not be cluttered with unneeded items. Properly store items not in use.

Ergonomic Guidelines

Eyes

- Position the monitor to minimize glare from overhead lights, windows, and other light sources. Reduce light intensity by turning off some lights or closing blinds and shades. You should be able to see images clearly without glare.
- Position the monitor so that it is 18″ to 30″ from your eyes. This is about an arm's length. To help reduce eyestrain, look away from the monitor every 15–20 minutes and focus on an object at least 20′ away for 1–2 minutes.

Wrists and Arms

- Forearms should be parallel to the floor.
- Periodically stretch your arms, wrists, and shoulders.
- Try using an ergonomic keyboard and mouse. The keyboard keeps the wrists in a normal body position and the mouse will fit your hand more comfortably.

Neck

- Adjust the monitor so that your head is level, not leaning forward or back. The top of the screen should be near your line of sight.

Back

- Use a chair that is comfortable and provides good back support. The chair should be adjustable and provide armrests.
- Sit up straight. This maintains good posture and reduces strain. Think about good posture until it becomes common practice.
- Try standing up, stretching, and walking every hour. This will also reduce strain.

Legs

- Keep your thighs parallel to the ground.
- Rest your feet flat on the floor or use a footrest.
- When taking a break, walk around. This will stretch the muscles and promote circulation through your body.

Test Your Knowledge

Please do not write in this book. Place your answers on another sheet of paper.

1. List two basic purposes of a T-square.

2. Why is a vinyl board cover sometimes attached to the working surface of a drawing board?

3. _____ are transparent plastic tools used to draw vertical lines and inclined lines at 30°, 45°, and 60° angles.

4. A compass is used in drafting to draw _____ and _____.

5. A pencil is repointed with a(n) _____.

6. The best way to attach a drawing sheet to the board is to use drafting _____.

7. A(n) _____ is a small mesh pouch filled with very fine eraser particles used to collect excess graphite from a drawing surface.

8. What is the purpose of a *protractor*?

9. What grade of lead pencil is recommended for layout work? What grade pencil is recommended for darkening lines and lettering?

10. Describe the different meanings of the term *scale* in relation to drafting.

11. The whole number divisions on an architect's scale are used to make measurements in _____.

12. A(n) _____ scale is a fully divided scale with inch divisions that are multiples of 10.
13. List five basic hardware components that make up a CAD system.
14. What type of memory is used by a computer to temporarily store and process unsaved data for later retrieval?
15. Describe the drafting concepts that are common to both traditional board drafting and computer-aided drafting.
16. How should a computer monitor be positioned to minimize eyestrain and strain on the neck?

Outside Activities

1. Examine the drafting equipment assigned to you and make a record of its condition. Notify your teacher if any of your tools need repair.
2. Prepare a bulletin board display on computer-aided drafting (CAD).
3. Using catalogs of available drafting equipment, make a comparison of the cost of a fully equipped drafting room using drafting boards, drafting machines, and triangles, etc., relative to the cost of the equipment used in a CAD system.

Basic drafting techniques, such as those shown here, are vital in creating high-quality drawings. Carefully note the hand positions shown.

Set a compass to a radius measurement by drawing a line and adjusting the setting to the length of the line. Do not allow the compass to make contact with the scale.

Draw vertical lines using the T-square and a triangle. Draw from the bottom of the sheet to the top.

Draw horizontal lines using the T-square.

Large arcs and circles can be drawn with a beam compass.

5 Drafting Techniques

OBJECTIVES

After studying this chapter,
you should be able to:

◆ Demonstrate basic drafting skills.

◆ Use basic drafting skills and
techniques when solving drawing
problems.

◆ Make accurate measurements using a
drafting scale.

◆ Draw horizontal, vertical, inclined,
and perpendicular lines.

◆ Identify common sheet size formats
for drafting.

DRAFTING VOCABULARY

Architect's scale
Border lines
Centerlines
Construction lines
Cutting-plane lines
Dimension lines
Engineer's scale
Erasing shield
Extension lines
Guidelines
Hidden lines
Line conventions
Mechanical drafter's
  scale
Metric scale
Object lines
Phantom lines
Primary centerline
Scale
Scale clip
Secondary centerline
Section lines
Symmetry centerline
Visible lines

You were introduced to the Alphabet of Lines in Chapter 3. The lines you sketched can be drawn more uniformly and accurately with drafting instruments. As you learned in Chapter 3, object lines and other types of lines are used to create drawings.

To understand the language of industry, it is necessary that you know the characteristics of the various line styles and the correct way to use them in a drawing. See **Figure 5-1**. The drawing guidelines that you learn in this chapter will be applied throughout the text.

In drafting room language, the physical characteristics of lines and their different standards for use are known as *line conventions*.

Each type of line has a specific meaning. It is essential that each line is drawn properly. Lines should be drawn opaque so that you cannot see through them. In addition, each line should have the correct length and spacing of dashes. Most importantly, each line should have proper line continuity. In other words, a line should be uniform in width and density throughout its entire length. Recommended standards for line quality and weight are given in **Figure 5-2**.

The line weights shown in **Figure 5-2** are based on guidelines provided in the ASME drafting standard (ASME Y14.2M, *Line Conventions and Lettering*). In this system, lines

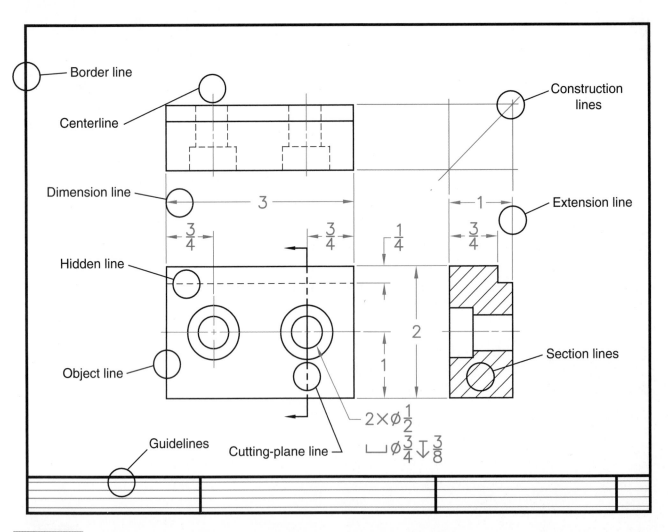

Figure 5-1 The lines in this drawing provide information about the dimensions, interior features, and construction of the object represented.

\multicolumn{5}{c}{Alphabet of Lines — Line Conventions}				
Line	Weight	Recommended grade pencil	Quality	Appearance
Construction	Very thin .012"	4H or 6H	Sharp	————————————————
Guideline	Very thin .012"	4H or 6H	Very sharp	————————————————
Border	Very thick .047"	H or 2H	Very sharp	━━━━━━━━━━━━━━━━
Object	Thick .024"	H or 2H	Very sharp	————————————————
Hidden	Thin .014"	4H or 6H	Very sharp	– – – – – – – – – – – – –
Dimension	Thin .014"	4H or 6H	Very sharp	⊢——— 2.50 ———⊣ Dimension line
Extension	Thin .014"	4H or 6H	Very sharp	⊢——— 2.50 ———⊣ Extension lines
Centerline	Thin .014"	4H or 6H	Very sharp	— – — – — – — – —
Cutting-plane	Thick .024"	H or 2H	Very sharp	↑— – — – — – —↑
Section	Thin .014"	4H or 6H	Very sharp	/////////
Phantom	Thin .014"	4H or 6H	Very sharp	— – – — – – —

Figure 5-2   Line conventions govern the manner in which lines are drawn. All lines should be continuous and sharp.

are drawn thick or thin, and thick lines are drawn approximately twice as thick as thin lines. However, drafting standards may vary depending on actual company or school practice. Notice that there are four different line weights specified in **Figure 5-2**. While actual line weights may vary, lines should range from very thin (construction lines and guidelines) to very thick (border lines). Visible lines are always drawn thick. These lines and other lines in the Alphabet of Lines are discussed in the following sections.

Line Conventions

Construction Lines and Guidelines

Construction lines are very thin, gray lines. They are drawn very lightly (approximately .012" thick) with very little pressure applied to the pencil. They are used to block in and lay out drawings. They may or may not be erased when the drawing is complete. Generally, they are erased on the final product.

Guidelines are drawn to the same weight as construction lines. They are used to specify and keep uniform the height of lettering on a drawing. They do not need to be erased and most generally are not. If they are drawn the proper weight, they will not show up on a print.

Both construction lines and guidelines need only to be dark enough so that the drafter can barely see them. They should be just dark enough to serve the purpose for which they are intended.

Border Lines

Border lines are the heaviest lines used in drafting. They are drawn approximately .047″ thick and may range in thickness from .031″ to .062″ depending on the size of the drawing sheet. It is important to have good contrast between border lines and the other lines on a drawing because border lines outline the area in which the drawing is to be created. If drawn properly, they create focus and draw the eye of the viewer to the object.

Object Lines

Object lines, also known as *visible lines*, are used to outline the *visible* edges and intersections of the object being drawn. They are drawn as thick, black lines (approximately .024″ thick) and should be drawn so that the views stand out sharply and clearly on the drawing.

Hidden Lines

Hidden lines, also known as *hidden object lines*, are used to outline the *invisible* edges and intersections of the object. They are

drawn thin (approximately .014″ thick) and are composed of short (.125″) dashes separated by .06″ spaces. The dashes and spaces may vary slightly according to the scale of the drawing. However, the dash sizes and spacing should be consistent throughout the drawing.

Cutting-Plane Lines

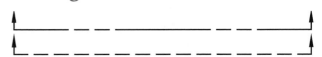

Cutting-plane lines are drawn to the same weight as object lines (approximately .024″ thick). They are used to indicate where the theoretical cut is taken for a sectional view.

There are two common ways to represent cutting-plane lines. In one method, the line is composed of a series of long (.75″ to 1.50″) dashes and two short (.125″) dashes. All dashes are separated by .06″ spaces. In the second method, the line is composed of a series of .25″ dashes separated by .06″ spaces. Cutting-plane lines and sectional views are discussed in Chapter 11.

Centerlines

Centerlines are used to represent the centers of round objects. Centerlines are classified as primary centerlines, secondary centerlines, and symmetry centerlines. These were introduced and illustrated in Chapter 3.

A *primary centerline* is used to indicate the center of a round object in the primary (true-shape) view of the object. It is composed of a small crosshair (.125″) with .06″ spaces around the crosshair and long lines that extend through the perimeter of the largest circle or arc for which the center point is valid.

A *secondary centerline* is made up of alternating long (.75″ to 1.50″) and short (.125″) dashes with .06″ spaces between. It is drawn in the secondary view of whatever is round. It should extend through the limits of the round object. It originates or is projected from the primary center in the primary view.

A *symmetry centerline* has the same dash components as a secondary centerline and is used to locate the center of an object that is symmetric.

All types of centerlines are thin lines (approximately .014″ thick). No centerline should ever start or stop at an object line. It should either stop short of or extend through the limits of whatever is round or cylindrical in shape.

Dimension Lines

Dimension lines are usually terminated at each end with arrowheads and placed between two extension lines. In some types of drafting, other styles of terminators are used. The arrow tips should always touch but not overlap the extension lines. With few exceptions, a dimension line is broken with the dimension number or fraction placed at the midpoint between the arrowheads. Dimension lines are drawn at the same weight as centerlines (approximately .014″ thick). There are specific rules for the correct placement and use of dimension lines. Dimensioning is discussed in Chapter 10.

Extension Lines

Extension lines extend dimensions beyond the outline of a view so that the dimensions can be read easily. They are drawn at the same weight as dimension lines and centerlines (approximately .014″ thick). These lines indicate the beginning and ending points of a linear distance. An extension line begins approximately .06″ away from the edge, intersection, or detail of the object and extends about .125″ past the last dimension line.

Section Lines

Section lines are used in sectional views when drawing the inside features of an object to indicate the surfaces exposed by a cutting plane. Section lines are also used to indicate general classifications of materials. General purpose section lines are parallel, inclined (45°) lines spaced approximately .125″ apart. They are drawn to the same line weight as centerlines (approximately .014″ thick).

Phantom Lines

Phantom lines are used to indicate alternate positions of moving parts, repeated details for parts such as threads and springs, or paths of motion of objects. Phantom lines are drawn to the same line weight as centerlines (approximately .014″ thick). They are composed of long (.75″ to 1.50″) dashes alternated with pairs of short (.125″) dashes, with .06″ spaces in between.

Using a Scale

There are three important words to remember when creating a drawing. These are accuracy, neatness, and speed. Drawings must be accurate, clean and legible, and completed rapidly. Since nearly every line on a mechanical drawing must be a measured line, you must be able to make accurate measurements if your drawings are to be made accurately.

Measurements are made in the drafting room with a *scale*, **Figure 5-3**. As discussed in Chapter 4, the term *scale* means both the device or tool for making measurements and the size to which the drawing is made. A large object such as a house may be scaled down in size to fit the drafting media. A small object such as a pager may be scaled up in size so that small details of the object may be seen more easily.

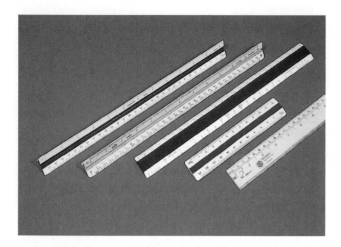

Figure 5-3 Various types of inch and metric scales.

There are four types of scales commonly used in drafting. These are the *architect's scale*, *engineer's scale*, *mechanical drafter's scale*, and *metric scale*.

Scales have graduations on the edges that show lengths used to indicate larger or smaller measurements. For example, a 1/4″ measurement on a 1/4″ architect's scale equals 1′-0″ on the actual object. While several different shapes of scales are available, **Figure 5-4**, triangular-shaped scales are most widely found in the school drafting room.

A *scale clip* provides a handle to lift and move a triangular scale. It also provides a way to keep track of the scale presently in use, **Figure 5-5**. Much time can be wasted by not marking the currently used scale. If a scale clip is not available, one can be created by using a strategically placed strip of drafting tape.

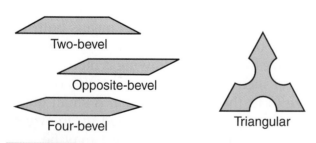

Two-bevel

Opposite-bevel

Four-bevel

Triangular

Figure 5-4 Scales are available in a number of different shapes.

Figure 5-5 The scale clip keeps the desired scale edge in an upright position. No time is wasted looking for the scale edge you are using.

Using an Architect's Scale

The triangular architect's scale has six faces with 11 different scales, **Figure 5-6**. Each face is graduated differently. There is one face where the inch divisions are each divided into 16 parts. This is the 16 scale. Each division is equal to 1/16 of an inch, **Figure 5-7**. To read the scale, imagine that the 1/16 divisions are numbered as shown in **Figure 5-8**. At first, you may find it easier to count the spaces when you measure. However, after some practice, this should not be necessary. First, measure the number of whole inches along the scale. Then, determine the remainder of the measurement by reading the 1/16 divisions. Reduce fractions to lowest terms. If you

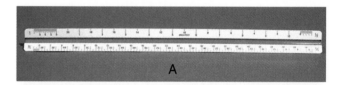

A

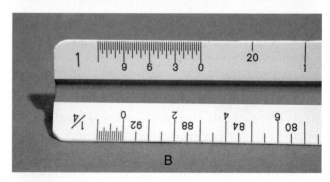

B

Figure 5-6 The architect's scale. A—The whole number divisions along the face of each scale represent feet. B—The divisions at the end of the scale represent portions of a foot (inches). Shown are the 1″ and 1/4″ scales.

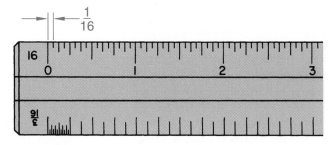

Figure 5-7 The 16 scale is graduated in sixteenths of an inch.

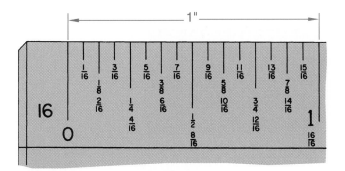

Figure 5-8 The 1/16 divisions of the 16 scale are numbered here for reference.

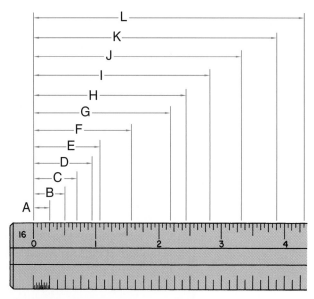

Figure 5-9 How many of these measurements can you answer correctly? On a piece of paper, write the letters *A* to *L*. After each letter, write the correct measurement. Reduce fractions to the lowest terms.

have difficulty reading the 16 scale, you must consult your instructor for help. It is absolutely essential that you understand this scale and can use it accurately.

A section of the 16 scale is shown in **Figure 5-9**. How many of the measurements can you read correctly?

After you can read and make measurements accurately and quickly to one-sixteenth of an inch, examine the other faces on the scale. Each division on the other scales, such as the 1/4″ scale, represents one foot (12″ or 1′-0″) of actual measurement. In other words, each division represents one foot on the actual object being drawn reduced to a particular length on the drafting media (paper). On the 1/4″ scale, for example, the foot divisions measure 1/4″ on the paper when drawn.

The architect's scale is commonly used to reduce the size of buildings so that they can be represented on a drawing. If the 1/4″ scale is used to measure distances on paper for the floor plan of a house, for example, each 1/4″

distance along the edge of the architect's scale, as measured on the paper, represents 1′-0″ of actual distance on the house to be built.

As discussed in Chapter 4, the architect's scale is an *open-divided scale*. This means that measurements are made by first reading the number of whole number divisions on the scale representing feet. The foot divisions are not subdivided. See **Figure 5-10**. The number of inches is then determined by reading the number of divisions at the end of the scale representing subdivisions of a foot (inches). See **Figure 5-11**. The number of subdivisions at the end of the scale corresponds to the specific scale used. For example, the 1/4″ = 1′-0″ scale has 12 subdivisions for the foot division, each representing 1″.

There are two scales on each face of the architect's scale. One scale is read from one end of the scale and the other is read from the opposite end. Each is marked on one end to identify the scale divisions corresponding to the specific scale. The scales on each face are grouped so that the divisions on one scale are twice as large as the divisions on the other

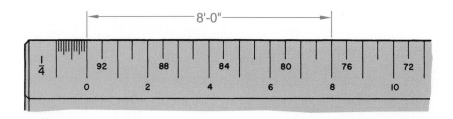

Figure 5-10 Measuring feet on the 1/4″ = 1′-0″ architect's scale. Count to the right of zero.

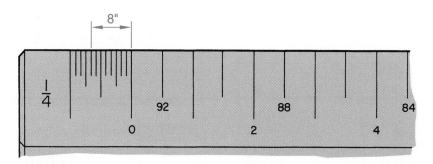

Figure 5-11 Measuring inches on an architect's scale. Count to the left of zero.

scale. These groupings are 3/32″ and 3/16″, 1/8″ and 1/4″, 3/8″ and 3/4″, 1/2″ and 1″, and 1-1/2″ and 3″. Referring to **Figure 5-10**, the upper divisions of the scale (those above the foot divisions for the 1/4″ = 1′-0″ scale) represent the foot divisions at the end of the 1/8″ = 1′-0″ scale.

The 3″ scale is used to make 3″ = 1′-0″ drawings. This means that 1′-0″ measurements have been reduced to 3″ along the edge of the scale. A drawing made using this scale would be one-quarter (1/4) actual size. Every 3″ distance measured on the paper would represent 1′-0″ on the actual manufactured or constructed object. See **Figure 5-12**.

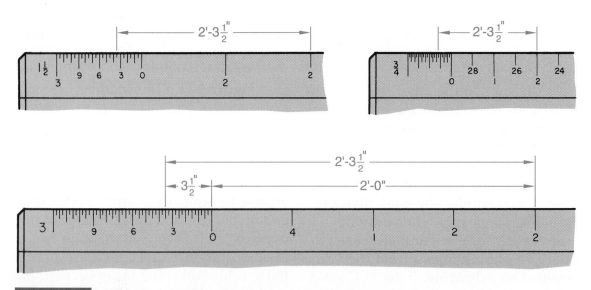

Figure 5-12 Reduction measurements made with architect's scales. The whole number graduations represent feet. The graduations at the end of each scale represent portions of a foot.

Using a Metric Scale

A metric scale is used to make measurements based on the metric system. Most drawings using this system are dimensioned in millimeters. As discussed in Chapter 4, a metric scale is expressed as a ratio. Full-size drawings are made with a 1:1 scale. A 1:2 scale is used when drawings are reduced to half size, **Figure 5-13**. Standard metric scales are shown in **Figure 5-14**. For architectural drafting, reduction scales above 1:10 are most often used. Architectural drafting is discussed in more detail in Chapter 24.

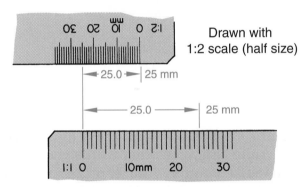

Drawn with
1:2 scale (half size)

Drawn with 1:1 scale (full size)

Figure 5-13 Metric scales are expressed in ratios. The full-size and half-size scales have graduations in millimeters.

Common Drafting Scales

Customary Inch		Nearest Metric Equivalent (mm)
1:2500	(1″ = 208′)	1:2000
1:1250	(1″ = 104′)	1:1000
1:384	(1/32″ = 1′)	1:500
1:192	(1/16″ = 1′)	1:200
1:96	(1/8″ = 1′)	1:100
1:48	(1/4″ = 1′)	1:50
1:24	(1/2″ = 1′)	1:20
1:12	(1″ = 1′)	1:10
1:4	Quarter-size (3″ = 1′)	1:5
1:2	Half-size (6″ = 1′)	1:2
1:1	Full-size (12″ = 1′)	1:1

Figure 5-14 A comparison of inch and metric scales.

Most metric drawings are created with a 1:1 metric scale. Each division is 1 mm, and the numbered graduations are multiples of 10 (0 mm, 10 mm, 20 mm, 30 mm, etc.). See **Figure 5-15**.

To make a measurement of 52.5 mm, read to the 50 mm division, and then add 2.5 mm. The .5 mm measurement falls midway between two divisions, **Figure 5-16**.

A section of a 1:1 scale is shown in **Figure 5-17**. How many of these measurements can you read correctly?

Making Measurements

To make a measurement, observe the scale from directly above. Mark the desired measurement on the paper by using a light perpendicular line made with a sharp pencil, **Figure 5-18**.

Keep the scale clean. Do not mark on it or use it as a straightedge. Scales are measuring devices. They are not intended to be used to draw lines. All straight lines on a drawing should be made along the edge of a T-square or a triangle—never along the edge of a scale.

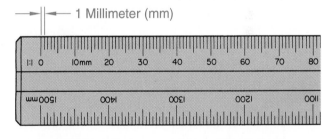

Figure 5-15 A section of a 1:1 metric scale. Each division is equal to 1 mm.

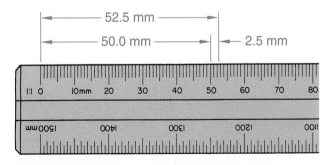

Figure 5-16 Making a measurement of 52.5 mm.

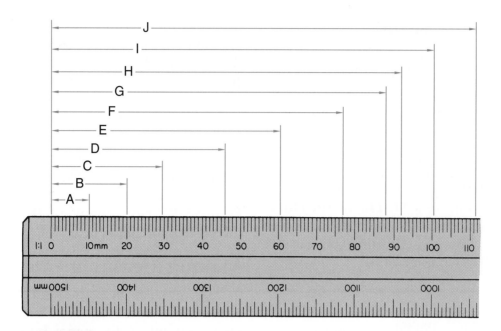

Figure 5-17 How many of these measurements can you answer correctly? On a piece of paper, write the letters *A* to *J*. After each letter, write the correct answer. Ask your instructor to check your answers.

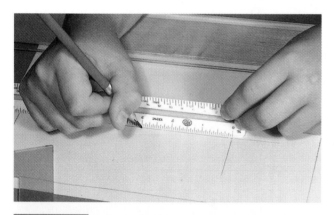

Figure 5-18 When making a measurement, observe the scale from directly above. Mark the desired measurement on the paper with a light perpendicular line using a sharp pencil.

Drawing Lines with Instruments

Care must be taken when drawing different types of lines. Object lines, hidden lines, and centerlines should have a distinct appearance and consistent quality throughout the drawing. In addition, all lines must be uniform in width and darkness throughout their entire length. In other words, they must have good continuity from end to end.

When lines are drawn using instruments, the pencil should form approximately a 30° angle with the paper and a 30° angle against the drawing edge. The pencil tip should intersect the straightedge "where the plastic meets the paper." The pencil should lean in the direction you are drawing the line. Lines should be "pulled" onto the paper, not "pushed." This is true regardless of whether the line is horizontal, vertical, inclined, or curved.

As you draw a line, you should be able to see the line go onto the paper. If you can't see the line, situate yourself so that you can. If you cannot see the line going onto the paper, there is a chance the line will not be accurate. It has been said that some people cannot draw a straight line with a straightedge. These people are the ones who allow the side of the pencil (instead of the tip) to follow the edge of the straightedge. Doing this can allow the tip to wander, causing the line to be crooked. Keeping your pencil constantly at the correct angle will eliminate this problem. Also, keep your wrist rigid as you pull the line onto the paper. Do not flex your wrist. If you flex your wrist, it causes the line to be "wiped" onto the paper and can cause inconsistency in line weight and accuracy.

To keep lines uniform in weight, especially if a long line is being drawn, rotate the pencil between your thumb and forefinger as you pull the line onto the paper. Rotating the pencil will keep the point sharper and therefore keep you from having to sharpen your pencil too often. Rotate the top of the pencil away from you (clockwise when looking at the unsharpened end of the pencil).

Horizontal lines are drawn with a T-square, **Figure 5-19**. If you are right-handed, draw from left to right. Hold the T-square head firmly against the *left* edge of the drawing board. If you are left-handed, use the right edge of the drawing board and draw lines from right to left. See **Figure 5-20**.

Figure 5-19   Using the T-square to draw horizontal lines. Note how the T-square head is held against the edge of the drawing board. The pencil should be inclined about 30°.

Note

Most instruction in this book reflects right-handed drafting. Left-handed drafters must reverse most of the procedures to be successful. Ask your instructor if you are uncertain as to whether you are drawing correctly.

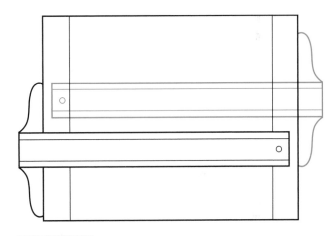

Figure 5-20   Left-handed drafters use the right edge of the drawing board to align the T-square.

Vertical lines are drawn using a triangle in combination with the T-square. They are drawn from the bottom to the top of the sheet using the overhand method, **Figure 5-21**. The base of the triangle must rest on the blade of the T-square. Use your left hand to hold the triangle in place. Try to extend the fingers of your left hand as far up the triangle as possible to eliminate the chance that the top end of the triangle will "lift" and the pencil will slip under it.

Inclined lines are not vertical or horizontal. The drawing procedure depends on the direction of the slope. Lines that incline

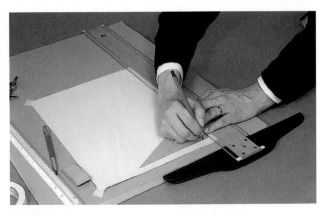

Figure 5-21   Vertical lines are drawn using a triangle. They are drawn from the bottom to the top of the sheet. Incline the pencil in the direction of travel.

to the left are drawn more easily from the top downward, **Figure 5-22**. Those that incline to the right should be drawn from the bottom upward, **Figure 5-23**. The movement of the pencil is still basically left to right even though the lines are inclined differently.

When drawing horizontal, vertical, and inclined lines, maintaining the proper pencil angle and using the drawing techniques discussed in this section are essential for achieving maximum accuracy. Apply these guidelines as you gain more drawing practice.

Drawing a Line Perpendicular to a Given Line

To draw a line perpendicular to a given line, place the hypotenuse (long edge) of any triangle parallel to the given line, **Figure 5-24**. Support the triangle on the T-square or another triangle. Rotate the first triangle about the 90° corner to draw a line perpendicular to the given line.

Another technique used to draw a line perpendicular to a given line requires that you place either leg of the triangle parallel to the given line, **Figure 5-25**. Support this triangle's

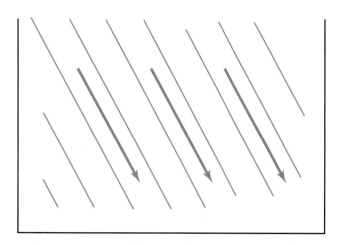

Figure 5-22 Lines that incline to the left are drawn from the top down.

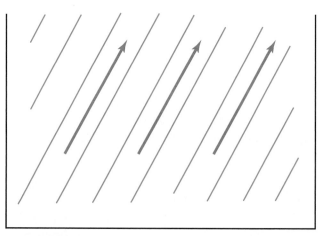

Figure 5-23 Lines that incline to the right are drawn from the bottom up.

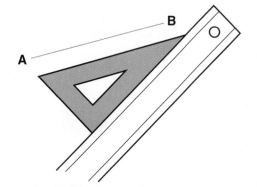

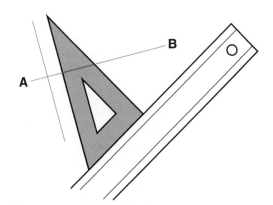

Figure 5-24 Drawing a line perpendicular to a given line using a T-square and triangle. Be sure to hold the base (T-square) firmly in place when the triangle is moved.

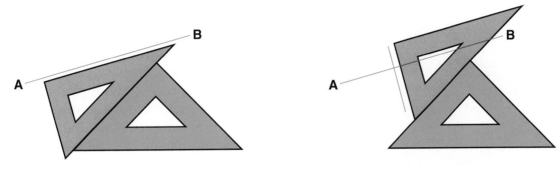

Figure 5-25 Drawing a line perpendicular to a given line using two triangles.

hypotenuse side on the T-square or another triangle. Slide the first triangle on the supporting triangle or T-square, then draw the line. It will be perpendicular to the given line.

There is another method that may be easier to remember for some drafters, **Figure 5-26**. Using the 45° and 30°-60° triangles, place the hypotenuse of the 45° triangle against the hypotenuse of the 30°-60° triangle. While keeping both triangles together, align the next longest edge of the 30°-60° triangle so that it is parallel to the given line. While holding the 45° triangle rigid, slide the 30°-60° triangle along the hypotenuse of the 45° triangle until the shortest side of the 30°-60° triangle crosses the given line. The resulting alignment creates a perpendicular intersection with the given line. Draw the perpendicular line along the short side of the 30°-60° triangle.

Erasing Errors

When drawing, every effort should be made to prevent mistakes. However, even the best drafter must occasionally make changes on a drawing. This will require erasing.

The following are some suggestions to follow when erasing:

1. Keep your hands and instruments clean. This will help to keep "smudges" to a minimum. Also, selecting an eraser that mixes well with the drafter's body chemistry will help eliminate smears and smudges. Some natural oils in the skin do not mix well with certain types of erasers. Trial and error will determine the best eraser for you.
2. Use an *erasing shield* whenever possible, **Figure 5-27**. Select an opening that will

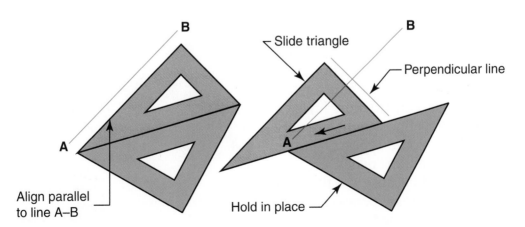

Figure 5-26 Using the 45° and 30°-60° triangles to draw a line perpendicular to another line.

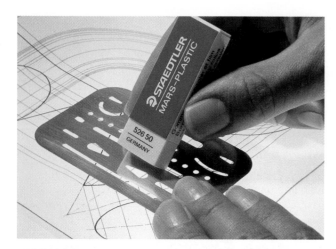

Figure 5-27   An erasing shield protects the area around where the correction or erasure is being made.

expose only the area to be erased. The shield will protect the rest of the drawing while the erasure is made. Learning to use the erasing shield correctly and consistently will result in saving vast amounts of time because lines will not be erased accidentally and need "touching-up." Such touch-ups take a lot of time.

3. Clean all eraser crumbs from the board immediately after making an erasure. Remove them with a brush or clean cloth. The preferred method is to use a brush. *Do not use your hands.*

4. Firmly hold the paper with your free hand when erasing. This will keep the paper from wrinkling or accidentally tearing.

5. Erasing will remove the lead but will not take the pencil grooves from the paper. Avoid deep, wide grooves by first blocking in all views with light construction lines. Using correctly drawn construction lines can all but eliminate neatness errors on drawings because construction lines, if drawn to the correct line weight, are very easily erased. On some types of paper, such as drafting vellum, pencil grooves cannot be removed because the fibers of the paper have been compressed. When the fibers are compressed, the paper is not as translucent and "ghost lines" will appear on the reproduction.

Using a Compass

In general drafting work, circles and arcs are drawn with a compass. Care must be taken so that lines drawn with the compass are the same weight as lines produced with the pencil. To accomplish this, the compass lead used should be one or two grades softer than that of the pencil. Also, it is recommended that circles and arcs are darkened on drawings first, to the proper object line weight, and then straight lines can be drawn to match the weight of circles and arcs drawn with the compass.

Sharpen the lead and adjust the point as shown in **Figure 5-28**. Do not forget to adjust the point after each sharpening. The correct way to hold the compass while sharpening the lead is shown in **Figure 5-29**.

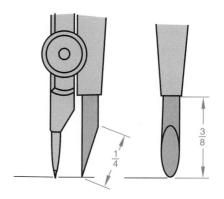

Figure 5-28   Sharpening and adjusting the compass lead. Readjust the point each time the lead is sharpened.

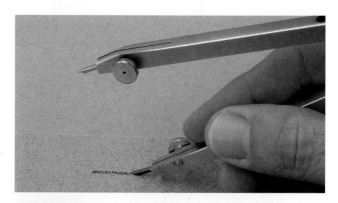

Figure 5-29   The correct method of holding the compass while sharpening the lead.

To set a compass, draw a line on scrap paper that is equal in length to the desired radius. Adjust the compass on this line, **Figure 5-30**. Avoid setting a compass on the scale. The point will eventually ruin the division lines on the scale.

To draw a circle, first locate the center of the circle by drawing vertical and horizontal intersecting lines (centerlines). Place the sharp tip of the compass at the intersection of the two lines (the center point). Rotate the compass in a clockwise direction between your thumb and forefinger, **Figure 5-31**. Incline the tool in the direction of rotation. Start and complete the circle on the centerlines. When drawing a series of concentric circles (circles with the same center), draw the smallest circle first and proceed to draw the rest of the circles in a smallest-to-largest sequence.

Darkening Lines

As previously discussed, a drawing begins by "blocking in" the entire object with construction lines of the proper weight. When creating a high-quality end product is your goal, the blocking-in procedure is absolutely

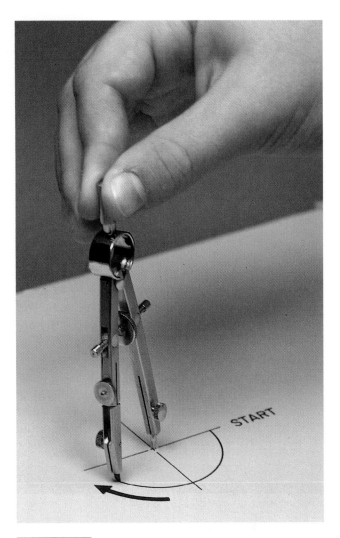

Figure 5-31 Drawing a circle. Note how the compass is inclined in the direction of rotation. Start drawing the circle on a centerline if one is available.

essential. Upon determining which lines need to be darkened to certain line weights and styles, using the following darkening sequence will result in improved accuracy, superior line continuity, and a neater, cleaner drawing. The key to neatness is to pass instruments back and forth across the drawing as few times as possible. This not only keeps the drawing clean, it also helps keep the instruments clean.

Always darken lines created with a compass first because it is much easier to draw black, sharp object lines against the edge of a drawing instrument. Work hard to create the best object lines for circles and arcs that

Figure 5-30 Adjust the compass to the desired radius size of a measured line. Never set it to size directly on the scale.

ACADEMIC LINK

Mathematics skills are very important in drafting. You will frequently encounter situations that require calculations when laying out drawings, drawing views, and placing dimensions. In order to properly use drawing tools such as the scale and triangle, you must understand basic mathematic concepts.

Using a scale requires the ability to work with fractions. You must be able to add, subtract, multiply, and divide fractions. For example, the fractional value of 1/4 is twice the fractional value of 1/8. Adding these two fractions results in a sum of 3/8. Also, the fractional value of 3/8 is half the fractional value of 3/4.

It is also important to be able to convert fractional values to decimal values. For example, 3/4 is equal to 0.75, 1/2 is equal to 0.50, 1/4 is equal to 0.25, and 1/8 is equal to 0.125.

You will frequently use formulas when working with geometric shapes. For example, if you know the diameter of a circle or arc, you can determine the radius by dividing the diameter in half ($R = D/2$). To find the area or perimeter of a rectangle, you must know the lengths of two sides. The area is found by multiplying the width of the rectangle by its height ($A = W \times H$). The perimeter is found by adding the four sides together (the opposite sides of the rectangle are equal.)

When measuring angles, you must be able to add and subtract angular values. If you are trying to determine a missing angular value within a triangular shape, you can subtract the sum of the known two angles from 180° to calculate the missing value (the three angles add up to 180°).

you can. Then match all other object lines to whatever line weight you produced with the compass. Contrast all other line weights to this object line weight. Border lines should be roughly twice as thick and hidden lines and centerlines should be roughly half as thick.

Proceed with darkening object lines in the following order. Start with irregular curves. Then, darken inclined lines. Finally, darken vertical and horizontal lines. Brush off excess graphite after each type is completed. It does not matter whether vertical or horizontal object lines are darkened last. However, they should be darkened after the other object lines because there are almost always more vertical and horizontal lines than any of the other types. Darken all horizontal lines by moving the T-square from the top of the drawing to the bottom, moving away from the line that was just darkened. Do the same with the vertical lines, moving the triangle away from the line just drawn. Regardless of the type of lines being drawn, always move away from the line you have just drawn.

When all object lines are darkened, proceed with the same sequence in darkening the thin weight lines. Upon completing the darkening procedure for the entire drawing, darken all lettering (including the title block information) working from the top of the drawing down. The last lines to be darkened before the drawing is completed for evaluation are the border lines. These are the widest, smeariest lines on any drawing and should be completed last to preserve the neatness and cleanliness of the final product.

Attaching a Drawing Sheet to the Board

The drawing sheet should be attached to the board with drafting tape. Tape is preferred because it does not damage the board. Before attempting to attach the paper, remove all eraser crumbs.

To attach the paper, place the sheet on the board as shown in **Figure 5-32**. Center the sheet vertically. Left-handed drafters should use the right-hand portion of the board.

Place the T-square on the board with the head firmly against the left edge. Slide it up until the top of the blade is in line with the top edge of the drawing sheet, **Figure 5-33**. Position the sheet so the top edge is parallel with the T-square blade. Fasten the sheet to the board by taping the top two corners. Larger or lighter weight sheets may also require fasteners on the bottom corners.

The following procedure is recommended when positioning and attaching A-size (8-1/2″ × 11″) and A4 (210 mm × 297 mm) size drawing sheets. Position the sheet on the board as shown in **Figure 5-32**.

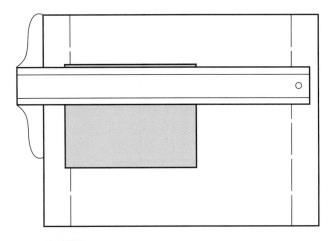

Figure 5-33   Aligning the top of the drawing sheet with the T-square.

Place the T-square head firmly against the left edge of the board. Align the drawing sheet by sliding the T-square blade until it contacts the bottom edge of the paper, **Figure 5-34**. Align the sheet with this edge. Fasten the sheet to the board.

Lightweight paper, like tracing vellum, is slightly more difficult to attach to the board. It has a tendency to wrinkle. This paper is aligned using the sequence shown in **Figure 5-35**.

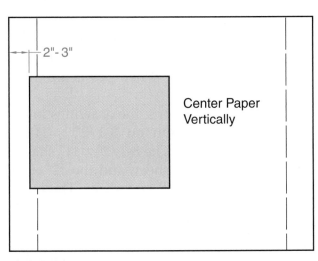

2″- 3″

Center Paper Vertically

Figure 5-32   Locating the drawing sheet on the board.

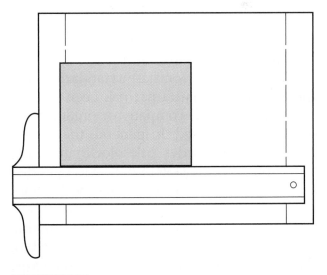

Figure 5-34   The drawing sheet can also be aligned on the board by placing the bottom edge of the sheet on the T-square blade.

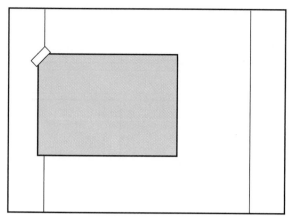

1. Use the T-square to align the sheet on the board. Fasten the upper-left corner of the sheet with the tape.

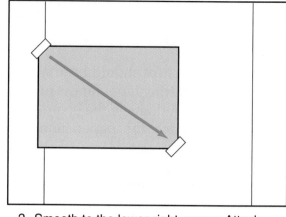

2. Smooth to the lower-right corner. Attach sheet.

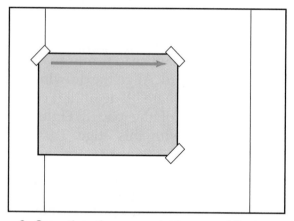

3. Smooth to the upper-right corner. Attach sheet.

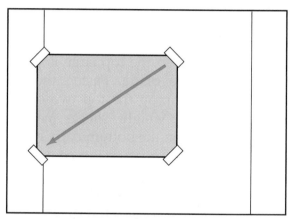

4. Smooth to the lower-left corner. Finish attaching the sheet.

Figure 5-35 Sequence recommended for attaching lightweight paper (such as tracing vellum) to the board.

Drafting Sheet Formats

Most drafting rooms use a standard layout format. Often, this format has been created specifically for the company or organization for which it is used. In general, the format consists of the border, title block, and standard notes, **Figure 5-36**. A border is included to define the drawing area of the sheet. A nice thick, black border causes the viewer's eye to focus and remain focused on the drawing within the border. The title block and standard notes provide information that is necessary for the manufacture and/or assembly of the object described on the drawing sheet. A sample preprinted title block is shown in **Figure 5-37**.

Most industrial firms employ standard drawing sheet sizes. Drawings made on standard sheet sizes are easier to file. They also present less difficulty when prints are made from them.

With few exceptions, the drawings in this text should be drawn on 8-1/2″ × 11″ or 11″ × 17″ size sheets. The 8-1/2″ × 11″ sheet is known as an A-size sheet, and the 11″ × 17″ sheet is known as a B-size sheet. The corresponding metric sheet sizes are the A4 (210 mm × 297 mm) and A3 (297 mm × 420 mm) size sheets.

Plan your work carefully. Avoid using a large sheet when a smaller size sheet will do.

ENGINEERS STAMP
DESIGNED BY
DRAWN BY
CHECKED BY
DATE
PROJECT NO.
SHEET NO.

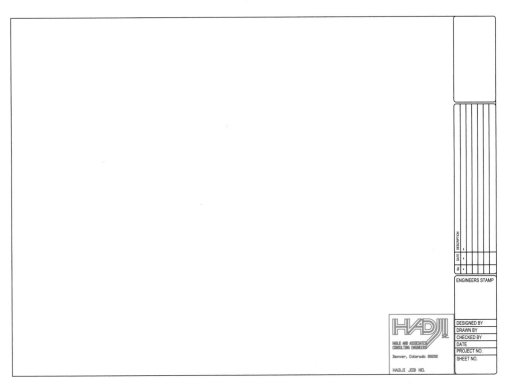

Figure 5-36 Preprinted drawing sheets save a great deal of time for the drafter.

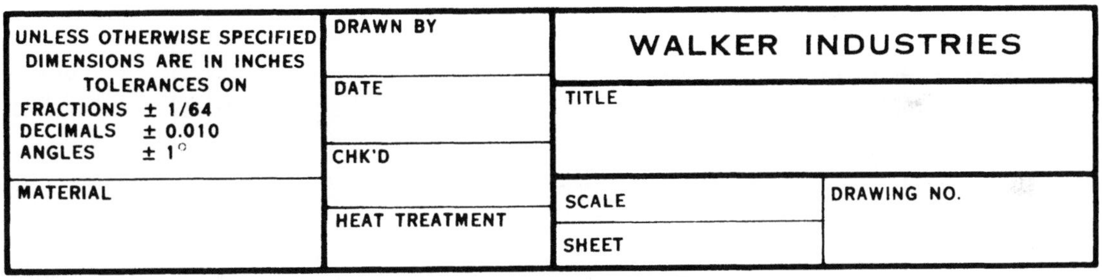

UNLESS OTHERWISE SPECIFIED
DIMENSIONS ARE IN INCHES
TOLERANCES ON
FRACTIONS ± 1/64
DECIMALS ± 0.010
ANGLES ± 1°
MATERIAL
DRAWN BY
DATE
CHK'D
HEAT TREATMENT
WALKER INDUSTRIES
TITLE
SCALE
SHEET
DRAWING NO.

Figure 5-37 A preprinted title block. When one is used, only the border has to be drawn.

Recommended Drawing Sheet Formats

The following drawing sheet formats are suggested for use, although these may be adjusted or customized by your instructor. These formats can be used for the drawing problems in this text. The first format is similar to the sketching sheet format presented in Chapter 3. See **Figure 5-38**. It should only be used when class time is limited or when a "quick" format is needed. To save time, your instructor may wish to use this format when assigning a practical test problem.

A more formal sheet format is prepared as follows. Draw a 1/2" (12.5 mm) border on the sheet, **Figure 5-39**. Use a short, light pencil stroke, not a dot, as the guide for locating the border line. The light mark should be covered when the border line is drawn. Allow another 1/2" (12.5 mm) for the title block. Divide the title block as shown in **Figure 5-40**. Layout for a vertical sheet is shown in **Figure 5-41**.

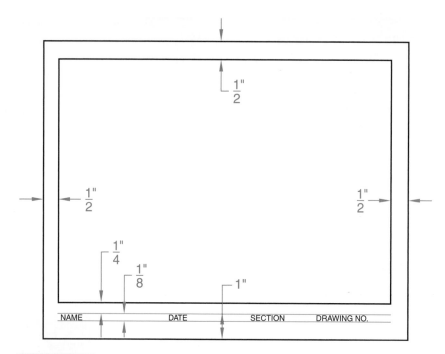

Figure 5-38 A basic drawing sheet format for quick setup.

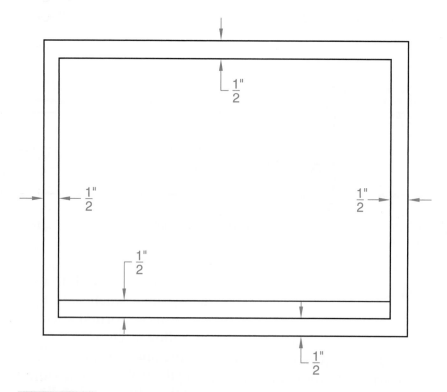

Figure 5-39 Begin the sheet layout by drawing a 1/2″ border and title block.

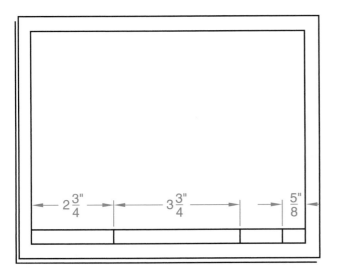

Figure 5-40 The title block is divided as shown.

Guidelines for the title block are then drawn, **Figure 5-42**. They should be drawn very lightly. Letter the necessary information when the drawing is completed and darkened to the correct line weights, **Figure 5-43**.

Note

It is suggested that you letter the title block after you complete the drawing because each letter is made up of object lines and should therefore be drawn with the object line weight. If the title block is lettered before beginning the drawing, there will be more graphite on the paper to smear when the drawing is made.

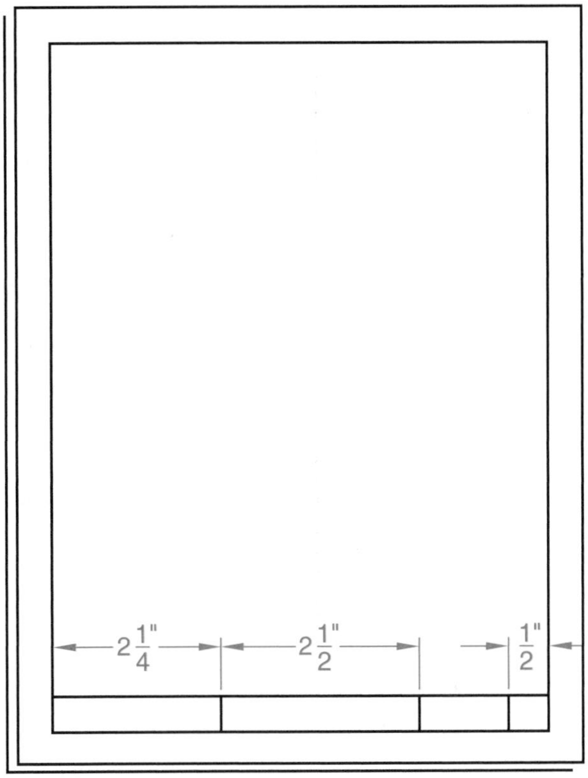

Figure 5-41 A vertical drawing sheet format.

It is recommended that duplicating equipment be used to prepare preprinted drawing sheets. The sheet format and the title block should be designed to meet the specific requirements of the drafting department and industry. Prescribed tolerances can be printed on the sheets. Preprinted drafting sheets will save a great deal of time by eliminating repetitive and time-consuming drawing operations.

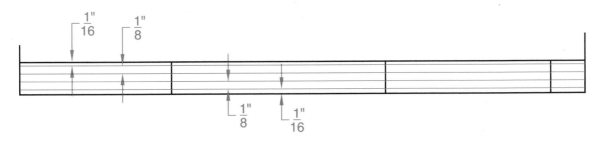

Figure 5-42 The layout of guidelines for lettering.

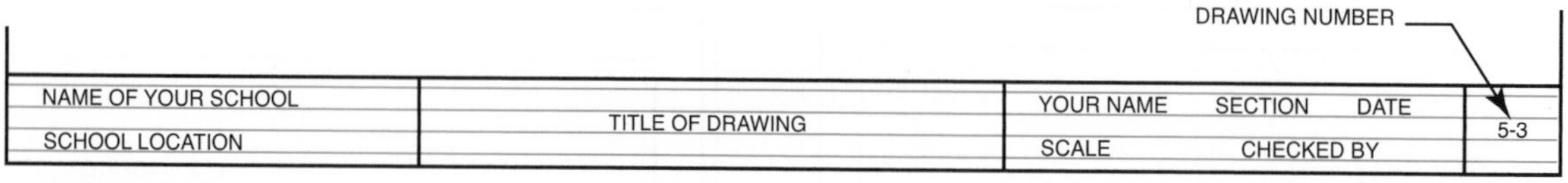

NAME OF YOUR SCHOOL	TITLE OF DRAWING	YOUR NAME SECTION DATE	DRAWING NUMBER
SCHOOL LOCATION		SCALE CHECKED BY	5-3

Figure 5-43 Suggested information to be lettered on drawing sheets. The title block should be filled in only after the drawing is completed.

Test Your Knowledge

Please do not write in this book. Place your answers on another sheet of paper.

1. Identify these lines:

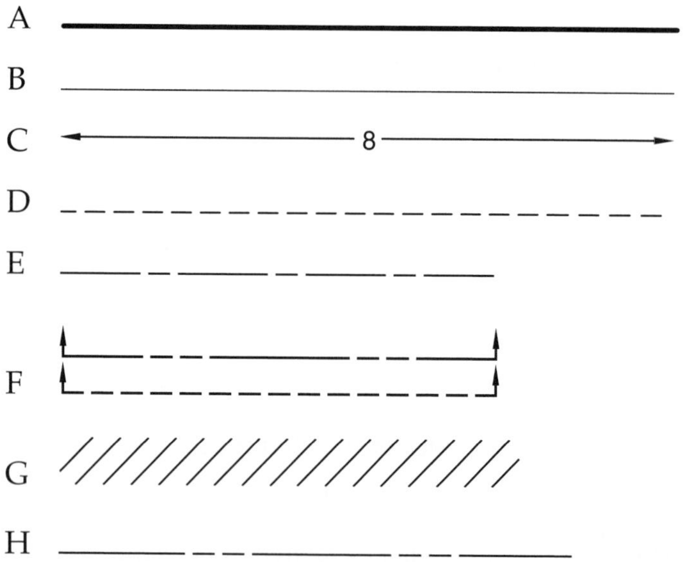

   A ————————————————

   B ————————————————

   C ◄————— 8 —————►

   D – – – – – – – – – – – – – – – –

   E —— – – —— – – ——

   F (bracket with dashed lines)

   G //////////////////

   H ——— – – ——— – – ———

2. In drafting room language, the physical characteristics of the lines in Question 1 and their different standards for use are known as line _____.

3. Identify four different types of scales that are commonly used for measuring drawings.

4. In manual drafting, a(n) _____ is most commonly used to draw horizontal lines.

5. The _____ and _____ are used in combination to draw vertical lines.

6. When erasing errors on a drawing, the erasing _____ is often used to protect surrounding areas while using an eraser.

7. Briefly discuss how to draw a circle with a compass.

8. Briefly discuss how to attach a drawing sheet to a board using drafting tape and a T-square.

9. What are the dimensions (in inches) of an A-size sheet and a B-size sheet?

10. Explain why a title block should be lettered after completing a drawing (and not before).

Outside Activities

1. Obtain samples of preprinted drawing sheets used in industry. After studying these industrial examples, design a sheet format for your school's drafting department.

2. Obtain a compass and demonstrate to the class the proper way to sharpen the lead, adjust the length of the point, set the compass to the proper radius, and draw a circle.

Drawing Problems

Duplicate the drawings shown on the problem sheets on the following pages. Use the dimensions provided. Follow the directions on each problem sheet.

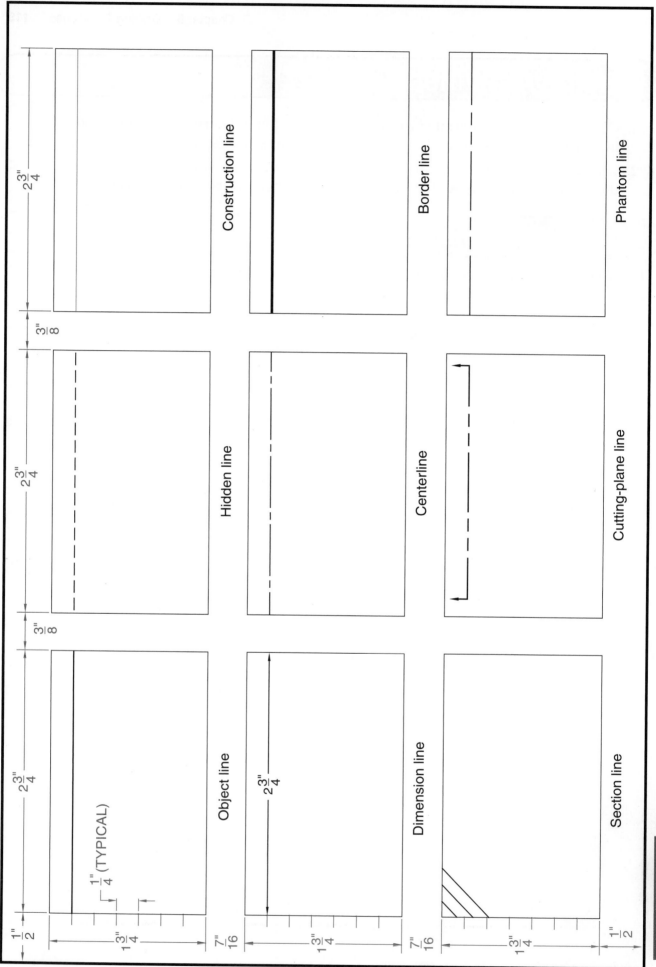

Problem Sheet 5-1 Alphabet of Lines. Using the examples shown, draw each type of line in the spaces provided.

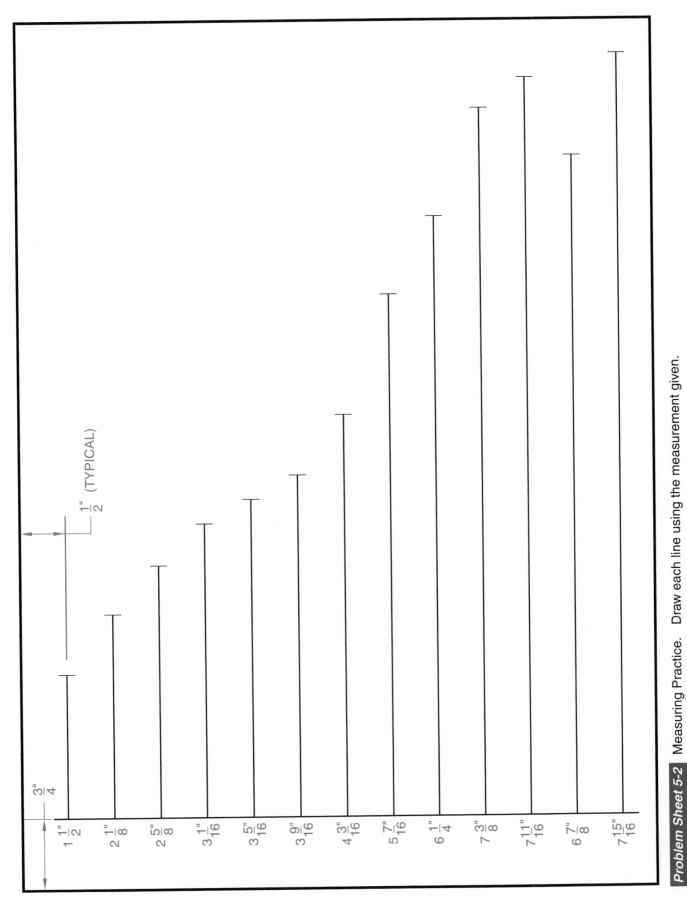

$\frac{3}{4}$"

$\frac{1}{2}$" (TYPICAL)

1 $1\frac{1}{2}$"
2 $2\frac{1}{8}$"
3 $2\frac{5}{8}$"
4 $3\frac{1}{16}$"
5 $3\frac{5}{16}$"
6 $3\frac{9}{16}$"
7 $4\frac{3}{16}$"
8 $5\frac{7}{16}$"
9 $6\frac{1}{4}$"
10 $7\frac{3}{8}$"
11 $7\frac{11}{16}$"
12 $6\frac{7}{8}$"
13 $7\frac{15}{16}$"

Problem Sheet 5-2   Measuring Practice.   Draw each line using the measurement given.

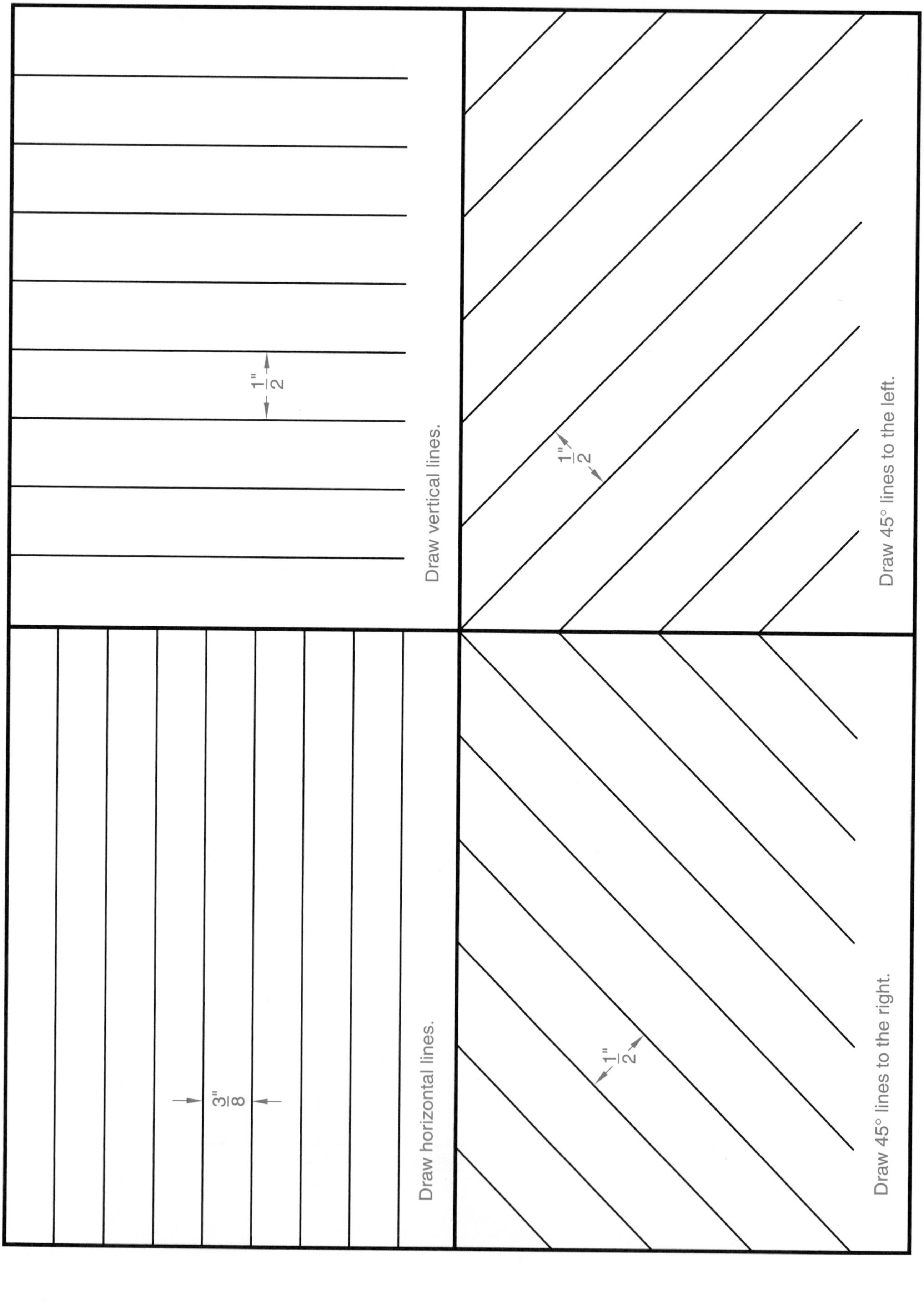

$\frac{1}{2}$"

Draw vertical lines.

$\frac{1}{2}$"

Draw 45° lines to the left.

$\frac{3}{8}$"

Draw horizontal lines.

$\frac{1}{2}$"

Draw 45° lines to the right.

Problem Sheet 5-3 Instrument Practice.

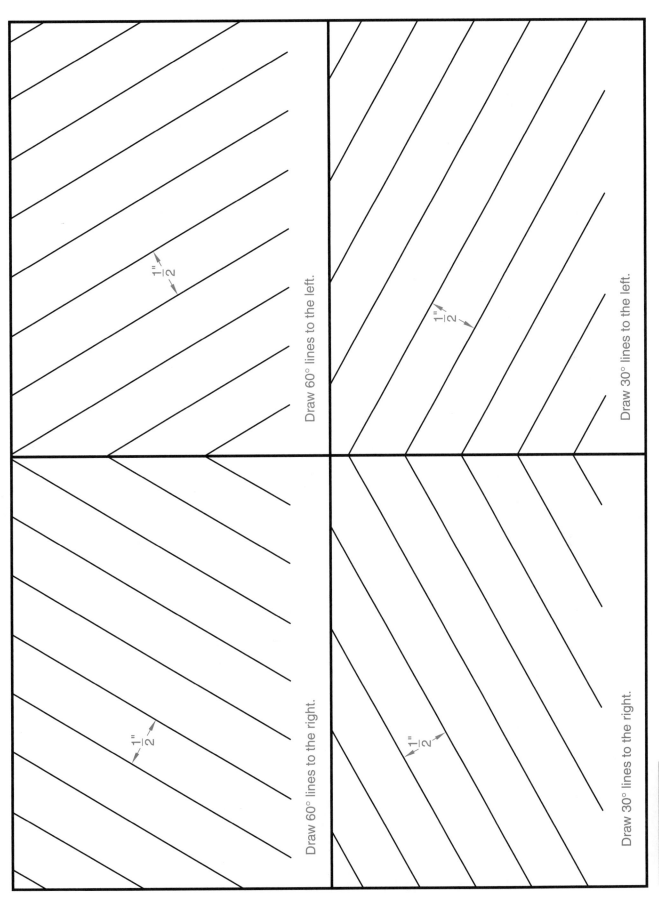

Draw 60° lines to the left.

$\frac{1"}{2}$

Draw 30° lines to the left.

$\frac{1"}{2}$

Draw 60° lines to the right.

$\frac{1"}{2}$

Draw 30° lines to the right.

$\frac{1"}{2}$

Problem Sheet 5-4 Instrument Practice.

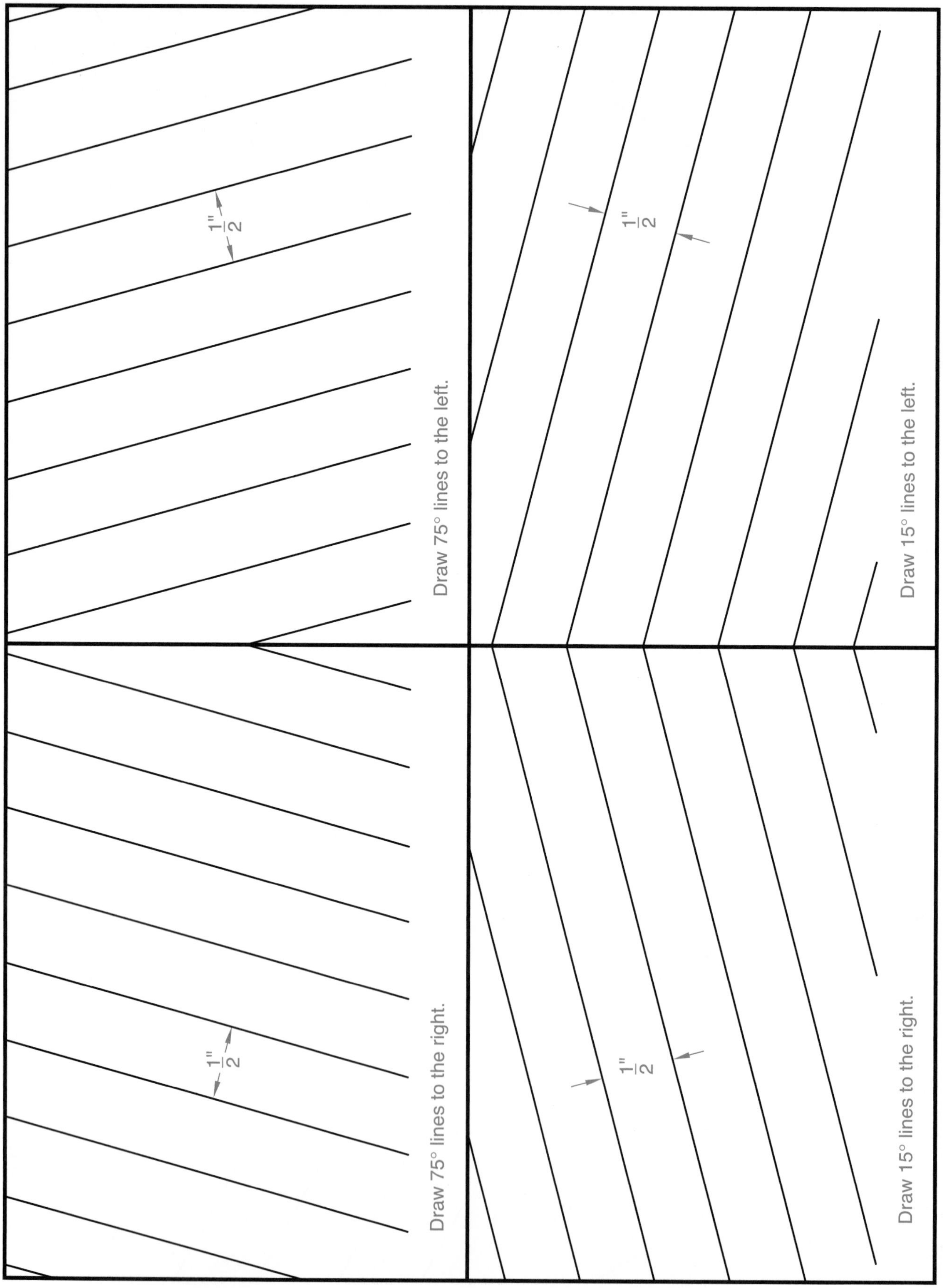

Draw 75° lines to the left.
1"/2
Draw 15° lines to the left.
1"/2
Draw 75° lines to the right.
1"/2
Draw 15° lines to the right.
1"/2

Problem Sheet 5-5 Instrument Practice.

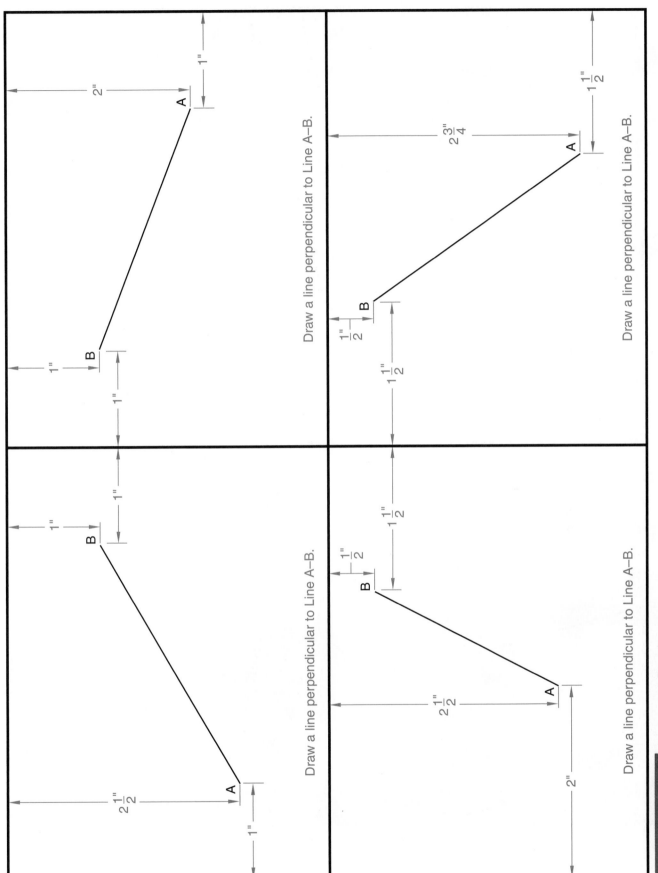

Draw a line perpendicular to Line A–B.

Draw a line perpendicular to Line A–B.

Draw a line perpendicular to Line A–B.

Draw a line perpendicular to Line A–B.

Problem Sheet 5-6 Instrument Practice.

6 Basic Geometric Construction

OBJECTIVES

After studying this chapter,
you should be able to:

- Identify basic geometric shapes.
- Bisect a line, arc, and angle.
- Transfer an angle.
- Construct various types of triangles.
- Construct a square given varying types of information about the square.
- Construct a pentagon, a hexagon, and an octagon.
- Draw an arc tangent to two lines at various angles.
- Draw an arc tangent to a straight line and a given arc.
- Draw arcs tangent to other arcs and circles.
- Divide a line into a given number of equal divisions.
- Construct an ellipse by several methods.

DRAFTING VOCABULARY

Bisect	Inscribed
Circumscribed	Octagon
Concentric	Pentagon
Ellipse	Regular polygon
Equilateral triangle	Tangent
Hexagon	

Whether we realize it or not, we see geometry in use every day, **Figure 6-1**. The design of the aircraft that flies overhead and the automobile that passes on the street is based on various geometric shapes. Buildings and bridges utilize squares, rectangles, triangles, circles, and arcs in their design and construction. Every drawing employed to construct a structure or manufacture a product is composed of one or more geometric shapes. Most utilize many different basic shapes.

Geometry is the basis of all computer-generated drawings, **Figure 6-2**. The first stage in developing a design is to generate a mesh or wireframe model using basic geometric shapes. CAD construction techniques are discussed in more detail in Chapter 7.

It is important that you acquire the ability to visualize and draw the basic geometric shapes presented in this chapter, **Figure 6-3**. This will aid you in solving drafting problems. It will also provide you an opportunity to improve your skill with drafting instruments.

Solving Basic Geometric Problems

Size does *not* matter when you are learning how to create basic geometric constructions. These are the basic tools used in solving most problems in drafting. It is more important to learn how to draw these basic shapes than to draw them at specific dimensions. For this reason, no dimensions are given for the

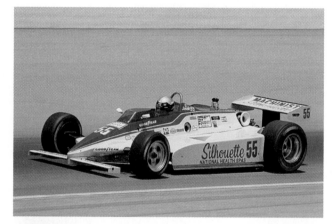

Figure 6-1 Geometric shapes are found in the design of most products and structures. Some are more obvious than others. How many geometric figures can you identify in these photos? (Top: Lockheed Advanced Development Company and Champion Spark Plug Company)

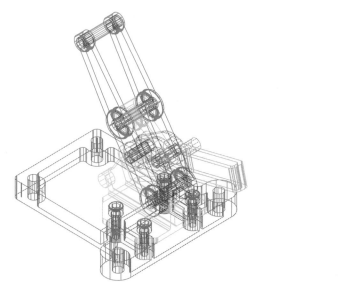

Figure 6-2 Geometry is the basis of all computer-generated drawings. Shown are a wireframe drawing of an assembly and a rendering of the final product. (Tom Short and Tony Dudek)

solutions of the basic geometric problems in this chapter. Most of them require little space for the solution. Therefore, several problems may be included on a single drawing sheet. A suggested sheet layout is shown in **Figure 6-4**.

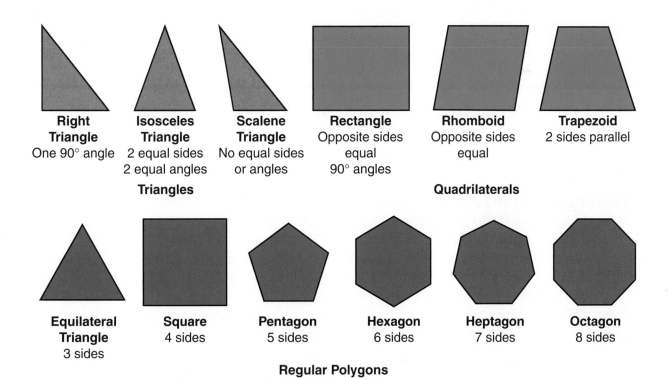

Figure 6-3 Basic geometric shapes on which drawings are based.

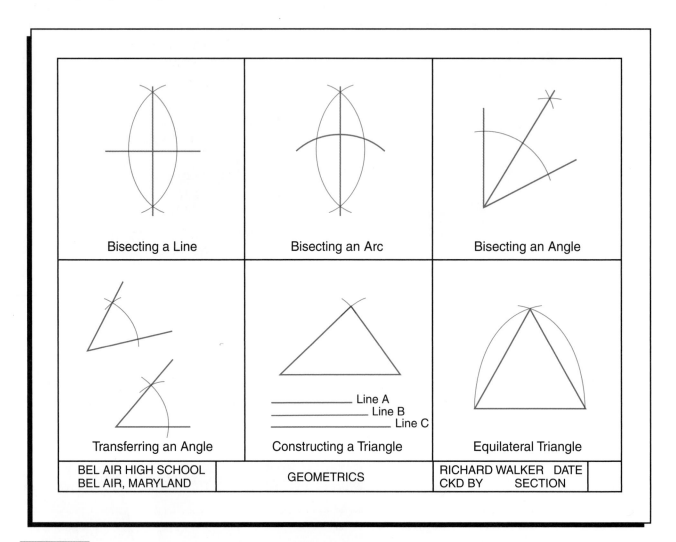

Figure 6-4   A suggested sheet layout for drawing basic geometric problems. Several figures may be placed on a single sheet.

Drawing sheets can be made more interesting and attractive if the geometric shapes are constructed with colored pencils. If you are using color in this manner, assign one specific color to each type of object so that the drawing appears consistent and accurate. The sections on the following pages discuss basic methods for constructing geometric shapes.

How to Bisect a Line

Bisecting an object divides the object into two equal parts of size or length. The midpoint of a line, for example, can be found by bisecting the line. Using the following method, the bisecting line will be at a right angle (90°) to the given line. Hence, it will be a perpendicular bisector of the line.

1. Draw a line similar to Line AB in the illustration. This is the line that will be bisected.

2. Set your compass to a distance slightly larger than one-half the length of the line. Using this setting as the radius and Point A as the center point, draw Arc CD. Using the same compass setting but Point B as the center point, draw Arc EF.

3. Draw a line through the resulting intersections that occur both above and below Line AB. This line will be at a right angle (90° or perpendicular) to Line AB and will bisect Line AB.

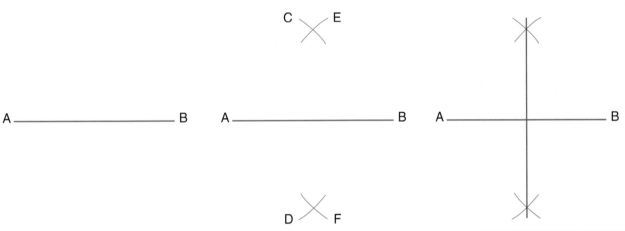

How to Bisect an Arc

1. Draw an arc similar to Arc AB in the illustration. This is the arc that will be bisected.

2. Set your compass to a distance slightly larger than one-half the length of the arc. Using this setting as the radius and Point A as the center point, draw Arc CD. Using the same compass setting but Point B as the center point, draw Arc EF.

3. Draw a line through the resulting intersections that occur above and below Arc AB. This line will bisect Arc AB.

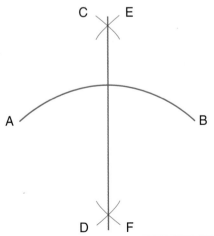

How to Bisect an Angle

1. Draw an angle similar to the angle formed by Lines AB and BC in the illustration.
2. With Point B (the vertex of the angle) as the center, draw an arc that intersects the sides of the angle at Points D and E.
3. Adjust a compass to a setting slightly larger than one-half the distance from Point D to Point E. Using Points D and E as center points, draw arcs that intersect in the interior of the angle. A line drawn through the resulting intersection and Point B will bisect the angle into two equal parts.

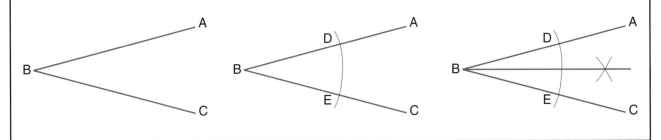

How to Transfer an Angle

1. Draw an angle that is similar to the angle formed by Lines AB and BC in the illustration. This angle will be transferred (copied).
2. Locate the new position of the angle by drawing Line A'B'.
3. Adjust a compass to a distance shorter than the length of the sides of Angle ABC. With Point B as the center point, draw an arc that intersects Angle ABC at Points D and E.
4. Using the same compass setting and using Point B' as the center point, draw Arc D'E'.
5. Reset the compass to a distance equal to Arc DE. With Point E' as a center, strike an arc that intersects the first arc at Point D'.
6. Draw a line through the resulting intersection to complete the transfer of the given angle.

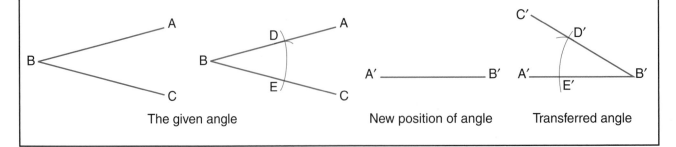

The given angle   New position of angle   Transferred angle

How to Construct a Triangle from Given Side Lengths

1. Lines A, B, and C will be the sides of the triangle.
2. Draw a line that is equal in length to Line A.
3. Set your compass to a length equal to Line B. Use one end of Line A as a center and draw an arc above Line A. Reset your compass to a length equal to Line C. With the other end of Line A as a center, draw another arc intersecting the first arc.
4. Draw lines originating from the ends of Line A to the resulting intersection to create the desired triangle.

Line C

Line B

Line A

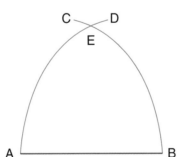

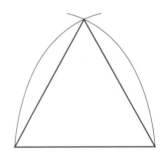

How to Construct an Equilateral Triangle

An *equilateral triangle* is one having all sides equal in length, with all interior and exterior angles equal.

1. Draw Line AB. This line will be equal to the length of each side of the triangle.
2. With Point A as the center and with the compass setting equal to the length of Line AB, strike Arc BC. Using the same compass setting, but with Point B as the center, strike Arc AD. These arcs intersect at Point E.
3. Complete the triangle by drawing lines from Points A and B to Point E.

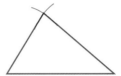

How to Construct a Square from a Given Diagonal Length

1. Draw a set of vertical and horizontal centerlines.
2. Using the resulting center point, draw a circle whose diameter is equal to the length of the diagonal.

3. Construct the square by connecting the points where the two centerlines intersect the circle. The square has been *inscribed* within the circle.

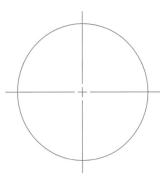
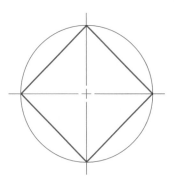

How to Construct a Square from a Given Side

1. Draw a set of vertical and horizontal centerlines.
2. Using the resulting center point, draw a circle whose diameter is equal to the desired length of the side.
3. Construct the square by drawing 45° lines that are tangent to the outside of the circle and whose endpoints rest on the centerlines. The square has been *circumscribed* about the outside of the circle.

Note

The term *tangent* refers to a line, arc, or circle that comes into contact with an arc or circle at a single point. A line drawn from the center point of an arc or circle to the tangency point of a tangent line is perpendicular to the tangent line. A line drawn between the center points of two tangent circles intersects the point of tangency. Creating tangent arcs is discussed later in this chapter.

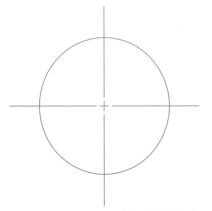
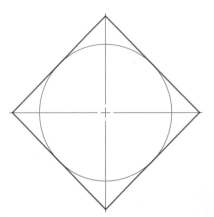

How to Construct a Regular Pentagon

A *regular polygon* is a geometric shape having all sides equal in length and all angles equal. An equilateral triangle is an example of a regular polygon. A square is a four-sided regular polygon. You can also draw pentagons, hexagons, and octagons as regular polygons. This procedure describes the construction of a regular pentagon. A *pentagon* is a five-sided geometric figure with each side forming a 72° angle. The resulting shape can be used to draw a five-point star.

1. Draw a set of vertical and horizontal centerlines (Lines AC and DB).
2. Using the resulting center point (Point O), draw a circle.
3. Bisect Line OB. This line is equal to the radius. This will locate Point E.

4. Adjust the compass to the radius EA. Using Point E as the center point, draw Arc AF.
5. Distance AF is equal in length to one side (or flat) of the regular pentagon. It is also the distance between the points of a five-pointed star. Set the compass to this distance. Using Point A as the center point, draw two arcs, one on either side of Point A and each intersecting the circle. Using the same compass setting, move the compass location to the resulting intersections and draw two more arcs intersecting the circle as illustrated below. Draw lines connecting these five points on the circle to construct the regular pentagon. The same points can be used to draw a five-point star. Refer to the illustration below.

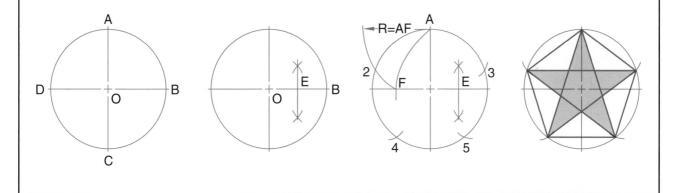

How to Construct a Regular Hexagon (First Method)

A *hexagon* is a six-sided figure with each side forming a 60° angle. Two methods can be used to construct a regular hexagon. The first method uses a compass with centerlines and arcs.

1. Draw a set of vertical and horizontal centerlines.
2. Using the resulting center point, draw a circle.
3. Set your compass equal to the radius of the drawn circle. Using Point A as the center, swing an arc to locate Points B and F. With Point D as the center, swing an arc and locate Points C and E.
4. Connect the points on the circle with lines to inscribe the regular hexagon.

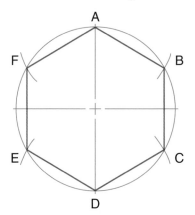

How to Construct a Regular Hexagon (Second Method)

The second method for constructing a regular hexagon uses construction lines with the 30°-60° triangle.

1. Draw a set of vertical and horizontal centerlines.
2. Using the resulting center point, draw a circle.
3. Circumscribe a hexagon around the outside of the circle by using the 30°-60° triangle. First, draw construction lines at 60° both to the left and to the right through the center of the circle and intersecting the perimeter of the circle. The resulting intersections are the exact tangent points on the circle where the flats of the hexagon will be drawn. Draw two vertical construction lines through the two points that mark the intersections between the horizontal centerline and the circle. Circumscribe the hexagon by drawing lines at 30° through the upper and lower tangent points. The lines should extend from the vertical centerline to the vertical construction lines on the sides of the circle. Darken the resulting hexagon using the desired linetype and weight.
4. Inscribe a hexagon within the circle by using the 30°-60° triangle. First, draw four 30° lines. The lines should originate from the upper and lower intersections of the vertical centerline and the circle. Extend the lines until they intersect the circle. Connect the resulting intersections with vertical lines. Darken the hexagon using the desired linetype and weight.

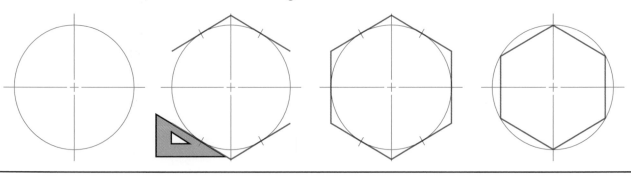

CAREERS IN DRAFTING

Interior Designer

What would I do if I were to become an interior designer? I would combine practical knowledge with creative ability to turn abstract ideas into formal designs for the spaces where people live and work. I would determine the needs of my client. Then, based on those needs, I would prepare sketches to illustrate my vision for the design. After consulting with my client, I would then prepare detailed drawings and possibly a structural model or computer simulation to present the final design.

What would I need to know? I would need to know how to enhance the function, aesthetics, safety, and quality of interior spaces for many types of buildings—including private homes, restaurants, hotels, retail establishments, hospitals, public buildings, and institutional facilities. I would also need to know how to efficiently redesign the interiors of existing structures for renovation or expansion purposes. I would need to know how to create the working drawings for my designs. I would need to know how to properly light, furnish, and finish the final product. I also would have to know how to conform to federal, state, and local laws and building codes as they relate to my designs.

Where would I work? I would work in my own home studio or in a business office. I would also frequently visit job sites, showrooms, markets, design centers, exhibit sites, or manufacturing facilities to gather information and ideas for my designs.

For whom would I work? I could be self-employed. Many interior designers do freelance work in addition to holding a salaried design job or other job. I could also work for an architectural firm, a specialized design firm, a retail furniture or interior design store, or a manufacturer.

What sort of education would I need? While in high school, I would want to take courses in art, drafting, mechanical drawing, computer-aided drafting (CAD), and business, along with general communications classes and core subject studies. Because most entry-level positions require a minimum of a bachelor's degree, I would want to acquire one through a program accredited by the Foundation for Interior Design Education Research (FIDER).

What are the special fields relating to this career? Residential design, commercial design, and business design. Some interior designers specialize in designing just one particular type of room (such as kitchens or bathrooms).

What are my chances of finding a job? My chances of finding a job should be very good. Over the next several years, the rising demand for professional interior design work in restaurants, offices, retail establishments, private homes, and institutions that care for the rapidly growing elderly population should provide accelerated growth in employment opportunities.

How much money could I expect to make? Recent statistics show that I could make an average of $39,180 as an entry-level interior designer. Salaries have ranged from less than $21,240 to more than $69,640 depending on the level of training and type of employer.

Where else could I look for more information about becoming an interior designer? See the US Department of Labor's Bureau of Labor Statistics Occupational Outlook Handbook (at www.bls.gov). For information about accredited programs for interior design, contact the National Association of Schools of Art and Design (www.arts-accredit.org) or the Foundation for Interior Design Education Research (www.fider.org). To obtain information on licensure programs in interior design, contact the American Society of Interior Designers (www.asid.org).

If I decide to pursue a different career, what other fields are related to interior design? Architecture, art, photography, commercial and industrial design, graphic design, set and exhibit design, and visual merchandising.

How to Draw an Octagon Using a Circle

An *octagon* is an eight-sided geometric figure with each side forming a 45° angle. Two methods can be used to construct a regular octagon. The first method uses centerlines and a circle.

1. Draw a set of vertical and horizontal centerlines.
2. Using the resulting center point, draw a circle with a diameter equal to the distance across the flats of the desired octagon.
3. Draw two construction lines at 45° through the center of the circle and

intersecting the perimeter of the circle. These locate the exact points where the octagon will be tangent to the circle. Use construction lines to draw two vertical and two horizontal lines tangent to the circle through the points located by the two centerlines intersecting the circle. Finish constructing the regular octagon by drawing 45° tangent lines through the final four tangent points and stopping at the vertical and horizontal construction lines. Darken the hexagon using the desired linetype and weight.

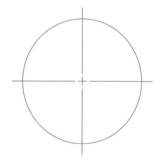 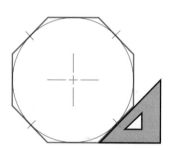

How to Draw an Octagon Using a Square

1. Draw a square with the sides equal in length to the distance across the flats of the required octagon. Draw diagonals similar to the diagonals AC and BD shown. The diagonals intersect at Point O.

2. Set your compass to radius AO. With Points A, B, C, and D as centers, draw arcs that intersect the square at Points 1, 2, 3, 4, 5, 6, 7, and 8.
3. Complete the octagon by connecting Point 1 to 2, 2 to 3, 3 to 4, 4 to 5, 5 to 6, 6 to 7, 7 to 8, and 8 to 1.

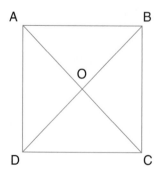 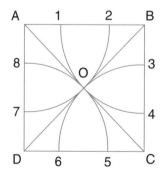 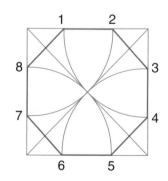

How to Draw an Arc Tangent to Two Straight Lines

The following procedure works for lines that intersect at obtuse and acute angles as well as right angles. Refer to each example as you follow the procedure. A simpler method for drawing arcs tangent to lines intersecting at right angles is covered in the next section.

1. Lines AB and CD in the examples shown are used as the two straight lines.
2. Set your compass to the radius of the arc to be drawn tangent to the lines. Selecting points near each end of Lines AB and CD as center points, scribe two arcs (one at each end of each line) inside the angle formed by the two lines.
3. Draw construction lines tangent to the arcs.
4. The point where the two lines intersect (Point O) is the center point for the tangent arc.
5. Locate the two tangent points where the arc becomes tangent to the two straight lines by drawing construction lines perpendicular to each line through the center of the tangent arc.
6. Draw the arc between the tangent points.

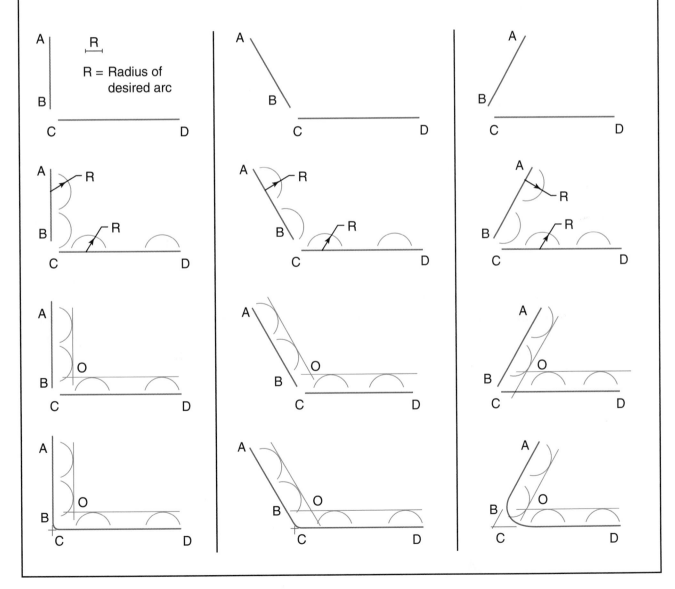

How to Draw an Arc Tangent to Two Lines That Form a Right Angle

The following procedure simplifies the method for drawing arcs tangent to lines intersecting at right angles. Use this procedure only for straight lines meeting at 90°.

1. Draw lines making up a 90° angle similar to Lines AB and BC shown.
2. Set a compass to a distance equal to the radius of the arc to be tangent.

Using Point B as the center point, scribe Arc DE. This arc intersects the two sides of the angle and locates two points that are equidistant from the vertex. Using Points D and E as center points and using the same compass setting, draw two arcs that intersect at Point O on the interior of the angle.

3. With Point O as the center and with the compass at the same setting, draw the tangent arc to the proper line weight from Point D to Point E.

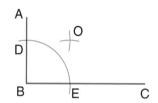

How to Draw an Arc Tangent to a Straight Line and a Given Arc or Circle

1. Draw an arc and a straight line similar to the ones illustrated. Draw the lines in proper relation to one another.
2. Draw Line AB parallel to Line ab and a distance away from Line ab equal to the radius (R) of the tangent arc.
3. Draw Arc CD by setting your compass to a radius equal to $R + r$ (the radius of the given arc plus the radius of the tangent arc). This arc should intersect Line AB at Point O.
4. Locate the tangent point where the arc becomes tangent to the original arc by

drawing a construction line connecting the centers of the two arcs. Where it crosses the original arc is the tangent point. Locate the tangent point between the arc and the line by drawing a construction line perpendicular to the straight line through the center of the arc (Point O). Where it crosses the straight line is the tangent point.

5. Using Point O as the center and with the compass set to the desired radius R, draw the new arc from tangent point to tangent point. Then darken the original arc to match the line weight of the new arc. Finally, darken the straight line.

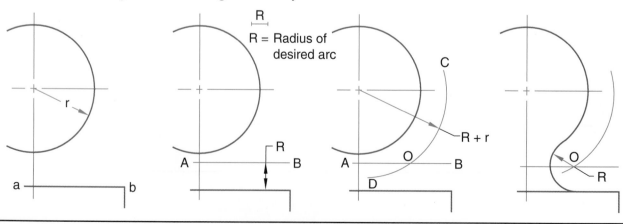

How to Draw Tangent Arcs

1. Draw two arcs similar to Arcs ra and rb. These arcs (portions of a circle) will be joined by the tangent arc. Points O and X (the circle center points) are the centers of these arcs.
2. Set the compass to a distance equal to the radius R + *ra* (the radius of the given arc plus the radius of the tangent arc). Using Point X as the center, draw Arc AB. Reset the compass to a distance

equal to the radius R + *rb*. Using Point O as the center, draw Arc CD. These arcs intersect at Point Y.

3. Set the compass to the radius of the required arc (R). With Point Y as the center, draw the desired arc to the desired line weight. This arc will be tangent to the given arcs. Finally, darken the original arcs to match the line weight of the new arc.

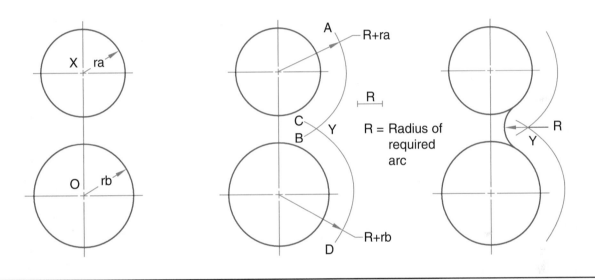

How to Divide a Line into a Given Number of Equal Divisions

Two methods can be used to divide a line into equal segments. The first method uses a scale with construction lines.

1. Draw a line similar to Line AB shown. This line will be divided into five equal parts.
2. With the T-square and triangle, draw Line BC. Use construction lines.

3. Locate the scale with one end at Point A. Adjust the scale until a multiple of the divisions required (in this case five 1″ divisions) lies between Point A and Line BC.
4. Make vertical points at each of the five 1″ divisions. Project vertical lines from these points parallel to Line BC. These vertical lines divide Line AB into five equal parts.

The second method for dividing a line into equal segments uses diagonal construction lines. Distances are transferred with a compass.

1. Draw a line similar to Line AB shown. This line will be divided into five equal parts.
2. With the T-square and triangle, draw two parallel construction lines sloping opposite directions and originating at Points A and B.
3. Set a compass to a small increment (1/4″ to 1/2″, depending upon the length of the given line).
4. Beginning at Point A and moving upward along the incline, transfer

distances with the compass equal in number to the desired number of divisions for Line AB.

5. Using the same compass setting, repeat the procedure beginning at Point B and moving downward along the incline.
6. Draw as many parallel construction lines as needed to connect points from the upper and lower divisions as illustrated.
7. When the construction lines cross Line AB, the line is divided into the desired number of parts.

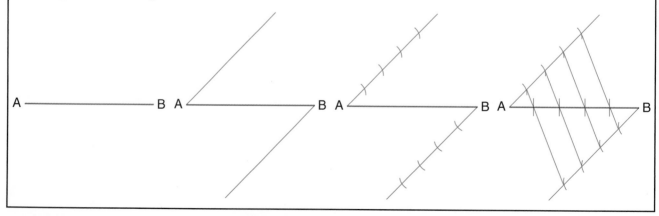

How to Construct an Ellipse Using Concentric Circles

An *ellipse* is a closed curve in the form of a symmetrical oval with four quadrants. The following procedure describes how to draw an ellipse using construction lines and concentric circles. Circles that are *concentric* have a common center.

1. Draw a set of vertical and horizontal centerlines. Using the resulting center point, draw two concentric construction line circles. The diameter of the large circle is equal to the length of the large (major) axis of the desired ellipse. The diameter of the small circle is equal to the length of the small (minor) axis of the desired ellipse.

2. Divide the two circles into 12 equal parts (30° increments) using construction lines. Use the 30°-60° triangle.

3. Draw horizontal construction lines originating from the points where the dividing lines intersect the small circle. These lines should extend into the area between the two circles.

4. Draw vertical lines originating from the points where the dividing lines intersect the large circle. These also should extend into the area between the two circles. These lines should intersect the horizontal lines just drawn.

5. Connect the points that are created by the intersections with a French curve to construct the ellipse. Find a curve that intersects the points for one quadrant of the ellipse, from one axis to the other. Use the same curve to finish the other three quadrants.

6. Care should be taken to have smooth transitions from quadrant to quadrant.

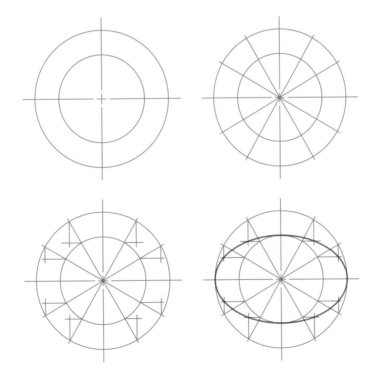

How to Construct an Ellipse Using the Parallelogram Method

This method is useful for drawing large ellipses.

1. Draw lines similar to Lines AB and CD. These represent the major axis and minor axis of the required ellipse.
2. Construct a rectangle with opposite sides equal in length and parallel to the two axes.
3. Divide Lines AO and AE into the same number of equal parts. In this example, four divisions are used. This may work well in most cases. However, any number of divisions will work.
4. From Point C, draw a line to Point 1 on Line AE. Draw a line from Point D through Point 1 on Line AO and through the line just drawn. The point of intersection of these two lines will establish the first point of the ellipse. The remaining points in this quadrant are then completed, as are the corresponding points in the other three quadrants.
5. Connect the points with a French curve to complete the ellipse. Find a curve that will intersect all of the points in one quadrant. The curve should also intersect the vertical axis horizontally and the horizontal axis vertically. Draw the curve in one quadrant and rotate the same curve into the other quadrants to complete the ellipse.

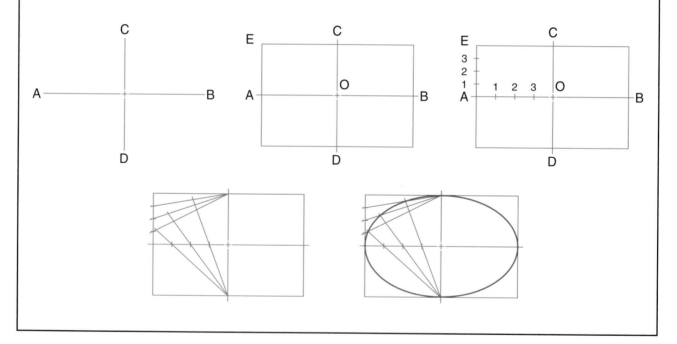

How to Construct an Ellipse Using the Four-Center Approximation Method

1. Draw lines similar to Lines AB and CD. These represent the major axis and minor axis of the required ellipse.
2. Draw a diagonal line for Line CB. With Point O as the center and Line OC as the radius, strike an arc. The arc will intersect Line OB at Point E.
3. Set the compass to a distance equal to the radius EB. Using Point C as the center, strike an arc that intersects Line CB at Point F.
4. Construct a perpendicular bisector of Line FB and extend it to intersect the major and minor axes at Points G and H.
5. Points G and H are the centers for two of the arcs needed to construct the ellipse. With Point O as the center, use a compass to locate Points J and K. They are symmetrical with Points G and H.
6. Draw a line from Point H extending through Point J. Draw lines extending from Point K through Points G and J.
7. Using Points G and J as centers, strike Arcs GB and JA.
8. With Points H and K as centers, strike Arcs HC and KD.

These four arcs will be tangent to each other and form a four-center approximate ellipse.

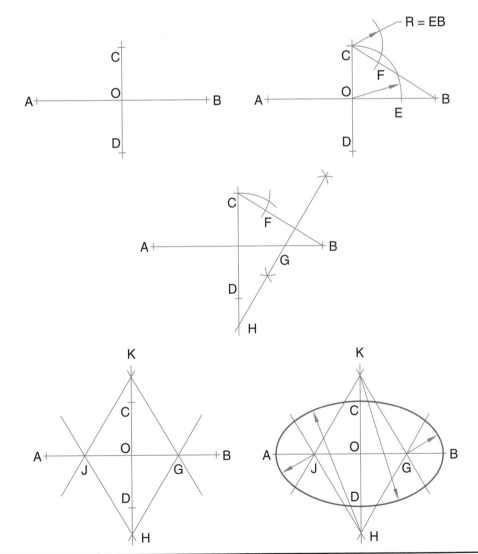

Outside Activities

Become aware of the many geometric shapes used in designing objects in your world by doing one or more of the following activities.

1. Prepare a bulletin board display or a notebook that illustrates the use of geometric shapes in buildings and bridges.
2. Develop a list of everyday items that make use of geometric shapes. For example, nut and bolt heads are round, square, and hexagonal.
3. Obtain a photo or a drawing of your favorite airplane or boat. Place a sheet of tracing vellum over it and sketch in the various geometric shapes used in its design.
4. Do the same using a photo or drawing of your favorite car, truck, or motorcycle.
5. Carefully examine a bicycle. Make a list of all the geometric shapes used in the design and construction of the bicycle. Be sure to look at all of the component parts.

Drawing Problems

Duplicate the drawings shown on the problem sheets on the following pages. Use the dimensions provided. Follow the directions on each problem sheet.

Bisect Angle ABC.

Construct an equilateral triangle.

Bisect Arc AB.

Construct a triangle.

Bisect Line AB.

New location

Transfer Angle ABC.

Problem Sheet 6-1   Geometric Shapes.

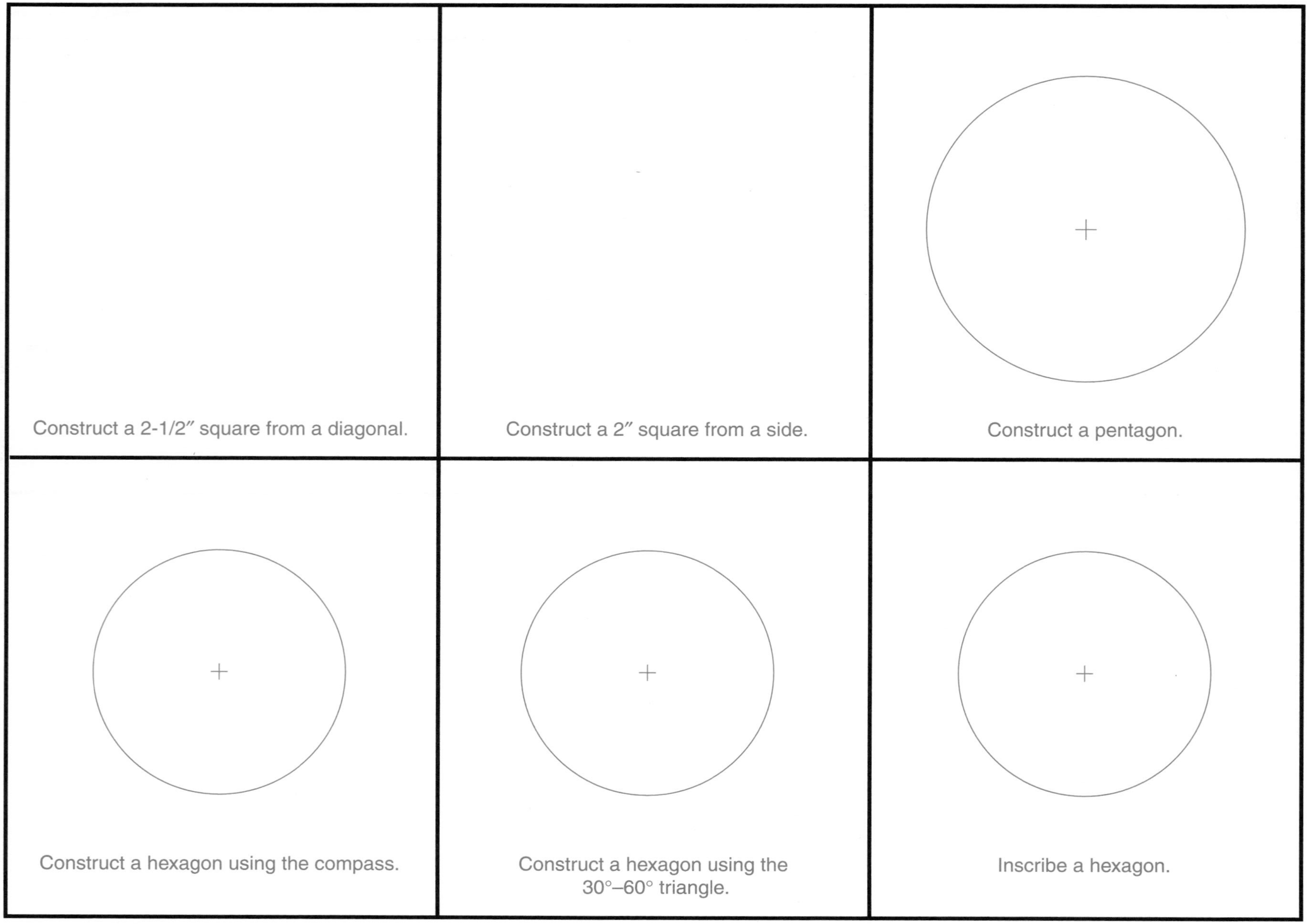

Construct a pentagon.

Inscribe a hexagon.

Construct a 2″ square from a side.

Construct a hexagon using the 30°–60° triangle.

Construct a 2-1/2″ square from a diagonal.

Construct a hexagon using the compass.

Problem Sheet 6-2 Geometric Shapes.

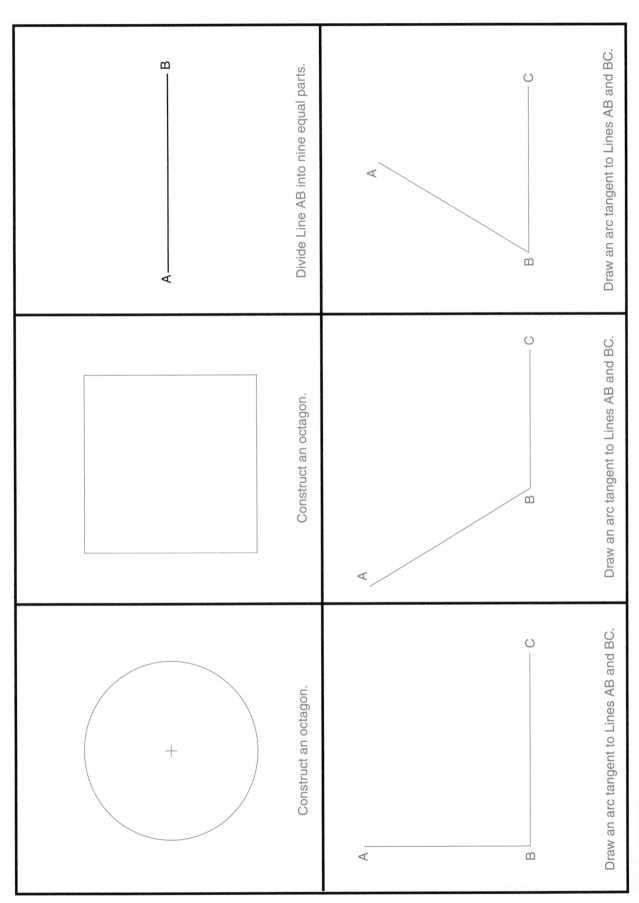

Divide Line AB into nine equal parts.

Construct an octagon.

Construct an octagon.

Draw an arc tangent to Lines AB and BC.

Draw an arc tangent to Lines AB and BC.

Draw an arc tangent to Lines AB and BC.

Problem Sheet 6-3 Geometric Shapes.

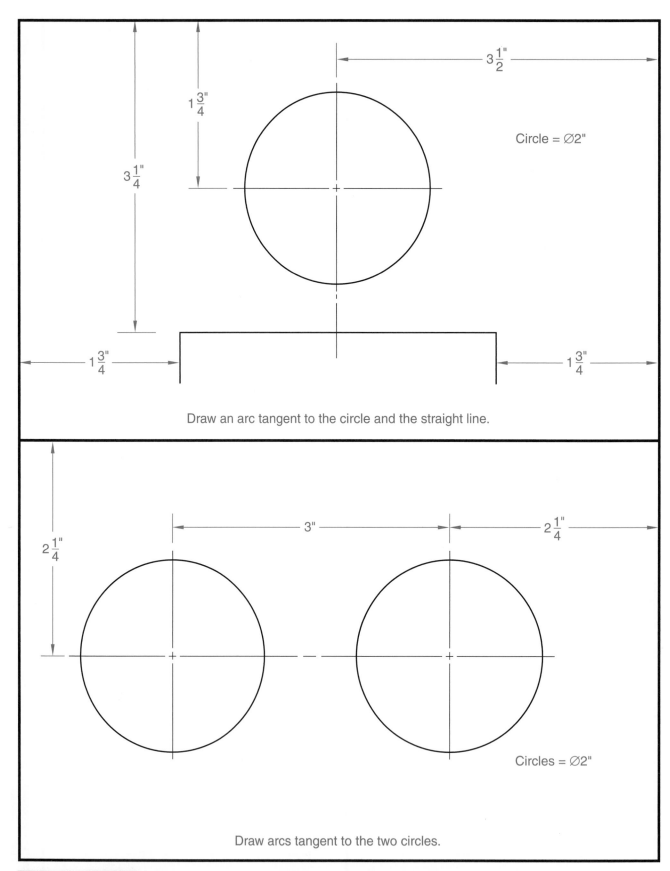

$3\frac{1}{2}"$

$1\frac{3}{4}"$

$3\frac{1}{4}"$

Circle = $\varnothing 2"$

$1\frac{3}{4}"$

$1\frac{3}{4}"$

Draw an arc tangent to the circle and the straight line.

$2\frac{1}{4}"$

$3"$

$2\frac{1}{4}"$

Circles = $\varnothing 2"$

Draw arcs tangent to the two circles.

Problem Sheet 6-4   Use a vertical sheet layout. Divide the work area as shown. Do not dimension.

Major axis = 5"

Minor axis = $3\frac{1}{2}$"

Center in block

Construct an ellipse using the parallelogram method.

Major axis = 5"

Minor axis = 3"

Center in block

Construct a four-center approximate ellipse.

Problem Sheet 6-5 Use a vertical sheet layout. Divide the work area as shown. Do not dimension.

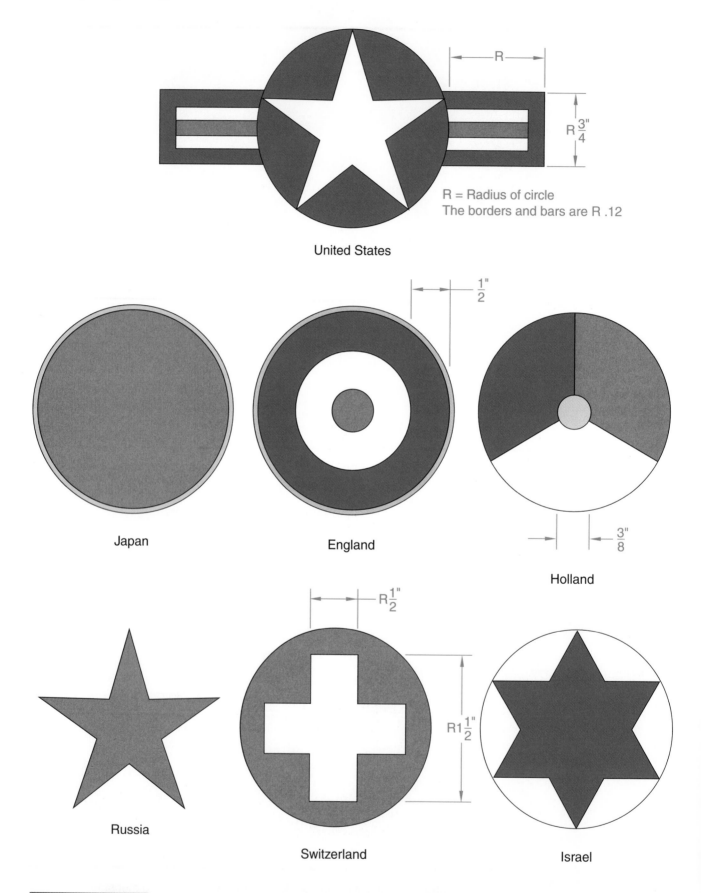

R = Radius of circle
The borders and bars are R .12

United States

Japan

England

Holland

Russia

Switzerland

Israel

Problem Sheet 6-6 Aircraft insignia of the world.

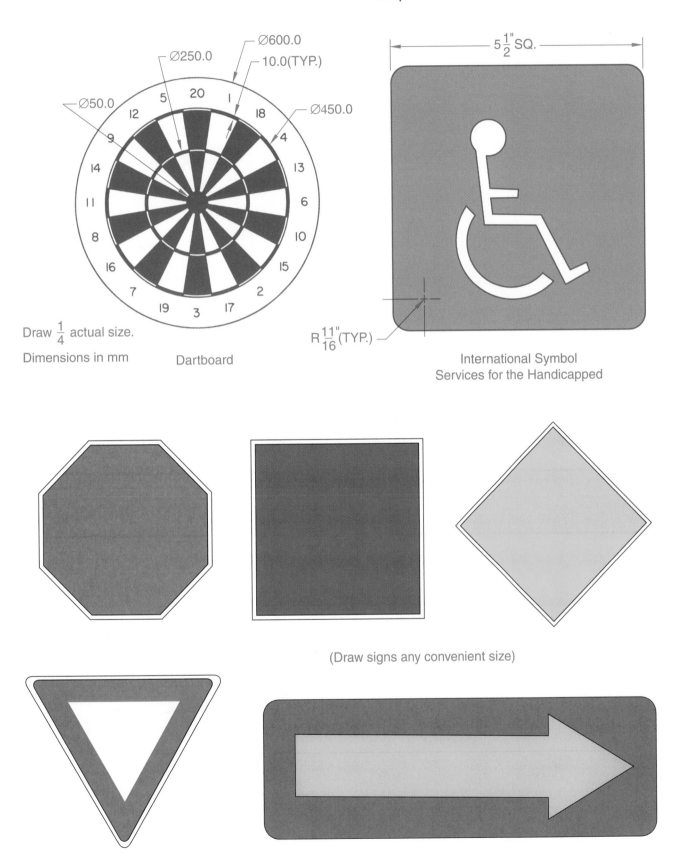

Ø600.0
Ø250.0
10.0(TYP.)
Ø50.0
Ø450.0

5
20
1
12
18
9
4
14
13
11
6
8
10
16
15
7
2
19
3
17

Draw $\frac{1}{4}$ actual size.

Dimensions in mm   Dartboard

$5\frac{1}{2}"$ SQ.

R $\frac{11}{16}"$ (TYP.)

International Symbol
Services for the Handicapped

(Draw signs any convenient size)

Traffic Warning Signs

Problem Sheet 6-7 Geometric Shapes. Draw each problem on a separate sheet.

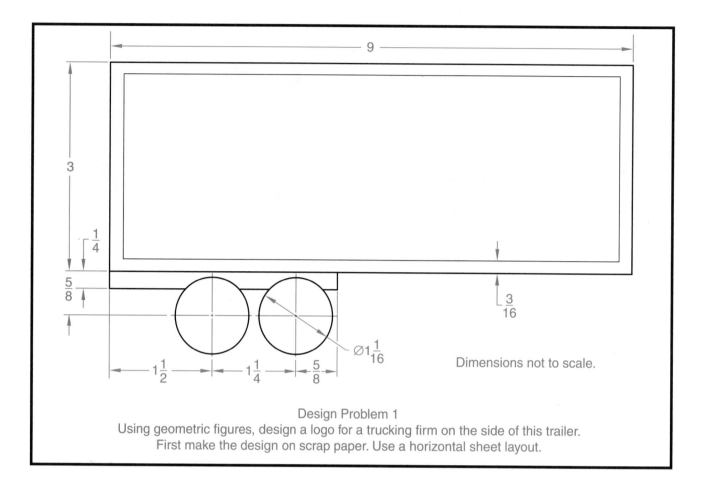

Design Problem 1
Using geometric figures, design a logo for a trucking firm on the side of this trailer.
First make the design on scrap paper. Use a horizontal sheet layout.

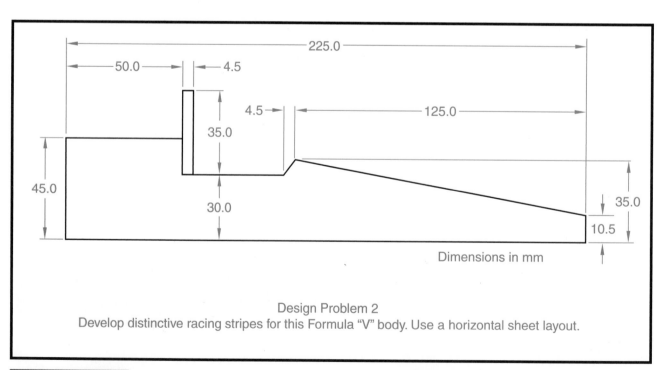

Design Problem 2
Develop distinctive racing stripes for this Formula "V" body. Use a horizontal sheet layout.

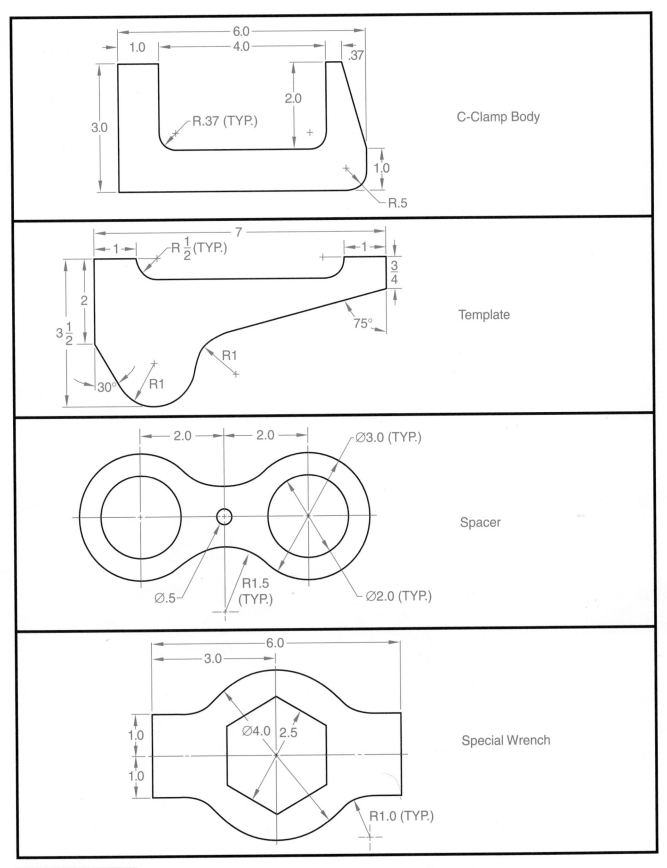

Problem Sheet 6-9   Make each drawing full size on a separate sheet. Do not dimension.

7 Computer-Aided Drafting and Design

OBJECTIVES

After studying this chapter,
you should be able to:

◆ Explain how computer technology is
revolutionizing drafting, design, and
engineering.

◆ Describe the basic features and
operation of a computer-aided
drafting program.

◆ Explain the various commands used to
create objects in CAD.

◆ Describe the tools used to modify
CAD drawings.

◆ Identify the various display functions
used in CAD programs.

◆ List different types of CAD software
and their applications.

DRAFTING VOCABULARY

Absolute coordinates
Array
Attributes
Bitmap graphics
Cartesian coordinate
    system
Chamfer
Computer-
    aided design/
    computer-aided
    manufacturing
    (CAD/CAM)
Coordinates
Fillet
Grid
Layers
Linetype
Menu
Object snap
Orthogonal mode
Parametric modeling

Pixels
Polar coordinates
Raster objects
Relative coordinates
Rendering
Resolution
Round
Scanner
Scene
Snap
Solid modeling
Surface modeling
Symbol library
Symbols
Template
User coordinate
    system
Vector objects
World coordinate
    system

Computer graphics continues to revolutionize drafting and engineering, **Figure 7-1**. Computer-aided drafting and design systems play an integral part in the entire engineering process, from design and drafting to analysis and presentation. They aid in designing mechanical products, buildings, and other structures.

There are many benefits to using CAD as a design and drafting tool. Traditional drafting tasks, such as drawing basic shapes, lettering, and creating views, are greatly simplified with the electronic tools of a CAD system. CAD programs provide setup tools, drawing and editing commands, and customization methods to maximize accuracy and proficiency. There is a wide range of programs to choose from depending on the nature of the work. This chapter introduces the various applications of CAD drafting and discusses the common tools used to create CAD drawings.

Overview of Computer Graphics and CAD

Computer graphics was first employed for aerospace design in the 1950s. It is now a required tool of industrial technology. Until the advent of CAD, engineers, designers, and drafters had to imagine and then evaluate a three-dimensional object that was drawn in two dimensions on a flat sheet of paper. The only way a design could be verified in three dimensions was to make a wood, clay, plaster, or plastic model. This is an expensive and time-consuming process.

The emergence of CAD provided designers with a dynamic new tool. CAD technology permits more time for creative work because it eliminates the repetitive tasks required in traditional drafting.

CAD is a computer graphics technology that allows users to generate 2D and 3D designs electronically on a display monitor, **Figure 7-2**. Many people are able to use a computer drawing program after a suitable training period. *However, the principles of drafting are fundamental to both traditional drafting and CAD.* A working knowledge of basic drafting standards, techniques, and procedures is absolutely necessary to be an effective CAD drafter.

The main function of a CAD designer or engineer is to define the basic shape of a part, assembly, or product in 2D or 3D form. The

Figure 7-1 Computer-aided drafting systems are used for a wide variety of applications in design and engineering. With the proper CAD program, it is possible to generate realistic three-dimensional models representing complex mechanical assemblies. (Autodesk, Inc.)

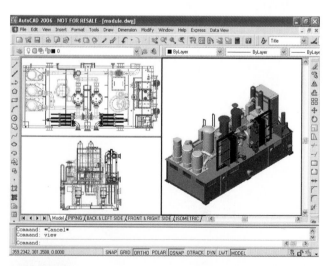

Figure 7-2 A 3D drawing created with a typical CAD system. With the proper tools, 2D and 3D images of the object being designed can be generated. (Autodesk, Inc.)

process involves many changes and refinements before a design is finalized. With a CAD system, design changes can be made and evaluated quickly.

Computer graphics programs fall into one of two classifications. These classifications are based on how the actual images are created. Images in a computer graphics program may be created with *vector objects* or *raster objects*. Drawings created in a CAD program are made up of vector objects. Vector objects are made up of lines (vectors) and arcs and are defined with point coordinates in space. See **Figure 7-3A**.

Raster objects are defined using tiny shapes of data called *picture elements*, or *pixels*. See **Figure 7-3B**. Pixels are arranged in a fixed, precise manner. Each pixel is the same size and shape. The number of pixels making up an image defines the *resolution*, or visual quality, of the image. Raster objects are also known as *bitmap graphics*. Image editing programs are commonly used to alter bitmap graphics. Televisions and computer monitors are examples of devices that use raster displays.

A vector-based drawing can be converted to bitmap form in several different ways. The most basic way is to export a drawing file from a CAD program as a bitmap file. The file can then be imported into a different program for editing. For example, a 3D model created with a CAD program may be converted to a bitmap file and edited for special effects, such as lighting and shadows. If a vector drawing is output as hard copy, it can be converted to bitmap form with a *scanner*. A scanner is an automatic digitizing device. It analyzes the lines, circles, and other graphic elements of the drawing and converts the objects into computer data.

Referring to **Figure 7-3**, vector images are edited by modifying the individual lines and arcs making up the drawing. Raster images are modified by editing the individual pixels making up the image. In creating or editing a vector object, such as a line, it can be helpful to visualize the object as an entity defined with coordinates. Most CAD programs provide a drawing grid that can be used to define objects with coordinates. This method of drawing is similar to the graph method used in manual

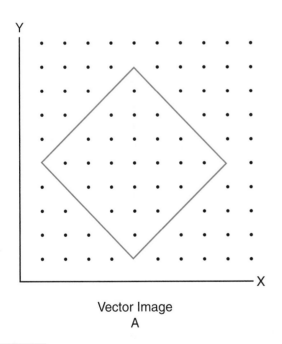

Vector Image
A

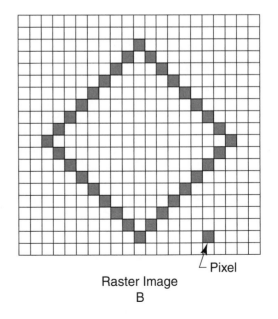

Raster Image
B

Figure 7-3   A comparison of vector and raster displays.

drafting. The graph method, discussed in Chapter 3, is used to enlarge or reduce drawings with coordinate grids. When using a CAD program, objects can be drawn to the desired size by defining coordinates or other parameters or by scaling an original object to a different size. Coordinate entry, scaling, and other types of drawing functions in CAD programs are discussed later in this chapter.

How CAD Works

A CAD drawing project starts with the generation of a geometric model of the proposed design on the display screen. The outline or profile of the design is created first and then details are added.

Instructions are given to a CAD program through the use of menus and commands. A *menu* is a list of options from which the drafter can select to execute the desired procedure. It can appear as a list of commands on a digitizing tablet or as a list of options on the monitor, **Figure 7-4**. Commands can also be entered at the keyboard or picked from toolbars.

Once objects are drawn, they can be altered as needed. For example, an object can be moved, rotated, copied, deleted, or mirrored. These operations are executed with editing commands. An object drawn in CAD can be manipulated in a variety of ways, making it unnecessary to draw the object again. CAD commands are discussed later in this chapter.

Dimensions and text can be added to a CAD drawing by selecting the appropriate menu function and entering the required information. The drafter can define the text size, style, and orientation as needed. CAD functions for creating text and dimensions are discussed later in this text.

After a drawing is completed, it can be output in a number of ways. Drawings converted into hard copy are typically printed on a plotter, **Figure 7-5**. Inkjet plotters are most commonly used to produce CAD drawings. CAD drawings may also be output to a printer, such as a laser printer.

Drawings made in a CAD program may also be converted to an appropriate file format for electronic viewing. For example, a drawing may be posted by a firm on a Web site for clients or for another engineer working on the project. If a drawing file is sent via

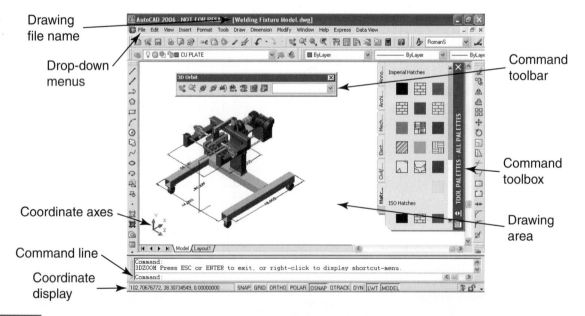

Figure 7-4 The drawing display of a typical CAD program includes drop-down menus, toolbars, and status displays. Commands can be accessed in a variety of ways to suit the user's needs. (Autodesk, Inc.)

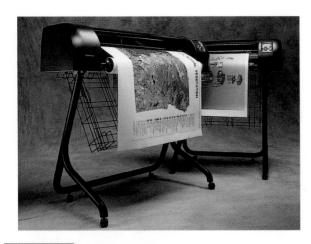

Figure 7-5   Plotters produce hard copy from CAD drawing files. (CalComp)

electronic mail to a client, a viewer configured for the software may be needed to display the drawing.

Regardless of the drawing and production methods used, CAD programs offer a variety of ways to manage projects from design to completion. The following sections discuss the basic features, tools, and commands used to generate CAD drawings.

Using Basic CAD Functions

One of the main benefits of CAD drafting is the added productivity and efficiency made possible by tools and commands in the software. Many of these tools are designed to automate the common tasks associated with traditional (manual) drafting. There are a number of basic features and functions common to most types of CAD software. These include coordinate systems, drawing aids, layers, linetypes, and symbols. These features are discussed in the following sections.

Coordinate Systems

As previously discussed, objects in a CAD drawing are defined with coordinates. *Coordinates* are points representing units of real measurement from a fixed point. Most CAD programs provide a basic coordinate system and the ability to create user-defined

coordinate systems. The most basic coordinate system in a typical program is the *world coordinate system*. This system is based on the *Cartesian coordinate system*. In this system, objects are defined by coordinates along the X axis (horizontal axis), Y axis (vertical axis), and Z axis (the axis projecting perpendicular from the XY plane). Coordinates are located in relation to the 0,0,0 origin. See **Figure 7-6**.

The horizontal and vertical axes of the Cartesian coordinate system divide the XY drawing plane into four quadrants. See **Figure 7-7**. Coordinates are entered as positive or negative, depending on the location from the origin. Referring to **Figure 7-7**, the coordinate (2,2) is located in the upper-right quadrant. This quadrant has positive X coordinates and positive Y coordinates. The coordinate (4,-3) is located in the lower-right quadrant. This quadrant has positive X coordinates and negative Y coordinates. The coordinate (-6,8) is located in the upper-left quadrant. This quadrant has negative

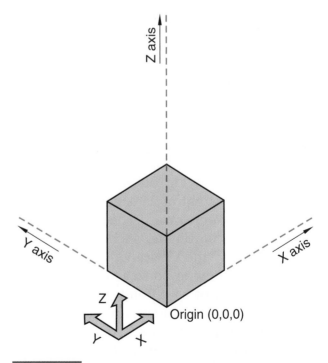

Figure 7-6   In the Cartesian coordinate system, coordinates establish points of measurement along the X, Y, and Z axes in relation to the 0,0,0 origin.

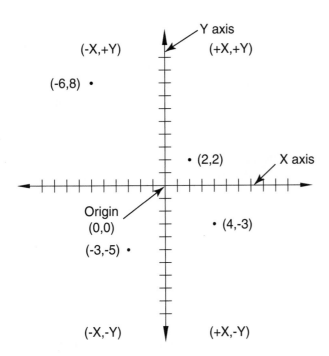

Figure 7-7 The XY axes of the Cartesian coordinate system divide the drawing plane into four quadrants. Coordinates have positive or negative X and Y values.

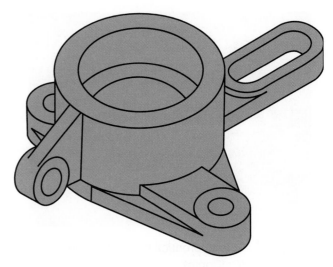

Figure 7-8 A third axis (the Z axis) is needed to generate three-dimensional images like the one shown. The ability to visualize objects in 3D space is fundamental to creating 3D drawings. (ROBO Systems)

X coordinates and positive Y coordinates. The coordinate (-3,-5) is located in the lower-left quadrant. This quadrant has negative X coordinates and negative Y coordinates.

Objects drawn with XY coordinates are sufficient for 2D drawings. A third coordinate axis, the Z axis, is required for 3D drawings. This axis is used for coordinate entry above or below the XY plane. A point with a positive Z coordinate, such as (0,0,1), is located "above" the XY drawing plane. When looking at a drawing on screen, this location can be thought of as a point projecting out of the monitor toward you. A point with a negative Z coordinate, such as (0,0,-1), is located "below" the XY drawing plane. When looking at a drawing on screen, this location can be thought of as a point projecting into the monitor away from you. In order to draw objects in 3D space with a CAD system, it is important to be able to visualize them in three dimensions with coordinates along each axis. See **Figure 7-8**.

There are three common forms of coordinate entry used in the Cartesian coordinate system. Coordinates may be entered as *absolute coordinates*, *relative coordinates*, or *polar coordinates*. See **Figure 7-9**. When using absolute coordinates, objects are drawn using points in relation to the coordinate system origin (0,0). The absolute coordinate (2,2) indicates that the point is located two units from the origin along the positive X axis and two units from the origin along the positive Y axis. When using relative coordinates, objects are drawn using coordinates in relation to the last coordinate specified (or the origin). For example, entering the relative coordinate (@5,4) after entering the absolute coordinate (2,2) places the next point five units along the positive X axis and four units along the positive Y axis at the coordinate (7,6). Refer to **Figure 7-9B**.

When using polar coordinates, coordinates are located at a given distance and angle from the origin or from the last coordinate specified. Polar coordinates are entered using a format such as *(distance<angle)*. This format

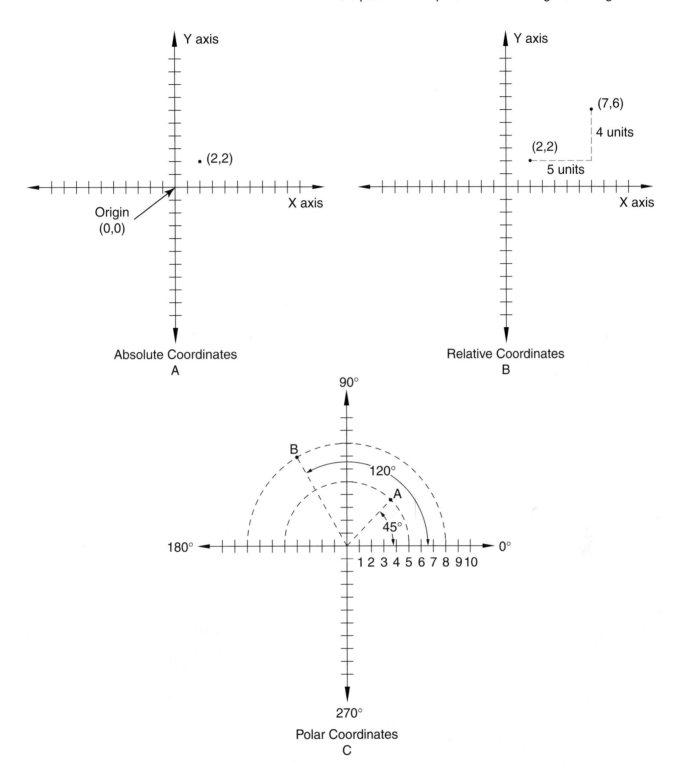

Figure 7-9 The three types of coordinate entry used in the Cartesian coordinate system. A—The absolute coordinate (2,2) is located 2 units along the positive X axis and 2 units along the positive Y axis from the 0,0 origin. B—Entering the relative coordinate (@5,4) locates the next point five units along the positive X axis and 4 units along the positive Y axis at the coordinate (7,6). C—Polar coordinates are located at a specified distance and angle from the origin or a given point. Angular values are measured counterclockwise. Point A represents the polar coordinate entry (@5<45) in relation to the origin. Point B represents the polar coordinate entry (@8<120) in relation to the origin.

specifies a linear distance and angle in the XY plane relative to the origin or another point. Angles are most commonly measured counterclockwise, with the positive X axis representing 0°. Referring to **Figure 7-9C**, the polar coordinate entry (5<45) locates the point five units away from the origin at an angle of 45° in the XY plane. The polar coordinate entry (8<120) locates the point eight units away from the origin at an angle of 120° in the XY plane.

Each of the different types of coordinate entry can be used when creating a drawing. The entry used typically depends on the object drawn. For example, it may be useful to use absolute coordinates when a given point is known, or when drawing straight lines. Relative coordinates may be used when locating points from a common feature. Polar coordinates are useful for drawing inclined lines and round objects.

User Coordinate Systems

As previously discussed, the default world coordinate system in a CAD program has the origin located at 0,0,0. This is typically sufficient for most 2D drawings, since coordinates for 2D objects can be drawn on the XY drawing plane without specifying a third coordinate along the Z axis.

When creating drawings in 3D, however, it is often useful to change the world coordinate system to a different coordinate system. This is because features in a 3D drawing are usually drawn in relation to surfaces on an object, rather than exact coordinates in 3D space. A *user coordinate system* is a relative drawing configuration that allows you to orient a drawing plane to a specific surface. Coordinates can then be located on the user-defined drawing plane in relation to a fixed origin. The origin used may be a specific point on the object, such as a corner or center point. See **Figure 7-10**.

User coordinate systems greatly simplify the 3D drawing process. There are also viewing tools and drawing commands that

Figure 7-10 A user coordinate system is used to establish a drawing plane in 3D space so that objects can be drawn on the surface of the plane. The XYZ coordinate axes identify the orientation of the drawing plane. In this 3D model of a phone, the XY drawing plane is oriented so that objects can be added to the mouthpiece. Note the direction of the axes.

are useful for 3D drawing. Viewing tools and 3D-based modeling methods are discussed later in this chapter. Commands used in 3D drawing are discussed in Chapter 13.

Drawing Aids

In addition to coordinate systems and the numerous commands used to create basic geometric shapes, CAD programs offer a number of drawing aids that simplify the drawing process. These features make it easy to specify distances and locate coordinates when drawing basic objects such as lines and circles. The typical drawing aids in a CAD program include grid and snap, object snap, and orthogonal mode.

In CAD, a *grid* is a network of uniformly spaced points used to determine distances. Displaying a grid is similar to using graph paper in manual drafting. The grid spacing may be set to any value that simplifies the process of locating points at specific increments. When used, the grid display is for

CAREERS IN DRAFTING

Drafting/CAD Teacher

What would I do if I were to become a drafting/CAD teacher? Because I would be a type of career and technical education teacher, I would use many different methods of presenting information and concepts relating to drafting and computer-aided drafting (CAD) in order to help students learn how to solve design problems. I would assist students in learning how to properly create drawings that are used to manufacture or construct objects.

What would I need to know? I would need to be able to properly organize a classroom and know how to present the information, concepts, and skills that I need to teach my students. I would need to know how to use (and instruct how to use) various manual drafting tools as well as computers and CAD software. I would need to be familiar with and competent using a variety of tools, techniques, and procedures as they relate to various specialized fields of drafting—such as mechanical, architectural, electrical, and civil drafting. I would need to know how to work effectively with diverse ethnic and socioeconomic groups of students. I would also need to know how to design classroom presentations; plan, evaluate, and assign lessons; prepare, administer, and grade tests; evaluate oral presentations; maintain classroom order and discipline; effectively work with and communicate with other staff and parents; assist students in setting career goals; and help with a wide variety of extracurricular activities.

Where would I work? I would spend a majority of my time in a classroom environment instructing students. However, my work could take me out of the classroom for field trips and other academic and extracurricular endeavors. Many teachers also have home offices where they spend many hours preparing for their classes.

For whom would I work? I could work for a public school district, usually at a secondary level. I could also work for a public or private technical school, trade school, college, or university. Some drafting/CAD teachers also work for large corporations to keep professional staffs current with the latest technologies, practices, and procedures.

What sort of education would I need? While in high school, I would need to take courses in drafting, mechanical drawing, CAD, and computer science, along with required high school courses. All 50 states require public school teachers to be licensed and have a minimum of a bachelor's degree from an approved teacher education program. Some states require that teachers earn a master's degree within a specified period of time after being hired. Also, many drafting/CAD programs are designated as vocational programs, and most states require that teachers of vocational programs be vocationally credentialed. Job experience as a drafter or CAD drafter is very helpful in acquiring a vocational credential.

What are the special fields relating to this career? There are many areas of study in which I can teach. Math, science, technology education, and computer science are probably the most closely related to drafting/CAD.

What are my chances of finding a job? In general, the overall job outlook for teachers over the next several years is good to excellent, depending on the subject matter, grade level, and locality. However, there are several factors regarding job opportunities for drafting/CAD teachers. First, many teachers now teaching drafting and CAD are nearing retirement age. Hence, new teachers are going to be needed to fill those positions. Second, at present, the job market is sorely lacking in qualified drafting/CAD teachers that are not already employed. And third, there are two realities

(continued)

Drafting/CAD Teacher *(continued)*

working against prospective drafting/CAD teachers. On a comparative basis, there are not as many drafting/CAD positions in existence as there are in other areas of study (such as math). Also, most positions are found in more densely populated areas with larger schools because many rural schools do not offer this kind of program. So, it could be concluded that drafting/CAD teachers will be in very high demand over the next several years—when existing positions become available.

How much money could I expect to make? Teacher pay varies greatly because of numerous variables. Generally speaking, I could expect to make more if I taught in a metropolitan area than if I taught in a rural setting. Recent statistics identify the average income of a public school teacher to be $44,367, but pay can range from $24,960 to $68,530. Private school teachers generally earn less than public school teachers. Degree held, locale, and amount of experience are the three largest contributing factors to the level of pay that I could expect. Also, if I taught in a technical school, trade school, college, or university, I could generally expect higher pay. I could also earn extra pay by coaching, teaching summer classes, or sponsoring various extra-curricular activities, clubs, or organizations.

Where else could I look for more information about becoming a drafting/CAD teacher? See the US Department of Labor's Bureau of Labor Statistics Occupational Outlook Handbook (at www.bls.gov) or visit the Recruiting New Teachers Web site (at www.rnt.org). A list of accredited teacher education programs can be obtained from the National Council for Accreditation of Teacher Education (at www.ncate.org). Information about vocational education can be acquired through the Association for Career and Technical Education (www.acteonline.org) and also through the International Technology Education Association (www.iteawww.org).

If I decide to pursue a different career, what other fields are related to drafting and CAD? Because teaching drafting and CAD is much like teaching applied geometry, teaching math would be similar. Some of the content in art classes is similar to that in drafting classes. General technology education also encompasses some of the content taught in drafting/CAD courses. Many projects completed in the average drafting program also have close ties to science. Thus, I could become a teacher of art, math, science, or technology education, and still be teaching in a related field.

reference only. It does not print when the drawing is plotted.

Snap is a function that allows the user to align ("snap") the cursor to specific increments, or snap points, in an invisible grid. Snap can be used with or without the grid display turned on. However, it is common to set the snap spacing in conjunction with the grid spacing. For example, if the grid spacing is set to .50", snap may be set to .25" so that the cursor can be "snapped" to the grid points as well as the midpoints between grid lines.

Object snap is a function that allows the cursor to be aligned, or snapped, to specific locations on an object. Object snap can be set to one or more modes that determine the type of location. This is useful for drawing objects using existing points on another object. For example, the Endpoint object snap mode allows you to attach the cursor to an endpoint of an object. The Midpoint object snap mode is used to attach the cursor to the midpoint of an object, such as a line. The Center object snap mode is used to attach the cursor to the center of a circle or an arc. Object snap can also be used to draw objects that are parallel, perpendicular, or tangent to other objects.

Orthogonal mode simplifies the task of drawing straight lines. When orthogonal mode is enabled, the movement of the cursor is confined to straight horizontal and vertical movement in relation to the drawing plane. Inclined lines cannot be drawn when using this mode. Orthogonal mode is useful for drawing lines at 90° angles, such as the outlines making up a drawing border.

Layers and Linetypes

In manual drafting, it is common to have several different views or plans on separate sheets for complex drawings, such as mechanical parts with section views or architectural plans for a building. When this is the case, the sheets are overlaid on top of each other so that the different drawings can be viewed separately. In CAD drafting, drawings can be managed in a similar way through the use of layers. *Layers* are user-defined object settings that can be displayed or "turned off" to distinguish the different types of content in a drawing. See **Figure 7-11**. Using layers, several different displays can be shown within a single drawing file. It is very common, for example, to create separate layers for object lines, construction lines, section lines, text, and dimensions. The display of each layer can be turned on or off as desired. In this way, certain portions of the drawing can be "hidden" while displaying other features. This helps drawing productivity because objects can be temporarily removed from the drawing without deleting them to free up drawing space. In architectural projects, different plans are commonly placed on different layers within a single drawing file. The floor plan, foundation plan, and plumbing plan, for example, may each be assigned to a separate layer. This provides a way to plot different displays from a single drawing.

Layers are typically named to reflect their content. For example, all of the dimensions on a drawing may be assigned to a layer named Dims. In addition, each layer may be assigned its own color. In many cases, company or school standards specify layer naming conventions and how to group drawing content.

Layers may also be assigned different linetypes to distinguish content. A *linetype* is a setting used to describe a line definition in the Alphabet of Lines. Examples of linetypes include the Object, Centerline, and Hidden linetypes. When a line is drawn with a specified linetype, it has the same characteristics as the equivalent line in the Alphabet of Lines. Each linetype may have its own lineweight setting to reflect the plotting thickness desired. When using a plotter with pens, the line thickness is determined by the size of the plotter pen.

Drawing specifications such as layer and linetype settings should be determined before starting a project. Saved settings for layers, linetypes, object snaps, and other CAD functions can be specified in a drawing template and used each time a new drawing is started. Templates and setup commands are discussed later in this chapter.

Symbols

One of the basic principles of CAD is to never draw the same object twice. For example, objects can be copied and reused once they are drawn. Copying objects is discussed later in this chapter. Another way to avoid drawing objects repeatedly is to use symbols. *Symbols* are saved or predrawn objects designed for multiple use in drawing projects. Once something is drawn and saved as a symbol, it can be inserted into a drawing as many times as needed. This is a powerful function that greatly increases drawing productivity. Symbols are commonly used in architectural and electrical drawings to represent items such as windows, doors, and outlets.

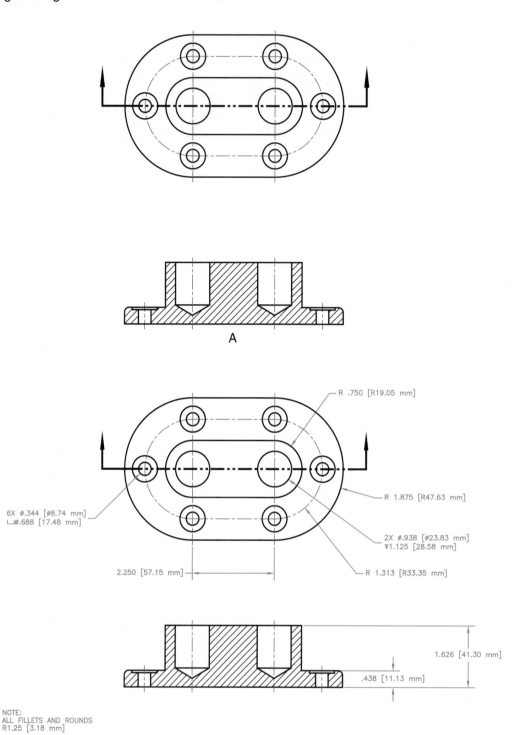

NOTE:
ALL FILLETS AND ROUNDS
R1.25 [3.18 mm]

R .750 [R19.05 mm]

R 1.875 [R47.63 mm]

6X ⌀.344 [⌀8.74 mm]
⌴⌀.688 [17.48 mm]

2X ⌀.938 [⌀23.83 mm]
⍋1.125 [28.58 mm]

2.250 [57.15 mm]

R 1.313 [R33.35 mm]

1.626 [41.30 mm]

.438 [11.13 mm]

A

B

Figure 7-11   Layers are used in CAD drawings to distinguish different content, such as different linetypes and dimensions. A—The object lines, centerlines, section lines, and cutting-plane line in this drawing are on different layers. Each layer has the appropriate linetype. The Centerline layer is assigned the color green. All other layers are assigned the color black. B—The dimension layer is turned on to show dimensions. This layer is assigned the color red.

Many companies store hundreds of symbols in symbol libraries. A *symbol library* is a collection of related drawing symbols. See **Figure 7-12**. To create a symbol, the shape is drawn and saved with a name. It can then be inserted into the drawing where it is stored or into other drawings. Many manufacturers and drafting firms provide symbols of their products that can be downloaded from Web sites on the Internet.

In some CAD programs, symbols may be saved with attributes. *Attributes* are text strings of information about the related symbol. Attributes may be created to identify a product number, price, size, or material. They can be displayed along with the symbol on the drawing, or they may be set invisible. Attributes are commonly used to create drawing schedules, which list manufacturing and purchasing information about parts and products on a drawing.

Drawing Setup Functions

As is the case with manual drafting projects, CAD drawings should be planned carefully prior to beginning work. Making drawing settings ahead of time increases efficiency and is important to being a successful CAD drafter. CAD programs provide a number of commands and features used to set up drawings. Applying these functions should become a normal routine when using a CAD system.

Most CAD programs base linear and angular measurements on the current unit settings. A drawing can be set to use decimal inch, architectural, metric, or engineer's units. Units are typically set with the **Units** command. The unit format selected depends on the drafting discipline.

Regardless of the unit format used, objects are drawn at full size in CAD drafting. This means that an object 2″ × 3″ is drawn at that size. The drawing scale determines the size of the drawing when it is plotted. The drawing scale is based on the size of the drawing media. It affects the size of dimensions and is determined before beginning a drawing along with the sheet size. A number of settings are typically made in a CAD drawing when specifying the scale factor, such as linetype scaling and text height.

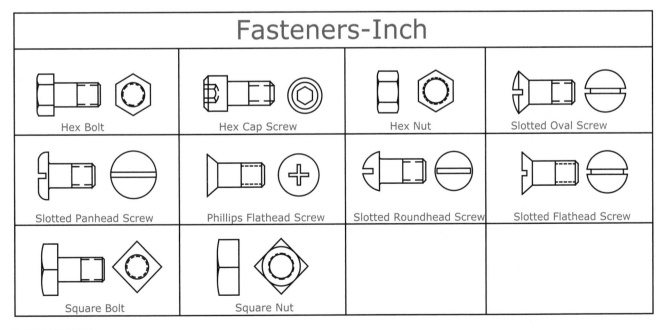

Figure 7-12   A symbol library of fasteners used in mechanical drafting.

As previously discussed, layers are normally created during the drawing setup process. Linetypes are defined and assigned to layers as needed. This provides a means to organize a wide variety of content.

Many of the drawing aids previously discussed can be saved in a drawing template. A *template* is a saved set of configurations used to start a drawing file. Different templates can be created for different drafting disciplines or applications requiring predefined entities such as symbols. They may include settings for the unit format, sheet size, and drawing scale. It is also common to have predefined text styles, dimension styles, and layer assignments in a template. The use of templates saves drawing time and allows drafters to focus on the drawing project at hand.

Creating Objects

As previously discussed in this chapter, there are a variety of ways to create objects using CAD. In most cases, the creation of an object begins with a command. Within a command sequence, objects may be created using coordinates, such as absolute coordinates, or parameters, such as radius values and linear measurements. Coordinates and parameters may be entered at the keyboard or specified with the cursor on screen.

Most of the basic geometric shapes discussed in Chapters 3 and 6 can be drawn quickly with drawing commands. The following sections discuss the common methods used to create basic geometric shapes in CAD.

Drawing Lines

Lines are most commonly drawn with the **Line** command. A line may be drawn straight or inclined by specifying coordinates at the keyboard or by using the cursor to pick points on screen. A line requires two coordinates, **Figure 7-13**. Additional coordinates may be entered within a single command sequence to create as many segments as needed. As

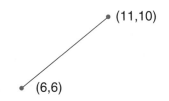

Figure 7-13 A line is created by drawing a segment between two endpoint coordinates.

previously discussed, lines may be displayed using different line conventions by applying the proper linetype. Before drawing the line, the layer or linetype must be set current.

Drawing Circles and Arcs

Curves making up CAD-generated circles and arcs are defined mathematically by the program based on the coordinates entered. Circles are typically drawn by specifying the center point and a radius or diameter, **Figure 7-14A**. A circle may also be drawn by specifying points along the perimeter of the circle or by entering a radius and selecting two lines or two circles to which the circle should be tangent. The **Circle** command is most commonly used to draw circles. The center point location and radius value may be entered at the keyboard or picked on screen.

Arcs can be drawn with the **Arc** command. A number of methods are usually available. Arcs typically require a center point, radius, and endpoint. See **Figure 7-14B**. Arcs may also be drawn by specifying three points, or a starting point, a center point, and a third entry, such as a chord length. As with circles, arcs may be drawn tangent to lines, other arcs, or circles.

Drawing Ellipses

Ellipses are drawn with the **Ellipse** command. An ellipse has a center point, a minor axis, and a major axis. See **Figure 7-15**. The axes divide the ellipse into four quadrants. Points for the axis endpoints and center point can be entered at the keyboard or picked on screen.

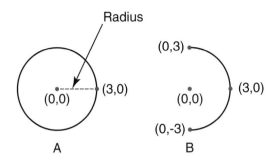

Figure 7-14 Drawing circles and arcs. A—Circles are defined with a center point and radius or diameter. B—Arcs are commonly defined with a center point, starting point, and endpoint, or with points along the arc.

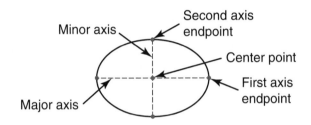

Figure 7-15 An ellipse is drawn by defining a center point and endpoints for the minor and major axes.

Elliptical arcs (portions of an ellipse) can also be drawn by specifying start and end angles after locating the center point or axis endpoints. The start and end angles represent points on the curve relative to the angular locations of the axis endpoints. The angles are measured counterclockwise from the first axis endpoint, which is designated as 0°. For example, an arc drawn with a 0° start angle and 180° end angle represents half an ellipse.

Drawing Polygons

The **Polygon** command can be used to draw regular polygons. After specifying a center point, the number of sides is entered. Specifying three sides draws an equilateral triangle. Specifying four sides draws a square. Regular pentagons, hexagons, and octagons can also be drawn.

After entering the number of sides, the command sequence includes prompts for the

user to inscribe or circumscribe the polygon. As you learned in Chapter 6, an inscribed polygon is drawn within a circle. A circumscribed polygon is drawn about a circle. After specifying the orientation of the polygon, the radius of the circle is entered.

Editing Objects

One of the most important advantages of a CAD program is the ability to easily modify objects once they are drawn. Objects can be moved, copied, rotated, and scaled using editing commands. In addition to these basic commands, there are a number of other editing methods that can be used to construct drawings. This provides great flexibility. Some of the most common editing commands in CAD programs are discussed in the following sections.

Moving Objects

It is often necessary to relocate objects after they are drawn. This can be done with the **Move** command. After selecting one or more objects to move, you must specify a base point for the selection set. This may be the corner point of a rectangle or the center point of a circle. You are then asked for a displacement point. The objects making up the selection set are then moved automatically to the new location using the distance specified. Distance values can be entered at the keyboard or picked on screen.

Copying Objects

Copying objects is similar to using the **Move** command, except the original objects are not altered by the operation. Objects can be copied using the **Copy** command. After selecting the objects to copy and the base point, a displacement point is specified. The selected objects are then copied to the new location.

The **Copy** command includes a **Multiple** option. This option allows you to copy the same object to several new locations. This option is entered before selecting the base point.

Rotating Objects

Rotating an object changes the angular position of the object with respect to the current orientation. Objects can be rotated using the **Rotate** command. When using this command, the selected objects are rotated about the base point specified. The objects may be rotated clockwise or counterclockwise. If the objects are already rotated to a given angle, the reference angle is entered, followed by the desired angle of rotation.

Scaling Objects

An object can be reduced or enlarged to a different size by a given scale factor. This is accomplished with the **Scale** command. After selecting the object to be scaled, the base point

and scale factor are specified. A scale factor of 0.5, for example, would be used to reduce the size of an object to one-half its original size.

Undoing a Command

CAD programs typically provide a command that allows you to "undo" a previous operation. If you enter an incorrect value for a scale or move operation, you can reverse the action by using the **Undo** command. This command typically allows you to undo several preceding commands, one by one. However, the commands must be undone in sequence.

Erasing Objects

The **Erase** command provides a quick way to remove unwanted objects from a drawing. After you select the objects to erase, the command automatically removes them from the drawing. The **Undo** command can

ACADEMIC LINK

The evolution of computer technology and electronic communication has had a major effect on the way drawings are made and presented. Not long ago, manual drawings were the primary means of communicating manufacturing information to trade workers. Today, drawings are created with computer-aided drafting programs and distributed with electronic media. They are used by workers to program computer-controlled machine tools. Computers then interpret the information and manufacture parts. This is accomplished through various phases of communication—including interaction between the drafter and the computer and the computer and a machine.

There are literally hundreds of CAD software programs that have been used to design

products for industrial use. Computer animation programs make it possible to communicate an entire design of a product before it is manufactured or built. Internet technology makes it possible to send, receive, evaluate, and modify drawings in a very short period of time.

When compared to manual drawing techniques, CAD tools have made it much simpler to communicate information. However, it is important to understand that as with other communication tools, CAD is *only* a tool. The same drawing skills, visualization techniques, and concepts practiced in manual drafting must be understood in order to use CAD accurately and successfully.

be used to restore an object that has been erased unintentionally.

Arraying Objects

An *array* of objects can be created by orienting multiple copies of a selected object in a pattern. This operation is useful when the same object appears in multiple locations in a regular pattern in the drawing (for example, when a pattern of holes is machined in a round part). Arrays may be created in rectangular or polar arrangements with the **Array** command. See **Figure 7-16**. A rectangular array is created by entering the base point, number of rows, number of columns, and the spacing between rows and columns. The number of columns and rows determines the number of objects in the array. A polar array is created by specifying a center point, the number of objects in the array, and an angular value determining the amount of rotation. Entering 360° creates a full rotation of objects about the center point.

Mirroring Objects

When drawing symmetrical objects, it is sometimes useful to create a mirror image. This operation allows you to select an object and make a mirror copy. This can save time when you want to draw half of an object and complete it by "mirroring" it. See **Figure 7-17**. The **Mirror** command is used to mirror an object. To use this command, the objects to be mirrored are first selected. Then, a mirror axis is specified. The axis represents a line about which the objects are "reflected." The command sequence typically allows you to keep or delete the original object selected before mirroring.

Creating Rounded and Angled Corners

Rounded and angled corners are often drawn in mechanical drafting. A *round* is an arc representing an outside rounded corner. A *fillet* is an arc representing an inside rounded corner. A *chamfer* is an angled line drawn where two straight lines would normally meet at a corner. Rounds, fillets, and chamfers are used to smoothen sharp edges. See **Figure 7-18**. Rounds and fillets can be drawn with the **Fillet** command. After entering the

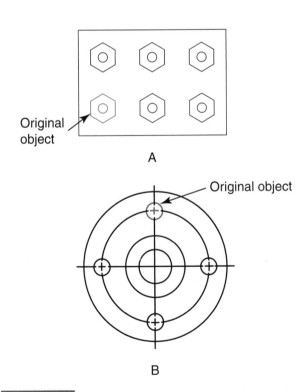

Figure 7-16 Arrays are created by orienting copies of original objects in a regular pattern.
A—Rectangular array. B—Polar array.

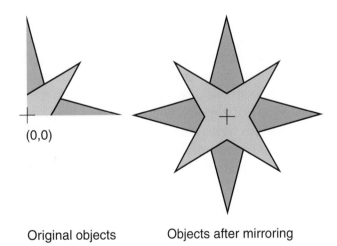

Figure 7-17 Mirroring an object creates a mirror copy about a mirror axis. In this example, the original image is mirrored twice using the X and Y axes.

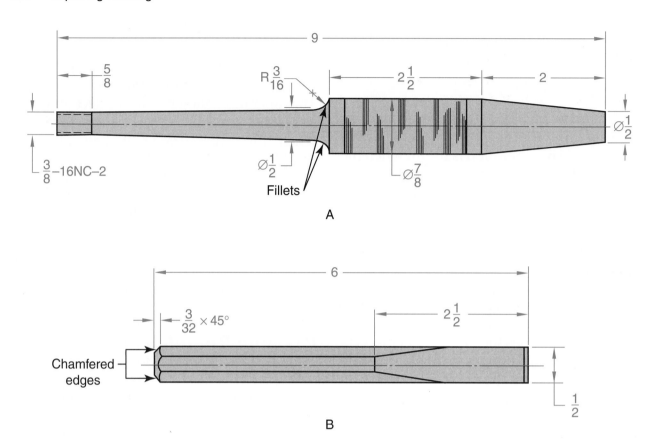

Figure 7-18 Creating rounded and angled features. A—Fillets are created by specifying a fillet radius and selecting the two objects forming the intersection. B—Chamfers are created by selecting two lines and entering the chamfer distances.

command, the fillet radius is set. Then, the two lines, circles, or arcs forming the intersection are selected. The original objects are then trimmed and the arc is automatically drawn.

A chamfer can be drawn with the **Chamfer** command. After entering the command, the chamfer distances from the two lines to the corner are set. A 45° chamfer is created with equal distances. Next, the two lines are selected. As with the **Fillet** command, the lines are trimmed automatically when the chamfer is drawn.

Trimming and Extending Lines

Many objects in a CAD drawing are made up of lines. During the drawing process, it is sometimes necessary to "clean up" areas of the drawing where lines must intersect accurately. Trimming is useful when two lines overrun past a corner. Extending is useful when a line must be lengthened to meet an edge.

The **Trim** command is used to trim lines, arcs, and circles. After entering the command, a cutting edge must be specified. This represents the point to where the object is to be trimmed. Next, the object to be trimmed is selected. The portion of the object extending past the cutting edge is automatically removed.

The **Extend** command is used to extend lines and arcs to meet other objects. After entering the command, a boundary edge must be specified. This represents the point to where the object is to be extended. Next, the object to be extended is selected. A segment connecting the object to the boundary edge is automatically drawn.

Using Display Commands

CAD programs provide a variety of ways to display drawing content on screen. Display commands are used to change the magnification of the drawing, reset the viewpoint, and establish views, such as multiviews in a 2D or 3D drawing. Multiview drawings are discussed in Chapter 9.

In a large drawing, it is often necessary to "zoom" into certain portions to view details. The **Zoom** command provides this capability. After entering the command, you can zoom into a portion of the drawing by windowing around the display. The windowed portion is then shown at a greater magnification scale. You can also enter a magnification scale factor to reduce or enlarge the display relative to the current display. A third option allows you to zoom the view in real time by using the pointing device to move the cursor upward (to enlarge the view) or downward (to reduce the view).

When you wish to move the drawing across the screen to view areas outside of the current display without changing the magnification, you can use the **Pan** command. Panning adjusts the view in real time. The drawing is panned by using the pointing device to move the cursor in the direction desired.

More advanced viewing commands are available with 3D drawing programs. The **Orbit** command is typically used when working with models in 3D space. This is a powerful command that allows you to rotate the model in three dimensions by using the pointing device. The view is changed in real time, allowing you to view different surfaces and features across the model dynamically.

CAD Systems and Software

CAD programs range in capability from simple 2D drawing to advanced 3D modeling and presentation. The type of program used normally depends on the application or drawing discipline for which it is used. While basic CAD programs require relatively inexpensive hardware to drive the system, higher-end programs may require computer equipment costing several thousands of dollars.

As discussed in Chapter 4, a basic CAD system consists of a computer, a monitor (display screen), keyboard, pointing device, and output device. Data is stored on the hard drive of the computer or on portable media, such as CDs. The primary component of a CAD system is CAD software. The software is the set of instructions that tells the computer what to do and when to do it.

CAD software programs can be classified in several different ways. Some CAD programs provide 2D drawing capability only. These programs have many of the functions discussed in this chapter, with the exception of 3D-based tools. Other CAD programs are based on a specific type of 3D modeling, such as solid modeling, surface modeling, or parametric modeling. Some CAD modeling software is specifically designed for mechanical drafting and manufacturing applications. There are also advanced modeling programs used to create photorealistic renderings and animation graphics. The following sections discuss some of the features provided by different types of CAD software.

CAD Modeling Programs

Modeling programs are used to create realistic definitions of objects using XYZ coordinates and a variety of 3D drawing methods. Commands in the software are used to construct a model in 3D space. The resulting model can then be shown in a pictorial view to display the various features and surfaces. Common 3D modeling commands are discussed in Chapter 13.

Three of the most common types of 3D modeling are solid modeling, surface modeling, and parametric modeling. In *solid modeling*, objects called *solids* or *solid models* are created to represent the entire mass of an object. See **Figure 7-19**. A solid model is considered to be defined from the actual material making up the object. Solid models are used in mechanical drafting applications because they can be analyzed for properties such as mass and volume.

Models created in *surface modeling* are similar to solid models, but the objects are not considered solid. *Surface models* have an outer "skin" to represent exterior surfaces. See **Figure 7-20**. While a surface model is not considered as realistic as a solid model, the quality of the representation is very similar. Therefore, surface models are primarily used for presentation purposes.

Parametric modeling is an advanced form of modeling that allows object dimensions, or parameters, to be modified during the construction of a model. This permits changes to be made to different portions of a model during the modeling process. See **Figure 7-21**. Parametric modeling programs are available for both solid modeling and surface modeling.

Figure 7-19 A solid model represents the entire mass of an object and the material used in its construction. (Designed with Solid Edge from UGS PLM Solutions)

Figure 7-20 A surface model is a representation of the outer "skin" of the various surfaces simulating the object. (Discreet, a division of Autodesk)

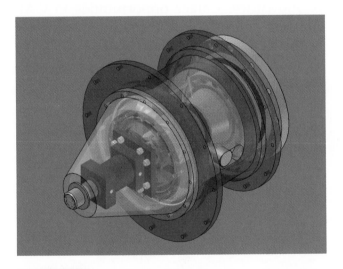

Figure 7-21 Parametric modeling programs provide powerful modeling tools that allow object dimensions to be changed throughout the modeling process. Any changes made affect the entire model. (Designed with Solid Edge from UGS PLM Solutions)

In more advanced programs, changing one parameter affects the entire model. These types of programs can simulate how a part will "work" with other parts in an assembly. This allows the engineer to determine whether possible conflicts exist (for example, if two parts are in the same place at the same time).

Solid modeling, surface modeling, and parametric modeling programs also typically provide rendering capability. In CAD terms, a *rendering* is a highly realistic representation of a model with lighting, shadows, and other visual effects applied. Renderings are common in mechanical and architectural drafting, because a mechanical assembly or an interior room can be shown in great detail to a potential client. The models shown in **Figures 7-19**, **7-20**, and **7-21** are rendered models.

CAD/CAM

Computer-aided design/computer-aided manufacturing (CAD/CAM) combines CAD with automated manufacturing operations. In this type of manufacturing, computer numerical control (CNC) machines control the manufacturing processes. Computer data that is input to the machine is used to control the movement of machine tools. After a part is drawn in the CAD program, the mathematical shape and size description of the part, or design data, is calculated by the program for manufacturing. The data is used to cut the material and make the part, **Figure 7-22**.

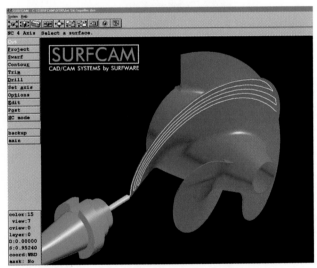

Figure 7-22 CAD/CAM programs use CAD-generated drawings to supply tool data for manufacturing processes. This display shows the generation of the cutter path for machining a personal watercraft impeller. (Courtesy of SURFCAM by Surfware)

Advanced Rendering and Animation Programs

In high-end applications, advanced rendering programs are used to create very realistic displays of complex models. See **Figure 7-23**. These programs provide lighting tools, material surface finishes, and environmental settings that can be used to greatly enhance the appearance of a model. A model set up for rendering in this manner is known as a *scene*. When the scene is rendered, material finishes and other effects are calculated based on the lighting used. Computer rendering programs require greater amounts of resources in order to perform the calculations needed. The original model may be created within the program, or it may be imported from a different modeling program with less rendering capability.

Some modeling and rendering programs allow you to animate models so that they can be shown in actual operation. Models created in this manner are assigned movement parameters for frame-by-frame animations. Animated models are useful in the architectural field. For example, an architectural project can be presented with an animated tour through a building for a design proposal.

One of the fastest-growing applications of CAD technology is the use of computer-generated animation and imaging for special effects in films. Computer drawing and animation programs are also used for imaging applications in the medical field. While originally conceived for engineering purposes, CAD-based graphics are now used in a variety of industries. Career opportunities in CAD drafting and design will continue to expand as the technology develops.

Figure 7-23 Realistic scenes such as this model of the Apollo spacecraft can be created with the lighting and surface finish controls of an advanced rendering program. (Discreet, a division of Autodesk)

Test Your Knowledge

Please do not write in this book. Place your answers on another sheet of paper.

1. Drawings created in a CAD program are made up of line and arc objects called _____ objects with defined point coordinates in space.
2. In the Cartesian coordinate system, _____ coordinates are located at a given distance and angle from another point.
3. Describe the difference between the world coordinate system and a user-defined coordinate system.
4. A network of uniformly spaced points used as a drawing aid to determine distances is known as what?
5. What are *layers* and what function do they serve in CAD drafting?
6. What is a *template*?
7. Circles are typically drawn by specifying a _____ and a radius or diameter.
8. What editing command is used to orient multiple copies of an object in a regular rectangular or polar pattern?
9. Describe how to create a round or fillet with the **Fillet** command.
10. What display command is used to create a magnified view by windowing a portion of a drawing?
11. What is the difference between a solid model and a surface model?
12. Define *rendering*.

Outside Activities

1. Obtain samples of various types of drawings prepared using a computer. Prepare a bulletin board display with these drawings.
2. Visit an industrial drafting firm that uses a CAD system. Interview a computer workstation operator. How does the CAD system save time? How does it assist with repetitive work? How does it improve productivity? What did the system cost the business? Report to the class what you observed and learned.
3. Visit a computer store that sells CAD equipment. Request literature on the equipment sold. Prepare a bulletin board display with the material.

8 Lettering

OBJECTIVES

After studying this chapter,
you should be able to:

- Produce neat, precise, and legible free-hand lettering.
- Demonstrate the difference between vertical and inclined lettering.
- Describe the use of common lettering aids and devices.
- Use preprinted lettering.
- Explain how lettering is generated in computer-aided drafting.

DRAFTING VOCABULARY

Alphanumeric
Ames lettering guide
Braddock lettering triangle
Burnishing tool
Dry transfer lettering
Leroy lettering instrument
Lettering
Single-stroke Gothic lettering
Text
Text styles

Lettering is used on drawings to show dimensions and other important information needed to describe objects. The lettering must be neat and legible if it is to be easily read and understood. Although text commands and styles in CAD software have simplified the lettering process in CAD drafting, the ability to produce exceptional freehand lettering is a valuable skill that can always be used as a quick communication tool.

A drawing is improved by good lettering. Likewise, a good drawing becomes sloppy and unprofessional if the lettering is poorly done. To become skilled at lettering, you must frequently practice doing it the right way. The old saying "practice makes perfect" is definitely true in reference to learning the skill of lettering. Conversely, you can also become extremely good at producing bad lettering by practicing it incorrectly and sloppily.

Single-Stroke Gothic Lettering

The ASME drafting standard (ASME Y14.2M, *Line Conventions and Lettering*) recommends *single-stroke Gothic lettering* as the accepted lettering standard. It can be drawn rapidly and is highly legible, **Figure 8-1**. It is called single-stroke lettering not because each letter is made with a single stroke of the pencil (most letters require several strokes to complete), but because each line is only as wide as the point of the pencil or pen.

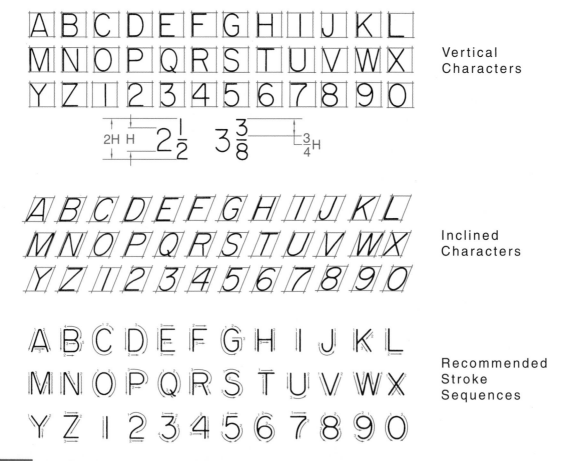

Figure 8-1 Single-stroke Gothic lettering should be drawn neatly and accurately. Characters may be drawn vertical or inclined. The characters are shown "blocked in" to the correct text height. Also shown are the recommended stroke sequences for letters and numerals.

Single-stroke lettering may be vertical or inclined. There is no definite rule stating that it should be one way or the other. However, mixing the two styles within individual words or sentences should be avoided, **Figure 8-2**.

You can produce excellent lettering if you learn the basic shapes of the letters, the proper stroke sequence for making them, and the recommended spacing between letters, words, and rows of lettering. As mentioned previously, you must also practice creating accurate and precise Gothic lettering. Do not practice doing lettering incorrectly. Practice doing it correctly. Do not expect to become good at lettering if you do not practice doing it correctly.

Lettering with a Pencil

Since each letter the drafter creates is an object, all letters should be drawn to object line weight. Hence, as discussed in Chapter 5, an H or 2H drafting grade pencil is used by most drafters for lettering. Do not attempt to letter a drawing with a standard 2H writing pencil.

Sharpen the pencil to a sharp conical (cone-shaped) point. Rotate it as you letter, **Figure 8-3**, to keep the point sharp and the lines that make up the letters uniform in weight and width. The pencil should rotate clockwise (when viewed from the unsharpened end) if the drafter is right-handed, and counterclockwise if left-handed. Re-sharpen the pencil when the lines start to become wide and "fuzzy." All letters should be black

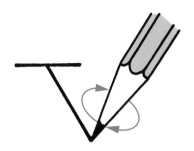

Figure 8-3 Rotate the pencil as you letter to keep the point sharp and lettering uniform in weight. Clockwise rotation is shown for right-handed drafters. Reverse the direction for left-handed drafting.

and sharp. Gray, fuzzy letters do not reproduce well on prints and detract from the readability of the print. Creating drawings that reproduce well is one of the most important goals of the drafter.

Guidelines

Good lettering requires the use of guidelines, **Figure 8-4**. Guidelines are very thin, gray lines made with a "needle-sharp" 4H or 6H pencil (refer to the pencil recommendations given in Chapter 5). Guidelines should be drawn so lightly that they will not appear on a print made from the drawing. If guidelines are drawn to the correct line weight, they need not be erased and they usually are not. Vertical guidelines, **Figure 8-5**, may be used to assure that the letters will be vertical. Use inclined guidelines where inclined lettering is to be used, **Figure 8-6**. Inclined guidelines are drawn at 67-1/2° to the horizontal line.

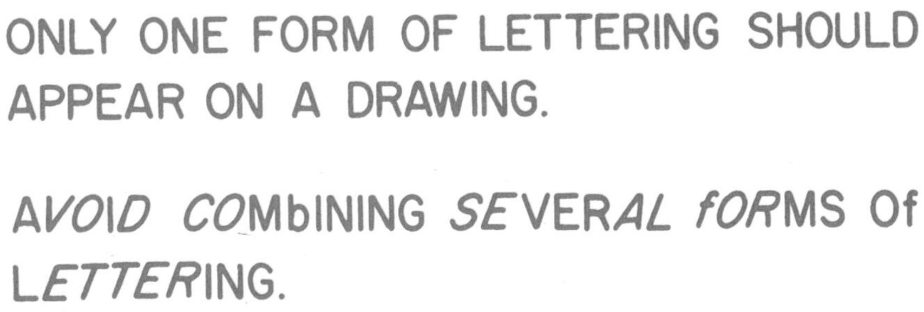

ONLY ONE FORM OF LETTERING SHOULD APPEAR ON A DRAWING.

AVOID COMBINING SEVERAL FORMS OF LETTERING.

Figure 8-2 Do not mix vertical and inclined lettering on a drawing.

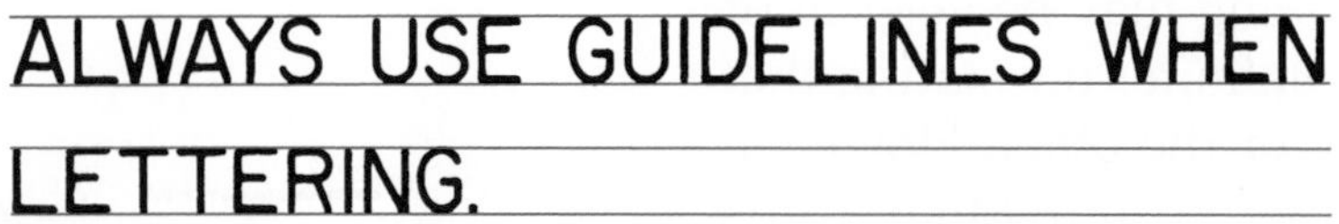

ALWAYS USE GUIDELINES WHEN

LETTERING.

Figure 8-4 Guidelines must be used when lettering to keep the letters uniform in height.

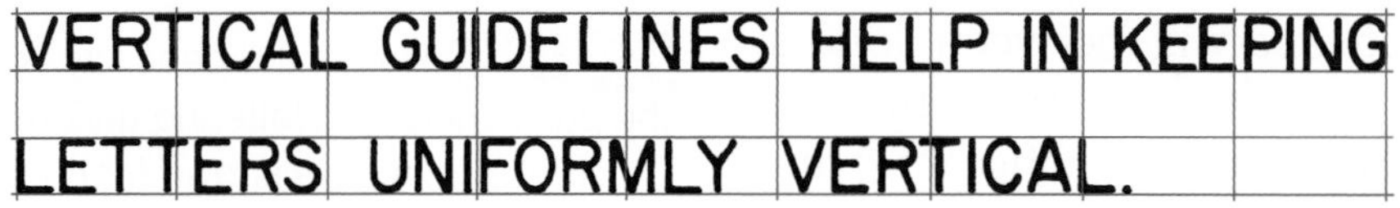

VERTICAL GUIDELINES HELP IN KEEPING

LETTERS UNIFORMLY VERTICAL.

Figure 8-5 Vertical guidelines.

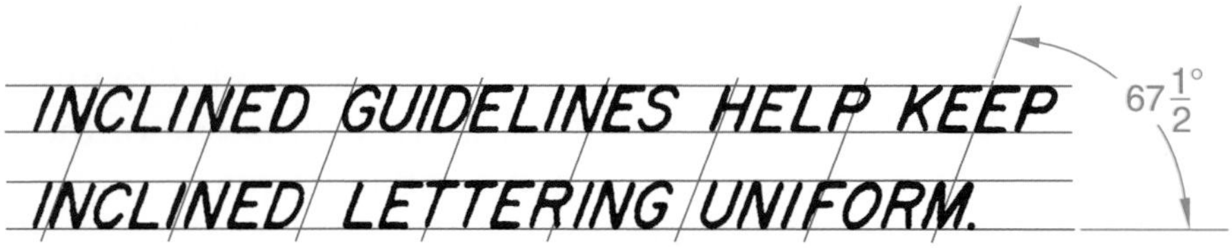

INCLINED GUIDELINES HELP KEEP

INCLINED LETTERING UNIFORM.

$67\frac{1}{2}°$

Figure 8-6 Inclined guidelines.

Lettering aids, discussed later in this chapter, help establish the inclined angle.

One very common error many novice drafters experience in using guidelines for lettering is not making letters uniform. The purpose of guidelines is to keep the height of the letters uniform. If the top and bottom of each letter does not touch the guidelines, the guidelines are useless. Also, no guideline should ever be used for two rows of lettering. There should always be space between rows of lettering.

Spacing

Proper spacing of letters is important in lettering. There is no hard and fast rule that indicates how far apart the letters should be spaced. The letters within individual words should be placed so spaces between the letters appear to be about the same. Adjacent letters with straight lines require more space than curved letters. Sloped letters (such as the *A* and the *W*) next to each other may appear to even overlap a bit. Letter spacing within words is judged by eye rather than by measuring, **Figure 8-7**.

Spacing between words and between sentences is another matter. The horizontal spacing between words and sentences should be roughly equal to the height of the letters used, **Figure 8-8**.

Vertical spacing between lines of lettering should be no more than the height of the letters, and no less than half the height of the letters, **Figure 8-9**.

DEVALUATION

Spaced visually

DEVALUATION

Spaced by measuring

Figure 8-7 Letter spacing is judged by eye rather than by measuring.

WORDS AND LETTERS MUST BE CLEARLY
SEPARATED. SPACING BETWEEN WORDS
AND SENTENCES IS EQUAL TO THE LETTER HEIGHT.

Spacing between words and sentences.

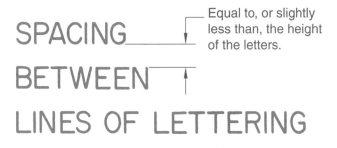

SPACING——————— Equal to, or slightly
less than, the height
of the letters.

BETWEEN

LINES OF LETTERING

Figure 8-9   Spacing between lines of lettering.

ACADEMIC LINK

Letter heights in manual drafting and CAD programs are expressed in inches. However, word processing programs and many printed materials (such as textbooks) use different forms of measurement for text. Letter heights are commonly expressed in points and picas. There are simple mathematic formulas you can use to convert these units of measure to inches.

A *point* is a unit of measure equal to 1/72″ (there are 72 points in 1″). Letter heights in a word processing document are typically expressed in points. For example, the body text in this book measures 11 points high. The headlines in a newspaper or magazine are also measured in points. Common sizes for headlines and subheads are 36 point, 24 point, and 18 point. Converted to inches, a 36-point headline measures 1/2″ (36 × 1/72 = 36/72 = 1/2″) and an 18-point headline measures 1/4″ (18 × 1/72 = 18/72 = 1/4″).

A *pica* is a unit of measure equal to 12 points. There are approximately six picas in 1″. You can convert inches to picas or picas to inches by multiplying or dividing by 6. For example, a 2″ measurement is equal to 12 picas (2 × 6 = 12 picas) and a measurement of 24 picas is equal to 4″ (24 ÷ 6 = 4″).

Another unit of measure used in the printing industry is the *agate*. One agate is approximately equal to 5-1/2 points. You can measure type sizes in agates, points, picas, and inches with a measuring instrument called a *line gauge*.

Letter Height

On most drawings, 1/8″ high lettering is satisfactory. This is the most common height of lettering on drawings. Most dimensioning and information in title blocks is completed in 1/8″ lettering. Titles are usually 3/16″ to 1/4″ in height.

On large drawings, lettering for dimensions, title blocks, and titles may be increased slightly to make the information easier to read.

Lettering Aids and Devices

To be done accurately and precisely, freehand lettering requires significant time and expense. There are a number of lettering aids and devices that help make the process easier and more efficient.

Two instruments are useful for drawing guidelines. These are the *Braddock lettering triangle*, shown in **Figure 8-10**, and the *Ames lettering guide*, **Figure 8-11**. Both devices help establish the correct letter height and spacing.

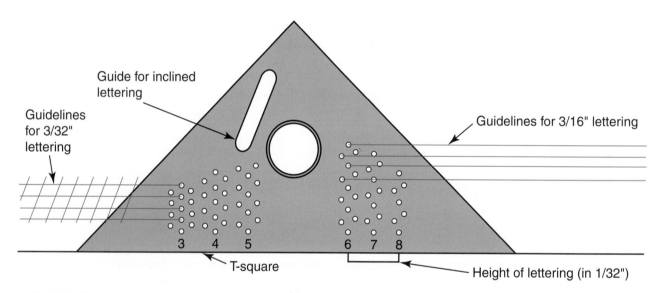

Figure 8-10 The Braddock lettering triangle. Shown are guidelines for 3/32″ and 3/16″ lettering. Lettering may be drawn vertical or inclined.

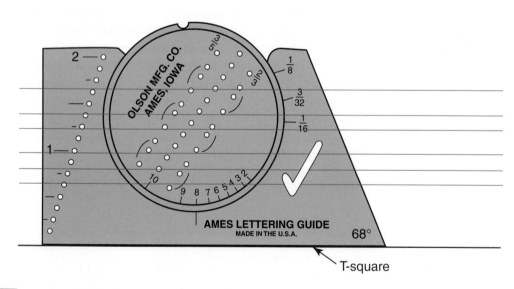

Figure 8-11 The Ames lettering instrument.

Each series of holes on the Braddock lettering triangle consists of three columns. The number appearing below each series of holes indicates the letter height in thirty-seconds of an inch. For example, when using the 3 series, guidelines are drawn 3/32″ apart. When using the 4 series, guidelines are drawn 4/32″ or 1/8″ apart. The center column of holes in each series is used to draw guidelines for the bottom edges of each row of letters. The left and right columns of holes are used to create guidelines for the top edges of lowercase letters and capital letters. The difference in height between a hole in the right column and an adjacent hole in the center column determines the vertical spacing between rows of letters. To use the triangle, align it with the T-square. The point of the pencil is placed in a hole and the triangle is slid while drawing the line lightly.

The Ames lettering guide is used to draw guidelines in a similar manner. The numbers labeled along the disk of the instrument indicate the spacing of guidelines in thirty-seconds of an inch. To set the guide, the disk is rotated until the inch setting is even with the vertical line on the base of the tool. The three-hole series are used to establish the height of lowercase and capital letters and the spacing between rows. The holes in the center column are equally spaced. This allows you to quickly draw guidelines with uniform line spacing. Every other hole represents the height of the current inch setting. For example, if the guide is set to draw 1/4″ guidelines, the distance from the first hole to the third hole is 1/4″. The distance from one hole to the next hole is 1/8″.

More detailed instructions on the complete and proper use of these instruments are provided by the manufacturers and included with the instruments when purchased.

Mechanical Lettering Device

For very precise lettering, a special mechanical lettering device may be used. See **Figure 8-12**. This device operates with a

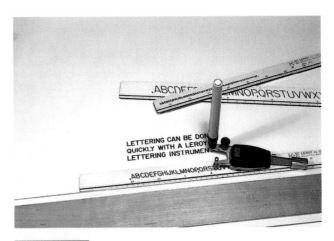

Figure 8-12 A mechanical lettering device. Many styles and sizes of letters, figures, and symbols are available with this tool.

stylus and template and is known as a *Leroy lettering instrument*. The stylus is used to guide a scriber along cuts in the template. Each cut represents an individual letter or pattern. Movement of the stylus controls the movement of an ink pen on the drawing. The lettering produced is very neat and accurate. There are many different letter and symbol templates available. This instrument is valuable for drawings that are enlarged or reduced for archiving, where the lettering must be highly legible.

Preprinted Lettering

Many types of preprinted lettering are available for use on drawings. With preprinted lettering, characters are removed or *transferred* from a printed sheet and adhered to a drawing surface. A wide selection of alphabets, symbols, and borders are available in preprinted form, **Figure 8-13**.

The use of *dry transfer lettering* is very common, **Figure 8-14**. Printed letters, symbols, and borders adhered to a plastic sheet are transferred from the sheet to the drawing media by lightly rubbing over the item with a *burnishing tool*. After burnishing, the character or symbol adheres to the media. Some transfer sheets have guidelines that are erased after an entire line of letters has been applied.

LEADERSHIP IN THE
18 leadership in the creat
LEADERSHIP IN
24 leadership in the
LEADERSHIP
24 leadership in
LEADERS
30 leadership

Leaders
LEADERSHi
leadership in
Leadership In T

LEADERSHIP IN THE
24 leadership in the cre
LEADERSHIP IN
36 leadership in
LEADERSHIP IN THE
24 leadership in the
LEADERSHIP

Figure 8-13 Examples of preprinted transfer lettering. Hundreds of lettering styles and sizes are available. (Formatt)

Figure 8-14 Drafters are sometimes called upon to produce work other than production drawings. These illustrations show a drafter completing an advertising sheet with transfer lettering. A—The lettering is applied by placing the letter in position and burnishing (rubbing) the back of the carrier sheet with a burnishing tool. B—The lettering sheet is carefully removed after the letter is applied.

Lettering in CAD

This chapter is aimed at helping you develop the manual freehand skills and dexterity needed to letter your drawings clearly, accurately, and eventually, rapidly. It is important to learn and practice good lettering skills.

In computer-aided drafting, the lettering process is automated with commands and lettering styles. Lettering in a CAD program is known as *text*. It consists of *alphanumeric* characters (letters and numbers) and symbols. Text is created with different lettering styles known as *text styles*. Some styles are similar to the single-stroke Gothic lettering style you are now learning.

However, text styles in a CAD program vary widely, **Figure 8-15**. Text can be created to appear in a number of ways. It may be drawn inclined, vertical, or backward. In addition, text can be easily edited once it is drawn.

Text on a CAD drawing is extremely accurate and readable. The ability to create or select a text style, type in text, and edit it on a drawing greatly simplifies the lettering process.

Typical commands used to create text are the **Text** and **Multiple Text** commands. The **Text** command is commonly used to create single lines of text, and the **Multiple Text** command is used to create text or notes consisting of one or more lines. These commands are used in conjunction with the **Style** command, which is used to create text styles.

Text styles are created with a number of settings. Common settings include the text font, justification, height, and rotation angle. The text justification controls the alignment of the text in relation to a text insertion point. For example, left-justified text is aligned so that the text is set from left to right with the starting point at the lower-left corner. Refer to **Figure 8-15**. Text can also be justified with center justification so that one or more lines of text are centered on a specified point. The text rotation angle controls the angular setting for inclined text.

Text is usually placed on a separate layer from other layers in the drawing. Once a style and text layer are created, text can be drawn by entering a specific command. A start point is typically selected with the pointing device, and text is entered at the keyboard. With some commands, text appears on screen as you type. After completing the command, the text is generated automatically by the program using the specified style. As previously discussed, the text can be edited as desired. Most CAD programs provide a spell check function to check the accuracy of the text.

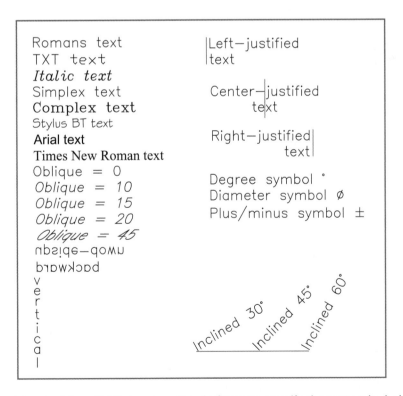

Figure 8-15 When adding text to a CAD drawing, the drafter can specify the text style, height, justification, and angular orientation. The Romans text font shown is a single-stroke font similar in appearance to single-stroke Gothic lettering.

Text can also be imported from other sources into a CAD program. For example, it may be useful to import text from a word processing document into a CAD drawing.

Text styles are normally used in creating dimensions on drawings. Dimensioning functions in CAD are discussed in Chapter 10.

Test Your Knowledge

Please do not write in this book. Place your answers on another sheet of paper.

1. What type of lettering is the accepted standard in manual drafting?
2. Why must lettering on a drawing be neat and legible?
3. Lettering should be drawn using the _____ line weight.
4. A(n) _____ or _____ pencil is usually used for lettering.
5. Why should guidelines be used when lettering?
6. Inclined guidelines should be drawn at what angle to horizontal?
7. Briefly discuss how to use an Ames lettering guide.
8. Briefly discuss how to use a mechanical lettering device (Leroy lettering instrument).
9. What is *dry transfer lettering?*
10. Lettering styles created in a CAD program are known as _____ styles.

Outside Activities

1. Using signs and posters from bulletin boards in your school, make a display of different lettering examples. Point out good spacing and poor spacing. Check to see if lettering styles are mixed in each example.
2. Research the variety of lettering styles, alphabets, and symbols available with mechanical lettering devices. The Internet is a good resource for this.
3. Freehand letter the following sentence: Good lettering technique requires practice and concentration. Use vertical single-stroke Gothic lettering. Letter the same sentence using a mechanical lettering device such as the Leroy lettering instrument. Time yourself and report to the class which method is faster and which lettering is easier to read.
4. Demonstrate the use of dry transfer lettering by producing a poster for another classroom or activity in your school.

Drawing Problems

Duplicate the drawings shown on the problem sheets on the following pages. Use the dimensions provided. Draw guidelines and duplicate the examples shown.

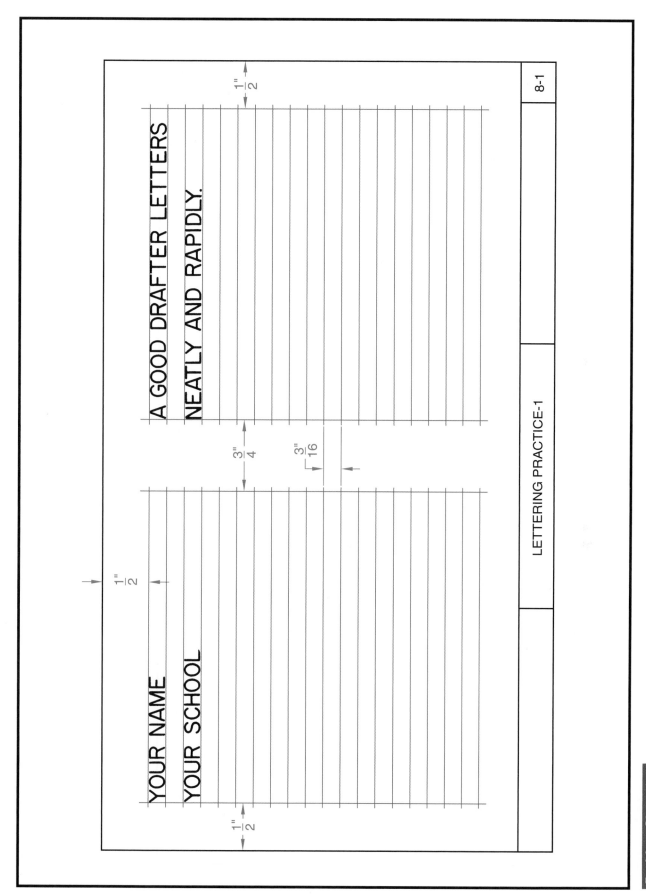

LETTERING PRACTICE-1

8-1

THE QUICK RED FOX JUMPED

OVER THE LAZY BROWN DOG.

1 2 3 4 5 6 7 8 9 0 $\frac{1}{2}$ $\frac{1}{16}$ $\frac{3}{8}$ $\frac{5}{32}$

LETTERING PRACTICE-2

8-2

"THE BEST THING ABOUT THE

FUTURE IS THAT IT COMES ONE

DAY AT A TIME."

MAKE THE MOST OF YOURSELF

FOR THAT IS ALL THERE IS OF

YOU.

8-3

LETTERING PRACTICE-3

PACK EACH BOX WITH SEVEN
DOZEN GIANT JUGS.

1 3 5 7
2 4 8 9

1 2 3 4 5 6 7 8 9 0

8-4

LETTERING PRACTICE-4

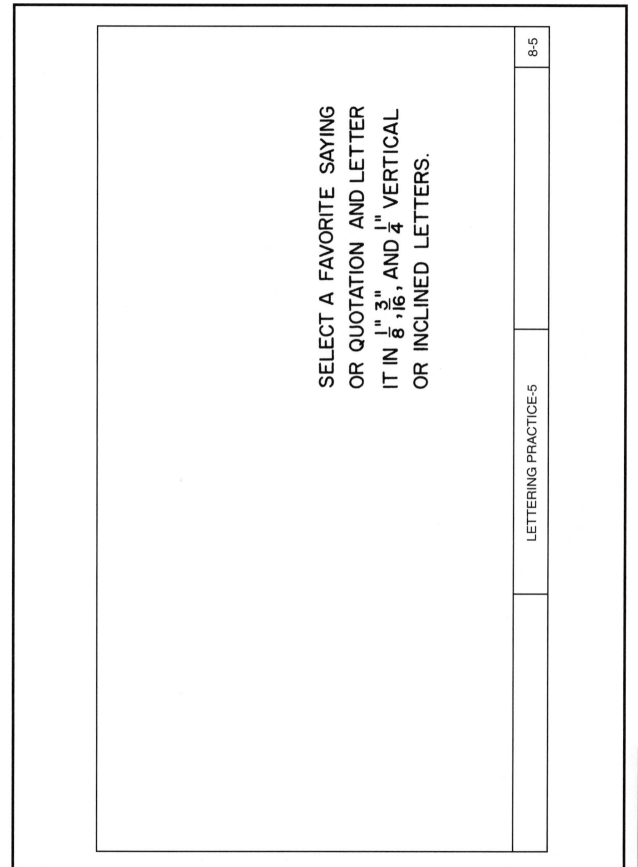

SELECT A FAVORITE SAYING OR QUOTATION AND LETTER IT IN $\frac{1}{8}$", $\frac{3}{16}$", AND $\frac{1}{4}$" VERTICAL OR INCLINED LETTERS.

LETTERING PRACTICE-5

8-5

Problem Sheet 8-5

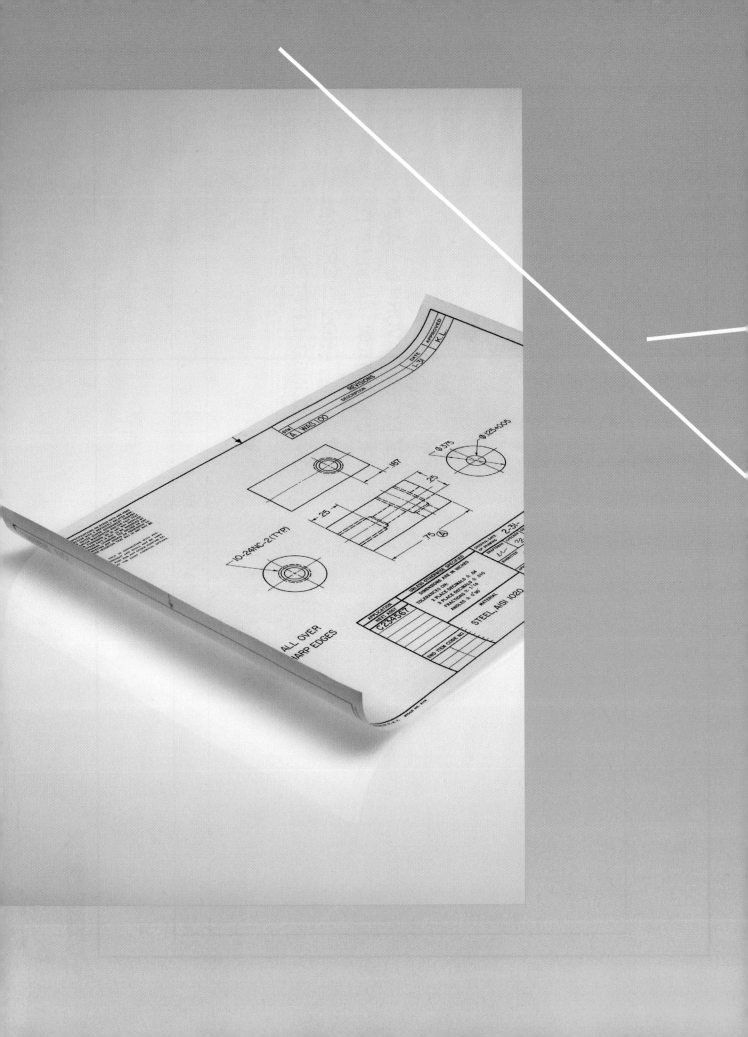

9 Multiview Drawings

OBJECTIVES

After studying this chapter, you should be able to:

◆ Explain why multiview drawings are used to represent objects.

◆ Understand the principles of orthographic projection.

◆ Use orthographic projection to develop multiview drawings.

◆ Identify and explain projection planes and how they relate to multiview drawings.

◆ Determine the views necessary to completely describe an object in a multiview drawing.

◆ Identify various types of features existing within objects.

◆ Identify and explain positive and negative mass as it relates to an object.

◆ Explain the difference between primary and secondary views of objects and features.

◆ Center a multiview drawing on the drawing sheet.

DRAFTING VOCABULARY

Blocking in
Depth
Engineering
  working drawings
First-angle
  projection
Foreshortening
Frontal plane
Height
Horizontal plane
Mechanical drawing
Multiview drawing
Negative mass
Object feature
Orthographic
  projection
Positive mass
Primary projection
  plane
Primary view
Principal planes
Principal views
Profile plane
Projection plane
Third-angle
  projection
True face
Width

When a drawing is made with the aid of instruments, it is called a *mechanical drawing*. Straight lines are made with a T-square, triangle, or drafting machine straightedge. Circles, arcs, and irregular curves are drawn with a compass, French curve, or the appropriate template for the object needed.

As discussed in Chapter 7, drawings are also generated with computer-aided drafting (CAD) software. While many drafting firms now use CAD for developing drawing projects, knowledge of manual drafting techniques and procedures is still extremely valuable in solving design problems.

Regardless of the technique, whether traditional (manual) or CAD drafting, the principles of drafting remain the same. The drafter must be familiar with the standards and procedures necessary to develop drawings that accurately describe objects.

Many drawings used by industry are created as multiview drawings. A *multiview drawing* is a drawing that requires more

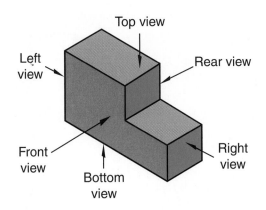

Figure 9-1 An object is normally viewed from six basic directions.

than one two-dimensional view in order to provide an accurate shape and size description of the object being produced. In developing the needed views, the object is normally viewed from six basic directions, as shown in **Figure 9-1**. These are the six *principal views*. They include the front, top, right side, left side, rear, and bottom views. See **Figure 9-2**.

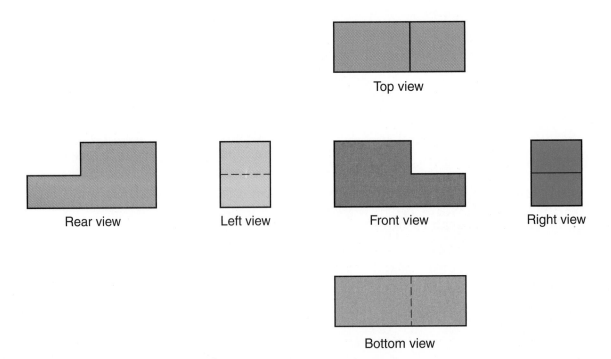

Figure 9-2 The six basic directions of sight provide the principal views for developing a multiview drawing. Shown are the principal views of the object in **Figure 9-1**.

Visualizing the Object and Projecting Views

Before a drafter can generate the necessary views for a multiview drawing, he or she must be able to visualize the object being drawn. In other words, the drafter must be able to see the object in three dimensions in his or her mind's eye. This is an essential skill in drafting. There are many methods and techniques that aid in the process of visualizing objects. The following approach should help the beginning drafter become successful at visualizing objects.

To obtain the two-dimensional views needed for a multiview drawing, the drafter should first think of the object as being enclosed in a hinged glass box. See **Figure 9-3**. The six surfaces of the glass box are the standard projection planes to which the individual views are projected. The process used in projecting the views to the projection planes is known as *orthographic projection*. This process allows three-dimensional objects (objects having

width, height, and depth) to be shown on a flat surface having only two dimensions. The flat surface may be a piece of paper or the screen of a computer monitor. Orthographic projection is the key tool used in developing multiviews for *engineering working drawings* (drawings used to manufacture or construct objects).

There are two ways to project views in orthographic projection, **Figure 9-4**. *Third-angle projection* is preferred in the United States. *First-angle projection* is typically used in most European countries.

The difference between the two types of projection relates to the placement of the imaginary box in one of the quadrants formed by the intersection of the three *principal planes*. Referring to **Figure 9-4**, these planes are the frontal plane, horizontal plane, and profile plane. The *frontal plane* represents the projection for the front view of an object. The *horizontal plane* represents the projection for the top view of the object. The *profile plane* represents the projection for the side view of the object. In third-angle projection, the imaginary box containing the object rests in the third quadrant (the lower-right or third-angle quadrant when looking at the profile plane). In this type of projection, the sides of the object are projected to the sides of the box and toward the viewer. In first-angle projection, the imaginary box containing the object rests in the first quadrant (the upper-left or first-angle quadrant when looking at the profile plane). In this type of projection, the sides of the object are projected to the sides of the box and away from the viewer.

A graphic explanation of third-angle projection is shown in **Figure 9-5**. In this method, the object is viewed from points of view that are perpendicular to the projection planes (the surfaces of the glass box). The drafter looks through the given projection plane and the surfaces, edges, and intersections that make up the object are then projected forward to the projection plane. That is, the views are projected to the six sides of the glass box.

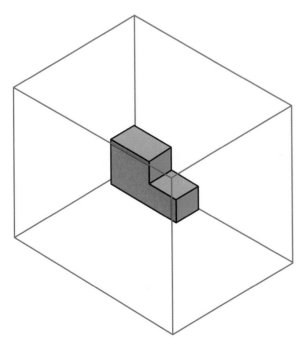

Figure 9-3 Visualizing a three-dimensional object inside a hinged glass box helps establish the planes of projection for projecting views.

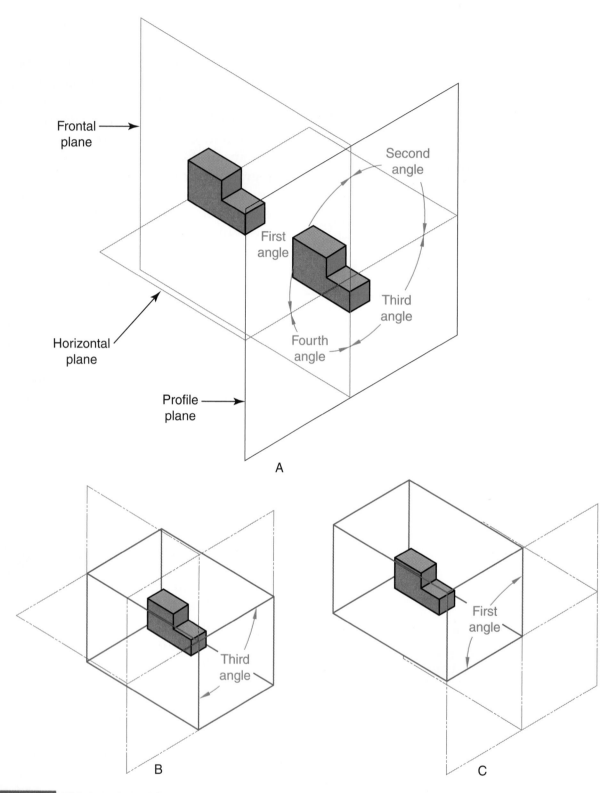

Frontal plane

Second angle

First angle

Horizontal plane

Third angle

Fourth angle

Profile plane

A

Third angle

B

First angle

C

Figure 9-4 Third-angle and first-angle projection. A—The principal planes used in orthographic projection divide the drawing space into four quadrants. B—An imaginary box containing the object is placed in the third quadrant for third-angle projection. C—An imaginary box containing the object is placed in the first quadrant for first-angle projection.

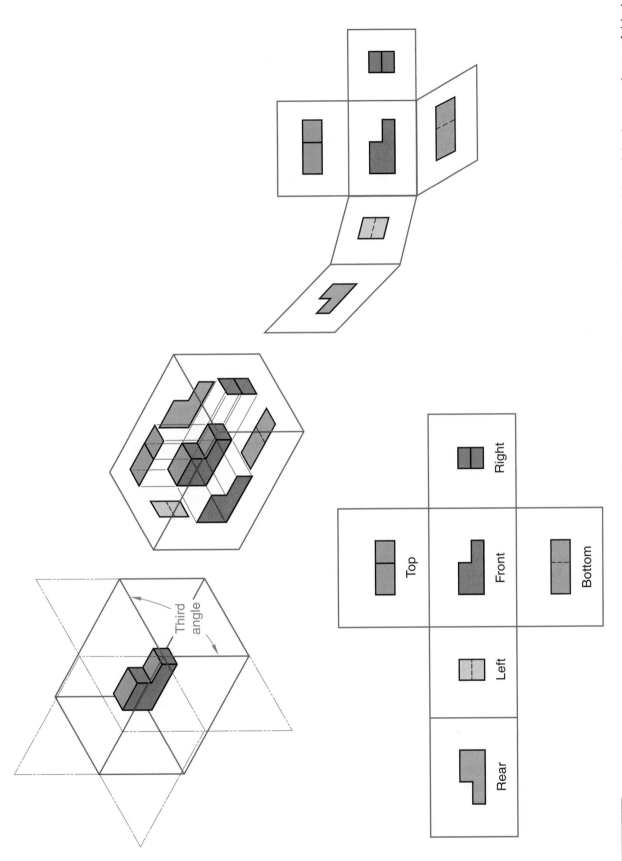

Figure 9-5   In third-angle projection, the sides of the object are projected to the sides of the imaginary box. The sides of the box are then unfolded toward the viewer.

CAREERS IN DRAFTING

Mechanical Engineer

What would I do if I were to become a mechanical engineer? I would design and develop power-producing machines such as generators, engines, and turbines. I would also design and develop power-using machines such as automotive vehicles, heating, ventilation, and air conditioning (HVAC) equipment, machine tools, manufacturing systems and components, elevators and escalators, and robots used in automation systems. I would also design and develop other types of machinery and products.

What would I need to know? I would need to know how to develop economical solutions to technical mechanical problems. I would have to know how to research, develop, design, manufacture, and test tools, engines, machines, and other mechanical devices by applying theories and principles of math and science. Also, I would need to know basic drafting skills, standards, and principles using both manual and computer-aided drafting (CAD) techniques and tools. All engineers need to be creative, inquisitive, analytical, and detail-oriented.

Where would I work? Generally, I would work in an office building, laboratory, or industrial plant.

For whom would I work? I most often would work in manufacturing. I would work for a manufacturer of machinery, transportation equipment, computer and electronics products, or fabricated metal products. I may also work for a government agency or a company in the architectural field.

What sort of education would I need? A bachelor's degree in mechanical engineering is required. To be admitted to an undergraduate engineering school, courses are required in math (through calculus), science (through physics), English, social studies, humanities, information technology, and mechanical drafting/CAD.

What are the special fields relating to this career? Mechanical engineering is a specialized field of engineering. Specialized fields of mechanical engineering include automotive design and plant engineering and maintenance. Mechanical engineering is also related to the design of energy systems, manufacturing systems, materials, pressure vessels and piping, and HVAC systems.

What are my chances of finding a job? The demand for mechanical engineers is not expected to grow quite as fast as the demand for some other engineering specialties over the next several years. However, new technologies relating to nanotechnology, materials science, and biotechnology should provide opportunities for mechanical engineers. Also, it is not uncommon for someone holding a degree in mechanical engineering to qualify for jobs in other special engineering fields.

How much money could I expect to make? The median salary for degreed mechanical engineers in recent years was $62,880. However, salaries ranged from $41,490 to $93,430 and up. Information from a recent survey showed that mechanical engineers with only a bachelor's degree received offers averaging $48,585. With a master's degree, that figure increased to $54,565. With a doctorate, it was $69,904.

Where else could I look for more information about becoming a mechanical engineer? See the US Department of Labor's Bureau of Labor Statistics Occupational Outlook Handbook (at www.bls.gov) or request information from the American Society of Mechanical Engineers (www.asme.org). Information relating to two special fields of mechanical engineering, HVAC and automotive, is available from the American Society of Heating, Refrigerating

(continued)

Mechanical Engineer *(continued)*

and Air-Conditioning Engineers (www.ashrae. org) and the Society of Automotive Engineers (www.sae.org), respectively. Special information for high school students about careers in engineering is available from the Junior Engineering Technical Society (www.jets.org).

If I decide to pursue a different career, what other fields are related to mechanical engineering? Mathematics, drafting, architecture, other types of engineering, and many types of science.

Then, the "sides" of the glass box are unfolded toward the drafter. The front is always the featured view with the other views oriented in the order obtained by unfolding the sides of the box. In other words, the right side view is always to the right of the front view, the top view is always above the front view, the bottom view is always below the front view, and so on.

A graphic explanation of first-angle projection is shown in **Figure 9-6**. In this method, the views are projected to the six sides of the box and the sides of the glass box are then unfolded *away from* the viewer. When viewing the object from the front, the surfaces, edges, and intersections of the object seen from that point of view are projected to a plane *behind* the object. In addition, the object is drawn *as if the object were placed on each side of the glass box*. When viewing the object from the top, what is seen is projected to a plane below the object. When viewing the object from the bottom, what is seen is projected to a plane above the object.

A very easy way to identify a drawing that has been generated using first-angle projection is to recognize that the views are in the opposite orientation of how they would appear in third-angle projection. That is, the views of the resulting multiview drawing are oriented so that the top view appears where the bottom view should be, the bottom view appears where the top view should be, and

so on. Compare the orientation of the views in **Figure 9-5** to the orientation of the views in **Figure 9-6**. Notice that regardless of the method of projection, all views are centered about and originate from the front view.

Different symbols are used in industry to identify third-angle and first-angle projection drawings. See **Figure 9-7**. The appropriate symbol typically appears next to the title block on the drawing sheet.

Identifying Object Features

An *object feature* may be defined as a physical characteristic of an object. It may be a hole that has been drilled, a notch that has been cut, or an angular cut. It is important for the drafter to be able to identify the features that exist in an object. This is because the size and location of each feature must be known for the object to be manufactured to the designer's specifications.

Features are physically represented as the *negative mass* of an object. Let us say that all objects begin as a solid mass of material. The solid block has what can be termed *positive mass*. Certain manufacturing operations must be performed on the solid mass to create the object's end product. These operations may include cutting, drilling, boring, and milling, among others. The important thing to remember about these operations is that they all remove material (positive mass) from

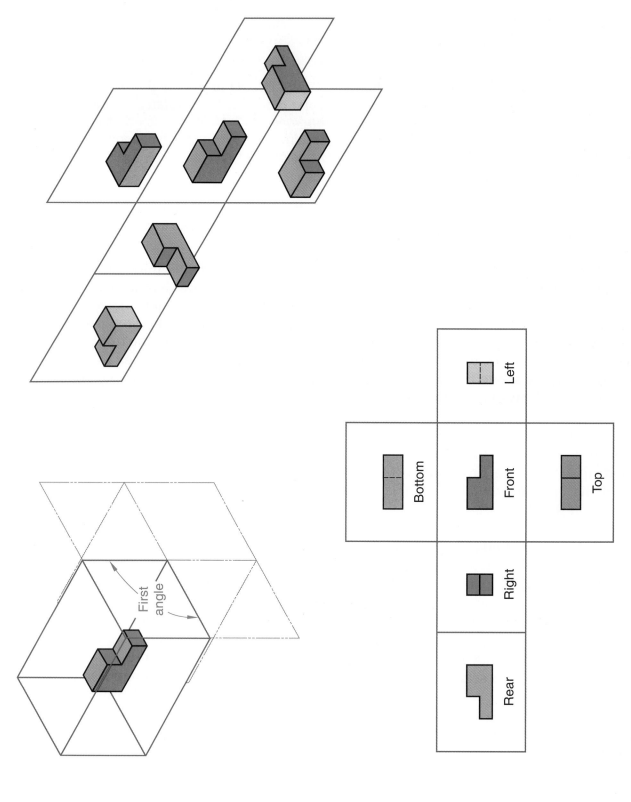

Figure 9-6 In first-angle projection, the sides of the object are projected to the sides of the imaginary box. The sides of the box are then unfolded away from the viewer. The views are projected to the rear.

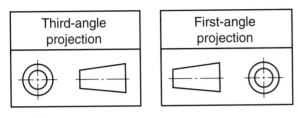

Figure 9-7 The appropriate symbol is placed on engineering drawings to show the method of projection used.

the original solid mass. The resulting subtractions created by these operations represent negative mass of the object. Hence, negative mass can be defined as the areas of unoccupied mass that exist within the overall limits of the original mass. See **Figure 9-8**.

For objects with more complex features, identifying the positive and negative mass becomes more difficult. Objects made from thin material, such as sheet metal, require

bending. This process does not remove material. However, the process of bending does create a feature in an object. There are other operations used to create features that do not require removing material. Regardless of what operations are required to create an object, a thorough understanding of positive and negative mass helps in identifying object features.

Primary and Secondary Views

When creating multiview drawings, every feature should be represented in every view. If the feature is visible in the given view, it is drawn with object lines. If the feature is invisible in the given view, it is drawn with hidden lines. Sometimes, in special situations, a feature may be partially visible and partially invisible from a particular point of

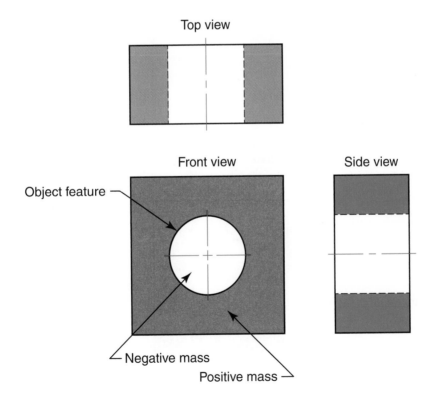

Figure 9-8 The entire solid object in this multiview drawing represents positive mass. The hole, which is the only feature of the object, represents the negative mass of the object.

view. In such cases, the feature is drawn partly with object lines and partly with hidden lines. Nevertheless, all features are represented in every view.

The view in which the feature appears in its true shape and size is the *primary view* of the feature. All other views then become secondary views of the feature, **Figure 9-9**. The primary view of a feature usually represents the feature with object lines, except in more complex situations. The secondary views usually represent the feature with hidden lines. In dimensioning multiview drawings, you will learn that, with few exceptions, the primary view is the view in which the drafter will both locate and give the size of any given feature. Dimensioning is discussed in Chapter 10.

The *primary projection plane* is the face of the glass box to which the primary view of a given feature is projected. The other faces then become the secondary projection planes for that feature, **Figure 9-10**.

True Faces and Foreshortening

When an object surface is drawn in its true shape and size within a view, it is said to be a *true face*. An object surface or feature is drawn true size when it is parallel to the projection plane. Multiview drawings of planar objects are normally made up of views representing true faces.

Orthographic drawings use different views to show the width, height, and depth of objects. These are the three most basic dimensions of any object. *Width* is defined as the horizontal distance measured across an object from side to side. *Height* is the vertical distance measured from the bottom to the top of an object. *Depth* is the horizontal distance measured from the front to the back of an object.

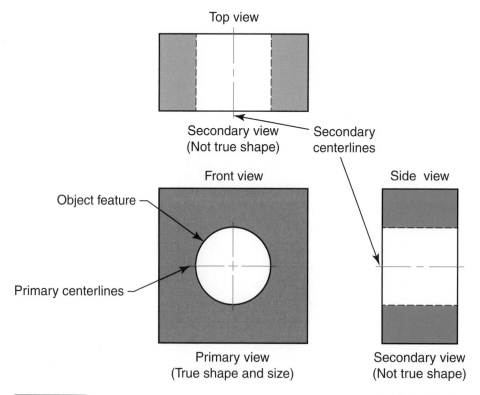

Figure 9-9 Primary and secondary views. Object lines are used to represent an object feature in its true size and shape in the primary view. Hidden lines are used to represent the feature in the secondary view.

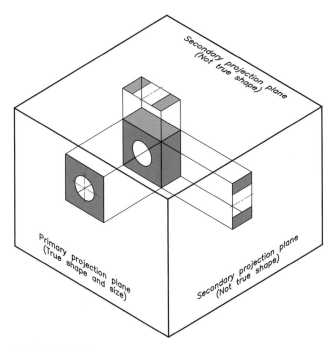

Figure 9-10 Primary and secondary projection planes. The primary view of a feature is projected in its true size and shape to the primary projection plane. Secondary views are projected to secondary projection planes.

When a surface is drawn as a true face in a given view, the surface is seen as true height and true width (in the front or back view), true height and true depth (in the right or left view), or true width and true depth (in the top or bottom view). See **Figure 9-11**. True faces do not have to be measured actual size. They may be drawn to scale. In other words, they may be drawn to a larger scale for easier viewing or to a smaller scale to fit on the drawing media.

An object surface that is not parallel to the projection plane is not drawn as a true face in the resulting view. This type of surface is drawn smaller than true size and shape. This is known as *foreshortening* and is common for objects with inclined surfaces. See **Figure 9-12**. Objects with inclined surfaces have at least one view where a face is at an angle to the projection plane. For this reason,

the surface does not appear in its true shape when drawn on a two-dimensional surface. For example, hole features on angled surfaces are not drawn in their true shape as circles when projected. They are drawn as ellipses because they are not perpendicular to the line of sight. The resulting features are said to be *foreshortened*.

Edges, Intersections, and Limiting Edges

When creating multiview drawings, the visualization of objects can be simplified by identifying what the lines in the different views should represent. In orthographic projection, all lines on multiview drawings represent one of three features of the object. Each line represents the edge view of a surface, an intersection between two surfaces, or the limiting edge of a round or elliptical detail. See **Figure 9-13**. Notice that most of the object features are described in the primary view. The secondary views use straight lines to show intersections

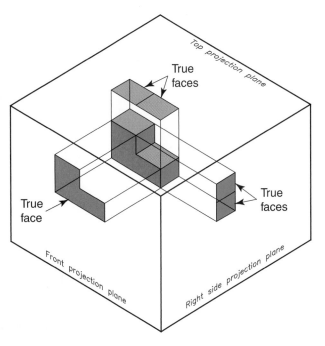

Figure 9-11 A surface that is parallel to the projection plane is drawn as a true face (in its true shape and size).

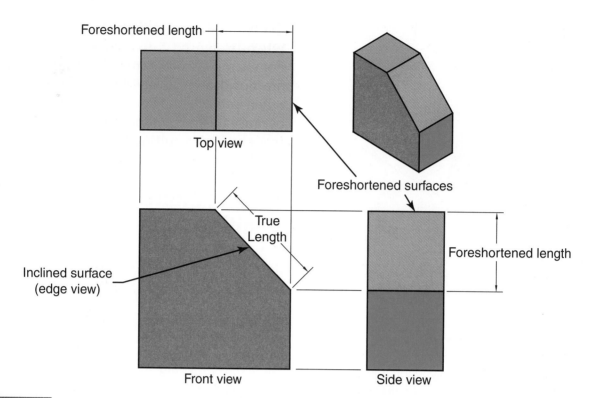

Figure 9-12 Objects with inclined surfaces have at least one view where the surface is not parallel to the projection plane. The inclined surface of this object does not appear in its true shape and size when projected to the top and side views. It instead appears foreshortened. The front view shows the inclined surface in its true size and shape.

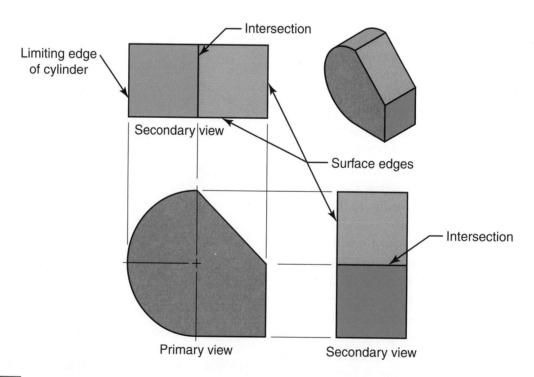

Figure 9-13 Lines in a multiview drawing represent edges of surfaces, intersections between surfaces, or limiting edges of round objects.

and edges. Thinking in these terms can help in the visualization process as well as the problem-solving process.

Selecting Views to Be Drawn

As previously discussed, there are six standard views of any object in orthographic projection. This does not mean that all six of the views must be used, or that they are needed to completely describe an object. Only the number of views needed to give a complete shape description of the object should be drawn. Any view that repeats the same shape description in another view (an identical view) can be eliminated, **Figure 9-14**.

In most instances, two or three views are sufficient to show the shape of an object. Objects that are basically cylindrical in shape can usually be drawn with just two views. Basic and complex prism-shaped objects generally require at least three views. In general, the front view should be the view that shows the most features (visible features) and the fewest hidden features of the object. The number of views needed is then decided in relation to the contents of the front view.

In general, the drafter should draw the views that show the fewest features as hidden lines. These are the views that should be used to create the multiview drawing. Views of objects showing a large number of hidden lines are normally used only when absolutely necessary for the complete understanding of the shape and size of the object. The use of too many hidden lines on a drawing tends to make the drawing confusing to the person reading the drawing or fabricating the part. Use another view without as many hidden lines, **Figure 9-15**. Sometimes it may be necessary to draw the left side or bottom of an object if the features are visible from one of those points of view instead of the standard right side or top. Regardless of the views shown, they should still be placed in proper ortho-

graphic order. As shown in **Figure 9-14B**, the top view is placed above the front view, and the right view is placed to the right.

When drawing hidden lines in multiviews, it is also important to draw them correctly in relation to other types of lines. Hidden lines should always start and end with a dash in contact with the object line, **Figure 9-16**. This illustration shows examples of how hidden lines are used and how they properly intersect or do not intersect other lines, depending on the situation.

It is important to remember with any drawing that the viewer wants to see as many visible features as possible, not invisible (hidden) features. The goal is to communicate the size and shape of the object as clearly and precisely as possible to the person making the part. Keep this in mind when laying out views for multiview drawings.

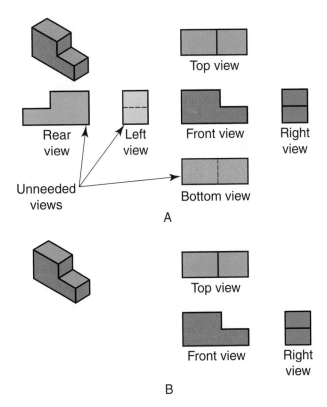

Figure 9-14 Not all views are needed in a multiview drawing. Eliminate any view that repeats the same shape description shown in another view. A—The six views of the object. B—Three views are sufficient for a complete description.

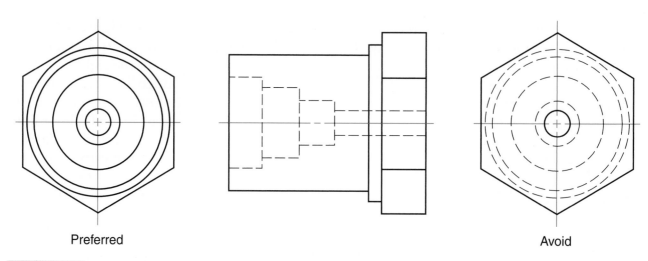

Preferred   Avoid

Figure 9-15   Views showing a large number of hidden lines are used only if absolutely necessary. Too many hidden lines tend to make the drawing confusing.

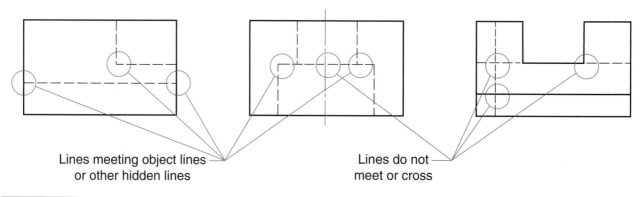

Lines meeting object lines
or other hidden lines

Lines do not
meet or cross

Figure 9-16   Correct uses of hidden lines.

Projecting Points and Edges

It is essential that the beginning drafter learn to properly use orthographic projection to project points and create views in multiview drawings. Each view will show a minimum of two dimensions. The front view will show the overall width and overall height, the side view will show the height and depth, and so on. Also, any two views of an object will have at least one dimension in common. For example, the front and side views will both have the overall height of the object in common.

The process of using orthographic projection in creating the views of a multiview drawing is known as *blocking in* the drawing. This process can save much time and eliminate many measurement errors. A good rule to follow when blocking in a drawing is to *measure each distance one time, double-check the measurement for accuracy, and project the distance to the adjacent view.* Do not "double-measure" distances. In other words, if a particular feature has a height of 1", do not measure that inch distance in the front view and then remeasure the same distance in the side view. Measure once and project. This rule should be followed for each measurement. If an object has seven different measurements associated with it, the seven distances are each measured *one time* and then projected between the views.

When projecting points, width measurements are projected between the front and top views. Height measurements are projected between the front and side views. See **Figure 9-17**. The depth distances are projected with either a 45° projection angle or a compass, **Figure 9-18**. Of the two, the projection angle method is probably more accurate than the compass method for most beginning drafters. However, if careful and precise compass placement and adjustment is followed and the compass is kept properly sharpened, both methods work very effectively.

All projection lines are drawn as construction lines. If these lines are drawn correctly, they are very easily erased with a quality eraser and erasing shield. Projection lines are generally erased after all lines are darkened to the proper line weights. Occasionally a drafting instructor may require the student to leave projection lines on a drawing to check for proper usage.

Centering a Multiview Drawing

In previous chapters of this text, you have learned that the keys to high-quality,

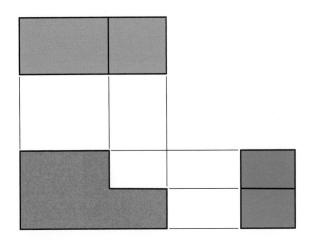

Figure 9-17   Projecting points from view to view.

efficient work are accuracy, neatness, and speed. A drawing looks neater and more professional if the views are evenly spaced and centered on the drawing sheet. Centering the views on a sheet is not difficult if one of two basic methods is used. These methods are discussed in the following sections.

Centering the Drawing with Construction Lines

1. Examine the object to be drawn. Observe its width, depth, and height dimensions, **Figure 9-19**. Determine the orientation in which the object will be drawn.
2. Measure the working area of the sheet *after* drawing the border and title block. It

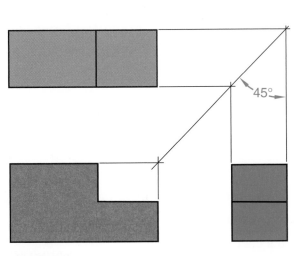

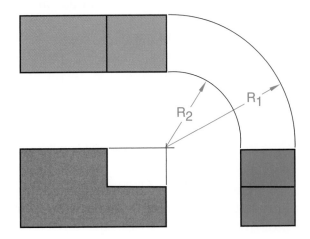

Figure 9-18   Two accepted methods used to transfer the depth of the top view to the side view.

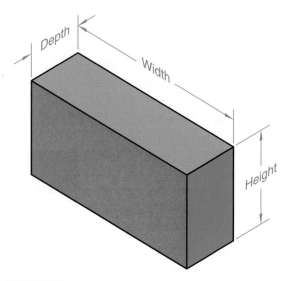

Figure 9-19 When centering views for a drawing, first determine the basic dimensions of the object.

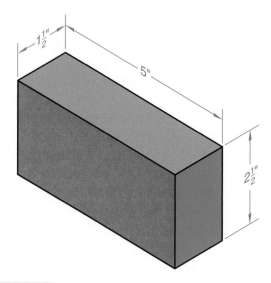

Figure 9-20 The object used as an example for centering views on a drawing sheet.

should measure 7″ × 10″ if you are using 1/2″ borders on a 8-1/2″ × 11″ drawing sheet and the title block measures 1/2″. Refer to Chapter 5 on how to prepare a drawing sheet.

3. Allow 1″ spacing between views.
4. To locate the front view, add the width of the front view, 1″ spacing between views, and the depth of the right view.

  Subtract this total from the horizontal width of the working surface (10″). Divide this total by 2. This will be the starting point for laying out the sheet horizontally.

  Using the object shown in **Figure 9-20**, for example, the calculations are as follows:

Width of front view	= 5″
Spacing between views	= 1″
Depth of right view	= 1-1/2″
Total	= 7-1/2″
Width of working area	= 10″
Total width of views	= −7-1/2″
Total	= 2-1/2″
Divide 2-1/2″ by 2	= 1-1/4″

This is the distance measured from the left border to locate the starting point for drawing.

5. Measure in 1-1/4″ from the left border line. Draw a vertical construction line through this point.
6. From this line, measure over a distance equal to the width of the front view. Draw another vertical construction line. See **Figure 9-21**.
7. The same procedure is followed to center the views vertically. The height of the front view and the depth of the top view are used. A 1″ space will separate the views. Add these distances together. Subtract the sum from the vertical working space (7″).

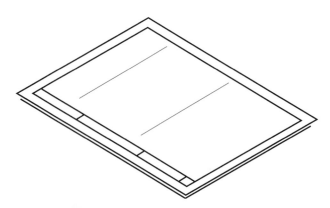

Figure 9-21 Vertical construction lines are drawn to locate the front view.

Divide this total by 2. The calculations are as follows:

Height of front view	= 2-1/2"
Space between views	= 1"
Depth of top view	= 1-1/2"
Total	= 5"
Height of working area	= 7"
Total height of views	= –5"
Total	= 2"
Divide 2" by 2	= 1"

This is the distance measured up from the lower border line to locate the starting point for drawing.

8. Measure up 1" from the lower border line. Draw a horizontal construction line through this point.

9. From this line, measure up the height of the front view and mark a point. Mark a point for the 1" spacing that separates the views. Mark one more point for the depth of the top view. Draw construction lines through these points. See **Figure 9-22**.

10. Use either the 45° angle method or the radius method to transfer the depth of the top view to the right side of the object, **Figure 9-23**.

11. Draw in the right view. Use construction lines.

12. Complete the drawing by going over the construction lines, **Figure 9-24**. Use the correct weight for the type of line drawn. Use the erasing shield when erasing the remaining construction lines.

This centering method and the next method discussed are intended for multiview drawings with three views. The calculations should be adjusted accordingly for drawings with one view, two views, or more than three views. Always leave at least 1" of space between any two given views for dimensioning purposes. The spacing may vary depending on the space available on the drawing sheet. However, regardless of the spacing used, it should be the same between all views.

Centering the Drawing with a Centering Rectangle

1. First, determine the maximum overall size of the object being drawn. See **Figure 9-25**. You must know the maximum overall

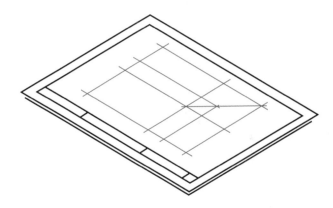

Figure 9-23 The depth of the top view is projected to the side view.

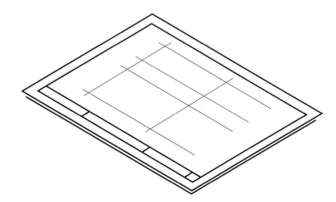

Figure 9-22 The top view is located with construction lines.

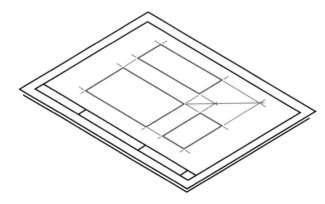

Figure 9-24 Object lines are drawn to complete the drawing. Construction lines may be erased.

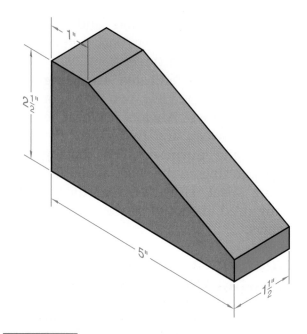

Figure 9-25 The object used as an example for centering views.

width, height, and depth of the object. Determine the orientation in which the object will be drawn.
2. Using the format of your choice, draw the border and title block on the sheet. This example uses an 8-1/2″ × 11″ drawing sheet.
3. Draw construction lines from corner to corner across the drawing area. See **Figure 9-26**. This locates the center of a rectangle representing the drawing area.
4. Lay out two construction lines, one horizontal and one vertical, intersecting the center point of the drawing area.
5. Add the width of the object (5″) to the depth (1-1/2″) plus 1″ for the distance between views to determine the horizontal space needed for the layout. Then add the height (2-1/2″) to the depth (1-1/2″) plus 1″ to determine the vertical

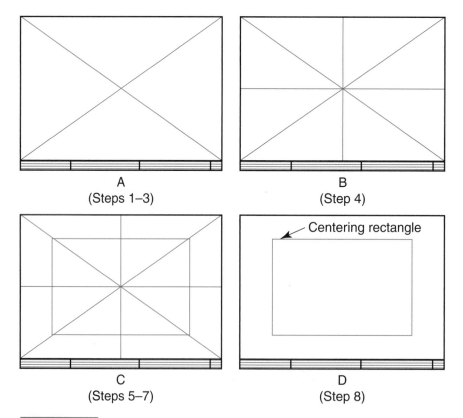

A
(Steps 1–3)

B
(Step 4)

C
(Steps 5–7)

D
(Step 8)

Figure 9-26 Laying out the centering rectangle for the drawing.

space of the layout. These dimensions are used to establish the width and height of a centering rectangle within the drawing area. For this example, the rectangle measures 7-1/2″ × 5″. The three views of the object will fit inside this rectangle. After completing the drawing, the views will be centered horizontally and vertically on the drawing sheet.

6. To draw the centering rectangle, divide the width (7-1/2″) by 2. Mark points for this measurement (3-3/4″) from the center point on each side along the horizontal construction line. Draw two vertical construction lines through the two measured points to create the sides of the centering rectangle.

7. In similar fashion, divide the height of the centering rectangle (5″) by 2. Mark points for this measurement (2-1/2″) from the center point on each side along the vertical construction line. Draw two horizontal construction lines through the two measured points to create the top and bottom of the centering rectangle.

8. Erase the diagonal construction lines used for locating the center of the drawing area. Also, erase the horizontal and vertical construction lines intersecting the center. These lines are no longer needed and could be misidentified as part of the object drawing. After erasing these lines, the centering rectangle can be used to block in the views.

9. To complete the drawing, measure horizontally from the lower-left corner of the centering rectangle. Lay out the overall width, the 1″ spacing between views, and the depth of the object. See **Figure 9-27**. Draw two vertical construction lines through the two measured points and extending the full height of the centering rectangle. These are Lines A and B in **Figure 9-27E**.

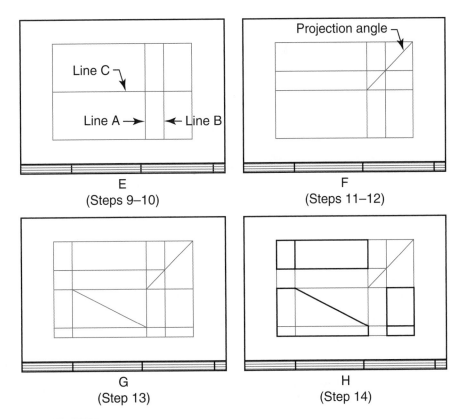

E
(Steps 9–10)

F
(Steps 11–12)

G
(Step 13)

H
(Step 14)

Figure 9-27 Completing the multiview drawing. After blocking in the views, the object lines are darkened.

10. From the lower-left corner, measure vertically along the left edge of the centering rectangle and lay out the overall height of the object. Draw a horizontal construction line through the measured point extending the entire width of the centering rectangle. This is Line C in **Figure 9-27E**.

11. Where Line A and Line C intersect, draw a 45° projection angle extending to the upper-right corner of the centering rectangle. If the angle does not intersect these points, check for incorrect measurements and adjust the layout as needed.

12. Draw a construction line through the intersection of the projection angle and Line B. This line should also extend the entire distance across the centering rectangle.

13. Measure and lay out the features of the object. When projecting points, measure each distance one time only and project the distance to the adjacent view. Do not double-measure features.

14. Complete the drawing by darkening lines. Use the correct weight for the type of line drawn. Recommended methods for darkening lines are discussed in Chapter 5.

Creating Multiview Drawings in CAD

Multiview drawings showing 2D views are developed in CAD programs using CAD commands and methods similar to those involved in manual drafting. CAD commands are introduced in Chapter 7. When using a CAD program to generate views, points are projected using construction lines, coordinate entry, and drawing aids such as orthogonal mode and snap. Object features in each view are drawn with basic drawing commands. Hidden features are drawn in the same manner using the hidden linetype.

Some CAD programs provide the ability to create multiview drawings from 3D models. For example, it is common to orient several 2D orthographic views of a 3D drawing along with a pictorial view, such as an isometric view. CAD-based pictorial drawing and modeling functions are discussed in more detail in Chapter 13.

Test Your Knowledge

Please do not write in this book. Place your answers on another sheet of paper.

1. Name the six viewing directions that define the principal views in a multiview drawing.

2. In orthographic projection, the _____ plane represents the projection for the top view of the object.

3. In the _____ method of orthographic projection, an imaginary glass box containing the object rests in the lower-right quadrant when looking at the profile view.

4. The view in which an object feature appears in its true shape and size is the _____ view of the feature.

5. Define *true face*.

6. Objects that are drawn smaller than true size and shape in a view because they are not parallel to the projection plane are said to be _____.

7. When selecting object views to be drawn, why is it recommended to use the views showing the fewest features as hidden lines?

8. A drawing that has views in the proper orthographic order shows the top view above the _____ view.

9. The process of using orthographic projection in creating the views of a multiview drawing is called _____ the drawing.

10. Identify two methods used to project depth distances between the top and side views in a multiview drawing.

Outside Activities

1. Collect objects for the class to draw multiviews using manual instruments. One object should require only two views; another object should require a three-view drawing. Find other objects that require more than three views to give a complete shape description.

2. Build a hinged box out of clear plastic that can be used to demonstrate the "unfolding" of the sides to show the front, top, bottom, and side views of an object. Place an object inside the box, trace the profiles of the object on the sides of the plastic with chalk or a marker, and then unfold the box to show the multiview projections.

3. Make a large poster for your drafting room showing the step-by-step procedure for centering a drawing on a sheet using one of the two methods explained in this chapter.

Drawing Problems

Draw the problems shown on the problem sheets on the following pages. Use the dimensions provided. Dimensions are in inches unless otherwise indicated. Follow the directions on each problem sheet.

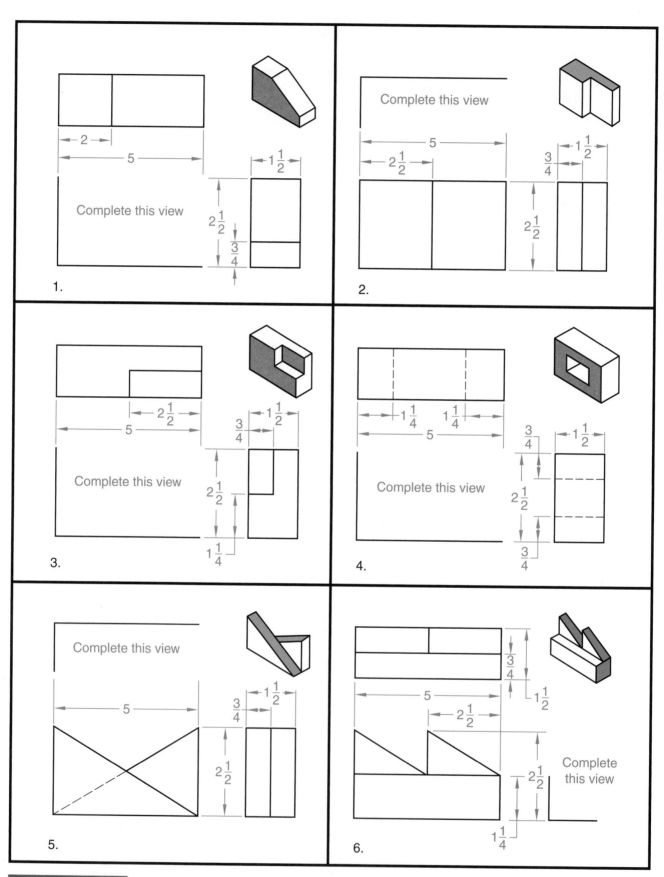

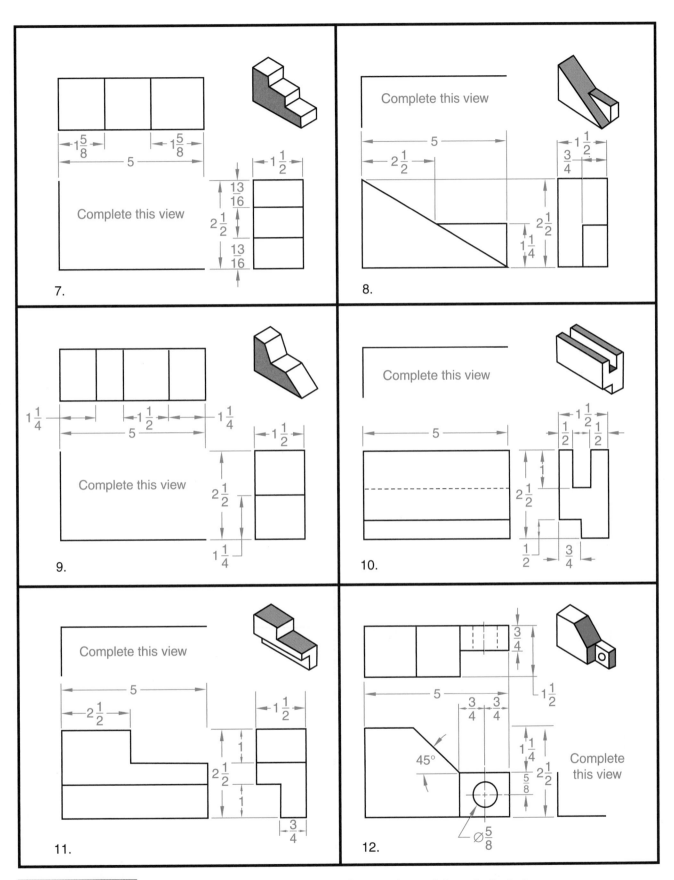

7.

Complete this view

$1\frac{5}{8}$ $1\frac{5}{8}$ 5

$1\frac{1}{2}$ $\frac{13}{16}$ $2\frac{1}{2}$ $\frac{13}{16}$

8.

Complete this view

5   $2\frac{1}{2}$ $1\frac{1}{2}$ $\frac{3}{4}$ $2\frac{1}{2}$ $1\frac{1}{4}$

9.

$1\frac{1}{4}$ $1\frac{1}{2}$ $1\frac{1}{4}$ 5

Complete this view

$1\frac{1}{2}$ $2\frac{1}{2}$ $1\frac{1}{4}$

10.

Complete this view

5   $1\frac{1}{2}$ $\frac{1}{2}$ $\frac{1}{2}$ 1 $2\frac{1}{2}$ $\frac{1}{2}$ $\frac{3}{4}$

11.

Complete this view

5   $2\frac{1}{2}$ $1\frac{1}{2}$ 1 $2\frac{1}{2}$ 1 $\frac{3}{4}$

12.

$\frac{3}{4}$ 5 $\frac{3}{4}$ $\frac{3}{4}$ $1\frac{1}{2}$ 45° $1\frac{1}{4}$ $\frac{5}{8}$ $2\frac{1}{2}$ Complete this view $\varnothing\frac{5}{8}$

Problem Sheet 9-2   Draw each problem on a separate sheet and complete as indicated.

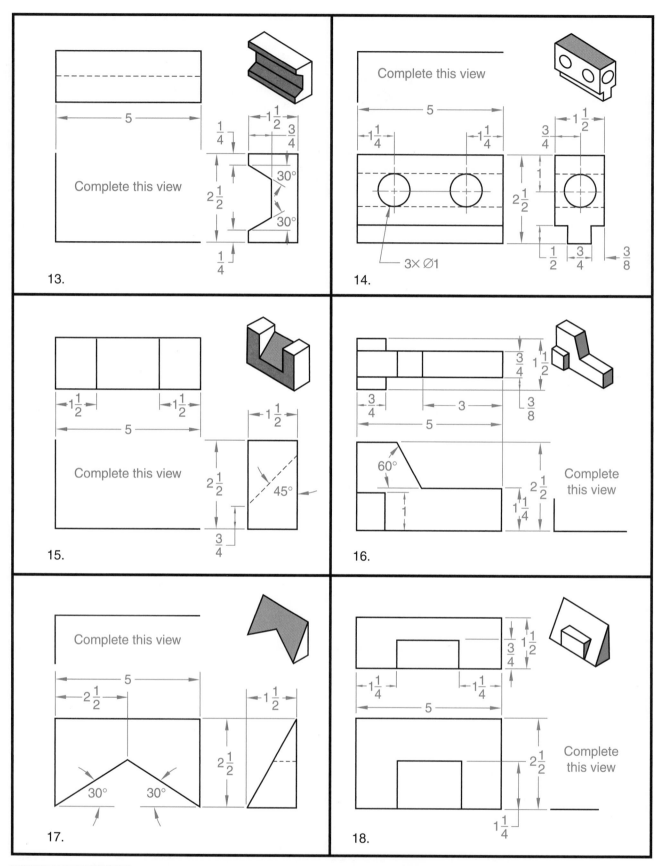

13. Complete this view

14. Complete this view — 3× Ø1

15. Complete this view

16. Complete this view

17. Complete this view

18. Complete this view

Problem Sheet 9-3 Draw each problem on a separate sheet and complete as indicated.

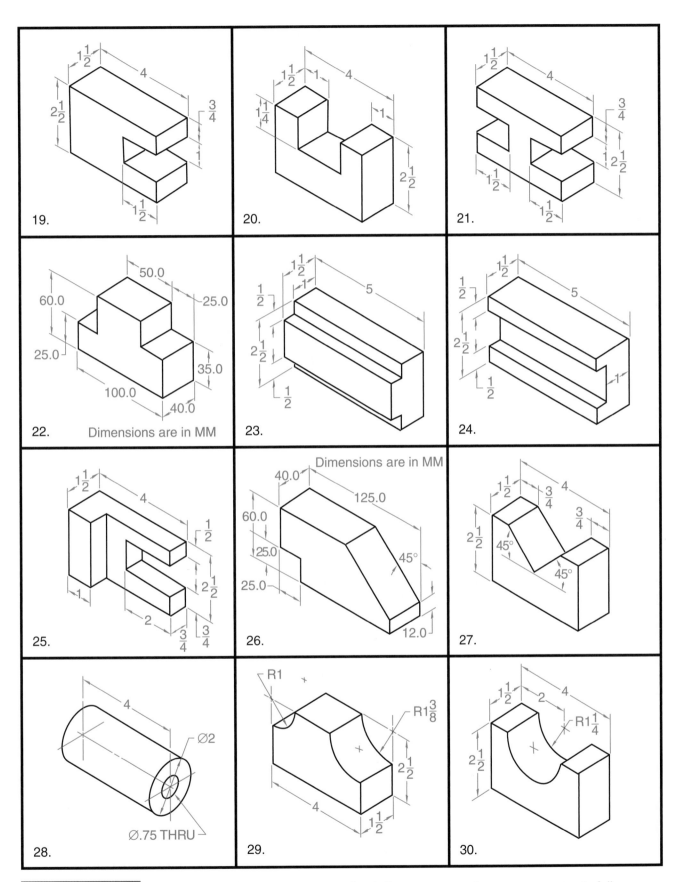

Problem Sheet 9-4   Draw each problem on a separate sheet. Draw as many views as necessary to fully describe each problem.

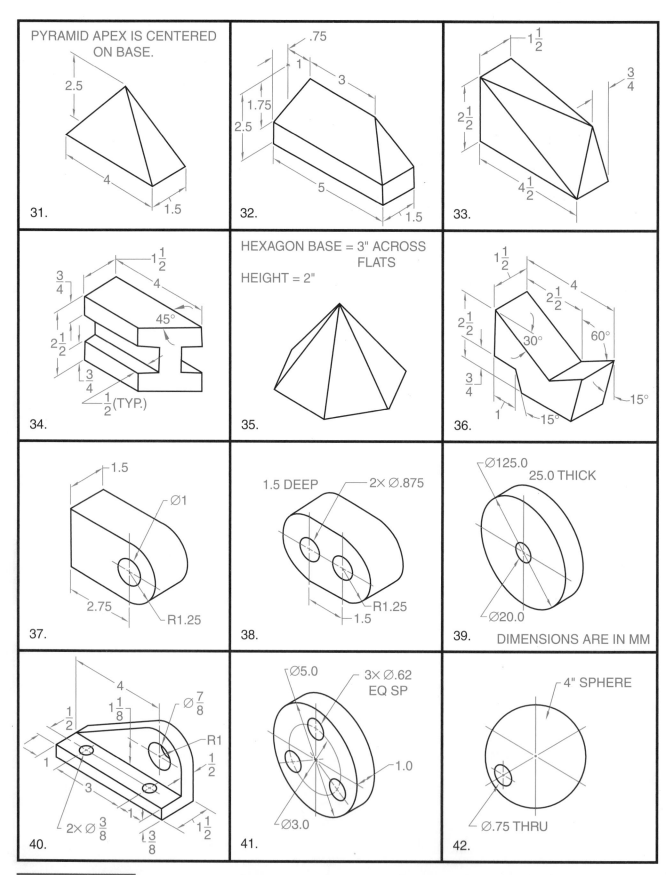

31. PYRAMID APEX IS CENTERED ON BASE.
2.5
4
1.5

32. .75
1
1.75
2.5
3
5
1.5

33. 1½
3/4
2½
4½

34. 1½
3/4
4
45°
2½
3/4
½ (TYP.)

35. HEXAGON BASE = 3" ACROSS FLATS
HEIGHT = 2"

36. 1½
4
2½
2½
30°
60°
3/4
1
15°
15°

37. 1.5
Ø1
2.75
R1.25

38. 1.5 DEEP
2× Ø.875
R1.25
1.5

39. Ø125.0
25.0 THICK
Ø20.0
DIMENSIONS ARE IN MM

40. 4
½
1⅛
Ø 7/8
R1
1½
1
3
1
1½
2× Ø 3/8
3/8

41. Ø5.0
3× Ø.62 EQ SP
1.0
Ø3.0

42. 4" SPHERE
Ø.75 THRU

Problem Sheet 9-5 Draw each problem on a separate sheet. Draw as many views as necessary to fully describe each problem.

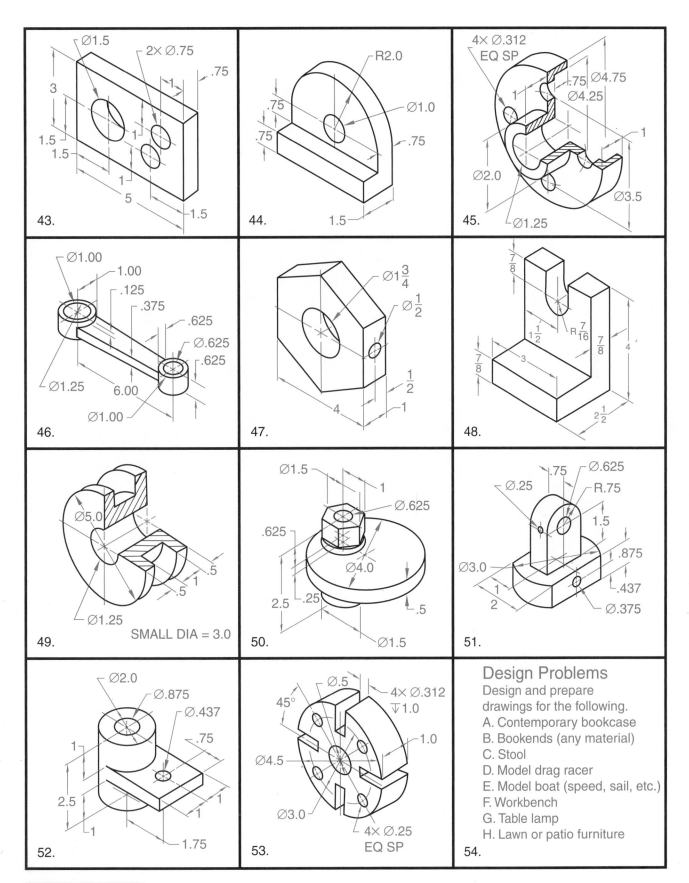

Problem Sheet 9-6   Draw each problem on a separate sheet. Draw as many views as necessary to fully describe each problem.

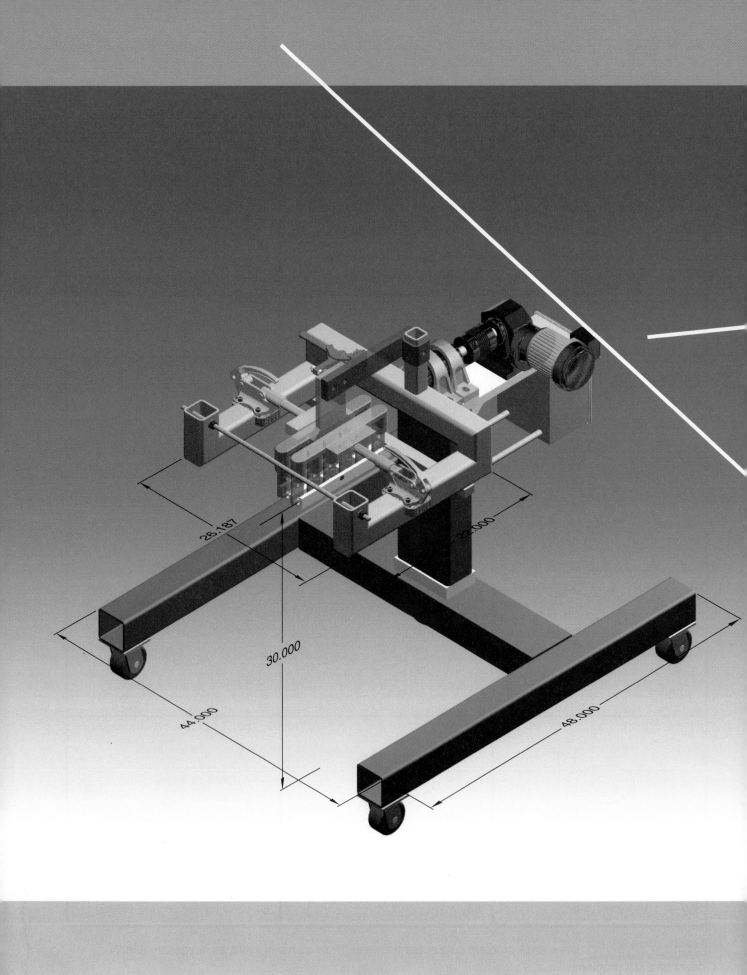

10 Dimensioning

OBJECTIVES

After studying this chapter,
you should be able to:

- ◆ Explain why dimensions and notes are needed on drawings.

- ◆ Identify, explain, and accurately use the two systems of linear measurement to dimension drawings.

- ◆ Describe the difference between unidirectional and aligned dimensioning.

- ◆ Identify and explain the three basic types of dimensions.

- ◆ Apply the general rules for dimensioning inch and/or metric drawings.

- ◆ Dimension circles, holes, arcs, and angles.

- ◆ Explain the methods used in the conversion to metric dimensioning from conventional inch dimensioning.

- ◆ Describe the basic principles of geometric dimensioning and tolerancing.

- ◆ Explain how dimensions are generated in computer-aided drafting.

DRAFTING VOCABULARY

Aligned
  dimensioning
Chain dimensioning
Counterbore
Countersink
Datum
Dimensions
Dual dimensioning
Feature control
  frame
Geometric
  characteristic
  symbols

Geometric
  dimensioning
  and tolerancing
  (GD&T)
Leader
Location dimensions
Notes
Overall dimensions
Size dimensions
Spotface
Tolerance
Unidirectional
  dimensioning

BASELINE
CONTINUOS
ORDINATE

If an object is to be manufactured according to the designer's specifications, the person making the product usually needs more information than that furnished by a scale drawing of its shape. Dimensions and drawing notes help provide this information, **Figure 10-1**.

It is important to realize that the main purpose for creating, dimensioning, and noting a drawing is to communicate the size and shape of the product so that the person making the product can do so as easily and accurately as possible. Hence, the most pertinent information needed for assembly must be provided. It is the job of the drafter to define what that information is and to provide it in the clearest and most efficient way.

Dimensions define the size and location of the details (geometric features) of an object and give the overall size of the object. *Notes* provide additional information not found in the dimensions. In manual drafting, dimensions and notes are added to a drawing by hand. In CAD drafting, drawings are dimensioned using CAD software commands and tools.

Systems of Measurement Used in Dimensioning

As discussed in Chapter 4, measurements on drawings are made in US Customary or SI Metric units. Dimensions are placed on drawings using the appropriate units in one of the two systems of measurement. Sometimes, drawings are dimensioned using both systems. In some cases, drawings are completed using one system for most of the dimensions and the other system for selected dimensions. When this occurs, special rules apply. This is discussed later in this chapter.

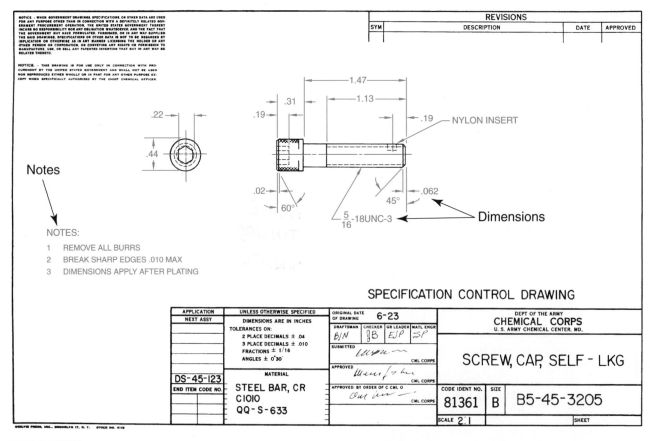

Figure 10-1 A typical drawing from industry with dimensions and notes.

When using the US Customary system, drawings are dimensioned in inches and feet. The dimensions may be represented in one of two ways. They may be decimal inch dimensions (such as 1.5 or 2.75) or fractional inch dimensions (such as 1-1/2 or 2-3/4). In mechanical drafting, drawings are most commonly dimensioned in decimal inches. This is the standard practice recommended by the ASME drafting standard. Decimal inch dimensioning is convenient because decimals are easier to add, subtract, multiply, and divide. However, fractional inch dimensioning is still widely employed. This type of dimensioning is primarily used in architectural drafting, but it is also sometimes used in engineering drawings. Decimal inch and fractional inch dimensioning are both used in examples in this text.

Fractional inch units are often used when making drawings of objects made from materials that typically cannot be machined to very fine tolerances (such as wood). Decimal inches are generally used for drawings of objects made from materials such as metal or plastic. These materials can be machined to very fine tolerances.

When using the SI Metric system, drawings are commonly dimensioned in millimeters (mm). There are special rules for dimensioning metric drawings. Metric dimensioning is discussed later in this chapter.

Unidirectional and Aligned Dimensioning

Dimensions are placed on the drawing in one of two orientations. They are drawn in either a unidirectional or aligned manner, **Figure 10-2**. Unidirectional dimensioning is preferred.

In *unidirectional dimensioning*, dimensions are placed horizontally so that they are read from the bottom of the drawing. In *aligned dimensioning*, dimensions are placed parallel to the dimension line. The numerals are read from the bottom and from the right side of the drawing.

Regardless of the method used, dimensions shown with leaders are lettered parallel to the bottom of the drawing. The same is true for all notes.

Dimensioning a Drawing

From your study of the alphabet of lines, you will remember that special lines are used for dimensioning, **Figure 10-3**. These include dimension lines, extension lines, and leaders.

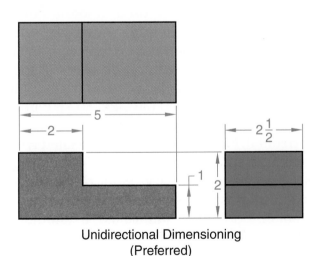

Unidirectional Dimensioning
(Preferred)

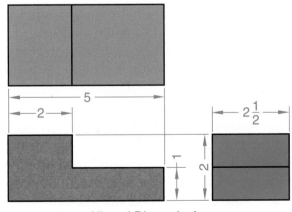

Aligned Dimensioning

Figure 10-2 The two accepted methods for dimensioning drawings. The unidirectional method is preferred.

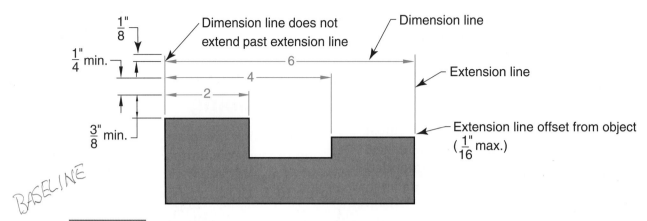

Figure 10-3 Lines used for linear dimensioning. Note how dimension and extension lines contrast in thickness with object lines.

The dimension line is a thin black line used to indicate linear distance as it relates to a given object. It is drawn to the same weight as a centerline. It should be thin enough to contrast with the object lines. It is usually broken near the center for the insertion of the actual lettered dimension. Although this is the most common practice, placement of the lettered dimension may vary. In some cases, the lettered dimension may be placed outside the extension lines. Refer to **Figure 10-1**.

The dimension line is capped at each end with arrowheads or some other type of terminator. The type of terminator used generally depends on the drafting discipline. For example, tick marks are used as dimension line terminators on architectural drawings.

Extension lines are drawn to the same weight as dimension lines. They extend the dimension beyond the outline of the view so that the dimension can be read easily. Extension lines indicate the beginning and ending points of linear distances. An extension line begins 1/16″ away from the point, edge, intersection, or detail of the object and extends about 1/8″ past the last dimension line it is used for. An extension line may originate within a view and extend across a view. However, it should not start or stop at an object line. Extension lines may cross any kind of a line except a dimension line. Hence, it is recommended that smaller dimensions

(size or location dimensions) should be placed nearest the view, while the larger dimensions (overall dimensions) should be placed farther from the view. If an extension line has to cross a dimension line (this may occur on more complicated objects), the extension line should be broken as it crosses.

Spacing between dimensions in a view may vary depending on the drawing. Generally, to avoid crowding, the dimension line for a dimension should be placed at least 3/8″ from the object. The spacing between dimensions should be at least 1/4″.

A *leader* is another type of dimension line. It is an angular line used to point out special characteristics of objects. Leaders are commonly used to specify sizes of circles and arcs. They are also used to locate notes. A leader does not require extension lines because it usually does not reference a linear distance. The arrowed portion of the leader is always angular. It is inclined at an angle ranging from 15° to 75° (30°, 45°, and 60° lines are common). A leader is never vertical or horizontal, **Figure 10-4**. When associated with a circle or an arc, the leader always points at or intersects the primary center of the round detail. In most cases, a leader is drawn with a small horizontal tail called a shoulder. When the leader is to the left of the note, the shoulder connects to the beginning of the first line of information associated with the leader.

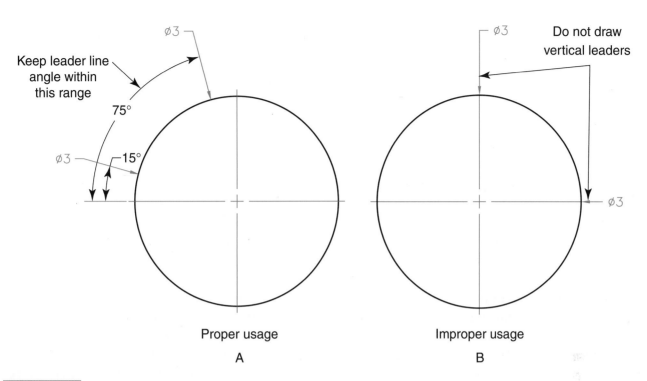

Proper usage

A

Improper usage

B

Figure 10-4 Leaders are used to connect dimensioning information to object features. A—Properly drawn leaders. Leader lines are drawn at an angle ranging from 15° to 75°. B—Leader lines should never be vertical or horizontal.

When the leader is to the right of the note, the shoulder connects to the end of the last line of information associated with the leader. The shoulder typically extends 1/4″ from the leader line. See **Figure 10-5**.

Arrowheads for leaders and dimension lines are drawn freehand and should be carefully made, **Figure 10-6**. The solid arrowhead is generally preferred. It is made narrower and slightly longer than the open arrowhead. For most applications, 1/8″ long arrowheads are satisfactory. To save time, preprinted (dry transfer) arrowheads may be applied by the drafter instead of manually constructing them. Also, when dimensioning linear distances, make certain that the tips of the arrows on the dimension lines touch the extension lines but do not extend past them. Refer to **Figure 10-3**.

Types of Dimensions

As previously discussed, the drafter's primary concern when dimensioning an object is to convey the basic information

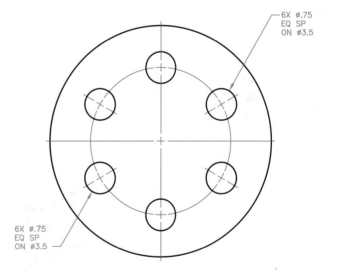

Figure 10-5 The leader shoulder connects to the first or last line of information depending on the placement of the leader with the note.

needed to manufacture the part. For the beginning drafter, a very basic and easy-to-understand way to determine this information is to identify all object distances as one of

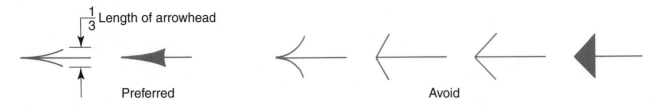

$\frac{1}{3}$ Length of arrowhead

Preferred

Avoid

Figure 10-6 Arrowheads are drawn 1/8″ long. The solid arrowhead is generally preferred.

three types—overall, location, and size. These object descriptions are known as overall, location, and size dimensions.

Overall dimensions provide the overall object size and tell the manufacturer how large a piece of material to use to make the object. *Location dimensions* indicate where particular details lie along or within the object. *Size dimensions* specify how large the particular details are, **Figure 10-7**. As objects become more complex, identifying these basic dimensions becomes more difficult. However, if a beginning drafter can visualize an object, analyze its features, and think in these terms,

he or she can learn to become very proficient and consistent in applying basic dimensions to drawings.

Simply put, when dimensioning an object, apply the following steps:
1. To identify the overall dimensions, tell how large the object is overall. Describe the positive mass. Provide the overall width, height, and depth dimensions.
2. To identify the location dimensions, tell where the details of the object are. Describe the negative mass.
3. To identify the size dimensions, tell how large the details (negative masses) are.

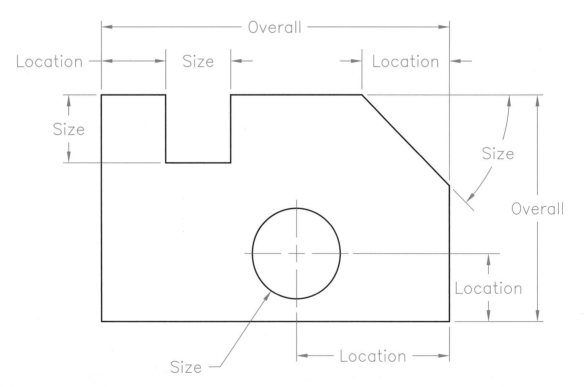

Figure 10-7 Object dimensions can be classified as overall, location, or size dimensions. The three features of this object are described by the size dimensions.

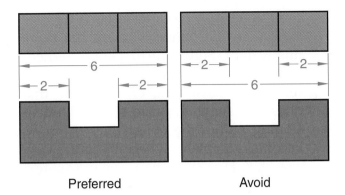

Note

When identifying location dimensions, try to locate the details as much as possible with respect to the original edges of the original mass of the object. Try *not to* locate them with respect to other details. Doing this has a tendency to either dictate the order of procedure for manufacturing or cause the person making the part to perform mental mathematics during the layout procedure.

Figure 10-8 Location and size dimensions are placed in views that show details in their true shape.

While following the previous steps, make accurate and consistent use of several fundamental dimensioning rules. These are discussed next.

Fundamental Rules for Dimensioning

For clarity, dimensions should conform to the following general rules:

1. Place location and size dimensions on the views that show the true shape of the detail being dimensioned (the primary views). See **Figure 10-8**. The true shape of the detail appears on the view that shows the detail as negative mass. Do not locate or give the size of details in secondary views. A secondary view is a view in which the feature is not visible (in other words, where it is hidden). In most cases, dimensioning to hidden lines is not an acceptable practice. Of course, as with some rules, there are exceptions. Your instructor will point these out when appropriate.

2. Unless absolutely necessary, dimensions should not be placed within the outlines (outer object lines) of the views, **Figure 10-9**. Instead, extension lines should be used to extend the profiles and features of the object to around the perimeter for the purpose of linear dimensioning. Primary

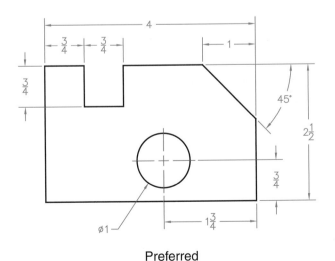

Preferred

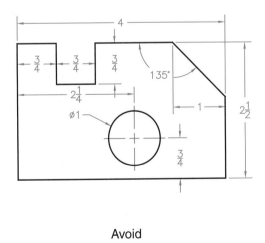

Avoid

Figure 10-9 Dimensions should not be placed within the object lines of views. They should be placed with extension lines around the perimeter.

centerlines may be extended and used as extension lines since they are the same line weight, **Figure 10-10**. Do not dimension to secondary centerlines. This would require dimensioning on the view that does not show the true shape. Dimensioning within the object lines of views becomes acceptable when objects are very complex. However, the focus of this text is to teach basic dimensioning. More complex examples will be part of your future drafting studies.

3. If possible, dimensions should be grouped together rather than scattered about the drawing. See **Figure 10-11**. The illustration shown is a good example of grouping linear distances between views or on two sides of a view. Grouping also applies to sizes and information attached to leaders. When grouping dimensions, try not to extend extension lines for linear distances more than halfway across any given view, **Figure 10-12**. If this is required, it is probably best to locate or give the size of the detail along the nearer side of the object.

4. Dimensions must be complete. No measuring or scaling of the drawing should be necessary for manufacturing the object. It should be possible to determine sizes and shapes without assuming any measurements.

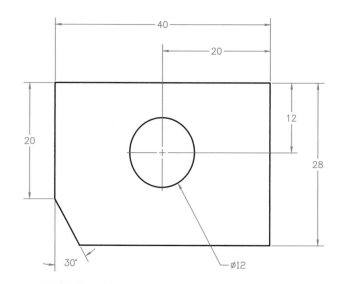

Figure 10-10 Notice how the primary centerlines are extended and used as extension lines for dimensioning.

5. Draw dimension lines parallel to the direction of measurement. If there are several parallel dimension lines, the numerals should be staggered to make them easier to read, **Figure 10-13**.

6. Dimensions should not be duplicated unless they are absolutely necessary to the understanding of the drawing. Omit all unnecessary dimensions, **Figure 10-14**. In mechanical drafting, it is common to provide an overall dimension and only enough location and size dimensions to

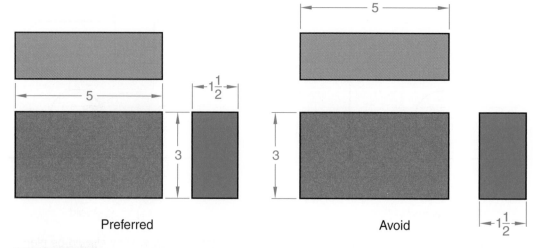

Preferred

Avoid

Figure 10-11 Keep dimensions grouped for easier understanding of the drawing.

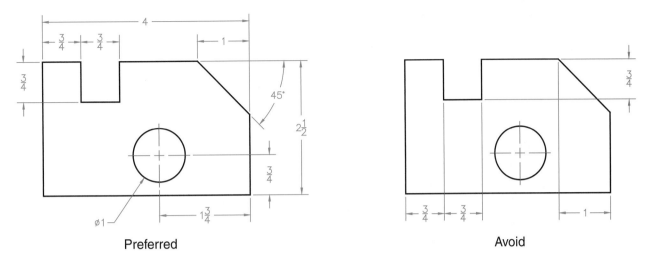

Preferred   Avoid

Figure 10-12   Do not extend extension lines more than halfway across a view.

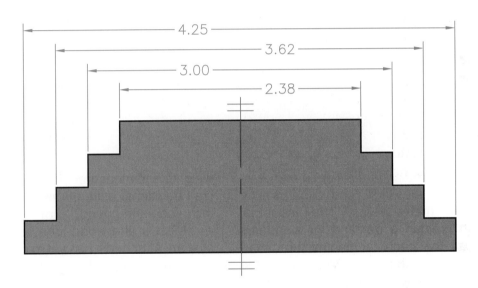

Figure 10-13   When there are several parallel dimension lines, numerals should be staggered for easier reading.

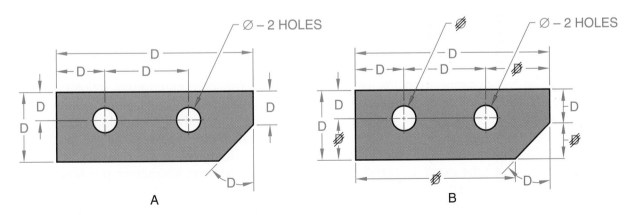

Figure 10-14   Avoid duplicating dimensions unless they are necessary to understand the drawing. A—Properly dimensioned object. B—Unnecessary dimensions are removed.

fully describe the object. When several continuous dimensions are drawn in a straight line or row, the least important distance is typically omitted. Placing several dimensions in a straight line along an object to describe successive features is known as *chain dimensioning*. Refer to **Figure 10-14**. In the example shown, three location dimensions are omitted from dimensional chains. Many times, an omitted dimension is a distance that relates one detail feature to another. If the information is not useful for the manufacture of the product, it is omitted.

7. Plan your work carefully so that the extension lines do not cross dimension lines, **Figure 10-15**. Smaller (size or location) dimensions should be placed nearest

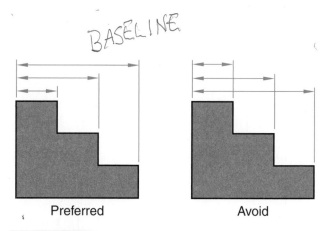

Preferred   Avoid

Figure 10-15 Crossing lines can be kept to a minimum if the shortest dimensions (size or location dimensions) are placed next to the object outline. Longer dimensions (overall dimensions) are placed farther from the drawing.

the view, while the larger (overall) dimensions should be placed farther from the view.

ACADEMIC LINK

The need for standardization in manufacturing, making drawings, and dimensioning dates back many years. The Industrial Revolution created a demand for standards because of the need to manufacture interchangeable parts and also because of the existence of many different manufacturers. Standards were adopted and used in Europe before they came into use in the United States.

In the late 1700s, the SI Metric system was developed by French scientists and instituted as the world standard. The system was based on the meter. It was made equal to one-ten millionth of the distance from the North Pole to the equator. Other units of measure in the metric system, such as the liter and gram, were based on the meter.

The SI Metric system was specifically developed to address the need for standardization. By contrast, the US Customary system had evolved from the English system of weights and measures. This system standardized traditional units of measure, such as the inch, foot, and pound.

Most of the world today uses the metric system. Although it has yet to gain widespread acceptance in the United States, there have always been efforts to bring metric standards into practice in the US. The SI Metric system was legalized as the weights and measures standard by the US in the late 1800s. Also, the Metric Conversion Act of 1975 was intended to facilitate the conversion of inch-based standards to metric standards.

The metric system is used today by the US in international commerce. Industry uses drawings in metric units, and automobile mechanics and other technicians must be able to use metric tools. In all US automobiles, speedometers have readouts in both miles per hour and kilometers per hour. Can you think of other examples where the metric system is used?

8. When all dimensions on a drawing are in inches, the inch symbol (") should not be used. However, the drawing should have a note stating "UNLESS OTHERWISE SPECIFIED, ALL DIMENSIONS ARE IN INCHES" (or "MILLIMETERS," as applicable). Dimensions on metric drawings are in millimeters (mm) unless otherwise noted. Special rules for dimensioning metric drawings are discussed later in this chapter.

9. Numerals and fractions must be drawn to the proper height in relation to one another, **Figure 10-16**. Proper sizes for lettering fractional numbers are discussed in Chapter 8.

General Rules for Inch Dimensioning

As previously discussed, mechanical drawings are dimensioned in decimal inches according to the ASME standard. Decimal inch dimensioning should conform to the following rules:

1. A zero should not be used before the decimal point for values less than 1". For example:

    .6, not 0.6

2. In drawings with geometric dimensioning and tolerancing, a dimension is expressed to the same number of decimal places as its tolerance. Geometric dimensioning and tolerancing is discussed later in this chapter. In inch tolerance dimensioning, zeros are added to the right of the decimal point for decimal inch values where necessary. Hence, if the tolerance is in three-place decimals, all dimensions will be in three places:

    .375 and .500, not .375 and .5

Fractional inch dimensioning is less common than decimal inch dimensioning in mechanical drafting. However, this type of dimensioning should conform to the following rule:

1. All fractions should be reduced to their lowest common denominator:

    1/2, not 4/8 or 8/16
    3/4, not 6/8 or 12/16

Dimensioning Circles, Holes, and Arcs

Many products are manufactured from parts that contain circles, cylindrical solids, round holes, or arcs in their design, **Figure 10-17**. These shapes are usually created using one or more manufacturing processes. Processes such as cutting, reaming, boring, turning, drilling, spotfacing, counterboring, and countersinking are used to produce round shapes, **Figure 10-18**.

$$2\frac{1}{4}$$

Preferred

$$21/4 \quad 2\frac{1}{4} \quad 2^{1\!/_4} \quad 2\tfrac{1}{4}$$

Avoid

Figure 10-16 Numerals and fractions must be drawn to the proper size and orientation.

Figure 10-17 These automobile castings are typical of manufactured parts that contain circles, round holes, and arcs in their design. (American Foundrymen's Society, Inc.)

Figure 10-18 Machining operations that produce hole features. A—Reaming produces a very accurately sized hole. The hole is first drilled slightly undersize before reaming. B—Boring is an internal machining operation. C—Turning work on a lathe. D—Spotfacing machines a surface that permits a bolt head or nut to bear uniformly over its entire surface. E—Drilling is an operation often performed on a drill press. F—Counterboring prepares a hole to receive a fillister or socket head screw. (Clausing Industrial, Inc.)

When dimensioning circles, holes, and arcs, it is important that the information given conveys the proper manufacturing procedure. The information may describe either a drilling or cutting procedure. If certain guidelines are followed, the correct procedure will be conveyed, and the correct tool will be chosen for the job.

When dimensioning an arc greater than 180°, dimension it as a diameter. This conveys a drilling procedure. When the drawing is used to make the part, the correct size and type of tool will be selected for manufacture. When dimensioning an arc 180° or smaller, dimension it as a radius. This conveys a cutting procedure. When the drawing is used to make the part, the correct layout will be completed and the appropriate cutting tool will be selected for the job.

The ASME drafting standard sets guidelines on how to "call out," or specify, a diameter or radius dimension. The Greek letter ⌀ (phi, pronounced "fi") indicates that the dimension is a diameter. The symbol is placed *before* the size.

Circles and round holes are dimensioned by giving the diameter. They should be dimensioned using one of the methods shown in **Figure 10-19**. The methods shown are recommendations based on the size of the feature. Note the different conventions used for placing the leader with the dimension. Each method corresponds to a specific diameter range for the feature. While dimensioning standards vary, these practices are common (the guidelines shown are not ASME standards).

The dimensioning method shown in **Figure 10-19A** is commonly used for diameters of 1-1/2" or greater. The method shown in **Figure 10-19B** is commonly used for diameters smaller than 3/4". The method shown in **Figure 10-19C** is commonly used for diameters ranging from 3/4" to 1-1/2". The methods shown in **Figures 10-19D** and **10-19E** are for use only when dimensioning sectional views. Sectional views are discussed in Chapter 11.

Different conventions may be used for dimensioning diameters depending on the situation. For instance, if several concentric circles are being dimensioned with diameters greater than 1-1/2" but increasing in size in relatively small increments, the drafter may choose not to use the common method for large diameters (diameters 1-1/2" and larger) but rather one of the others to improve clarity. The key is to select the convention that most clearly does the job in any given situation.

Where it is not clear that a hole goes through the part, the abbreviation THRU follows the dimension. See **Figure 10-20A**. In cases where the hole does not go through the

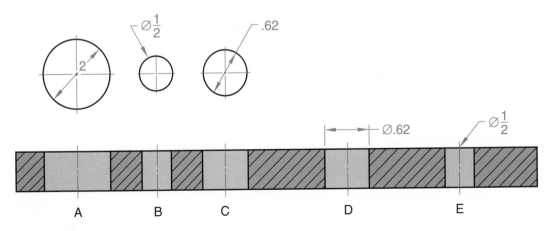

Figure 10-19   Circles and holes are dimensioned by giving the diameter. Different conventions are shown.

entire part, the depth of the hole is provided. See **Figure 10-20B**. A special symbol is placed before the depth size.

Symbols are also used to show whether the hole is to be countersunk, spotfaced, or coun- terbored in manufacturing. See **Figure 10-21**. A *countersink* is a chamfered recess at the end of a smaller hole used to receive the head of a fastener. A *spotface* is a recess at the end of a smaller hole used to provide a bearing surface

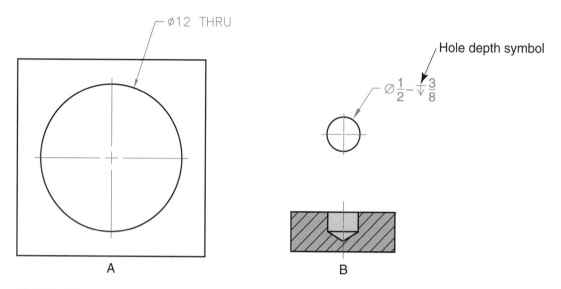

Figure 10-20 Conventions for dimensioning holes. A—The abbreviation THRU is used with the hole size in views where it is not clear that the hole goes through the part. B—The hole depth size is provided in cases where the hole does not go through the entire part.

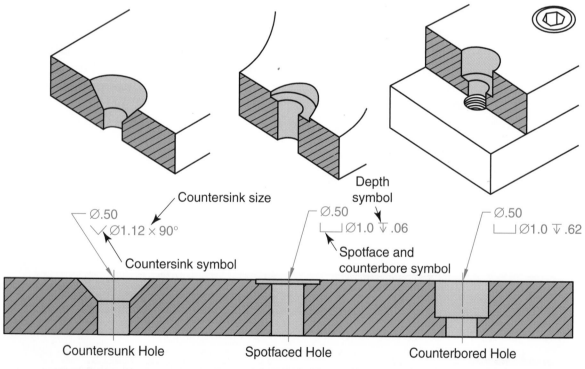

Figure 10-21 Symbols and notes used to identify countersunk, spotfaced, and counterbored holes.

for the head of a bolt or nut. A *counterbore* is similar to a spotface, but the depth of the recess is larger. See **Figure 10-22**.

When dimensioning a multiview drawing of a cylinder, the diameter and length of the cylinder should be dimensioned on the same view (the secondary view), **Figure 10-23A**. In other words, the diameter and length of the cylinder should both be represented as linear distances. If the diameters of several concentric circles must be dimensioned on a drawing, it may be more convenient to show them on the front view, **Figure 10-23B**.

The correct way to use a leader to indicate a diameter is shown in **Figure 10-24**. The leader always points to the primary center of the diameter. When the leader is placed "inside" the circular feature, it intersects the primary center of the diameter. Refer to **Figure 10-19**. The tip of an arrowhead for any leader never *touches* the primary center point, **Figure 10-25**.

When dimensioning arcs, the radius of the arc is given, **Figure 10-26**. The capital letter *R* indicates that the dimension is a radius. It is placed *before* the dimension. The methods shown in **Figure 10-26** are common. Each method corresponds to a specific range of radii for the feature. While dimensioning standards vary, these practices are typical (the guidelines shown are not ASME standards).

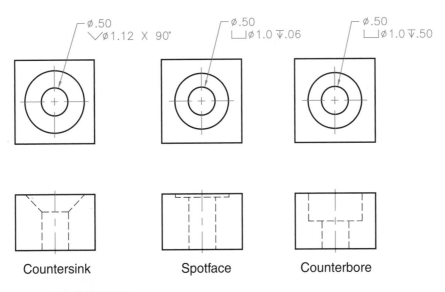

Countersink   Spotface   Counterbore

Figure 10-22 Multiview drawings of hole features for manufacturing processes.

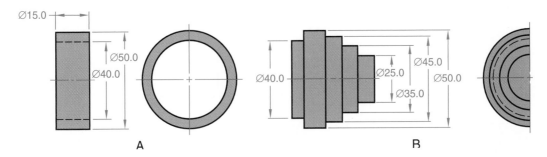

A   B

Figure 10-23 Recommended ways to dimension cylindrical objects and concentric circles. A—Dimensions for a cylinder are placed in the side view. B—When placing dimensions in this manner, only half a view is needed for the side view.

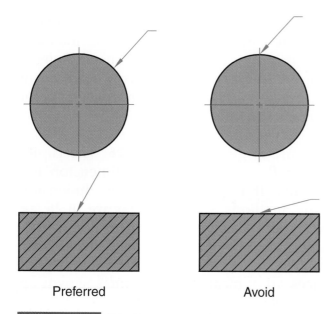

Preferred · Avoid

Figure 10-24 Placing leaders to dimension circles. The leader should radiate from the center of the object.

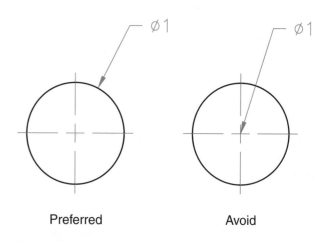

Preferred · Avoid

Figure 10-25 The tip of an arrowhead for any leader never touches a primary center point.

The dimensioning method shown in **Figure 10-26A** is commonly used for radii of 1″ or greater. The method shown in **Figure 10-26B** is commonly used for radii ranging from 3/8″ to 1″. The methods shown in **Figure 10-26C** are commonly used for radii smaller than 3/8″.

Different conventions may be used for dimensioning radii depending on the situation. For instance, if several concentric arcs are being dimensioned with radii greater than 1″ but increasing in size in relatively small increments, the drafter may choose not to use the common method for large radii (radii 1″ and larger) but rather one of the others to improve clarity. As with diameter dimensioning, the key is to select the style that most clearly does the job in any given situation. There are many acceptable conventions for radius dimensioning. The conventions in **Figure 10-26** are not the only ones that can be used. Consult your instructor for advice on whether one you have created is acceptable.

When placing location and size dimensions on parts, the sizes of round holes and cylindrical parts are dimensioned with respect to primary center points, *never* with respect to the edges of the round detail, **Figure 10-27**. However, as previously discussed, it is best to locate the center points of round details with respect to the original edges of the original mass of the object.

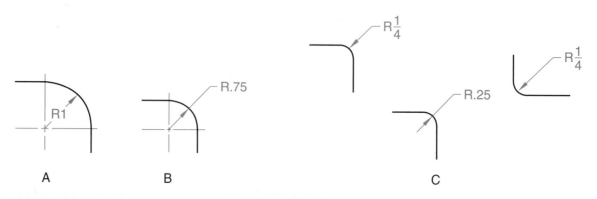

A · B · C

Figure 10-26 Recommended methods for dimensioning arcs.

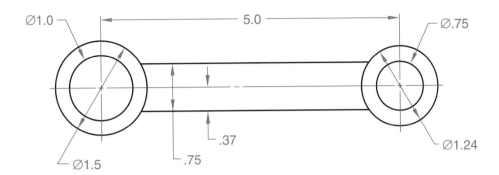

Figure 10-27 Round holes and cylindrical parts are dimensioned from the centers when placing location dimensions.

When it is necessary to dimension a series of holes that lie in a radial (circular) pattern, a special note (grouping statement) is created to designate the number of holes, their size, and the diameter of the circle on which they are located. See **Figure 10-28**. If the holes are equally spaced in the circular pattern, the information should be included in the grouping statement. Refer to **Figure 10-28A**.

Dimensioning Angles

Angular dimensions are expressed either in degrees and decimal parts of a degree or in degrees (°), minutes ('), and seconds ("). Where degrees are indicated alone, the numerical value is followed by the symbol. Where only minutes or seconds are specified in an angular dimension, 0° should precede the number of minutes or seconds.

Angles are dimensioned as shown in **Figure 10-29**. The origin (vertex) of the angle must be located and the size given. Whenever possible, locate the vertex with respect to an original edge of the original mass, not with respect to another detail. See **Figure 10-30**.

Dimensioning Small Portions of an Object

There are many cases where the size of object features limits the space available to place dimensions. When the space between extension lines is too small for both the numbers of the dimension and the arrowheads,

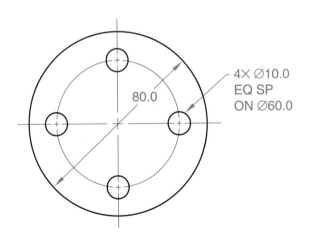

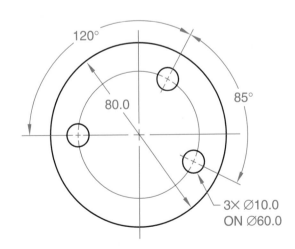

Figure 10-28 A—The correct way to dimension equally spaced holes in a radial pattern. B—Holes that are not equally spaced are dimensioned as shown.

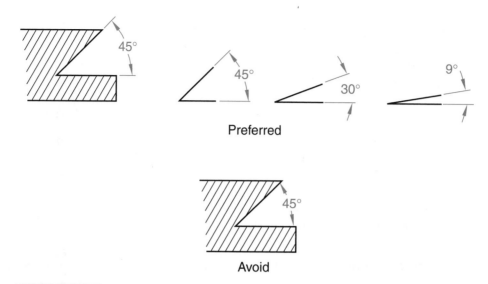

Figure 10-29 Conventions for dimensioning angles. As with dimensioning linear distances, dimension angles to extension lines, not object lines.

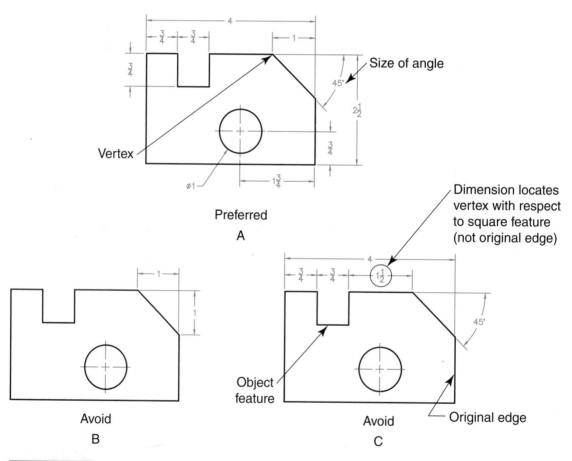

Figure 10-30 Dimensioning angles. A—Locate the vertex of the angle and give its size. B—If the angle is unknown, providing a linear distance (as shown) is acceptable. C— Locate angles with respect to the original edges of the object, not with respect to other details.

dimensions are placed as shown in **Figure 10-31**. These are just several alternatives. There are other options that are also acceptable. See your instructor for recommendations.

Adapting US Customary Conventions to Metric Dimensioning

Many companies use metric measurement extensively. Some companies have started changing to the SI Metric system to compete successfully in the international market.

It is important that industries working together on projects use the same measurement system. As previously discussed, metric drawings are dimensioned in millimeters. On drawings made with US Customary units, the standard practice is to use decimal inches. One problem encountered in the transition from the US Customary system to the SI Metric system has been at the *interface* of a part (a surface where parts come together). It is difficult to interface an object designed to metric standards to fit an existing object that was designed to inch standards.

Five methods have been devised for drafters to provide the information necessary to make metric parts that must interface with existing parts dimensioned using conventional measurement. These methods are listed as follows and discussed in the next sections:
- Dual dimensioning
- Dimensioning with a tabular chart

- Metric dimensioning with a conversion chart
- Metric dimensioning (metric units only)
- Undimensioned master drawings

Dual Dimensioning

The use of *dual dimensioning* was the first method devised to dimension engineering drawings with both inch and metric units. See **Figure 10-32**.

Dual dimensions are presented using one of two methods, the position method or the bracket method. See **Figure 10-33**. The inch dimension is placed first on drawings of products to be made in the United States. The metric dimension is placed first on drawings of products to be made where the SI Metric system is the basic form of measurement.

Dual dimensioning is the most complicated dimensioning system. It is seldom used today. However, large numbers of dual-dimensioned drawings are still in use. This method is presented in this text so that you will be aware of its existence.

Dimensioning with a Tabular Chart

When a drawing is shown with both inch and metric dimensions, a tabular chart is sometimes used. See **Figure 10-34**. With this technique, the dimensions are labeled with letters (A, B, C, etc.) rather than sizes. The letters are listed in the chart, and the chart shows the metric and inch equivalents of each

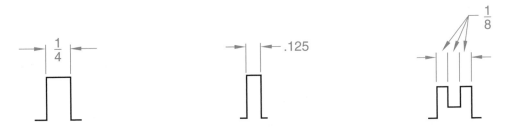

Figure 10-31 Depending on the space available between extension lines, the arrowheads, dimension numeral, or entire dimension may be placed outside the extension lines.

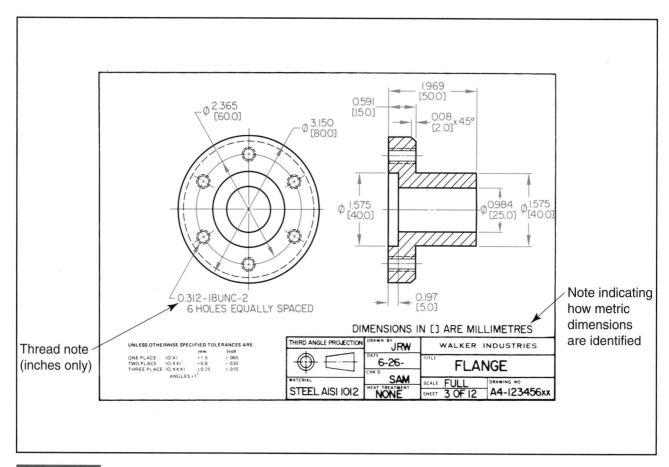

Figure 10-32 A dual-dimensioned drawing. Inch dimensions are given first. The thread size is not given in metric units because there is no metric thread this size.

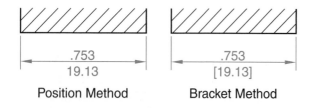

Position Method   Bracket Method

Figure 10-33 Methods of indicating inches and millimeters on a dual-dimensioned drawing.

dimension.

Metric Dimensioning with a Conversion Chart

When a part is designed to metric standards, the engineering drawing is made with metric dimensions. A drawing labeled "Metric" tells the person reading the drawing that all dimensions are in metric units. Some

metric drawings provide a conversion chart, **Figure 10-35**. The chart shows metric dimensions in the left column and the inch equivalents in the right column. This method permits a comparison of values.

Metric Dimensioning (Metric Units Only)

Some metric drawings provide metric dimensions only, **Figure 10-36**. This method is the quickest way to get engineers, designers, drafters, and craft workers to "think metric." In the example shown, the drawing is labeled "Metric" and no conversion values are given.

Undimensioned Master Drawings

When designing parts to meet different

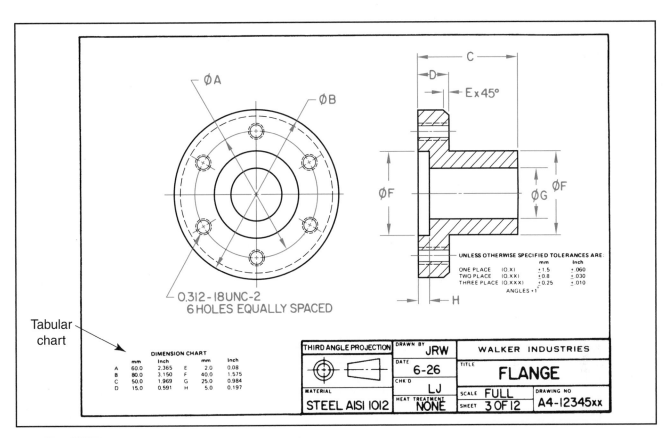

Figure 10-34 Dimensioning with a tabular chart. The chart shows the inch and millimeter equivalents for each dimension.

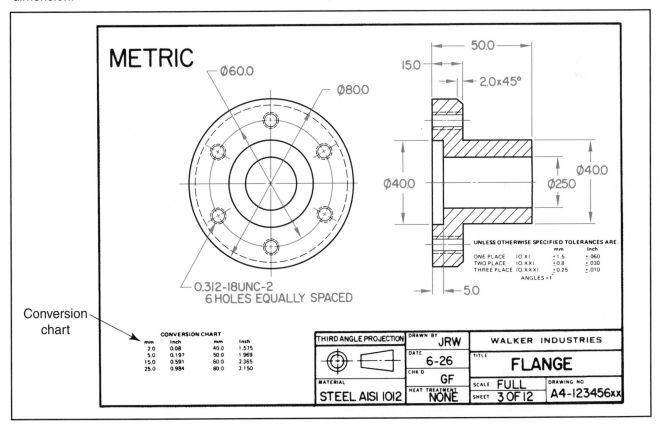

Figure 10-35 A metric drawing with a conversion chart.

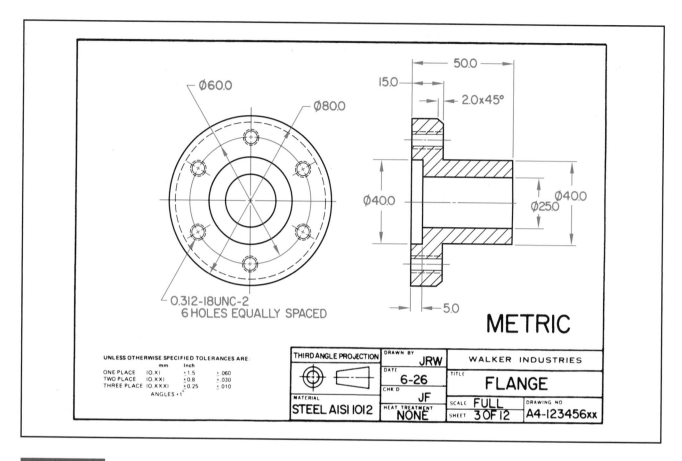

Figure 10-36 A metric drawing dimensioned in metric units only. Since there is no metric equivalent for the thread indicated on the drawing, the thread size is given in decimal inch units.

measurement standards, drawings may be made without dimensions so that the dimensions can be added later in the different formats. When this is the case, a master drawing is first made without dimensions, **Figure 10-37**. Next, prints are made. Metric dimensions may be added to one print, inch dimensions to another print. Notes and details can be added in whatever language is needed to produce the part—German, French, English, Japanese, etc.

Whatever dimensioning method is used, drafting personnel must have both scales and templates on hand. They must also have a thorough knowledge of the metric system.

The drafter, engineer, or designer will find that he or she cannot specify a 9/16 bolt by merely listing the metric equivalent of 9/16″ (15.29 mm). There is no metric bolt that corresponds to this diameter. The same problem will occur if a 1.0″ diameter is specified as a 25.4 mm diameter. There is no metric-sized shaft 1.0″ in diameter. The closest size would be 25.0 mm. To get the 25.4 mm diameter shaft, an expensive machining operation would be necessary to turn a larger shaft to the required 25.4 mm diameter.

General Rules for Metric Dimensioning

As previously discussed, most metric drawings are made in millimeters. This is standard practice. Millimeter dimensioning should conform to the following rules:

1. When a millimeter dimension is a whole number, the decimal point and following zero are not shown. This holds true unless tolerances are shown.

125, not 125.0

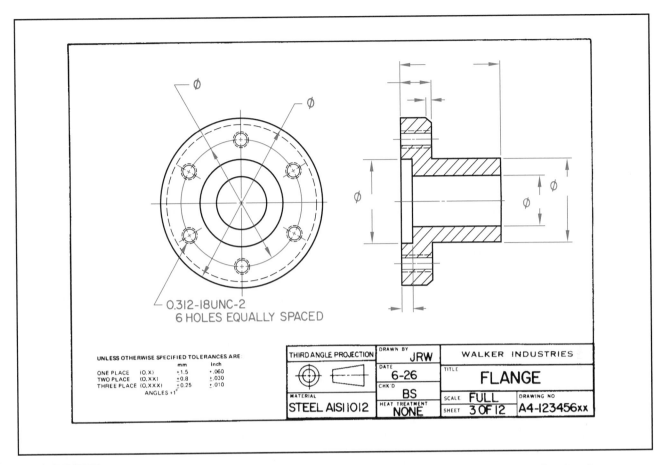

UNLESS OTHERWISE SPECIFIED TOLERANCES ARE

		mm	Inch
ONE PLACE	(0.X)	±1.5	±.060
TWO PLACE	(0.XX)	±0.8	±.030
THREE PLACE	(0.XXX)	±0.25	±.010
ANGLES ±1°			

THIRD ANGLE PROJECTION	DRAWN BY JRW	WALKER INDUSTRIES
	DATE 6-26	TITLE FLANGE
	CHK'D BS	
MATERIAL STEEL AISI 1012	HEAT TREATMENT NONE	SCALE FULL SHEET 3 OF 12 DRAWING NO A4-123456xx

0.312-18UNC-2
6 HOLES EQUALLY SPACED

Figure 10-37 When parts are designed to conform to different standards of measurement, the drawing may be completed without dimensions. Except for the thread size, no dimensions are shown on this master drawing. After the print is made, dimensions in either inch or metric units are added.

2. When a dimension is less than one millimeter, a zero is shown to the left of the decimal point:

0.5, not .5

3. All metric drawings should be clearly identified as such. The symbol for millimeter (mm) does not have to be added to every dimension if a note is placed on the drawing. See **Figure 10-38**.

4. A space (or comma) is not used to separate digits for dimensions into groups:

125mm, not 125 000

5. When the dimension exceeds a whole number by a decimal fraction of one millimeter, a zero does not follow the last digit to the right of the decimal point.

125.5, not 125.50

METRIC

ALL DIMENSIONS ARE IN MILLIMETERS.

Figure 10-38 Metric drawings should be clearly identified by use of a note.

Note

Where some millimeter dimensions are shown on an inch-dimensioned drawing, the symbol "mm" follows the millimeter values.

Geometric Dimensioning and Tolerancing (GD&T)

The design of parts for many complex applications requires a highly precise system of specifying dimensions and tolerances on drawings. A *tolerance* is an allowable variance from the original dimension. Tolerances permit allowances in size from the specified dimension that may occur during manufacturing. Machining processes have improved to the point where highly accurate definitions of tolerances for *form* (shape and size) and *position* (location) are needed to design products.

Geometric dimensioning and tolerancing (GD&T) is a standard system devised to control

interpretation of the form, profile, orientation, location, and runout of features on drawings. This type of tolerancing provides the necessary precision for the most economical manufacture of parts and *interchangeable* parts. Different dimensioning standards exist and a common drawing language must be applied because components for specialized products are typically manufactured in a number of locations and often in different countries. The GD&T system provides an international *language* that standardizes the dimensioning and tolerancing process.

GD&T uses *geometric characteristic symbols* to specify and explain form and positional tolerances, **Figure 10-39**. These symbols relate to such variables as the form

Type of Tolerance	Geometric Characteristic	Symbol
Form	Straightness	—
	Flatness	▱
	Circularity	○
	Cylindricity	⌭
Profile	Profile of a line	⌒
	Profile of a surface	⌓
Orientation	Angularity	∠
	Perpendicularity	⊥
	Parallelism	//
Location	Position	⊕
	Concentricity	◎
	Symmetry	=
Runout	Circular runout	↗ or ↗
	Total runout	↗↗ or ↗↗

Geometric Tolerance Specification	Symbol
At maximum material condition	Ⓜ
At least material condition	Ⓛ
Diameter	⌀
Radius	R
Basic dimension	30
Reference dimension	(30)
Counterbore/spotface	⌴
Countersink	⌵
Depth/deep	⌇
Square (shape)	□
Dimension not to scale	25
Number of times/places	6X
Datum feature	A◀
Between	↔

Figure 10-39 The drafter uses various symbols to identify geometric characteristics in the application of geometric dimensioning and tolerancing. The table on the left shows the five standard types of geometric characteristic symbols applied to communicate form, profile, orientation, location, and runout. The table on the right shows additional symbols used in the GD&T system, including maximum material condition, least material condition, datum feature, and other practical items. The application of GD&T symbols on drawings supports precision manufacturing and the global economy.

of an object, the profile or *outline* of an object, the orientation of features, the location of features, and the *runout* of surfaces or relationship of features to an axis.

Geometric tolerances are often used to specify the location or relationship of features that originate from a *datum*. A **datum** is an exact point, axis, plane, or surface from which features of a part are located. Datums are identified by symbols. The symbol consists of a reference letter enclosed in a box attached to a triangle, **Figure 10-40**. Datum feature symbols are positioned next to the datum point or surface, on an extension line, or under a dimension, along with a note.

Characteristic symbols, datums, and other geometric tolerance specifications are often indicated in a *feature control frame*. A **feature control frame** is a rectangular compartment that contains a divided series of symbols identifying geometric tolerance. See **Figure 10-41**. The characteristic symbol is typically given first and is followed by the allowable toler-

ance and a datum reference letter. (Datums are also identified by squares containing a reference letter.) Feature control frames may be shown along with the dimension or attached to a dimension line or extension line.

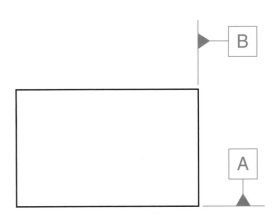

Figure 10-40   A datum is identified by a letter inside a box attached to a solid triangle. A datum is used to indicate an exact point, axis, plane, or surface from which features are located.

Dimensioning in CAD

As is the case with lettering a drawing, dimensioning a drawing manually can be a very time-consuming process. In CAD drafting, dimensions can be created very quickly and accurately with commands and drawing aids such as object snaps. A number of common commands are typically available.

As discussed in Chapter 8, lettering is known as *text* in CAD. Text is created with text styles. In similar fashion, dimensions in CAD are drawn with dimension styles. Typically, each dimension style has a text style assigned to it. There are also settings for the unit format. A dimension style can be created for decimal inch, fractional, metric, or dual dimensioning. When creating a dimension style, it is important to set the correct scale for dimensions in relation to the drawing scale. This ensures that the dimensions will be drawn to the proper size in relation to object features.

Dimension styles also provide controls for the extension line and dimension line format, spacing, tolerancing, and orientation. Dimensions can be placed in a number of ways with CAD, depending on the size of the feature and proximity to other dimensions. For example, the dimension text and dimension line can be placed inside or outside the extension lines. Also, as with manual drafting, dimensions may be placed using unidirectional, aligned, or chain dimensioning.

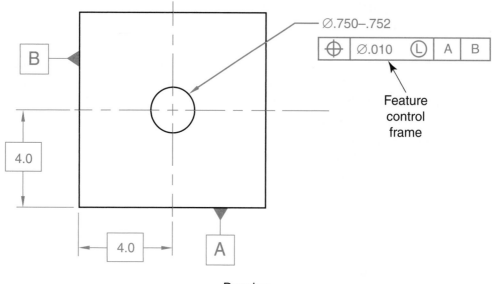

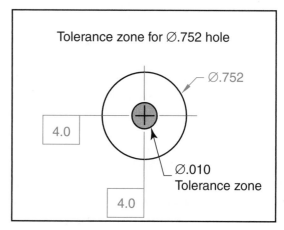

Drawing

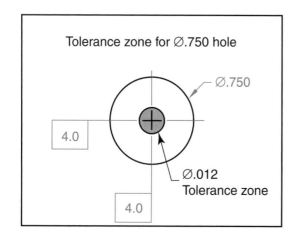

Interpretation

Figure 10-41 The feature control frame on this drawing provides precise information to manufacture the component part. It specifies the tolerance for the position of the hole at least material condition. The interpretation of the information is shown below the drawing. By learning the GD&T system, you will be able to interpret the exact location and form of features.

Dimensions are usually placed on a separate layer from other layers in the drawing. After creating a dimension style, it can be set current and used with various dimensioning commands. There are normally different commands for linear, aligned, angular, diameter, radius, and leader dimensioning. See **Figure 10-42**. In linear dimensioning, object points (such as corners or center points) are selected for the extension line origins. The placement of the dimension line and text is then specified. In angular dimensioning, the lines making up the angle are selected for the extension line origins. When placing a diameter or radius dimension, the circle or arc is first selected, followed by locations for the leader line and text. The diameter or radius symbol is generated automatically, and the dimension value is calculated automatically by the program.

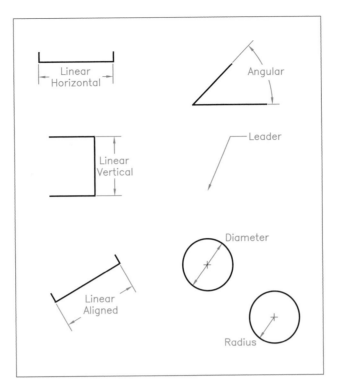

Figure 10-42 Different types of dimensioning are associated with commands in CAD programs.

Leaders are drawn in a similar manner. Points are selected for the placement of the arrowhead, line, and text. When creating a note, the text is entered manually. The text can include a variety of symbols, such as the counterbore or countersink symbol.

As is the case with text, special editing functions are commonly available for modifying dimensions. Editing commands may be used to reposition dimension text, specify different text, or change the dimension style.

Some CAD programs have special functions for geometric tolerancing and dimensioning. When this is the case, commands are normally available for drawing datum symbols, feature control frames, and geometric characteristic symbols. When placing tolerance dimensions, there are options for setting the tolerance method, limits, and precision.

The same rules used in manual dimensioning apply to dimensioning in CAD. To save drawing time, create different dimension styles based on the drafting discipline used. As with other drawing conventions, dimension styles should observe ASME, school, or company standards.

Test Your Knowledge

Please do not write in this book. Place your answers on another sheet of paper.

1. Explain why it is important to provide the most pertinent information in the clearest way possible when dimensioning a drawing.

2. Mechanical drawings dimensioned in inches are most commonly dimensioned in _____ inches.

3. Metric drawings are most commonly dimensioned in _____.

4. In unidirectional dimensioning, dimensions are placed _____ so that they are read from the bottom of the drawing.

5. The dimension line is a _____.
   A. heavy black line
   B. thin black line
   C. heavy dashed line
   D. thin dashed line

6. An extension line begins 1/16" away from the point, edge, intersection, or detail of the object and extends about _____ past the last dimension line it is used for.

7. A(n) _____ is an angular dimension line used to specify sizes of circles and arcs or to point out special characteristics of an object.

8. For most applications, _____ long arrowheads are satisfactory for dimensioning.
   A. 1/8"
   B. 1/4"
   C. 1/2"
   D. 3/4"

9. The three basic types of dimensions are overall, _____, and size dimensions.

10. Dimensions are placed on the views that show the true _____ of the detail being dimensioned.

11. Which of the following is true of dimensions?
    A. Dimensions should be placed within the outlines of the views.
    B. Overall dimensions should be placed nearest the view, while the smaller dimensions should be placed farther from the view.
    C. Dimensions should be placed so that no scaling of the drawing is necessary.
    D. Dimensions should be duplicated across views.

12. Define *chain dimensioning*.

13. Give the symbols used to indicate the diameter of a circle and the radius of an arc.

14. On your answer sheet, sketch the following hole symbols.
    A. Hole depth
    B. Countersunk hole
    C. Counterbored or spotfaced hole

15. When associated with the diameter of a circle, a leader always points to what?

16. When dimensioning the multiview drawing of a cylinder, the diameter and length should be dimensioned in which view?

17. Explain the different types of units used to express angular dimensions.

18. Define *dual dimensioning*.

19. A(n) _____ is an exact point, axis, plane, or surface from which features of a part are located.

20. Briefly describe some of the factors to consider when creating a dimension style for use in a CAD drawing.

Outside Activities

1. Contact several industrial drafting departments. If possible, obtain copies of the standards they use for dimensioning. Compare how similar or dissimilar they are. Do they vary by industry?

2. Obtain copies of several industrial prints. Study how they are dimensioned and how notes are used. Are there any provisions for foreign components to be used with the items on the prints? Will the parts be exported?

Drawing Problems

Draw the problems shown on the following pages. Follow the directions in each problem.

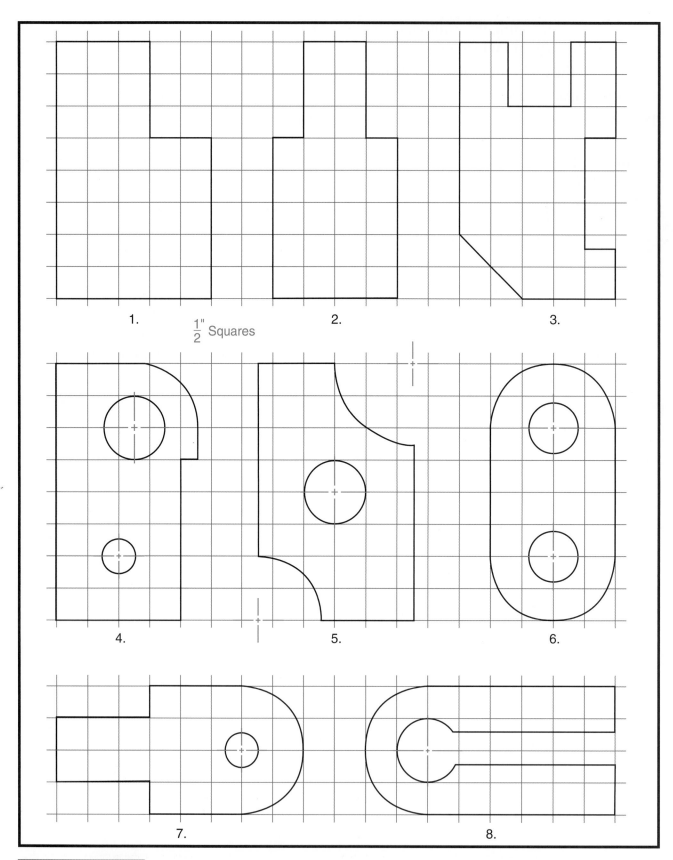

1.

$\frac{1}{2}"$ Squares

2.

3.

4.

5.

6.

7.

8.

Problem Sheet 10-1 Redraw and dimension. Draw only the view shown. Draw two problems per sheet. Grid squares are 1/2″.

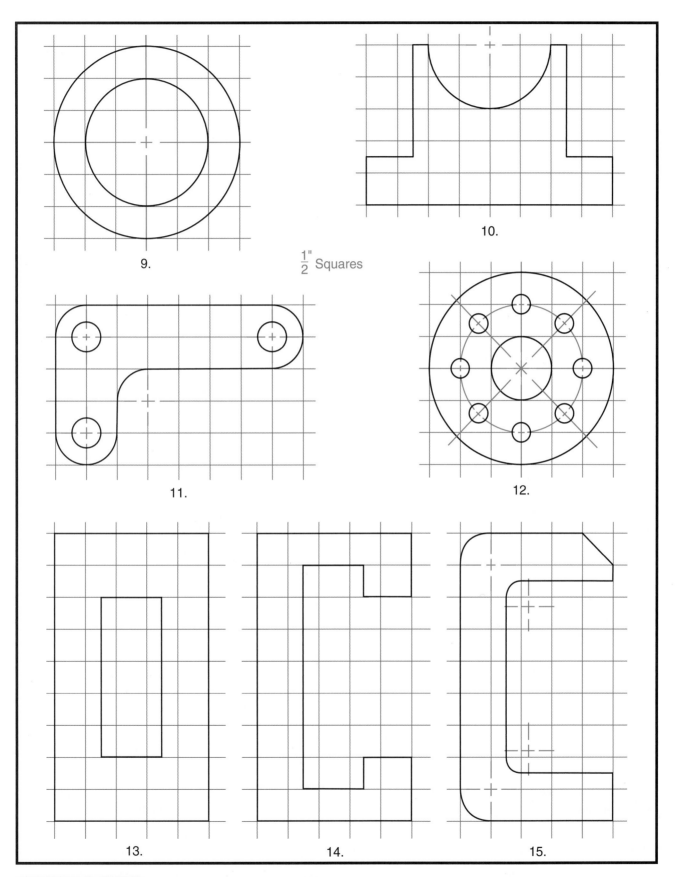

$\frac{1}{2}$" Squares

9.

10.

11.

12.

13.

14.

15.

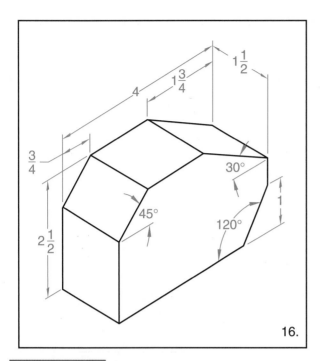

16.

Problem 10-16 **Shim.** Draw the necessary views and correctly dimension them.

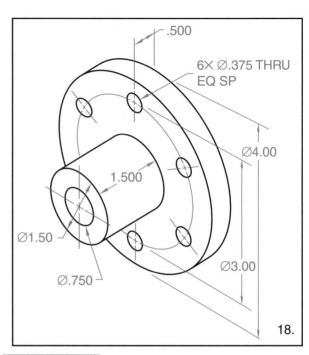

18.

Problem 10-18 **Face Plate.** Draw a two-view drawing and dimension correctly.

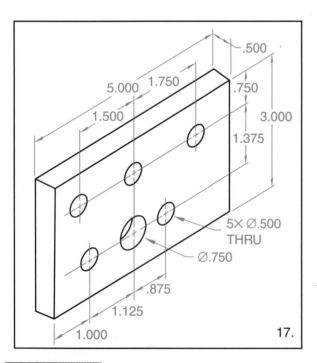

17.

Problem 10-17 **Alignment Plate.** Draw the necessary views and correctly dimension them.

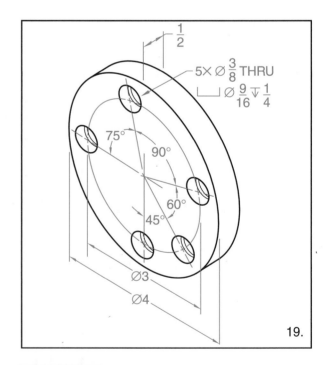

19.

Problem 10-19 **Cover Plate.** Draw the necessary views and correctly dimension them.

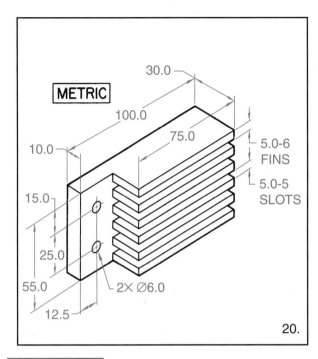

Problem 10-20   **Heat Sink.** Draw the necessary views and correctly dimension them.

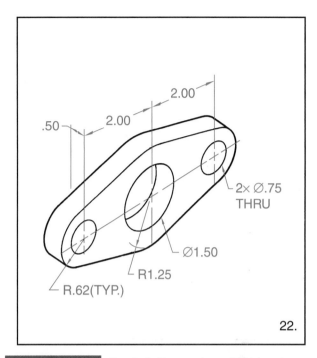

Problem 10-22   **Gasket.** Draw a two-view drawing and dimension correctly.

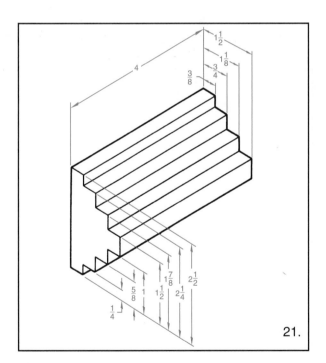

Problem 10-21   **Step Block.** Draw the necessary views and correctly dimension them.

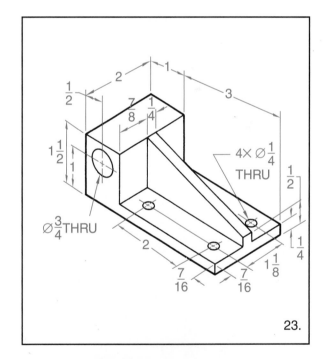

Problem 10-23   **Motor Bracket.** Draw the necessary views and correctly dimension them.

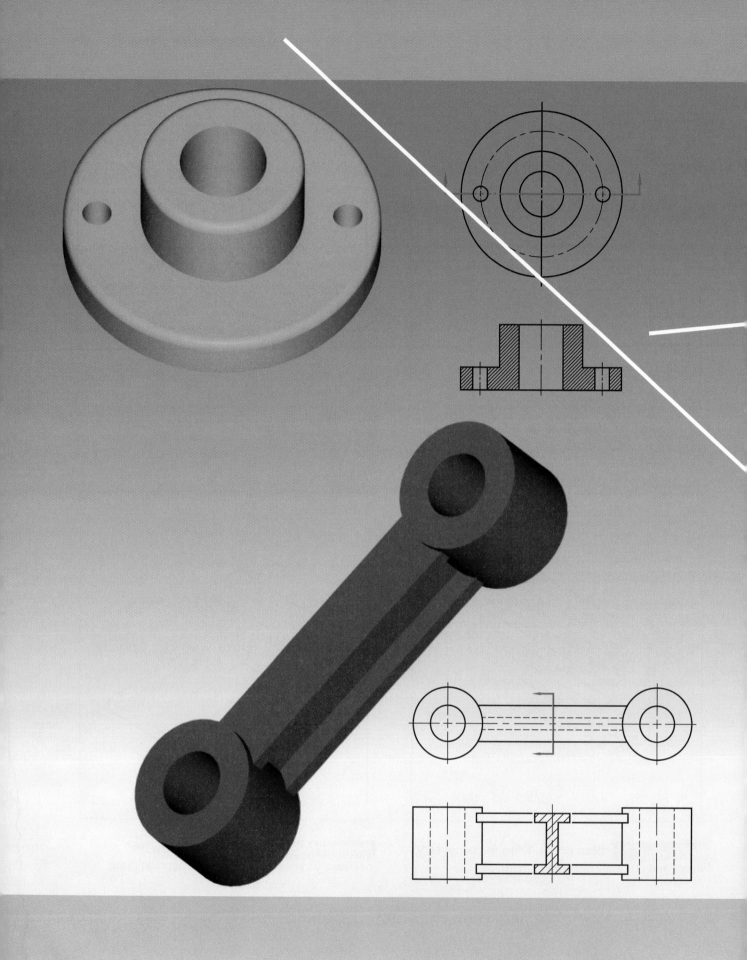

11 Sectional Views

OBJECTIVES

After studying this chapter,
you should be able to:

- Describe what a sectional view is and why it is used.
- Explain when a sectional view is needed.
- Describe the different types of sectional views.
- Draw sectional views.
- Explain how sectional views are generated in computer-aided drafting.

DRAFTING VOCABULARY

Aligned section
Broken-out section
Conventional break
Crosshatch patterns
Cutting-plane line
Full section
Half section

Offset section
Outline sectioning
Removed section
Revolved section
Sectional view
Symmetrical

The purpose of a sectional view is to show interior features of an object in an orthographic or pictorial view as visible edges and intersections (as opposed to hidden edges and intersections). In other words, sectional views permit interior features to appear as object (visible) lines rather than hidden (invisible) lines. This text focuses on creating sectional views of multiview drawings. You will learn how to construct sectional views of pictorials in more advanced studies of drafting. See **Figure 11-1**.

Many features of objects that are basically simple in design can be shown in regular multiview drawings. However, when an object has many complicated interior features that are hidden from the exterior view, it is difficult to show the interior structure without using a "jumble" of hidden lines. When this is the case, drawing sectional views helps clarify the interior of the object. Sectional views allow the drafter to eliminate the confusion of too many hidden lines. When used properly, they make drawings easier to understand. Sectional views are also useful when explaining interior construction or hidden features that cannot be shown clearly by using various exterior views and hidden lines. Another advantage of sectional views is that they often allow the drafter to eliminate one of the regular views of the multiview projection, **Figure 11-2**.

A *sectional view* shows how an object would look if a theoretical (not actual) cut were made through the object perpendicular to the drafter's direction of sight, **Figure 11-3**. The cut is known as the *cutting plane*. It is important for the drafter to understand that the cut made with the cutting plane is imaginary, not actual. There is only a theoretical removal of material, not actual. The end product is still whole when manufactured. The cut is only created to make the interior features of the object visible. Basically, a sectional view says that "If you cut the object at the location indicated (the cutting plane), look in the direction indicated (the direction of sight), and remove the portion of the object that is nearest you (the part in front of the cutting plane), it will appear like this (the sectional view)." The sectional view is beyond the imaginary cut. Sectional view drawings are often necessary in order to provide a clear understanding of the shape of complicated parts.

Cutting-Plane Lines

A *cutting-plane line* indicates the location of the imaginary cut that is made through the object to show the interior features or structure of the object. The ends of the cutting-plane line typically extend past the physical limits of the object or part of the object being

Figure 11-1 A pictorial sectional view showing the interior details of a four-cylinder, dual overhead cam automobile engine. Note where "cuts" are made to show internal features. (Ford)

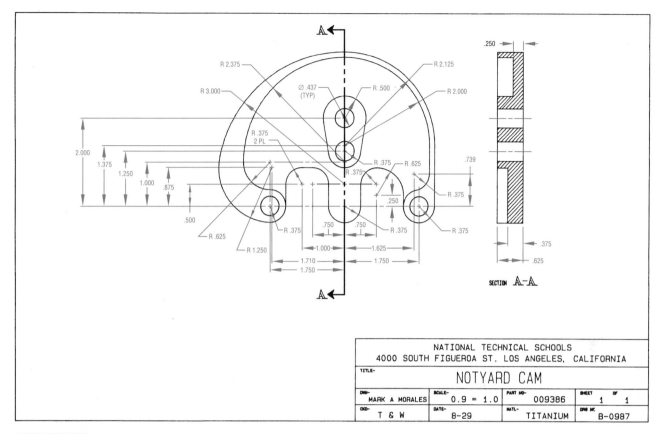

NATIONAL TECHNICAL SCHOOLS
4000 SOUTH FIGUEROA ST. LOS ANGELES, CALIFORNIA

TITLE-				
	NOTYARD CAM			
DWN- MARK A MORALES	SCALE- 0.9 = 1.0	PART NO- 009386	SHEET 1	OF 1
CKD- T & W	DATE- 8-29	MATL- TITANIUM	DWG NO. B-0987	

SECTION A-A

Figure 11-2 A computer-generated drawing with a sectional view. Only a front view and sectional view are shown. The student developing this drawing had to have a good working knowledge of basic drafting procedures and techniques.

sectioned. The ends of the line are then capped with arrowheads pointing in the direction of sight. That is, they point in the direction the drafter is looking when viewing the sectional view. Refer to **Figure 11-3**.

Cutting-plane lines may be drawn in three basic forms, **Figure 11-4**. Line drawing conventions for each type are discussed in Chapter 5. Some drafters prefer to use the simplified version of the cutting-plane line, which employs only two ends of the line with arrows. This method helps reduce the number of lines in views where many other lines are close to the cutting plane. As you continue to study sectional views, you will also find that not all types of section drawings require the use of a cutting-plane line. Some drawings do not require any kind of line indicating where the cut is to be made, while others require just a simple break line.

Often, cutting-plane lines are drawn with letters identifying the corresponding sectional view, **Figure 11-5**. The sectional view may be identified as A-A, B-B, etc. Refer to **Figure 11-2**. This is done when the sectional view is moved to another position on the drawing sheet, or when several sections are used on a single drawing.

As shown in **Figures 11-2** and **11-3**, the cutting-plane line is placed on the primary view in the multiview projection. This is the view showing the features that are being sectioned as object lines.

Section Lines

Section lines are used to indicate the positive mass (solid portion) of the object that has been theoretically cut by the cutting plane. Areas where the cutting plane passes through

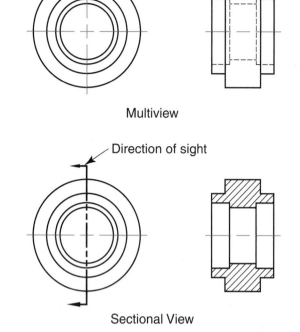

Multiview

Direction of sight

Sectional View

Figure 11-3 A comparison of a conventional multiview drawing and a section drawing. The sectional view describes the object's interior structure.

negative mass (open areas within the object where material has been removed, such as holes) do not receive section lines. As shown in **Figures 11-2** and **11-3**, the section lines are placed on the secondary view of the multiview projection. This is the view showing the hidden features that are being sectioned. Normally, these features would be drawn with hidden lines. Remember, the purpose of the sectional view is to make these hidden features visible.

General-purpose section lines are often used in drawings where the material specifications

Figure 11-5 Cutting-plane lines with letters identify the corresponding sectional view on the drawing.

("specs") are shown elsewhere on the drawing. General-purpose section lines are usually 45° lines, **Figure 11-6**. Spacing is done by eye and is somewhat dependent on the drawing size or the area to be sectioned. Spacing of 1/8″ (3.0 mm) is commonly used. However, larger spacing or outline sectioning, discussed later in this section, is suggested when large areas must be sectioned.

Section lines may be drawn in many different ways. They are commonly used as symbols to specify a particular type of material. General-purpose section lines are used to represent cast iron. Other common sectioning symbols are shown in **Figure 11-7**. Some drafters use general-purpose section lines in place of more complicated symbols and specify the type of material in a note on the drawing. When representing certain materials, this method saves time. Sectioning symbols are also available in dry transfer form.

General-purpose section lines should be drawn to the same line weight as centerlines. Do not make them too thick. They should contrast with the thicker object lines on the view. Good line contrast is a necessity for creating clear, easy-to-understand sectional views. Also, do not space section lines too closely. The lines should be uniformly spaced.

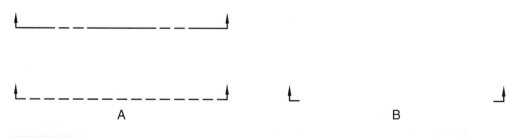

A

B

Figure 11-4 Cutting-plane lines. A—Two common types. B—A simplified version employs only the ends.

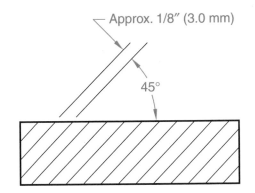

Approx. 1/8″ (3.0 mm)

45°

Figure 11-6 General-purpose section lining is spaced by eye and usually drawn at 45°. Spacing of 1/8″ (3.0 mm) is commonly used.

Do not draw section lines in different directions on a single part, **Figure 11-8**.

When drawing 45° section lines will make them parallel, or nearly parallel, to the outline of an object, they should be drawn at some other angle (such as 30° or 60°). See **Figure 11-9**. When two or more pieces are assembled and shown in section, the section lines should be drawn in opposite directions and/or with different angles to provide contrast, **Figure 11-10**.

When indicating large sections, *outline sectioning* is a permissible and timesaving technique. See **Figure 11-11**. With this method,

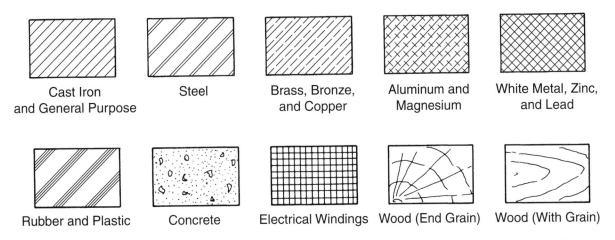

Cast Iron
and General Purpose

Steel

Brass, Bronze,
and Copper

Aluminum and
Magnesium

White Metal, Zinc,
and Lead

Rubber and Plastic

Concrete

Electrical Windings

Wood (End Grain)

Wood (With Grain)

Figure 11-7 Standard symbols used for common materials shown in section.

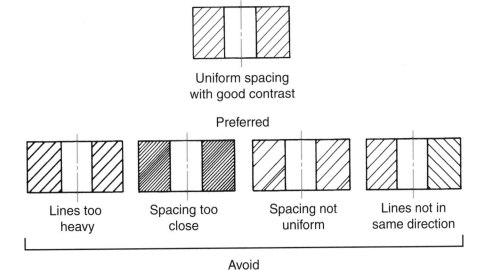

Uniform spacing
with good contrast

Preferred

Lines too
heavy

Spacing too
close

Spacing not
uniform

Lines not in
same direction

Avoid

Figure 11-8 Conventions for drawing section lines.

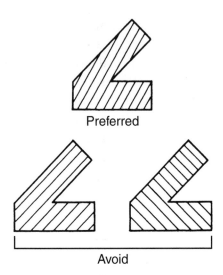

Preferred

Avoid

Figure 11-9 The outline shape of the section may require the section lines to be drawn at an angle other than 45°.

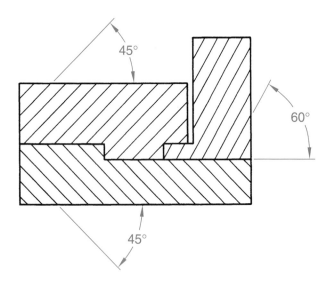

Figure 11-10 When several parts in the same section are adjacent (next to each other), draw the section lines in different directions or at different angles.

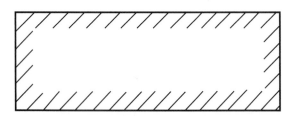

Figure 11-11 Outline sectioning saves time when large areas must be sectioned.

section lines are only drawn near the boundary of the sectioned area. The interior portion is left clear.

Hidden lines that depict features beyond the cutting plane that are still not visible even after the sectioning is done are omitted. This is the case unless they are absolutely necessary for a complete understanding of a view, or when they are needed for dimensioning purposes, **Figure 11-12**.

Types of Sections

Different sectioning techniques may be used to show object details depending on the characteristics of the drawing. Some objects require more than one sectional view to describe the interior. As is the case with views in a multiview drawing, sectional views should be drawn to provide the clearest shape description in the simplest manner possible. The common types of sections include full, half, revolved, aligned, removed, offset, and broken-out sections. These are discussed next.

Full Sections

A *full section* view is developed by making the theoretical cut through the entire object. See **Figure 11-13**. The part of the object between the drafter's eye and the cut is removed to reveal the interior features of the object. The resulting features are drawn as part of the regular multiview projection. Interior features that were invisible (hidden

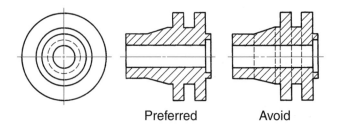

Preferred   Avoid

Figure 11-12 Unless absolutely necessary for a complete understanding of a view, hidden lines behind the cutting plane are omitted.

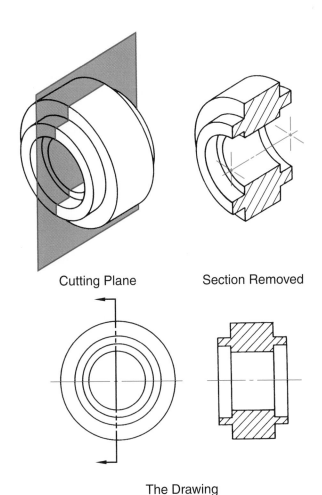

Cutting Plane   Section Removed

The Drawing

Figure 11-13 A full section. The cutting plane passes completely through the object. The section behind the cutting plane is exposed.

lines) in the multiview projection become visible (object lines) in the sectional view.

Half Sections

Half section views typically show one-half of the interior features and one-half of the exterior features of the object, **Figure 11-14**. In this type of section, one-quarter of the object is considered removed to show a half section of the interior structure. Half sections are best suited for objects that are *symmetrical* (objects having the same size, shape, and relative position on opposite sides of a dividing line or plane). In other words, if you were to divide the object in half, what appears on one side of the object would be the mirror image of what

appears on the other side. The cutting-plane line of a half section has a right-angle bend in it, usually occurring at the primary center of the object. Refer to **Figure 11-14**. The cutting-plane line has only one arrow pointing in the direction of sight. Unless needed for clarity or dimensioning, hidden lines are not shown on either the interior or the exterior portions of half section views.

Revolved Sections

Revolved section views are primarily utilized to show the shapes of objects such as spokes, ribs, and stock metal shapes. A revolved section is also known as a *rotated section*. The sectional view is created by revolving the cutting plane about an axis. The resulting view shows the cross section of the object. See **Figure 11-15**. The procedure is described as follows.

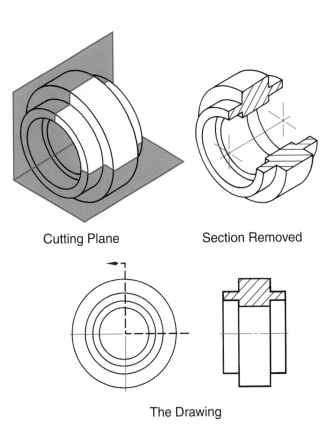

Cutting Plane   Section Removed

The Drawing

Figure 11-14 A half section. The internal details of a symmetrical object can be fully described by removing one-quarter of the object.

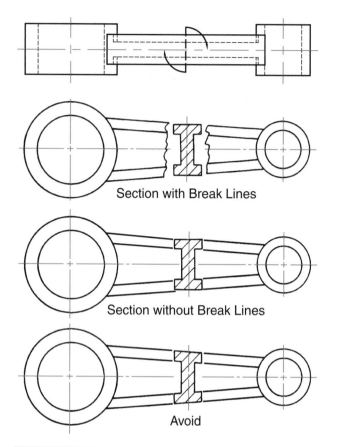

Section with Break Lines

Section without Break Lines

Avoid

Figure 11-15 A revolved section. The sectional view may be presented with or without break lines. Note that object lines do not pass through the revolved section when the break lines are omitted.

The normal multiview projection of the object is drawn first. Then, the cutting plane is located in one view at some point along the shape being sectioned. In **Figure 11-15**, it is located in the top view. The cutting-plane line in the example shown is the dashed line. It indicates where the section is to occur. The directional arrows indicate the direction of

revolution of the sectioned surface. The axis of revolution is established at the midpoint of the cutting-plane line (also the midpoint of the shape being sectioned). The sectioned surface is then revolved about the axis to a position that is parallel to the adjacent plane of projection. This plane is the front view in **Figure 11-15**. The sectional view is drawn "on top of" the view. The sectioned surface should be aligned with (centered on) the cutting-plane line. The sectional view may be drawn with or without break lines.

The multiview projection "behind" the sectional view should not touch the sectioned view in front. Also, the lines representing edges and intersections associated with the original view should not be drawn through the sectional view. See **Figure 11-16**.

Aligned Sections

It is not considered good drafting practice to make a full section of a symmetrical object that has an odd number of holes, webs, or ribs. For objects with irregular features, the cutting plane may pass through only one of the features. In such cases, an *aligned section* may be used. In this type of section, the conventional practice is to show two of the holes, webs, or ribs depicted on the secondary view, with one of them aligned into the same plane as the other. See **Figure 11-17**. The actual or true projection in a full section may be misleading or confusing. Notice in **Figure 11-17** that an aligned section drawing generally does not require a cutting-plane line in the primary view.

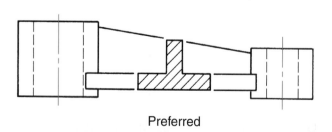

Preferred

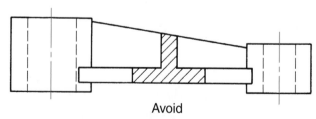

Avoid

Figure 11-16 A revolved section must show the true shape of the object at the cutting plane. Lines showing the outline of the object in section are never drawn through the revolved section.

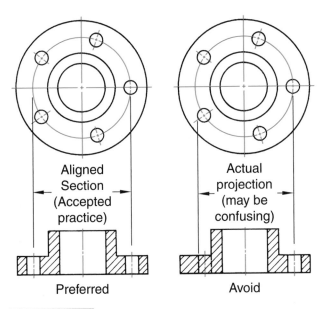

Aligned
Section
(Accepted
practice)

Actual
projection
(may be
confusing)

Preferred

Avoid

Figure 11-17 An aligned section.

Removed Sections

When a sectional view is needed, there are times when it is not possible to draw the view on top of one of the regular views of the multiview projection (as with a revolved section). When this occurs, a *removed section* is generally used, **Figure 11-18**. A removed section is nothing more than a revolved section with the sectional view or multiple sectional views placed elsewhere on the drafting sheet instead of on top of the regular view. Removed sections usually employ a simplified cutting-plane line as in **Figure 11-18**. Use reference letters at the ends of the cutting-plane lines and label the views.

A removed section is also employed when the section must be enlarged (drawn

ACADEMIC LINK

Drawing symbols are important communication devices. They allow the drafter to communicate information in a manner that is easily understood. You will often find the need to use symbols in drafting.

There are many standard symbols used for various devices and other items in different types of drafting, including electrical, welding, piping, and architectural drafting. There are also many types of symbols used to represent materials in the building trades. In addition to the sectioning symbols for concrete and wood shown in this chapter, there are symbols for brick, insulation, roofing materials, and other products. Standard graphic symbols for drafting are given in standards published by the American Society of Mechanical Engineers (ASME). In each case, the designated symbol is used to communicate the needed information.

Abbreviations for terms are also important in drafting. Many abbreviations used in industry are given on drawings to communicate information. Abbreviations are useful to drafters because they deliver the necessary message without taking up valuable space on the sheet. They are commonly used in notes and dimensions. For example, you may encounter the following note on a drawing with specifications for screw threads:

6-32UNC × 1/2 LG.
F.H. MACH. SCW.
2 REQ'D

This note specifies two 1/2″ long flat-head machine screws in the Unified National Coarse (UNC) thread series. The first line indicates the thread size (6) and the number of threads per inch (32).

Drawings are intended to communicate information clearly and concisely. Symbols and abbreviations are commonly used to achieve this objective. Common abbreviations and drafting symbols are presented in the Useful Information section of this text.

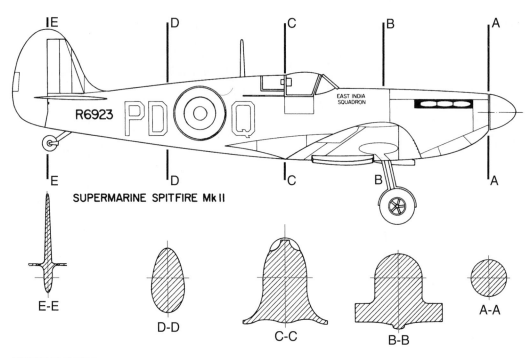

SUPERMARINE SPITFIRE Mk II

E-E   D-D   C-C   B-B   A-A

Figure 11-18 A drawing showing the use of removed sections.

to a larger scale) for clarity and better understanding of the drawing.

Offset Sections

While the cutting plane is ordinarily taken straight through an object, it may be necessary at times to section interior features that do not lie on the same straight cutting plane. An *offset section* employs a stepped or "offset" cutting plane in the primary view so that it passes through the required features, **Figure 11-19**. The conventional practice is to draw the features in the secondary (sectioned) view as if they were aligned on the same straight cutting plane.

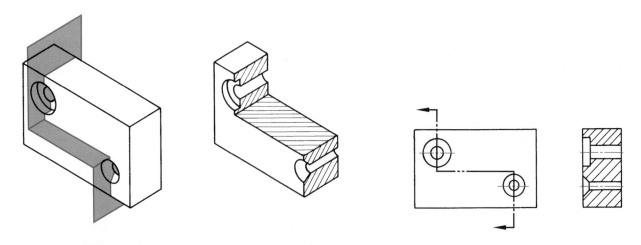

Figure 11-19 An offset section.

Offsets in the cutting plane are *not* shown in the sectional view as object line edges because the cut is theoretical, not actual, as with all sections. The sectional view appears as if all features lie on the same plane.

Broken-Out Sections

A *broken-out section* is employed when sectioning only a small portion of the object will provide the required information. Broken-out sections, as with all sectional views, may be done on single parts or on assembly views, where multiple pieces have been assembled together.

A broken-out section utilizes an irregular "break" line instead of a cutting-plane line to define the sectioned area. It is drawn freehand to the object line weight. The sectional view appears as though a portion of the object has been "eaten away," with the sectioned area showing the interior detail.

The rules for drawing broken-out sections vary according to whether the section is made on a single part or on an assembly. A broken-out section on an assembly generally does not require that the drafter show hidden edges and intersections on the portion not sectioned, **Figure 11-20**. However, when breaking out a single part, the multiview projection is drawn first, complete with object lines, hidden lines, and centerlines as required. Then the section is broken out where just the interior features to be shown are made visible, **Figure 11-21**. As a result, the interior features are visible on

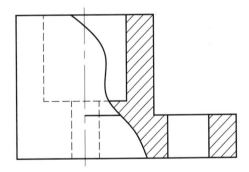

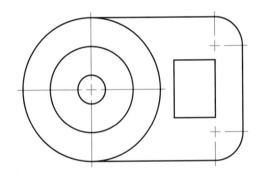

Figure 11-21 A broken-out section of a single part.

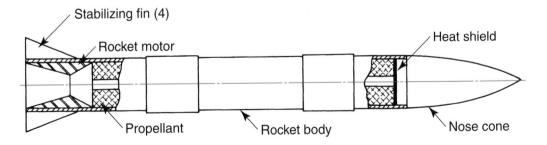

Figure 11-20 Broken-out sections of a rocket assembly.

one side of the break line, as in a full section drawing, and the rest of the view appears as a normal multiview (with hidden lines).

Conventional Breaks

Some objects have a small cross section but a long, continuous shape along a portion of their length. When this type of object must be drawn, the drafter is faced with a difficult situation. If the drawing is drawn full size, it probably will not fit on the drawing sheet. If a scale is used to reduce the size of the object so it is small enough to fit on the sheet, the features of the object may be so small they cannot be seen clearly or easily dimensioned.

In such cases, the object can be fit to the sheet by reducing its length by means of a *conventional break*, **Figure 11-22**. In this type

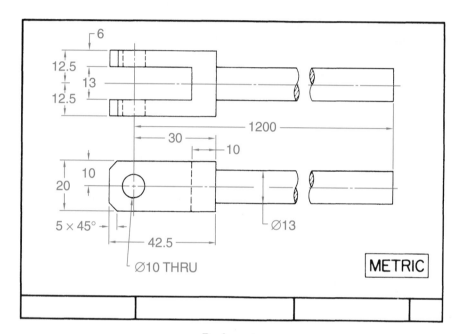

Preferred

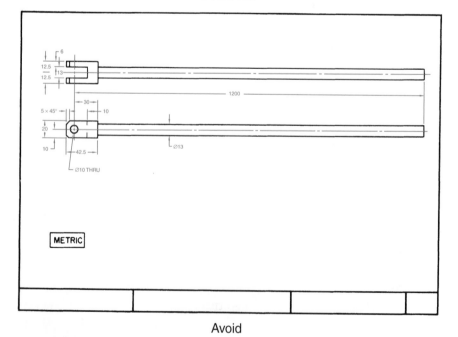

Avoid

Figure 11-22 A round conventional break.

of sectional view, a portion of the object is deleted (cut out) from the drawing and the two ends of the object are slid together. There is no set length or amount that is deleted. The amount deleted is determined solely by the drafter and is decided strictly on the basis of whether the drawing will fit effectively on the sheet. A conventional break can only be used when the cross section of an object or portion of an object is uniform in size and shape its entire length.

Conventional breaks for round and tubular shapes may be drawn freehand or with instruments, such as a compass or small French (irregular) curve. See **Figure 11-23**.

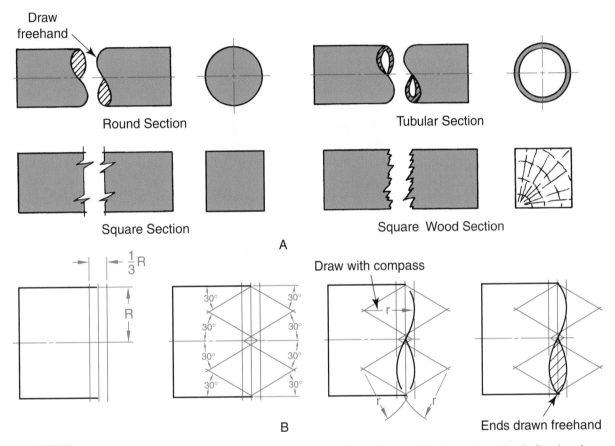

Figure 11-23 Conventional breaks. A—Sample breaks for various shapes. B—Layout methods for drawing break symbols.

Drawing Sectional Views in CAD

Many of the same techniques used to create different types of sectional views in manual drafting apply in CAD drafting. The drafter must have the same basic visualization skills, as well as the ability to arrange and depict accurate views. However, the process used in drawing section lines and sectioning symbols is greatly simplified. Section symbols are applied to views using special fill objects called *crosshatch patterns*.

Once the necessary views are drawn, the sectioned areas are identified. The areas to receive section lines are known as boundary areas. When a specific area is picked, it is automatically filled with the specified crosshatch pattern. Many different types of patterns are available. In addition to general purpose section lines, there are patterns for construction materials, metals, and other common symbols used in drafting. Users typically have the option to create custom patterns and vary the common settings for patterns, such as the line spacing, thickness, and rotation angle. This is a much faster and accurate process than drawing section lines manually.

In more advanced CAD programs, sections can be created from three-dimensional models. After the 3D part or assembly is drawn, a cutting-plane location or view is specified. Once the cutting plane is oriented correctly, the sectional view is generated and labeled automatically. See **Figure 11-24**. This function is particularly useful for creating sections other than full sections, such as offset sections.

Other types of views, such as details, can be created quickly and accurately using CAD functions. Details are similar to sectional views, but they provide more information. There are also similar CAD functions for creating auxiliary views. Auxiliary views are discussed in Chapter 12.

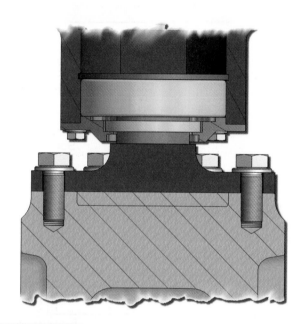

Figure 11-24 A CAD-generated section drawing of a 3D model. (Autodesk, Inc.)

Test Your Knowledge

Please do not write in this book. Place your answers on another sheet of paper.

1. What is the purpose of a sectional view?
2. A _____ line indicates the location and extent of an imaginary cut that is made through an object to create a sectional view.
3. Sectional views are identified by the use of _____ lines to indicate the positive mass (solid portion) of an object that has been theoretically cut.
4. General-purpose section lines are typically drawn at a _____ angle.
5. What is *outline sectioning*?

6. A _____ section is developed by making the cut through the entire object.

7. In a _____ section, one-quarter of the object is considered removed to show one-half of the interior and one-half of the exterior features of an object.

8. What is a *revolved section*?

9. A _____ section is a type of revolved section in which the sectional view is placed elsewhere on the drafting sheet rather than on top of the regular view.

10. The sectioned area of a _____ section is defined with a break line and appears as though a portion of the object has been "eaten away."

11. What is a *conventional break* and when is it typically used?

12. Section symbols are applied to views in CAD drawings with special fill objects called _____ patterns.

Outside Activities

1. Obtain an industrial drawing that uses one or more sectional views to describe the features of an object. With colored pencils, highlight the different component sections in the plan to demonstrate how the various parts fit together.

2. Using an actual object that has been cut away from a solid object, draft a sectional view showing the internal features. Display both the object and the completed drawing in class.

3. Create sectional view drawings of common drafting tools such as a drawing pencil, a T-square head, or a bow compass.

4. On a separate sheet of paper, answer the following questions about the drawing shown in **Figure 11-2** in this chapter.
   A. What are the overall width, height, and depth dimensions of the cam?
   B. What type of sectional view is drawn?
   C. What is the typical diameter of the four holes?
   D. What type of dimensioning technique is used to locate the center points horizontally?
   E. What type of dimensioning technique is used to locate the center points vertically?

Drawing Problems

Draw the problems shown on the following pages. Follow the directions in each problem and use the dimensions provided. Dimensions are in inches unless otherwise indicated.

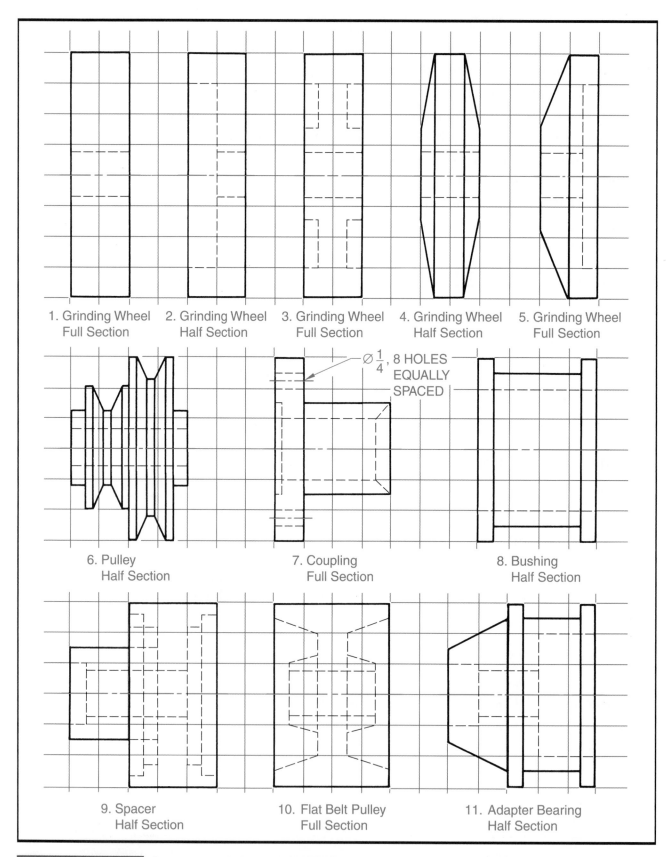

1. Grinding Wheel
   Full Section

2. Grinding Wheel
   Half Section

3. Grinding Wheel
   Full Section

4. Grinding Wheel
   Half Section

5. Grinding Wheel
   Full Section

$\varnothing\frac{1}{4}$, 8 HOLES
EQUALLY
SPACED

6. Pulley
   Half Section

7. Coupling
   Full Section

8. Bushing
   Half Section

9. Spacer
   Half Section

10. Flat Belt Pulley
    Full Section

11. Adapter Bearing
    Half Section

Problem Sheet 11-1   Draw the views necessary to show the shape of each object. Make one view a full section or half section as indicated. Draw the cutting-plane line on the primary view. Use a horizontal sheet format. Draw two problems per sheet. Do not dimension. Grid squares are 1/2".

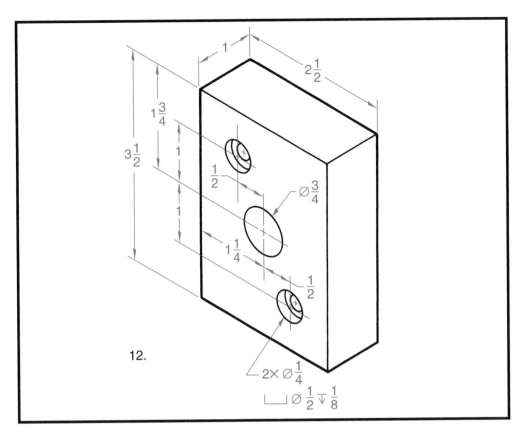

12.

Problem 11-12 **Spacer.** Draw the views necessary to show the shape of the spacer. Draw one view as an offset section through the three holes. Draw the cutting-plane line on the primary view. Do not dimension.

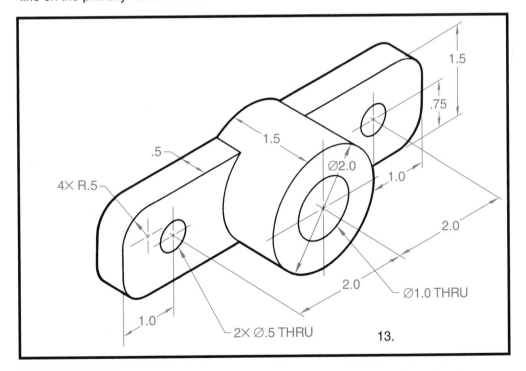

13.

Problem 11-13 **Special Bushing.** Draw the views necessary to show the shape of the bushing. Draw one view as a full section along the horizontal plane. Draw the cutting-plane line on the primary view. Do not dimension.

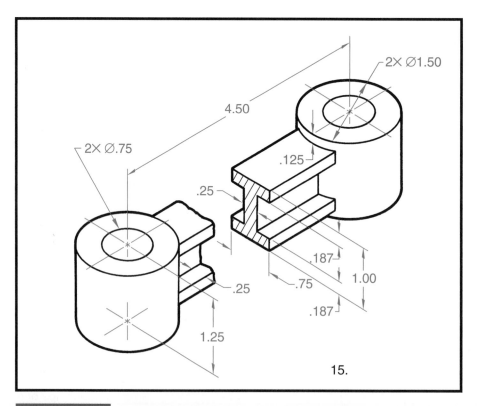

Ø 3/4 THRU
⌴ Ø1 1/8 ▽ 1/4

Ø2

1 1/8   1/2

Ø 1/4

1 3/4

2× R 9/16

1 3/4

3/8

2× Ø 1/2

14.

Problem 11-14 **Bracket.** Draw the views necessary to show the shape of the bracket. Include a broken-out section through the 1/4″ diameter hole on one view. Do not dimension.

2× Ø1.50

4.50

2× Ø.75

.125

.25

.25

.187

.75

.187

1.00

.25

1.25

15.

Problem 11-15 **Connecting Rod.** Draw the views necessary to show the shape of the rod. The cross section of the rod may be shown as a revolved section or as a removed section. Do not dimension.

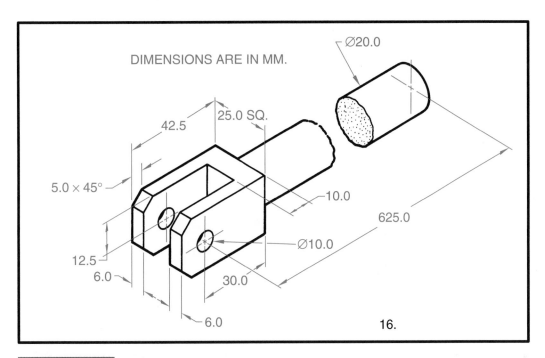

DIMENSIONS ARE IN MM.

Ø20.0

42.5

25.0 SQ.

5.0 × 45°

10.0

625.0

12.5

Ø10.0

6.0

30.0

6.0

16.

Problem 11-16 **Torque Rod.** Draw the views necessary to show the shape of the rod. Use a conventional break to fit the object on the drawing sheet. Do not dimension.

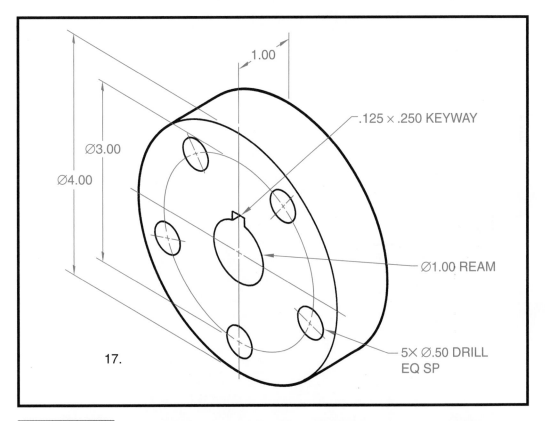

1.00

.125 × .250 KEYWAY

Ø3.00

Ø4.00

Ø1.00 REAM

17.

5X Ø.50 DRILL
EQ SP

Problem 11-17 **Adapter Plate.** Draw the views necessary to show the shape of the plate. Draw one view as an aligned section. Do not dimension.

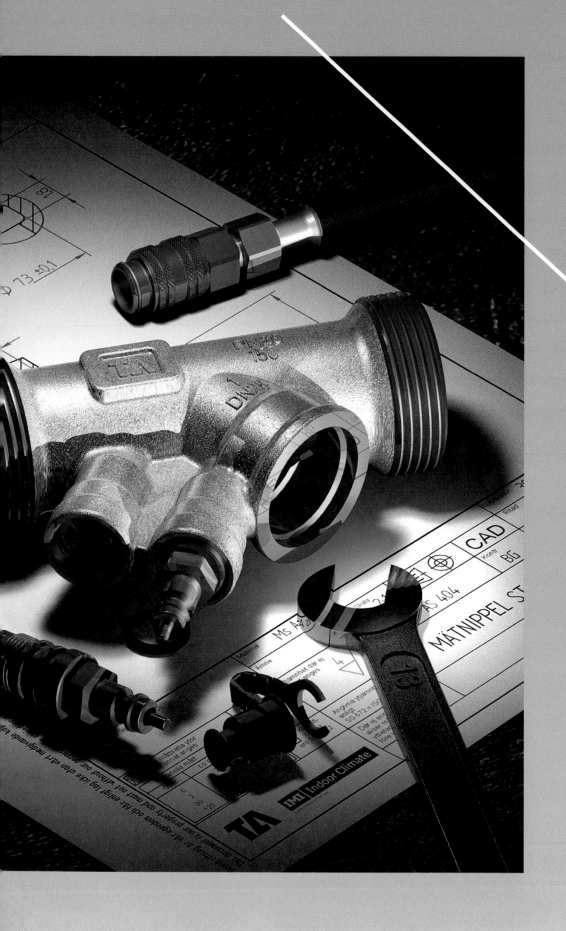

12 Auxiliary Views

OBJECTIVES

After studying this chapter,
you should be able to:

◆ Describe what an auxiliary view is.

◆ Determine when an auxiliary view is
needed to fully describe an object.

◆ Explain why an auxiliary view is
constructed perpendicular to an
angular surface.

◆ Develop and draw simple auxiliary
views.

DRAFTING VOCABULARY

Auxiliary view
Complete auxiliary
view
Front auxiliary view
Partial auxiliary
view

Right-side auxiliary
view
Secondary auxiliary
view
Top auxiliary view

Introduction

The true shape and size of inclined surfaces cannot be drawn using the regular views that are the result of a standard multi-view projection (the front, side, and top views). This is because an inclined surface appears at an angle to two of the principal planes of projection. (Multiview projection is introduced in Chapter 9.) When projecting an inclined surface, it appears as an edge in the front, side, or top view. In the other two views, it appears foreshortened. The surface is perpendicular to the primary projection plane of the angular feature created by the inclined surface. That is why, in that plane, it appears as an edge. The surface is inclined with respect to both secondary planes of the feature and therefore foreshortened in those views.

Surfaces with features that are not parallel to the principal planes of projection in multi-view drawings can be shown in their true size and shape in auxiliary views. This chapter discusses how to construct auxiliary views for objects with inclined surfaces.

Projecting Inclined Surfaces and Drawing Auxiliary Views

The object shown in **Figure 12-1** has an inclined surface. The true length of the angular surface is shown on the front view (where it appears as an edge). However, this view does not show the true width of the surface (actually, the true depth of this object because the width of the surface is measured from front to back). The true width (depth) of the surface is shown on the top and right-side views, but neither view shows the true length because the incline is foreshortened in both views.

In order to show the true length and true width of the angular (inclined) surface, an *auxiliary view* must be constructed,

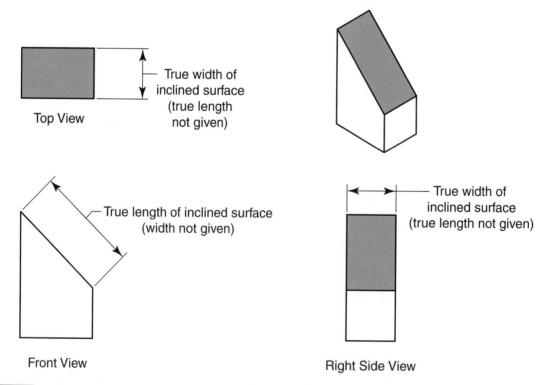

Figure 12-1 Auxiliary views are necessary to show the true shape and size of objects with inclined surfaces. The single orthographic views of this object do not show the true shape (length and width) of the angled portion.

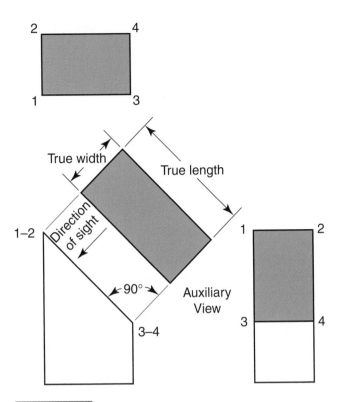

Figure 12-2 The auxiliary view shows the true shape of the angled surface.

size and shape on two-dimensional media. The auxiliary view in **Figure 12-2** represents the true size and shape of the inclined surface.

The view shown in **Figure 12-2** is called a *front auxiliary view*, because it is projected from the front view. A *top auxiliary view* is projected from the top view. A *right-side auxiliary* view is projected from the right-side view.

It is important to remember that the auxiliary view is *always* projected from the regular view of the multiview projection where the true length (edge view) of the inclined surface is shown. This could be the front, top, side, or some other orthographic view. Also, the construction lines projecting from the inclined surface are *always* drawn at right angles (90°) to that surface. In other words, if the angular feature created by the incline slopes at 45°, the projection lines will also be sloped at 45°. Similarly, if the incline is at 60°, the projection lines are drawn at 30° because the sum of the two angles must equal 90°. Auxiliary views are *always* perpendicular to the inclined surface.

It is often possible to eliminate one of the standard views of the multiview projection when using an auxiliary view, **Figure 12-3**. In this example, the top view has been eliminated. Also, the usual practice with auxiliary views is to project and show only the inclined portion of the object in its true shape and size.

Figure 12-2. An auxiliary view is viewed as if it is perpendicular to the inclined surface. To create the view, an auxiliary projection plane is created parallel to the edge view of the incline and the surface is projected in its true shape and size to that plane. The view is projected at 90° so that it is perpendicular to the incline. This allows the view to be drawn in its true

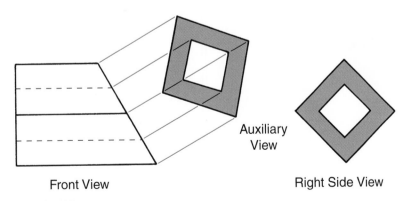

Front View   Right Side View

Figure 12-3 One view may often be eliminated when using an auxiliary view to describe an object. In this example, the top view is not shown.

See **Figure 12-4**. Notice that the surface with the two holes is not included in the view. This can be referred to as a *partial auxiliary view*. It is seldom necessary to draw a complete projection of the object to indicate what the entire object looks like from a point of view that is perpendicular to the incline. A view drawn in this manner can be referred to as a *complete auxiliary view*. A complete auxiliary is seldom drawn because, in that view, the only surface that appears in its true shape and size is the inclined surface. All other surfaces appear foreshortened. In most cases, there is little value in a view of this nature.

In more complicated situations, where the incline slopes with respect to all three primary planes of projection, it may be necessary to create a *secondary auxiliary view* to determine the true shape of the oblique surface. This is an auxiliary of an auxiliary view. The true shape and size of these types of surfaces may also be determined with a process called successive revolution. If you continue in your drafting studies, you will learn how to construct both secondary auxiliary views and revolutions.

Drawing Circular Features in Auxiliary Views

As discussed in Chapter 9, circular features on surfaces that are not parallel to the projection plane (such as holes) cannot be drawn in their true size and shape. In such cases, they are foreshortened and drawn as elliptical shapes. Referring to the latch plate in **Figure 12-4**, the two holes are drawn as circles in the right-side (orthographic) view because they are parallel to the line of sight in that view. In the pictorial view, they are drawn as ellipses because they are at an angle to the line of sight. Pictorial views are discussed in more detail in Chapter 13.

Special techniques are used to draw circular features and round surfaces in auxiliary views. With certain objects, such as symmetrical objects, considerable time can be saved by drawing one-half of the view, **Figure 12-5**. Referring to the right-side view, the upper hole feature is drawn as an ellipse. This feature is projected from the front view to the auxiliary view in its true size and shape, but

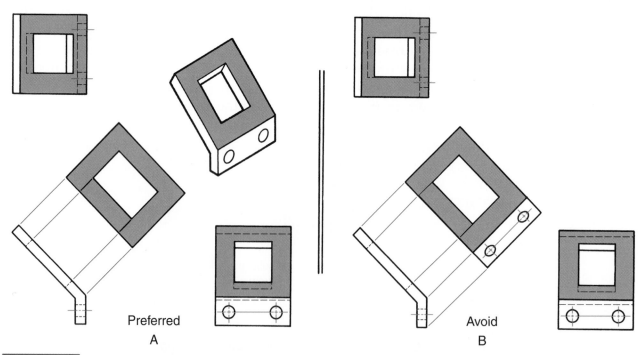

Preferred
A

Avoid
B

Figure 12-4 It is not necessary to draw a full projection of the object in an auxiliary view. A—Partial auxiliary view. B—Complete auxiliary view.

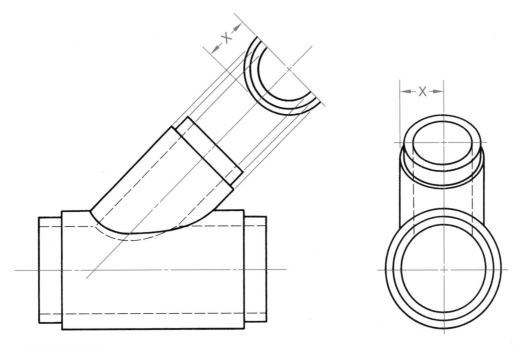

Figure 12-5 A half auxiliary view can be used to describe certain symmetrical objects.

only half the view is drawn. This is a conventional practice (it is not only acceptable, but recommended). However, this method only works with symmetrical objects.

Objects with round, inclined surfaces are somewhat difficult to represent in auxiliary views. An auxiliary view of an inclined surface with a cylindrical shape is shown in **Figure 12-6**. This cylindrical object is said to be *truncated*. The following procedure describes how to project to and develop an auxiliary view for this type of object.

1. Draw the required orthographic views. These include the primary (round) view of the cylinder and the secondary (adjacent) view, where the inclined surface appears as an edge. Remember, cylinders generally only require two views in a multiview projection.

2. Divide the primary (circular) view into 12 equal parts (using 30° increments). This is easily done with a 30°-60° triangle and the horizontal baseline provided by the T-square.

3. Project the intersections from where the divisions intersect the perimeter of the circular view to the edge view of the inclined surface on the secondary view. In the primary (circular) view, identify the intersections of the divisions with letters as shown. Use A-A for the lateral centerline.

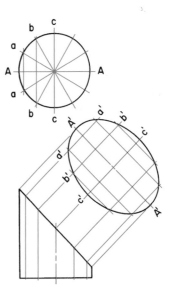

Figure 12-6 Drawing an auxiliary view of a circular object.

4. At any convenient distance from the inclined surface, draw the lateral centerline A'-A' for the auxiliary view. The centerline must be parallel to the inclined edge.

5. Project the necessary points from the inclined edge through centerline A'-A'. These lines are at right angles (90°) to the edge view of the inclined face. (To determine the angle of projection for the auxiliary plane, subtract the angle of the inclined edge from 90°. The resulting angle is the projection angle for the auxiliary view.)

6. Use dividers (or a compass) to transfer the depth distances that exist in the primary view (a-a, b-b, and c-c) to the auxiliary view. To do this, adjust the dividers to the distances that exist from the lateral centerline A-A in the primary view to points a, b, and c, both in front of and behind A-A. Use the dividers to transfer these distances to the auxiliary view. The points should be located along the projection lines extending from the edge of the incline and equidistant both in front of and behind centerline A'-A'. This procedure will locate distances a'-a', b'-b', and c'-c'.

Note

The critical factor in locating points in the auxiliary view is that distances a'-a', b'-b', and c'-c' equal the true depth distances a-a, b-b, and c-c in the primary view. Also, it is essential that the points are equidistant from the centerlines.

7. Complete the auxiliary view by drawing object lines through the points with a French curve. It is suggested that one-fourth (one quadrant) of the resulting ellipse be drawn at a time, taking care to create smooth transitions from quadrant to quadrant.

Drawing Auxiliary Views in CAD

Auxiliary views can be projected from normal views with inclined features in CAD programs using many of the same drawing methods involved in manual drafting. The same concepts and visualization skills used in manual drafting apply when creating auxiliary views in CAD. However, CAD commands and functions are used to project features and orient the views. This can greatly reduce the time spent in creating auxiliary views, particularly those with more complex features. In some CAD programs, special functions for drawing ellipses and elliptical arcs for circular features in their true size are available.

In more advanced CAD programs, auxiliary views can be automatically generated from an orthographic view. After entering the appropriate command, an angled line representing the inclined surface is selected in the normal view. The auxiliary view of the surface is then created automatically, with the features shown in their true shape and size. The user simply specifies the location of the view in relation to the normal views.

With some programs, secondary auxiliary views can be created in a similar manner. This may require several additional steps, such as specifying the surface or plane to be projected (instead of simply selecting a line representing the edge view). Automatic view generation functions are typically provided in CAD programs with 3D modeling capability. Modeling and pictorial drawing commands are discussed in Chapter 13.

Test Your Knowledge

Please do not write in this book. Place your answers on another sheet of paper.

1. What is the purpose of an auxiliary view?

2. An auxiliary view is always projected from the view that shows the inclined surface as a(n) _____. The construction lines projecting from the inclined surface are always drawn at an angle of _____.

3. What is a *front auxiliary view*?

4. A(n) _____ auxiliary view shows only the inclined portion of the object in its true shape and size, while a(n) _____ auxiliary view shows what the entire object would look like when viewed from a point of view that is perpendicular to the incline.

5. An auxiliary of an auxiliary view is known as a(n) _____ auxiliary view.

6. Describe how auxiliary views are typically drawn in a CAD program.

Outside Activities

1. Make a sketch of an original object that would require an auxiliary view.

2. Make a collection of items from your school that would need auxiliary views to show their true shape and size. Examples would be starting blocks from the track or your milk carton at lunch. Draw the views needed to create such an object.

3. Make a sketch of the inclined roof of a home or garage as an auxiliary view. Add appropriate dimensions. Explain the relationship between the area of the roof (or the number of shingles needed) and the steepness of the roof.

Drawing Problems

Draw the problems shown on the problem sheets on the following pages. Follow the directions on each problem sheet and use the dimensions provided. Dimensions are in inches unless otherwise indicated.

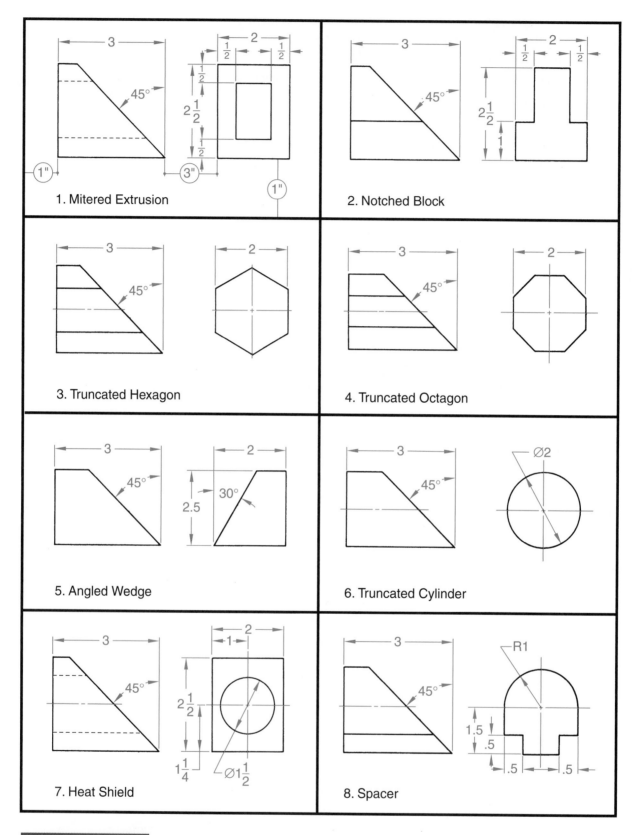

1. Mitered Extrusion

2. Notched Block

3. Truncated Hexagon

4. Truncated Octagon

5. Angled Wedge

6. Truncated Cylinder

7. Heat Shield

8. Spacer

Problem Sheet 12-1 Using the views shown, draw an auxiliary view for each problem. Space drawings according to the circled dimensions. Use a horizontal sheet format. The top views may be eliminated. Draw one problem per sheet. Do not dimension.

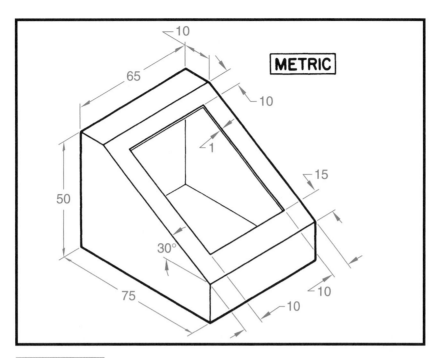

Problem 12-9 **Instrument Case.** Draw the orthographic and auxiliary views needed to describe the object. Use a vertical sheet format. Allow 4″ between the front and top views. Locate the auxiliary view 1-1/2″ from the front view. Locate the front view 1″ from the left border. Do not dimension.

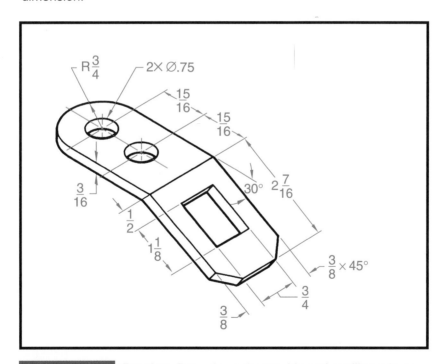

Problem 12-10 **Bracket.** Draw the orthographic and auxiliary views needed to describe the object. Use a horizontal sheet format. Allow 3″ between the front and top views. The top view is 3/4″ from the top border (draw the top view first). Locate the auxiliary view 1″ from the front view. Locate the front view 2-3/4″ from the left border. Do not dimension.

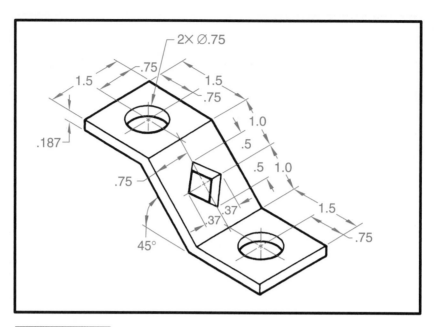

Problem 12-11 **Hanger Clamp.** Draw the orthographic and auxiliary views needed to describe the object. Use a horizontal sheet format. Allow 3″ between the front and top views. Locate the auxiliary view 1-1/2″ from the front view. Allow 2-1/2″ between the front and right-side view. Locate the front view 3/4″ from the left border. Do not dimension.

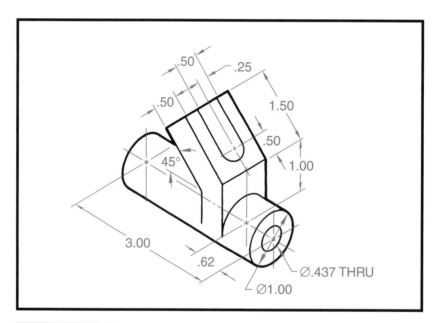

Problem 12-12 **Shifter Bar.** Draw the orthographic and auxiliary views needed to describe the object. Use a horizontal sheet format. Allow 2″ between the front and top views. The top view is 1/2″ from the top border. Locate the auxiliary view 1″ from the front view. Allow 2″ between the front and right-side view. Locate the front view 2-1/2″ from the left border. Do not dimension.

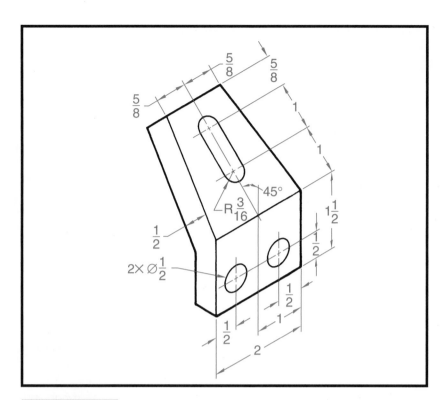

Problem 12-13 **Support.** Draw the orthographic and auxiliary views needed to describe the object. Use a vertical sheet format. Allow 2-1/2″ between the front and top views. Locate the auxiliary view 1-1/2″ from the front view. Locate the front view 1-1/4″ from the left border. Do not dimension.

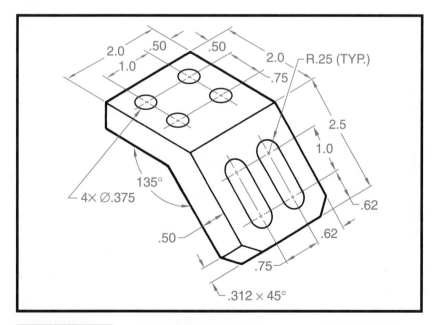

Problem 12-14 **Adjustable Bracket.** Draw the orthographic and auxiliary views needed to describe the object. Use a horizontal sheet format. Allow 2-1/8″ between the front and top views. The top view is 9/16″ from the top border. Locate the auxiliary view 1″ from the front view. Allow 2-3/4″ between the front and right-side views. Locate the front view 3/4″ from the left border.

13 Pictorials

OBJECTIVES

After studying this chapter,
you should be able to:

◆ Describe what a pictorial drawing is
   and why it is used.

◆ Identify the basic types of
   pictorial views.

◆ Construct pictorial views from
   multiview drawings.

◆ Correctly dimension isometric and
   oblique drawings.

◆ Develop and construct simple
   perspective drawings.

◆ Center pictorial drawings on a
   drawing sheet.

DRAFTING VOCABULARY

Angular perspective
Cabinet oblique
Cavalier oblique
Cutaway pictorial
   drawing
Exploded assembly
   drawing
General oblique
Horizon line
Isometric axes
Isometric drawing
Isoplanes

Nonisometric lines
Oblique drawing
One-point
   perspective
Parallel perspective
Perspective drawing
Pictorial drawing
Primitive objects
Two-point
   perspective
Vanishing point

A *pictorial drawing* shows a likeness (shape) of an object as viewed by the human eye. In other words, it shows the object in three dimensions, as opposed to the two-dimensional views that have been developed as multiview drawings in previous chapters of this book. All three basic overall dimensions—width, height, and depth—are represented in a single view.

The pictorial view of the automobile engine in **Figure 13-1** shows many features of its exterior and interior construction. This type of drawing is called a *cutaway pictorial drawing*. The exterior is shown by the pictorial view and the interior is shown by the "sectioned" views of the individual parts of the assembly.

In this chapter, you will learn how to generate pictorial drawings using manual methods and techniques. When objects get more and more complex, generating pictorials can become a time-consuming process.

Figure 13-1 Pictorials have many uses. This one shows the internal details of a V-6 automobile engine. (Buick, Div. of GMC)

See **Figure 13-2**. However, it is important for the drafter to learn these manual processes.

Figure 13-2 A drafter must have considerable skill to create pictorial drawings of complex objects. This perspective of a downtown street required a significant amount of drawing time. (Clem Cizewski)

The basic theory and techniques associated with manual drawing are "built into" CAD software. Having practiced the manual routines will make the drafter more appreciative of the power and ability of CAD. Manual drawing skills also give the drafter a greater ability to unleash the full power of CAD software, and the knowledge of what pictorial drawings should look like. Pictorial drawing applications in CAD are discussed later in this chapter.

Types of Pictorial Drawings

If you have ever purchased a computer desk or other furniture requiring assembly, you are familiar with pictorial drawings. See **Figure 13-3**. The assembly instructions for many products are composed of pictorial views. Technical illustrators, who generally work almost entirely with pictorial views, create pictorials for use with assembly instructions. These drawings show the assembler

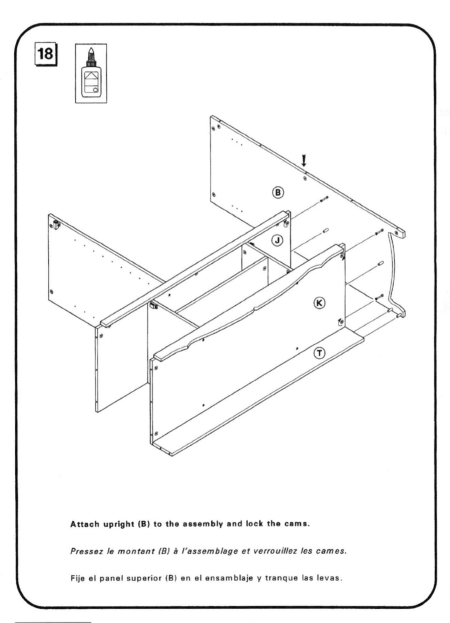

Attach upright (B) to the assembly and lock the cams.

Pressez le montant (B) à l'assemblage et verrouillez les cames.

Fije el panel superior (B) en el ensamblaje y tranque las levas.

Figure 13-3 Pictorial drawings commonly accompany written instructions for assembling products.

what needs to be done and the order in which it should be completed. They provide a visual map of how the parts are to go together.

All beginning drafters need to become familiar with several basic types of pictorial drawings. The most widely used types of pictorial drawings are isometric, oblique, and perspective drawings. The oblique and perspective drawing types can be further classified into cavalier oblique, cabinet oblique, parallel (one-point) perspective, and angular (two-point) perspective. See **Figure 13-4**. This chapter discusses the principles used in creating each type.

Only the basics of pictorial drawing will be covered in this text. As you continue further in your study of drafting, you will become familiar with many more types of pictorial views that are routinely used to describe objects in three dimensions.

One characteristic that applies to all pictorial drawings is that they are designed to illustrate the visible features of objects, whether they are exterior features on regular pictorial views or interior features on cutaway pictorial views. Interior views of buildings are commonly drawn as perspective views, **Figure 13-5**. Since pictorials are designed to show visible features, hidden lines are seldom shown on any type of pictorial view.

Isometric Drawings

An *isometric drawing* is a representation of an object in which two horizontal axes at 30° to horizontal and a vertical (straight) axis are used to show the object's width, length, and depth. The horizontal and vertical axes are known as the *isometric axes*. When drawn properly, the axes intersect at 120° angles. See **Figure 13-6**. An isometric drawing appears as if it is tilted toward the viewer. The 30° rotation of the horizontal axes corresponds to tilting the object forward 35°16′ in the normal

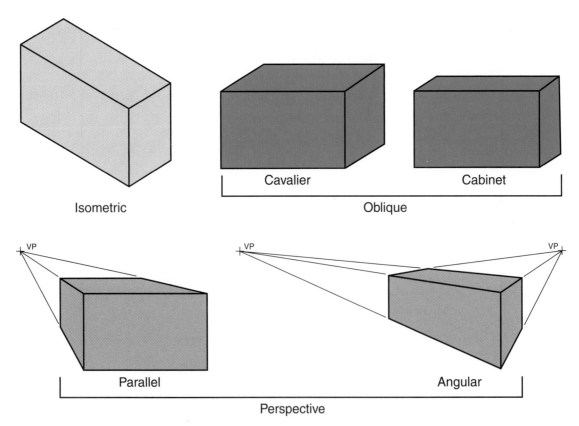

Isometric

Cavalier   Cabinet

Oblique

VP   VP   VP

Parallel   Angular

Perspective

Figure 13-4 The basic types of pictorial drawings.

Figure 13-5 Interior views of buildings are commonly presented as perspective drawings in architectural drafting. (SoftPlan Architectural Design Software)

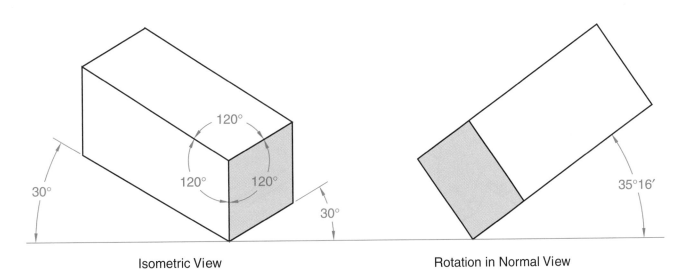

Isometric View

Rotation in Normal View

Figure 13-6 An isometric view is drawn with horizontal and vertical axis lines. It appears as if it is rotated 35°16′ toward the viewer.

view. This is the angle of sight that is formed with the paper in the isometric view.

Isometric drawings are created using a very simple, easy-to-learn process. Isometric lines can be drawn using the T-square, the 30°-60° triangle, and the appropriate scale for measurement. The isometric method of drawing is easier than some of the other pictorial drawing methods. It is a fairly simple way to show how the viewer's eye actually sees the width, length, and depth of an object.

First, the drafter must locate and draw a set of three baselines. The baselines represent the isometric axes. The baselines may be drawn in one of two orientations, **Figure 13-7**. When using the regular orientation, the viewer looks down and sees the object from above. When using the reversed orientation, the viewer looks up and sees the object from below. This view is used to show exterior features underneath the object, **Figure 13-8**. The regular orientation of baselines is used, on the average, more often than the reversed orientation.

The true length distances of the object (the overall width, height, and depth) are then measured along their respective baselines. All distances are measured full size unless the object is being scaled up or down in size.

Next, the object is blocked in to form a three-dimensional box equal in size to the overall dimensions. In blocking in the object, all lines that are horizontal on the front and side views of the multiview projection are drawn at 30°. They are drawn either to the left or the

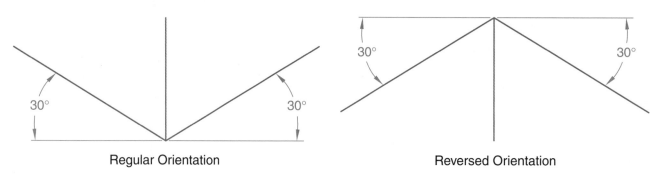

Regular Orientation   Reversed Orientation

Figure 13-7 Baselines used to make isometric drawings. Two orientations are shown.

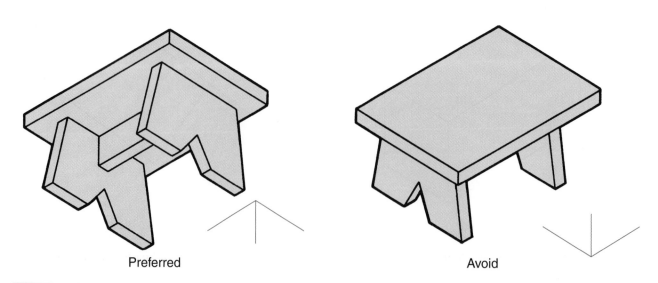

Preferred   Avoid

Figure 13-8 Reverse the orientation of the isometric baselines if more information can be shown. Note the underside features are visible in the reversed (preferred) orientation.

right, depending on whether they represent a width distance or a depth distance. If the object has more features that are visible from the right front corner, the width is measured to the left and the depth to the right. If the object has more features that are visible from the left front corner, the width and depth measurements are reversed. Vertical edges and intersections that exist on the multiview remain vertical in the isometric view. Refer to **Figure 13-4**. Just remember, object lines that are parallel on the multiview projection are still parallel on the isometric drawing.

Lines that form the inclined edges of inclined surfaces on isometric drawings are known as *nonisometric lines*, **Figure 13-9**. They are called nonisometric lines because they do not appear in their true length in the isometric view. Only lines that lie parallel to the primary planes of projection appear in their true length in an isometric view.

To draw nonisometric lines in an isometric view, the endpoints of the lines are transferred from the multiview and located in the planes where the endpoints exist in the isometric view. Lines are then drawn to connect the endpoints. Again, a nonisometric line is *not* true length, as is the case with the line representing the same edge in the multiview drawing.

Drawing Isometric Circles

Round features that appear as circles and arcs in a multiview projection are elliptical in the isometric view. Special ellipses called isometric circles are used to represent circular shapes in isometric views. It is important to understand that isometric ellipses are not true ellipses. They must appear in the proper orientation because of the viewing angle. On an isometric ellipse template, the ellipses are adjusted to the proper angle of sight.

On surfaces that are parallel to the projection plane, there are three common orientations for isometric ellipses. See **Figure 13-10**. These orientations correspond to the normal horizontal and vertical isometric planes formed by the isometric axes. On vertical isometric planes, ellipses are drawn in one of two ways, depending on whether the surface is inclined to the left or right. In **Figure 13-10**, notice the orientations of the primary centerlines for each isometric ellipse. In each case, they are parallel to the axis lines forming the isometric plane. On horizontal isometric planes, centerlines for isometric ellipses are drawn at 30° angles. On vertical isometric planes, the centerlines are drawn vertical (straight) and at 30°.

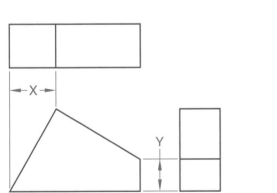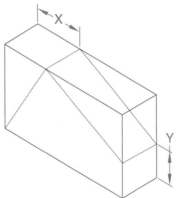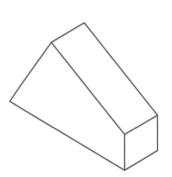

Figure 13-9 Nonisometric lines are made by locating the endpoints of the inclined surfaces in the planes where they exist and connecting them with object lines.

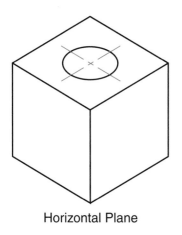

Horizontal Plane

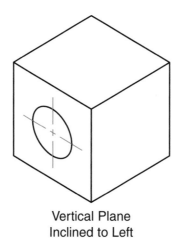

Vertical Plane
Inclined to Left

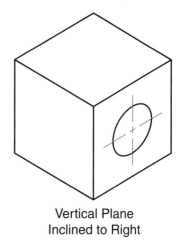

Vertical Plane
Inclined to Right

Isometric Ellipses

Figure 13-10 Common orientations for isometric ellipses, with centerlines shown.

Isometric ellipses can be constructed using a compass and 30°-60° triangle. The following procedure is used to construct isometric ellipses lying on a horizontal plane. See **Figure 13-11**.

Using the 30° angle on the 30°-60° triangle, create a construction line isometric square whose sides are equal in length to the diameter of the isometric circle being constructed. Using the 60° angle on the 30°-60° triangle, draw construction lines from the two closest corners of the isometric square to the centers of the opposite sides. The resulting intersections of these lines provide the center points for drawing radius R'. Radius R is determined and drawn by setting the compass as described in **Figure 13-11**. Arcs are then drawn

tangent to the sides of the isometric square and between the 60° construction lines.

Isometric ellipses on vertical planes are constructed using very similar methods. See **Figure 13-12**.

> ## Note
>
> Extreme accuracy in measurement and instrument placement is required when constructing isometric ellipses. Small errors can result in the procedure being very frustrating. Be very precise when making measurements.

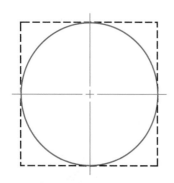

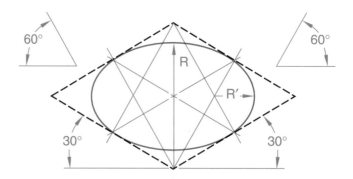

Figure 13-11 Drawing an isometric ellipse on a horizontal isometric plane with a compass.

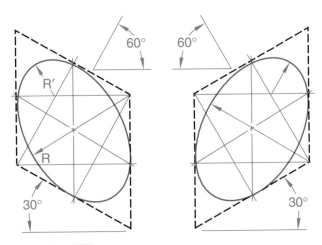

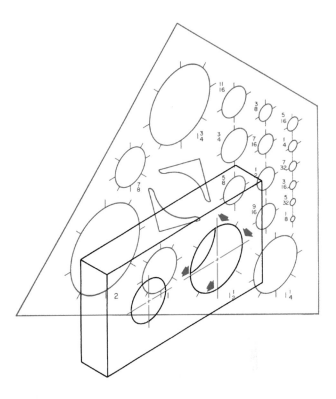

Figure 13-12 Drawing isometric ellipses on vertical isometric planes with a compass.

It is essential to know how to construct isometric ellipses with drafting instruments. However, as mentioned previously, an easier way to draw isometric ellipses is to use an isometric ellipse template. See **Figure 13-13**. A template may be used if the correct size is available. To use an ellipse template effectively, the drafter must first draw the appropriate isometric centerlines on the plane to which the template is aligned.

Figure 13-13 Using a template is a quick way to draw isometric ellipses. Be sure to create the appropriate centerlines first and then align the crosshairs on the template with the centerlines to accurately draw the ellipse.

Oblique Drawings

Although oblique views are not as natural to the viewer's eye as isometric views, the oblique method of pictorial drawing is often used as a quick and easy alternative to other methods. An *oblique drawing* is a representation in which the longest dimension (usually the width) or front surface is parallel to the projection plane. Refer to **Figure 13-4**. Because it is parallel to the projection plane, the front surface is shown in its true shape and size. The top and side are projected "behind" the front surface to show the depth of the object.

All measurements, except depth, are true distances. The depth varies according to the type of oblique drawing being created. Parallel lines from the multiview projection are still parallel on the oblique view. Horizontal lines representing widths are still horizontal, vertical lines are still vertical, and horizontal lines representing depth are drawn to an angle determined by the type of oblique drawing being created.

There are three common types of oblique drawings, **Figure 13-14**. These are cavalier, cabinet, and general. In each type, the front face appears in its true shape and size, unless the object is to be scaled to a larger or smaller size. The angle used to draw the depth axis may be any angle, but 15°, 30°, and 45° axis angles are generally used.

A *cavalier oblique* is an oblique drawing in which the depth axis lines are drawn at full scale (full size). A *cabinet oblique* is an oblique drawing in which the depth axis lines are drawn at one-half scale. A *general oblique* is an oblique drawing in which the scale of the depth axis lines varies from one-half to

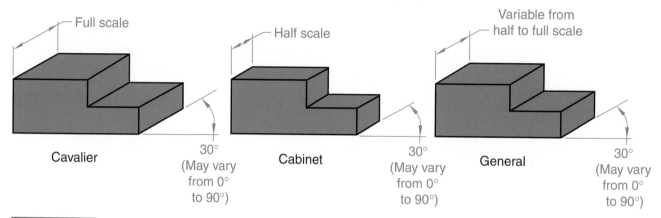

Figure 13-14 The three types of oblique drawings.

full scale. The cavalier and cabinet oblique types are most commonly used.

Even though cavalier oblique drawings have a tendency to exaggerate depth to the human eye, they are still often used where quick representations are needed. However, in situations where an oblique drawing is the best way to show an object but there is concern for not exaggerating depth, both cabinet and general oblique views are good options.

Dimensioning Pictorial Drawings

When dimensioning pictorial drawings, the same basic rules of dimensioning normal orthographic views apply. Dimensioning is introduced in Chapter 10. However, there are a few guidelines specific to pictorial dimensioning. The same basic dimensions required in a multiview projection of an object are required in the pictorial view. The difference

ACADEMIC LINK

Later in this chapter, you will learn some of the common methods for creating pictorial views in CAD drafting. There are different ways to draw and represent objects as pictorials in CAD. One method, modeling, provides applications beyond representation.

If you are using a CAD program with modeling capability to create 3D solids, you may find it useful to calculate various mass properties of the objects you are drawing. Some CAD programs with modeling tools allow you to calculate this type of information for prisms, cylinders, spheres, cones, and other solids. For instance, you can typically enter a command that automatically calculates the mass and volume of a prism, cylinder, sphere, or

cone after picking the object. You can also quickly find coordinate information, such as the center of an object. Mathematical formulas for finding the volume of prisms, cylinders, spheres, and cones are presented in the Useful Information section of this text.

CAD programs normally also provide commands for calculating design data for 2D geometry. You can typically find the area, perimeter, or circumference of an object by entering the appropriate command and picking the object. Line lengths can also be quickly determined by picking endpoints. These functions can be very helpful when you are trying to calculate distances or other geometric information for objects.

is that the dimensions are placed in pictorial planes instead of orthographic planes.

As with normal orthographic views, the overall size of the object should, in most cases, be given. The size of all features of the object should be specified. Finally, the location of those features should be given. The following are some general rules for dimensioning pictorial drawings. If needed, refer to Chapter 10 for a complete discussion on dimensioning. The rules that follow apply to isometric and oblique views. (Perspective drawings are usually not dimensioned.)

1. Place dimensions along the edge of the pictorial view where the feature being dimensioned is visible (not hidden).
2. Unless absolutely necessary, dimensions should not be placed on top of (or within) the pictorial view. Also, extension lines should not cross the view any more than necessary.
3. If possible, linear dimensions should be grouped together rather than placed randomly about the drawing. Grouping also applies to leadered information for duplicate features, such as multiple holes of the same size.

4. Dimensions should be complete, so that no scaling of the drawing is required by the viewer. It should be possible to determine sizes and shapes without assuming any measurements.
5. Draw dimension lines parallel to the direction of measurement.
6. Dimensions should not be duplicated unless they are absolutely necessary for a complete understanding of the object.
7. Extension lines should not cross dimension lines. Place smaller distances nearer the view than larger ones.
8. When all dimensions on a drawing are in inches, the inch symbol (") should not be used. Dimensions on metric drawings are in millimeters unless otherwise noted.
9. Whole numbers and fractions should be in proper relation to one another with respect to size.

Spacing of linear dimensions that specify the overall size, location of features, and size of features should follow the same guidelines that apply to normal orthographic views. It is permissible for the same extension line to be used for multiple dimensions that lie on adjacent planes, **Figure 13-15**.

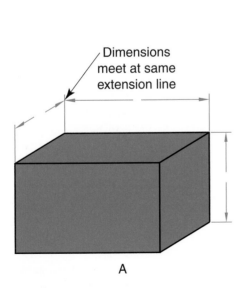

Dimensions meet at same extension line

A

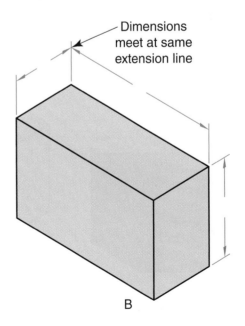

Dimensions meet at same extension line

B

Figure 13-15 Examples of dimensioned pictorial views. Dimensions on adjacent planes can use the same extension line. A—Oblique view. B—Isometric view.

When providing information with leaders, the same recommended guidelines for orthographic views apply. The same styles of leaders (with a few minor modifications) are acceptable for use on pictorial views as well.

Lettering that appears on dimensions in pictorial views may be presented in one of two ways. The preferred method is to orient numbers and fractions so that they are unidirectional, as is common with multiview drawings. This method places all numbers and fractions in the same orthographic plane that is parallel to the projection plane. See **Figure 13-16**.

The other method of lettering dimensions in pictorial views places numbers and fractions in the same pictorial plane as the dimension and extension lines used for the dimension. See **Figure 13-16B**. In order to create the lettering, the drafter must make all horizontal elements of the numbers and fractions parallel to either the dimension line (if a horizontal distance) or the extension lines (if a vertical distance). For example, the horizontal line in the numeral *4* should be parallel to the dimension line or extension lines. If the dimension is in a vertical plane, all vertical elements within the numbers

(such as the vertical line in the numeral *4*) are still vertical.

> **Note**
>
> You may wish to orient dimensions in pictorial views so that they align with the pictorial planes rather than the direction of sight when looking at the drawing. This will challenge you to create "pictorial" lettering (numbers and fractions) and even arrowheads, thereby making you think more about how objects appear in three-dimensional space. This will help you become a better drafter because many drawing applications require the ability to think in three dimensions. It will also help in your transition to pictorial drawing in CAD because the most effective use of CAD requires the ability to think in three dimensions.

It is critical to understand that all dimensions on pictorial views should be given full size, even if the drawing is completed to a smaller or larger scale. This is because the drawing is intended to tell the manufacturer the exact information needed to

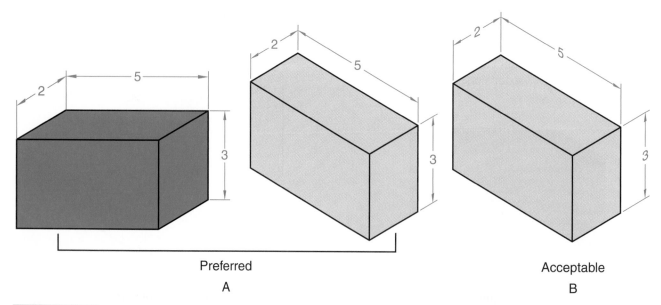

Preferred

A

Acceptable

B

Figure 13-16 Methods of lettering dimensions in pictorial views.

make the "full size" product. Scaled dimensions on a drawing would be useless to the manufacturer.

There are some additional guidelines and recommendations that are specific to isometric and oblique dimensioning. These are discussed in the following sections.

Isometric Dimensioning

It is recommended that, when the drafter is dimensioning an isometric drawing, all linear distances be specified in vertical planes, **Figure 13-17**. This can easily be done by making certain that either the dimension line is vertical or the extension lines are vertical on any given linear dimension. If dimensions are specified in horizontal isometric planes, lettering becomes much more difficult if the dimension numbers are to be parallel to the pictorial planes. See **Figure 13-18**.

All extension lines and dimension lines on isometric views should be either vertical or drawn at 30°. Remember, on isometric drawings, all lines that are horizontal (specifying width or depth distances) in the multiview

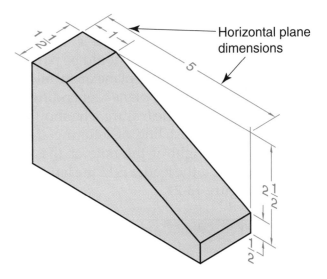

Figure 13-18 Avoid drawing linear dimensions in horizontal isometric planes.

projection become 30° lines in the isometric view. Do not dimension parallel to nonisometric lines. These lines are not true length lines on isometric views, **Figure 13-19**. If this is done, the dimension will specify a given distance and not actually measure what it says.

> ## Note
>
> All dimensions should measure, arrowhead to arrowhead, exactly what they say.

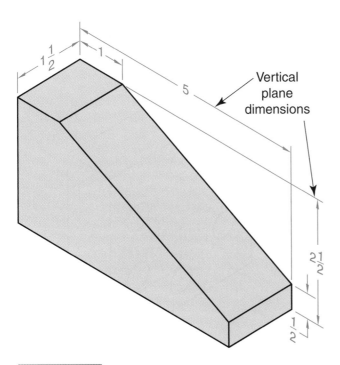

Figure 13-17 Specifying linear distances in vertical isometric planes.

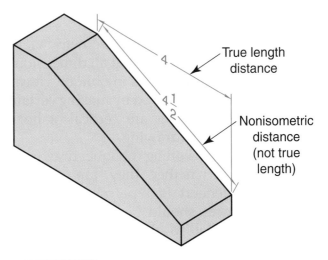

Figure 13-19 Do not dimension parallel to nonisometric lines. They are not true length lines.

When creating leaders in isometric planes, the leader shoulder should be a 30° line, **Figure 13-20**. The shoulder should be parallel to the top edge of the front plane or parallel to the top edge of the side plane, depending on the plane location of the feature. The shoulder should meet the last line of lettering if the leader is to the right of the note or the first line of lettering if the leader is to the left of the note. See **Figure 13-21**.

> ## Note
>
> Try to dimension width, height, and all related feature locations and sizes in the vertical back plane of the object being dimensioned (refer to **Figure 13-17**). This will not only group the linear distances, it will also prevent dimensions and extension lines from being placed within the limits of the isometric view. By doing this, the drafter will have satisfied several of the basic rules of dimensioning all at once. Dimensions for depth and depth-related features can then be easily drawn parallel to the top of the far end or the bottom of the near end of the isometric view. Sometimes, a combination of the two locations is required, depending on the individual features of the object.

Oblique Dimensioning

As with dimensioning an isometric view, it is highly recommended that all dimensions be given in vertical planes in oblique views. This can easily be achieved by making certain that all extension lines are vertical or horizontal on the entire drawing.

When dimensioning oblique drawings, regardless of whether they are cavalier, cabinet, or general in type, all width and height distances should be given in planes that are parallel to the projection plane, **Figure 13-22**. These dimensions will appear much like they would in a correctly dimensioned multiview projection of the object.

Horizontal lines from the multiview will still be horizontal in the oblique view, and vertical lines from the multiview will still be vertical in the oblique view.

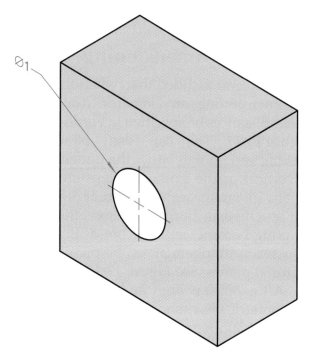

Figure 13-20 A sample leader and note in an isometric plane.

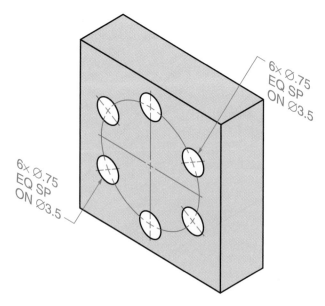

Figure 13-21 Proper orientations for leaders and notes in an isometric view.

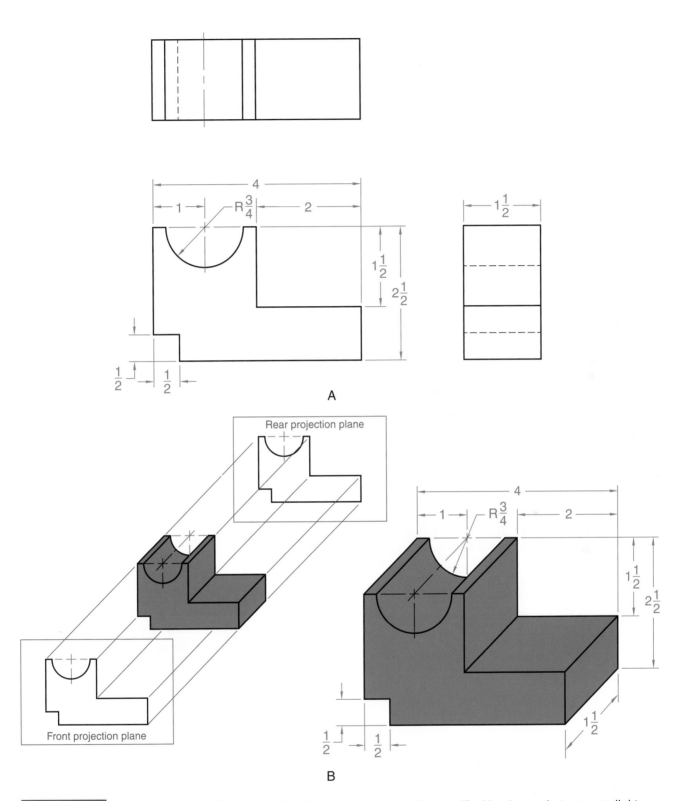

Figure 13-22 Width and height dimensions in oblique views should be specified in planes that are parallel to the projection plane. A—A properly dimensioned multiview drawing of the object. B—A cavalier oblique view. Notice how the dimensions are grouped on the front and back surfaces of the object.

When dimensioning depth on an oblique drawing, the extension lines should be vertical and the dimension lines should slope at the same angle used for the depth axis. Lettering for overall and feature-related depth dimensions may be drawn parallel to the projection plane or the pictorial plane. If the lettering is drawn parallel to the pictorial plane, the vertical internal elements are still made vertical because the dimension is lying in a vertical plane. Depth dimensions should *not* be placed in horizontal oblique planes, **Figure 13-23**. Finally, the depth on oblique drawings is always specified to full size regardless of the type of oblique view used. The manufacturer needs to know the full depth of the object, *not* the reduced depth

created by drawing a cabinet or general oblique view. The only value in using these two types of oblique views is they make the object look a little more natural to the human eye (in comparison to using a cavalier oblique for the same object).

> ## Note
>
> As is the case with dimensioning isometric views, try to dimension width, height, and all related feature locations and sizes in oblique views in the vertical back plane of the object being dimensioned (refer to **Figure 13-22**). Depth and depth-related features can then be easily dimensioned parallel to the depth angle axis at the top or bottom of the oblique view. Sometimes, a combination of the two locations is required, depending on the individual features of the object.

Perspective Drawings

Perspective drawings are used by architects, interior designers, artists, and drafters to represent large objects such as buildings. A *perspective drawing* is a drawing in which lines are projected to one or more vanishing points to show the depth of an object as it would appear when viewed from a certain position (point of view). See **Figure 13-24**. Refer to **Figure 13-4** for a comparison of the perspective, isometric, and oblique drawing types.

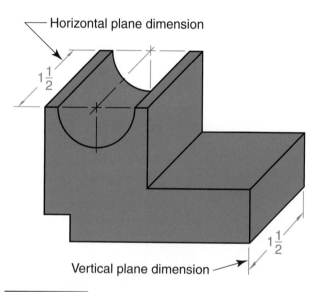

Horizontal plane dimension

$1\frac{1}{2}$

$1\frac{1}{2}$

Vertical plane dimension

Figure 13-23 Avoid drawing linear dimensions in horizontal oblique planes.

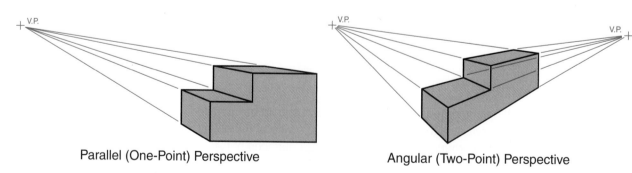

Parallel (One-Point) Perspective

Angular (Two-Point) Perspective

Figure 13-24 Perspective drawings with vanishing points indicated.

There are two basic types of perspective drawings. A *parallel perspective*, also known as a *one-point perspective*, has lines that converge to a single vanishing point. An *angular perspective*, also known as a *two-point perspective*, has lines that converge to two vanishing points. Angular perspective is what our eye actually sees in nature. For this reason, it is the most accurate method of drawing an object in three dimensions. Objects in perspective appear to become smaller the farther away they are from the eye. The closer we are to an object, the more exaggerated the perspective will be. The further we are away from an object, the more naturally it appears and the less exaggerated the perspective.

The way we perceive objects in perspective can be understood by trying the following. Next to the corner of a very tall building, stand up and look straight up at its corner without standing back. See **Figure 13-25**. The sensation you will get is that the building is going to fall over on top of you. You may get dizzy, so be careful and don't fall down. (You will probably have other people looking up, too, wondering what you are looking at.) This dizzy sensation is caused by you being so close to the structure. Your perspective of the structure is extremely exaggerated from this point of view.

Next, go to the top of a hill or the top of another large building several miles away. The original building must be visible from this location. View the building from the new point of view. See **Figure 13-26**. Viewing the same building from this location will not give you the same, dizzy sensation because you have improved your perspective in relation to the building. It will appear much more natural because you are further away and the perspective is more natural to your eye.

Another way that perspective drawing can be understood is by imagining that you are landing a jet aircraft. As you approach the runway, you notice that the parallel sides of the runway appear to converge (intersect), **Figure 13-27**. The point where the runway edges appear to intersect is called the *vanishing point (V.P., or VP)*. This point is said to be located on the horizon. In a perspective drawing, the horizon is called the *horizon line*.

A one-point perspective drawing is simpler and quicker to draw than a two-point perspective drawing but not as natural looking. A two-point perspective is often

Figure 13-25 A photo taken next to the corner of a large building. The perspective is very exaggerated because of the closeness of the photographer (viewpoint).

Figure 13-26 A photo taken of the same building from a distance away provides more natural perspective.

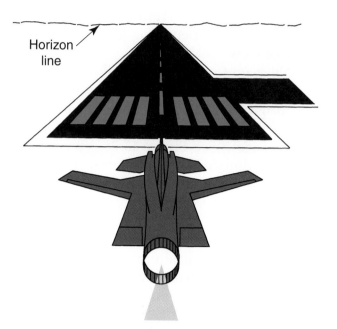

Horizon line

Figure 13-27 Lines in a perspective drawing converge as they project to the horizon line. Notice how the parallel sides of the runway appear to converge in the distance at the horizon.

more time-consuming to draw, but it is a much more accurate representation of what the human eye actually sees.

In drawing a one-point perspective, lines representing horizontal edges of an object that lie in a plane parallel to the front projection plane remain horizontal. The features that extend toward the back of the object are the depth features. If extended far enough, they will converge or intersect at a vanishing point on the horizon. Perspective drawings are based on the principle of parallel lines converging in the distance. Refer to **Figure 13-24**. Lines representing edges and intersections that are vertical remain vertical in the perspective view regardless of which plane they lie in. A one-point perspective drawing has a true size front face much like the front view of an oblique drawing. All lines that make up the true size face are true length. All lines beyond the true face making up the object depth become smaller because they project closer to the vanishing point.

In drawing a two-point perspective, the only lines that appear true size are edges representing vertical features that are parallel to the projection plane. All other lines (representing horizontal edges) are projected to the horizon, where they appear to intersect at the vanishing points. Horizontal features representing width are projected in one direction to the horizon. Features representing depth are projected in the opposite direction to the horizon. All vertical edges and intersections remain vertical. All features become progressively smaller as they project to the vanishing points.

Creating One-Point Perspectives

The following method for creating one-point perspective drawings is simplified for easy understanding by beginning drafters. There are much more precise and complex methods of creating both one-point and two-point perspectives. However, the purpose of this text is to introduce beginning drafters to the basic concepts of perspective drawing with simple objects. More complex procedures in a beginning drafting course may hinder immediate progress toward gaining basic skills.

To create a simple one-point perspective, the front surface is first drawn in its true shape to full or scaled size, **Figure 13-28**. Then the vanishing point is selected.

Placement of the vanishing point with respect to the front surface determines what the final perspective drawing will look like. A perspective drawing may be located in any position relative to the vanishing point, **Figure 13-29**. As previously discussed, the vanishing point is located on the horizon line. If the vanishing point is placed close to the front surface, the perspective will be very exaggerated. The further the vanishing point is placed from the front surface, the more natural the object will appear. The vanishing point can also be placed above or below the object. Placing the vanishing point above the front surface orients the view so that the viewer

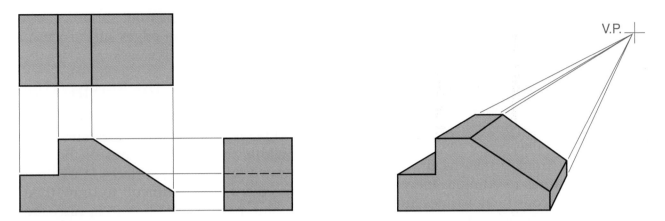

Figure 13-28   On one-point perspective drawings, the front view is shown in its true shape at full or scaled size.

is looking down at the object. The higher the vanishing point is placed with respect to the front surface, the more aerial the perspective view becomes. Placing the vanishing point and horizon line below the front surface orients the view so that the viewer is looking up at the object. The lower the vanishing point is placed with respect to the front surface, the more "underground" the perspective view

becomes. Finally, if the vanishing point is placed more above the front surface instead of to one side or the other, you will see more of the top of the object and less of the side. If at first you do not obtain a pleasing effect, try another vanishing point location.

Determine the best location for the vanishing point by first identifying the features of the object and their relative loca-

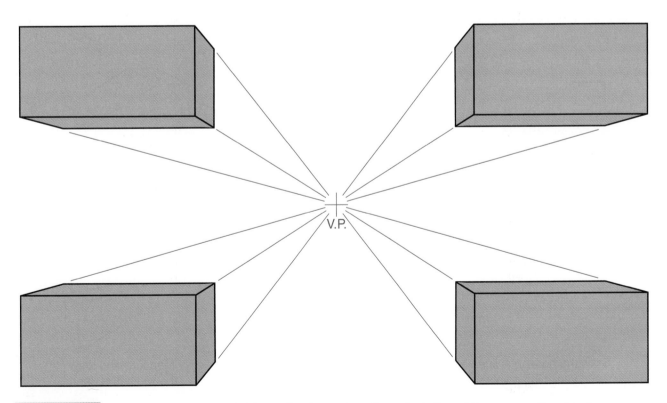

Figure 13-29   The location of the vanishing point determines the orientation of the perspective drawing.

tions on the object. Remember, your goal is to create a perspective view of the object that makes as many features visible as possible. The purpose for creating the view is to present the object in three dimensions in the clearest, most descriptive way possible so that the viewer can understand exactly what the object looks like.

After the front surface is drawn, draw the depth features receding to the vanishing point. Project construction lines from each point (intersection) on the front surface to the vanishing point, **Figure 13-30**. Then measure the full depth of the object along one of the projection lines. Measure the depth along one line only. Then, assuming that the front and back surfaces are parallel, draw lines parallel to the front surface edges originating from the back end of the depth line. The relative lengths of the lines forming the back surface are determined by where intersections occur with the construction lines projected from

the intersections on the front surface. Darken the visible object line edges of the view to complete the perspective view.

Creating Two-Point Perspectives

A two-point perspective is created by projecting features to two vanishing points. The width and depth features of the object are drawn on receding surfaces. A two-point perspective is more difficult to draw than a one-point perspective, but it is also more realistic. The simple two-point perspective shown in **Figure 13-31** is drawn by using the following procedure.

1. Locate the horizon line and two vanishing points. Use the same criteria outlined for one-point perspective drawings.
2. Locate and draw a vertical line representing the true height of the object. This line should represent a primary vertical feature. For some objects, there may be two or more lines that lie in the same

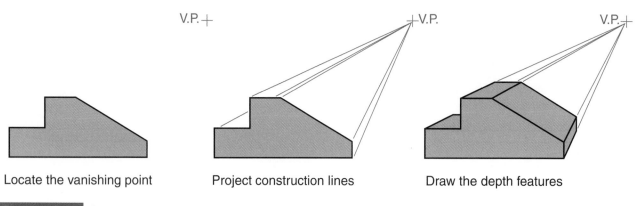

Locate the vanishing point   Project construction lines   Draw the depth features

Figure 13-30 Drawing a simple one-point perspective.

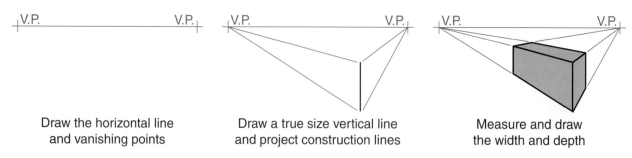

Draw the horizontal line
and vanishing points

Draw a true size vertical line
and project construction lines

Measure and draw
the width and depth

Figure 13-31 Drawing a simple two-point perspective.

plane parallel to the projection plane. In **Figure 13-31**, only the front vertical corner represents a true size feature.

3. Project construction lines from the top and bottom of the true size vertical line to each of the vanishing points. Along one of the lines projected to the left vanishing point, measure the width (full size). Do likewise to the right for the depth. This procedure may be reversed if the left side of the object is to be visible instead of the right side. For simplified two-point perspectives such as this example, it is permissible to orient the width and depth in a way that gives the most pleasing visual effect.

4. "Block in" the view and darken the necessary lines to object line weight.

Manual development of perspective drawings can be very time-consuming. These types of views can typically be generated automatically from 3D models with CAD software designed for 3D drawing. However, it is still important for the drafter to understand and know how to draw more complex pictorial views manually. CAD drawing and modeling methods are discussed later in this chapter.

Exploded Assembly Drawings

An *exploded assembly drawing* is a series of pictorial drawings (usually isometric drawings) that show how the parts of a disassembled object fit together. See **Figure 13-32**.

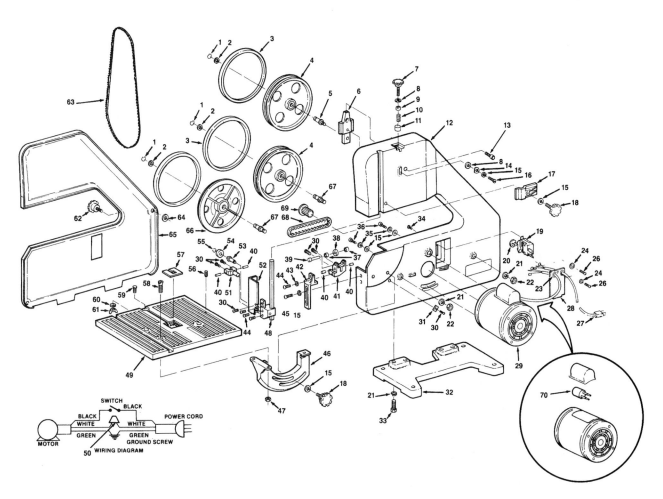

Figure 13-32 An exploded assembly drawing. (Sears-Roebuck)

Exploded assembly drawings are commonly found in various types of assembly instruction manuals. They show the parts that make up the assembled object in proper relation to one another and in what order they are to be assembled.

Well-organized exploded assembly drawings are easy to read and can be understood without having an extensive knowledge of print reading. Industry makes extensive use of exploded assembly drawings, especially in areas where semiskilled workers are employed.

Assembly drawings are also used in many hobby areas. You are probably familiar with them if you build model cars, planes, boats, or rockets, or if you have ever assembled a piece of furniture, such as a computer desk.

Cutaway Pictorial Drawings

A *cutaway pictorial drawing* shows the interior features of an assembled product, **Figure 13-33**. This type of drawing is typically used in instructional manuals where the

Figure 13-33 A cutaway pictorial drawing of a four-cylinder engine. (Saturn)

interior features of the product and how they go together are important for the complete understanding of the assembly.

Centering Pictorial Drawings

There are several ways to center a pictorial drawing on a drawing sheet. The methods include approximating the placement of the view, tracing an existing drawing, and using specific centering methods for different pictorial drawing types.

One widely used method is known as "eyeballing it." The drafter estimates, by sight, the approximate location of the starting point and develops the drawing from that point. An experienced drafter with a trained eye can probably be successful in using this method.

Another method involves creating the drawing anywhere within the limits of the sheet. When the drawing has been checked for accuracy, a piece of tracing vellum is then centered over it and the drawing is traced onto the vellum. Or, if regular drawing paper is used instead of vellum, the total width and height of the pictorial is determined. After locating the center of the drawing area (the starting point), the drawing is then redrawn using the center point of the drawing and the overall size.

A third method used to center pictorial drawings establishes the center point of the sheet and then a starting point based on the dimensions of the object. This method works well with most isometric and oblique drawings. The centering method for isometric drawings is shown in **Figure 13-34**. The centering method for oblique drawings is shown in **Figure 13-35**. Most beginning drafters should probably use these methods to improve their accuracy of placement.

The first step is to locate the center of the drawing area. The easiest and quickest way to find the center of a rectangular drawing

1.   Sketch or draw the isometric view.

2.   Locate the center of the drawing area.

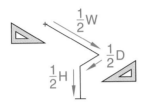

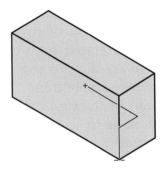

3.   Plot the starting point of the drawing.

4.   Complete the drawing.

Figure 13-34   An easy, accurate method for centering isometric drawings.

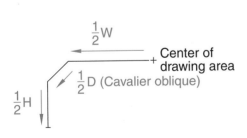

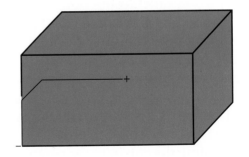

1.   Plot the starting point of the drawing.

2.   Complete the drawing.

Figure 13-35   An easy, accurate method for centering cavalier oblique drawings.

area is to draw diagonal construction lines between the opposite corners of the drawing area. Where the lines intersect is the center of the drawing area. This center point provides the starting point for centering the drawing. The starting point is determined by drawing construction lines for half the width, depth, and height as shown in **Figure 13-34** and **Figure 13-35**. The lines should be drawn parallel to the pictorial axes.

The method shown in **Figure 13-34** is used for a regular orientation of isometric baselines with the end product showing the front, right side, and top of the object. The direction of measurement may be reversed for drawings using a reversed orientation of baselines (where the bottom of the object is shown instead of the top). Similar adjustments may be made to show the left side of the object if appropriate.

The method shown in **Figure 13-35** is used for a cavalier oblique drawing with a regular orientation of baselines and a 45° depth axis. The final product displays the front, right side, and top of the object. The direction can be adjusted to show the left side or bottom of the object as needed. In addition, the depth scale or axis angle may be varied for different types of oblique drawings. If you are centering a cabinet oblique drawing, for example, the depth centering measurement should be changed from one-half to one-quarter because the depth axis for a cabinet oblique is drawn to one-half scale.

Drafters may wish to use the oblique centering method for the approximate centering of a one-point perspective. This is because both types of drawings originate from the true face of a front surface.

Drawing Pictorials in CAD

CAD systems offer a variety of ways to develop pictorial drawings. As discussed earlier in this chapter, CAD programs with 3D drawing capability can be used to construct models, which can then be displayed in a perspective view. There are also 2D-based drawing functions for creating isometric and oblique drawings.

Many CAD programs provide drawing commands and tools specifically designed for isometric drawing. For example, the drawing grid can be configured so that lines are automatically drawn parallel to the normal isometric axes. In isometric drawing mode, the isometric planes formed by the isometric axes are known as *isoplanes*. A special cursor indicates the current isoplane and drawing direction. See **Figure 13-36**. This greatly simplifies the isometric drawing process because distances from an orthographic view can be entered to construct different sides of the object. Nonisometric lines can be drawn by using existing points on isometric surfaces as reference points and constructing with object snaps.

As previously discussed, circular features in isometric views are created as ellipses. In CAD, the same cursor orientations used to draw isometric lines are used to draw isometric circles. After orienting the cursor to the proper horizontal or vertical isometric plane, the desired ellipse can be generated at the proper angle by specifying a center point and radius or diameter.

One useful viewing tool in CAD systems is the ability to display an isometric view as a multiview projection is being developed. See **Figure 13-37**. This helps in visualizing the various features making up the object during the drawing process. It is particularly useful in 3D drawing.

Similar CAD drawing techniques can be used to create oblique views. If the depth axis is oriented at 30°, the depth features can be drawn using isometric mode. If the depth axis is

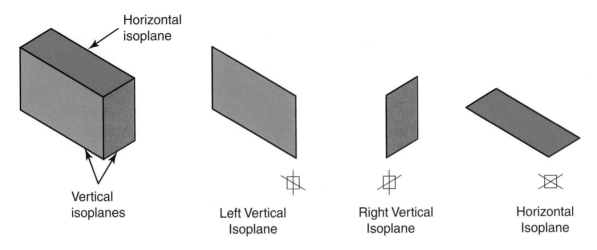

Figure 13-36 Drawing cursor orientations in isometric drawing mode. The three normal isometric planes are known as isoplanes.

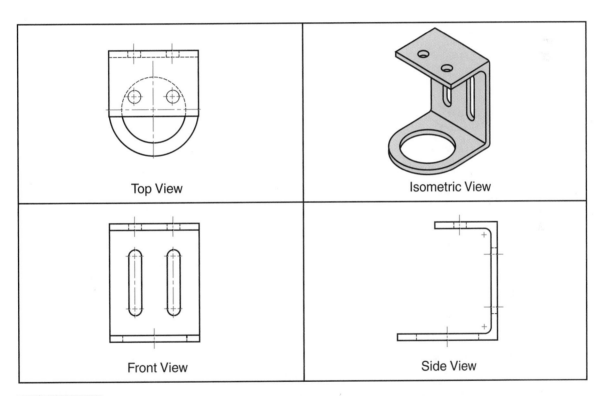

Figure 13-37 Pictorial and orthographic views can be displayed simultaneously in the course of developing a drawing.

oriented at a different angle, the drawing grid and snap configuration can be set to the angle so that lines are drawn at proper angular distances.

CAD systems with 3D drawing capability allow the designer to develop pictorial views in varying degrees of detail and realism. CAD-generated pictorial views range in complexity from basic "wireframe" models to solid models and surface models. When creating a model, objects are generated using 3D coordinates and special modeling commands.

A variety of commands and methods are used to create solid models. The most common way to create solid models is to extrude 2D shapes into solid objects. This is typically done with the **Extrude** command. Extruded solids can be created from objects such as circles, rectangles, and polygons. After the 2D geometry is created, it is extruded to a given thickness. See **Figure 13-38**.

Solids can also be created by revolving a profile about a centerline axis. Revolutions are typically created with the **Revolve** command. This type of modeling is useful for symmetrical objects. See **Figure 13-39**.

Most CAD programs provide simple geometric shapes that can be used to develop solid models or surface models. These shapes are called *primitive objects*. Common primitives include boxes, cylinders, cones, spheres, wedges, and pyramids. See **Figure 13-40**. These basic

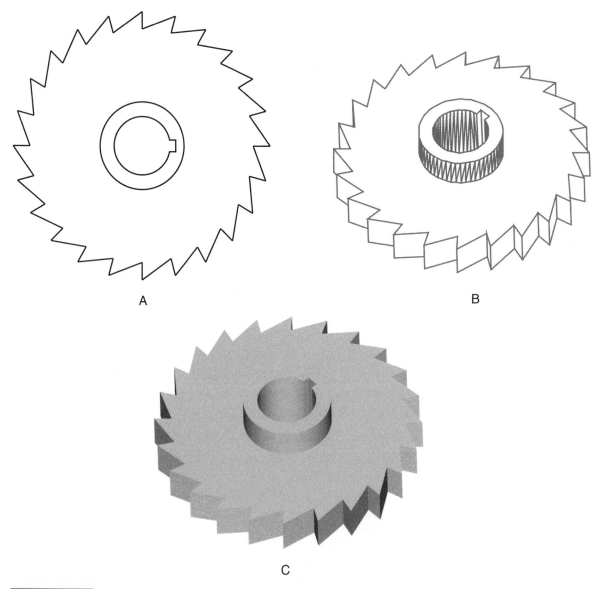

A

B

C

Figure 13-38 Solid models are commonly created by extruding 2D shapes with the **Extrude** command. A—The geometry for the model is drawn using 2D-based commands and coordinates. B—After extruding, the model appears "solid." C—A rendering of the model.

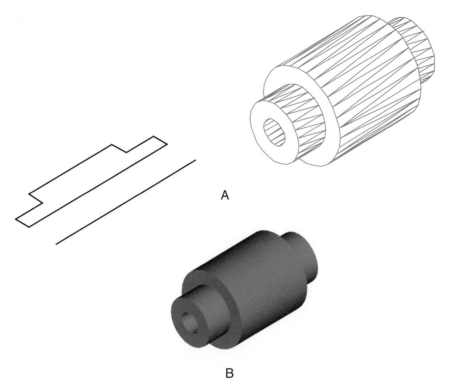

A

B

Figure 13-39 Creating a solid model with the **Revolve** command.
A—A profile and revolution axis for the model (at left) are drawn using
2D-based commands and coordinates. After revolving, the model appears
"solid." B—A rendering of the model.

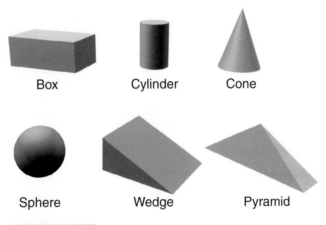

Box   Cylinder   Cone

Sphere   Wedge   Pyramid

Figure 13-40 Basic shapes, called primitives,
are used in solid modeling and surface modeling
applications.

shapes can be used in many different modeling applications. Different shapes are available
depending on the software and whether the program is based on solid modeling or surface
modeling. The commands used are normally based on the name of the object. For example, a
sphere is typically created with the **Sphere** command.

After a solid or surface model is created, it is common to generate a perspective view for shading or rendering purposes. This is often a powerful tool for the drafter or designer to help the client visualize the product quickly and easily before it is manufactured or built. See **Figure 13-41**. Higher-end CAD programs provide the ability to create lights, shadows, and other effects to improve the quality of the presentation. The complexity of a computer-generated pictorial is determined by the computing power of the hardware and the type of software used.

More powerful CAD systems are capable of not only generating pictorial views, but also creating animated, visual tours of the product. See **Figure 13-42**. Some programs can also generate exploded assembly views of a product and animate and test it for accuracy and functionality before construction or manufacturing.

A

B

Figure 13-41 A CAD model of a hotel. A—A 2D representation shows the basic geometry used to create the model. B—A realistic representation of the model results from rendering a perspective view. (Autodesk, Inc.)

Figure 13-42 A CAD-generated scene of a gallery developed for an animated walkthrough. Animations of buildings are commonly shown to clients in order to present a virtual portrayal of the project. (Discreet, a division of Autodesk)

CAD is an amazingly powerful tool that substitutes commands and modeling methods for manual drawing techniques. However, it is better to learn to walk before you run when it comes to generating pictorial views. Learning to manually generate these types of views is the walking process.

Test Your Knowledge

Please do not write in this book. Place your answers on another sheet of paper.

1. What is a *pictorial drawing* and how is it different from a multiview drawing?

2. List the three basic types of pictorial drawings.

3. Isometric pictorial drawings are drawn about three baselines called the isometric axes. Sketch these baselines in both the regular and reversed orientation. Label each set of baselines and identify the angles formed by the axes.

4. Lines that represent edges of inclined surfaces in an isometric drawing are known as _____ lines.

5. What types of shapes are used to represent circular features in isometric views?

6. What object surface is parallel to the projection plane in an oblique drawing?

7. Prepare a sketch of an object that shows the difference between a cavalier and a cabinet oblique drawing.

8. Oblique drawings may be drawn using any angle for the depth axis, but _____, _____, and _____ angles are generally used.

9. Describe two methods for placing lettering in dimensions when dimensioning pictorial views.

10. When dimensioning isometric and oblique views, it is recommended to place as many linear dimensions as possible in _____ planes.

11. When dimensioning oblique drawings, the depth axis is always specified to _____ size regardless of the type of oblique view used.

12. The points at which lines converge in perspective drawings are known as _____ points.

13. In a one-point perspective drawing, at what size is the front surface drawn?

14. What is an *exploded assembly drawing*?

15. When centering a cabinet oblique drawing, the centering measurement for the depth axis should be _____ the actual depth of the manufactured object.
    A. 1/4
    B. 1/2
    C. 3/4
    D. the same as

16. Identify three methods that can be used to create solid models in CAD programs with 3D drawing capability.

Outside Activities

1. Collect pictorial drawings that are used to advertise real estate. Find both residential and commercial examples. Explain to the class why you think pictorials are used to "sell" real estate.

2. Make a bulletin board display of pictorial drawings such as exploded assembly views of models that you and your classmates have built. Explain why the pictorial views assisted in constructing the models.

3. Search through old magazines (not library copies) and find examples of cutaway pictorial drawings. Make a comparison of drawings using fill color and drawings printed in black and white. Try to make sharp black and white photocopies of the full-color cutaway views. Does color help explain, or "sell"? Why or why not?

Drawing Problems

Draw the problems shown on the problem sheets on the following pages. Using the views shown, draw an isometric, oblique, or perspective view for each problem as indicated. Add dimensions for the problems where indicated. Dimensions are in inches unless otherwise indicated. Draw one problem per sheet. Use a horizontal sheet format.

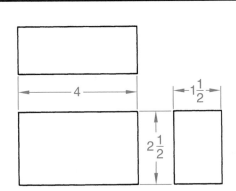

1. Sanding Block
   Draw in isometric.

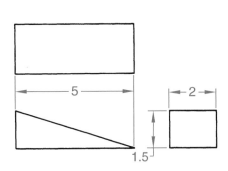

2. Doorstop
   Draw in isometric and dimension.

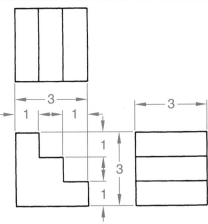

3. Step Block
   Draw in isometric or cavalier oblique.

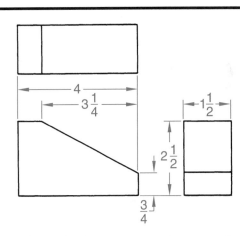

4. Gage Block
   Draw in isometric and dimension.

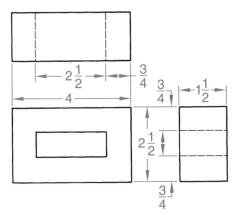

5. Spacer
   Draw in isometric or cavalier oblique.

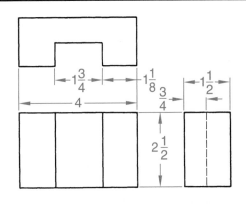

6. Slide
   Draw in isometric or cabinet oblique.

Problem Sheet 13-1

DIMENSIONS ARE IN MM.

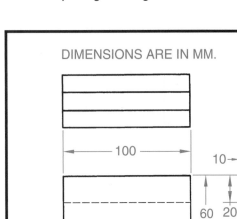

7. Guide
   Draw in isometric.

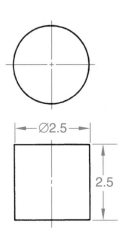

8. Canister
   Draw in isometric.

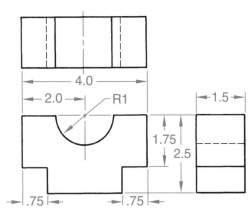

9. Support
   Draw in cabinet or cavalier oblique
   and dimension.

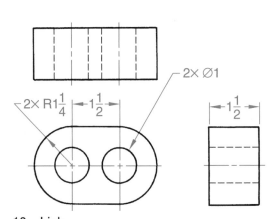

10. Link
    Draw in cabinet oblique.

DIMENSIONS ARE IN MM.

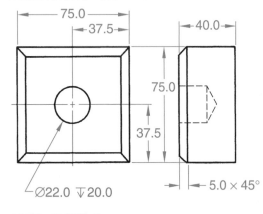

11. Candlestick Holder
    Draw in isometric.

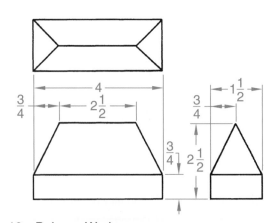

12. Balance Wedge
    Draw in isometric and dimension.

Problem Sheet 13-2

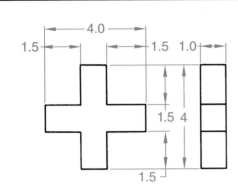

13. Cross
    Draw in one-point perspective.

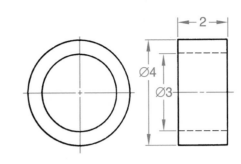

14. Bearing
    Draw in isometric or one-point perspective.

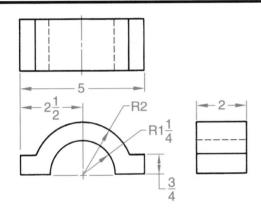

15. Bearing Cap
    Draw in isometric and dimension.

16. Hexagonal Base
    Draw in isometric or cabinet oblique.

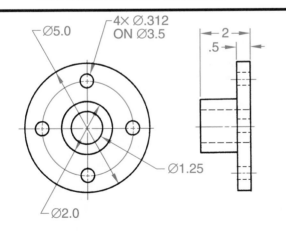

17. Face Plate
    Draw in isometric.

Pictorial Drawing Problems
1. Book rack
2. Shoe shine box
3. Modern birdhouse
4. Coffee table
5. End table

Exploded Pictorial Drawing Problems
1. Picture frame
2. Bookcase
3. Jewelry box
4. Wall storage shelf
5. Desk, computer table, or stereo equipment stand

18. Design Problems
    Draw each problem on a B-size or C-size sheet.

14 Pattern Development

OBJECTIVES

After studying this chapter,
you should be able to:

◆ Define pattern development.

◆ Describe the parallel line and radial
line development methods.

◆ Explain what a wired edge, hem, and
seam are and why they are used.

◆ Develop patterns for cylinders,
prisms, pyramids, and cones.

DRAFTING VOCABULARY

Edges
Hems
Lofting
Parallel line
    development
Pattern
Pattern development

Radial line
    development
Seams
Sheet metal drafting
Stretchout
Surface development

Introduction

A *pattern* is a full-size drawing of the various outside surfaces of an object stretched out on a flat plane, **Figure 14-1**. A pattern is frequently called a *stretchout*. It is a two-dimensional representation that can be bent or folded into a three-dimensional shape.

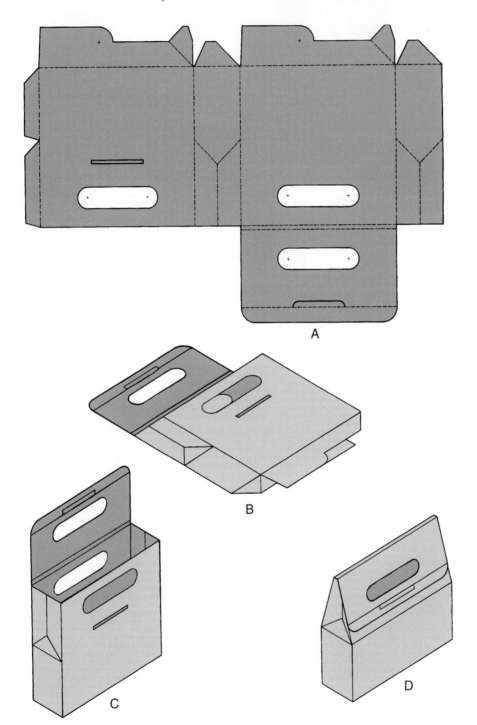

Figure 14-1 A—A pattern of a container used to introduce a sample of a new product. B—After printing and die cutting, the container is flattened for shipping. Only four points are glued, reducing waste to a minimum. C—The package is opened for loading. D—After being filled with samples, the container is folded for easy shipment.

Patterns or stretchouts are produced by utilizing a form of drafting called *pattern development*. This method is also known as *surface development* and *sheet metal drafting*. Pattern development is important to many occupations and hobbies.

Patterns were required to make the clothing and shoes you wear. Wallets and handbags are cut to shape using patterns as guides. This chapter discusses the various applications of patterns and how to develop them from basic geometric shapes.

Pattern Development and Manufacturing

Patterns are used in many types of product designs and forms of manufacturing. For example, pattern development plays an important part in the fabrication of sheet metal ducts and pipes needed in the installation of heating and air conditioning units. Stoves, refrigerators, and other appliances are fabricated from many sheet metal parts. Accurate patterns have to be developed for the parts before the appliance can be put into production.

The packaging industry makes extensive use of patterns. The packages for all kinds of dry and canned foods require pattern development. First the volume of the container to hold the product is determined. Then the surface of the container is developed and the graphic design is created to cover the outer surface of the package. Examples of packages created using pattern development include cereal boxes, tissue boxes, milk containers, and cans for canned foods.

Drafters in the aerospace industry must be familiar with pattern development techniques. Manufacturing space-age materials into components for airplanes, rockets, and hot air balloons requires many patterns, **Figure 14-2**. The technique used is called *lofting*. In this process, the fabrication of materials is derived directly from production drawings.

Figure 14-2 Very accurate patterns must be developed for the manufacture of hot air balloons. Each panel must be precisely shaped so the stress of the ropes that support the basket is shared equally around the circumference of the vehicle.

Every plate on a ship's hull and superstructure started with a pattern. Otherwise, the components would have required extensive cutting and fitting before they could be used. This would be very costly.

If you have ever built a model boat or flying model airplane, **Figure 14-3**, you know that many patterns are needed to cut the parts to shape for assembly.

Pattern developments can be prepared with CAD systems using the same methods involved in manual drafting. See **Figure 14-4**. However, before the drafter can use CAD for this type of work, he or she must have a thorough knowledge of pattern development techniques.

As you can see, patterns play an important part in the manufacture of many products. How many items in the drafting room can you name that use pattern development in their manufacture?

Drawing Patterns

Regular drafting techniques, as described in previous chapters of this text, are used to draw patterns. Basic pattern development falls into the two categories of parallel line development and radial line development. See **Figure 14-5**.

In *parallel line development*, the lines used to develop the pattern are parallel or at right angles to each other. This method is used to make patterns for prisms and cylinders.

In *radial line development*, the lines used to develop the pattern radiate out from a single point. This method is used to make patterns for regular tapering forms such as cones and pyramids.

Combinations and variations of these basic developments are used to draw patterns for more complex geometric shapes.

While regular drafting techniques and line conventions are used in pattern development, some lines have additional meanings. Sharp folds or bends are indicated on the stretchout by object lines. For an example of this, refer to the *Pattern Development of a Rectangular Prism* section later in this chapter.

Figure 14-3 A flying model airplane requires accurate patterns to construct the wing ribs, fuselage, formers, and tail sections.

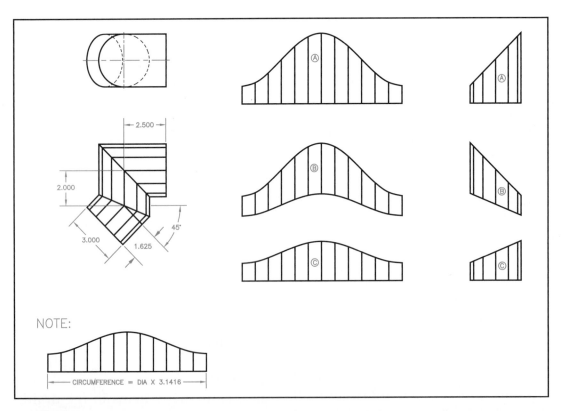

Figure 14-4 A CAD-generated pattern drawing for a three-piece elbow. Note how the components are drawn separately.

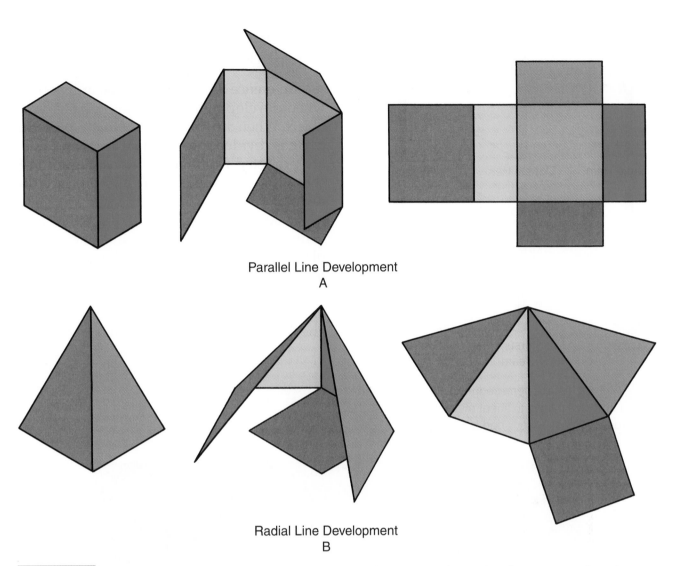

Parallel Line Development
A

Radial Line Development
B

Figure 14-5 Pattern development methods. A—Parallel line development is used to draw patterns for prisms and cylinders. B—Patterns for objects with regular tapering, such as cones and pyramids, are developed using radial line development.

Curved surfaces are shown on the pattern with construction lines or centerlines. For an example of this practice, refer to the *Pattern Development of a Cylinder* section later in this chapter.

Pattern drawings are seldom dimensioned. Instead, reference numbers or letters may be used to identify surfaces.

Drawing Sheet Metal Patterns

When developing a pattern or stretchout for a sheet metal product, it is often necessary to allow additional material for *hems, edges,*

and *seams*. See **Figure 14-6**. Examples of how these types of joints are used in actual sheet metal products are shown in **Figure 14-7**.

Hems are folds that strengthen the lips of sheet metal objects. They are made in standard fractional sizes, such as 3/16″, 1/4″, and 3/8″. Standard metric sizes are 4.0 mm, 6.0 mm, 10.0 mm, etc.

Edges provide extra strength and rigidity to sheet metal edges. *Seams* make it possible to join sheet metal sections. They are usually finished by soldering, spot welding, or riveting.

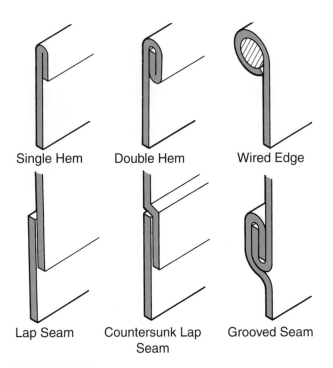

Single Hem Double Hem Wired Edge

Lap Seam Countersunk Lap Seam Grooved Seam

Figure 14-6 Typical hems, edges, and seams used to join and give rigidity to sheet metal. Extra material is required and must be included in the design.

Drawing Patterns for Circular Objects

Reference lines and points are needed when developing the stretchout of a circular object. When drawing patterns of this type, the circle is divided into 12 equal parts and lines are projected from the divisions. **Figure 14-8** shows how to divide a circle to produce the reference points.

Irregular curves in patterns are drawn using a French curve. The points of the irregular curve are first plotted. The points may then be connected with lightly sketched lines. Match the French curve to the sketched line or points, taking care to make the curve of the line flow smoothly. See **Figure 14-9**.

Figure 14-7 Many types of sheet metal products use common joints such as hems and seams in their manufacture.

CAREERS IN DRAFTING

Sheet Metal Worker

What would I do if I were to become a sheet metal worker? I would fabricate, install, and maintain heating, ventilation, and air conditioning (HVAC) systems, roofs, siding, rain gutters and downspouts, and many other products made from sheet metal. I might specialize in fabrication, installation, or maintenance, but more than likely, I would do all three as most sheet metal workers do. I might also work with fiberglass or plastics.

What would I need to know? I would need to know about the materials, tools (both manual and machine tools), processes, and techniques necessary to work with sheet metal and similar materials. I would also need to know about the various technologies that are used in the industry more and more each day. I would need to know how to read plans, specifications, and various types of blueprints. I would need to know about pattern development and how to make an accurate "stretchout" (pattern) for a variety of products. I would need to know about and be able to perform proper fastening methods and procedures. I would need to be able to produce seams, hems, and joints using screws, rivets, and welding, soldering, and brazing processes. I would need to be familiar with safe practices, codes, and requirements.

Where would I work? If I worked in fabrication, I may work in a factory or shop. Sometimes, it may be necessary for me to fabricate an object on the job site, but most of my work would be completed indoors. If I worked in installation or maintenance, I would work predominantly on the job site.

For whom would I work? My chances of working in the construction industry would be very good since almost 67% of all sheet metal workers do. If I didn't work in construction, I could work in a manufacturing industry such as the automotive industry or aerospace industry.

I could also work for the federal government. It is not likely that I would be self-employed, but possible.

What sort of education would I need? While in high school, I would need to take courses in algebra, geometry, trigonometry, drafting, mechanical drawing, and computer-aided drafting (CAD), along with vocational courses and any required courses. Apprenticeship is generally considered the best way to learn this trade. Hence, I would be involved in an apprenticeship program, which would probably consist of approximately four to five years of on-the-job training and an average of 200 hours of classroom instruction.

What are the special fields relating to this career? HVAC, automotive manufacturing, aerospace and aeronautical manufacturing, appliance manufacturing, roofing, and plumbing.

What are my chances of finding a job? My chances of finding a job in the construction industry are good in the next several years due to trade workers retiring. The demand for skilled workers is always very good. Of course, the level of activity in the construction industry would determine whether I am working or not at any given time. This can vary from locale to locale. My chances of finding a job in the manufacturing industry are not expected to be as good. Jobs in maintenance of existing facilities and equipment are always in demand. Also, jobs involving installation of new, more energy-efficient equipment are always in high demand as well.

How much money could I expect to make? As an apprentice, I could expect to earn 40% to 50% less than experienced workers. Average hourly wages for sheet metal workers vary by industry and employer. Recent statistics indicate that I could earn as little as $9.50 per hour or less and as high as $29.53 or

(continued)

Sheet Metal Worker *(continued)*

more depending on my years of experience, my employer, and the industry I am involved in. Workers in architectural and structural metals manufacturing have earned an average salary of $14.60 per hour, where those doing sheet metal work for various federal government agencies have enjoyed a higher average salary of $19.73 per hour.

Where else could I look for more information about becoming a sheet metal worker? See the US Department of Labor's Bureau of Labor Statistics Occupational Outlook Handbook (at www.bls.gov). For general information, contact the International Training Institute for the Sheet Metal and Air Conditioning

Industry (www.sheetmetal-iti.org), the Sheet Metal and Air Conditioning Contractors National Association (www.smacna.org), or the Sheet Metal Workers International Association (www.smwia.org). The US Department of Labor's National Apprenticeship system (www.doleta.gov) provides information about becoming an apprentice.

If I decide to pursue a different career, what other fields are related to sheet metal work? Tool and die making, machining, assembling, and fabrication. Professionals doing related work in the construction industry include glaziers, HVAC mechanics, and installers.

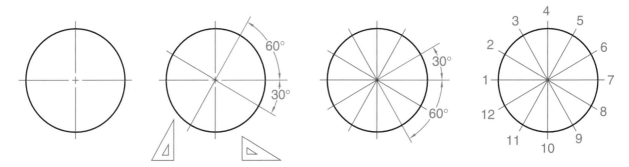

Figure 14-8 Dividing a circle into 12 equal parts.

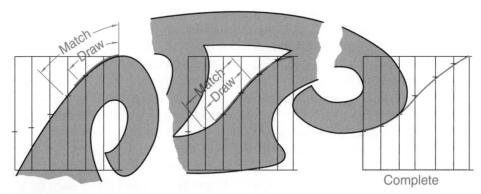

Figure 14-9 Using a French curve to draw an irregular curve. When drawing curved lines, take care to make the curve of the line follow smoothly to produce one continuous line.

Pattern Development of a Rectangular Prism

1. Draw the front and top views. Number the points as shown.
2. The height of the pattern is the same as the height of the front view. Project construction lines from the top and bottom of the front view.
3. Measure over 1″ from the front view and draw a vertical line between the construction lines to locate Line 1.
4. Set your compass or dividers to the distance from Point 1 to Point 2 on the top view, and transfer this distance to the same points on the stretchout. Locate the other distances using the reference points shown.
5. Construct the top and bottom of the prism as shown. Allow material for the seams.
6. Go over all outlines and folds with object lines.

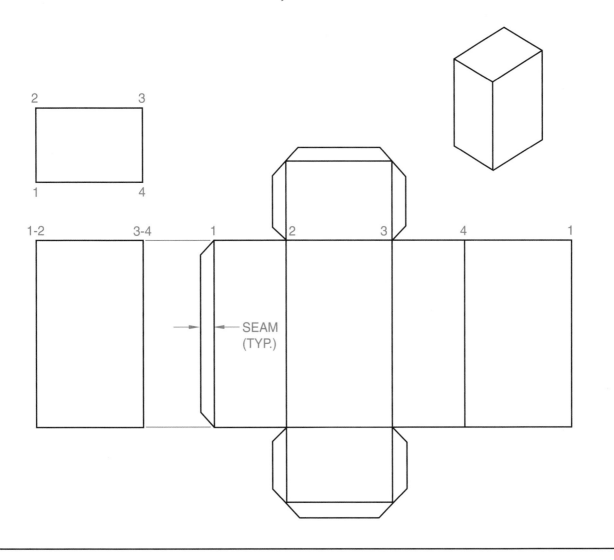

Pattern Development of a Cylinder

1. Draw the front and top views of the cylinder. Divide the top view into 12 equal parts and number as shown. Project lines to the front view as shown.
2. The height of the pattern or stretchout is the same as the height of the front view. Project construction lines from the top and bottom of the front view to the stretchout (pattern).
3. Allow sufficient space (1″ is adequate) between the front view and the pattern, and draw a vertical line. This will locate Line 1 of the pattern.
4. Calculate the circumference of the circle in the top view (top of the cylinder). Use the formula $C = \pi d$, where $\pi = 3.14$ and d equals the diameter of the circle. From Line 1 of the pattern, draw a straight line the length of the circumference, and divide it into 12 equal parts. Set your compass or dividers to one of the equal parts on the line. Transfer this distance to the extended lines of the pattern to locate reference lines 2, 3–12, and 1.
5. Draw the top and bottom of the cylinder tangent to the extended lines.
6. Add material for the seam shown. Allow 1/4″. Draw the inclined lines at 45°.
7. Go over all outlines with object lines. The lines that represent the curves or circular lines may be left as construction lines.

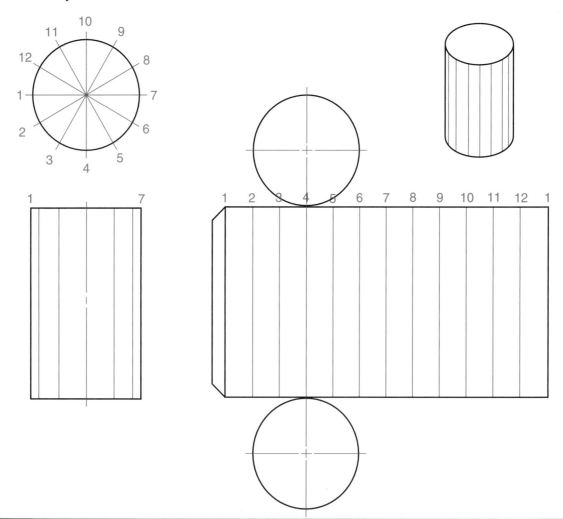

Pattern Development of a Truncated Prism

1. Draw the front and top views. Number the points as shown.
2. Proceed as in the previous examples of pattern development.
3. Mark off and number the reference points and then project Point 1 on the front view to Line 1 of the stretchout.
4. Project Points 2, 3, and 4 to Lines 2, 3, and 4.
5. Connect Points 1 to 2, 2 to 3, 3 to 4, and 4 to 1.
6. Draw the top and bottom of the object in position as shown. Allow material for the seams.
7. Go over all outlines and folds with object lines.

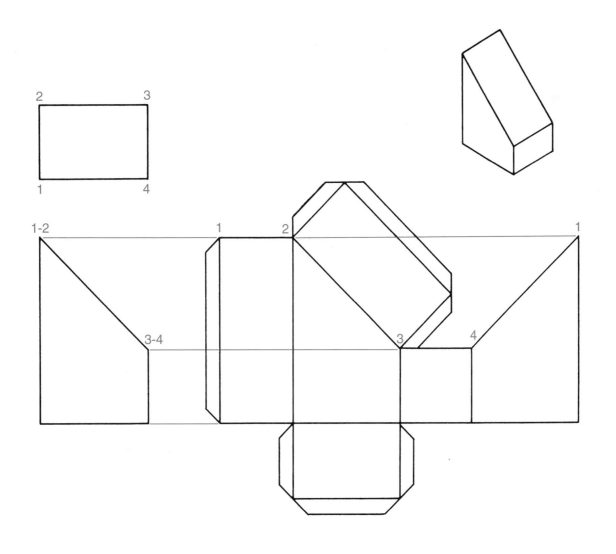

Pattern Development of a Truncated Cylinder

1. Draw the front and top views. Divide the circle in the top view and project lines to the front view. Number the points as shown.
2. Extend lines from the top and bottom of the front view to the stretchout.
3. Allow 1″ between the front view and the stretchout and draw Line 1.
4. Calculate the circumference of the circle in the top view. Use the formula $C = \pi d$, where $\pi = 3.14$ and d equals the diameter of the circle. From Line 1 of the pattern, draw a straight line the length of the circumference, and divide it into 12 equal parts.
5. Draw a vertical construction line at each of the divisions.
6. The curve of the pattern is developed by projecting lines from the points on the front view. Point 1 is projected until it intersects Line 1 on the pattern. Repeat this with Points 2–12 and Lines 2–12. When all of the points are located, connect them with a curved line using a French curve.
7. Add material for the seam.
8. Complete by adding the top and bottom of the object. The top is developed as an auxiliary view.
9. Go over all outlines with object lines.

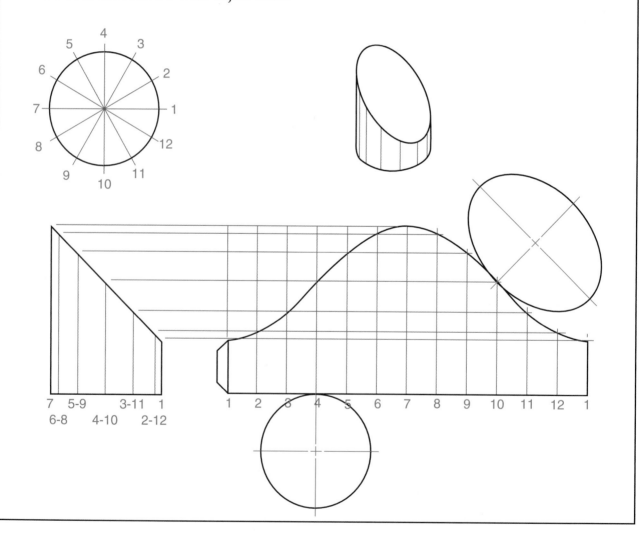

Pattern Development of a Pyramid

1. Draw the front and top views as shown. Number the points as shown.
2. Locate Center Point X of the stretchout.
3. Set your compass to a radius equal to Line X-1 on the front view. Using Point X in the stretchout as the center, draw Arc A-B.
4. Draw a vertical line through Point X and Arc A-B.
5. Set your compass to the distance from Point 1 to Point 2 on the top view. At the point where Line 1 intersects the arc as the starting point in the stretchout, step off four divisions (Points 1-2, 2-3, 3-4, and 4-1 on the stretchout).
6. Connect the points, draw the bottom of the object in place, and add seams.
7. Go over all outlines and folds with object lines.

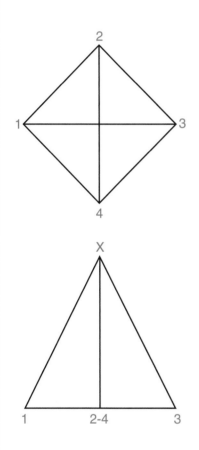

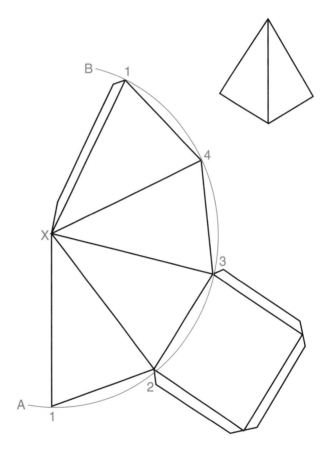

Pattern Development of a Cone

1. Draw the front and top views. Divide the circle in the top view and project lines to the front view. Number the points as shown.
2. Locate Center Point X of the stretchout.
3. Set your compass to a radius equal to Line X-1 on the front view. Using Point X in the stretchout as the center, draw Arc A-B.
4. Draw a vertical line through Point X and Arc A-B.
5. Set your compass to the distance from Point 1 to Point 2 on the top view. At the point where Line 1 intersects the arc as the starting point in the stretchout, step off 12 divisions along the arc (Points 1-2, 2-3, etc.).
6. Connect the points, draw the bottom of the object in place, and add the seam.
7. Go over all outlines with object lines. The lines that represent the curved portion may be left as construction lines.

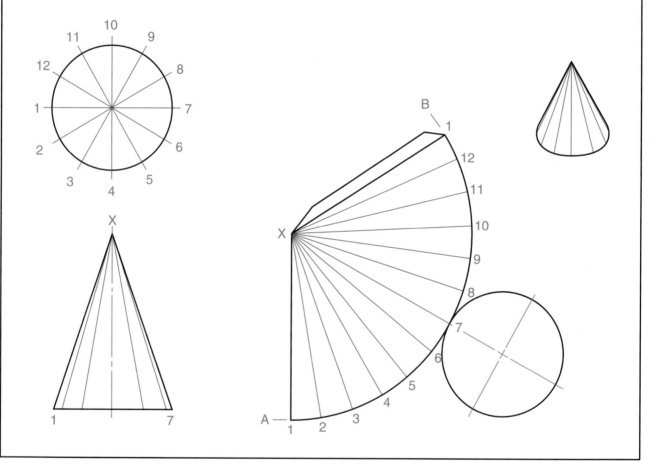

Pattern Development for a Right Rectangular Pyramid

1. Draw the front and top views. Number the points as shown. A right rectangular pyramid has a rectangular base and a vertical axis that is perpendicular to the base.
2. To create the pattern, you must establish the true length of the pyramid edges. Neither view shows a true length distance for the edges. To find the true length, rotate one edge as shown and project it to the front view. Where this line intersects a horizontal line from the base, establish a new projected point. The edge appears in true length when the projected point is connected with Point X.
3. Locate Center Point X of the stretchout.
4. Set your compass to a radius equal to the true length of the pyramid's edge. With Point X as the center point in the stretchout, draw Arc A-B.
5. Draw a vertical line through Point X and Arc A-B.
6. Set your compass to the distance from Point 1 to Point 2 on the top view. At the point where Line 1 intersects the arc as the starting point in the stretchout, step off Side 1-2 of the pyramid.
7. Reset your compass to the distance from Point 2 to Point 3 on the top view. Step off Side 2-3 on Arc A-B.
8. Repeat the sequence and step off Sides 3-4 and 4-1 on Arc A-B.
9. Connect the points, draw the bottom of the object in place, and add the seams.
10. Go over all outlines with object lines.

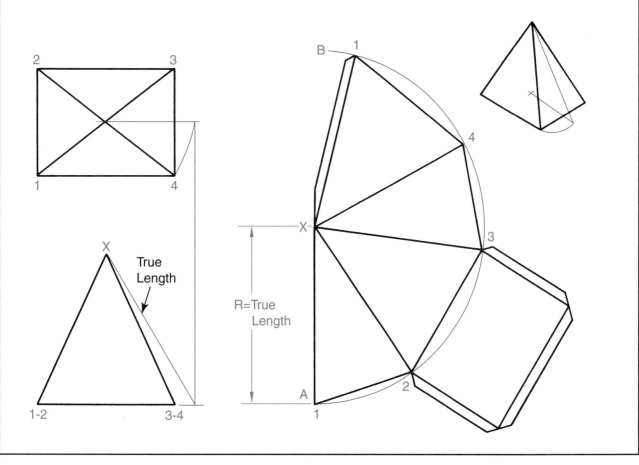

Test Your Knowledge

Please do not write in this book. Place your answers on another sheet of paper.

1. Define *pattern*.
2. Patterns are also known as _____.
3. List four products that use patterns in their development.
4. Explain the difference between parallel line development and radial line development.
5. Prisms are developed using what type of pattern development method?
6. What are *hems*?
7. Briefly describe how to develop a pattern for a cylinder.
8. Briefly describe how to develop a pattern for a pyramid.

Outside Activities

1. Obtain illustrations of products that require pattern development in their manufacture. They may be cut from discarded magazines and newspapers. Label each product with the method used to develop its pattern (parallel line development or radial line development).
2. Using a discarded product such as a paper cup, milk carton, or snack food package, carefully unfold the product. Draw a full-size pattern for the product.

Drawing Problems

Develop patterns for the problems shown on the problem sheets on the following pages. Use the dimensions shown. Dimensions are in inches unless otherwise indicated. Draw the stretchout where indicated. Draw seams as appropriate. Use a horizontal sheet format.

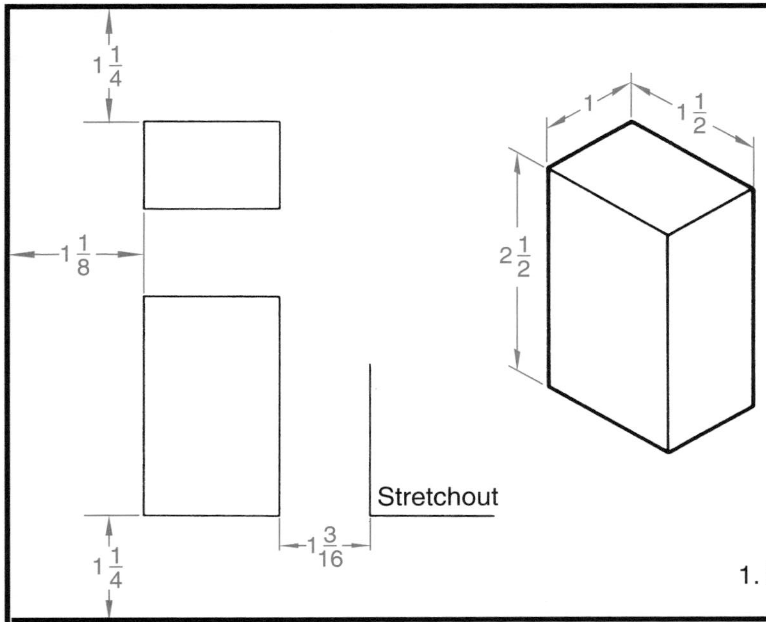
1 1/4
1 1/8
1 1/4
1 3/16
Stretchout
1
1 1/2
2 1/2

1. Prism

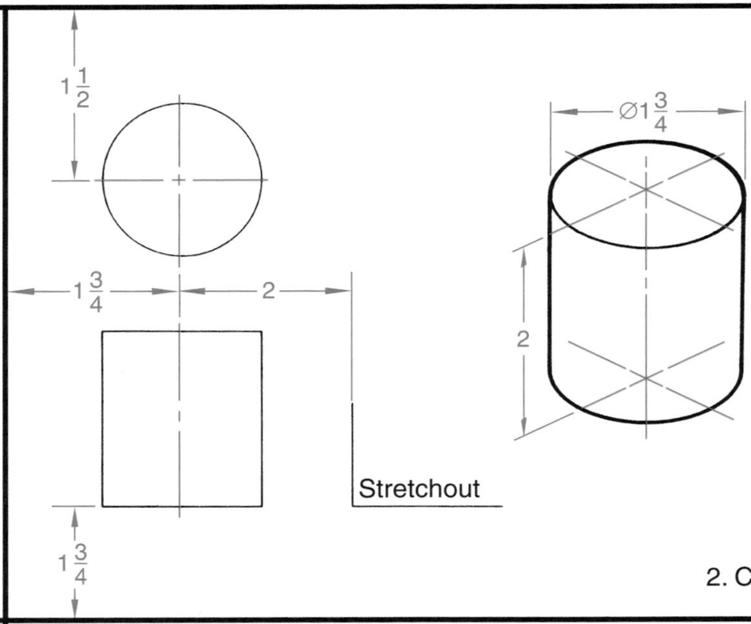
1 1/2
1 3/4
2
1 3/4
Stretchout
Ø1 3/4
2

2. Cylinder

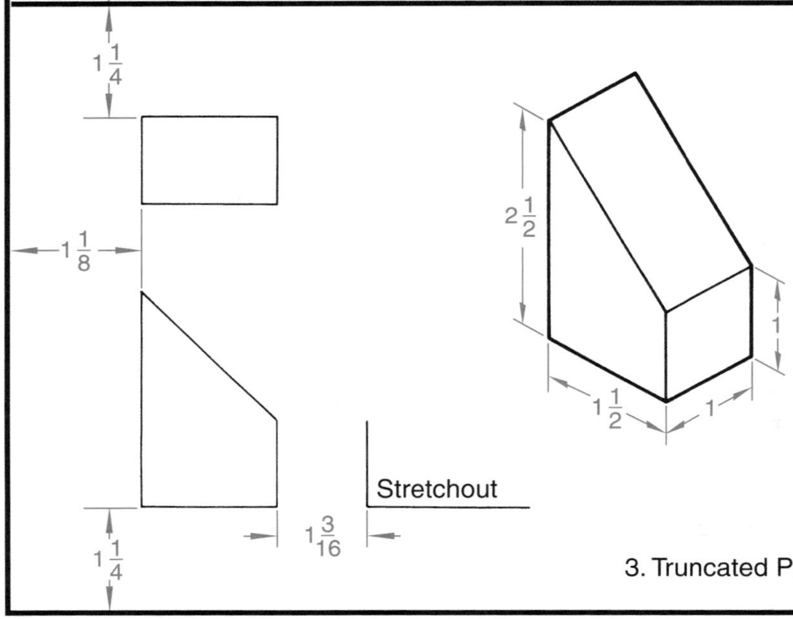
1 1/4
1 1/8
1 1/4
1 3/16
Stretchout
2 1/2
1
1 1/2
1

3. Truncated Prism

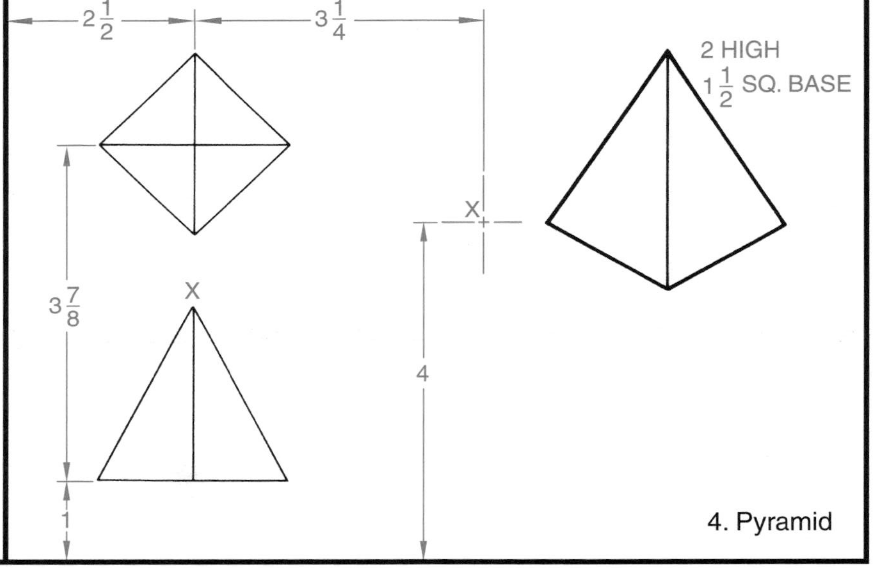
2 1/2
3 1/4
3 7/8
X
X
4
1
2 HIGH
1 1/2 SQ. BASE

4. Pyramid

Problem Sheet 14-1

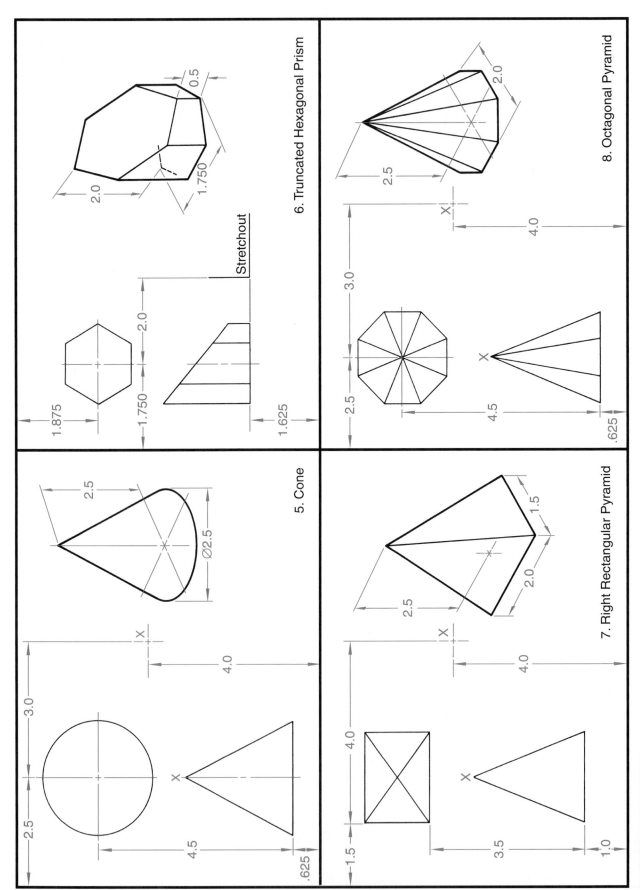

6. Truncated Hexagonal Prism

Stretchout

5. Cone

8. Octagonal Pyramid

7. Right Rectangular Pyramid

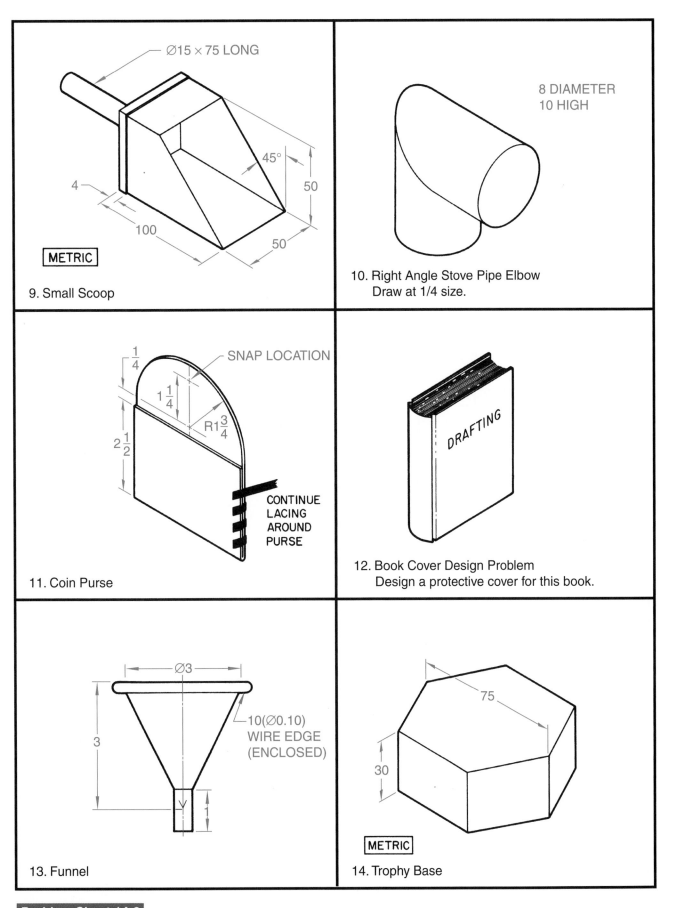

Ø15 × 75 LONG

45°

50

4

100

50

METRIC

9. Small Scoop

8 DIAMETER
10 HIGH

10. Right Angle Stove Pipe Elbow
    Draw at 1/4 size.

$\frac{1}{4}$

SNAP LOCATION

$1\frac{1}{4}$

$R1\frac{3}{4}$

$2\frac{1}{2}$

CONTINUE
LACING
AROUND
PURSE

11. Coin Purse

DRAFTING

12. Book Cover Design Problem
    Design a protective cover for this book.

Ø3

3

10(Ø0.10)
WIRE EDGE
(ENCLOSED)

13. Funnel

75

30

METRIC

14. Trophy Base

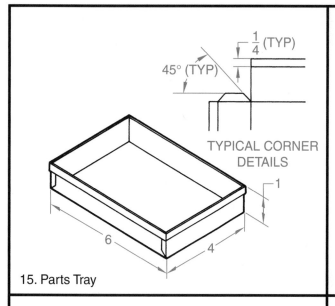

$\frac{1}{4}$ (TYP)

45° (TYP)

TYPICAL CORNER
DETAILS

1

6

4

15. Parts Tray

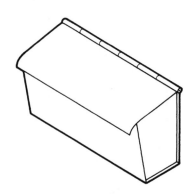

With ideas and dimensions from mail order catalogs and home improvement magazines, design a mailbox for your home.

16. Mailbox Design Problem

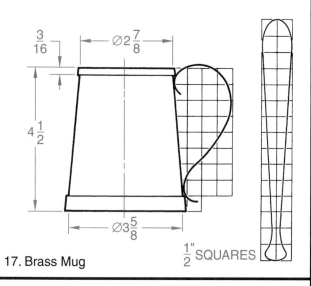

$\frac{3}{16}$

$\varnothing 2\frac{7}{8}$

$4\frac{1}{2}$

$\varnothing 3\frac{5}{8}$

$\frac{1}{2}$" SQUARES

17. Brass Mug

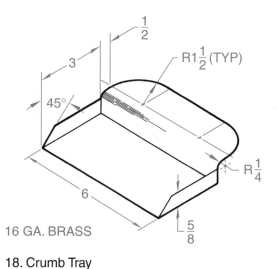

$\frac{1}{2}$

3

45°

R1$\frac{1}{2}$ (TYP)

6

R$\frac{1}{4}$

$\frac{5}{8}$

16 GA. BRASS

18. Crumb Tray

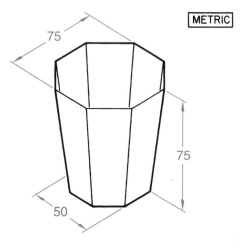

METRIC

75

75

50

19. Octagonal Planter

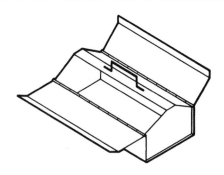

Design and develop patterns for a sheet metal toolbox.

20. Toolbox Design Problem

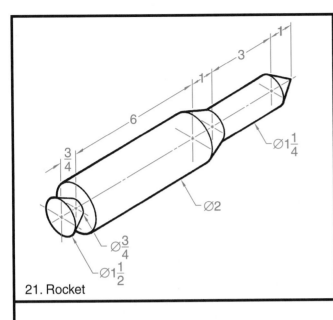

21. Rocket

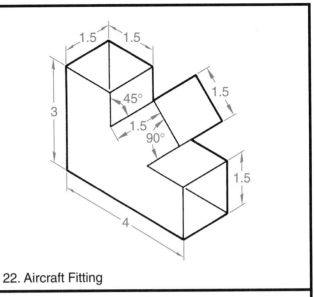

22. Aircraft Fitting

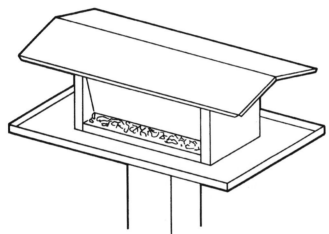

23. Bird Feeder Design Problem
Design and develop patterns
for a bird feeder. The roof
must be hinged for easy
loading of feed. Construct
a cardboard model of
your design.

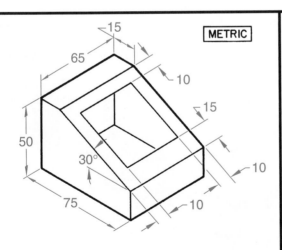

METRIC

24. Instrument Case

25. Design Problems

Design and develop patterns for the
following projects. Make a cardboard
model of your choice.
A.   Wastebasket
B.   Planter
C.   Dustpan
D.   Charcoal scoop
E.   Bookends
F.   Leather hand or wallet
G.   Jewel box

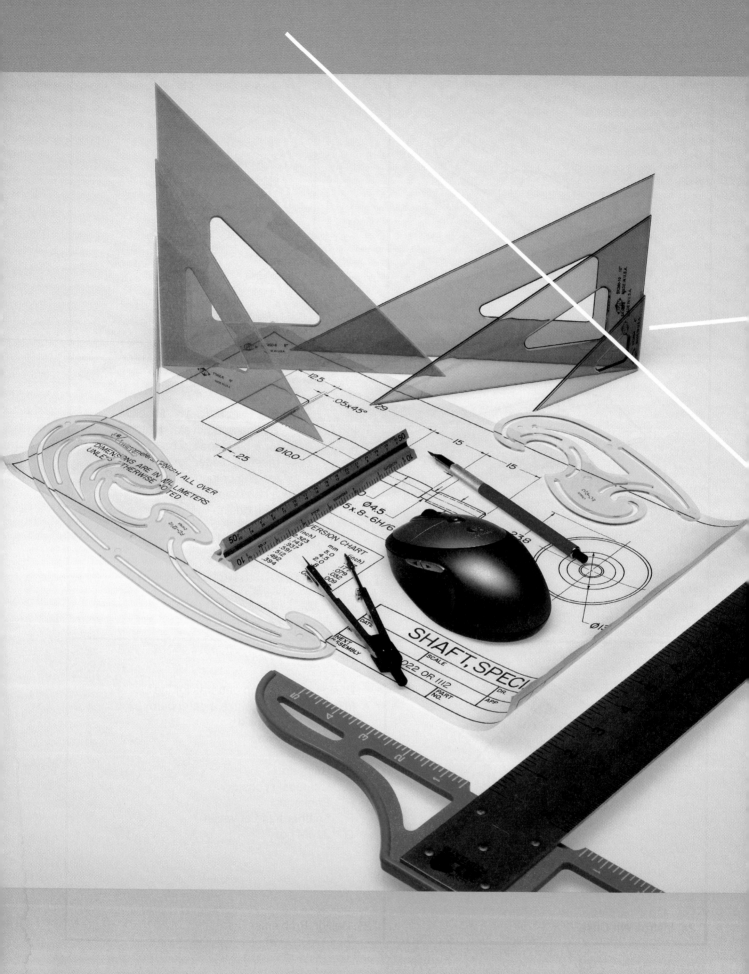

15 Working Drawings

OBJECTIVES

After studying this chapter,
you should be able to:

◆ Explain why working drawings
are needed.

◆ Discuss the differences between detail
drawings and assembly drawings.

◆ Identify the information provided on
working drawings.

◆ Prepare simple detail and assembly
drawings.

DRAFTING VOCABULARY

Assembly drawing
Bill of materials
Continuous quality
  improvement
Detail drawing

Parts list
Quality control
Subassembly
  drawing
Working drawing

It would not be practical for industry to manufacture products without using design drawings that provide complete manufacturing details. Required drawings range from a single freehand sketch for a simple part to thousands of drawings needed to manufacture a complex product like an aircraft design. A *working drawing* tells the craftworker what to make and establishes the standards to which he or she must work. See **Figure 15-1**.

Industry greatly depends on the accuracy of working drawings. For many reasons, *quality control* is critical in the production of drawings for manufacturing. Drawings prepared by a drafter are checked by the designer or engineer, and any inaccuracies are corrected and rechecked. The design process must include a method of *continuous quality improvement*. This includes a systematic method of identifying drawing errors and a procedure for implementing changes that can prevent future occurrences of errors.

Working drawings fall into two categories, *detail drawings* and *assembly drawings*. This chapter discusses these two classifications and the various components making up different types of drawings.

Detail Drawings

A *detail drawing* includes a view (or views) of the product, with dimensions and other pertinent information required to make the part. The drawing shown in **Figure 15-1** is a detail drawing.

In addition to the actual sizes and dimensions of the part, detail drawings provide other types of information. This information may appear in the title block, revision block, or elsewhere on the drawing. Common information found on a detail drawing includes the following (refer to **Figure 15-1**):

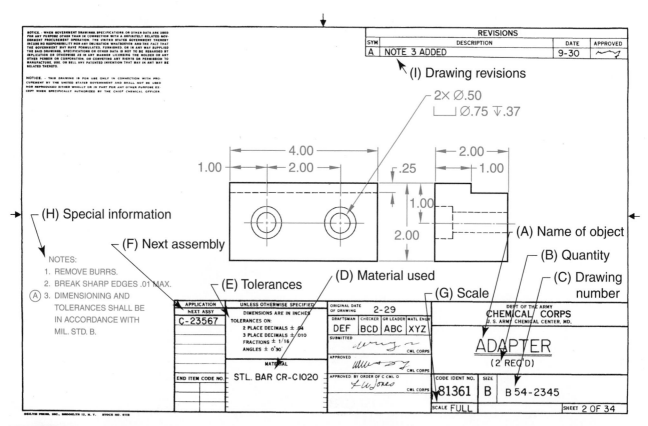

Figure 15-1 A typical working drawing with its components identified.

A. **Name of the object**. The name assigned to the part. This should appear on all drawings making reference to the piece.

B. **Quantity**. The number of units needed for each assembly.

C. **Drawing number**. The number assigned to the drawing for filing and reference purposes.

D. **Material used**. The exact material specified to make the part.

E. **Tolerances**. The permissible deviation, either oversize or undersize, from a basic dimension.

F. **Next assembly**. The name given to the major assembly for which the part is to be used.

G. **Scale**. The scale at which the drawing was made.

H. **Special information**. Information pertinent to the correct manufacture of the part that is not shown on the various views of the object.

I. **Revisions**. Changes that have been made on the original drawing.

In most instances, a detail drawing provides information about a single part. See **Figure 15-2**. It is also permissible to draw all of the parts and assembly details of a small or simple mechanism on the same sheet, **Figure 15-3**. Study **Figures 15-2** and **15-3**. Can you identify all of the different types of information found in each drawing?

Assembly Drawings

An *assembly drawing* contains views that show where and how the various parts fit into the assembled product. **Figure 15-4** is an example of a typical assembly drawing. Assembly drawings provide object sizes and also show how the complete object will look.

When the object is large or complex, it may not be possible to present all of the information on one sheet. A *subassembly drawing* illustrates the assembly of only a small portion of the complete object, **Figure 15-5**. A subassembly drawing solves the problem of not

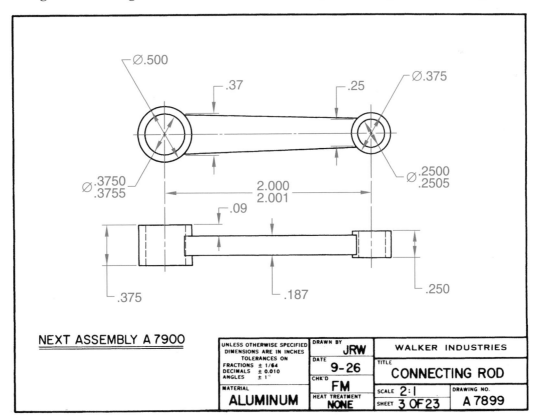

Figure 15-2 A detail drawing usually contains information for making one part.

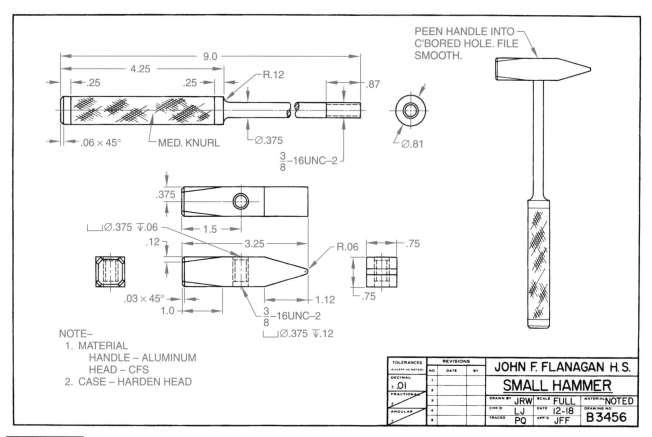

Figure 15-3 If the object is small enough, it is permissible to draw the details and assembly on the same drawing sheet.

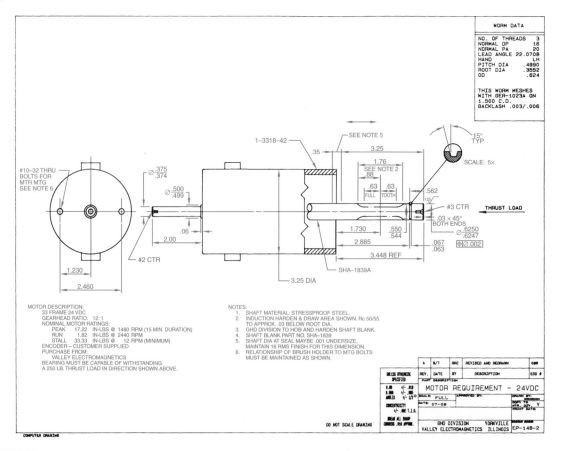

Figure 15-4 A CAD-generated assembly drawing for a motor. The dimensions are placed on this drawing for reference purposes for quality control. (T & W Systems, Inc.)

being able to fit all the drawing information on a single sheet.

Assembly and subassembly drawings may also be drawn in pictorial form, **Figure 15-6**. These types of drawings are common in manuals used to install products or build assemblies, such as installation and operation manuals.

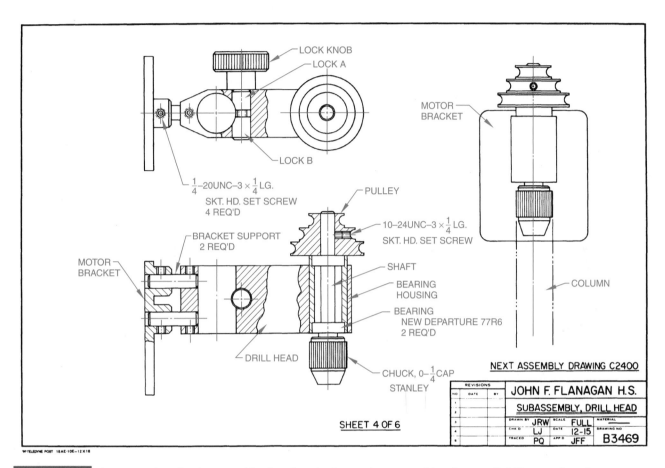

Figure 15-5 A conventional subassembly drawing. It shows the assembly of a small drill press head.

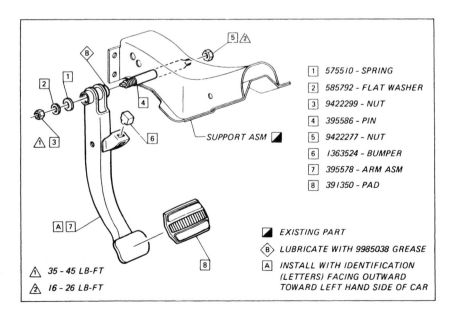

Figure 15-6 A pictorial subassembly drawing. This type of drawing is often used with semiskilled workers who have received a minimum of training in print reading. (General Motors Corp.)

CAREERS IN DRAFTING

Carpenter

What would I do if I were to become a carpenter? I would cut, fit, and assemble wood and other materials for the construction of buildings, highways, bridges, docks, industrial plants, boats, and many other structures and products.

What would I need to know? I would have to know how to read blueprints of structures, how to make proper and correct applications of local building codes, how to accurately measure and lay out all types of building materials, how to safely use a variety of hand and power tools, how to properly join all types of materials together, and how to properly install all types of prefabricated building products.

Where would I work? A majority of my time would be spent at the job site working either indoors or outdoors regardless of the weather conditions. Working as a carpenter can be strenuous and dangerous but very rewarding when admiring a job well done.

For whom would I work? I could work for a wide variety of employers, such as a general building contractor, a specialty trades contractor, a manufacturing firm, a government agency, or a retail establishment. My chances of working for myself are about 30%.

What sort of education would I need? I could learn to be a carpenter through on-the-job training, formal training, or both. I could get on-the-job training through an apprenticeship program or by just working with an experienced carpenter. I could get formal training through a vocational carpentry program at a high school, community college, or trade school. It would be desirable for me to have training in carpentry, woodworking, drafting, and general math at the high school level.

What are the special fields relating to this career? Many carpenters specialize in one or two carpenter-type tasks. They may specialize in setting forms for concrete construction, framing a structure, erecting scaffolding, doing finish carpentry work, installing interior or exterior building materials, or some other specific task.

What are my chances of finding a job? My chances of finding work as a carpenter in the next several years are excellent. This is due to two basic reasons. First, there are many carpenters retiring and/or leaving the profession each year. Second, many prefer work that is less strenuous and offers more comfortable working conditions.

How much money could I expect to make? The median hourly wage for carpenters in recent years was $16.44. Per-hour wages ranged from $9.95 to $27.97 and up. Higher wage rates may be found in commercial construction rather than residential construction. Prospects for maintaining employment are greatly enhanced by being a skilled "all-around" worker as opposed to a specialist with only a few specific skills.

Where else could I look for more information about becoming a carpenter? See the US Department of Labor's Bureau of Labor Statistics Occupational Outlook Handbook (at www.bls.gov) or request information from the Associated General Contractors of America (www.agc.org), the Home Builders Institute (www.hbi.org), the National Association of Home Builders (www.nahb.org), the United Brotherhood of Carpenters and Joiners of America (www.carpenters.org), or the US Department of Labor's National Apprenticeship System (www.doleta.gov).

If I decide to pursue a different career, what other fields are related to carpentry? Carpenters are skilled construction workers who work or come into contact with other skilled workers in related fields—including brick, block, stone, stucco, and cement masons; concrete finishers; electricians; plumbers; pipefitters; steamfitters; and plasterers.

Pictorial assembly drawings are also commonly used for small building projects, such as models, **Figure 15-7**. The assembly is typically broken down visually into a series of steps that detail the required procedure.

Using Information on Working Drawings

Under certain situations, a working drawing may include additional elements to provide reference information. A *parts list* is

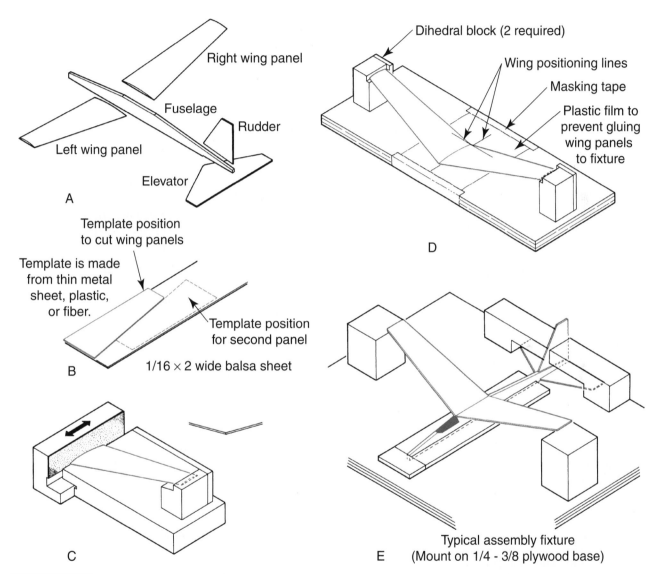

Figure 15-7   An assembly drawing for a model glider. This drawing shows jigs, fixtures, and other information helpful in mass-producing the assembly developed in Problem 15-2 of this chapter. A—The glider is made of five different parts. B—A template is planned carefully for the wing panels so that the parts can be cut with a minimum of waste. C—A jig for sanding the dihedral angle where the wing panels meet. D—Blocks are aligned on a fixture for holding the wing panels in place while the glue dries. The required dihedral angle (necessary for flight stability) is set automatically. E—The completed fixture for assembling the glider. If properly made, all parts will be perfectly aligned.

used to spell out part numbers and names, **Figure 15-8**. Drawings with manufacturer information may include a *bill of materials*, **Figure 15-9**. A bill of materials is similar to a parts list, but it includes additional information, such as the material needed for manufacture, manufacturer names, and pricing. The information on a parts list or bill of materials is read from the top down (when the list is located at the upper-right corner of the drawing sheet) or from the bottom up (when it is located above the title block). Either position is acceptable. The parts are usually listed according to size or order of importance.

As discussed in this chapter, a drawing number is placed on each sheet to identify the product shown. See **Figure 15-10**. Numbering makes the filing or rapid location of a drawing more convenient. The drawing number is also usually the part number stamped or printed on the object after it is manufactured.

Developing Working Drawings

Working drawings use a variety of orthographic, sectional, auxiliary, and other views to describe objects. The methods for developing these types of views have been covered in previous chapters of this text. Refer to a specific chapter if you need to review certain drawing conventions.

PARTS LIST		
No.	Name	Quan.
1	CRANKCASE	1
2	CRANKSHAFT	1
3	CRANKCASE COVER	1
4	CYLINDER	2
5	PISTON	2

Figure 15-8 A sample parts list.

A1776	NUT	BRASS	6
A1985	BOLT	BRASS	6
B1765	PLATE	ALUMINUM	2
B1767	CYLINDER	CAST IRON	2
Pt. No.	Name	Material	Quan.
BILL OF MATERIALS			

Figure 15-9 A sample bill of materials.

When developing detail drawings and assembly drawings, it is important to remember that CAD drafting uses the same drawing and dimensioning concepts that are practiced in manual drafting. Regardless of which method you use, it is essential to learn proper orthographic and pictorial drawing skills in order to create working drawings.

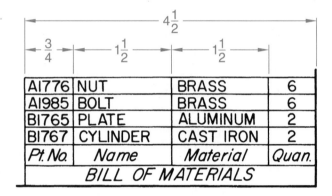

UNLESS OTHERWISE SPECIFIED DIMENSIONS ARE IN INCHES TOLERANCES ON FRACTIONS ± 1/64 DECIMALS ± 0.010 ANGLES ± 1°	DRAWN BY JRW	WALKER INDUSTRIES	
	DATE 9-23	TITLE BRACKET	
	CHK'D FM		
MATERIAL STEEL AISI-1020	HEAT TREATMENT NONE	SCALE FULL	DRAWING NO. A 123456-1
		SHEET 1 OF 5	

Figure 15-10 Each drawing is numbered to simplify the storage of drawings or to identify parts.

Test Your Knowledge

Please do not write in this book. Place your answers on another sheet of paper.

1. Why are working drawings used?
2. Name five types of information provided on a detail drawing.
3. How does an assembly drawing differ from a detail drawing?
4. What is a *subassembly drawing*?
5. What is the purpose of a bill of materials?
6. Name two reasons why drawings are numbered.

Outside Activities

1. From a local company in industry, try to obtain samples of detail drawings. Include samples of assembly drawings and subassembly drawings. Prepare a bulletin board display using the theme *working drawings*.
2. Design a suitable title block for the drawing sheets of a company that you are planning to start. Make sure there are blanks to include all pertinent information required.
3. Obtain a piston and rod assembly from a small single-cylinder gasoline engine. Prepare detail drawings for these parts. Indicate all dimensions in decimal units. It may be necessary for you to learn how to read a micrometer to make accurate measurements.
4. Design a product with sales appeal. Prepare the drawings necessary to mass-produce it in the school laboratory. Make your drawings on tracing vellum so that a number of prints can be made.
5. Research the principles of geometric dimensioning and tolerancing (GD&T). Report to the class how industry uses GD&T in preparing assembly drawings. Show some examples.

Drawing Problems

Draw the problems shown on the following pages. Draw detail and assembly drawings as indicated. Draw the orthographic and sectional views necessary to describe each object. Follow the directions in each problem and use the dimensions provided. Dimensions are in inches unless otherwise indicated.

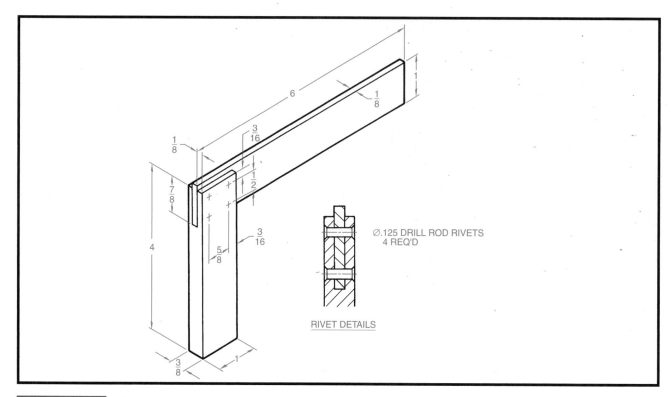

Problem 15-1 **Machinist's Square.** Make detail and assembly drawings.

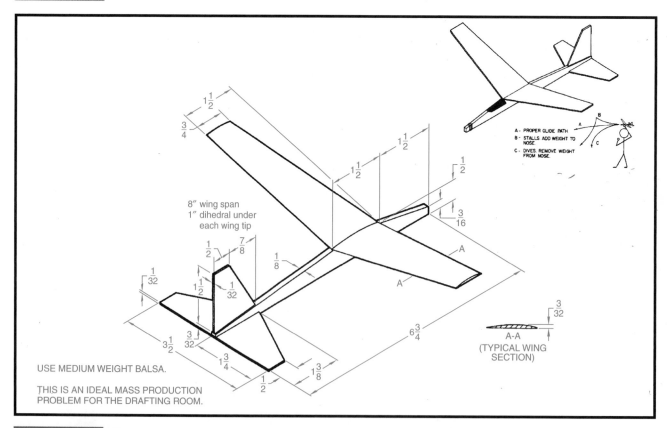

Problem 15-2 **Model Glider.** Make detail and assembly drawings and construct the model. Design the necessary patterns, fixtures, and other components needed to mass-produce the glider. Refer to Figure 15-7 for jigs, fixtures, and other helpful assembly information.

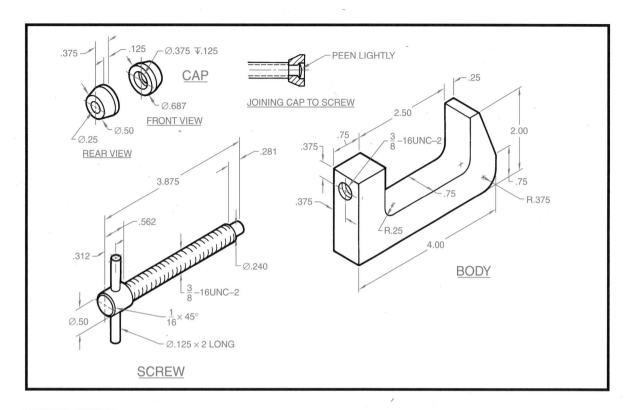

Problem 15-3   **C-Clamp.** Make detail and assembly drawings.

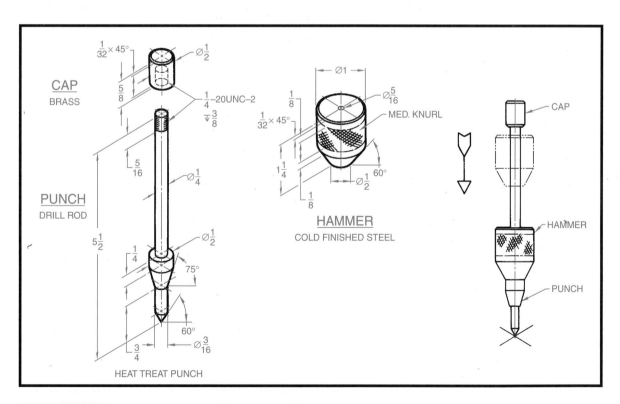

Problem 15-4   **Gravity Center Punch.** Make detail drawings of the three components.

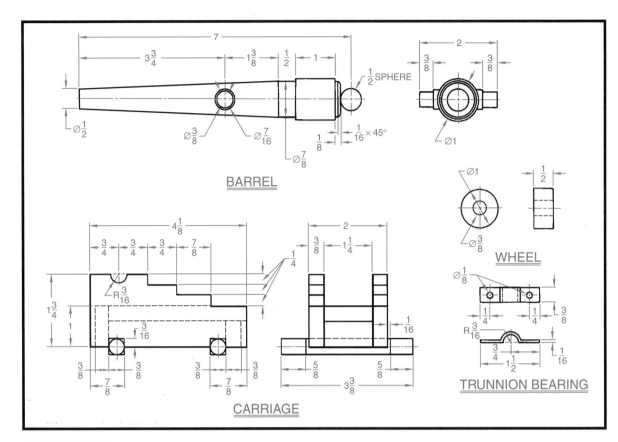

Problem 15-5 **Deck Gun.** Make an assembly drawing.

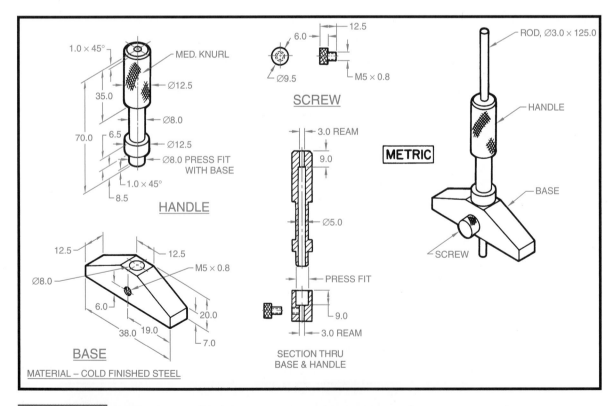

Problem 15-6 **Depth Gage.** Make detail and assembly drawings.

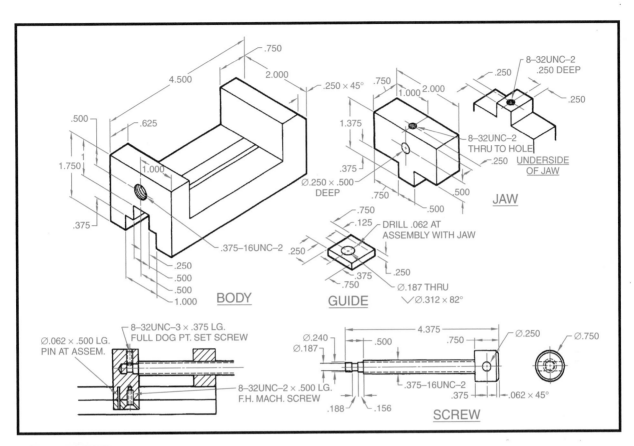

Problem 15-7 **Small Vise.** Make detail and assembly drawings.

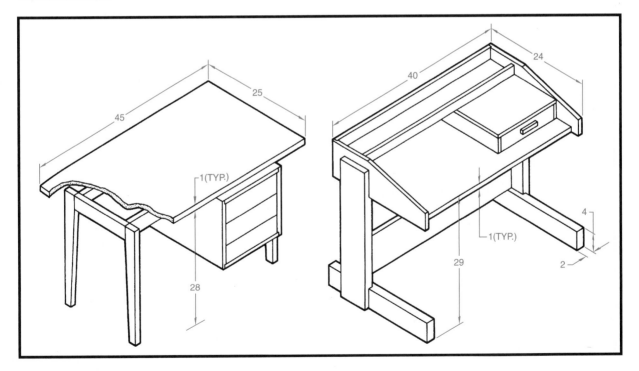

Problem 15-8 **Contemporary Desk Design Problem.** Design a desk using the basic dimensions given. The desk does not have to look like either example shown. Study furniture and mail order catalogs for ideas if necessary. Make the drawings required to build your design.

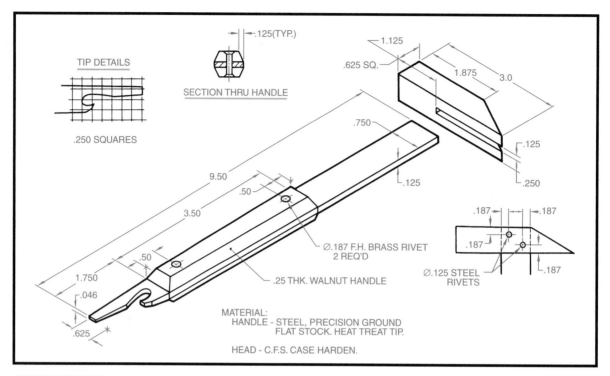

TIP DETAILS

.250 SQUARES

.125(TYP.)

SECTION THRU HANDLE

1.125

.625 SQ.

1.875

3.0

.125

.250

.750

9.50

.50

3.50

.125

.187 F.H. BRASS RIVET
2 REQ'D

.50

.187

.187

.187

.187

1.750

.25 THK. WALNUT HANDLE

Ø.125 STEEL
RIVETS

.046

.625

MATERIAL:
HANDLE - STEEL, PRECISION GROUND
FLAT STOCK. HEAT TREAT TIP.

HEAD - C.F.S. CASE HARDEN.

Problem 15-9 **Handy Helper.** Make detail and assembly drawings.

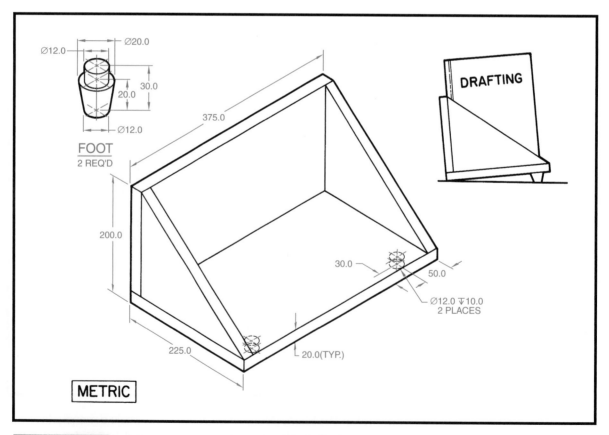

Ø12.0

Ø20.0

30.0

20.0

Ø12.0

FOOT
2 REQ'D

375.0

DRAFTING

200.0

30.0

50.0

Ø12.0 ▼10.0
2 PLACES

225.0

20.0(TYP.)

METRIC

Problem 15-10 **Book Rack.** Make a fully dimensioned assembly drawing.

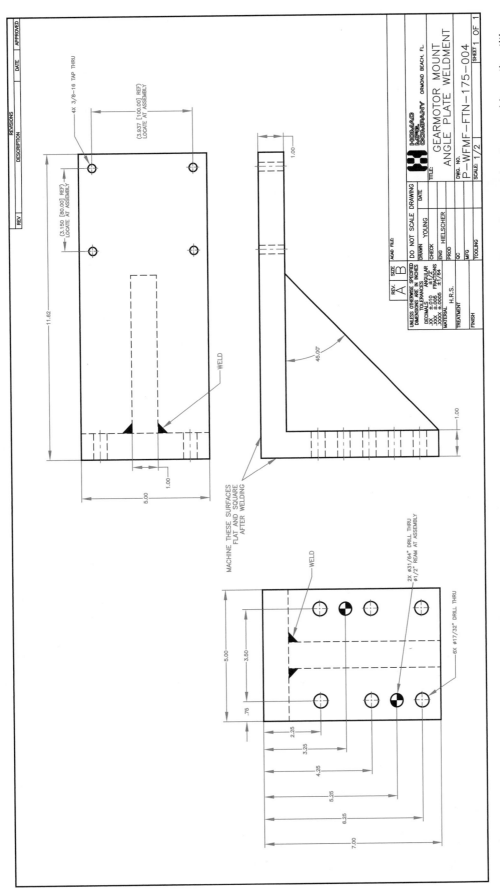

When designing working drawings in a CAD program, there are special tools for arranging views, placing dimensions and notes, and inserting title block information. Shown is a subassembly drawing included in the plans for a welding fixture model. (Autodesk, Inc.)

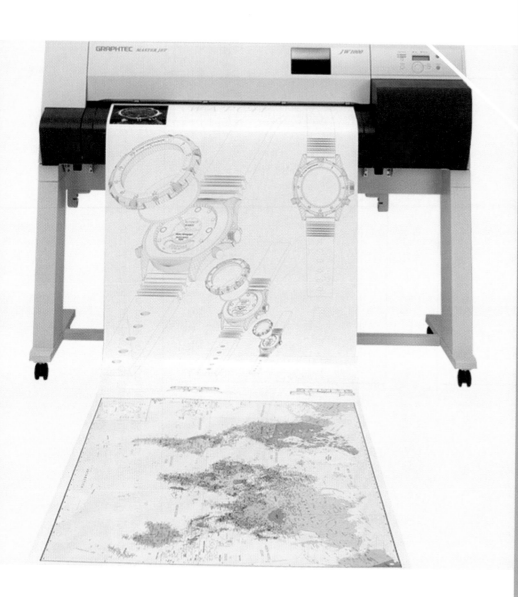

16 Making Prints

OBJECTIVES

After studying this chapter,
you should be able to:

- ◆ Identify the reasons why prints are used in place of original drawings.
- ◆ List the typical ways to print and distribute CAD drawings.
- ◆ Demonstrate how to make a pencil tracing or an ink tracing.
- ◆ Describe traditional printmaking processes.
- ◆ Observe guidelines for material safety.

DRAFTING VOCABULARY

Blueprint
Blueprint process
Diazo process
Drafting film
Drawing ink
Electrostatic
  reproduction
Inkjet plotters
Inkjet printer

Laser printer
Pen plotters
Plotter
Print
Technical pen
Tracing
Tracing paper
Vellum
Xerography

Original drawings are seldom found on a job site. They would soon become worn or soiled, and difficult to read. Also, workers at different locations producing the various parts of a product or structure need different sets of prints. This means that several sets of identical drawings are needed at the same time. Drawing up a set of plans for each person who needs them is impractical because of the costs. Creating new originals to replace plans that are damaged or ruined is also costly. Reproductions of the original drawings are used in these situations. These reproductions are called *prints*.

When several sets of prints are needed, the original drawings are reproduced or duplicated. The method used must produce accurate copies of the originals, must not destroy the original drawings, must be quick, and must be cost effective. Common printing and duplicating processes are discussed in this chapter.

Making Original Drawings

Before a print can be made, a high-quality original must first be drawn. It can be drawn using computer-aided drafting (CAD) techniques or manual techniques. No matter which method is used, original drawings must have lines that are dense and uniform for good reproduction.

There are a number of ways to make prints from original drawings. The following sections discuss methods used to print and reproduce CAD drawings. Reproduction methods for manual drawings are discussed later in this chapter.

Printing and Distributing CAD Drawings

Many of the drawings produced by drafting departments today are created on CAD systems. As computers become less expensive, so do the means used to output and distribute work created electronically. Personal computer packages, for example, are often purchased with a printer or similar output device.

In most cases, printers and plotters are used to produce CAD drawings. However, there are other ways to print and distribute CAD drawings.

Sometimes, printing or plotting multiple copies is the least expensive way to reproduce CAD drawings. However, in situations where dozens of prints must be made, using electrostatic reproduction or a traditional printmaking process is best. These processes are discussed later in this chapter.

Printers and Plotters

Printers and plotters are the primary output devices used in CAD applications. High-quality printing and plotting devices are capable of producing dense lines at the correct thickness and color. In many drafting firms, CAD systems are networked to several output devices so that drawings can be printed in different sheet formats or grades of resolution.

There are several types of printers and plotters. The main difference between the two types of devices is that printers are used for printing smaller sheet sizes, and plotters are used for large-format work. Printers can be classified as *inkjet* or *laser*.

An *inkjet printer* is an inexpensive device that produces good quality. Most inkjet printers are small enough to fit on a desktop, **Figure 16-1**. They are capable of creating hard copy on A-size, B-size, and sometimes C-size sheets. Inkjet printers form images by depositing droplets of ink onto the sheet.

A *laser printer* uses electrostatic reproduction to produce prints. This process is also known as *xerography* and is discussed later in this chapter. Laser printers typically produce a very high-quality color image. Many are capable of printing large-size drawings while maintaining high-quality resolution, **Figure 16-2**.

Figure 16-1   An inkjet printer. (Epson America, Inc.)

Figure 16-3   Inkjet plotters produce large-format prints at a good rate of speed. (Graphtec)

The *plotter* is very common in CAD systems. There are two main types: *inkjet* and *pen*. The main advantage to inkjet plotters is the speed with which they create hard copy.

Inkjet plotters are capable of printing D-size and E-size drawings, **Figure 16-3**. Most inkjet plotters can print thousands of colors. Inkjet plotters have become popular

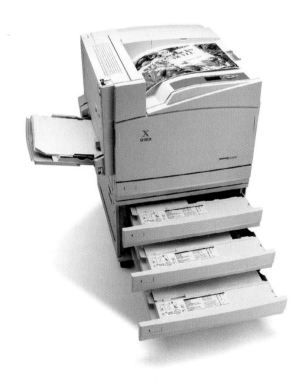

Figure 16-2   A large-format laser printer. (Xerox)

because they are faster than pen plotters in large-production environments. While a pen plotter has to plot each line individually, an inkjet plotter prints the entire drawing with one pass of the paper.

Pen plotters are available in two basic types—*rotary-drum* and *flatbed*. Both types duplicate the motion that a human hand might make while drawing. In other words, these devices draw lines instead of printing "dots" on the page. Each line and letter is drawn individually. Rotary-drum plotters operate by moving both the pen and paper back and forth to create the drawing. Flatbed plotters hold the paper stationary while the pen is directed across the paper. A flatbed plotter is shown in **Figure 16-4**.

Pen plotters produce very high-quality drawings. In many cases, lines are drawn accurate to within 1/100 of an inch. However, these devices are not very good at drawing large quantities of text because each letter has to be drawn individually, line by line. This makes pen plotters much slower than inkjet plotters.

Pen plotters can also create plots with color very easily. Even though they are slower, they are especially nice for school environments where hard copies are not necessarily

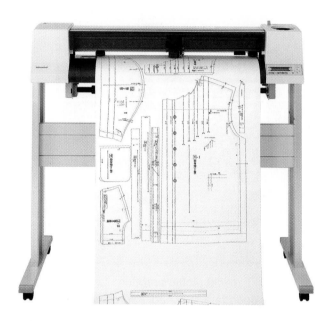

Figure 16-4 An eight-pen plotter. (Graphtec)

needed every day. It is very easy to cap the pens to keep them from drying out when the plotter is not in use. Inkjet plotters require more constant use to keep the ink from drying up. In smaller production environments, this may require more attention to keep the plotter operating properly.

Distributing Drawings Electronically

Because many drawings are created electronically using CAD software, drawing distribution is not limited to printing and plotting. To reach clients or other drafters more quickly, drafting firms typically transmit drawing files electronically using the Internet. The recipient can then download the file onto his or her computer and print or edit the drawing as desired. If the recipient does not have the same software used to create the drawing, the drawing may be viewed using free viewer software. The viewer software permits the user to view files and insert comments or minor changes without owning the actual software.

Drafting firms that operate Web sites can display their work online. This provides another way for clients to access drawings, since the files can be downloaded electronically. In cases where user security is important, the company may use password protection to prevent downloads from the general public.

Reproducing Drawings

As with CAD drawings, there are a number of ways to reproduce manual drawings for distribution or storage. Drawings may be traced, reproduced using xerography, or preserved on microfilm. Special printmaking processes may also be used to duplicate original drawings. These methods are discussed in the following sections.

Making Tracings for Reproduction

A *tracing* is commonly made for manual drafting when prints are to be made. The first step in making a tracing is to draw it on a translucent (somewhat see-through) material. There are different types of translucent material available in sheet or roll form.

Tracing paper is frequently used because it is less expensive than film or cloth. Tracing paper is used for making preliminary plans or sketches.

Vellum is treated, moisture-resistant tracing paper. It is stronger than regular tracing paper and is used for pencil and ink drawings.

Drafting film made from acetate, mylar, or polyester is ideally suited for work requiring print stability. Film will not expand or contract in heat, cold, or high humidity. Drafting film is tough and tear-resistant. It does not become discolored or brittle with age.

Pencil Tracings

Sharp, clear reproductions can be made from pencil tracings with conventional reproduction equipment and materials. Many

CAREERS IN DRAFTING

Civil Engineer

What would I do if I were to become a civil engineer? I would design and supervise the development and construction of highways, tunnels, bridges, airports, dams, sewage systems, and water supply systems, among other large-scale projects.

What would I need to know? I would need to know how to use the principles of math and science to intelligently and accurately design various large-scale projects. Also, I would need to know how to use drafting and computer-aided drafting (CAD) skills to create concept drawings for these projects so that working drawings could be generated and used to construct the projects.

Where would I work? Part of my day would be spent on the job site gathering information and supervising the project. Another part of my day would be spent in an office processing the information retrieved from the job site, creating reports related to the job, and consulting with clients.

For whom would I work? Civil engineers often hold positions as supervisors or administrators. I could work for a city government as a city engineer, or I could work as a construction site supervisor. I could also work for a variety of industries in research, design, construction, or even teaching.

What sort of education would I need? I would need a minimum of a bachelor's degree in civil engineering. To gain admission to an undergraduate engineering school, courses are required in math (through calculus), science (through physics), English, social studies, humanities, information technology, and mechanical drafting/CAD.

What are the special fields relating to this career? Civil engineering students may specialize in several types of engineering while getting their degree. These could include transportation, construction, geotechnical, environmental, structural, and water resources engineering.

What are my chances of finding a job? The demand for civil engineers is not expected to grow as fast as that for other engineering specialties over the next several years. Job opportunities will vary by geographic area, but engineers trained in the design of mass-transit systems, water and pollution control systems, and large buildings and building complexes will see the greatest availability of positions.

How much money could I expect to make? The median salary for civil engineers in recent years was $60,070. However, salaries ranged from $39,960 to $91,010 and up. Also, engineers employed by federal and local government agencies have consistently drawn higher wages than those in private business.

Where else could I look for more information about becoming a civil engineer? See the US Department of Labor's Bureau of Labor Statistics Occupational Outlook Handbook (at www.bls.gov) or request information from the American Society of Civil Engineers (www.asce.org). Special information for high school students about careers in engineering is available from the Junior Engineering Technical Society (www.jets.org).

If I decide to pursue a different career, what other fields are related to civil engineering? Professionals involved in related fields include architects, landscape architects, drafters, city planners, engineering and natural science managers, engineering technicians, science technicians, and various types of scientists.

drafters make original drawings on the tracing material that will be used to produce the copies. For more complex jobs, the layout is usually "traced" from the original drawing. This is where the term *tracing* comes from.

Tracings for reproduction are made the same way as the conventional drawings you have been making. Complete the drawing, add notes, and dimension the drawing. Keep the lines uniformly sharp and dense to reproduce well.

Every effort must be made to keep the tracing clean. Work with clean hands. Also place a piece of clean paper under your hand when you letter, dimension, or add notes.

Inked Tracings

Inked tracings are more difficult to prepare than pencil tracings. Much patience, knowledge of inking techniques, and lots of practice are required to produce acceptable inked tracings.

A dense, black, waterproof ink called *drawing ink* is used for inking. Lines are drawn with a *technical pen*, **Figure 16-5**. Technical pens are available in different widths. A technical pen must be held vertically to obtain the best line.

Most of the difficulties you will encounter when starting to ink are shown in **Figure 16-6**. Many of these difficulties can be avoided if you keep the pen clean. Use great care so you do not accidentally slide your instruments or hand into freshly inked lines.

Figure 16-5 Technical pens are used to ink drawings. They come in many different sizes. (Koh-I-Noor Rapidograph, Inc.)

Reproduction Methods for Drawings

After an original drawing is completed, it may then be reproduced. Reproduction methods include xerography and making microfilm from drawings. These methods are discussed next.

Xerography

Xerography (pronounced ze-rog'-ra-fee) is a printmaking process that uses an electrostatic charge to duplicate an original, **Figure 16-7**. Xerography is commonly known as *electrostatic reproduction*. It is based on the scientific principle that like electrical charges repel and unlike charges attract, **Figure 16-8**.

Correctly inked line

Pen not held vertically

Instrument accidentally pushed into freshly inked line

Ink ran under edge of instrument, pen not held vertically

Figure 16-6 A correctly inked line, and incorrectly inked lines with the probable causes.

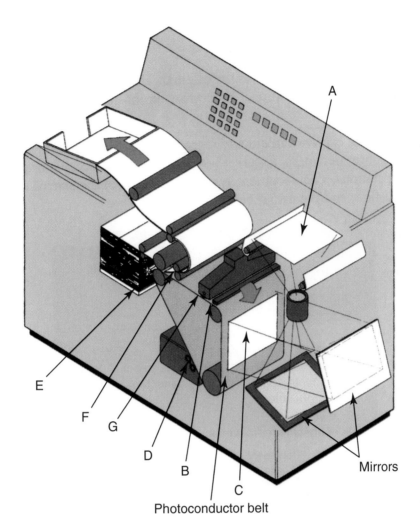

A

E

F

G

D

B

C

Mirrors

Photoconductor belt

Figure 16-7 The various parts of an electrostatic (xerographic) printer. A—The original drawing. B—A positive charge is placed on the photoconductor as the belt travels. C—The positive charge is removed from the nonimage areas on the photoconductor. D—Negatively charged toner is placed on the photoconductor. E—The photoconductor presses against the copy paper. F—Rollers fuse the toner to the paper. G—Brushes and a vacuum remove remaining toner.

Electrostatic reproduction exactly duplicates the original. The copy can be enlarged or reduced in size from the original if needed. The original drawing can be a manual or CAD drawing.

Large-format engineering copiers can quickly reproduce from original drawings. Some computer networks are connected to imaging systems, **Figure 16-9**. These systems receive drawing information from electronic files created with CAD software or special graphics software. The imaging system is able to prepare the printing materials and control the size and resolution of the reproduction.

Full-color copies can be made on color copiers. This is an important capability in CAD drafting, because color may be used on final prints to identify items such as wiring and piping. Color is also frequently used in CAD-generated renderings and other presentation work.

Microfilm Storage

Microfilm was originally designed to reduce storage facilities and to protect prints from loss. With this technique, the original

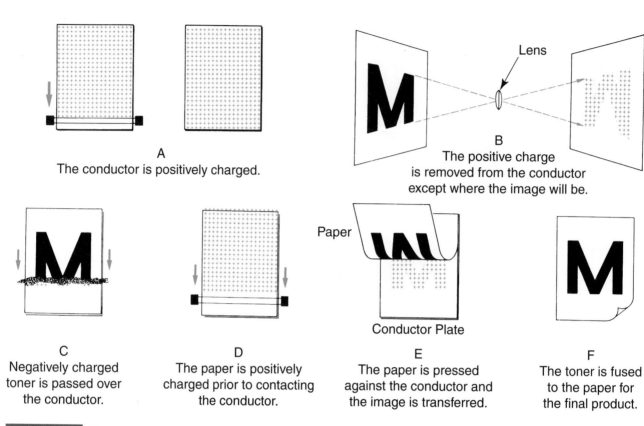

A
The conductor is positively charged.

B
The positive charge is removed from the conductor except where the image will be.

C
Negatively charged toner is passed over the conductor.

D
The paper is positively charged prior to contacting the conductor.

E
The paper is pressed against the conductor and the image is transferred.

F
The toner is fused to the paper for the final product.

Figure 16-8 The sequence for electrostatic reproduction.

Figure 16-9 An imaging system can produce printing materials directly from CAD drawings. (basysPrint)

drawing is reduced by photographic means to negative form. The finished negative can then be stored in roll form or on a card, **Figure 16-10**. Cards or film are easier to store than full-size drawings. To produce a working print, the microfilm image is retrieved from the files and printed on photographic paper. The print is often discarded or destroyed when it is no longer needed. Microfilm can also be viewed on a microfilm reader to check details without making a print.

Traditional Printmaking Processes

There are two traditional printmaking processes that are still used in drafting to duplicate drawings. These are the diazo process and the blueprint process. The term *blueprint* is often used generically to refer to any print in drafting. However, there is a special process that is used to make actual blueprints.

In comparison to other printmaking methods, the diazo and blueprint processes employ a chemical reaction to produce prints. As CAD drafting becomes more prevalent, more prints are generated electronically by computer. This has caused a decline in the use of traditional processes. However, you should be familiar with these processes. They are covered in the next sections.

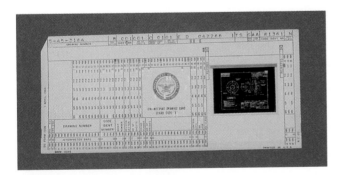

Figure 16-10 Microfilmed drawings can be stored on cards. The drawings can be enlarged and printed later.

Safety Note

Many printmaking processes use hazardous materials and machines that can cause injury. Be aware of any hazardous materials used by the specific equipment. Always follow the manufacturer's instructions and requirements for handling and disposing of all materials that may be hazardous. When operating a machine or mechanical device, always follow the manufacturer's instructions and guidelines for safety.

Diazo Process

The *diazo process* is a reproduction method for making direct positive prints, **Figure 16-11**. Positive prints consist of dark lines on a white background. The copies are produced quickly and inexpensively. In order to use this process, the drawing must first be made on translucent material. This material is usually vellum or film.

A diazo print is made by placing the drawing in contact with light-sensitive paper or film, and exposing the paper or film to light. The light does not penetrate the opaque lines that are on the original drawing. Exposure takes place when light strikes the light-sensitive coating of the print paper or film. After exposure, the print paper is developed by passing it through ammonia vapors.

Blueprint Process

The *blueprint process* is the oldest of the drawing duplication methods. A *blueprint* has white lines on a blue background.

The process is similar to the diazo process. First, a tracing or drawing is made. The drawing is placed in contact with light-sensitive paper and the two sheets are exposed to light. The print is then developed in a chemical solution, washed, and dried.

Material Safety

As a drafter, you may not think about material safety. However, there are many types of materials that you come in contact with, and some may be considered hazardous. Precautions must be taken when working with chemicals, inks, and other materials used when producing or printing drawings. The Occupational Safety and Health Administration (OSHA) requires the following:

- A list of all hazardous materials used is kept on the premises.
- A file containing material safety data sheets (MSDS file) for each hazardous material is maintained.
- Employees are trained in the proper use of hazardous materials.

Some materials that you may handle or come in contact with include ammonia, cleaning fluids, inks, and toner. In addition to proper handling of these materials, they must be properly disposed of when you are done using them. For example, spent toner cartridges should not be placed in the garbage. They should be returned to a recycling facility for recharging and eventual reuse. When in doubt, check your facility's master list of hazardous mate-

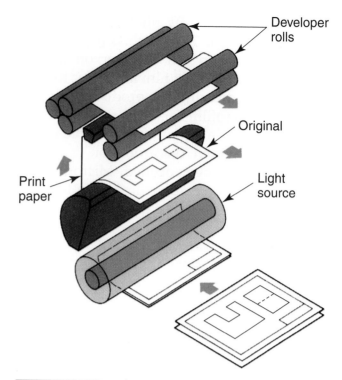

Figure 16-11 For diazo process prints, the original drawing is placed with light-sensitive paper into the printing machine. The two sheets are exposed to light, and the image is transferred to the print paper. The exposed image is developed with ammonia vapors.

rials. If the material is listed as hazardous, check the material's MSDS for hazards. Finally, check with the manufacturer or the Environmental Protection Agency (EPA) for disposal procedures.

Test Your Knowledge

Please do not write in this book. Place your answers on another sheet of paper.

1. List three reasons why prints are used instead of original drawings.
2. Name two types of printers used to output computer-generated drawings.
3. What advantage do inkjet plotters present over pen plotters?
4. Name two types of translucent materials used to make drawings.
5. Describe two methods of creating tracings.
6. Briefly describe the sequence of steps involved in electrostatic reproduction.
7. In diazo printing, prints consist of dark lines on a _____ background. In the blueprint process, prints consist of white lines on a _____ background.
8. What does *MSDS* stand for?

Outside Activities

1. Make a pencil tracing of one of your drawings and make a print. Make an ink tracing of the same drawing and make a print using the same process. Compare the results. How do they differ?
2. Make a CAD drawing of the drawing from the previous activity. Make a print using a pen plotter and a laser printer (or inkjet printer, depending on what is available). Compare the results. How do these prints compare to the prints you made in the previous activity?
3. Obtain prints made using each of the reproduction processes described in this chapter. Obtain photos of the devices used for each of the processes. Prepare a bulletin board display. Label each method.
4. Obtain a sample printed microfilm card and a print made from it. How does the quality compare to a full-size reproduction?
5. Survey industries in your local area. What types of reproductions are used by architects, contractors, and manufacturers?

17 Design

OBJECTIVES

After studying this chapter,
you should be able to:

◆ Describe the role of the industrial
designer.

◆ Explain why product design requires
so much research and development.

◆ Cite the qualities that help identify
good design.

◆ Recognize that a design may have
several solutions.

◆ Know how to apply basic design
guidelines when developing your
projects.

DRAFTING VOCABULARY

Concurrent design
  process
Design
Design problem

Industrial designers
Research and
  development
  (R&D)

Design is a plan for the simple and direct solution to a technical problem. Good design is the orderly and interesting arrangement of an idea to provide certain results and/or effects, **Figure 17-1**.

A well-designed product is functional (it does what it is supposed to do and does it well). It is also efficient and dependable. Such a product is less expensive than a similar product that is poorly designed, or one that does not function properly and must constantly be repaired.

The men and women who plan designs for industry are called *industrial designers*, **Figure 17-2**.

In addition to a creative imagination, skilled designers must have knowledge of engineering, production techniques, tools, machines, and materials. They must be able to design a new product or improve an existing product for manufacture. See **Figure 17-3**.

Design Guidelines

Product design requires much *research and development (R&D)*. It starts out as an idea, **Figure 17-4**. Many concepts of that idea must be studied, tried, refined, and then either used or discarded. The same technique is followed whether designing a company

Figure 17-1 A design is a plan to solve a problem. Many drawings and engineering tests are required in the design and manufacture of modern automobiles. (Pontiac Div., General Motors Corp.)

Figure 17-2 Industrial designers, in addition to having a creative imagination, must have a knowledge of engineering, manufacturing processes, and materials. (Ford Motor Company)

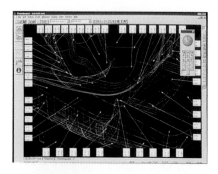
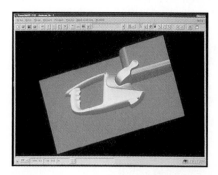
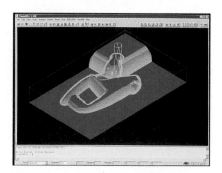

Figure 17-3 The computer software shown is being used to analyze the plastic housing for a chainsaw. The mold used for the part is being tested by the software and a coordinate measuring machine (CMM). The inspection data is fed from the CMM probe to a computer along with corresponding data from the original CAD file. From this point, the system refines the mold's geometry and is ultimately used to finish-machine the mold. (Delcam International Inc.)

Figure 17-4 After the design problem is identified, many techniques are used to put the design into visual form for further study. In the automotive industry, full-size tape drawings are made to see if the idea is feasible after design sketches have been made. Shown is a tape outline of a small car under study. (General Motors Corp.)

Figure 17-5 While this trademark logo appears to be simple, it was a challenging problem for its designer. The "mark" of a company or product has great commercial value. People may not remember the company name, but they remember its trademark. Can you name familiar trademarks?

trademark, **Figure 17-5**, a complex product, **Figure 17-6**, or a student learning experience for class.

The design process is not an exact science. There is no special formula that, if followed, 1, 2, 3... will guarantee a successful product. However, there are certain qualities that can help you identify a good design. These qualities serve as guidelines and are listed and described next.

ACADEMIC LINK

The design of materials plays a key part in many areas of science and engineering. For years, automotive and aerospace engineers have worked on developing new materials to help make vehicles more aerodynamic and lightweight. Plastic composites, for example, have been engineered to make automobiles lighter and more fuel efficient. They are also used in the manufacture of aircraft bodies, golf club shafts, and boat hulls.

Metal parts used in aircraft engines must be able to sustain strength at very high temperatures. They must also be lightweight. Therefore, metallurgy is an important area of study in aerospace engineering. Metallurgy is the science of developing metals with special properties. Metallurgists design *alloys* (mixtures of two or more metals fused or melted together to form a new metal). Examples include aluminum and titanium alloys. Some aluminum and titanium alloys are as strong as structural steel.

Metals are also designed to be suitable for certain manufacturing processes and for applications where resistance to water or corrosion is important. Can you think of other design characteristics that are important in certain metals?

Figure 17-6 Product design requires considerable work. Many people are responsible for the design of components, no matter how complex. Proper product design will help increase productivity and reduce cost while improving quality. (General Electric)

- **Functional**. A well-designed product "works." It does what it is designed to do and does it efficiently. Function often dictates many design results, such as product shape. Some design problems have several solutions to arrive at a certain function, **Figure 17-7**.
- **Honest**. In a good design, the true qualities of the materials used (strength, weight, texture, etc.) are emphasized. One material is not made to look like another material, **Figure 17-8**.
- **Appealing**. The elements of a good design create interest. The product is visually pleasing, **Figure 17-9**.
- **Reliable**. A well-designed product is not always malfunctioning (breaking down) or failing. It should be easy to service and economical to maintain. See **Figure 17-10**.

A

B

Figure 17-7 A design problem may have several solutions. Here are how two companies designed a vertical take-off and landing (VTOL) aircraft. Can you explain how each aircraft operates? (A—Bell Helicopter Textron/ Boeing Helicopters; B—Robert Walker)

- **Safe**. When used properly, a successfully designed product is safe. Protection from possible injury to the user is part of the basic design, **Figure 17-11**.
- **Colorful**. Color plays an important role with some products and is included in

the design process. The automotive industry does much research before selecting the interior and exterior colors for new models, **Figure 17-12**. A well-designed product can be further enhanced in appearance when completed in carefully selected colors. However, the addition of color, no matter how carefully chosen, will not improve a poorly designed product.

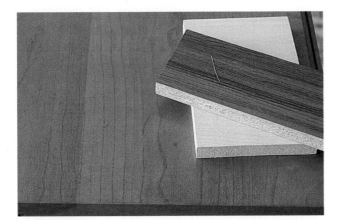

Figure 17-8   A well-designed product does not have one material masquerading as another. Shown is a table made of cherry wood. Included on the tabletop is a material made of compressed sawdust and covered with a thin plastic sheet on which a wood grain pattern has been printed. It has been scratched to show how thin the imitation wood covering is. The scratch cannot be sanded out and the finish cannot be repaired. The plastic sheet also has a tendency to blister and peel, ruining the item made from the material.

Figure 17-10   A well-designed product is dependable; it is not always in need of repair. Here an auto body from the production line is being checked to ensure it meets design specifications. Production units are selected at random and actually "torn apart" to check whether they have been welded properly. (Ford Motor Company)

Figure 17-9   A good design generates interest and visual appeal. This Dodge Sidewinder concept truck is designed to attract truck enthusiasts. (DaimlerChrysler)

Figure 17-11   A well-designed product is safe. This "thrill ride" was designed to provide certain results and effects. What things do the designers have to consider when planning such rides to make them safe?

CAREERS IN DRAFTING

Landscape Architect

What would I do if I were to become a landscape architect? I would design functional and attractive outdoor areas that are compatible with their natural environment. These would include golf courses, residential areas, public parks and playgrounds, school campuses, amusement parks, water parks, industrial parks, and shopping centers. I would determine where buildings, roads, and walkways would be constructed and where bushes, trees, and flowers would be planted.

What would I need to know? I would need to know how to identify the purpose of a project and how to best utilize the funds available to create the most functional and aesthetically pleasing design possible. I would need to know how to analyze the nature of a site. Analysis could include identifying and examining both natural and human-made features, local climate conditions, and soil characteristics. I would need to know how to integrate my design into the existing surroundings in a natural and unobtrusive way. Also, I would need to be familiar with local, state, and federal regulations such as those protecting wildlife, wetlands, and other historic resources. Finally, I would need to know basic drafting skills and standards using both manual and computer-aided design (CAD) techniques. From personal computing CAD software to GIS (geographic information systems), CAD has become a valuable tool for landscape architects, not only in the design process but also in the presentation of the design to clients.

Where would I work? I would spend most of my time in an office creating designs and plans, preparing cost estimates, doing research, and preparing models of my designs. I would also spend a portion of my indoor time meeting with clients and other professionals with whom I would collaborate. My outdoor time would be spent on the job site gathering information that I would utilize in the design process. Later, I would spend more outdoor time observing and supervising the construction of my design.

For whom would I work? Approximately 23% of all landscape architects are self-employed. Hence, I would be working for whoever contracted me to do work. This could be a private homeowner, architect, surveyor, engineer, contractor, or agency needing landscaping design work done. Many landscape architects work for real estate development firms and government agencies.

What sort of education would I need? At the high school level, I would need to take courses in English, history, art, social studies, math, physics, and computer science, as well as any drafting and CAD courses available. To become a licensed or registered landscape architect, I would need to acquire a minimum of a bachelor's degree in landscape architecture—preferably from a school accredited by the Landscape Architectural Accreditation Board of the American Society of Landscape Architects. Also, many employers prefer hiring landscape architects who have some internship experience.

What are the special fields relating to this career? Landscape architecture, being a specialized field in itself, has many areas of specialization. A landscape architect may specialize in designing golf courses, amusement or water parks, residential development, municipal parks and playgrounds, shopping centers, or street and highway beautification projects.

What are my chances of finding a job? The demand for landscape architects is
(continued)

Landscape Architect *(continued)*

expected to increase due to the need to meet environmental restrictions, as well as the demand for incorporating natural elements into human-made environments. This career is expected to be one of the faster-growing careers over the next several years. Opportunities will be best for those who have acquired strong CAD and communication skills. Knowledge of environmental codes and regulations will also greatly enhance job opportunities.

How much money could I expect to make? Salaries for landscape architects have in recent years ranged from $28,730 to more than $79,620. Those demanding the highest average salaries were employed in the federal government sector. As with most careers of this nature, those contracted by larger corporations or organizations have seen greater levels of compensation than those who work for themselves or smaller firms.

Where else could I look for more information about becoming a landscape architect? See the US Department of Labor's Bureau of Labor Statistics Occupational Outlook Handbook (at www.bls.gov), visit the American Society of Landscape Architects web site (at www.asla.org), or request information from the Council of Landscape Architectural Registration Boards (at www.clarb.org).

If I decide to pursue a different career, what other fields are related to landscape architecture? Architecture, surveying, cartography, civil engineering, urban and regional planning, conservation science, and forestry.

- **Made with quality**. Quality is a basic part of good design. It cannot be added after the product is made. Good design should be a guarantee of quality, **Figure 17-13**. Quality is designed and built into items.

Simply stated, good design is characterized by certain qualities. All of them are necessary. Overlooking or eliminating one can potentially destroy the entire design.

When a product is designed, the designer should apply a *concurrent design process.* In this process, the designer takes into account all aspects of the product life cycle. The design

Figure 17-12 The selection of colors is very important in the design of certain products. Colors must be carefully chosen to attract buyers. (Ford Motor Company)

Figure 17-13 Quality results from good design. This hardwood mahogany stool is well designed and constructed, and it looks that way.

process includes input from those who will be manufacturing the product, those who will be selling the product, and those who will be using the product. This process results in the best product for all involved.

Designing a Project

How should *you* go about designing a project? One way is to employ a method used by professional designers. Think of your project as a *design problem* with specific steps to follow:

1. **Begin with an idea**. What kind of a project do you want to make? Keep your first few design problems simple. How will the product be used? Will its use affect the nature or shape of the project? Are there cost limitations?

2. **Develop your idea**. What must your product do? How can it best be created? Study and research similar products. How did other designers solve the problem? Make sketches of your ideas. Select the best of the ideas. When possible, submit your design for class critique (review).

3. **Make models**. Construct models of your best ideas, **Figure 17-14**. Evaluate them. Select the best. You may want to make refinements (changes) in your design when you see it in three dimensions.

4. **Make working drawings**. When satisfied that you have done the best you can to solve the problem, prepare working drawings for the project. If practical, make the drawings full size.

5. **Construct the project**. Make the product to the best of your ability. Do a job you will be proud to show to others, **Figure 17-15**. Do not be afraid to ask for help from your instructor if you encounter a problem.

Developing a well-designed project takes time. Do not be discouraged if your first attempts fall short of your goals. It takes practice and effort to acquire the skill and ability to solve design problems. The only way to succeed is by doing.

Keep a notebook of your design efforts. Include your sketches, drawings, and photos or projects you have designed. It will make it easier to evaluate your progress.

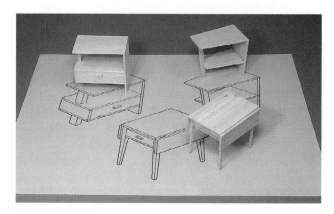

Figure 17-14 Develop your ideas by making many sketches and constructing models. Make models of your best ideas to determine how they will look in three dimensions. The sketches shown were made with drafting instruments and ink so they would photograph well. Your drawings can be drawn in pencil.

Figure 17-15 The proof of a design is how it looks when it is constructed and put into use. This student-designed and made table is nicely designed and has been constructed using approved cabinetmaking techniques. The only metal fasteners were the screws used to hold the top to the body.

Test Your Knowledge

Please do not write in this book. Place your answers on another sheet of paper.

1. Define *design*.
2. Describe the specific areas in which industrial designers must have knowledge and explain their role in industry.
3. List four qualities that can be identified in a good design.
4. List the steps you would follow to solve a design problem. Briefly describe each.

Outside Activities

The design problems listed below are presented to give you practice in design activities. You may also develop your own ideas for products you wish to design.

1. Hand-launched glider
2. Jet-propelled (CO_2 cartridge engine) model automobile
3. Book rack
4. Storage box for compact discs/tapes
5. Toolbox
6. Turned bowl
7. Clock
8. Nightstand table
9. Stereo cabinet
10. Bicycle rack
11. Storage container for DVDs/video cassettes
12. Display cabinet for awards and trophies
13. Fiberglass model boat
14. Cutting board
15. Metal base for a table lamp
16. Coffee table
17. Tray
18. Turned wooden lamp
19. Plastic soft food spreader
20. Salad server (laminated wood, wood, metal, or plastic)
21. Wall shelf
22. Shoeshine box
23. Disposable wastebasket (made from corrugated cardboard)
24. Desktop pencil holder
25. Storage folder for drawings
26. Carrying case for drafting tools

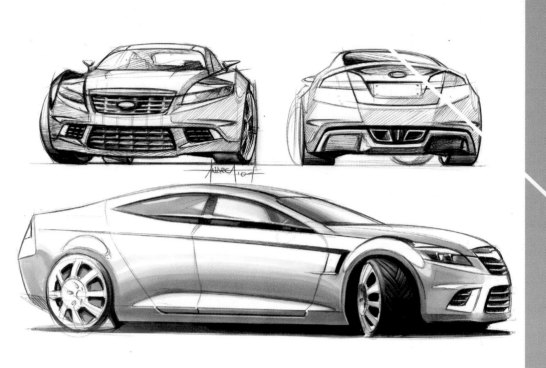

18 Models, Mockups, and Prototypes

OBJECTIVES

After studying this chapter,
you should be able to:

- ◆ Explain why industry uses models, mockups, and prototypes.
- ◆ Define the terms *model*, *mockup*, and *prototype*.
- ◆ Describe how different industries use models, mockups, and prototypes.
- ◆ Construct simple models.
- ◆ Use modelmaking equipment and supplies safely.

DRAFTING VOCABULARY

Mockup
Model
Production fixtures
Prototype

Surface model
Solid model
Wireframe model

To many people, modelmaking is an interesting and challenging hobby. You have probably made models of famous planes, boats, or cars from wood or plastic.

Industry makes extensive use of modeling. Models are constructed for engineering, educational, and planning purposes, as well as for merchandising. Models help solve design problems and verify the workability of designs and ideas before they are put into production.

Models used in industry can be classified as one of three types. These are *models*, *mockups*, and *prototypes*. This chapter discusses common modeling applications and the ways in which models are used in product design and development.

Models

Industry's definition of a *model* is a reduced scale replica of a proposed, planned, or existing product. Even though computer-aided drafting (CAD) is a great help in developing a new product design, a model may be constructed to see how the product will look in three dimensions, to verify scientific theory,

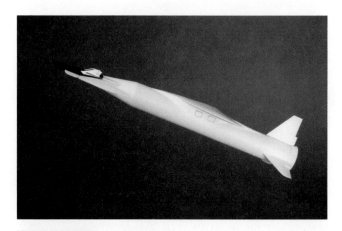

Figure 18-1 Modelmaking is an important part of the design process in aerospace engineering. Shown is a 3-foot-long scale model of the Hyper-X flight vehicle used in research for developing hypersonic aircraft. (NASA)

to demonstrate ideas, to aid in training, or to use for advertising purposes. See **Figure 18-1**.

Computer-Generated Models

Computers and CAD software are commonly used to create models in industry. There are three types of models that can be created with CAD software to represent objects. See **Figure 18-2**. These are *wireframe*

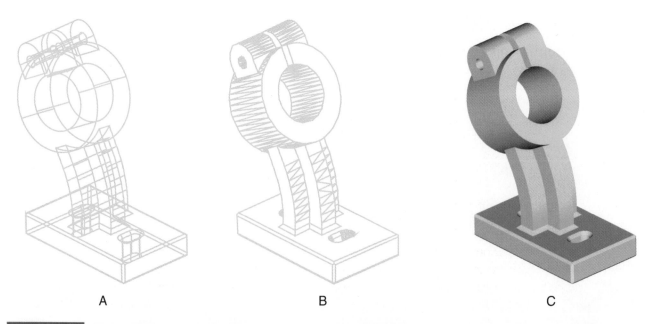

A   B   C

Figure 18-2 CAD models can be constructed as wireframes, surface models, or solid models. A—Wireframe representation. B—Surface model. C—Rendered solid model.

models, surface models, and *solid models.* A *wireframe model,* **Figure 18-2A,** looks like it is made of wire. You can easily see through it. Wireframe models are sometimes hard to visualize since you cannot tell which is the front or the back. A *surface model,* **Figure 18-2B,** is easier to visualize. A surface model is basically a wireframe with a thin "skin." Many times surface models look like solid models, but surface models are *not* solid. As its name implies, a *solid model* is defined as "solid" all the way through. See **Figure 18-2C.** When a section is made through a part represented as a solid model, the interior features are seen.

One advantage of computer-generated models is that they can be analyzed using computer programs. For example, the stress in an automotive engine component can be evaluated before an actual part is manufactured.

Mockups

A *mockup* is a full-size, three-dimensional copy of a product, **Figure 18-3.** The mockup is usually made of plywood, plaster, clay, or a combination of materials.

Prototypes

A *prototype* is a full-size operating model of the production item, **Figure 18-4.** It is often handcrafted to check for and eliminate possible design and production "bugs."

How Models, Mockups, and Prototypes Are Used

Many industries employ models, mockups, and prototypes as design tools. A few of the more important industrial applications for models, mockups, and prototypes are in automotive engineering, aerospace engineering, architecture, shipbuilding, city planning, and construction engineering. See **Figure 18-5.** These applications are discussed in the following sections.

Automotive Applications

The automotive industry places great importance on the use of models, mockups, and prototypes. Mistakes in marketing and

Figure 18-3 A full-size mockup of the front seat and controls of a concept car. Such design features often find their way into future production vehicles. (Pontiac Div., General Motors Corp.)

Figure 18-4 When designing this 200 mph (320 km/h) train, it was important to know how it would handle actual operating conditions. Before it was put into production, a prototype was constructed and run more than a million miles. Only a few changes had to be made. (French National Railroad)

Figure 18-5 A cutaway of a turbo fan jet engine. It is used for sales and training purposes in the aerospace industry. (Pratt & Whitney Canada)

production can be very costly. An automobile starts "life" as a series of sketches, **Figure 18-6**. These are usually developed around specifications supplied by management. Promising sketches are usually drawn full size for additional evaluation. Clay models are employed for three-dimensional studies. In some cases, three-dimensional, computer-drawn models are created to evaluate the design.

Upon completion of further design development, a full-size mockup is constructed, **Figure 18-7**. If it is decided that the design has potential, a fiberglass prototype is generally

Figure 18-7 Final smoothing of the vinyl sheets coating the full-size clay model of this automobile takes place before review by company officials. Modeled exactly to scale from the full-size line drawing on the wall, this clay body eventually will be destroyed after a two-part epoxy/fiberglass mold is made. The resulting mold will be used to shape the body for the prototype vehicle. (Ford Motor Company)

fabricated, **Figure 18-8**. This is the concept car you see at auto shows where autos are displayed for evaluation by the public. If the comments are favorable, the concept car may

Figure 18-6 The automotive industry uses sketches to develop ideas. Scale models are made of promising designs for future study and development. (Pontiac Div., General Motors Corp.)

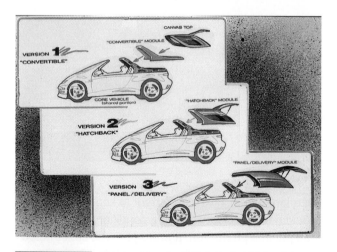

Figure 18-8 A prototype of the concept car shown in **Figure 18-6**. While only a few "idea" vehicles go into production, they are used for design studies. Many proposed innovations are utilized on production vehicles. (Pontiac Div., General Motors Corp.)

CAREERS IN DRAFTING

Aerospace Engineer

What would I do if I were to become an aerospace engineer? I would design, develop, test, and supervise the manufacture of all types of flight machines. These machines would include aircraft if I were an aeronautical engineer and spacecraft if I were an astronautical engineer.

What would I need to know? I would need to know how to develop new technologies for aviation applications using principles of math and science. Because I may specialize in structural design, guidance, navigation and control, or other areas, I would need to know how to effectively use drafting and computer-aided drafting (CAD) skills. I would also need to be familiar with robotics, laser technology, and advanced optics systems.

Where would I work? Part of my day would be spent in a manufacturing facility supervising various projects that I have had a hand in designing. I would also spend a portion of my day at my desk researching, designing, and developing concepts, materials, and processes as they relate to the project I am currently involved with. I may also spend some time consulting with clients or other members of my design team.

For whom would I work? If I were an aeronautical engineer, I would work for an aircraft manufacturer on either commercial or government projects. If I were an astronautical engineer, I would either work for a private corporation that did consulting design and development work for various government agencies—such as the department of defense or NASA—or I would work directly for one of those agencies. I could also work for an automobile manufacturer designing aerodynamic cars (those that have a lower resistance to air) for greater fuel efficiency.

What sort of education would I need? I first would need to get a bachelor's degree in aerospace engineering. To gain admission to an undergraduate engineering school, courses are required in math (through calculus), science (through physics), English, social studies, humanities, information technology, and mechanical drafting/CAD.

What are the special fields relating to this career? Aerospace engineers may specialize in a particular product area, such as commercial airliners, military aircraft, helicopters, or various types of spacecraft. They may also be specialists in fields such as thermodynamics, acoustics, guidance, aerodynamics, propulsion, celestial mechanics, or control systems.

What are my chances of finding a job? Because of a perceived lack of opportunity in the aerospace industry, job prospects over the next several years are good due to a lack of degrees granted in recent years. In fact, there could even be a shortage due to many in the field nearing retirement and leaving the profession.

How much money could I expect to make? The median salary for aerospace engineers in recent years was $72,750. Salaries ranged from $49,640 to $105,060 and up. Also, the prevailing trend has been that engineers employed by the government have consistently drawn higher wages than those in private business.

Where else could I look for more information about becoming an aerospace engineer? See the US Department of Labor's Bureau of Labor Statistics Occupational Outlook Handbook (at www.bls.gov) or request information from the Aerospace Industries Association (www.aia-aerospace. org) or the American Institute of Aeronautics and Astronautics, Inc. (www.aiaa.org). Special information for high school students about
(continued)

Aerospace Engineer *(continued)*

careers in engineering is available from the Junior Engineering Technical Society (www.jets.org).

If I decide to pursue a different career, what other fields are related to aerospace engineering? Professionals involved in related

fields include control systems specialists, aerospace drafters, CAD specialists, engineering and natural science managers, engineering technicians, science technicians, and various types of scientists.

be put into production. After many more months of development and production planning, the vehicle is manufactured and made available to the public. The mockup is also used to develop *production fixtures*. These are devices to hold body panels in position while they are welded together. Dies to shape other parts, as well as other production tools, are developed from the mockup.

Aerospace Applications

The tremendous cost of aerospace vehicles makes it mandatory that they first be developed in model and mockup form, **Figure 18-9**.

Flight characteristics can be determined with considerable accuracy, without endangering human life, by subjecting test aircraft to structural testing. See **Figure 18-10**. Prototype aircraft are the first two or three production planes (they are usually handcrafted). They are flown to check the data obtained from wind tunnel and computer research, **Figure 18-11**.

Architectural Applications

You have seen photos or illustrations of proposed buildings in the real estate section of your newspaper. Some of these illustrations are models that are very accurate replicas

Figure 18-9 An artist's rendering of the X-38 technology demonstrator, an emergency crew return vehicle (CRV) test model used for design studies. (NASA)

Figure 18-10 A modified F/A-18A Hornet research aircraft undergoing structural loads testing in a NASA flight laboratory. The purpose of the testing is to determine wing flexibility of the Active Aeroelastic Wing F-18 design. (NASA)

Figure 18-11 A prototype of the advanced Boeing 777. It is used for flight testing and crew and maintenance technician training. Commercial aircraft must undergo hundreds of hours of rigorous testing before the aircraft can be put into passenger service. (The Boeing Company)

of the proposed buildings, **Figure 18-12**. Many people use models when planning new homes, **Figure 18-13**. This helps them visualize how the house will look when completed. The model enables the owner to see the completed design in three dimensions and how paint colors and shrubbery plantings will look. Models of buildings are also used for advertising purposes, **Figure 18-14**. Photos of models for advertising are used in magazines, newspapers, and brochures.

Shipbuilding

Ship hulls are tested in model form before designs are finalized and construction begins, **Figure 18-15**. Special equipment designed for the project tows the model hull through a water test basin. The model hull behaves

Figure 18-12 A computer-generated architectural model of a proposed house. (SoftPlan Architectural Design Software)

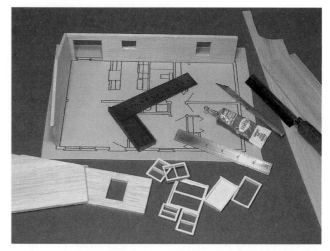

Figure 18-13 Many potential homebuilders make scale models so they can see how their home will look before starting to build.

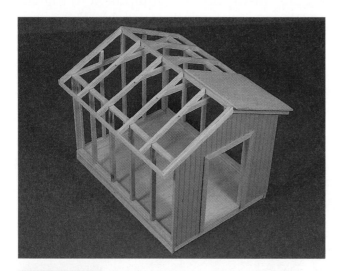

Figure 18-14 A student-designed and constructed storage shed. Models like this are often used for advertising purposes.

like the full-size ship so design faults can be located and corrected. The models test a proposed ship's sea worthiness, power requirements, resistance as it travels through water, and stability characteristics.

City Planning

Many towns and cities use scale models to show city officials and planners how proposed changes and future developments will look, **Figure 18-16**. Models, while costly, permit intelligent decisions to be made before large sums of money are spent acquiring land and before existing buildings are torn down. The models help designers plan for the movement of vehicles and people to avoid

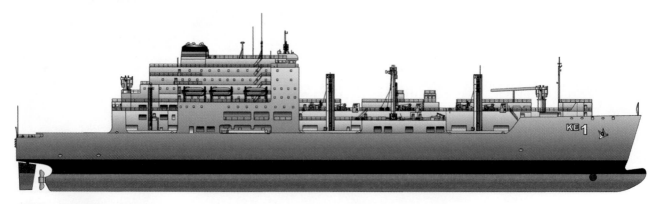

Figure 18-15 A rendered model profile of the Lewis and Clark T-AKE 1 Class ship, a US Navy Combat Logistics Force vessel under study for production. (NAVSEA/Naval Sea Systems Command)

Figure 18-16 An architectural scale model showing the details of a proposed condominium development. The model is used for planning purposes. (Scale Reproductions, LLC)

congestion after the plan is built. The models can be used to help "sell" the future development so financing can be obtained.

Construction Engineering

Many construction projects are designed from carefully constructed models, **Figure 18-17**. By working from models, engineers can see how space can best be utilized. In some instances, they can determine how the proposed project will affect surrounding communities and the environment. This helps minimize field problems and changes during construction.

Constructing Models

Modelmaking materials are readily available commercially, **Figure 18-18**. Many products made for the model railroader are ideally

Figure 18-17 Computer-generated models for industrial projects can be used to determine the best way to utilize space.

suited for making architectural models. Kits are available for the small homebuilder who wants to design his or her own home. A professional touch can be added to models by using accurately scaled furniture, automobiles, and figures. These items can be purchased at toy and hobby shops.

Walls and partitions in a model home are usually constructed of balsa wood. Preprinted sheets of brick and stone can be glued to the wood sections to represent exterior walls.

Various types and grades of abrasive paper are suitable for roofing, driveways, and walkways. Simulated window glass can be made from transparent plastic sheet. Several different scale sizes of window frames and door frames are available molded in plastic. Most model shops can supply brushes, paints, and trees in various types and sizes.

Other types of models—autos, planes, and boats—are made from basswood, mahogany, balsa wood, metal, plaster, and various kinds of plastics, **Figure 18-19**. Regular model-making paint is produced in hundreds of colors and is ideal for painting all types of models, **Figure 18-20**. However, care must be exercised when painting models that have plastic in their construction. Be sure the paints are designed for plastics. If you are not sure, paint a scrap portion of similar plastic or a small portion of the plastic that is hidden from view. This will help determine whether the paint is compatible with the material.

Figure 18-19 A plastic model of a helicopter to be used in constructing a hangar.

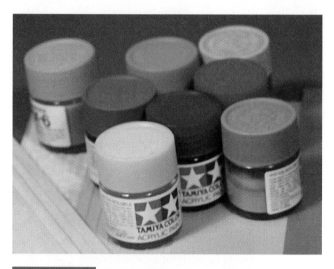

Figure 18-20 Modelmaking paints are available in hundreds of colors. Be sure to select the right types for your models.

Figure 18-18 A sampling of modelmaking materials available at hobby shops.

Safety Note

Carefully read the instructions on modelmaking paint and adhesive containers. Use these products only as specified. Wear a dust mask if you are sanding wood or plastic. Wash your hands after cleaning any brushes and the work area. Models may be assembled with model airplane cement, Elmer's® Glue, Titebond®, cyanoacrylates, or epoxies. Use care when using these products and follow all safety directions according to the manufacturer's directions.

Test Your Knowledge

Please do not write in this book. Place your answers on another sheet of paper.

1. Define the term *model* as it relates to industry.
2. What is a CAD-generated *wireframe model* and how is it different from a *surface model*?
3. What is a *mockup*?
4. What is a *prototype*?
5. List four industries that employ models, mockups, and prototypes as design tools. Briefly describe how each industry listed uses them.
6. Walls and partitions in a model home are usually constructed of _____ wood.
7. Roofs, driveways, and walkways can be made from different kinds and grades of _____.
8. Models of cars, planes, and boats may be made from what kinds of materials?

Outside Activities

1. Visit a model or hobby shop, then prepare a list of available materials that may be used for building architectural models.
2. Review technical magazines and clip illustrations that show models, mockups, and prototypes being used for engineering, educational, planning, or other purposes. (Do not cut up library copies.)
3. Make a collection of materials suitable for building model homes.
4. Visit a professional modelmaker in your community. With permission, make a series of slides showing examples of various models and how these models are made. Then, give a talk to your class on professional modelmaking.
5. Make a scale model of your drafting room. Discuss alternate layouts.
6. Construct a model helicopter similar to the one shown in **Figure 18-19**. Design and construct from balsa wood a minimum building that would protect the helicopter from the elements.

19 Maps

OBJECTIVES

After studying this chapter,
you should be able to:

- ◆ Explain why maps are used.
- ◆ Identify and describe various types of maps.
- ◆ Explain how maps are developed.
- ◆ Read a map.
- ◆ Describe the use of CAD programs in mapping applications.

DRAFTING VOCABULARY

Bearings	Plat plan
Cartographer	Plot plan
City maps	Real estate maps
Contour lines	Site plan
Elevation	Spatial data
Field notes	Surveyor
Hectare	Tape
Location maps	Topographic maps
Map	Transit
Map symbols	Vicinity maps

A *map* is a graphic representation, usually on a flat plan, of a portion of the earth's surface, **Figure 19-1**. Maps are used to communicate ideas, illustrate concepts, and provide direction. A typical map of a community is shown in **Figure 19-2**.

Figure 19-1 Maps are important to many people. They use them on the job and to plan business trips and vacations. Many types of maps are available for reference and everyday use.

There are many types of maps. General reference maps show elevations, roads, cities, and towns of an area. Maps published by the United States Geological Survey show the exact location of features of the earth. Surveyors rely on these precision maps whenever they need data or facts.

Aeronautical and marine maps provide navigational information for those using the air and sea-lanes. These types of maps are often called *charts*.

Road maps show the roads and highways in a region and aid in planning business and vacation trips. Other maps show or emphasize some particular features or surface characteristics of the earth (or planets).

A professional mapmaker is called a *cartographer*. He or she has the specialized skills to combine data from many sources to design and prepare accurate maps.

Maps are generated using computers and software or manual drawing methods. In both cases, there are times when drafters are called upon to draw maps. This chapter discusses the types of maps they would be expected to prepare.

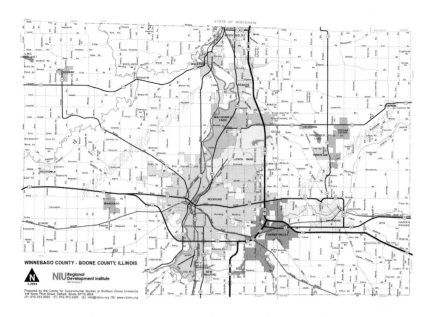

Figure 19-2 A well-designed map showing the area surrounding Rockford, Illinois. (Regional Development Institute at Northern Illinois University)

Preparing Maps

Aerial photography, space satellites, and computer-aided drafting (CAD) methods have reduced the time needed to map large areas of land and sea. Because of these methods, accuracy has also been greatly improved. However, a great deal of "legwork" is still necessary to map small areas. Information for a map used in civil engineering or construction is collected by a *surveyor*. In traditional surveying, the surveyor uses an instrument called a *transit* to establish the boundaries of the area being mapped. Distances are measured with a *tape*. Measurements are made in both linear and angular units, and angular measurements are expressed as *bearings*. These are the angles that boundary lines make with due north and south. These and other surveyor's measurements are recorded in the form of *field notes*. With this information, a map or drawing is developed and drawn. A drawing that shows property and boundary lines is called a *plat plan*, **Figure 19-3**. Notice that the measurements for the surveyed lots are given in feet and acres.

In metric surveying, the areas of the surveyed land are given in hectares (ha) instead of acres, **Figure 19-4**. A *hectare* is an area that is 100 meters long and 100 meters wide. Linear distances on metric maps are given in meters and kilometers.

Maps are always drawn to scale because it is not possible to draw them full size. The size of the land area being mapped determines the scale.

In most towns, cities, and counties or parishes, a drawing of a building lot or farm may be drawn at a scale of 1″ = 30′-0″. Metric drawings for building lots typically use a drawing scale of 1:300. That is, 1.0 mm on the drawing equals 300.0 mm of the actual lot.

Many maps use a graphic scale to indicate the map scale, **Figure 19-5**.

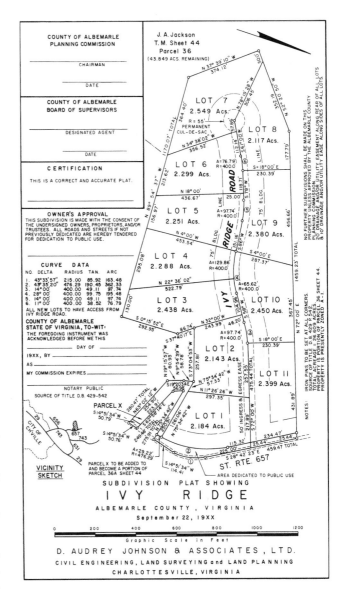

Figure 19-3 A typical plat plan developed from information gathered by a surveyor. This is a plat showing a housing subdivision.

Maps Drawn by Drafters

Plot plans, city maps, topographic maps, location maps, and vicinity maps are some of the types of plans and maps that drafters are asked to prepare. These are discussed in the following sections. When drawing a map, it is very important to draw it at the proper scale. Plan ahead so that you select an appropriate sheet size for the scale used.

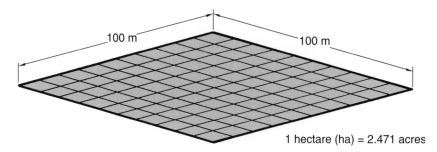

1 hectare (ha) = 2.471 acres

Figure 19-4 A hectare (ha) is 100 meters long and 100 meters wide. (It equals about 2.5 acres.)

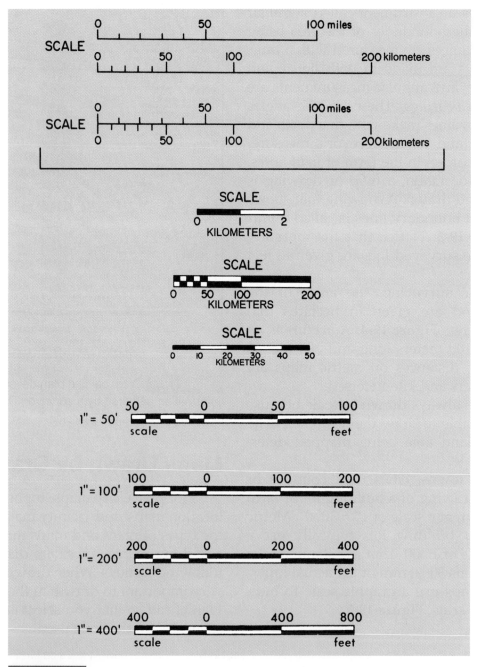

Figure 19-5 Typical graphic scales used on maps.

Plot Plans

The drawing of a lot on which a house or building is to be constructed is called a *plot plan* or *site plan*. See **Figure 19-6**. It shows site dimensions, the exact location of the lot, and the location where the structure is to be situated on the lot. It may also show topographical features and elevations. Elevations on a

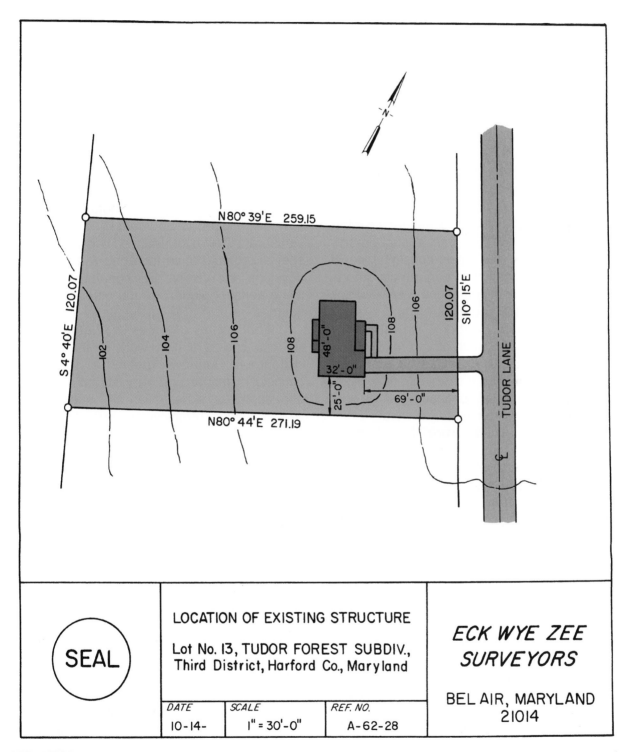

Figure 19-6 A plot plan. Differences in elevation are shown by a series of curved lines called contour lines. They are drawn at regular intervals.

CAREERS IN DRAFTING

Cartographer

What would I do if I were to become a cartographer? I would collect geographical, cultural, and political information and data and create maps of large areas. Simply put, a cartographer is a mapmaker. I would measure, chart, and map the earth's surface.

What would I need to know? I would need to know how to collect, analyze, and interpret both spatial data (concerning latitude, longitude, elevation, and distance) and nonspatial data (including demographic characteristics, land-use patterns, annual precipitation levels, and population density). I would also need to know how to perform geographical research, compile data, and prepare maps in either electronic or graphic form.

Where would I work? A majority of my time would be spent in an office creating various types of maps using data acquired from a surveyor or surveying technician. The work of the cartographer is predominantly indoor work (cartographers seldom go to job sites).

For whom would I work? I would probably work for an architectural or engineering firm (or a related service firm). I could also work for a local, state, or federal agency. Private sector positions could also be available with construction firms, mining companies, and oil and gas extraction companies. I could also work for a private company that produces maps for consumer use.

What sort of education would I need? While in high school, I would need to take courses in algebra, geometry, trigonometry, drafting, mechanical drawing, computer-aided drafting (CAD) and computer science. I would also need to have, at a minimum, some sort of postsecondary school training. Many cartographers have a bachelor's degree in engineering, forestry, geography, or a physical science. With the development of GIS (geographic information systems), it has become increasingly important to acquire as much technical and computer skill training as possible.

What are the special fields relating to this career? One specialized field of cartography is photogrammetry. A photogrammetrist is a cartographer that specializes in creating maps from data acquired from aerial photographs—usually of areas that are inaccessible, difficult, or not cost effective to survey by conventional means. A photogrammetrist may be required to be licensed as a professional land surveyor. Map editing is another specialized field of cartography. A map editor develops and verifies the contents of maps using aerial photographs and other reference sources.

What are my chances of finding a job? My chances of finding work in the field of cartography improve greatly if I have a bachelor's degree and very strong technical and computer skills. Over the next several years, average employment growth is projected. Knowledge of GPS (global positioning systems) and GIS will enhance employment opportunities as well.

How much money could I expect to make? In recent years, salaries for cartographers have ranged from $25,810 to more than $69,320. Levels of compensation for cartographic work in the private sector have traditionally not been as lucrative as those in local government. Likewise, positions in state government have paid better than those in local government, while federal government positions have paid the best.

Where else could I look for more information about becoming a cartographer? See the US Department of Labor's Bureau of Labor Statistics Occupational Outlook

(continued)

Cartographer *(continued)*

Handbook (at www.bls.gov), visit the American Congress on Surveying and Mapping Web site (at www.acsm.net), or request information from the Imaging and Geospatial Information Society (at www.asprs.org).

If I decide to pursue a different career, what other fields are related to cartography? Geodetic surveying, geography, urban and regional planning, photogrammetry, and map editing.

plot plan are commonly shown with *contour lines*. Refer to **Figure 19-6**. *Elevation* refers to the height of the land above sea level. *Contour lines* are irregular lines spaced at intervals to show differences in elevation on the lot. Each contour line shows all points where the ground has a single elevation.

City Maps

City maps show street and lot layouts. They are similar to plat plans. See **Figure 19-7**.

Topographic Maps

Topographic maps provide information about the physical features and land characteristics in a specific area. Crops, streams,

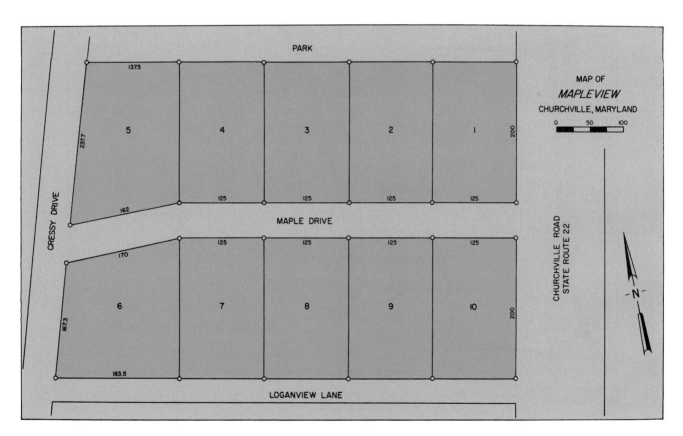

Figure 19-7   A map of a section of a city showing the layout of streets and lots.

airports, roads, bridges, buildings, and other features are shown. Contour lines are often included on topographic maps to show differences in elevation.

Special Maps

Special-purpose maps such as *location maps* and *vicinity maps* help you find your way around a specific area, **Figure 19-8** and **Figure 19-9**. Other special maps aid in determining travel time and calculating distances. These maps are used to plan trips when traveling on vacations or for business, **Figure 19-10**.

Special maps are often provided at historical sites to guide visitors to the various points of interest. See **Figure 19-11**.

Other types of maps include *real estate maps*. These show available home sites to potential buyers, **Figure 19-12**.

Map Symbols

Map symbols make it possible to include a large amount of information on a map. See **Figure 19-13**. Map symbols use a simple graphic to describe a location or activity. Each symbol is often an icon resembling the feature it represents.

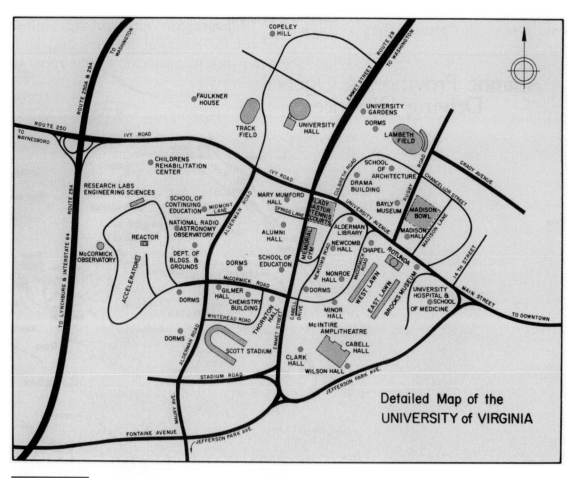

Figure 19-8 A location map showing the locations of the various facilities of the University of Virginia in Charlottesville, Va.

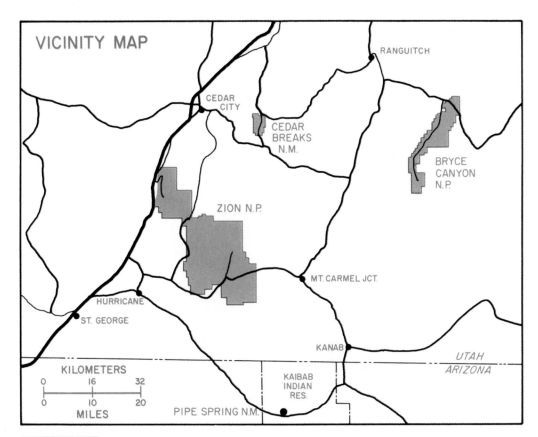

Figure 19-9 A vicinity map of Zion National Park in Utah.

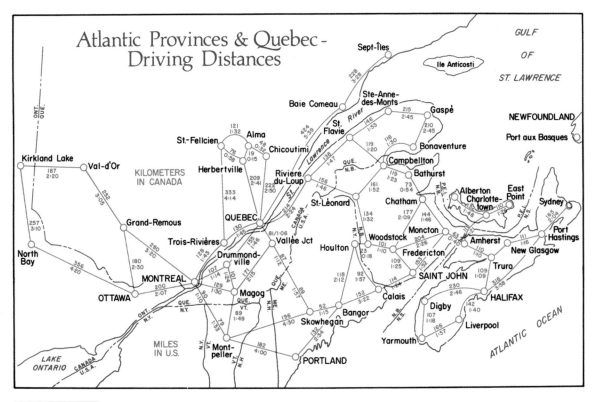

Figure 19-10 A regional map used to determine traveling distances between cities.

Figure 19-11 A map of historic Jamestown in Virginia posted at the National Park entrance. It shows the various points of interest.

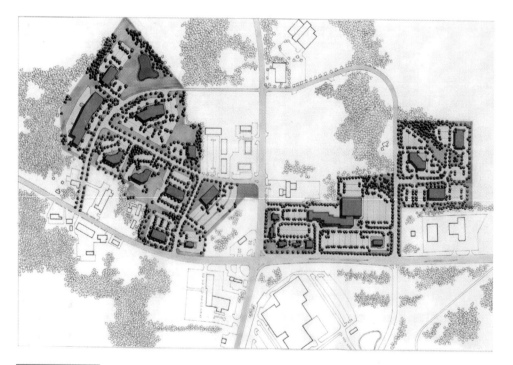

Figure 19-12 A map showing a planned housing area. It will help home buyers select sites for their new homes. (Clem Cizewski)

Figure 19-13 A few of the hundreds of types of symbols used on maps. How many can you identify?

CAD-Generated Mapping

Computer technology plays a major role in mapping applications. There are many types of software programs designed specifically for creating maps. These programs use geological, physical, and demographic data to generate maps automatically. Geographic information system (GIS) programs are used by utilities, transportation companies, and local and national governments to generate maps for community planning and economic development. In some cases, software programs import data directly from global positioning satellite (GPS) systems to create maps. The drawing data from the map is then used for analysis and planning.

CAD programs with map-drawing capability provide special design tools for developing 2D maps and 3D models. See **Figure 19-14**. There are tools for drawing contours, waterways, boundaries, and other graphic objects such as symbols and legends. Because CAD models consist of coordinates and objects defined with *spatial data*, modifications can be made quickly as physical conditions change. These capabilities make CAD mapping functions important to cartographers, landscape architects, and civil engineers.

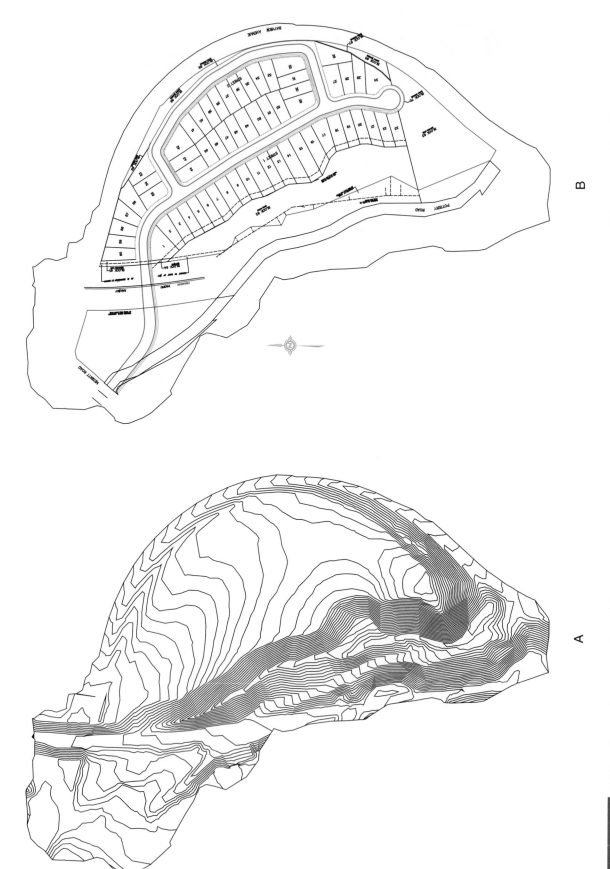

Figure 19-14 CAD software is commonly used to make drawings that show land characteristics such as physical conditions and terrain. A—A plot plan with contour lines showing changes in elevation for a parking lot design. B—The same land area shown with streets, lot lines, and boundary lines. (Autodesk, Inc.)

Test Your Knowledge

Please do not write in this book. Place your answers on another sheet of paper.

1. What is a *map*?
2. List at least three reasons why maps are used.
3. A professional mapmaker is called a(n) _____.
4. A surveyor uses an instrument called a(n) _____ to gather data to prepare a map.
5. What are *bearings*?
6. In metric surveying, the areas of the surveyed land are given in _____ instead of acres.
7. Why must maps be drawn to a scale less than full scale?
8. What is a *plot plan* and what does it show?
9. Differences in elevation on a drawing or map are often shown with _____ lines.
10. What is a *topographic map*?

Outside Activities

1. Obtain samples of special-purpose maps and make a bulletin board display.
2. Prepare a map showing the school grounds of your school. Label all athletic fields.
3. Make a plot plan of the property on which your home is located. Show the street and make sure that the north direction is facing "up."
4. Prepare a map of your neighborhood. Label all businesses, churches, and schools.
5. Draw a map showing the route you take in coming to school.
6. Obtain a road map of your state. Plot the shortest route between your hometown and the capital of your state. If you live in the capital city, plot the shortest route between it and the next largest city in the state.
7. Prepare a special map that shows the locations of the various schools in your school district.

Group Activities

1. Draw a map of the surrounding community. Have each student draw in the route traveled in coming to school.
2. If survey equipment is available, divide into groups and have each group survey the school grounds. Compare the results of each group. Also, compare the results with an actual survey of the grounds.

20 Graphs and Charts

OBJECTIVES

After studying this chapter,
you should be able to:

◆ Explain why graphs and charts
  are used.

◆ Describe the most commonly used
  graphs and charts.

◆ Create simple graphs and charts.

◆ List the advantages of using a
  computer to create graphs and charts.

DRAFTING VOCABULARY

Area graph
Bar graph
Circle graph
Composite bar
  graph
Curves
Flow chart
Horizontal bar
  graph
Key

Line graph
Organization chart
Pictorial bar graph
Pictorial chart
Pie chart
Pie graph
Vertical bar graph
100 percent bar
  graph

Industry and education have many uses for graphs and charts. A few of the more widely used types are described and shown in this chapter.

Graphs and charts explain information visually. They are used to show trends, make comparisons, and measure progress quickly without studying a mass of statistics and information.

Drafters are often asked to prepare graphs and charts. They take the statistical information and determine the most effective way to present the material. The end result should be interesting, accurate, and easily understood.

Graphs

There are three common types of graphs used to illustrate information. These are *line graphs*, *bar graphs*, and *circle* or *pie graphs*. These are discussed in the following sections.

Line Graphs

A *line graph* may be used to make comparisons between data, **Figure 20-1**. Typically, the graph is made up of two axes with plotted data to show a relationship between the data (such as changes in a function over a period of time). Lines that represent the plotted information are called *curves*. When only one curve appears on the graph, it should be drawn as a solid line.

When more than one curve is employed, each line should be clearly labeled and a *key* included with the graph to show what each curve represents.

A line graph may be used to show trends; that is, what has happened or what may happen. See **Figure 20-2**. In designing line graphs, be sure to use an appropriate scale for each of the axes.

Bar Graphs

Comparisons between quantities or conditions can also be made with a bar graph. A *bar graph* uses one or more rectangular bars to represent and compare data. Several different types of bar graphs are available to the graph maker.

A *horizontal bar graph* presents information in a horizontal format, **Figure 20-3**.

A *vertical bar graph* presents information in a vertical or upright format, **Figure 20-4**.

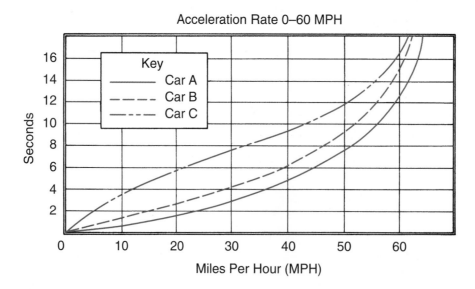

Figure 20-1 A line graph that compares the times needed by three different cars to reach 60 mph.

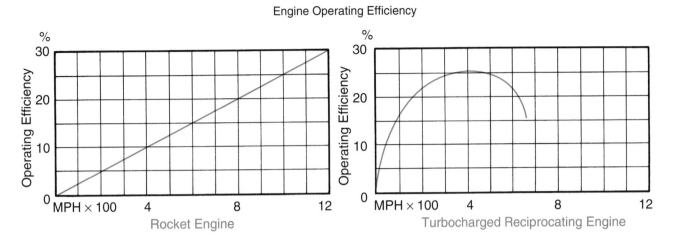

Figure 20-2   A line graph showing that a rocket engine's efficiency increases the faster it travels while a turbocharged internal combustion engine's efficiency drops off at high speed.

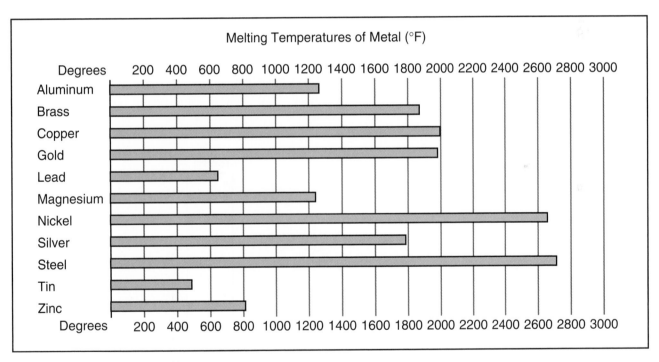

Figure 20-3   A horizontal bar graph used to indicate melting temperatures of metal.

A *composite bar graph* can be drawn in either a vertical or horizontal format, **Figure 20-5**. This type of graph compares information by combining the different data within bars.

A *100 percent bar graph* consists of a single rectangular bar, **Figure 20-6**. The information is broken down into percentages that add up to 100 percent.

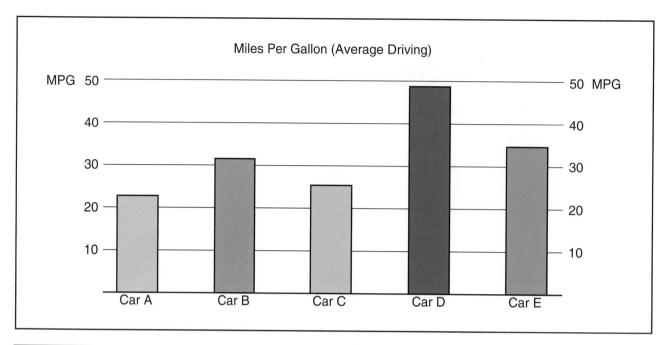

Figure 20-4 Car economy is shown in this vertical bar graph.

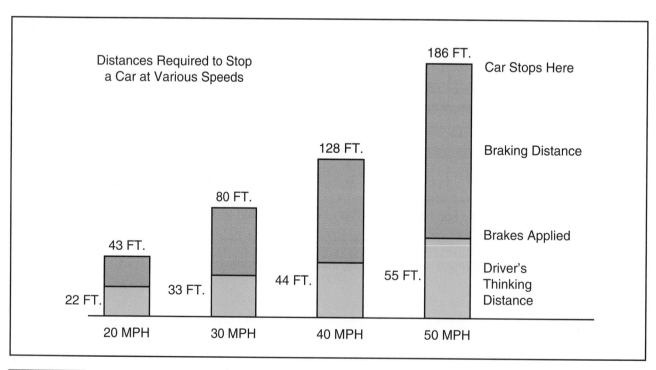

Figure 20-5 A composite bar graph showing stopping distances at various speeds.

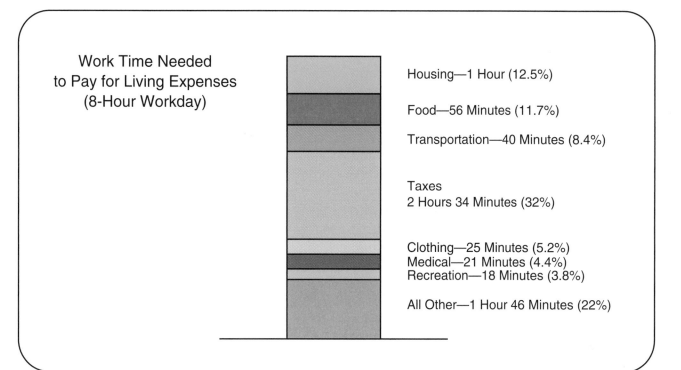

Work Time Needed
to Pay for Living Expenses
(8-Hour Workday)

Housing—1 Hour (12.5%)

Food—56 Minutes (11.7%)

Transportation—40 Minutes (8.4%)

Taxes
2 Hours 34 Minutes (32%)

Clothing—25 Minutes (5.2%)
Medical—21 Minutes (4.4%)
Recreation—18 Minutes (3.8%)

All Other—1 Hour 46 Minutes (22%)

Figure 20-6 A 100 percent bar graph indicating the amount of time a person works to pay for living expenses.

ACADEMIC LINK

Graphs and charts are very important communication tools. Used in the right manner, they can effectively convey messages that would normally be difficult to explain verbally. They often simplify the explanation of complex data or trends.

Pie charts are commonly used to break down comparisons between data based on percentages because the reader can instantly interpret the information. By focusing on the largest shaded or bordered area of the circle, the reader can quickly determine what component is associated with the greatest percentage or amount.

Organization charts help clarify the chain of command in a company because the most important members are listed above others. This makes it easy to determine which employees report to each manager. If you are a new employee at a company, this information can be very useful and would be much more difficult to learn through verbal communication.

Assume you are working for a company that is implementing a local area network (lan) computer system. By looking at a schematic diagram of the network, you can quickly determine the location of the server computer(s) and individual workstations. Likewise, electrical drawings are often presented as schematics because the components of a circuit and their functions can be easily identified.

A *pictorial bar graph* is a variation of the bar graph. It employs pictures or drawings to represent the information instead of bars, **Figure 20-7**. Pictorials tend to make a graph more interesting.

Circle (Pie) Graphs

A *circle graph* or *pie graph* is a segmented circle showing an entire unit divided into comparable parts. See **Figure 20-8**. This type of graph commonly breaks down data into percentages or fractional units of a whole. It is also known as a *pie chart* or an *area graph*.

Charts

Charts are similar to graphs. They provide another means to convey information

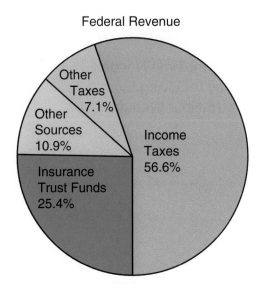

Figure 20-8 A circle graph breaks down information into percentages of a whole. It is also known as a pie graph, pie chart, or area graph.

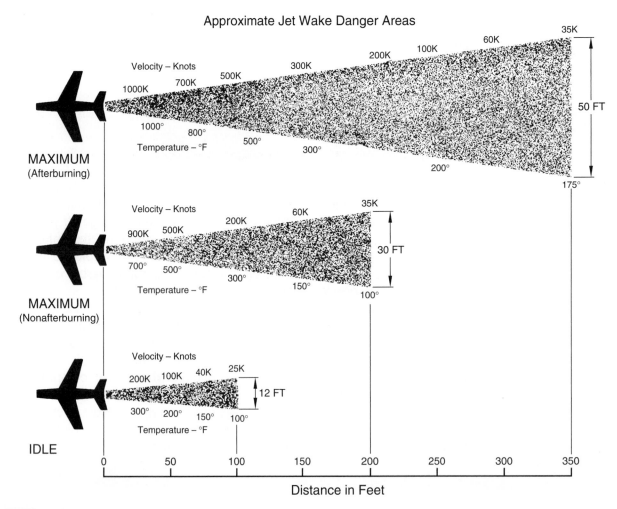

Figure 20-7 A pictorial bar graph showing jet wake danger areas in combination with the temperature and speed of exhaust gases.

CAREERS IN DRAFTING

Urban and Regional Planner

What would I do if I were to become an urban and regional planner? I would develop plans, both short-term and long-term, for the use of land. These plans would be aimed at the growth and revitalization of the community in which I work. This could be a rural, urban, or suburban community. I would also help local officials in making decisions about social, economic, and environmental problems. My job would be to make recommendations for the best use of the land for recreational, commercial, and residential purposes.

What would I need to know? I would need to be familiar with zoning codes, building codes, environmental regulations, pollution control, wetlands preservation, forest conservation, and landfill specifications and requirements. I would need to know how to make informed recommendations for public transportation systems, natural resource development, and changes in community infrastructure. I would need to know how to develop reports and communicate information to planning commissions, civic leaders, and the general public on community demographics, commercial and industrial growth, characteristics of populations, and employment and economic trends. I would need to be able to confer with land developers and public officials and (at times) act as mediator in community disputes. I also would need to be able to utilize technology to its full extent in order to carry out the requirements of my job.

Where would I work? I would work both indoors and outdoors. I would visit land sites to gather data that I would use in generating reports that would rationalize my recommendations. I would also work in an office generating my recommendations and plans for community changes, and I would attend meetings, forums, and public hearings with citizens' groups.

For whom would I work? There is about a 70% chance I would work for a rural, suburban or urban community as the city or community planner. In the private sector, I may work for an architectural or engineering firm or a management, scientific, or technical consulting service group or organization. In the government sector, I may work for a housing, transportation, or environmental protection agency.

What sort of education would I need? To gain employment by a government agency, I would most likely need to have a master's degree in urban and regional planning or a related program from an accredited institution. While in high school and college, I would need to take courses in making and reading blueprints, architecture, finance, health administration, economics, law, earth sciences, GIS (geographic information systems), management, marketing, public relations, and demography. There are many colleges and universities that offer advanced degrees in urban and regional planning.

What are the special fields relating to this career? Transportation, demography, housing, historic preservation, urban design, environmental science, regulatory development, and economic development. Planners in smaller venues are usually generalists and cannot specialize in any one field.

What are my chances of finding a job? Employment for urban and regional planners is expected to grow at an average rate. Expanding population and its needs (in regard to transportation, commercial and residential development, and the environment) will create future openings. Also, nongovernment initiatives

(continued)

Urban and Regional Planner *(continued)*

for redevelopment and historical preservation will provide opportunities as well. The number of openings in the private sector is expected to grow at a more rapid rate in comparison to government positions. Affluent and rapidly growing communities will also provide opportunities. If I have an accredited degree, I will have a distinct advantage in getting hired. With some background in marketing and public relations, I could end up working for a tourism bureau or a local chamber of commerce.

How much money could I expect to make? Yearly earnings for urban and regional planners vary from job to job. However, I could earn from less than $31,830 to more than $76,700 depending on whether I work in the private sector or for a government body. Private sector earnings in recent years have averaged $49,880, while government positions have averaged $48,950.

Where else could I look for more information about becoming an urban and regional planner? See the US Department of Labor's Bureau of Labor Statistics Occupational Outlook Handbook (at www.bls.gov). For information about accredited programs for urban and regional planning, contact the Association of Collegiate Schools of Planning (www.acsp.org). To learn about careers, salaries, and certification in urban and regional planning, contact the American Planning Association (www.planning.org).

If I decide to pursue a different career, what other fields are related to urban and regional planning? Geography, environmental engineering, landscape architecture, civil engineering, and architecture.

rapidly. There are several types of charts. The most common is the *organization chart*, **Figure 20-9**. It illustrates the order of responsibility in an organization by showing the relation of persons and/or positions in the organization.

A *pictorial chart* uses pictorial drawings or symbols to compare information. See **Figure 20-10**. In some cases, this type of chart is ideal for presenting comparisons in an interesting and easily understood manner.

A *flow chart* is used to show a sequence of steps or events in the order in which they occur. It is useful for showing the order of operations for how a product is manufactured and/or distributed, **Figure 20-11**.

Preparing Graphs and Charts

There are many variations of the graphs and charts presented in this chapter. It is up to the ingenuity and creativity of the person preparing the material to decide which type will be best for the job.

Do *not* start a graph or chart until *all* of the information has been gathered. A rough layout should be prepared first to determine what size and proportion will be best for the presentation.

Use color whenever possible to brighten your presentation and to make the information stand out. If you are creating the work

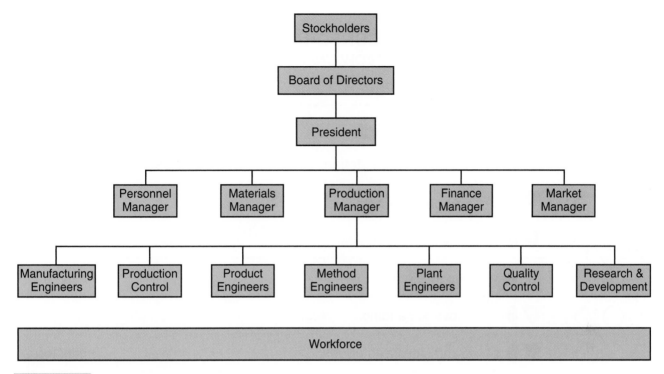

Figure 20-9   An organization chart.

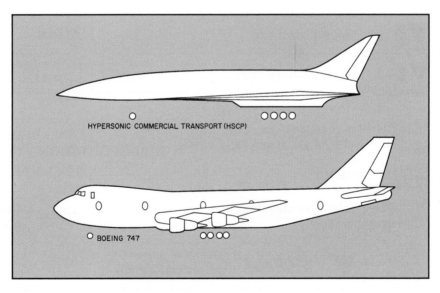

Figure 20-10   A pictorial chart showing how the size of a hypersonic commercial transport compares with present-day commercial aircraft. (Pratt & Whitney Aircraft)

XYZ CORPORATION
FLOW CHART

PRODUCT: #610 Birdhouse **PART:** Side

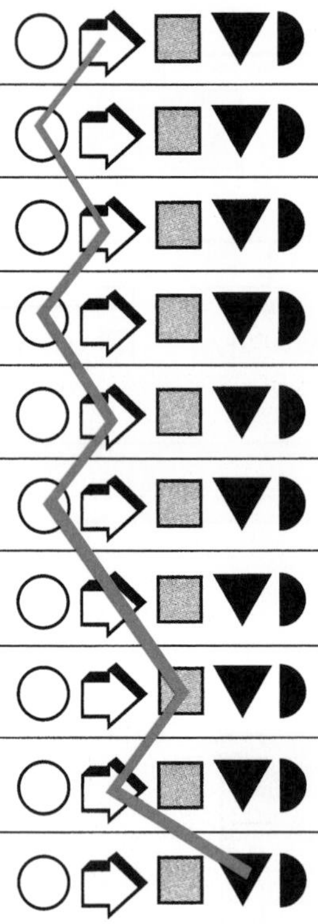

TASK	DESCRIPTION	DISTANCE	RATE
○⇨■▼◗	Move to cut-off station.	10 feet	
○⇨■▼◗	Cut part to length.		50 min/100
○⇨■▼◗	Move to ripping station.	12 feet	
○⇨■▼◗	Rip to width.		55 min/100
○⇨■▼◗	Move to sanding.		
○⇨■▼◗	Sand sides and edges.		95 min/100
○⇨■▼◗	Move to inspection.		
○⇨■▼◗	Inspect size and sanding.		20 min/100
○⇨■▼◗	Move to storage.	20 feet	
○⇨■▼◗	Store for assembly.		

SYMBOLS

○ **OPERATION** Object is changed in its chemical or physical makeup. It is assembled or disassembled.

⇨ **TRANSPORTATION** Object is moved from one place to another.

◗ **DELAY** Object is held awaiting the next operation.

■ **INSPECTION** Quality of the object is checked.

▼ **STORAGE** Object is placed in a protected location.

Figure 20-11 A flow chart showing the tasks involved in making the sides of a birdhouse in a mass-production operation.

manually, use predrawn graphics or symbols whenever possible to save time and make the graph or chart more interesting. There are many styles of transfer lettering, symbols, and figures available commercially, **Figure 20-12**.

Computer-Generated Graphs and Charts

Computer software programs have greatly reduced the amount of time spent preparing graphs and charts. There are many types of graphics programs, including CAD programs, that can be used to create bar graphs and other visual material. See **Figure 20-13**. With the proper program, any type of graph or chart can be developed in two-dimensional and three-dimensional form. Multicolor 2D and 3D presentations created electronically are widely used in industry, **Figure 20-14**.

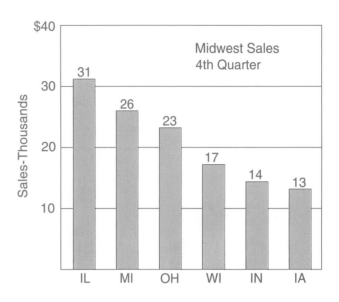

Figure 20-13   A computer-generated bar graph.

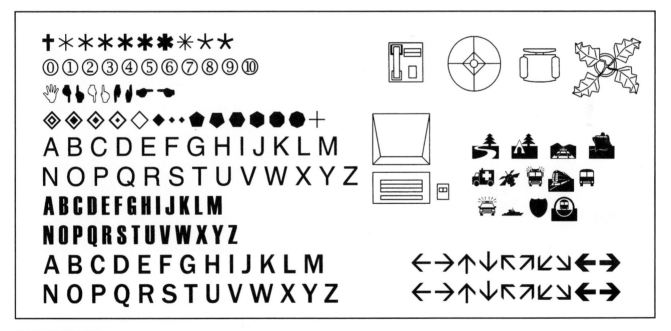

Figure 20-12   A sampling of transfer symbols and lettering. Predrawn symbols can be used to make professional-looking graphs and charts.

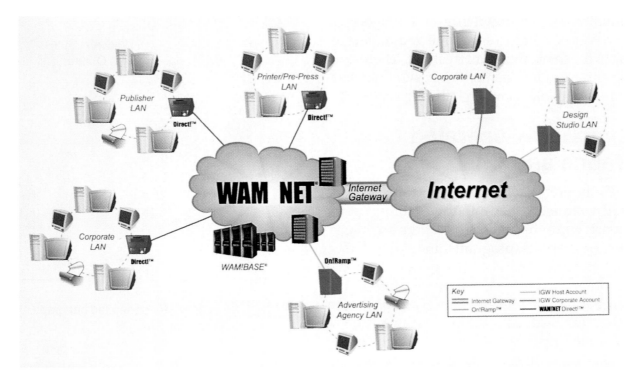

A

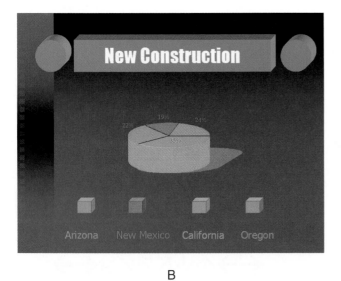

B

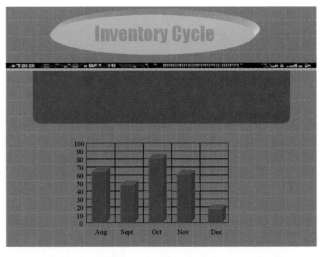

C

Figure 20-14 Computer-generated graphics are widely used by industry in sales, production planning, and evaluation. With electronically created presentations, the information can always be up-to-date. Can you identify the types of graphs shown? (A—WAM!NET, Inc.)

Test Your Knowledge

Please do not write in this book. Place your answers on another sheet of paper.

1. Why are graphs and charts used?
2. Lines that present plotted information on a graph are called _____.
3. Of what use is a key when more than one line is used on a graph?
4. Briefly describe each of the following types of graphs.
   A. Horizontal bar graph
   B. Vertical bar graph
   C. Composite bar graph
   D. 100 Percent bar graph
   E. Pictorial bar graph
5. A _____ graph is also known as an *area graph*.
6. Briefly describe each of the following types of charts.
   A. Flow chart
   B. Organization chart
   C. Pictorial chart

Outside Activities

1. Create a pie graph to illustrate how you spend your money.
2. Create a bar graph to show the approximate increase in horsepower in a particular make of automobile from 1940 to the present time. Use five-year steps.
3. Create a line graph showing how the price of the automobile chosen for Activity 2 has risen in the same periods of time.
4. Make a 100 percent bar graph showing a breakdown of the cost of a gallon of gasoline. Include the cost of the gasoline and state, federal, and local taxes.
5. Draw a pictorial bar graph showing how far an automobile will travel after the brakes are applied at 25 mph, 45 mph, 55 mph, and 65 mph.
6. Make an organization chart of your school's pupil personnel system.
7. Create a pictorial chart showing how the size of a particular make of automobile has increased or decreased in the past 20 years.
8. Make a pictorial graph showing the enrollment in each grade of your school. Let each symbol represent 25 students.
9. Design a flow chart showing how a simple product could be manufactured in the Industrial Technology lab.

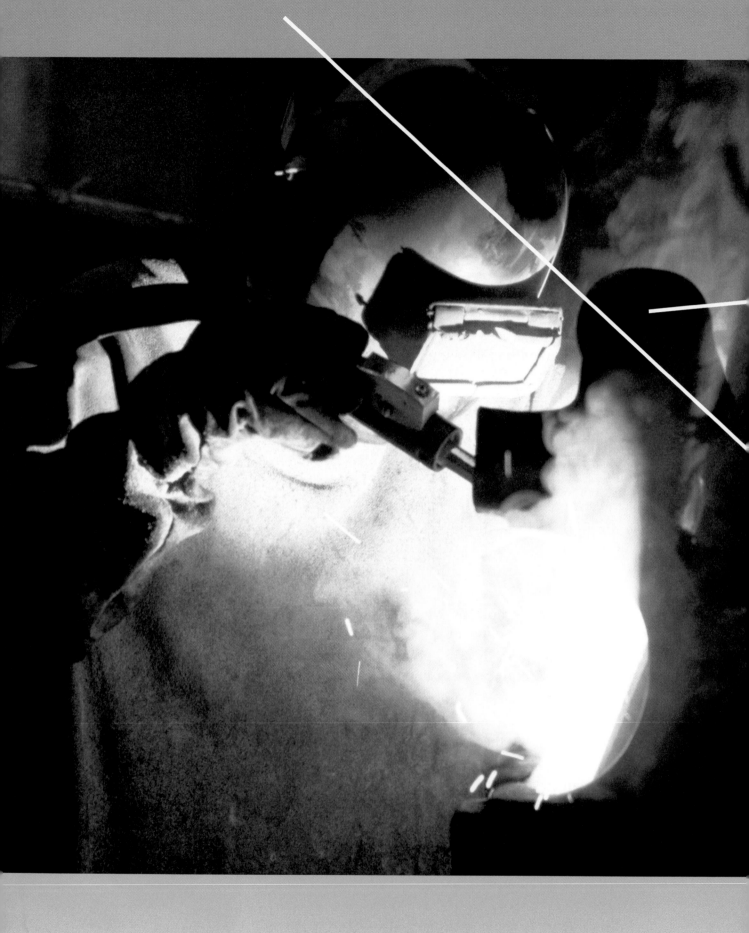

21 Welding Drafting

OBJECTIVES

After studying this chapter,
you should be able to:

◆ Describe the welding process.

◆ Explain why weld symbols are used on drawings.

◆ Identify what the various weld symbols indicate.

◆ Use weld symbols on drawings to provide exact weld specifications.

DRAFTING VOCABULARY

Arrow side   Weld symbol
Field weld   Welding
Other side   Welding symbol

Welding is a widely used industrial process for *fabricating* (joining) metal pieces. It is a method of joining by heating metals to a high temperature, which causes them to melt and fuse together. The high temperatures are generated by electricity (in arc welding, for example) or by burning gases (oxygen and acetylene, in most cases). Some common welding processes are shown in **Figure 21-1**.

In order to tell the welder what type of weld the engineer wants on the job, standard drawing symbols are used. Weld symbols developed and standardized by the American Welding Society (AWS) are shown in **Figure 21-2**. These symbols provide a means of giving complete and specific welding information on the drawing of the part to be welded.

A

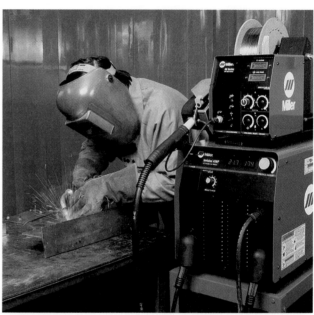

B

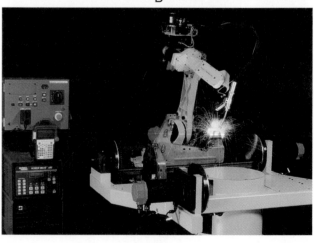

C

Figure 21-1 There are many welding processes. All welding processes join metals by heating them to a suitable temperature where they melt and fuse together. (A—Nederman, Inc.; B—Miller Electric Mfg. Co.; C—Fanuc Robotics North America, Inc.)

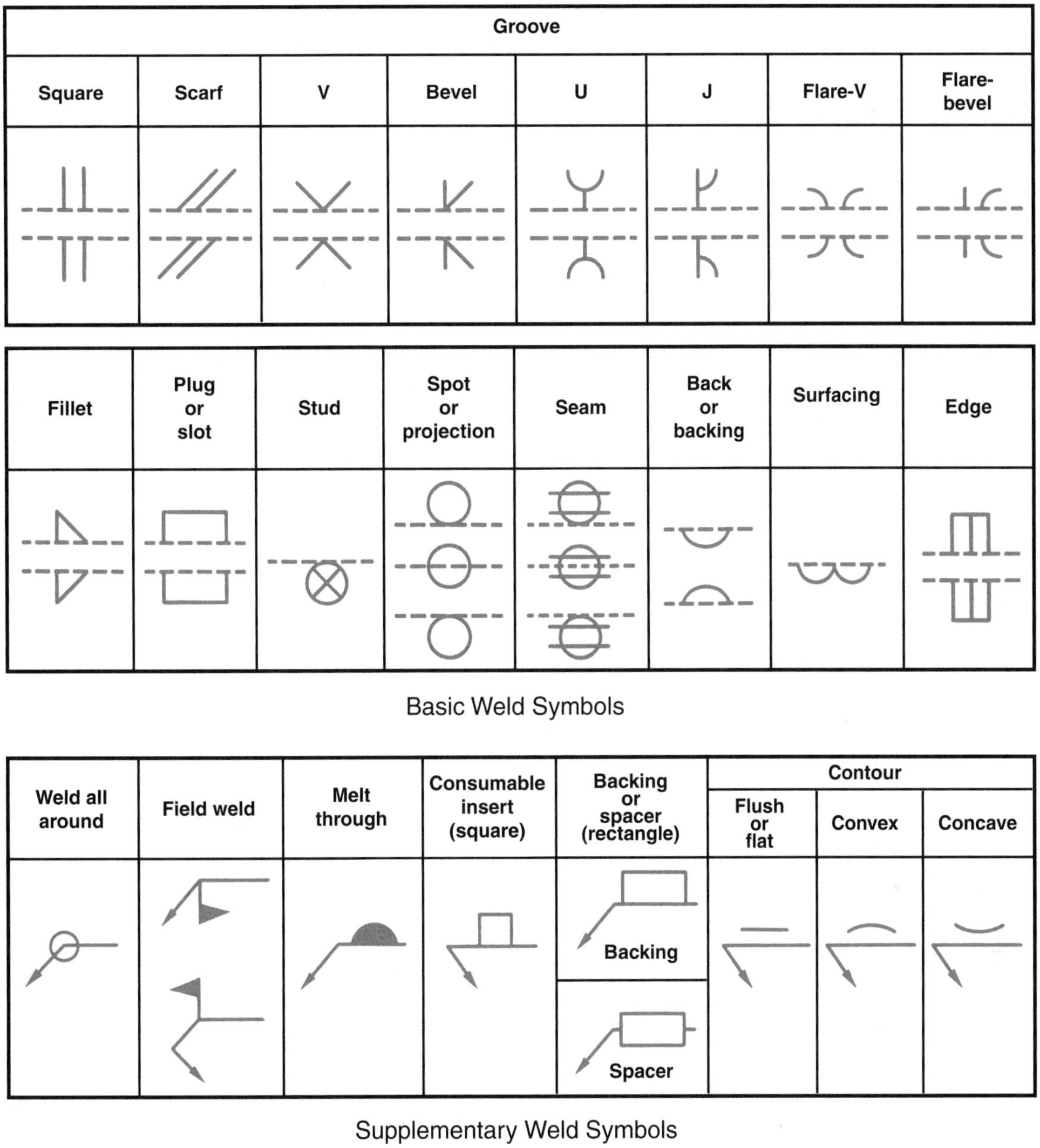

Groove							
Square	Scarf	V	Bevel	U	J	Flare-V	Flare-bevel

Fillet	Plug or slot	Stud	Spot or projection	Seam	Back or backing	Surfacing	Edge

Basic Weld Symbols

Weld all around	Field weld	Melt through	Consumable insert (square)	Backing or spacer (rectangle)	Contour		
					Flush or flat	Convex	Concave
				Backing / Spacer			

Supplementary Weld Symbols

Figure 21-2 Standard weld symbols.

A welding symbol placed on the drawing consists of several elements that represent specific information. See **Figure 21-3**. A welding symbol is made up of basic and supplementary weld symbols. The terms "welding symbol" and "weld symbol" have distinct meanings. A *welding symbol* is the symbol on the drawing. A *weld symbol* describes a specific type of weld. The weld symbol is included as part of the welding symbol on the drawing when used to identify a required weld. Refer to **Figure 21-2** for standard weld symbols.

Using Welding Symbols

Before welding symbols can be employed effectively, the drafter must be familiar with the various types of joints used in welding. These include butt, tee, lap, corner, and edge joints. See **Figure 21-4**.

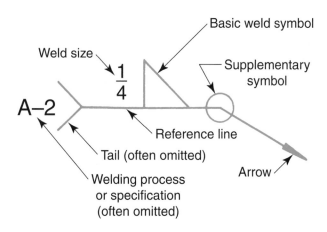

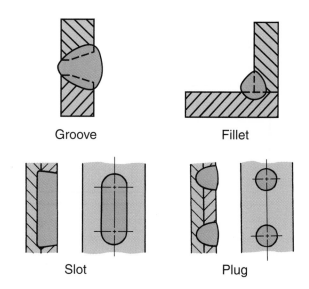

Figure 21-3 A welding symbol is made up of several elements. It gives complete information to the welder. This symbol indicates a fillet weld.

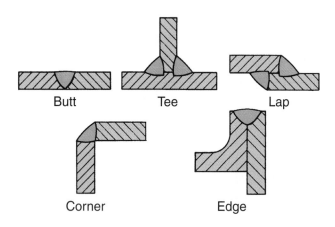

Figure 21-4 Basic joints used in welding.

Figure 21-5 Basic weld types.

A drafter should also be familiar with the basic types of welds that are applied to joints. The basic types of welds include groove, fillet, slot, and plug welds. See **Figure 21-5**. The type of weld used depends on the type of joint to be formed, the material, and the strength required under load.

Drawing Welding Symbols

When drawing welding symbols, the placement and orientation of elements provides important information. The location of the symbol arrow with respect to the joint specifies how the required weld is made. The side of the joint indicated by the arrow is considered to be the *arrow side*. The side

opposite the arrow side of the joint is considered to be the *other side* of the joint.

When the weld is to be made on the arrow side of the joint, the weld symbol is placed below the reference line *toward the reader*, **Figure 21-6**.

To specify a weld on the other side of the joint, the weld symbol is placed above the reference line *away from the reader*, **Figure 21-7**.

Welds on both sides of the joint are specified by placing the symbol on both sides of the reference line, **Figure 21-8**.

A weld that is made all of the way around the joint is specified by drawing a circle at the

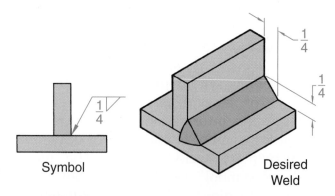

Figure 21-6 A welding symbol indicating that the weld is to be made on the *arrow side* of the joint. Note the weld symbol is below the reference line *toward* the reader.

point where the arrow is bent, **Figure 21-9**. A weld that is to be made on the job rather than in the shop is referred to as a *field weld*. Field welds are specified as shown in **Figure 21-10**.

The weld size is placed to the left of the symbol. The figure indicating the length of the weld is placed to the right of the symbol, **Figure 21-11**.

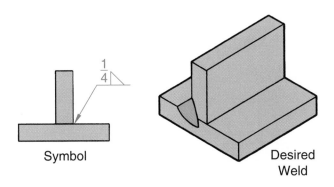

Symbol   Desired Weld

Figure 21-7 A welding symbol indicating that the weld is to be made on the *other side* of the joint.

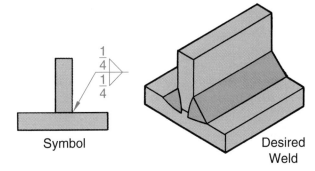

Symbol   Desired Weld

Figure 21-8 A welding symbol indicating that the weld is to be made on *both sides* of the joint.

ACADEMIC LINK

Welders must be able to identify metals and metal characteristics for several reasons. They must understand how metals behave under certain conditions (such as when heat is applied) in order to perform a suitable welding process. They must also understand the physical properties of important metals (such as steel) so that they can assess the strength or other requirements of their work. A basic understanding of chemistry and the compositions of different metals helps welders identify certain material properties (such as strength and hardness). Drafters should also be familiar with these concepts because welding drawings convey information about welding processes and weldments.

Steel is made from iron. Steel also contains carbon. Iron and carbon are both *elements* (pure substances). On the periodic table, iron is identified with the symbol Fe. Carbon is identified with the symbol C. It is important to know the carbon content of steel because different levels of carbon have an effect on the properties of steel. For example, low-carbon steels are not as strong as high-carbon steels, but they are easier to work in manufacturing. If the composition of a certain metal is not known, the welder may conduct different tests to identify the material.

Other metals can be added to carbon steel to produce desirable properties. The resulting material is an alloy (a mixture of two or more elements). Metals can be added to steel to produce strength and ductility (the ability to stretch or change in shape without breaking). Alloy steels are created from metals (elements) such as nickel, titanium, chromium, and manganese. Each metal is used for bringing about a specific property. Knowing the composition of metal and the effects of alloying elements gives welders the ability to determine the most suitable welding processes in a given situation.

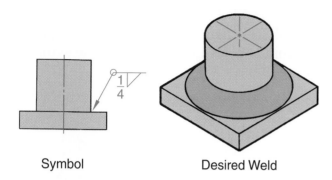

Symbol   Desired Weld

Figure 21-9 A welding symbol indicating that the weld is to be made *all around* the joint.

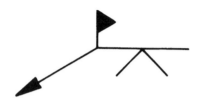

Figure 21-10 A field welding symbol. This indicates the welding is to be done on the job and not in the fabrication shop.

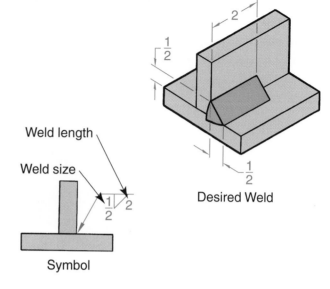

Weld length

Weld size

Symbol   Desired Weld

Figure 21-11 How weld size and length are indicated.

Planning Welding Drawings for Assemblies

Parts that are to be assembled by welding are usually composed of several pieces. See **Figure 21-12**. Since the individual pieces are seldom cut to size, welded, and machined in the same general shop area, several drawings are often required for welded assemblies. Each drawing provides information on a specific operation. Multiple drawings may also be required in cases where complex jobs must show a considerable amount of information and a single drawing is not sufficient. For simple jobs, all of the needed information can be included on a single drawing, **Figure 21-13**.

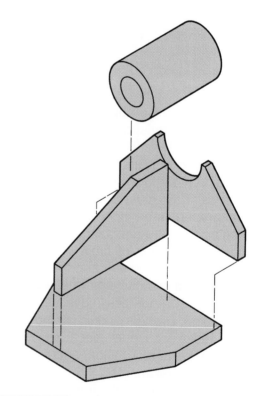

Figure 21-12 Welded assemblies composed of several different pieces require several drawings for manufacturing information.

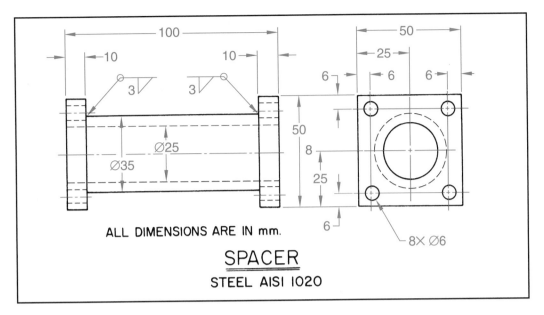

Figure 21-13 Information for cutting, welding, and machining is included on this drawing. Note the dimensions are in millimeters.

Test Your Knowledge

Please do not write in this book. Place your answers on another sheet of paper.

1. How are the high temperatures needed for welding generated?
2. Explain the purpose of weld symbols.
3. What is the difference between a *welding symbol* and a *weld symbol*?
4. List five basic types of joints used in welding.
5. Sketch the symbol for a fillet weld on the arrow side of the joint.
6. Sketch the symbol for a fillet weld on the other side of the joint.
7. Sketch the symbol for a fillet weld on both sides of the joint.
8. Sketch the symbol for a fillet weld all of the way around the joint.
9. What is a *field weld*?
10. Why are several different drawings needed for a job that is made up of several pieces and assembled by welding?

Outside Activities

1. Obtain samples of welded joints and mount them on a display board. Label the samples and add the proper drafting symbol to the display.

2. Visit a local industry that makes extensive use of welding and get samples of the work produced.

3. Invite a professional welder to the school shop to demonstrate the safe and proper way to weld using gas and electric processes.

4. Report for the class on the welding processes known as gas tungsten arc welding and gas metal arc welding.

Drawing Problems

Draw the problems shown on the following pages. Draw the orthographic views necessary to describe how to assemble and fabricate each object. Use the correct symbols for the welding information specified. Follow the directions in each problem and use the dimensions provided. Dimensions are in inches unless otherwise specified.

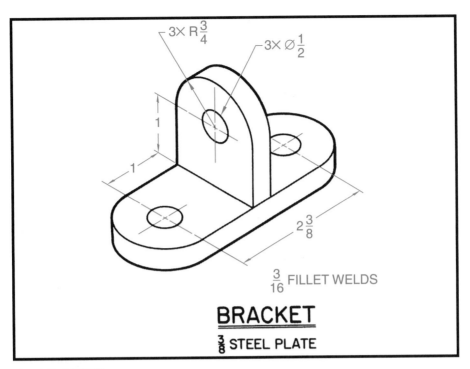

3× R$\frac{3}{4}$

3× Ø$\frac{1}{2}$

1

1

2$\frac{3}{8}$

$\frac{3}{16}$ FILLET WELDS

BRACKET

$\frac{3}{8}$ STEEL PLATE

Problem 21-1   **Bracket.** Welds are to be made on both sides of the joint.

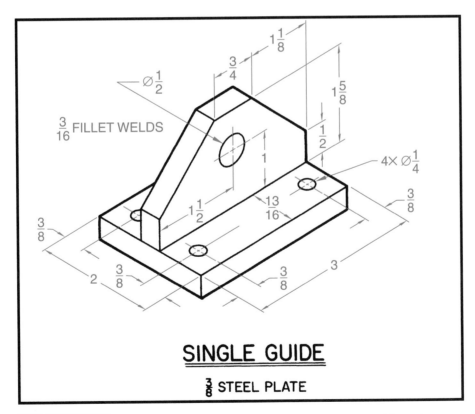

Ø$\frac{1}{2}$

$\frac{3}{4}$

1$\frac{1}{8}$

1$\frac{5}{8}$

1$\frac{1}{2}$

$\frac{3}{16}$ FILLET WELDS

4× Ø$\frac{1}{4}$

1

$\frac{3}{8}$

1$\frac{1}{2}$

13$\frac{1}{16}$

$\frac{3}{8}$

2

$\frac{3}{8}$

$\frac{3}{8}$

3

SINGLE GUIDE

$\frac{3}{8}$ STEEL PLATE

Problem 21-2   **Single Guide.** Welds are to be made on both sides of the joint.

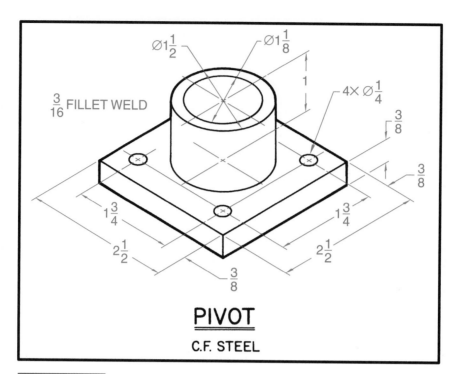

PIVOT
C.F. STEEL

Problem 21-3 **Pivot.** The weld is to be made all around the joint.

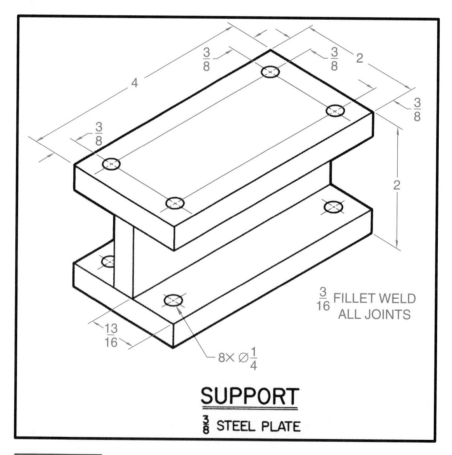

SUPPORT
3/8 STEEL PLATE

Problem 21-4 **Support.** Welds are to be made on both sides of each joint.

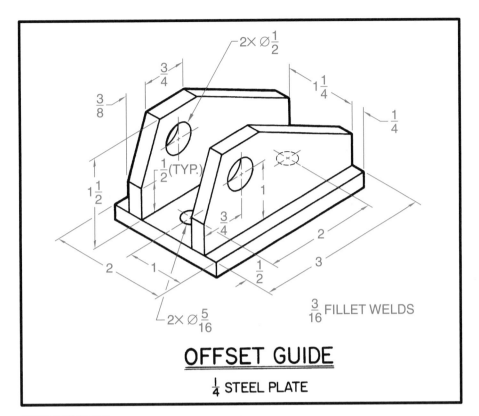

OFFSET GUIDE

$\frac{1}{4}$ STEEL PLATE

Problem 21-5 **Offset Guide.** Welds are to be made on both sides of each vertical piece.

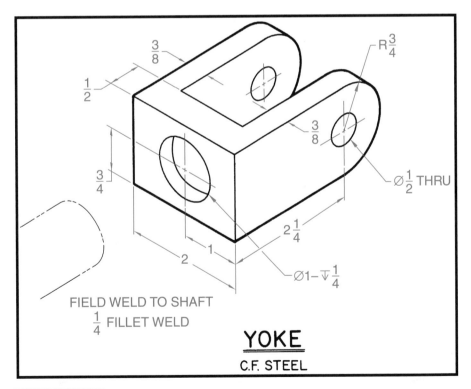

YOKE

C.F. STEEL

Problem 21-6 **Yoke.** The part is to be welded to a 1″ diameter shaft at the job site.

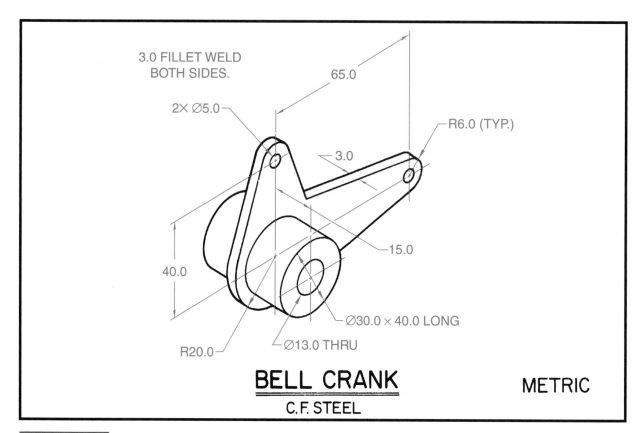

3.0 FILLET WELD
BOTH SIDES.

65.0

2X Ø5.0

R6.0 (TYP.)

3.0

40.0

15.0

Ø30.0 × 40.0 LONG

R20.0

Ø13.0 THRU

BELL CRANK

C.F. STEEL

METRIC

Problem 21-7   **Bell Crank.** A 3 mm weld is to be made on both sides of the joint.

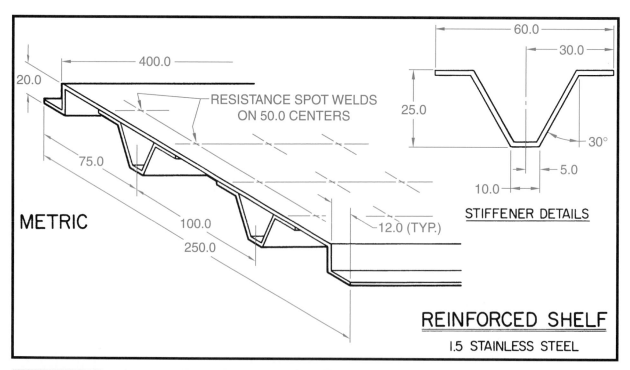

400.0

20.0

RESISTANCE SPOT WELDS
ON 50.0 CENTERS

75.0

METRIC

100.0

250.0

12.0 (TYP.)

60.0

30.0

25.0

30°

5.0

10.0

STIFFENER DETAILS

REINFORCED SHELF

1.5 STAINLESS STEEL

Problem 21-8   **Reinforced Shelf.** Stiffeners are spot welded to the shelf.

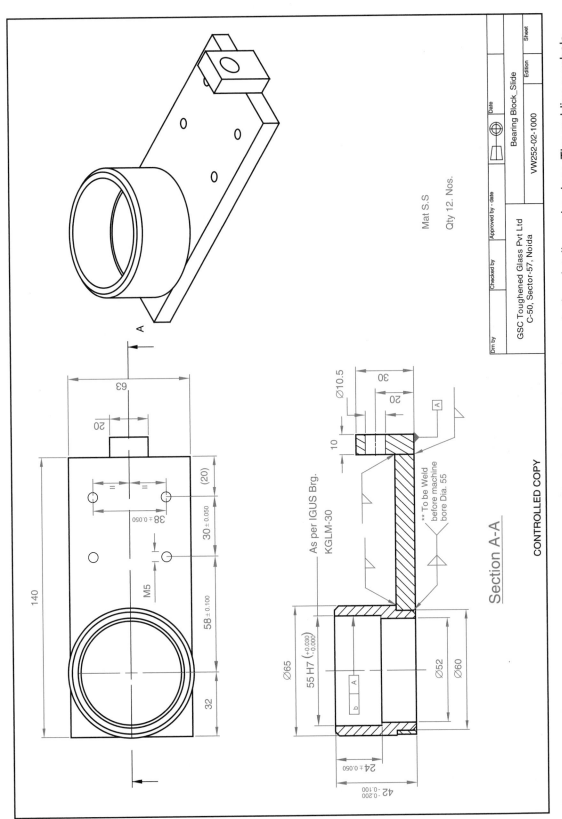

Section A-A

CONTROLLED COPY

Mat S.S

Qty 12. Nos.

As per IGUS Brg.
KGLM-30

** To be Weld
before machine
bore Dia. 55

GSC Toughened Glass Pvt Ltd
C-50, Sector-57, Noida

Bearing Block_Slide

VW252-02-1000

Dim by | Checked by | Approved by - date | Date

Edition | Sheet

CAD software programs simplify the process of placing welding symbols, notes, and other details on drawings. The welding symbols shown can be modified for use from one or more predrawn symbols. Can you identify the types of welds that this part will require? (Autodesk, Inc.)

22 Fasteners

Manufactured products are assembled by many different kinds of fasteners, **Figure 22-1**. A *fastener* is a device used to hold two or more parts together. Fasteners include screws, nuts and bolts, rivets, nails, etc. Since fasteners are so important to industry, drafters, engineers, and designers must be familiar with them. They must know what types to use for a particular application, and they must know how to draw them.

Threaded Fasteners

There are many applications that make use of threaded fasteners. Threaded fasteners are employed to:
- Make adjustments between parts.
- Transmit motion.
- Assemble parts.
- Apply pressure.
- Make measurements.

How many examples of each application can you name?

Threaded fasteners employ the wedging action of the screw thread to hold items together. They are found extensively in manufactured products, **Figure 22-2**. Threaded fasteners vary in cost. For products such as large aircraft, they range up to several thousand dollars apiece for special bolts that attach

Figure 22-2 Many types of fasteners and adhesives are used in manufacturing boats. When selecting fasteners, what important factor had to be considered? (Champion Spark Plug Co.)

the wings to the fuselage. By comparison, a small machine screw costs a fraction of a penny. (One auto manufacturer uses more than 11,000 fasteners of various types and sizes.)

Standard specifications for threads fall under two classification systems—*inch-based threads* and *metric threads*. Standards for inch-based and metric threads have been developed by the American Society of Mechanical Engineers (ASME). Industry must be familiar with both systems. In each system, threaded fasteners are classified under **screw-thread series**. Inch-based threaded fasteners are classified under the **Unified Inch Screw Thread Series** system. The thread designations include

Figure 22-1 A few of the thousands of different types and sizes of fasteners used by industry. How many can you identify?

coarse and *fine* threads, **Figure 22-3**. Coarse threads are identified as ***Unified National Coarse (UNC)*** threads. Fine threads are identified as ***Unified National Fine (UNF)*** threads. As shown in **Figure 22-3**, fine thread has more threads per inch than coarse thread.

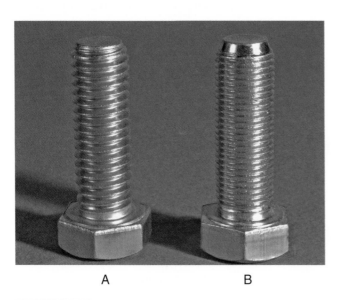

Figure 22-3 It is easy to tell the difference between fasteners in the UNC (coarse thread) and UNF (fine thread) series. The bolts have the same diameter and are the same length. A—Coarse threads. B—Fine threads.

Metric-based threaded fasteners are classified under the ***Metric Screw Thread Series*** system. Like inch-based fasteners, metric fasteners are also made in coarse and fine threads.

Inch-based and metric-based screw threads have the same basic *profile* (shape). The parts of a screw thread are shown in **Figure 22-4**. This figure shows the common terms used to describe screw threads. The basic shape of a screw thread is formed by a point curve that wraps around a cylinder in a spiral. This shape is known as a ***helix***. The ***helix angle*** is the angle formed by the incline of the helix and a line perpendicular to the vertical axis of the screw thread. The ***pitch*** of a screw thread is defined as the distance from a point on one thread to a corresponding point on the next thread. For inch-based screw threads, the pitch is measured in relation to the number of threads per inch. It is expressed using the formula *1/number of threads per inch*. For metric-based screw threads, the pitch is indicated as the actual pitch measurement and is measured in millimeters. The ***length of engagement*** is the length of the threads engaged in the nut when a screw and nut are mated together.

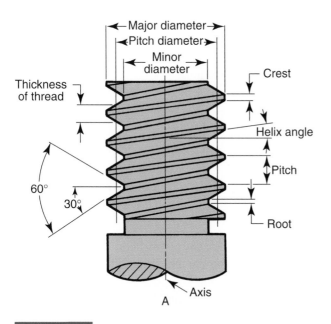

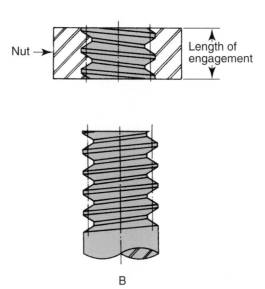

Figure 22-4 Inch-based and metric-based screw threads have the same shape. A—The basic parts of a screw thread. B—Nuts are machined to mate with specific types and sizes of screw thread.

More than 2 million different kinds, shapes, and sizes of inch-based threaded fasteners are made. Added to this number are the many types of metric-based threaded fasteners. Both inch-based and metric-based fasteners will have to be kept in inventory for many, many years. Inch-based and metric-based wrenches will also be needed.

A comparison of metric and inch-based coarse thread sizes is shown in **Figure 22-5**. While some inch-based and metric-based threaded fasteners may appear to be the same size, *they are not interchangeable*. A metric-based bolt cannot be used with an inch-based nut that appears to have the same thread size as the bolt.

A user may have trouble telling a metric bolt from a similar inch-based fastener. Different methods to identify metric fasteners have been proposed. Two possible designations for metric fasteners are shown in **Figure 22-6**.

Drawing Threads

It is very time-consuming to show threads on a drawing as they would actually appear. For this reason, there are alternate methods for representing threads. These include the *schematic* and *simplified* representations. Approved methods of thread representation are shown in **Figure 22-7**.

Metric Thread Series	UNC Thread Series
	1-8UNC
M24 x 3	7/8-9UNC
M20 x 2.5	3/4-10UNC
M16 x 2	5/8-11UNC
M14 x 2	9/16-12UNC
	1/2-13UNC
M12 x 1.75	7/16-14UNC
M10 x 1.5	3/8-16UNC
M8 x 1.25	5/16-18UNC
M6.3 x 1	1/4-20UNC
	12-24UNC
M5 x 0.8	10-24UNC
M4 x 0.7	8-32UNC
M3.5 x 0.6	6-32UNC
	5-40UNC
M3 x 0.5	4-40UNC
M2.5 x 0.45	3-48UNC
	2-56UNC
M2 x 0.4	

Figure 22-5 A comparison of metric and inch-based coarse thread sizes. Even though several of them seem to be the same size, they are not interchangeable.

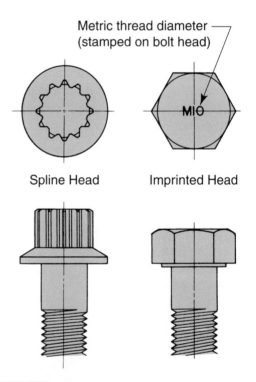

Metric thread diameter (stamped on bolt head)

Spline Head   Imprinted Head

Figure 22-6 Much study has been done to devise an easy way to identify metric-based fasteners from inch-based fasteners. Two possible methods are the 12-element spline head and the imprinted hexagonal head (where the thread diameter is stamped on the head).

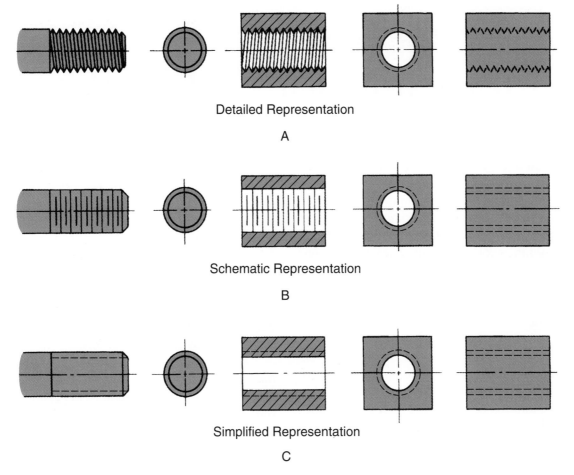

Detailed Representation

A

Schematic Representation

B

Simplified Representation

C

Figure 22-7 Approved ways of representing threads on drawings.

The *detailed representation*, illustrated in **Figure 22-7A**, looks like the actual screw thread. It is sometimes employed in cases where confusion might result when using the simplified representation.

The *schematic representation* of a screw thread, **Figure 22-7B**, is easier to draw. It uses schematic symbols to represent the threads. This method should not be used for hidden threads or sections of external threads.

The *simplified representation* of a screw thread, **Figure 22-7C**, is a fast and easy method used to draw threads. For this reason, it is widely used in drafting. A simplified representation uses regular object and hidden lines to show the thread details. It should be avoided where there is a possibility of confusing the representation with other details on a drawing.

The best method should be chosen when drawing threads. Avoid mixing the various methods on the same drawing.

Regardless of which thread representation the drafter decides to draw, the thread size and series must be shown on the drawing. The thread size should include the major diameter, number of threads per inch or pitch, and class of fit or tolerance. The *class of fit* is a thread designation that determines the allowable difference in size from the actual size. A *tolerance* is an allowable variance from a specific size or position. There are different conventions used for specifying the class of fit and tolerance for screw threads.

Other information, such as whether the thread is external or internal, is also given in thread notes. External thread is identified with the letter *A*. Internal thread is identified

CAREERS IN DRAFTING

Woodworker

What would I do if I were to become a woodworker? I would work in an industry that produces or uses wood. I would be involved in the manufacturing of products such as doors, windows, building construction members, furniture, kitchen cabinets, musical instruments, sporting goods, toys, or numerous other wooden products.

What would I need to know? I would have to know how to make and read plans for the products that I would be making. I would also have to be familiar with standard woodworking hand tools and machines—as well as manual, machine, and computer-assisted procedures, adhesives and finishing materials, fasteners, and all woodworking-related products.

Where would I work? I could work in a saw mill or plywood mill producing wood products. I could also work in a plant producing furniture, kitchen cabinets, musical instruments, sporting goods, toys, or other wood products. Depending on my skill level, I could also work in a custom woodworking shop.

For whom would I work? I could work for a furniture and fixture manufacturer, a wood product manufacturer, a wholesale or retail lumber company, a furniture store, a furniture repair and reupholstery shop, a construction company, a custom woodworking shop, or for myself.

What sort of education would I need? Like many woodworkers, I could receive training on the job by learning skills and procedures from experienced workers. I could also become a woodworker by receiving training through a vocational education program in high school or by acquiring a bachelor's degree at a college or university.

What are the special fields relating to this career? Woodworking specialists include skilled workers such as sawing machine operators and tenders, woodworking machine operators and tenders, cabinetmakers, bench carpenters, modelmakers, patternmakers, upholsterers, and furniture finishers.

What are my chances of finding a job? My chances of finding work as a woodworker in the next several years are good. This is due primarily to anticipated job openings occurring because of long-time experienced workers retiring or leaving the labor force.

How much money could I expect to make? The median hourly wage for cabinetmakers and bench carpenters in recent years was $11.54. Per-hour wage rates ranged from $7.70 to $18.11 and up. My chances of a higher wage rate will be enhanced slightly if I work in furniture and cabinet manufacturing.

Where else could I look for more information about becoming a woodworker? See the US Department of Labor's Bureau of Labor Statistics Occupational Outlook Handbook (at www.bls.gov) or request information from local furniture manufacturers, sawmills or planing mills, cabinetmaking or millwork firms, lumber dealers, or the nearest office of the state employment service.

If I decide to pursue a different career, what other fields are related to woodworking? Woodworkers work with wood, follow blueprints and drawings, and use machines to shape and form raw materials into a final product. Other professionals who perform similar tasks include sheet metal workers, computer-control programmers and operators, machinists, and tool and die makers.

with the letter *B*. See **Figure 22-8** for accepted ways to present thread information.

Threads are understood to be right-hand threads. Left-hand threads are represented by the letters *LH* following the class of fit (for inch-based thread) or thread tolerance (for metric-based thread).

Types of Threaded Fasteners

The fasteners described in this chapter can usually be found in the school laboratory, a typical hardware store, or an automotive parts supply store. The majority of them are made of steel, brass, or aluminum. Special applications may require them to be made of other materials.

Machine Screws

Machine screws are available with single-slotted, cross-slotted (Phillips), and hexagonal heads, and round, flat, fillister, pan, truss, and oval head shapes, **Figure 22-9**. Nuts are not furnished with machine screws and must

Figure 22-9 A few of the many styles of machine screws available, classified by head type. A—Fillister. B—Round. C—Flat. D—Socket. E—Pan. F—Truss.

be purchased separately (they are available in square and hexagonal shapes). Machine screws have many applications in general assembly work where screws less than 1/4″ (6.0 mm) in diameter are needed. Machine screws are available in many sizes starting as small as No. 0 80UNC (0.06″ diameter) for inch-based applications and 1.4 × 0.3 mm for metric-based applications.

Machine Bolts

Machine bolts are manufactured with hexagonal and square heads, **Figure 22-10**.

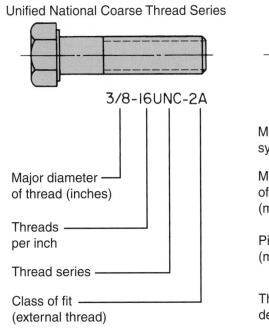

Unified National Coarse Thread Series

3/8–16UNC–2A

Major diameter of thread (inches)

Threads per inch

Thread series

Class of fit (external thread)

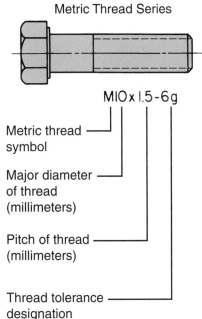

Metric Thread Series

M10 × 1.5–6g

Metric thread symbol

Major diameter of thread (millimeters)

Pitch of thread (millimeters)

Thread tolerance designation

Figure 22-8 How thread notes are given for inch-based and metric-based thread.

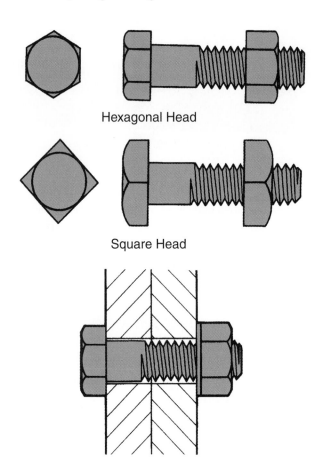

Hexagonal Head

Square Head

Figure 22-10 Machine bolts.

They are used to assemble machinery and other items that do not require close-tolerance fasteners, which are more expensive. Machine bolts are secured by tightening the matching nut.

Cap Screws

Cap screws are used when the assembly requires a stronger, more precise fastener with a fine finish, **Figure 22-11**. Cap screws are primarily employed to bolt two pieces or sections together. The screw passes through a *clearance hole* in one part and screws into a threaded hole in the other part, **Figure 22-12**. Machine tools are usually assembled with cap screws.

Set Screws

Set screws prevent slippage of pulleys and gears on shafts, **Figure 22-13**. They are available in many different head types and point styles. Set screws are made of heat-treated steel to make them stronger and less likely to fail.

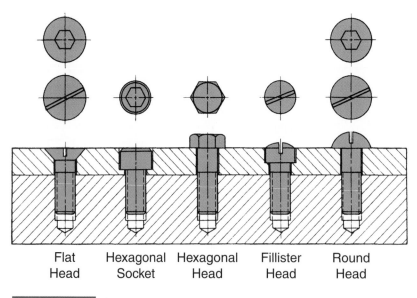

| Flat Head | Hexagonal Socket | Hexagonal Head | Fillister Head | Round Head |

Figure 22-11 Common types of cap screws.

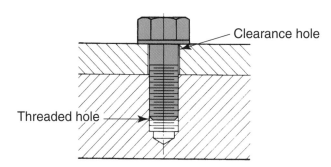

Figure 22-12 How a cap screw works. What type of thread representation is used on this drawing?

Figure 22-13 A typical set screw application.

Stud Bolts

Stud bolts are threaded on both ends. One end is threaded into a tapped (threaded) hole. The piece to be clamped is fitted over the stud bolt and the nut screwed on to clamp the two sections tightly together. See **Figure 22-14**.

Nuts

Nuts are screwed down on bolts or screws to tighten or hold together the sections through which the fastener passes. There are many types of nuts, including square, semifinished, slotted, acorn, and wing. See **Figure 22-15**.

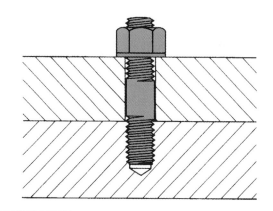

Figure 22-14 A stud bolt. What type of thread representation is used on this drawing?

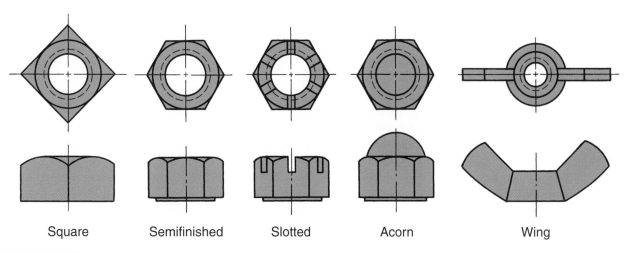

Square   Semifinished   Slotted   Acorn   Wing

Figure 22-15 Common types of nuts.

A square nut is typically used with a machine bolt with the same head shape to provide a uniform bearing surface. Semi-finished nuts have a machined bearing surface to provide a truer surface for a washer. Slotted nuts are used to prevent movement in parts. After the nut has been tightened, a cotter pin is fitted in one set of slots and through a hole in the bolt shaft. The cotter pin prevents the bolt from turning loose. Acorn nuts are applied when the appearance is important or exposed sharp edges on the bolt must be avoided. Wing nuts provide for rapid tightening without the use of a wrench.

Washers

Washers are used with nuts and bolts to distribute the clamping pressure over a larger area. They also prevent the fastener from marring the work surface when the nut is tightened. Many types are manufactured, **Figure 22-16**.

Nonthreaded Fasteners

Nonthreaded fasteners comprise a large group of holding devices. They include rivets, pins, and keys. These are discussed in the following sections.

Rivets

Permanent assemblies are made with *rivets*, **Figure 22-17**. These are headed pins used to hold two or more sections of material together. In riveting, holes are drilled through the material to be riveted. The rivet shank passes through the hole. After aligning the sections, the plain end of the rivet is upset or headed by hammering to form a second head. The parts are drawn together by the heading operation.

Blind rivets are mechanical fasteners that are used for applications where the joint is accessible from one side only. They require special tools to put them in place, **Figure 22-18**. Blind rivet types are shown in **Figure 22-19**.

Cotter Pins

Cotter pins are used to prevent movement in fastened parts, **Figure 22-20**. The pin is fitted into a hole drilled crosswise in a shaft. The ends are bent over after assembly to prevent parts from slipping or turning off the shaft.

A   B   C   D   E   F

Figure 22-16 Washer types. A—Plain (flat). B—Split lock. C—External lock. D—Internal lock. E—Internal-external (used when the mounting holes are oversize). F—Countersunk.

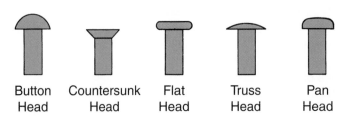

Button Head   Countersunk Head   Flat Head   Truss Head   Pan Head

Figure 22-17 Rivet types.

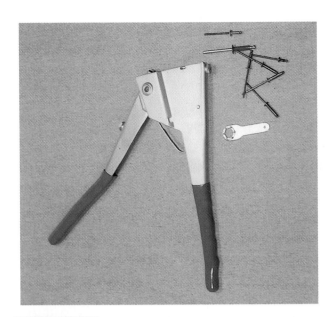

Figure 22-18 A riveting tool used to insert one type of blind rivet.

Figure 22-20 Cotter pin.

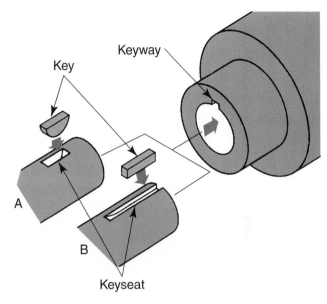

Figure 22-21 Keys are used to prevent a gear, wheel, or pulley from rotating on a shaft. A—Woodruff key assembly. The key is half-round in shape. B—Rectangular key assembly.

Keys, Keyways, and Keyseats

A *key* is a small piece of metal partially fitted into a shaft and partially into a hub to prevent rotation of a gear, wheel, or pulley on the shaft, **Figure 22-21**. The *keyway* is the slot cut in the hub of the mating part. The *keyseat* is the slot cut in the end of the shaft. It mates with the keyway and accepts half the thickness of the key when the key is inserted. Different types of keys are used for special applications. A Woodruff key and a rectangular key are shown in **Figure 22-21**.

Fasteners for Wood

Threaded and nonthreaded fasteners are used to assemble products made from wood. The most common fasteners used for wood are nails and screws.

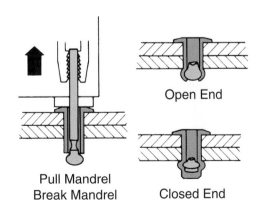

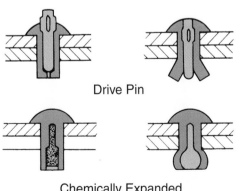

Figure 22-19 Types of blind rivets.

Nails

Nails provide an easy way to fasten wood pieces together, **Figure 22-22**. They are usually made of mild steel. For exterior work, nails made from mild steel are *galvanized* (coated with zinc) so they will not rust. Nail size is given as "penny" size and is abbreviated with the lowercase letter *d*.

Wood Screws

Wood screws are manufactured from many kinds of metal. Screw size is indicated by the shank diameter and length. The length

Figure 22-22 The building trades industry uses vast quantities of nails. More than a thousand different kinds are available.

is measured in different ways depending on the style of screw, **Figure 22-23**. Standard wood screws are available in lengths from 1/4″ to 5″ (6.5 mm to 125.0 mm).

How to Draw Bolts and Nuts

Bolts and nuts are drawn manually by projecting views. A top or front view is drawn to show the head of the bolt. A front or side view is drawn to show the diameter and length of the bolt. Normally, bolts and nuts are not drawn manually unless the drawing must show specific details. Templates for drawing bolt heads and nuts are available and make the job faster and easier.

Hexagonal and square head bolts are drawn as shown in **Figure 22-24**. The dimensions given are approximations, but they are acceptable for most drafting applications. The following information is needed to draw a bolt and nut:

- Bolt diameter
- Bolt length
- Type of bolt head and/or nut

As shown in **Figure 22-24**, the bolt head and nut dimensions are drawn in relation

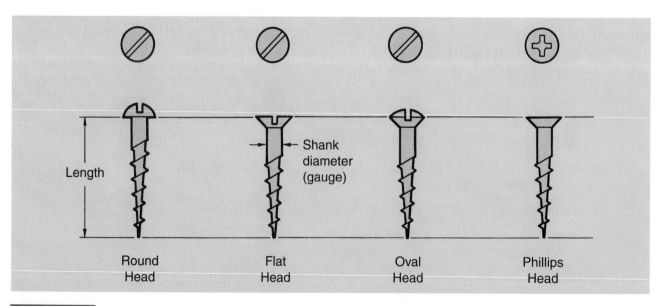

Figure 22-23 Common types of wood screws. Note how they are measured.

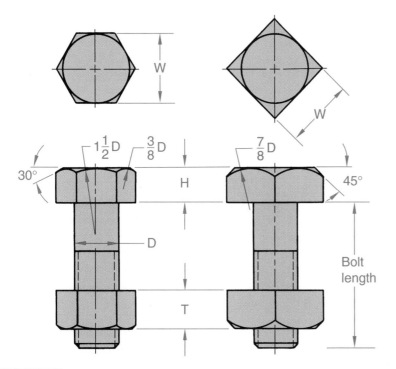

Bolt and Nut Formulas	
Width of bolt head (W)	$W = 1\frac{1}{2}D$
Height of bolt head (H)	$H = \frac{3}{4}D$
Thickness of nut (T)	$T = \frac{7}{8}D$
Diameter $= D$	

Figure 22-24   Approximate dimensions and formulas used to draw hexagonal and square bolts and nuts.

to the bolt diameter. In the formulas shown, the diameter is represented with the letter D. The width of the bolt head (across the flats of the shape) is represented by the letter W. The height of the bolt head is represented by the letter H. The thickness of the nut is represented by the letter T.

The drawing procedure for hexagonal and square bolts and nuts is as follows. See **Figure 22-25**.

1. Draw object lines and centerlines representing the bolt diameter.
2. Using the construction lines, draw a circle representing the width of the bolt head (W = 1-1/2D).
3. Using a 30°-60° triangle, circumscribe a hexagon about the circle. If drawing a square bolt, use a 45° triangle to circumscribe a square about the circle.
4. Develop the side view of the bolt.
5. Draw arcs in the bolt head and nut using the radii indicated in **Figure 22-24**.
6. Complete by drawing the chamfered corners on the bolt head and nut. Draw threads (either simplified or schematic) on the bolt. Dimensions and formulas for drawing schematic and simplified threads for Unified inch-based thread forms are shown in **Figure 22-26**.

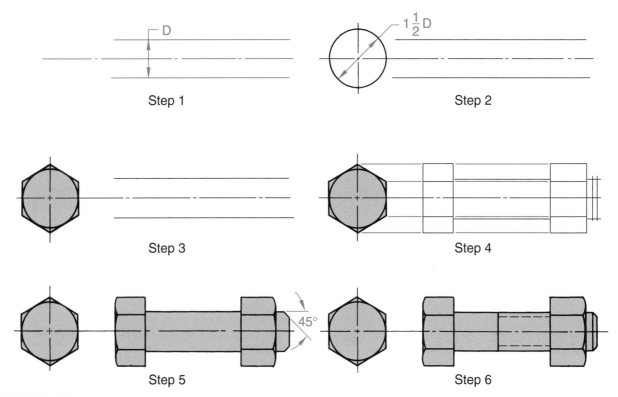

Figure 22-25 Steps used in drawing a bolt and nut. The same procedure is followed whether the bolt or nut is to have a square or hexagonal head.

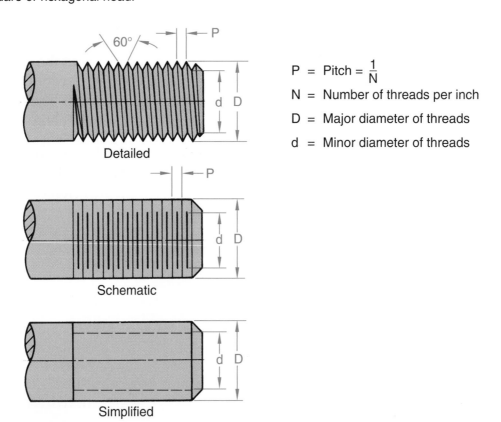

$P = \text{Pitch} = \frac{1}{N}$

$N = \text{Number of threads per inch}$

$D = \text{Major diameter of threads}$

$d = \text{Minor diameter of threads}$

Figure 22-26 Dimensions used when drawing detailed, schematic, and simplified representations for Unified inch-based thread forms.

Test Your Knowledge

Please do not write in this book. Place your answers on another sheet of paper.

1. Define *fastener*.
2. Identify 10 different types of fasteners. Underline the threaded fasteners.
3. List five applications that make use of threaded fasteners.
4. What is the difference between coarse and fine thread?
5. What is the *pitch* of a screw thread and how is it expressed for inch-based screw threads?
6. Make sketches of screw threads that show how a detailed, schematic, and simplified representation differ.
7. Explain the meaning of the inch-based screw thread note 1/2-20UNF-3LH.
8. What types of fasteners are most commonly used to assemble products made of wood?

Match each of the following statements with the correct lettered fastener term.

9. Threaded on both ends.
10. Fitted on a bolt.
11. Distributes clamping pressure of a nut or bolt.
12. Used for any general assembly work where screws less than 1/4″ in diameter are needed.
13. A fastener that passes through a clearance hole in one part and screws into a threaded hole in the other part.
14. A small piece of metal fitted into a shaft and hub to prevent turning on a shaft.

A. Machine screw
B. Cap screw
C. Stud bolt
D. Nut
E. Washer
F. Key

15. Briefly explain the information and procedures needed to draw hexagonal and square bolts and nuts.

Outside Activities

1. Obtain samples of machine screws, cap screws, machine bolts, set screws, stud bolts, nuts, washers, rivets, cotter pins, nails, and wood screws. Make a display for use in the drafting room. Label all samples.
2. Choose an assembly that uses a key, keyseat, and keyway in its operation. Describe how the components are assembled.
3. Identify an example of a set screw application. How does this differ from the use of a key?

Drawing Problems

1. Draw 4″ long hexagonal and square head bolts and nuts with 3/4-10UNC-2 threads. Draw the bolts and nuts on the same sheet. Allow 3″ between the drawings. Use a simplified thread representation.
2. Draw 3″ long hexagonal and square head bolts and nuts with 1-8UNC-2 threads. Draw the bolts and nuts on the same sheet. Allow 3″ between the drawings. Use a schematic thread representation.

23 Electrical and Electronics Drafting

OBJECTIVES

After studying this chapter,
you should be able to:

◆ Demonstrate a basic understanding of
electrical and electronics drafting.

◆ Explain why electrical and electronics
drafting is diagrammatic in nature.

◆ List and describe the common types of
diagrams used in drafting.

◆ Describe the use of CAD in electrical
and electronics drafting.

DRAFTING VOCABULARY

Block diagram
Connection diagram
Diagram
Integrated circuit
  (IC)

Pictorial diagram
Schematic diagram
Wiring diagram

Our world, as we know it today, could not exist without electricity and electronic devices. You can see how true this is by listing the electrical appliances and electronic devices you may depend on in your home. Electricity and electronics enables the use of products such as TV sets, radios, stereos, DVD players, personal computers, washing machines, refrigerators, ranges, and lighting systems. See **Figure 23-1**.

There are many other types of electrical devices that are found outside the home or school. Examples include the computer-controlled devices that are important to business and medicine, as well as the programmable devices that control the machines that make, inspect, assemble, and test so many of the products we use. See **Figure 23-2**. Many hobbies are electronically oriented, **Figure 23-3**.

Overview of Electrical and Electronics Drafting

Electrical and electronics drafting is done in much the same manner as conventional drafting. The same equipment is used. The

Figure 23-2 Drafters preparing drawings for machines such as this robotic welder must have an extensive knowledge of electrical/electronics drafting techniques and standards. Electronic sensors on the robot "read" a code on the fixture holding the auto body components. The robot's computer adapts the welding sequence for the body design moving into position. This means that different automobile models can be welded on the same assembly line. (Ford Motor Company)

same types of skills are required, regardless of whether drawings are made manually or with a computer. However, the actual drawings differ from those in other types of drafting.

Instead of using regular multiview drawings, a large portion of electrical and electronic drafting is *diagrammatic* in nature. That is, there is considerable use of symbols. A typical drawing of an electrical/electronic circuit is made up of symbols representing the various components and wires that make up the circuit, **Figure 23-4**. Symbols are easier and quicker to draw than the actual parts. An electrical circuit drawing made up of schematic symbols is known as a *diagram*. The symbols are combined on the diagram to show the function and relation of each component in the circuit. A typical diagram of a circuit is shown in **Figure 23-5**. This type of diagram is known as a *schematic diagram* and is discussed in the next section.

Figure 23-1 There are many products that are powered by electricity and electronics in a typical home. How many can you identify?

Figure 23-3 Many hobbies are dependent on electronics. Shown are radio-controlled model aircraft. The controls are activated electronically by radio signals. In flight, the models can duplicate the flight patterns of the real aircraft. These models have the power source completely enclosed in the fuselage; they have no propellers. (Frank Fanelli, *Flying Models*)

Types of Diagrams Used in Drafting

A drafter working in electrical and electronics drafting must be familiar with different types of diagrams. The common types include schematic diagrams, wiring (or connection) diagrams, block diagrams, and pictorial diagrams.

A *schematic diagram*, **Figure 23-6**, is a drawing with symbols and single lines to show electrical connections and functions of a specific circuit. The various components that make up the circuit are drawn without regard to their actual physical size, shape, or location.

A *wiring* or *connection diagram* has several uses. First, this type of diagram is commonly used to show the distribution of electricity on architectural drawings, **Figure 23-7**. Wiring and connection diagrams may also be drawn to show the general physical arrangement of

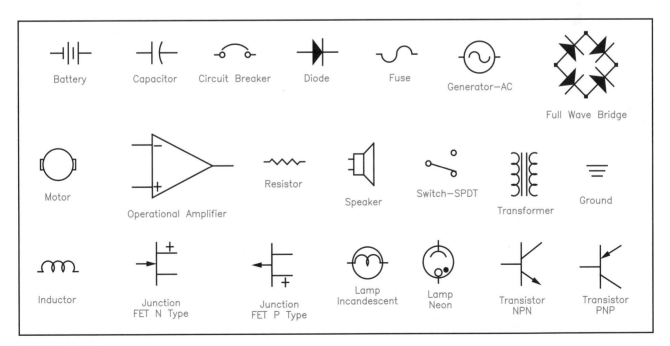

Figure 23-4 Common symbols used in electrical and electronics drafting. These are just a few of the hundreds of types of symbols used. (Autodesk, Inc.)

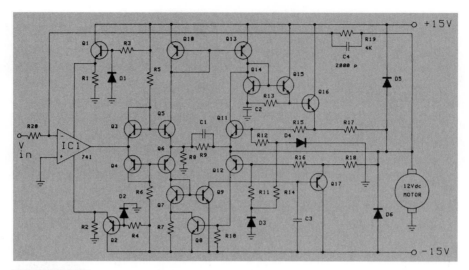

Figure 23-5 A schematic diagram. (ROBO Systems)

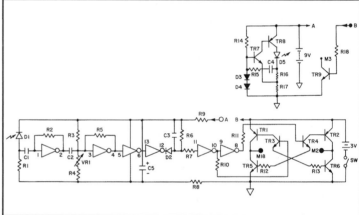

Figure 23-6 An all-terrain robot with a schematic diagram shown. This miniature, six-legged robot walks in a straight line until it "sees" an object in its path. The robot's state-of-the-art infrared beam detects the obstruction and alerts the motor control circuits, which alter the robot's course to avoid the obstacle. (Graymark International, Inc.)

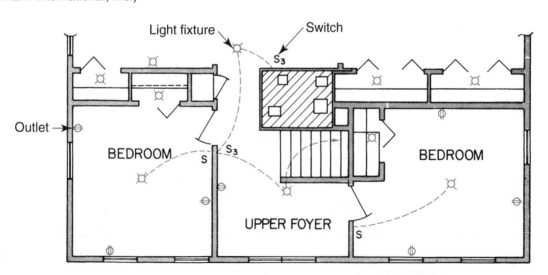

Figure 23-7 A wiring diagram showing the location of switches, outlets, and lighting in a residence.

ACADEMIC LINK

Scientific advances in electricity and electronics are responsible for many of the products we depend on today. Devices such as semiconductors and integrated circuits have brought about computer technology and many developments in manufacturing, automation, and medicine. The study of matter is directly related to these advances.

Electrical flow (current) is based on the action of charged particles of matter. The most basic unit of matter is the *atom*. Atoms are made up of subatomic particles that include electrons, protons, and neutrons. Electrons are negatively charged. Protons are positively charged. Neutrons have a neutral charge. The nucleus of an atom consists of protons and neutrons. The electrons of an atom orbit around the nucleus in rings; they are attracted to the positively charged protons and this attraction holds the electrons in orbit.

An atom can become charged (lose its normal state) when one of its electrons leaves the outer ring of the orbit. When this occurs, the charged atom is said to be *ionized*. An ion can be a negative ion or a positive ion. Ionization is caused by forces such as friction, mechanical pressure, heat, and magnetism. Ionization is the basic source of electrical energy.

Materials are considered good or poor conductors of electricity based on their atomic structure. Atoms that have fewer electrons in their outer orbit (such as those in metals) are more easily ionized. For example, copper is a good conductor of electricity because a copper atom has only one electron in its outer structure. This allows ionization to occur fairly easily because an outside force (such as heat) can free the outer electron from its orbit.

Poor conductors of electricity are known as insulators. Examples of insulators are rubber and glass. Materials that are neither good nor poor conductors of electricity are known as semiconductors. The conduction and resistivity properties of semiconductors can be enhanced in a great number of ways. Typically, impurities are added to the semiconductor material to influence the behavior of free electrons. The way semiconductors function is the basis behind the operation of modern electronic devices.

the transistors, diodes, resistors, switches, and other components that make up an electronic circuit. See **Figure 23-8**.

A *block diagram*, **Figure 23-9**, provides a simplified way to show the operation of an electronic device. This type of diagram uses "blocks" (squares, rectangles, triangles, etc.) to show the various components. The block shapes are joined by a single line and the diagram reads from left to right.

In a *pictorial diagram*, the components are drawn in pictorial form and in their proper location, **Figure 23-10**. Pictorial diagrams are used extensively by electronic kit manufacturers because they are so easy to understand.

Drawing Electrical and Electronic Symbols

Symbols in circuit diagrams need not be drawn to any particular scale. However, they should be drawn accurately, large enough to be seen clearly, and in correct

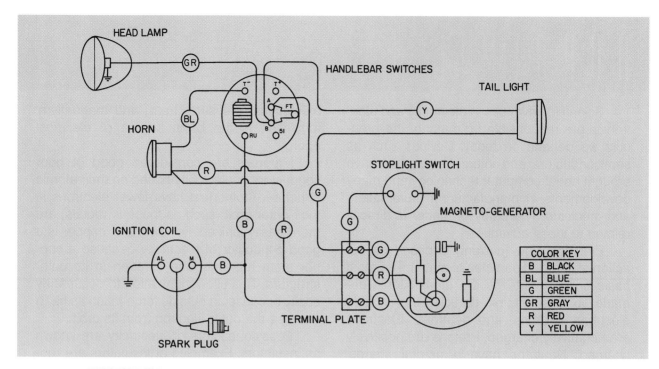

Figure 23-8 A wiring diagram for a motorcycle light. (Harley-Davidson)

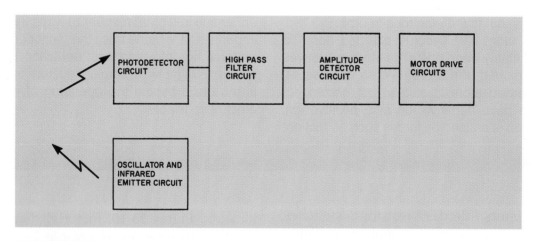

Figure 23-9 A block diagram of the all-terrain robot shown in **Figure 23-6**. (Graymark International, Inc.)

proportion, **Figure 23-11**. The easiest way to draw electrical and electronic symbols in proportion manually is to use a symbol template, **Figure 23-12**.

Symbols and lines are drawn to the same weight as object lines. Darker lines may be employed when a portion of the diagram must be emphasized.

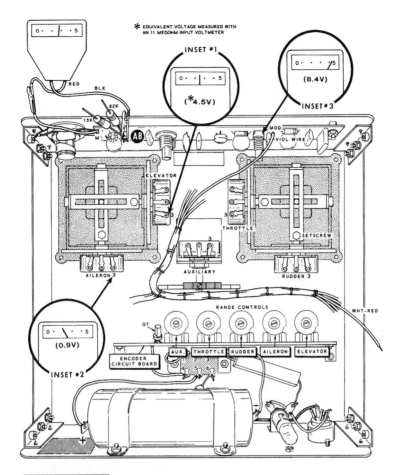

Figure 23-10 Pictorial diagrams are commonly used by electronic kit manufacturers. You do not have to be an expert to construct most of these kits.

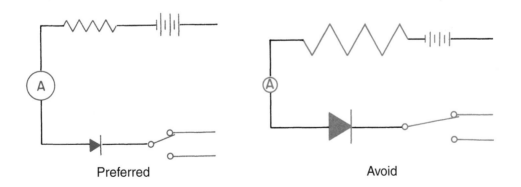

Preferred   Avoid

Figure 23-11 Symbols on a schematic diagram should be drawn in proportion to one another.

CAREERS IN DRAFTING

Electrical and Electronics Engineer

What would I do if I were to become an electrical and electronics engineer? I would design, develop, test, and supervise the manufacture of electrical and electronics equipment. I would not only design new equipment but would also write performance requirements, develop maintenance schedules, test equipment, solve operating problems, and estimate the time and cost of engineering projects.

What would I need to know? I would need to know how to develop new technologies using principles of math and science as they relate to the field of electricity and electronics. I would also need to know how to use drafting and computer-aided drafting (CAD) skills to create the concept drawings for the products I am designing.

Where would I work? As with most engineering positions, part of my day would be spent in a manufacturing facility supervising various projects that I have had a hand in designing. Another portion of my day would be spent at my desk and computer researching, designing, and developing concepts, materials, and processes as they relate to my current project.

For whom would I work? I would work for a professional, scientific, or technical service firm, a government agency, a manufacturer of computer and electronics products or machinery, or a wholesale trade, communications, or utilities firm.

What sort of education would I need? A bachelor's degree in electrical and electronics engineering is required. To gain admission to an undergraduate engineering school, courses are required in math (through calculus), science (through physics), English, social studies, humanities, information technology, and mechanical drafting/CAD.

What are the special fields relating to this career? Electrical and electronics engineers may specialize in different areas, such as power generation, transmission and distribution, communications, electronics equipment manufacturing, industrial robotic control systems, aviation electronics, or other specialties.

What are my chances of finding a job? Graduates from electrical and electronics engineering programs should have very favorable employment opportunities over the next several years. Job growth will be especially attractive in service industries—in particular with consulting firms that provide electronics engineering expertise.

How much money could I expect to make? The median salary for electrical and electronics engineers in recent years was $68,180. Salaries ranged from $44,780 to $100,980 and up. Also, engineers employed by federal and local government agencies have consistently drawn higher wages than those in private business.

Where else could I look for more information about becoming an electrical and electronics engineer? See the US Department of Labor's Bureau of Labor Statistics Occupational Outlook Handbook (at www.bls.gov) or request information from the Institute of Electrical and Electronics Engineers (www.ieee.org). Special information for high school students about careers in engineering is available from the Junior Engineering Technical Society (www.jets.org).

If I decide to pursue a different career, what other fields are related to electrical and electronics engineering? Professionals involved in related fields include control systems specialists, electrical and electronics drafters and CAD specialists, engineering technicians, science technicians, and various types of scientists.

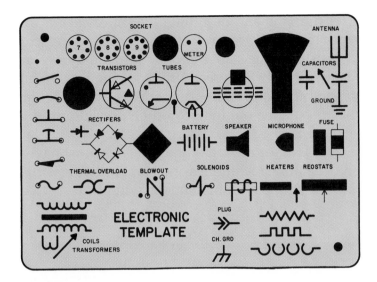

Figure 23-12   A typical electrical/electronics symbol template. This is only one template of a set. Using templates is the easiest way to manually draw symbols in proper proportion.

CAD Applications in Electrical and Electronics Drafting

Computer-aided drafting has extensive use in electrical and electronics drafting. Depending on the program used, predrawn electrical symbols are typically provided in 2D or 3D form. Other drawing tools help simplify the creation of complex parts. CAD is commonly used in the design and layout of printed circuit drawings for printed circuit boards, **Figure 23-13**. CAD

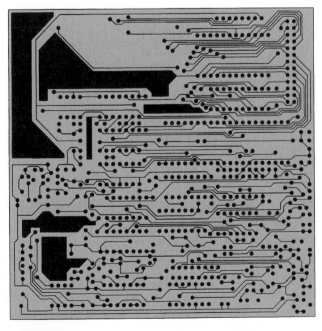

Figure 23-13   A computer-designed printed circuit board. (ROBO Systems)

is also commonly used for drawing and designing *integrated circuits* for electronic assemblies, **Figure 23-14**. An *integrated circuit (IC)* is an electronic device made up of multiple components such as transistors and resistors. Integrated circuits are commonly manufactured into *chips* for use on circuit boards. CAD software greatly reduces the time required to make drawings of chips, circuit boards, and other electronic components by hand. Many complex integrated circuit designs would be obsolete before they could be put into production if the design and layout work were done manually.

In order to use CAD to its fullest potential, the designer must have a thorough knowledge of electrical and electronics drafting techniques and standards. As with other types of drafting, the designer must have a strong grasp of manual drawing skills before he or she can become skilled in using CAD.

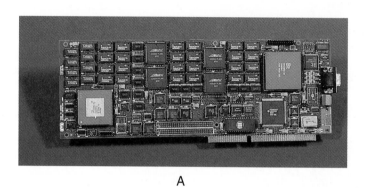

A

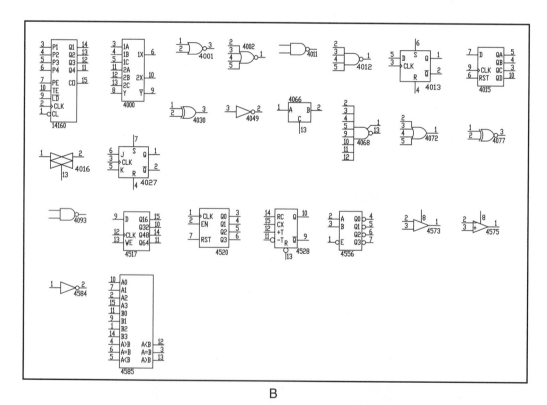

B

Figure 23-14 A—A circuit board made up of integrated circuits. Complex assemblies such as this one are commonly designed with CAD systems. B—A sample 2D-based CAD drawing of integrated circuits.

Test Your Knowledge

Please do not write in this book. Place your answers on another sheet of paper.

1. How do drawings made in electrical and electronics drafting differ from those made in conventional drafting?
2. What is a *schematic diagram*?
3. How does a block diagram differ from a wiring diagram?
4. What is a *pictorial diagram*?
5. Symbols and lines used in electrical and electronics drafting are drawn to the same weight as _____ lines.
6. Electrical diagrams used to show the distribution of electricity on architectural drawings are called _____ diagrams.
7. Name two applications in which computer-aided design has been used extensively by the electronics industry.

Outside Activities

1. Make a schematic diagram of a desk lamp or light used on a drafting table.
2. Prepare a schematic diagram of a two-cell flashlight.
3. Make a complete wiring diagram of your bedroom.
4. Obtain a small battery-powered toy. Examine how it operates. Make a suitable electronics diagram showing your findings.
5. Prepare a pictorial diagram of an inexpensive transistor radio.
6. Make a suitable diagram showing four batteries, a switch, and a lamp wired in series.
7. Make a suitable diagram showing four batteries, a switch, and a lamp wired in parallel.
8. Prepare a wiring diagram showing how to connect a stereo receiver, CD player, and two speakers.

24 Architectural Drafting

OBJECTIVES

After studying this chapter,
you should be able to:

◆ Explain the importance of
architectural plans.

◆ List the types of information required
when building a home.

◆ Describe common framing and
construction methods.

◆ Identify the types of plans in a set of
architectural drawings.

◆ Read and use an architect's scale.

◆ Identify common architectural
abbreviations.

◆ Apply architectural dimensioning rules.

◆ List and explain general guidelines to
follow when planning a home.

◆ Describe some of the advantages
in using CAD to prepare architectural plans.

◆ Produce plans for a simple structure.

DRAFTING VOCABULARY

Architect
Architect's scale
Architectural
   drawings
Balloon framing
Basement plan
Building codes
Building permit
Contour lines
Details
Elevations
Floor plan
Foundation plan
Header
Joists

Module
Nosing
Plan
Platform framing
Plot plan
Rise
Riser
Sections
Schedule
Sill Plate
Site plan
Specifications
Spec sheets
Tread
Truss

Plans that provide trade workers with the information needed to construct buildings in which people live, work, and play are called *architectural drawings*. See **Figure 24-1**. Architectural drawings or plans are created, designed, and produced by an *architect*.

Buying a home is probably one of the largest investments you will make in your lifetime. An understanding of the basic principles of architectural drafting will be a great help if you plan to design or construct a new home, remodel an existing home, or judge the soundness and value of a home offered for sale.

The ability to read and interpret architectural drawings is essential to those in the construction industry. Drawings by architects and drafters working for architects are used by carpenters, masons, plumbers, electricians, roofers, and others involved in residential and commercial construction. They are designed to represent the final product in an accurate and appealing manner. The ability to read architectural drawings is also useful to workers in lumberyards or in hardware and building supply stores.

Building a Home

To make sure your home is built to your specific requirements, it is important that you have a good plan and a well-defined contract with your builder. Plans provide the vast amount of information needed to construct a modern home.

Building Codes

A set of plans should observe all applicable aspects of the local and state building codes. *Building codes* are laws that provide for the health, safety, and general welfare of the people in the community. Building codes are based on standards developed by government and private agencies.

Building Permit

In most communities, the building contractor or owner must file a formal application for a *building permit*. Plans and specifications are submitted for the proposed structure. The plans are reviewed by building officials to determine whether they meet local building code requirements.

An inspection card is usually posted on the building site and work is inspected by local building officials as construction progresses. The card is signed as each phase of construction is approved.

Types of Framing and Construction

A basic knowledge of framing and construction methods is helpful in understanding how plans are drawn for structures. There are common methods for framing floors, walls, and roofs in wood-based construction.

Floor Framing

There are three basic floor framing methods used to build structures. These are platform framing, balloon framing, and post and beam framing. Platform framing and balloon framing are most common. In *platform framing*, the wall studs and flooring are supported by a box-shaped platform. This type of construction is also known as

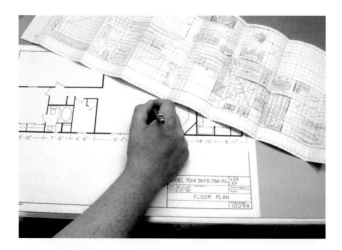

Figure 24-1   Floor plans and other types of architectural plans are drawn by architects.

box sill construction. This is because a *sill plate* and *header* rest on the foundation wall to serve as the framework for construction. See **Figure 24-2**. In this system, each floor of the structure is framed separately. *Joists* rest on the sill plate and provide support for the subfloor. A sole plate resting on the subfloor provides support for the wall studs. The wall studs are one-story high. On two-story structures, the second-floor wall studs rest on a top plate above the second-floor subfloor, which is supported by ceiling joists spanning above the first-floor walls.

In *balloon framing*, box sill construction is used, but the wall studs rest directly on the sill plate and run two stories high. The first-floor framework is made up of joists and studs and rests on a sill plate on the foundation wall. See **Figure 24-3**. The second-floor subfloor is supported by joists. The joists are nailed to the sides of the studs and supported by a ribbon, which is inserted into cuts in the studs. This type of framing is more common in older structures.

Wall Construction

A typical example of wall construction (with box sill construction) is shown in **Figure 24-4**. For the corners, studs are grouped as shown. They provide support for the structure and nailing for the interior walls. Bracing is used for the exterior walls, **Figure 24-5**. Three common bracing methods are shown.

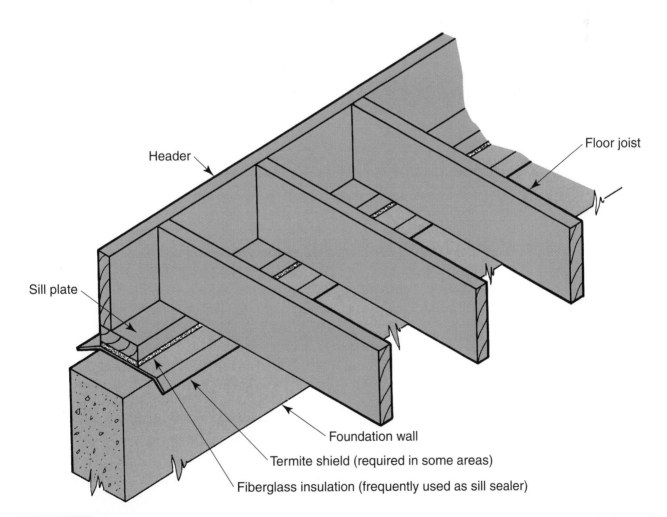

Header

Floor joist

Sill plate

Foundation wall

Termite shield (required in some areas)

Fiberglass insulation (frequently used as sill sealer)

Figure 24-2 Box sill construction used in platform framing. The sill plate and header rest on the foundation wall and make up the box-shaped platform.

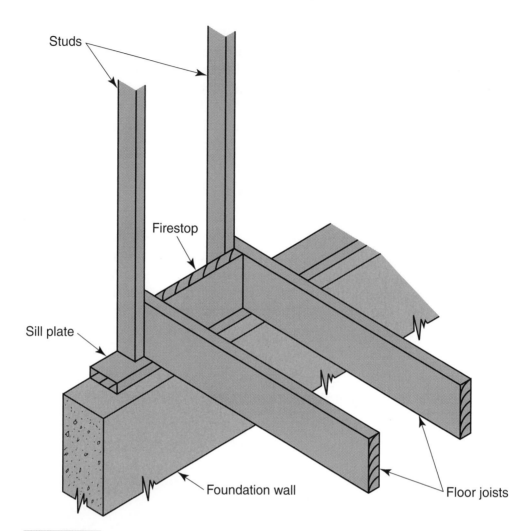

Studs

Firestop

Sill plate

Foundation wall

Floor joists

Figure 24-3 In balloon framing, the wall studs run two stories high and rest directly on the sill plate with the joists.

With horizontal bracing, plywood sheathing is nailed to the exterior side of the studs at the wall corners. See **Figure 24-5A**. With diagonal bracing, metal strips or lumber braces are notched into the studs between the sole plate and the top corner. See **Figure 24-5B**. Another horizontal bracing method uses horizontal framing members notched into the studs. See **Figure 24-5C**.

Openings in walls for windows and doors require additional framing members. When framing an opening for a window, two framing members are nailed together to provide a header. This supports the window from above. Below and above the opening,

studs known as *cripples* are used. These are studs that are less than full length. Inside the opening, vertical *trimmers* are added to each side to support the header. Refer to **Figure 24-4**.

Openings in walls for doors use the same types of framing members as window openings. See **Figure 24-6**. Different types of headers are used, depending on the width of the opening. A trussed header is used for large openings or in cases where support is required for a heavy load. A **truss** is a triangular framing support designed for long spans.

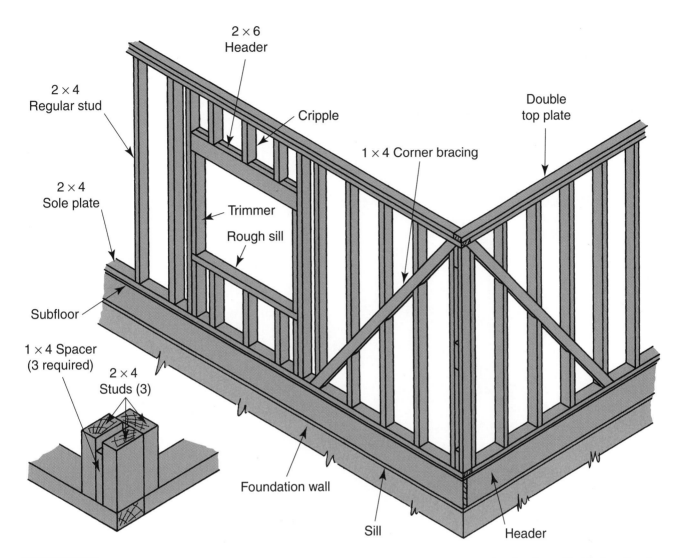

2 × 6
Header

2 × 4
Regular stud

Cripple

1 × 4 Corner bracing

Double
top plate

2 × 4
Sole plate

Trimmer

Rough sill

Subfloor

1 × 4 Spacer
(3 required)

2 × 4
Studs (3)

Foundation wall

Sill

Header

Figure 24-4 The components of wood stud wall construction. Shown are corner details. Box sill construction is used in this example.

Stair Construction

Stairs provide access to different levels or floors in a structure. The most common types of stairways are straight run, platform (such as L and U), and winding. There are common terms used to describe the components of stairs, **Figure 24-7**. Stairs are made up of treads and risers. A *tread* is the horizontal surface of one step. A *riser* is the vertical surface between treads. The *nosing* is the portion of the tread that extends past the riser. The *rise* of a flight of stairs is equal to the vertical distance from one floor to the next floor. There are recommended methods for calculating riser heights and tread widths. Added together, the riser height and tread width should equal 17" to 18". In addition, the sum of two risers and one tread should equal 24" to 25". Stairs should slope at an angle between 30° and 35°. Recommended dimensions for laying out stairs are shown in **Figure 24-7**.

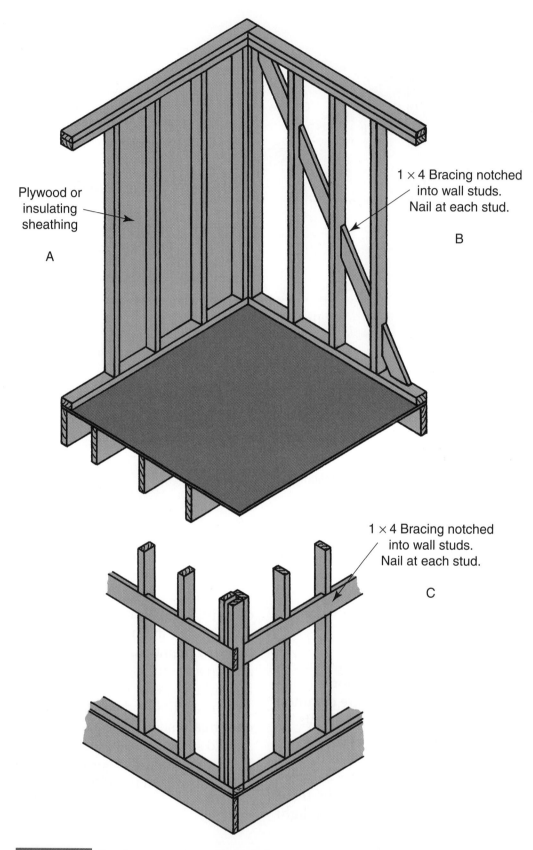

Plywood or
insulating
sheathing

A

1 × 4 Bracing notched
into wall studs.
Nail at each stud.

B

1 × 4 Bracing notched
into wall studs.
Nail at each stud.

C

Figure 24-5 Bracing methods for wall section corners. A—Plywood sheathing nailed
to the exterior walls. B—Notched wood bracing or metal strip may be nailed diagonally.
C—Wood bracing notched and nailed horizontally.

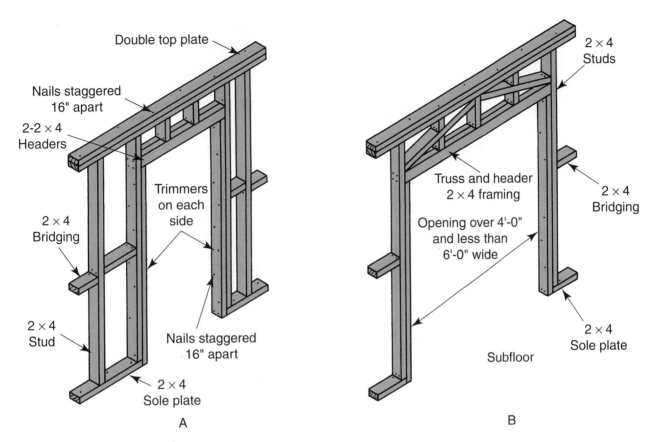

Figure 24-6 Framing methods for wall openings. A—Interior door framing. B—A trussed header used for a large wall opening.

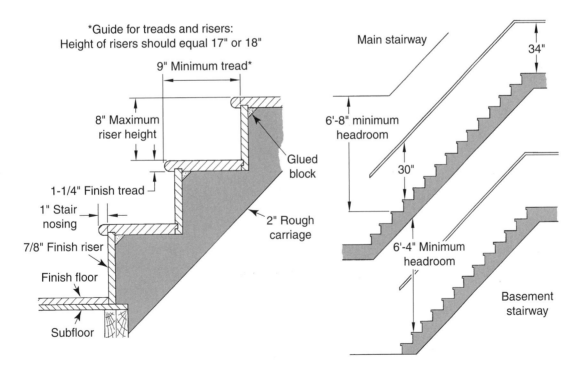

Figure 24-7 Common stair details, including handrail heights, required headroom clearances, and riser and tread dimensions.

ACADEMIC LINK

Stair calculations, room size calculations, and other types of measurements are frequently made in architectural drafting. If you are drawing plans for a structure, you will often find it necessary to apply mathematic formulas and ratios to determine dimensional information.

When designing a roof, there are recommended standards to use when calculating the roof pitch. The roof pitch relates to the *slope* of the roof and is expressed as a ratio between the rise and run. The total *rise* is the vertical measurement from the top plate elevation to the center of the rafters (the ridge). The total *run* is the horizontal distance equal to one-half the clear span. The *clear span* is the horizontal distance between the interior stud walls. The roof pitch is expressed as a ratio between the rise and clear span (Pitch = rise/clear span). The pitch calculation is usually based on a run of 12″. In other words, it represents the vertical rise of the roof over a horizontal distance of 12″. Since the clear span is twice the run, the pitch describes the rise of the roof over 24 units. If the rise is 12″ over a run of 12″, then the pitch is 1/2.

There are common ratios used for roof pitches. These include 5/24, 1/4, and other ratios. The pitch determines the angle of the rafters or trusses and usually appears on the drawing with a triangular pitch symbol.

There are also recommended standards for determining the spacing between rafters, rafter spans, and number of vents for a given square footage of roofing. In each case, proper mathematic calculations must be made.

Roof Construction

A roof design is directly related to the style of home or structure being built. Basic types of roofs are shown in **Figure 24-8**. Roofs are framed using one of two systems. These are conventional rafter construction and truss construction. In rafter construction, the rafters are diagonal members made with cuts to fit the structure. The rafters have a ridge cut at the top to meet at the ridge (top) of the roof. At the other end, where the rafter meets the top plate of the structure, a square notch is cut in the rafter to allow the rafter to fit over the plate. If the rafter extends past the structure, the end has a tail cut. An example of this type of construction with a gable roof is shown in **Figure 24-9**. Notice that the roof extends past the front of the structure. Framing members called *lookouts* permit this extension to be made.

Truss construction simplifies the process of framing a roof. This is because trusses are available in preassembled units from manufacturers. Common types of trusses are shown in **Figure 24-10**.

Types of Plans

A *plan* is a drawing showing the top view of something relatively large, such as a building or plot of land. Since it is not possible to include all construction details on a single sheet, a set of typical house plans will include a site (or plot) plan, a foundation and/or basement plan, floor plans, elevations, and wall sections or entire house sections. A set of plans for a house will also typically include details, such as built-in cabinets, fireplace details, and any other details necessary to completely explain the structure. The

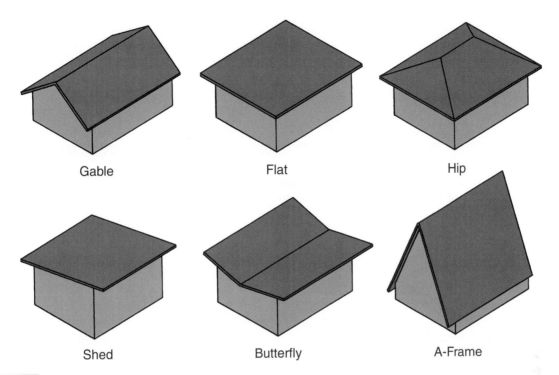

Figure 24-8   Basic roof styles.

Gable

Flat

Hip

Shed

Butterfly

A-Frame

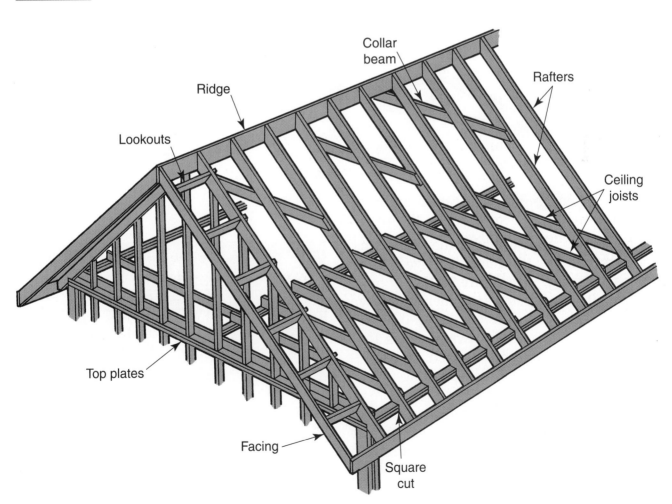

Collar beam

Ridge

Rafters

Lookouts

Ceiling joists

Top plates

Facing

Square cut

Figure 24-9   Rafter construction for a gable roof.

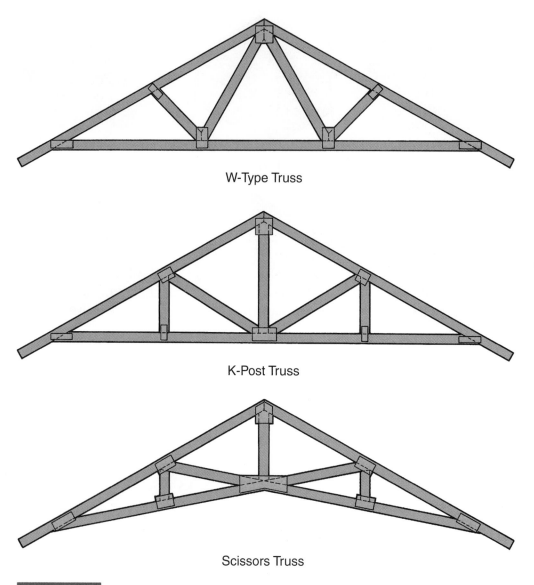

W-Type Truss

K-Post Truss

Scissors Truss

Figure 24-10 Basic types of trusses.

more detail that is specified in the set of plans, the less latitude the builders have to "do things their way." See **Figure 24-11**.

Architectural plans are generally drawn to one-fourth inch scale (1/4″ = 1′-0″). This means that 1/4″ on the drawing equals 1′-0″ on the building being constructed.

Other scales are used depending on the drawing contents. A larger scale, such as 1″ = 1′-0″, is used when greater visibility of details is needed on detail drawings (such as structural details). Framing plans are often drawn to the scale 1/8″ = 1′-0″.

Figure 24-11 A successfully constructed home requires accurately designed plan drawings and details. Drawings for this home are presented in this chapter. (Don Nelson, South Central Technical College; North Mankato, Minn.)

Site Plan

A *site plan* or *plot plan* shows the location of the structure on the building site, **Figure 24-12**. Site plans also show walks, driveways, and patios. Overall building and lot dimensions are included. *Contour lines* are sometimes shown on a site plan. These are lines indicating the slope of the site surface.

Elevations

Elevations are the front, rear, and side views of the house, **Figure 24-13**. They are made up of lines showing visible features that are seen when the building is viewed from various positions. Included on the elevations are the floor levels, grade lines, window and door heights, roof slope, and the types of materials to be used in building the walls and roof. Foundation and footing lines below grade level are indicated with hidden lines.

Floor Plan

A *floor plan* shows the size and shape of the building, as well as the interior arrangement of the rooms. See **Figure 24-14**. Additional information, such as the location and sizes of interior partitions, doors, windows, stairs, and utility installations (plumbing fixtures, electrical fixtures, etc.) is also included. The floor plan is nothing more than a horizontal

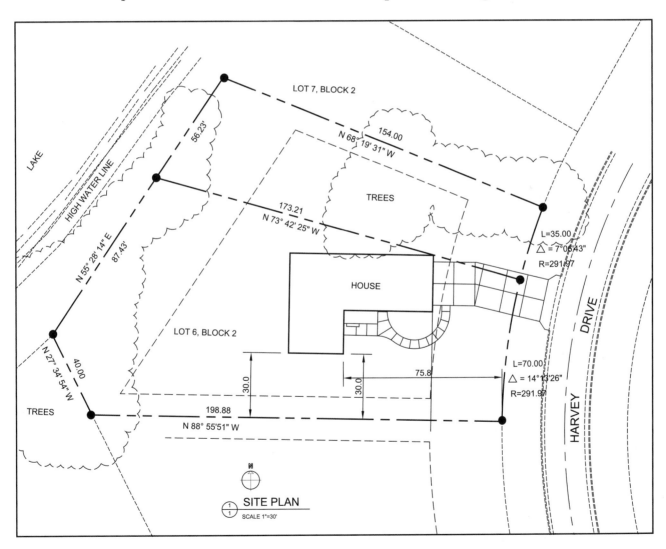

Figure 24-12 A site plan for the house shown in **Figure 24-11**. (KMA Design & Construction/Walter Cheever)

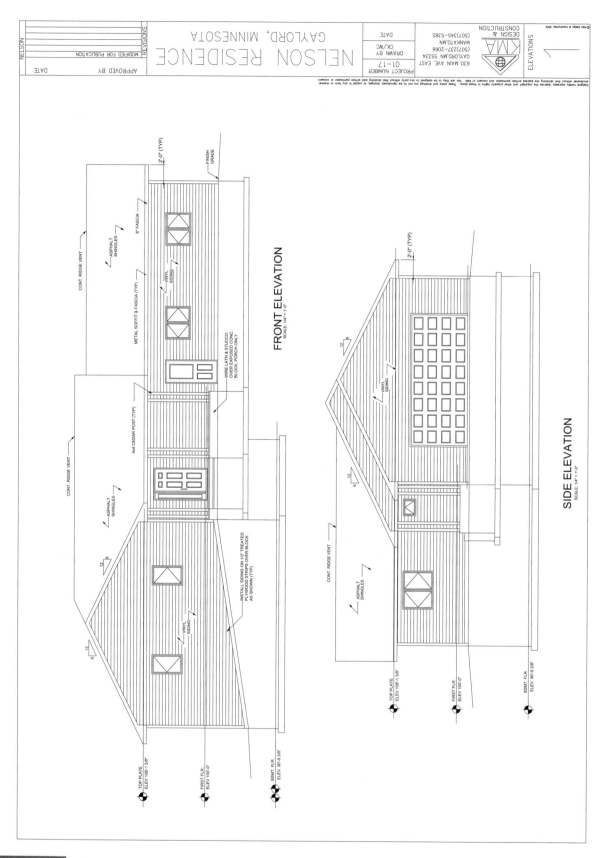

Figure 24-13 Front and side elevation drawings for the house shown in **Figure 24-11**. (KMA Design & Construction/Walter Cheever)

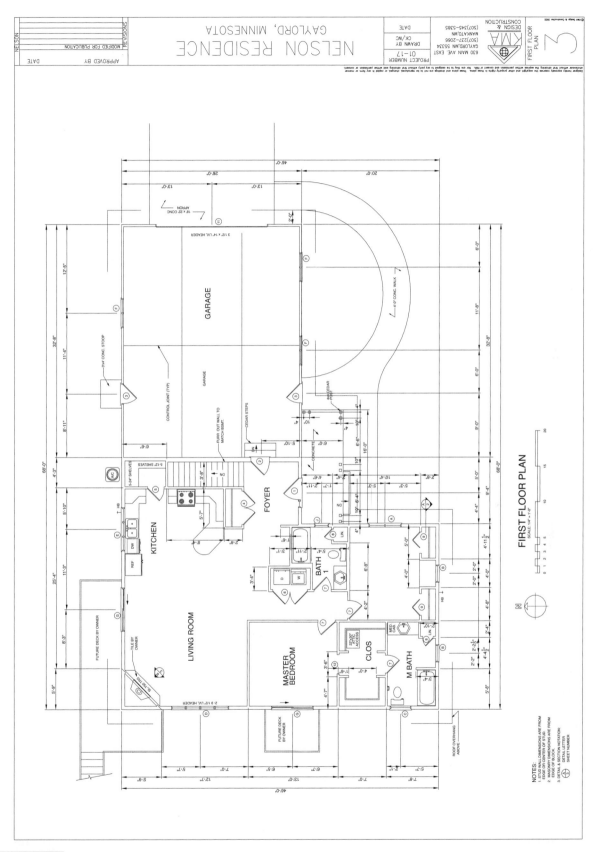

Figure 24-14 The house floor plan. Shown are appliances and plumbing fixtures for the main level.
(KMA Design & Construction/Walter Cheever)

full section of the structure, without structural members shown. An imaginary horizontal cutting plane is created through the structure at a point approximately four feet above the finished floor. The top portion is removed and the building components that are seen from a point of view perpendicular to the cutting plane (from the top) are drawn to create the floor plan.

Other types of plans are developed in relation to the floor plan so that the location of features can be shown "on top" of the floor plan. These include electrical plans and heating, ventilation, and air conditioning (HVAC) plans. These drawings are made on separate sheets without dimensions. They show the location of components such as electrical circuits, light fixtures, heating and cooling units, and ductwork.

Foundation Plan

A *foundation plan* shows the structural components of a building, such as beams, posts, and footings. It is drawn as a section through the structure and shows details "below" the floor plan (as viewed from above). Foundation and basement plans are sometimes combined on a single sheet, **Figure 24-15**.

Sections

Sections are used to give construction details by making an imaginary "cut" through the structure, **Figure 24-16**. Break lines are often incorporated into the section to reduce the drawing size and save time in drawing the plan.

Sections are commonly used to show building information for roofs, walls, and stairs. They show the sizes of the framing materials, as well as information about the types and kinds of materials to be used for sheathing, insulation, and interior and exterior wall surfaces. They are usually referenced on floor plan and foundation drawings with a cutting-plane symbol.

Details

Details are similar to sections. They are sectional views that provide more detailed information about a given area or feature of the building. They assist the trade worker in constructing such things as built-in cabinets and fireplaces, **Figure 24-17**.

Specifications

Sheets of specifications usually accompany house plans. These sheets provide additional information that cannot be easily indicated on the plans. These sheets are known as *specifications* or *"spec" sheets*. These sheets describe, in writing, details about the project, such as quality of materials, how specific items are to be installed, and other work standards.

Drawing Architectural Plans

Architectural plans consist of plan views and sectional views, rather than the types of views in other forms of drafting (multiviews). As is the case with electrical and electronics drafting, drawings are made with lines and graphic symbols. However, most conventional drafting techniques apply to architectural drafting. The same drawing tools and visualization techniques are required, whether plans are drawn manually or by computer.

There are slightly different dimensioning standards used in architectural drafting in comparison to other forms of drafting. In addition, there are certain drawing scales and other specific conventions used when drawing architectural plans. Drawing conventions for architectural plans are discussed in the following sections.

Drafting Symbols

Symbols are used extensively in architectural drafting. Symbols are employed on plans because it is not practical to show items such as doors, windows, and plumbing fixtures as they would actually appear in the structure.

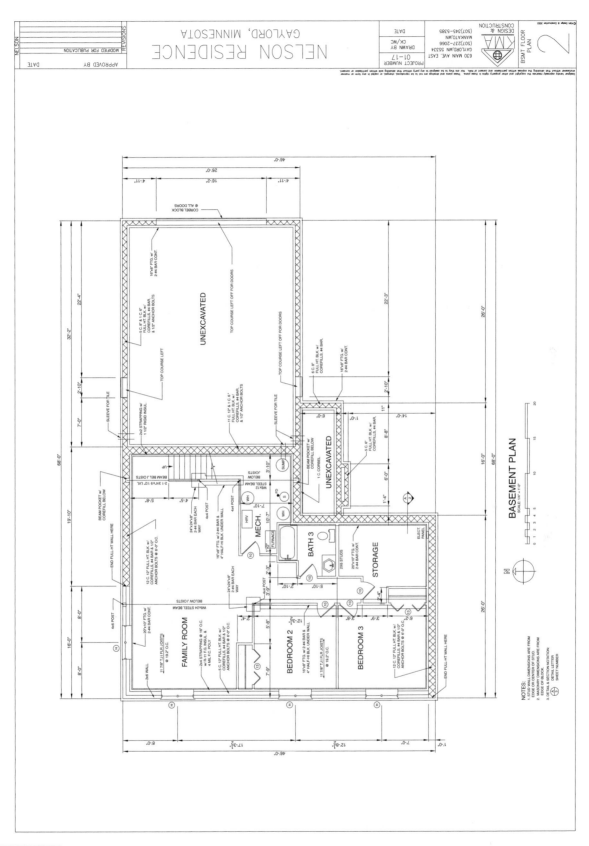

Figure 24-15 A basement/foundation plan for the house. (KMA Design & Construction/Walter Cheever)

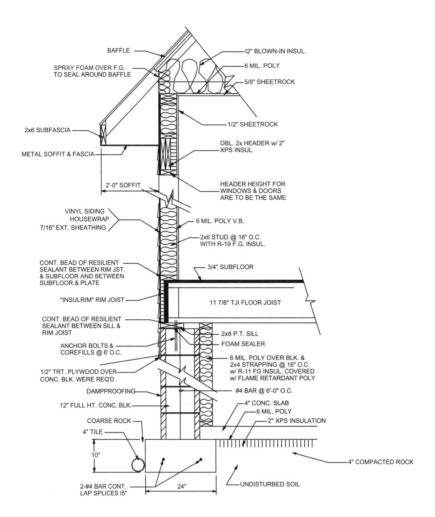

BAFFLE

12" BLOWN-IN INSUL.

SPRAY FOAM OVER F.G. TO SEAL AROUND BAFFLE

6 MIL. POLY

5/8" SHEETROCK

2x6 SUBFASCIA

1/2" SHEETROCK

METAL SOFFIT & FASCIA

DBL. 2x HEADER w/ 2" XPS INSUL.

2'-0" SOFFIT

HEADER HEIGHT FOR WINDOWS & DOORS ARE TO BE THE SAME

VINYL SIDING
HOUSEWRAP
7/16" EXT. SHEATHING

6 MIL. POLY V.B.

2x6 STUD @ 16" O.C. WITH R-19 F.G. INSUL.

CONT. BEAD OF RESILIENT SEALANT BETWEEN RIM JST. & SUBFLOOR AND BETWEEN SUBFLOOR & PLATE

3/4" SUBFLOOR

"INSULRIM" RIM JOIST

11 7/8" TJI FLOOR JOIST

CONT. BEAD OF RESILIENT SEALANT BETWEEN SILL & RIM JOIST

2x8 P.T. SILL

FOAM SEALER

ANCHOR BOLTS & COREFILLS @ 6' O.C.

6 MIL. POLY OVER BLK. & 2x4 STRAPPING @ 16" O.C. w/ R-11 FG INSUL. COVERED w/ FLAME RETARDANT POLY

1/2" TRT. PLYWOOD OVER CONC. BLK. WERE REQ'D

DAMPPROOFING

#4 BAR @ 6'-0" O.C.

4" CONC. SLAB

12" FULL HT. CONC. BLK.

6 MIL. POLY

COARSE ROCK

2" XPS INSULATION

4" TILE

10"

4" COMPACTED ROCK

UNDISTURBED SOIL

2-#4 BAR CONT. LAP SPLICES 15"

24"

A / 2 TYP. WALL SECTION

SCALE: 3/4" = 1'-0"

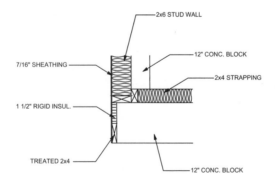

2x6 STUD WALL

12" CONC. BLOCK

7/16" SHEATHING

2x4 STRAPPING

1 1/2" RIGID INSUL.

TREATED 2x4

12" CONC. BLOCK

B / 2 TYP. WALL SECTION

SCALE: 3/4" = 1'-0"

Figure 24-16 Wall sections for the house. (KMA Design & Construction/Walter Cheever)

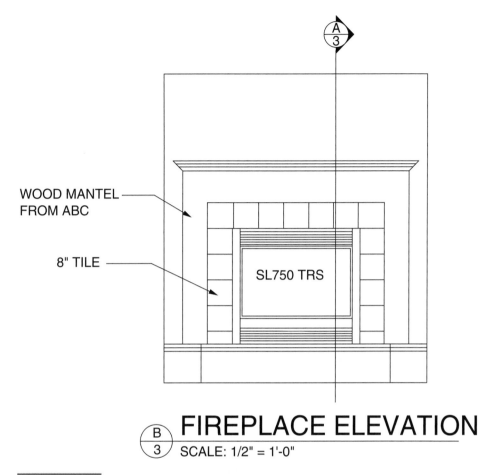

FIREPLACE ELEVATION
SCALE: 1/2" = 1'-0"

WOOD MANTEL
FROM ABC

8" TILE

SL750 TRS

Figure 24-17 An elevation detail drawing showing construction details for the fireplace on the main floor. (KMA Design & Construction/Walter Cheever)

Common floor plan symbols are shown in **Figure 24-18**. These include doors, windows, appliances, fixtures, and cabinets. Examples of their actual use are shown in **Figure 24-14**.

On electrical drawings, there are common symbols used to represent outlets, electrical devices, and switches. See **Figure 24-19**.

Symbols are also used to represent building materials on architectural plans. These types of symbols are commonly found on framing plans, building sections, and elevations. See **Figure 24-20**.

Drawing to Scale

As with other types of drawings, it is very important to draw architectural plans to the correct scale. When drawn to scale, the plans are shown in accurate proportion in relation to the full-sized structure. A floor plan drawn at 1/4" = 1'-0" scale means that 1/4" on the drawing equals 1'-0" in the structure to be built.

Scale drawings are relatively easy to make by using an *architect's scale*. Using this scale is discussed in detail in Chapter 5. The scale is divided into major and minor units, with each major unit representing a distance of 1'-0". The minor units at the end of the scale represent inches. A 1/4" = 1'-0" scale is shown in **Figure 24-21**.

When using the architect's scale to make a measurement, readings are first made in feet, then in inches. For example, to make a reading of 8'-8" (eight feet, eight inches), start at the 0 and go to the right to locate 8'-0" (eight feet). Then, move in the opposite direction from 0 to locate 8" (eight inches).

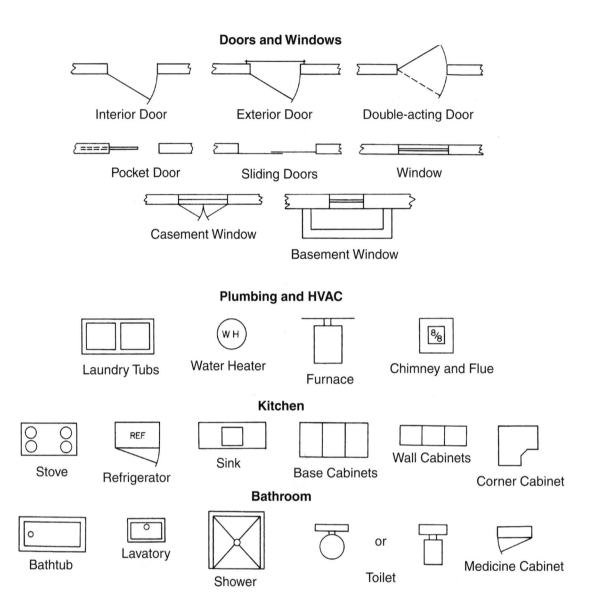

Figure 24-18 Common floor plan symbols.

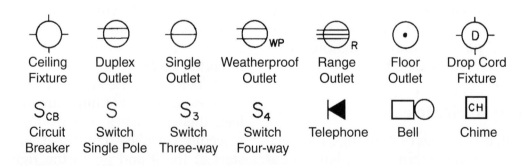

Figure 24-19 Common electrical symbols.

Plan/Section Symbols

Face Brick	Concrete	Firebrick	Rough Wood Framing	Wood
Earth	Tile	Insulation	Slate	Cinders

Elevation Symbols

Brick	Concrete	Wood Siding	Wood	Glass
Concrete Block	Metal	Plaster	Wood-End Grain	Stone

Figure 24-20   Symbols used to indicate building materials.

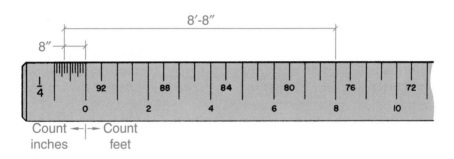

Figure 24-21   Measuring both feet and inches on an architect's scale.

The combined measurement is 8'-8". This is shown in **Figure 24-21**.

Practice reading the architect's scale by making the measurements in **Figure 24-22**. List your answers on a sheet of notebook paper.

Drawing a Title Block

An architectural title block, **Figure 24-23**, provides important information. It should include the following items:

- Type of structure (house, garage, shed, etc.).
- Where the structure is to be located.
- Name of the architect (and/or drafter).
- Date.
- Drawing scale(s) used.
- Sheet number and number of sheets making up the full set of drawings (Sheet 1 of 10, etc.).

The title block may be any convenient size. However, 2" × 4" is a suitable size for most home plans. It is usually located in the lower-right corner of the drawing sheet.

Lettering Architectural Plans

Most architectural lettering differs in appearance from the single-stroke Gothic

CAREERS IN DRAFTING

Architect

What would I do if I were to become an architect? I would design buildings or complexes in which people live, work, play, learn, worship, meet, govern, shop, and eat. Along with designing, I would manage projects while communicating effectively with clients and builders.

What would I need to know? I would have to know how to communicate my ideas persuasively with clients. I would also need to know how to develop designs for buildings while addressing the client's budget constraints and following building codes, zoning laws, fire codes, and American Disabilities Act (ADA) regulations. I would need to know basic drafting skills and standards using both manual and CAD techniques.

Where would I work? I would work in a comfortable environment that would allow me to develop drawings and reports while consulting with clients, other designers (including interior designers), and engineers. I would also frequently visit construction sites to check on the progress of my projects and evaluate the quality of the work being done.

For whom would I work? About 1 in 5 architects are self-employed. Therefore, I could be working for myself. However, I could work with a group of architects, a building construction firm, or a government agency.

What sort of education would I need? At the high school level, I would need to take courses in English, history, art, social studies, math, physics, and computer science, as well as any drafting and CAD courses available. To become a licensed architect, I would need to acquire a professional degree in architecture— preferably from a school accredited by the National Architectural Accrediting Board (there

are approximately 115 in the United States). I would also need to intern, most likely for three years, and pass all divisions of the Architect Registration Examination (ARE).

What are the special fields relating to this career? Because architecture is a specialized field, specialization may occur in one of the phases of architecture. An architect may specialize in designing sports facilities, museums, churches, schools, or medical facilities.

What are my chances of finding a job? Employment of architects is expected to show average growth over the next several years. Because of considerable competition, those who acquire CAD skills as well as experience at an architectural firm while still in school have a distinct advantage in employability after graduation from a professional program.

How much money could I expect to make? Salaries in recent years have ranged from $36,280 to $92,350 or more. Earnings for partners in established firms fluctuate with business conditions.

Where else could I look for more information about becoming an architect? See the US Department of Labor's Bureau of Labor Statistics Occupational Outlook Handbook (at www.bls.gov), visit the American Institute of Architects Web site (at www.aia.org), or request information about the Intern Development Program of the National Council of Architectural Registration Boards (at www.ncarb.org).

If I decide to pursue a different career, what other fields are related to architecture? Landscape architecture, urban and regional planning, civil engineering, and design (interior design, commercial and industrial design, and graphic design).

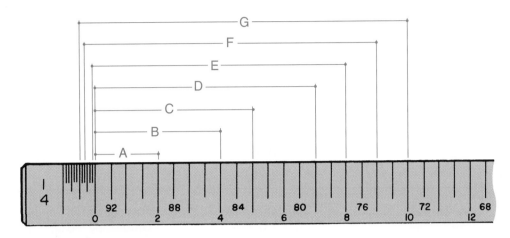

Figure 24-22 How many of these measurements can you read correctly? Do not write in the book. Place your answers on a piece of notebook paper.

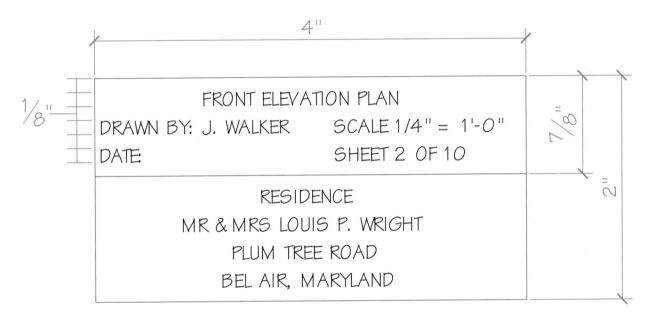

Figure 24-23 Sample title block for an architectural drawing.

lettering used in mechanical drafting. See **Figure 24-24**. Conventional single-stroke Gothic lettering is sometimes used on architectural drawings. However, many architects and drafters develop their own distinctive style of lettering. Custom styles are usually based on the single-stroke Gothic style, but they always have a unique theme or set of features. Whether you decide to use the single-stroke Gothic letter form or develop a style of your own, remember that your lettering must be legible.

Using Architectural Abbreviations

Considerable drawing time and sheet space can be saved when lettering architectural drawings by using abbreviations that are standard in industry. Some of the most commonly used abbreviations on plan drawings are shown in **Figure 24-25**. Refer to the *Useful Information* section of this text for a more extensive list of standard abbreviations.

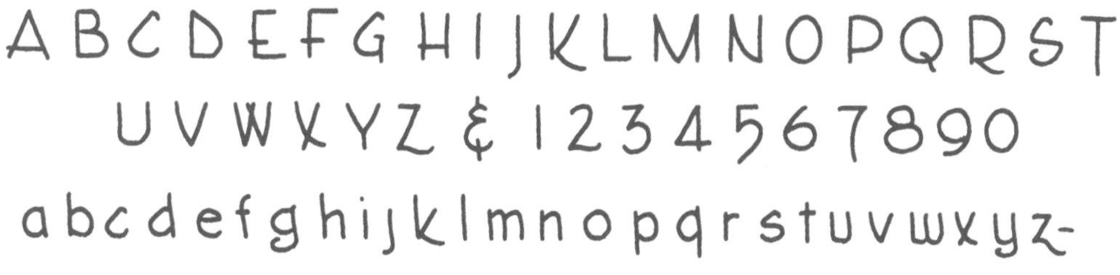

A B C D E F G H I J K L M N O P Q R S T
U V W X Y Z & 1 2 3 4 5 6 7 8 9 0
a b c d e f g h i j k l m n o p q r s t u v w x y z

Figure 24-24 One style of architectural lettering.

Asphalt Tile—AT	Concrete—CONC	Footing—FTG
Beam—BM	Drawing—DWG	Grade Line—GL
Bedroom—BR	Door—DR	Lavatory—LAV
Brick—BRK	Elevation—EL, ELEV	Living Room—LR
Ceiling—CLG	Exterior—EXT	Plaster—PLAS
Center Line—CL or ℄	Floor—FLR	Room—RM

Figure 24-25 Common abbreviations used on architectural plans.

Obtaining Information

A great deal of research must be made by the student in order to complete an accurate set of plans. There are many drawing conventions, such as the use of standard sizes, that are essential to practice when producing architectural drawings. Research can be conducted by obtaining catalogs, reference books, and other published materials. The Internet is also a good source of information about architectural drafting and the building trades. Organizations such as the American Institute of Architects (AIA) and the Construction Specifications Institute (CSI) are useful sources of information.

Additional information may be found in mail order catalogs, lumber and building supply company literature, and copies of your local building ordinances. Specialized textbooks in architecture, carpentry, and plumbing are other excellent sources of information when planning a home or other structure.

Dimensioning Architectural Plans

There are only slight differences between the dimensioning techniques used on architectural drawings and in other forms of drafting. As is the case with mechanical drafting, the dimensions are read from the bottom and right sides of the drawing sheet. However, measurements over 12″ are expressed in feet and inches. Foot marks and/or inch marks (′ and ″) are used on all dimensions.

Architectural dimensions may be placed on all sides of the drawing as well as within the drawing itself. Dimension text, usually 1/8″ high, is written above the dimension line (in most cases) or in a break in the dimension line. The dimension line may be capped with arrowheads, small dark circles, or short 45° slash marks known as architectural tick marks. See **Figure 24-26**.

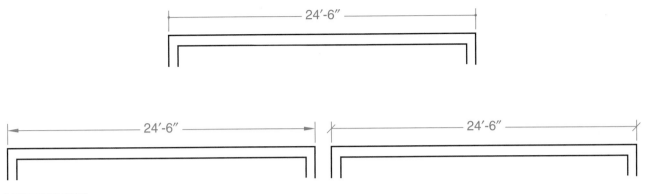

Figure 24-26 Conventions for dimension lines and text in architectural drafting.

Architectural Dimensioning Rules

The following rules should be applied when drawing dimensions for architectural drawings:

1. Make sure that the dimensioning is complete. A builder should never have to assume or measure a distance on the drawing for a dimension. Dimensions are not omitted from dimensional chains in architectural dimensioning (as they are in mechanical dimensioning). All dimensions in the chain are shown, and they must all add up to the sum of the overall dimensions of the structure.
2. *Always* dimension features full size regardless of the drawing's scale.
3. Dimensions and notes should be placed at least 1/4″ away from the drawing.
4. Align dimensions across the drawing whenever possible. In other words, create dimensional chains where they will work without interfering with too many features of the structure.
5. Place overall dimensions outside the overall features of the drawing.
6. Overall dimensions are determined by adding the location dimensions in the chain. Do not measure (scale) the drawing to determine overall sizes.
7. Dimension partitions center-to-center or from center to outside wall. They may also be dimensioned stud-face to stud-face.
8. Room size may be indicated by specifying the width and length of the room.
9. Windows, doors, and beams on frame structures are dimensioned to their centers.
10. Window and door sizes and types are given in a *schedule*. This is a table that accompanies the drawing and lists information about dimensions and materials. See **Figure 24-27**.

WINDOW SCHEDULE				
MARK	REQ'D	OVERALL SASH SIZE		DESCRIPTION
		WIDTH	HEIGHT	
W-1	4	5'-4"	x 4'-0"	ALUMINUM SLIDING WINDOW WITH INSULATED SASH-FIBERGLASS SCREEN
W-2	3	5'-4"	x 2'-0"	SAME AS ABOVE
W-3	1	4'-0"	x 3'-0"	"
W-4	1	2'-7"	x 5'-8"	1/4" PLATE GLASS
W-5	1	9'-6"	x 2'-4"	FIXED, SAME AS ABOVE

Figure 24-27 A typical window schedule.

Note

Exterior dimensions on structures that have one or more exterior offsets typically have three rows (chains) of dimensions. The closest chain to the structure gives the most distances. This chain links from the outside of the exterior stud-face to the centers of the openings to the outside of the stud-face at the offset to the centers of the openings to the outside of the stud-face on the opposite end of the structure. The second chain usually links from the outside stud-face to the outside stud-face at the offset to the outside stud-face. This chain shows the overall size of each offset of the structure. The third chain usually is the overall size of the structure and equals the sum of each of the other chains.

Planning a Home

When planning a home, you must determine how much money will be available for building purposes. Most people building homes must borrow a major portion of the construction money. Lending institutions use formulas based on the cash available for a down payment and the owner's income (salary, etc.) to establish how much money they will lend to build or purchase a home.

The amount of money available for building a home helps dictate the size and type of home to be built. One way to ascertain the size of a home you plan to build based on the money available is to use the square foot method. A local contractor can give you the approximate cost per square foot of construction in your community.

Divide the money available to build the house by the cost of construction per square foot, and you will find the floor area of a home you can afford to build.

After determining the approximate size of the proposed house, you should try to develop a suitable floor plan. Say, for example, calculations show that you can afford a home with an area of 1200 square feet. Outlines of homes having 1200 square feet of floor space are shown in **Figure 24-28**. Room use and space available must be carefully considered and balanced.

Be sure to include closet and storage facilities in your calculations. Using scale cutouts of the furniture and appliances you plan to use in the various rooms will aid in your planning. The preliminary floor plan can be drawn on graph paper. Make each square equal to one foot. Changes can be made easily on the grid as you create the floor plan.

The cutouts *must* be made to the same scale used for the floor plan. Your drawing should also show all openings and the amount of space doors will require when opened. By placing the cutouts, it is easy to find out whether each room is large enough for the intended use.

Sizes of common appliances, fixtures, and furniture are given in **Figure 24-29**. Dimensions of items not shown may be found in manufacturer catalogs, home magazines, and mail order catalogs.

Cutout planning for a typical room on a floor plan is shown in **Figure 24-30**.

US Customary and Metric Measurement in Architecture

The building trades industry probably is one of the last business enterprises to "go metric" in the United States. Inch-based measurement is the standard in US residential construction. However, some companies (such as those that manage international projects) use the metric system for design and dimensioning. In some cases, architectural drawings use dual dimensioning.

Lumber producers have decided upon a "soft" metric conversion of existing lum-

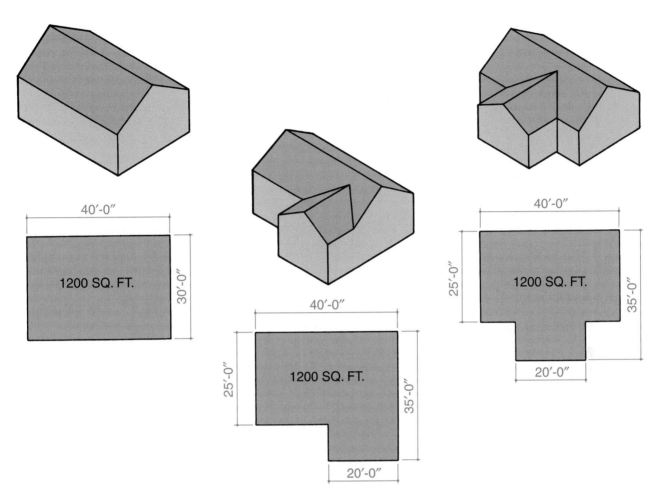

Figure 24-28   Examples of homes with floor areas of 1200 square feet.

ber sizes. This does not require a basic re-dimensioning of lumber sizes (as would a "hard" metric conversion). A "soft" metric conversion simply means that inches have been converted to millimeters, pounds to kilograms, etc., without changing the basic size of the product. A "hard" conversion with metric engineering standards is one in which all of the designing is done in metric sizes.

In the United States, most buildings are designed to a 4″ base module. See **Figure 24-31A**. A *module* is a standard unit size used for determining sizes of construction materials. All lumber, blocks, bricks, panel stock (products such as plywood and hardboard) and components such as windows and doors are specified in multiples of the 4″ module. Windows, for example, usually are 2′-8″ or 3′-0″ wide.

A 100 mm module has been established as the basic metric module. See **Figure 24-31B**. All metric-based building materials and components are based on multiples of this module.

A 100 mm module is almost, *but not quite,* the same size as the customary 4″ module. The difference is small, but it is enough to cause major problems in a building project. *All* materials used in constructing a building must be designed to the same basic module. See **Figure 24-32**.

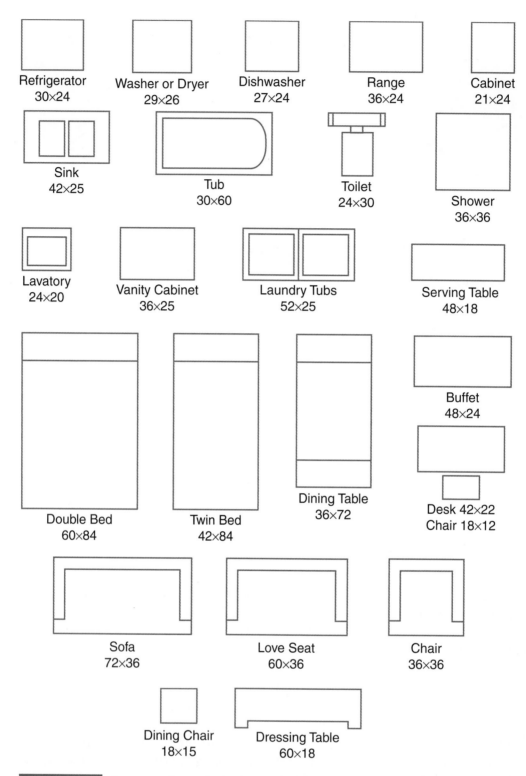

Figure 24-29 Common dimensions of appliances, fixtures, and furniture used in home planning. All dimensions are width × depth.

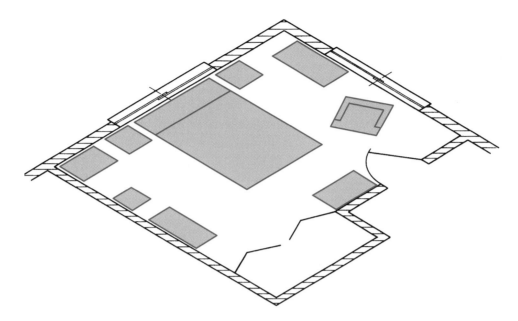

Figure 24-30 How cutouts may be used to plan a bedroom.

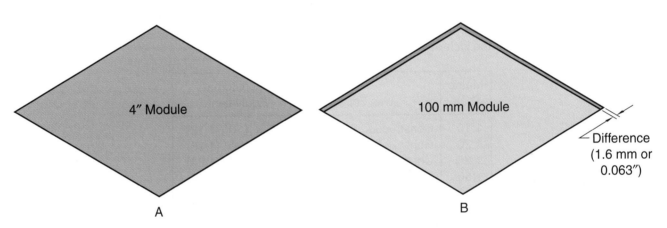

Figure 24-31 Building dimensions and product sizes for construction are based on modules. A—In the United States, the 4″ module is most common. This module measures 4″ × 4″. In this system, product sizes in multiples of 4″ are used. B—A comparison between the 4″ module and the metric-based 100 mm module. The metric module measures 100 mm × 100 mm.

Metric Architectural Drafting

Outside of the use of different measurement systems, there is little difference between metric and conventional (inch-based) architectural drafting. In metric-based architectural drafting, all structures are designed and constructed using the 100 mm module. Dimensions are given in meters and millimeters instead of feet and inches.

Scales for use in metric-based architectural drafting are shown in **Figure 24-33**. The equivalent inch-based scales are also shown.

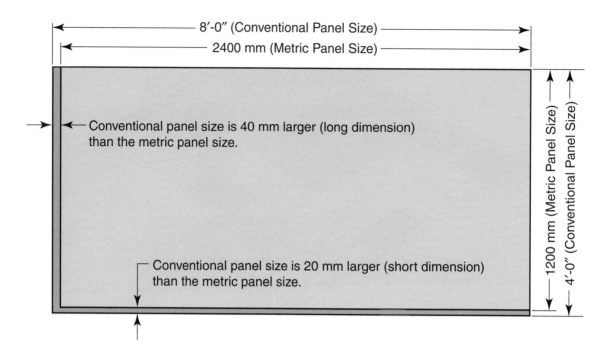

Figure 24-32 A comparison between a conventional size building panel based on the 4″ module and a metric size panel based on the 100 mm module. The metric-size panel is too small to use as a replacement for the inch-based panel.

Metric Scale	Use For	US Customary Equivalent
1:10	Construction Details	1″ = 1′-0″ (1:12)
1:20	Construction Details	3/4″ = 1′-0″ (1:16)
1:25	Construction Details	1/2″ = 1′-0″ (1:24)
1:50	Floor and Foundation Plans, Elevations	1/4″ = 1′-0″ (1:48)
1:100	Plot Plans	1/8″ = 1′-0″ (1:96)
1:200	Plot Plans	1/16″ = 1′-0″ (1:192)
1:500	Site Plans	1/32″ = 1′-0″ (1:384)

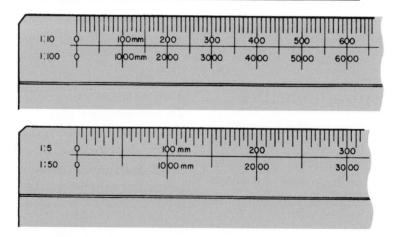

Figure 24-33 Recommended metric scales for use in metric-based architectural drafting.

Computer-Aided Drafting in Architecture

As with other areas of industry, computer-aided drafting (CAD) is changing the field of architecture. Talented people working with computers are able to produce quality work faster and more profitably than ever before. Time is greatly reduced throughout the phases of concept, design, working drawings, and construction scheduling of a building project.

There are many special architectural CAD software programs available that allow the drafter to design using architectural objects instead of basic CAD drafting objects. In other words, drawings can be made using windows, doors, and walls instead of lines, circles, and arcs. Some of these software programs are special add-ons that run with basic graphics engines. These are powerful, expensive industry-standard programs used by designers and engineers. Others are standalone design and build programs that are much less expensive (and used more by contractors than designers). Some of the design and build programs are more powerful and used by industry, while others are more suitable for consumer and home use (and less expensive).

An important advantage of CAD over manual drafting in architecture is that two- and three-dimensional drawings can be developed and combined to create new structures and layouts, **Figure 24-34**. Designs can be viewed and rotated in 3D space and seen from any angle. Walkthroughs may be designed to allow the designer and client to tour the structure while it is still in its soft form (in the computer's memory). Design flaws can be viewed and changes may be made immediately, even as the client watches if the designer desires.

Figure 24-34   A rendered model of a home generated with CAD software. This model can help plan room layout and show the home owner how it will look in 3D. Using the same software, plan drawings, building sections, and details can be generated. (Chief Architect)

Architectural CAD programs are designed to reduce repetitive work to a minimum. See **Figure 24-35**. Specific tasks, such as the outlining of a structure with the windows and doors located, can be quickly accomplished. Structural details, as well as window and door details meeting engineering standards, can be generated automatically from other drawings. For each project, a bill of materials and estimated cost of materials can be computed using the same information.

New architectural CAD programs are under continual development. As these types of programs evolve, they will offer architects and interior designers more advanced design and management capabilities.

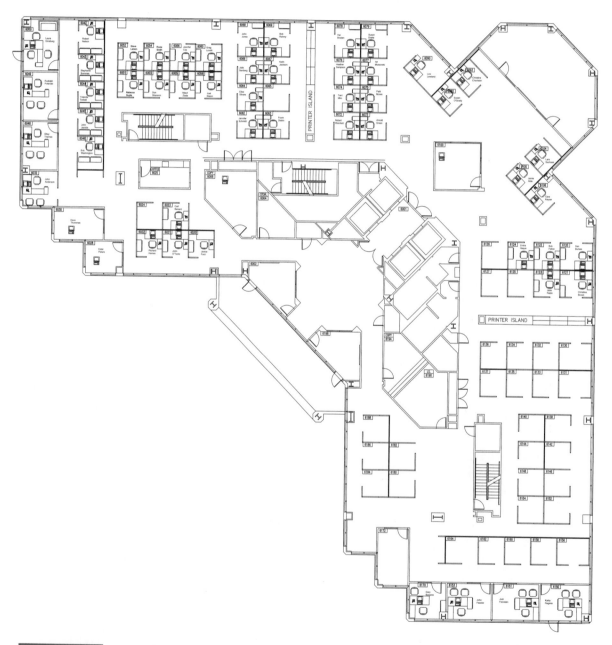

Figure 24-35 Architectural CAD programs are designed to reduce drafting time. Shown is a CAD-generated floor plan for an office building with predrawn symbols used for doors, windows, workstations, and other multiple-use objects. (Autodesk, Inc.)

Test Your Knowledge

Please do not write in this book. Place your answers on another sheet of paper.

1. What are architectural drawings?
2. List five occupations to which the ability to read and interpret architectural drawings is essential.
3. What are *building codes*?
4. What is the basic difference between platform framing and balloon framing?
5. When framing an opening for a window, two framing members are nailed together to form a _____ to support the window from above.
6. What is a *truss*?
7. Stairs are made up of horizontal surfaces known as _____ and vertical surfaces known as _____.
8. Architectural plans (such as floor plans) are usually drawn to a scale of _____.
9. The location of the building(s) on the construction site is shown on the _____ plan. This drawing also shows walks, driveways, and patios.
10. Drawings that show the various views of the structure (the front, rear, and side views) are called _____.
11. What type of plan drawing shows the structural components of a building, such as beams, posts, and footings?
12. Make a sketch showing three recommended methods for dimensioning architectural drawings. Refer to **Figure 24-26**.
13. Explain how to use the square foot method to determine the size of a home that can be built based on the amount of money available.
14. Define *module* and identify the most common module used for residential construction in the United States.
15. Describe several advantages presented by computer-aided drafting (CAD) programs over manual drafting in preparing architectural drawings.

Outside Activities

1. Make a scale drawing of the school drafting room. Use a scale of 1/4″ = 1′-0″. Use cutouts to determine an efficient layout for the furniture in the room.
2. Prepare a drawing of your bedroom showing the location of the furniture in the room. Use a scale of 1/2″ = 1′-0″.
3. Draw a floor plan of a two-car garage with a workshop at one end.
4. Design and draw a full set of plans for a two-room summer cottage or hunting cabin.
5. Draw the plans necessary to convert your basement or other space into a workshop, a recreation room, or a darkroom.

6. Design and draw the plans needed to construct a toolshed. See **Figure 24-36**.

7. Design a small two-bedroom house that can be constructed at minimum cost. Construct a model of it.

8. Plan a structure to house a sports car agency.

9. Obtain samples of computer-generated architectural drawings. Label each type of drawing.

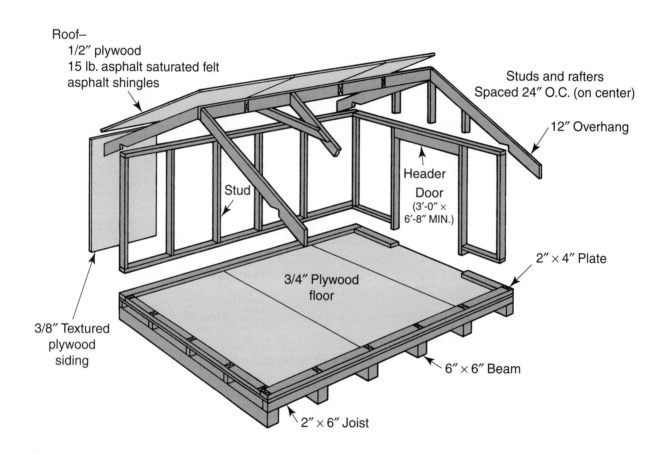

Figure 24-36 Framing and structural details for a toolshed. Use the information shown for completing Outside Activity #6.

A well-designed structure requires drawings that specify construction details and building information such as electrical locations. Can you identify the types of floor and wall framing used in the design of this building?

25 Manufacturing Processes

OBJECTIVES

After studying this chapter,
you should be able to:

◆ Identify and describe basic manufacturing processes.

◆ Name and describe the different types of machines and tools used to manufacture products.

◆ Explain and illustrate methods of cutting, shaping, forming, molding, and fabricating metals and plastics.

DRAFTING VOCABULARY

Bench grinder
Blanking
Bore
Broach
Casting
Composites
Computer numerical
   control (CNC)
Compression
   molding
Cope
Countersinking
Cylindrical grinder
Die
Die casting
Direct shell
   production casting
   (DSPC)
Drag
Drilling
Drill press
Flask
Forming
Gates
Grinding
Horizontal milling
   machine
Injection molding

Lathe
Machine tool
Milling
Milling machine
Mold
Numerical control
   (NC)
Pattern
Permanent mold
Planer
Ream
Reinforced plastics
Risers
Sand casting
Servos
Shearing
Sprue
Stamping
Stereolithography
Surface grinder
Tapping
Transfer molding
Turning center
Turret
Turret lathe
Twist drill
Vertical milling
   machine

The purpose of most drawings is to describe a part or a product that is to be manufactured. Therefore, it is important that the drafter have an understanding of how the materials can be cut, shaped, formed, and fabricated. Metals, plastics, and other materials are made in a variety of shapes and sizes for use in manufacturing. See **Figure 25-1**. By understanding manufacturing processes, the drafter can better visualize how objects are drawn to represent manufactured parts.

Machine Tools

The world of today could not exist without machine tools. They produce the accurate and uniform parts needed for the many products we use.

A *machine tool* is a power-driven machine that holds a workpiece and cutting tool and brings them together so that material is drilled, cut, shaved, or ground. Machine tools are used to *machine* metal and other materials. They use cutting, impact, pressure, and electrical techniques (or a combination of processes) to manufacture products.

There are many types and sizes of machine tools. Only basic tools and manufacturing techniques are covered in this chapter.

Lathe

The *lathe* is one of the oldest and most important of the machine tools, **Figure 25-2**. It operates on the principle of the workpiece being rotated against the edge of a cutting

Figure 25-2 A lathe with manual operation controls.

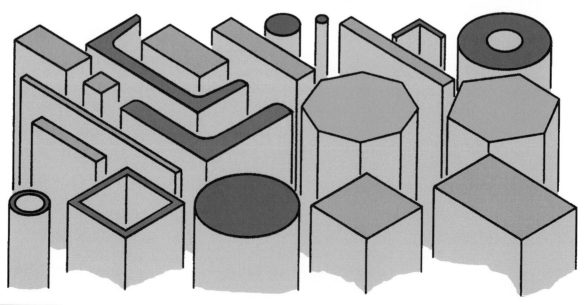

Figure 25-1 Metals, plastics, and other materials used in manufacturing are made in many sizes and shapes.

tool. See **Figure 25-3**. The cutting tool can be controlled to move lengthwise and across the face of the material being machined (turned). The major parts of a lathe are shown in **Figure 25-4**.

Operations other than turning can also be performed on the lathe. It is possible to *bore* (enlarge a hole to exact size), **Figure 25-5**. It is also possible to *ream* (finish a hole to exact size), as well as cut threads and tapers.

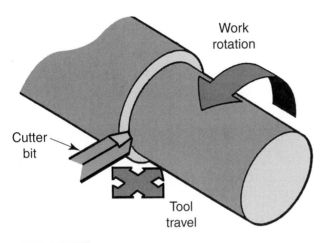

Figure 25-3   The operating principle of the lathe.

Figure 25-5   Boring (internal machining) on a lathe. (Clausing Industrial, Inc.)

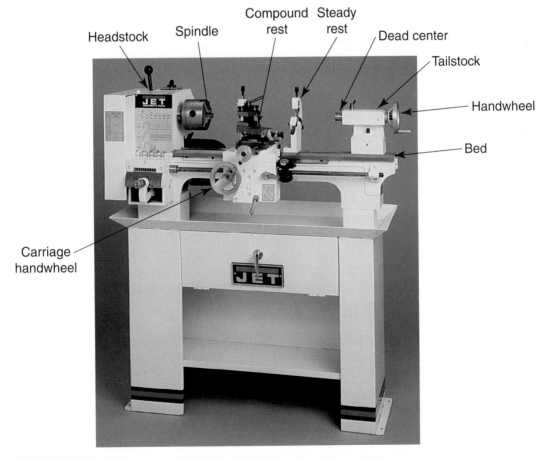

Figure 25-4   The lathe and its major parts. (Jet Equipment & Tools)

There are many variations of the basic lathe. One of the most complex is the *turning center*, **Figure 25-6**. It is capable of automated machining without operator intervention (involvement). This type of lathe operates using *computer numerical control (CNC)*. CNC machine tools perform computer-automated machining functions. In CNC machining, the tool movement and workpiece operations are controlled by a computer. After the turning center is set up and programmed, it changes parts and tools, monitors tool condition, and determines when tools need to be changed. The finished machined parts are *gaged* (measured) automatically and the data is fed back into the machine's CNC controls, which makes necessary adjustments to maintain consistent machining accuracy. Material that is machined is commonly loaded and unloaded robotically.

Figure 25-6 A multifunction CNC horizontal turning center. All machining functions are computer controlled. (Okuma America Corporation)

The *turret lathe* is used when a number of identical parts must be turned. It is a conventional lathe fitted with a six-sided tool holder called a *turret*. Different cutting tools fitted in the turret rotate into position for machining operations.

ACADEMIC LINK

Machine tools can be defined as the class of machines which, taken as a group, can reproduce themselves (manufacture other machine tools). Many machine tools have evolved from the lathe.

Two of the earliest machine tools, used as early as about 1200 BC, were the handmade bow lathe and bow drill. They were human-powered and used for making parts for plows and wagons. Up to the late 17th century, the lathe could be used to manufacture parts from soft materials (such as wood). Tools during this period were powered by hand, foot, animals, or water.

A major advance in the development of machine tools was the invention of the boring mill by John Wilkinson in 1774. This tool, a type of lathe powered by a waterwheel, made it possible to bore metal cylinders. Soon after, James Watt used this technology to produce the first steam engine. The introduction of steam power was important because it enabled tools to be powered at any location (rather than near a source of water). This period was the beginning of the Industrial Revolution.

A lathe used to cut screw threads in metal was introduced in the early 1800s. This brought about further advances. The milling machine also evolved from the lathe and was used by Eli Whitney to mass-produce interchangeable parts for muskets beginning around 1820.

By the late 1800s, machine tools were capable of machining parts to accuracies within 1/1000″. Much of the progress from that time can be traced to the lathe. The development of the lathe and other machine tools is responsible for many of the products we enjoy today.

Other lathes range in size from the small lathe needed by the instrument and watchmaker, **Figure 25-7**, to the large lathes that machine forming rolls for steel mills, **Figure 25-8**.

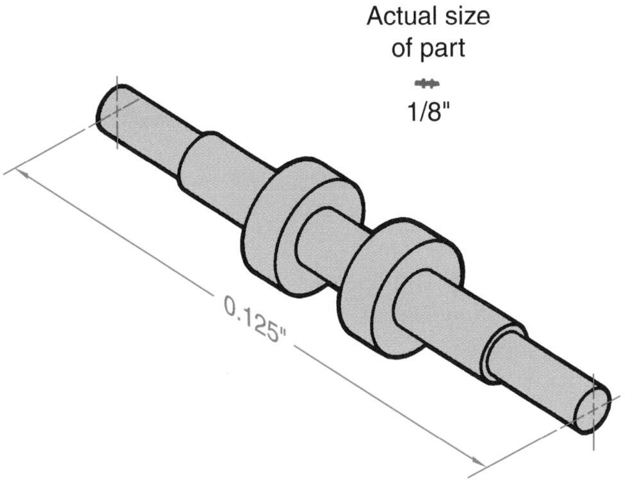

Drill Press

The *drill press* is probably the best known of the machine tools, **Figure 25-9**. In *drilling*, a cutting tool called a *twist drill* is rotated

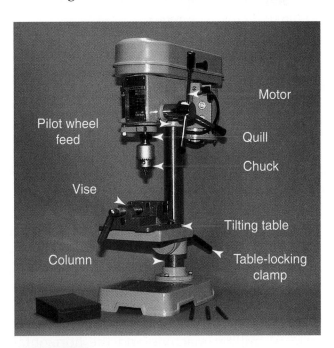

Figure 25-9   A bench-model drill press with major parts identified.

Actual size
of part

1/8"

0.125"

Figure 25-7   A part made on a lathe used by instrument and watchmakers.

Figure 25-8   A lathe for machining forming rolls for a steel mill.

against the workpiece with sufficient pressure to cut its way through the material, **Figure 25-10**. The spiral flutes on the twist drill do not pull the drill into the workpiece. Pressure must be applied to the rotating drill to make it cut.

Other operations that can be performed on a drill press include reaming, countersinking, and tapping. *Countersinking* is cutting a chamfer on a hole so a flat head fastener can be inserted. *Tapping* is cutting internal threads in a drilled hole.

Milling Machine

A *milling machine* is a very versatile machine tool. It can be used to machine flat and irregularly shaped surfaces. It can also be used to drill, bore, and cut gears.

In *milling*, metal is removed by means of a rotating cutter that is fed into the moving workpiece. See **Figure 25-11**. There are two basic types of milling machines. These are the vertical milling machine and the horizontal milling machine.

The *vertical milling machine* uses a cutter mounted *vertically* in relation to the worktable, **Figure 25-12**. With this type of machine, the cutter spindle is perpendicular to the

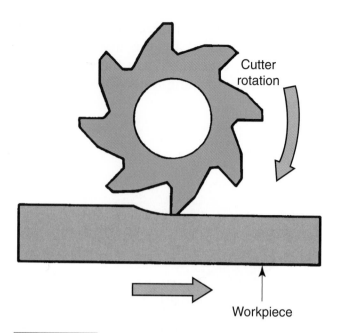

Figure 25-11 The operating principle of a milling machine. Shown is the operation of a horizontal milling machine.

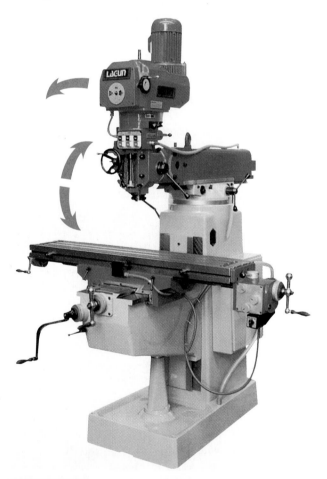

Figure 25-12 A vertical milling machine. (Republic-Lagun Machine Tool Co.)

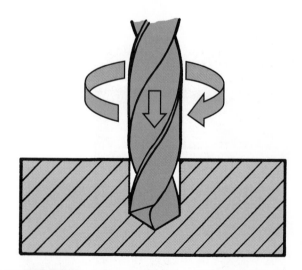

Figure 25-10 The operating principle of the drill press. The tool rotates while pressure is applied to force the drill into the material.

work surface, **Figure 25-13**. The *horizontal milling machine* uses a cutter mounted *horizontally* in relation to the worktable, **Figure 25-14**. With this type of machine, the cutter spindle is parallel to the work surface. See **Figure 25-15**. There are other types of milling machines. They vary in size and by types of automatic controls. The main parts of a horizontal milling machine are shown in **Figure 25-16**.

Planer and Broach

Large, flat surfaces are machined on a *planer*, **Figure 25-17**. This is a very large type of milling machine. It operates by moving the workpiece against a cutting tool or tools, **Figure 25-18**.

A *broach* employs a multi-tooth cutting tool. Each successive tooth has a cutting edge that increases in size by a few thousandths of an inch. The teeth increase in size to the exact finished size required. See **Figure 25-19**. The teeth are grouped into roughing teeth, semi-finishing teeth, and finishing teeth. The teeth of the cutting tool are pushed or pulled over the surface being machined.

Many flat surfaces on automobile engines are broached. Broaching can also be used to perform internal machining operations, such as the removal of material for keyways, splines, and irregularly shaped openings, **Figure 25-20**.

Figure 25-13 The cutter position of a vertical milling machine.

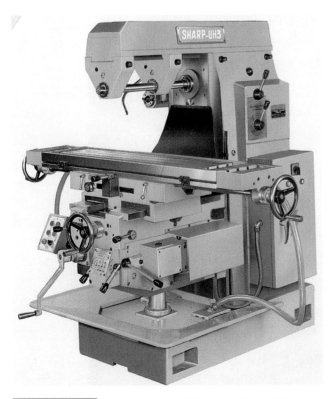

Figure 25-14 A horizontal milling machine. (Sharp Industries, Inc.)

Figure 25-15 The cutter position on a horizontal milling machine.

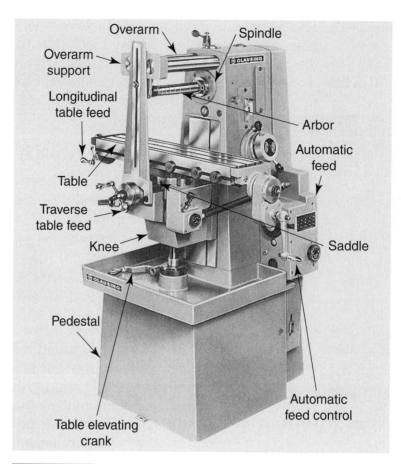

Figure 25-16 A horizontal milling machine and its main parts.

Figure 25-17 A large, multispindle fixed-bed planer mill. This machine is shaping upper wing skins for commercial aircraft. (Northrop-Grumman Aerospace Corp.)

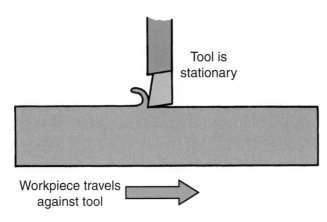

Figure 25-18 The operating principle of the planer.

Tool is stationary

Workpiece travels against tool

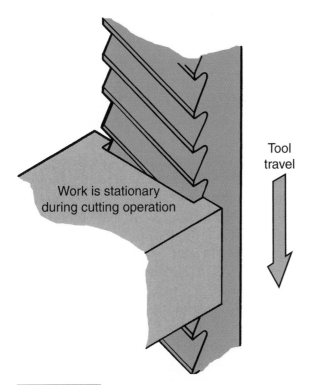

Work is stationary during cutting operation

Tool travel

Figure 25-19 How a broach operates. A multi-tooth cutter moves against the workpiece. The operation may be on a vertical or horizontal plane.

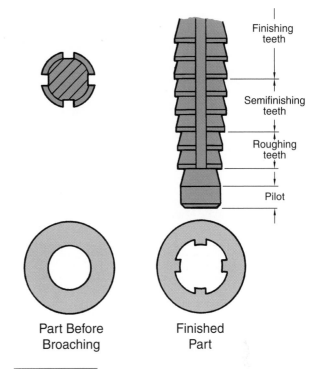

Finishing teeth

Semifinishing teeth

Roughing teeth

Pilot

Part Before Broaching

Finished Part

Figure 25-20 A typical broaching cutter tool and the work it produces. In this internal broaching operation, the pilot (front end) of the tool guides the cutter into an opening previously made in the work. The teeth cut the part to the specified size.

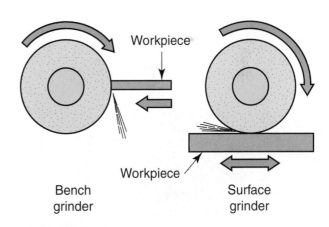

Workpiece

Workpiece

Bench grinder

Surface grinder

Figure 25-21 Operating principles for grinders.

Grinder

Grinding is an operation that removes material by rotating an abrasive wheel against the workpiece, **Figure 25-21**. A *bench grinder* is the simplest and most widely used grinding machine, **Figure 25-22**.

Flat surfaces are ground to very close tolerances on a *surface grinder*, **Figure 25-23**.

It is possible to surface grind hardened steel parts to tolerances of 1/100,000 (0.00001″ or 0.0002 mm) with very fine (almost mirror-like) surface finishes.

Round work can be ground to the same tolerances and finishes on a *cylindrical grinder*, **Figure 25-24**.

Figure 25-22 Bench grinder.

Figure 25-24 A closeup of a cylindrical grinder. Note the part being ground and the abrasive wheel doing the work. (Landis Division of Western Atlas)

Other Machining Techniques

In addition to the conventional machining methods previously discussed, industry employs many unusual techniques to shape metal and other materials. These include electrical discharge machining (EDM), electrochemical machining (ECM), electron beam machining, laser machining, and ultrasonic machining. These are just a few of the more modern methods. These methods are usually used to machine materials that are difficult or impossible to machine by conventional methods. If interested, you might want to refer to other published materials or online resources to research these newer machining techniques.

Machine Tool Operations

Machining technology has evolved over many years. There are many types of operations that have been used to control machine tools. They range from manual methods to modern-day operations using automated equipment. The most common machine tool operations have been based on manual, numerical control, and computer numerical control methods. This section discusses these types of methods.

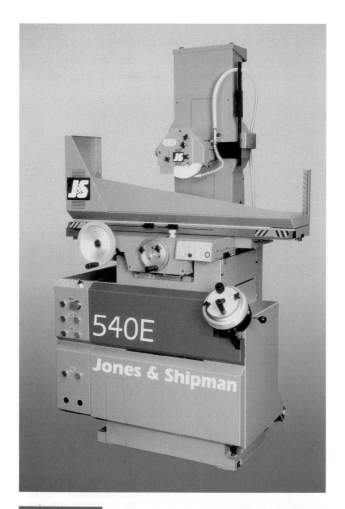

Figure 25-23 Surface grinder. (Jones & Shipman, Inc.)

CAREERS IN DRAFTING

Machinist

What would I do if I were to become a machinist? I would use machine tools, such as lathes, milling machines, and machining centers, to produce precision metal parts. I would plan and prepare the operations needed to make each part. I would also review blueprints or written specifications for the part, determine what machines or tools would be necessary to create the part, calculate the precise operations required, and perform the operations with accuracy and precision.

What would I need to know? I would have to know how to read plans for the products that I would be making and possibly make the plans. I would also have to be familiar with standard metalworking hand tools and machines, manual and computer numerical control (CNC) procedures, metal fasteners and fastening methods, and all metalworking-related products and procedures.

Where would I work? I would work in a machine shop equipped with hand tools and machine tools necessary to do various types of work.

For whom would I work? I would work for a small privately owned machine shop or for a manufacturer, such as a machinery manufacturer or a transportation equipment manufacturer. If I do well in my profession and I am fortunate enough, I may be able to open my own machine shop.

What sort of education would I need? I could receive training to become a machinist in several different ways. I could train in an apprenticeship program, informally on the job, or in high school, at a vocational school, or at a community or technical college. High school courses in math (especially trigonometry), blueprint reading, metalworking, and drafting are highly recommended.

What are the special fields relating to this career? Some specialized fields of machining include CNC programming, tool and die making, and moldmaking.

What are my chances of finding a job? My prospects for finding a job are excellent. This is due to a projected shortage of workers able to fill positions left vacant by experienced machinists who leave the profession or retire.

How much money could I expect to make? The median hourly wage for machinists in recent years was $15.66. Per-hour wages ranged from $9.57 to $23.17 and up. My chances of a higher wage rate will be enhanced slightly if I work in the metalworking machinery manufacturing industry.

Where else could I look for more information about becoming a machinist? See the US Department of Labor's Bureau of Labor Statistics Occupational Outlook Handbook (at www.bls.gov) or request information from the Precision Machined Products Association (www.pmpa.org), the National Tooling and Machining Association (www.ntma.org), or the Precision Metalforming Association Educational Foundation (www.pmaef.org).

If I decide to pursue a different career, what other fields are related to machining? Professionals in related fields include tool and die makers; machine setters, operators, and tenders; and CNC programmers and operators. Welding, soldering, and brazing are also closely related to machining.

- **Manual**. Although computer-based machining methods have replaced manual methods in many cases, manual-based equipment is still used to machine parts. In manual-based machining, the operator feeds the cutter into the workpiece and manually guides it through the operations that will produce the part specified on the drawing. See **Figure 25-25**.
- **Numerical control** (**NC**). Before computer processing was integrated into manufacturing, numerical control systems made automated machine tool operations possible. *Numerical control (NC)* is a system of controlling a machine tool by means of numeric codes that direct commands to electric motors and devices attached or built into the machine. The motors are called *servos*. Instructions from magnetic tape (or data from a computer) control electronic impulses that tell the servos when to start, where to move, and how far they are to move, as well as the cutter speed and depth, **Figure 25-26**.
- **Computer numerical control** (**CNC**). Numerical control systems have evolved into computer numerical control

systems. As previously discussed, CNC machine tools are controlled by computer programs. Using one of the many CNC languages, the machining instructions are entered into the system and sent directly to one or more tools, **Figure 25-27**.

Figure 25-26 A numerically controlled (NC) machine tool. Instructions from magnetic tape or computer memory tell the servos (motors) when to start and how to move the work being machined. Shown is a plasma cutter, which produces parts with little waste. (Cybernation Cutting Systems, Inc.)

Figure 25-25 The controls on this vertical milling machine are manually operated. (U.S. Army)

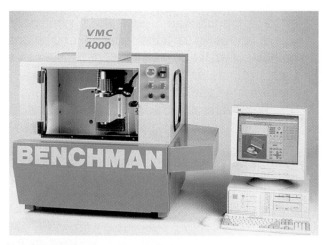

Figure 25-27 A CNC bench-type vertical machining center. This machine is capable of all types of milling and drilling operations. (Light Machines Corp.)

CNC machine tools are commonly used in conjunction with CAD/CAM (computer-aided design/computer-aided manufacturing) systems. With CAD/CAM software, it is possible for an engineer, designer, or drafter to design a part and see how it will fit and work with the other parts that make up a product. After the design has been confirmed, the computer can be programmed to analyze the geometry and calculate the tool paths required to make the part. The program is verified by machining a sample part from inexpensive material (such as plastic or special wax). An example of CAD/CAM machining is shown in **Figure 25-28**.

Metal Cutting and Forming Operations

In addition to the machining processes previously discussed, there are a number of other common operations used in metalworking. Metal sheet can be given shape

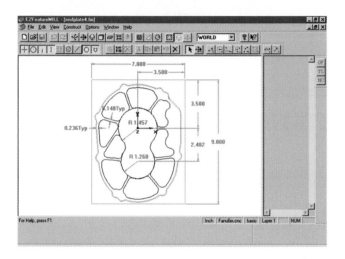

A

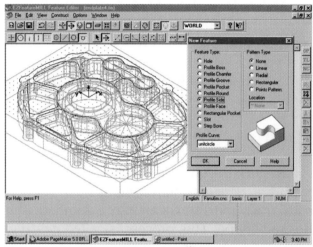

B

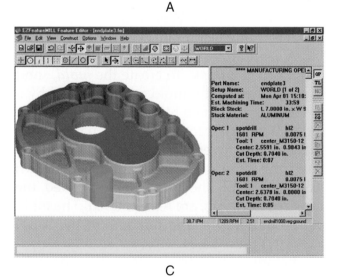

C

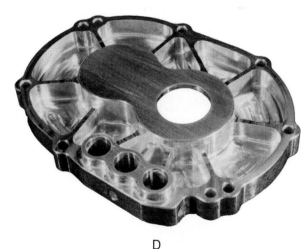

D

Figure 25-28 Machining a part with CAD/CAM software. A—The geometry of the part is created at the machine tool or imported from files. B—The software defines the surfaces and features of the part. C—The software produces ready-to-use operations sheets and tool lists for the machinist. D—A program generated by the software is used to machine the part. (EZFeatureMILL—Engineering Geometry Systems)

and form through shearing, stamping, and forming. These operations are used to cut and form metal to finished shapes or to prepare metal for further machining.

Shearing is a cutting process in which the material (usually in sheet form) is cut to shape using actions similar to cutting paper with scissors.

Stamping is a general metalworking term used to describe different operations. Stamping can be divided into two separate classifications: *cutting* and *forming*. A cutting operation known as *blanking* involves cutting flat sheets to the shape of the finished part. Holes and openings in the metal are cut with punches and dies. See **Figure 25-29**. *Forming* is a process where flat metal is given three-dimensional form using a press and die. See **Figure 25-30**.

Casting Processes

Materials can also be given shape and form by reducing them to liquid in a molten state and pouring them into a mold of the desired shape. This process is called *casting*. Metal casting methods include sand casting, permanent mold casting, and die casting.

Figure 25-30 A forming operation gave flat metal sheet three-dimensional form for use in this panel. It also added strength and rigidity. (Laserdyne Div., Lumonics Corp.)

Sand Casting

In *sand casting*, the mold that gives the molten metal the desired shape is made of sand, **Figure 25-31**. This is one of the oldest metal forming techniques known.

A sand mold is made by packing sand in a box called a *flask*. To create the *mold*, sand is packed around a mold cavity formed by a *pattern* of the shape to be cast, **Figure 25-32**. Since metal contracts as it cools, patterns are made slightly oversize to allow for shrinkage. After the pattern has been drawn (removed) from the sand, the mold halves, called the *cope* and the *drag*, are reassembled. The mold of the required shape remains in the sand. Refer to **Figure 25-31**.

Before assembling the mold, openings are made in the mold to allow molten metal to reach and fill the mold. These openings are called *sprues*, *risers*, and *gates*. A *sprue* is an opening into which the molten metal is poured. *Risers* allow the hot gases to escape.

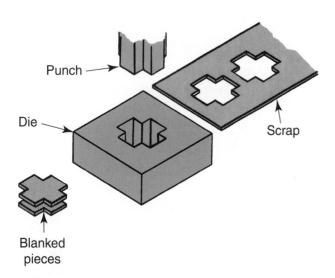

Figure 25-29 A blanking operation.

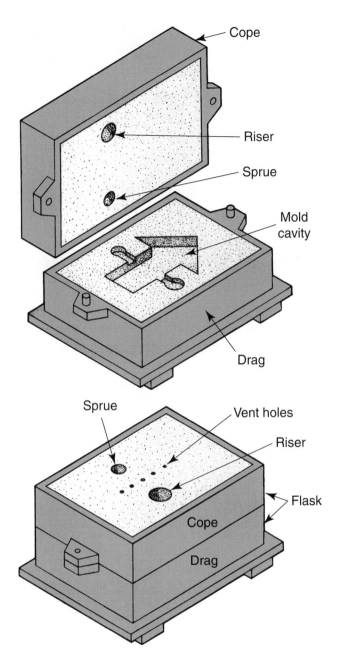

Figure 25-31   The parts of a typical sand casting mold.

Gates are trenches that run from the sprues and risers to the mold cavity. After the metal is poured, the casting is allowed to cool and solidify. Sand molds must be destroyed to remove the casting.

Permanent Mold Casting

Some molds used for casting metal are made from metal. These molds are called *permanent molds* because they do not have

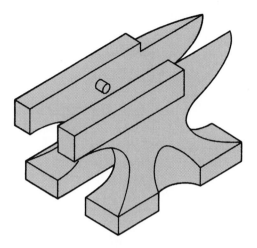

Figure 25-32   A two-piece pattern used to make a cavity in a sand mold.

to be destroyed (like sand molds) to remove the casting. A *permanent mold* is used for the repeated production of similar castings. The process produces castings with a fine surface finish and a high degree of accuracy.

Auto pistons and fishing sinkers are common products made using the permanent mold process. See **Figure 25-33**.

Die Casting

Die casting is a process in which molten metal is forced into a *die* (mold) under pressure, **Figure 25-34**. The pressure is maintained until the metal solidifies. The mold is then opened and the casting is ejected. The mold or die is made of metal.

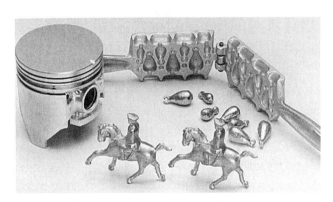

Figure 25-33   Common metal products made from permanent mold casting.

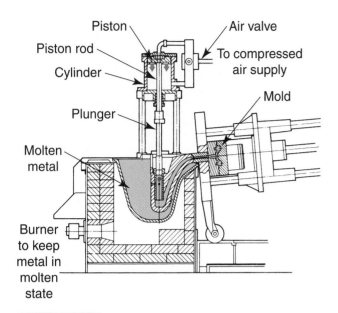

Piston
Piston rod
Cylinder
Plunger
Molten metal
Burner to keep metal in molten state
Air valve
To compressed air supply
Mold

Figure 25-34 A diagram of a die casting machine. The molten metal is forced into the die (mold) under pressure. (American Die Casting Institute)

Figure 25-35 A finished die cast part being checked to determine whether specifications have been achieved. (American Foundrymen's Society, Inc.)

Die castings are denser than sand castings. The castings are usually very accurate, **Figure 25-35**.

Plastics and Molding Processes

Plastics are made into usable products by many different processes. Some plastics can be shaped directly into final form. Other plastics require several operations to transform them into usable products. Many of the processes for forming plastics are similar to those used to shape metal.

Compression Molding

In *compression molding*, a measured amount of plastic is placed in a two-part mold. See **Figure 25-36**. The mold is heated and closed, and pressure is applied. The plastic, melted by the heat and pressure, flows into all parts of the mold cavity. The mold is then opened and the molded plastic is removed for trimming.

Transfer Molding

Transfer molding is similar to compression molding. It differs in that the plastic is heated in a separate section of the mold before it is forced into the mold cavity, **Figure 25-37**.

Injection Molding

Injection molding is similar to transfer molding in that the plastic is heated before it is forced into the mold. See **Figure 25-38**. Plastic granules are placed in the injection molding machine and heated until they are soft enough to flow. The softened plastic is then injected into the mold cavity. When cooled, the mold is opened, and the part is ejected. Plastic model kits are one of the many plastic products made by injection molding, **Figure 25-39**.

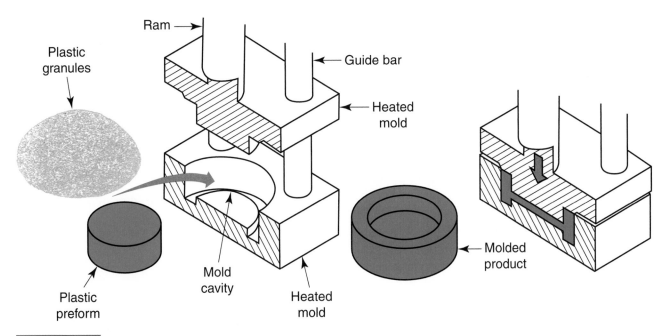

Figure 25-36 The compression molding process.

Reinforced Plastics

Reinforced plastics are resins that have been strengthened with fiberglass, carbon, or organic fibers. Reinforced plastics are also known as *composites*. See **Figure 25-40**.

Resin-saturated fibers can be formed mechanically using heat and pressure. Body parts for automobiles are made this way. Reinforced plastic products are usually formed in polished metal molds.

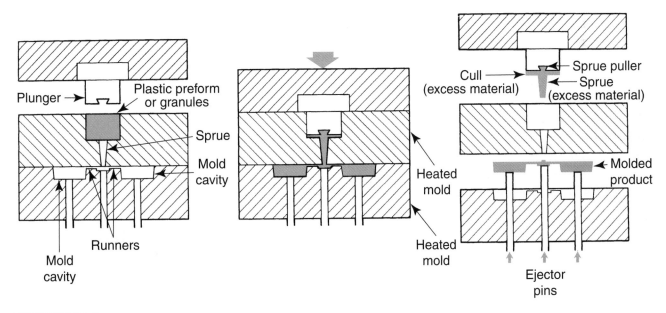

Figure 25-37 The transfer molding process.

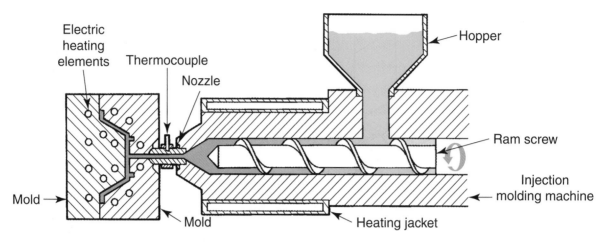

Figure 25-38 The injection molding process.

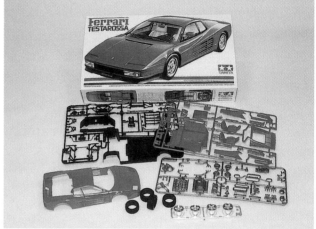

Figure 25-39 Plastic model kits are typical products made by injection molding.

Figure 25-40 An aircraft made from composites. The plane's strong, lightweight airframe is made primarily of a honeycomb of Nomex® aramid fiber sandwiched between skins of Kevlar® aramid fiber. The plane's maximum weight is 5500 pounds, less than half that of most aluminum turboprop aircraft. (Avtek Corp.)

Stereolithography

Stereolithography is a plastics technology capable of producing complex design prototypes of castings and other components. This process is a useful alternative to other prototyping processes because three-dimensional models can be generated in several hours (instead of days or weeks). The hard plastic models can be viewed and studied to determine whether they are the best solution to the design problem. Since new models can be made quickly, design changes and modifications can be evaluated without the expense of making new patterns or molds.

The stereolithography process starts by creating the required design as a 3D model using a CAD system. The resulting electronic file is then used by a machine to generate a physical model. The operation is similar to that of a CNC machine tool. The stereolithography machine contains a vat of liquid photo-curable polymer plastic. The machine uses a computer-guided, low-powered laser beam to harden a shape from the polymer, **Figure 25-41**. A support platform in the vat holds the model as it is built up.

The machine's computer defines the part for production by "slicing" the design into thin cross sections of 0.005″ to 0.020″ (0.12 mm to 0.50 mm). The design data is used to construct the part section by section.

The machine's control unit guides the laser to generate each section. The first section is generated on the support table, which is positioned just below the vat surface. The liquid solidifies wherever it is struck by the laser. After the first section is generated, the platform drops a programmed distance. The model is constructed from the bottom up, with the platform dropping after each section is completed. The process continues until the entire model is formed. The model is then removed from the vat. When it is removed, the excess plastic drains off.

The finished part requires ultraviolet curing. When completely cured, the model can be finished by filing, sanding, and polishing, **Figure 25-42**. Paint or dye can be applied.

A variation of the stereolithography process produces parts made of ceramic material instead of plastic. The model is built up with layers of a special ceramic powder generated by an inkjet-style printer. The printer sprays a quick-hardening binder to solidify each layer. The technology has been used to quickly produce shell molds for casting metals. The moldmaking process is called *direct shell production casting (DSPC)*.

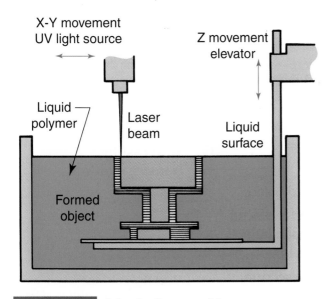

Figure 25-41 A basic diagram of the stereolithography process. The machine uses a laser to generate a model from liquid polymer.

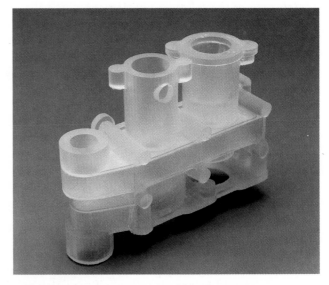

Figure 25-42 A complex part produced for evaluation by the stereolithography process. (Garrett Engine Division, Allied Signal Aerospace)

Test Your Knowledge

Please do not write in this book. Place your answers on another sheet of paper.

1. Define *machine tool*.
2. Briefly describe the operating principle of a lathe.
3. Make a sketch showing how a lathe operates.
4. A _____ lathe has a six-sided tool holder used for different machining operations.
5. List three operations that can be performed on a drill press.
6. Make a sketch showing how a drill press operates.
7. What is the difference between a vertical milling machine and a horizontal milling machine?
8. Make a sketch showing how a horizontal milling machine operates.
9. Briefly describe how a broach operates.
10. Make a sketch showing how a planer operates.
11. Make a sketch showing how a surface grinder operates.
12. A turning center is an example of what type of machining?
13. In sand casting, a _____ is an opening in the mold into which molten metal is poured.
14. Briefly describe the stereolithography process.

Match each of the following statements with the correct lettered term.

15. A metalworking operation in which sheet metal is given a three-dimensional shape.
16. A process in which the mold must be destroyed to remove the casting.
17. A process in which the mold is not destroyed when the casting is removed.
18. The upper half of a sand casting mold.
19. The object used to make the mold cavity in a sand mold.
20. A process in which a measured amount of plastic is placed into a two-part mold, the mold is heated and closed, and pressure forces the plastic into all parts of the mold.
21. A process in which plastic is heated in a separate section of the mold before it is forced into the mold cavity.
22. A metalworking operation that involves cutting sheet metal to the shape of the finished part.

A. Blanking
B. Compression molding
C. Cope
D. Forming
E. Pattern
F. Permanent mold casting
G. Sand casting
H. Transfer molding

Outside Activities

1. Prepare a bulletin board with clippings that illustrate basic machine tools.

2. Obtain samples of work manufactured with various machine tools, including the lathe, drill press, milling machine, and surface grinder. Make a display and label the advantages of using the different machines.

3. Bring into class examples of products that were cast in sand molds, die castings, and permanent molds. Describe the differences among the products.

4. Report to the class, using visual aids, the newest developments in flexible manufacturing systems.

Drafting standards play a critical role in the development of drawings for prototype models in the automotive industry. Before vehicles such as this Ford Iosis concept car are considered for production, engineering drawings that observe standards must be developed to accurately show manufacturing details and other product information. (Ford)

Useful Information

This section contains a number of tables, charts, and other resources that can be used for reference for a variety of drafting applications. These resources are listed below by page number to simplify locating them.

ASME Drafting and Dimensioning Standards

The American Society of Mechanical Engineers (ASME) *Dimensioning and Tolerancing* drafting standard (ASME Y14.5M) includes revisions to standards for placing notes and dimensions on drawings. The following is a very brief description of the standards and practices recommended for use.

Symbols are used in place of certain terms that were used on older drawings. The symbols are intended to make drafting a more international language. They include symbols for placing diameter dimensions, radius dimensions, and other notes for holes. These practices are outlined in the following charts. The current standards are compared against older conventions. As older drawings are

revised, drafters will incorporate the symbols into the revisions.

When dimensioning drawings, unidirectional dimensioning is preferred over aligned dimensioning. Decimal dimensions (in inches or millimeters) are the preferred practice. Fractional inch dimensions are only recommended for special fields that do not require decimal accuracy (such as furniture making, sheet metal fabrication, or other types of manufacturing where materials are not machined to fine tolerances).

Drawings dimensioned to ASME standards should contain a note such as "Drawn in accordance to ASME Y14.5M." Additional information about drafting standards can be obtained from the American Society of Mechanical Engineers at 345 East 47th Street, New York, NY 10017 or at www.asme.org.

Designation	ASME Standard Practice	Old Practice
Not to scale	12	12 or NTS
Diameter	Ø26	26 DIA
Radius	R13	13 R
Reference dimension	(14)	14 REF
Times/places	6X	6 PLACES
Counterbore	⌴Ø7	7 CBORE
Countersink	⌵Ø3	3 CSK
Deep	▽14	14 DP
Square	□14	14 SQ
Sample Notes	4X 1/2–12 UNC–3B Ø.4062 ▽1.25 ⌴Ø.50 ▽.062 ⟶	1/2–12 UNC—3B–4 HOLES 13/32 DRILL—1 1/4 DP 1/2 C BORE–1/16 DP⟶

Standard Symbols Used in Dimensioning

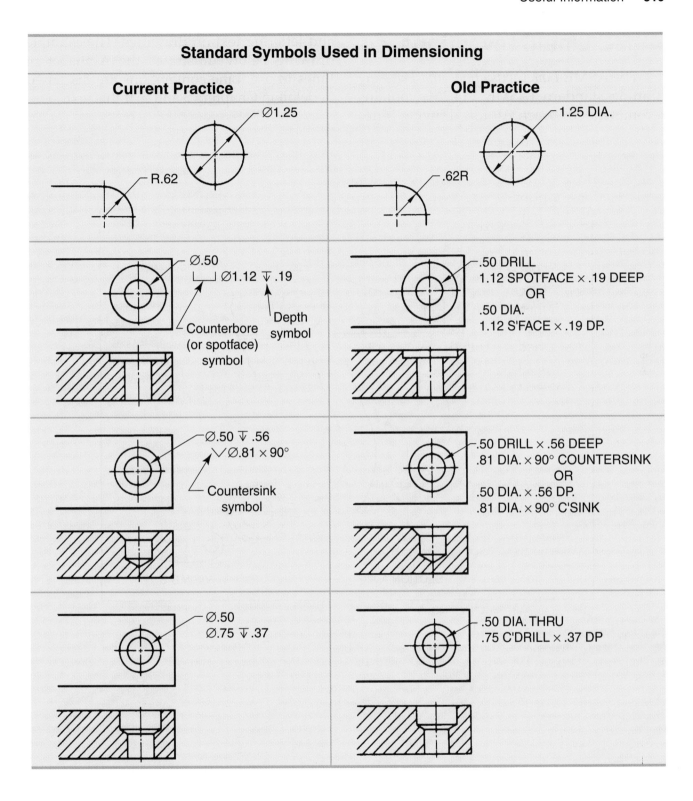

ASME Line Conventions

The ASME *Line Conventions and Lettering* drafting standard (ASME Y14.2M) contains recommended practices for drawing lines and lettering text on drawings. The example drawing below illustrates the Alphabet of Lines in use. Line conventions are discussed in detail in Chapters 3 and 5 of this text.

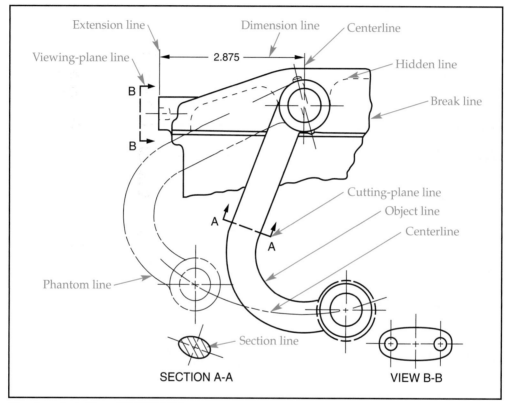

(Drawing adapted from ASME Y14.2M)

Measurement Systems

English System	Metric System

English System

Measures of Time

60 sec. = 1 min.
60 min. = 1 hr.
24 hr.   = 1 day
365 dy. = 1 common yr.
366 dy. = 1 leap yr.

Dry Measures

2 pt.   = 1 qt.
8 qt.   = 1 pk.
4 pk.   =1 bu.
2150.42 cu. in. = 1 bu.

Measures of Length

12 in.   = 1 ft.
3 ft.   = 1 yd.
5 1/2 yd. = 1 rod
320 rods = 1 mile
5280 ft. = 1 mile
1760 yd. = 1 mile
6080 ft. = 1 knot

Liquid Measures

16 fluid oz. = 1 pt.
2 pt.   = 1 qt.
32 fl. oz. = 1 qt.
4 qt.   = 1 gal.
31 1/2 gal. = 1 bbl.
231 cu in. = 1 gal.
7 1/2 gal. = 1 cu. ft.

Measures of Area

144 sq. in.   = 1 sq. ft.
9 sq. ft.   = 1 sq. yd.
30 1/4 sq. yd. = 1 sq. rod
160 sq. rods   = 1 acre
640 acres   = 1 sq. mile

Measures of Weight (Avoirdupois)

7000 grains (gr.) = 1 lb.
16 oz.   = 1 lb.
100 lb.   = 1 cwt.
2000 lb.   = 1 short ton
2240 lb.   = 1 long ton

Measures of Volume

1728 cu. in. = 1 cu. ft.
27 cu. ft.   = 1 cu. yd.
128 cu. ft. = 1 cord

Metric System

The basic unit of the metric system is the meter (m). The meter is exactly 39.37" long. This is 3.37" longer than the English yard. Units that are multiples or fractional parts of the meter are designated as such by prefixes to the word "meter." For example:

1 millimeter (mm) = 0.001 meter or 1/1000 meter
1 centimeter (cm) = 0.01 meter or 1/100 meter
1 decimeter (dm)   = 0.1 meter or 1/10 meter
                     1 meter (m)
1 decameter (dkm) = 10 meters
1 hectometer (hm) = 100 meters
1 kilometer (km)   = 1000 meters

These prefixes may be applied to any unit of length, weight, volume, etc. The meter is adopted as the basic unit of length, the gram for mass, and the liter for volume.

In the metric system, area is measured in square kilometers (sq km or km^2), square centimeters (sq cm or cm^2), etc. Volume is commonly measured in cubic centimeters, etc. One liter (1) is equal to 1000 cubic centimeters.

The metric measurements in most common use are shown in the following tables:

Measures of Length

10 millimeters = 1 centimeter
10 centimeters = 1 decimeter
10 decimeters = 1 meter
1000 meters   = 1 kilometer

Measures of Weight

100 milligrams = 1 gram
1000 grams   = 1 kilogram
1000 kilograms = 1 metric ton

Measures of Volume

1000 cubic centimeters = 1 liter
100 liters   = 1 hectoliter

Metric Prefixes, Exponents, and Symbols

Decimal Form	Exponent or Power	Prefix	Pronunciation	Symbol	Meaning
1 000 000 000 000 000 000	$= 10^{18}$	exa	ex'a	E	quintillion
1 000 000 000 000 000	$= 10^{15}$	peta	pet'á	P	quadrillion
1 000 000 000 000	$= 10^{12}$	tera	tĕr'á	T	trillion
1 000 000 000	$= 10^{9}$	giga	ji'gá	G	billion
1 000 000	$= 10^{6}$	mega	mĕg'á	M	million
1 000	$= 10^{3}$	kilo	kĭl'ō	k	thousand
100	$= 10^{2}$	hecto	hĕk'to	h	hundred
10	$= 10^{1}$	deka	dĕk'a	da	ten
1					base unit
0.1	$= 10^{-1}$	deci	dĕs'i	d	tenth
0.01	$= 10^{-2}$	centi	sĕn'ti	c	hundredth
0.001	$= 10^{-3}$	milli	mĭl'ĭ	m	thousandths
0.000 001	$= 10^{-6}$	micro	mi'krō	μ	millionth
0.000 000 001	$= 10^{-9}$	nano	nănʼō	n	billionth
0.000 000 000 001	$= 10^{-12}$	pico	pécō	p	trillionth
0.000 000 000 000 001	$= 10^{-15}$	femto	fĕm'tō	f	quadrillionth
0.000 000 000 000 000 001	$= 10^{-18}$	atto	ăt'tō	a	quintillionth

Most commonly used

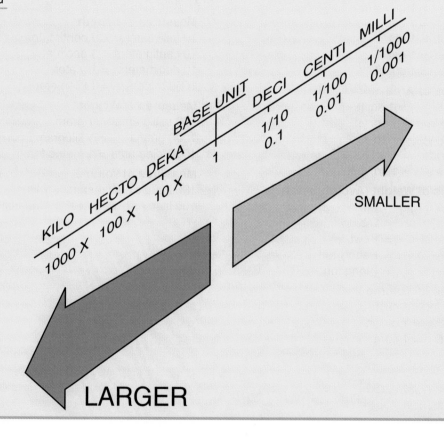

Conversion Table: US Conventional to SI Metric

When You Know ↓	Multiply By: Very Accurate	Multiply By: Approximate	To Find ↓
Length			
inches	* 25.4		millimeters
inches	* 2.54		centimeters
feet	* 0.3048		meters
feet	* 30.48		centimeters
yards	* 0.9144	0.9	meters
miles	* 1.609344	1.6	kilometers
Weight			
grains	15.43236	15.4	grams
ounces	* 28.349523125	28.0	grams
ounces	* 0.028349523125	.028	kilograms
pounds	* 0.45359237	0.45	kilograms
short ton	* 0.90718474	0.9	tonnes
Volume			
teaspoons		5.0	milliliters
tablespoons		15.0	milliliters
fluid ounces	29.57353	30.0	milliliters
cups		0.24	liters
pints	* 0.473176473	0.47	liters
quarts	* 0.946352946	0.95	liters
gallons	* 3.785411784	3.8	liters
cubic inches	* 0.016387064	0.02	liters
cubic feet	* 0.028316846592	0.03	cubic meters
cubic yards	* 0.764554857984	0.76	cubic meters
Area			
square inches	* 6.4516	6.5	square centimeters
square feet	* 0.09290304	0.09	square meters
square yards	* 0.83612736	0.8	square meters
square miles		2.6	square kilometers
acres	* 0.40468564224	0.4	hectares
Temperature			
Fahrenheit	* 5/9 (after subtracting 32)		Celsius
Density			
pounds per cubic feet	1.602×10	16	kilograms per cubic meter
Force			
ounces (F)	2.780×10^{-1}		newtons
pounds (F)	4.448×10^{-3}		kilonewtons
Kips	4.448		meganewtons
Stress			
pounds/square inch (psi)	6.895×10^{-3}		megapascals
kips/square inch (ksi)	6.895		megapascals
Torque			
ounce-inches	7.062×10^{3}		newton-meters
pound-inches	1.130×10^{-1}		newton-meters
pound-feet	1.356		newton-meters

* = Exact

Conversion Table: SI Metric to US Conventional

When You Know ⬇	Multiply By:		To Find ⬇
	Very Accurate	**Approximate**	
Length			
millimeters	0.0393701	0.04	inches
centimeters	0.3937008	0.4	inches
meters	3.280840	3.3	feet
meters	1.093613	1.1	yards
kilometers	0.621371	0.6	miles
Weight			
grains	0.00228571	0.0023	ounces
grams	0.03527396	0.035	ounces
kilograms	2.204623	2.2	pounds
tonnes	1.1023113	1.1	short tons
Volume			
milliliters		0.2	teaspoons
milliliters	0.06667	0.067	tablespoons
milliliters	0.03381402	0.03	fluid ounces
liters	61.02374	61.024	cubic inches
liters	2.113376	2.1	pints
liters	1.056688	1.06	quarts
liters	0.26417205	0.26	gallons
liters	0.03531467	0.035	cubic feet
cubic meters	61023.74	61023.7	cubic inches
cubic meters	35.31467	35.0	cubic feet
cubic meters	1.3079506	1.3	cubic yards
cubic meters	264.17205	264.0	gallons
Area			
square centimeters	0.1550003	0.16	square inches
square centimeters	0.00107639	0.001	square feet
square meters	10.76391	10.8	square feet
square meters	1.195990	1.2	square yards
square kilometers		0.4	square miles
hectares	2.471054	2.5	acres
Temperature			
Celsius	* 9/5 (then add 32)		Fahrenheit

* = Exact

Decimal Inch Conversion Chart

Fraction	Decimal Inches	Millimeters	Fraction	Decimal Inches	Millimeters
1/64	0.0156	0.3967	33/64	0.5162	13.0968
1/32	0.0312	0.7937	17/32	0.5312	13.4937
3/64	0.0468	1.1906	35/64	0.5468	13.8906
1/16	0.0625	1.5875	9/16	0.5625	14.2875
5/64	0.0781	1.9843	37/64	0.5781	14.6843
3/32	0.0937	2.3812	19/32	0.5937	15.0812
7/64	0.1093	2.7781	39/64	0.6093	15.4781
1/8	0.125	3.175	5/8	0.625	15.875
9/64	0.1406	3.5718	41/64	0.6406	16.2718
5/32	0.1562	3.9687	21/32	0.6562	16.6687
11/64	0.1718	4.3656	43/64	0.6718	17.0656
3/16	0.1875	4.7625	11/16	0.6875	17.4625
13/64	0.2031	5.1593	45/64	0.7031	17.8593
7/32	0.2187	5.5562	23/32	0.7187	18.2562
15/64	0.2343	5.9531	47/64	0.7343	18.6531
1/4	0.25	6.5	3/4	0.75	19.05
17/64	0.2656	6.7468	49/64	0.7656	19.4468
9/32	0.2812	7.1437	25/32	0.7812	19.8437
19/64	0.2968	7.5406	51/64	0.7968	20.2406
5/16	0.3125	7.9375	13/16	0.8125	20.6375
21/64	0.3281	8.3343	53/64	0.8281	21.0343
11/32	0.3437	8.7312	27/32	0.8437	21.4312
23/64	0.3593	9.1281	55/64	0.8593	21.8281
3/8	0.375	9.525	7/8	0.875	22.225
25/64	0.3906	9.9218	57/64	0.8906	22.6218
13/32	0.4062	10.3187	29/32	0.9062	23.0187
27/64	0.4218	10.7156	59/64	0.9218	23.4156
7/16	0.4375	11.1125	15/16	0.9375	23.8125
29/64	0.4531	11.5093	61/64	0.9531	24.2093
15/32	0.4687	11.9062	31/32	0.9687	24.6062
31/64	0.4843	12.3031	63/64	0.9843	25.0031
1/2	0.50	12.7	1	1.0000	25.4

Drawing Sheet Sizes

US Conventional

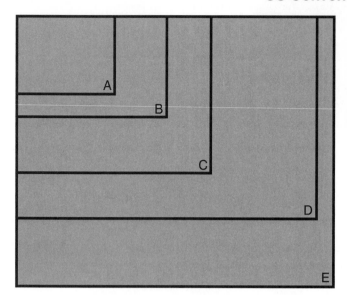

Conventional (Inch-based) Sheet Sizes

Size	Dimensions (inches)	Dimensions (mm)
A	8 1/2 × 11	215.9 × 279.4
B	11 × 17	279.4 × 431.8
C	17 × 22	431.8 × 558.8
D	22 × 34	558.8 × 863.6
E	34 × 44	863.6 × 1117.6

ISO (Metric)

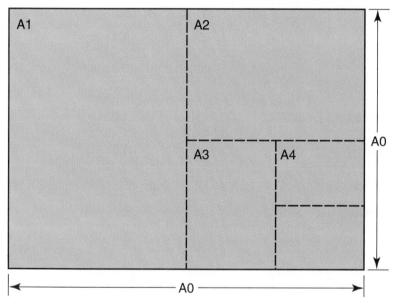

ISO Sheet Sizes

Size	Dimensions (mm)	Dimensions (inches)
A0	841 × 1189	33.11 × 46.81
A1	594 × 841	23.39 × 33.11
A2	420 × 594	16.54 × 23.39
A3	297 × 420	11.69 × 16.54
A4	210 × 297	8.27 × 11.69

Formulas

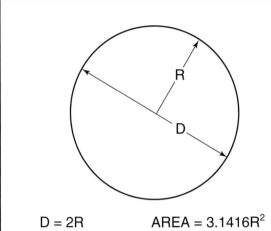

D = 2R   AREA = 3.1416R^2

CIRCLE

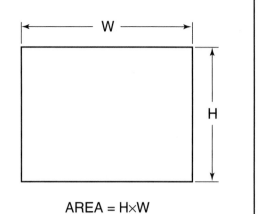

AREA = H×W

RECTANGLE

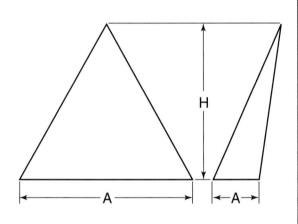

AREA = 0.5A × H

TRIANGLE

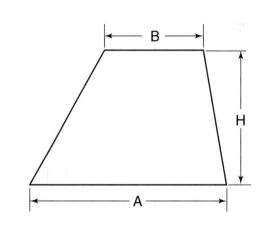

AREA = 0.5 (A+B)H

TRAPEZOID

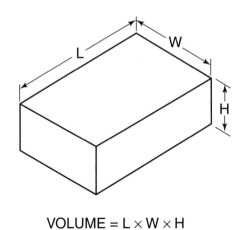

VOLUME = L × W × H

RECTANGULAR PRISM

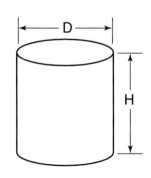

D = 2R
VOLUME = 3.1416R^2 × H

CYLINDER

Formulas

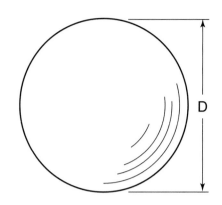

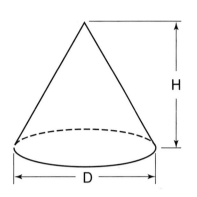

$$D = 2R$$

$$\text{VOLUME} = \frac{3.1416R^2 \times H}{3}$$

CONE

$$D = 2R$$

$$\text{VOLUME} = \frac{4 \times 3.1416R^3}{3}$$

SPHERE

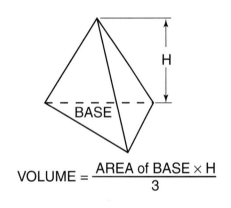

$$\text{VOLUME} = \frac{\text{AREA of BASE} \times H}{3}$$

TRIANGULAR PYRAMID

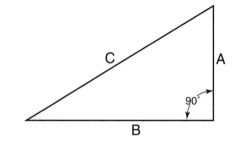

$$A = \sqrt{C^2 - B^2}$$
$$B = \sqrt{C^2 - A^2}$$
$$C = \sqrt{A^2 + B^2}$$

PYTHAGOREAN THEOREM

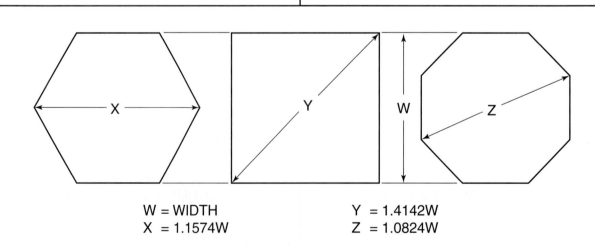

W = WIDTH
X = 1.1574W

Y = 1.4142W
Z = 1.0824W

Standard Abbreviations Used on Drawings

A

Abrasive	ABRSV
Accessory	ACCESS
Accumulator	ACCUMR
Acetylene	ACET
Across Flats	ACR FLT
Actual	ACT
Actuator	ACTR
Addendum	ADD
Adhesive	ADH
Adjust	ADJ
Advance	ADV
Aeronautic	AERO
Alclad	CLAD
Alignment	ALIGN
Allowance	ALLOW
Alloy	ALY
Alteration	ALT
Alternate	ALT
Alternating Current	AC
Aluminum	AL
American National Standards Institute	ANSI
American Society of Mechanical Engineers	ASME
American Wire Gage	AWG
Ammeter	AMM
Amplifier	AMPL
Anneal	ANL
Anodize	ANOD
Antenna	ANT
Approved	APPD
Approximate	APPROX
Arrangement	ARR
As Required	AR
Assemble	ASSEM
Assembly	ASSY
Automatic	AUTO
Auxiliary	AUX
Average	AVG

B

Babbitt	BAB
Baseline	BL
Battery	BAT
Bearing	BRG
Bend Radius	BR
Bevel	BEV
Bill of Material	B/M
Blueprint	BP or B/P
Bolt Circle	BC
Bracket	BRKT
Brass	BRS
Brazing	BRZG
Brinell Hardness Number	BHN
Bronze	BRZ
Brown & Sharpe (Gage)	B&S
Burnish	BNH
Bushing	BUSH

C

Cabinet	CAB
Calculated	CACL
Cancelled	CANC
Capacitor	CAP
Capacity	CAP
Carburize	CARB
Case Harden	CH
Casting	CSTG
Cast Iron	CI
Cathode Ray Tube	CRT
Celsius	C
Center	CTR
Center to Center	C to C
Centerline	CL
Centimeter	CM
Centrifugal	CENT
Chamfer	CHAM
Circuit	CKT
Circular	CIR
Circumference	CIRC
Clearance	CL
Clockwise	CW
Closure	CLOS
Coated	CTD
Cold-Drawn Steel	CDS
Cold-Rolled Steel	CRS
Color Code	CC
Commercial	COMM
Concentric	CONC
Condition	COND
Conductor	CNDCT
Contour	CTR
Control	CONT
Copper	COP
Counterbore	CBORE
Counterclockwise	CCW
Counterdrill	CDRILL
Countersink	CSK
Countersunk Head	CSK H

Cubic	CU
Cylinder	CYL

D

Datum	DAT
Decimal	DEC
Decrease	DECR
Degree	DEG
Detail	DET
Detector	DET
Developed Length	DL
Developed Width	DW
Deviation	DEV
Diagonal	DIAG
Diagram	DIAG
Diameter	DIA
Diameter Bolt Circle	DBC
Diametral Pitch	DP
Dimension	DIM
Direct Current	DC
Disconnect	DISC
Double-Pole Double-Throw	DPDT
Double-Pole Single-Throw	DPST
Dowel	DWL
Draft	DFT
Drafting Room Manual	DRM
Drawing	DWG
Drawing Change Notice	DCN
Drill	DR
Drop Forge	DF
Duplicate	DUP

E

Each	EA
Eccentric	ECC
Effective	EFF
Electric	ELEC
Enclosure	ENCL
Engine	ENG
Engineer	ENGR
Engineering	ENGRG
Engineering Change Order	ECO
Engineering Order	EO
Equal	EQ
Equivalent	EQUIV
Estimate	EST

Standard Abbreviations Used on Drawings (continued)

F					
Fabricate	FAB	Independent	INDEP	Meter	M
Figure	FIG	Indicator	IND	Middle	MID
Fillet	FIL	Information	INFO	Military	MIL
Finish	FIN	Inside Diameter	ID	Millimeter	MM
Finish All Over	FAO	Installation	INSTL	Minimum	MIN
Fitting	FTG	International Standards	ISO	Miscellaneous	MISC
Fixed	FXD	Organization		Modification	MOD
Fixture	FIX	Interrupt	INTER	Mold Line	ML
Flange	FLG			Motor	MOT
Flat Head	FHD	J		Mounting	MTG
Flat Pattern	F/P	Joggle	JOG	Multiple	MULT
Flexible	FLEX	Junction	JCT		
Fluid	FL			N	
Forged Steel	FST	K		Nickel Steel	NS
Forging	FORG	Keyway	KWY	Nomenclature	NOM
Furnish	FURN	Kilowatt	KW	Nominal	NOM
				Normalize	NORM
G		L		Not to Scale	NTS
Gage	GA	Laboratory	LAB	Number	NO.
Gallon	GAL	Lacquer	LAQ		
Galvanized	GALV	Laminate	LAM	O	
Gasket	GSKT	Left Hand	LH	Obsolete	OBS
Generator	GEN	Length	LG	Opposite	OPP
Grind	GRD	Letter	LTR	Oscilloscope	SCOPE
Ground	GRD	Limited	LTD	Ounce	OZ
		Limit Switch	LS	Outside Diameter	OD
H		Linear	LIN	Over-All	OA
Half-Hard	1/2H	Liquid	LIQ		
Handle	HDL	List of Material	L/M	P	
Harden	HDN	Long	LG	Package	PKG
Head	HD	Low Carbon	LC	Parting Line (Castings)	PL
Heat Treat	HT TR	Low Voltage	LV	Parts List	P/L
Hexagon	HEX	Lubricate	LUB	Pattern	PATT
Hexagonal Head	HEX HD			Piece	PC
High Carbon Steel	HCS	M		Pilot	PLT
High Frequency	HF	Machine, Machining	MACH	Pitch	P
High Speed	HS	Magnaflux	M	Pitch Circle	PC
Horizontal	HOR	Magnesium	MAG	Pitch Diameter	PD
Hot-Rolled Steel	HRS	Maintenance	MAINT	Plan View	PV
Hour	HR	Major	MAJ	Plastic	PLSTC
Housing	HSG	Malleable	MALL	Plate	PL
Hydraulic	HYD	Malleable Iron	MI	Pneumatic	PNEU
		Manual	MAN	Port	P
I		Manufacturing (ed, er)	MFG	Positive	POS
Identification	IDENT	Mark	MK	Potentiometer	POT
Inch	IN	Master Switch	MS	Pounds Per Square Inch	PSI
Inclined	INCL	Material	MATL	Pounds Per Square	PSIG
Include, Including,	INCL	Maximum	MAX	Inch Gage	
Inclusive		Measure	MEAS	Power Amplifier	PA
Increase	INCR	Mechanical	MECH	Power Supply	PWR
		Medium	MED		SPLY

Standard Abbreviations Used on Drawings *(continued)*

Pressure	PRESS	American Standard	NPSF	Temperature	TEM
Primary	PRI	Straight (Dryseal)		Tensile Strength	TS
Process, Procedure	PROC	Unified Screw Thread	UNC	Thick	THK
Product, Production	PROD	Coarse		Thread	THD
		Unified Screw Thread	UNF	Through	THRU
Q		Fine		Tolerance	TOL
Quality	QUAL	Unified Screw Thread	UNEF	Tool Steel	TS
Quantity	QTY	Extra Fine		Torque	TOR
Quarter-Hard	1/4H	Unified Screw Thread	8UN	Total Indicator Reading	TIR
		8 Thread		Transformer	XFMR
R		Section	SECT	Transistor	XSTR
Radar	RDR	Sequence	SEQ	Transmitter	XMTR
Radio	RAD	Serial	SER	Tungsten	TU
Radio Frequency	RF	Serrate	SERR	Typical	TYP
Radius	RAD or R	Sheathing	SHTHG		
Ream	RM	Sheet	SH	**U**	
Receptacle	RECP	Silver Solder	SILS	Ultra-High Frequency	UHF
Reference	REF	Single-Pole	SPDT	Unit	U
Regular	REG	Double-Throw		Universal	UNIV
Regulator	REG	Single-Pole	SPST	Unless Otherwise	UOS
Release	REL	Single-Throw		Specified	
Required	REQD	Society of Automotive	SAE		
Resistor	RES	Engineers		**V**	
Revision	REV	Solder	SLD	Vacuum	VAC
Revolutions Per Minute	RPM	Solenoid	SOL	Vacuum Tube	VT
Right Hand	RH	Speaker	SPKR	Variable	VAR
Rivet	RIV	Special	SPL	Vernier	VER
Rockwell Hardness	RH	Specification	SPEC	Vertical	VERT
Round	RD	Spotface	SF	Very High Frequency	VHF
		Spring	SPG	Vibrate	VIB
S		Square	SQ	Video	VD
Schedule	SCH	Stainless Steel	SST	Void	VD
Schematic	SCHEM	Standard	STD	Volt	V
Screw	SCR	Steel	STL	Volume	VOL
Screw Threads		Stock	STK		
American National	NC	Support	SUP	**W**	
Coarse		Switch	SW	Washer	WASH
American National	NF	Symbol	SYM	Watt	W
Fine		Symmetrical	SYM	Weatherproof	WP
American National	NEF	System	SYS	Weight	WT
Extra Fine				Wide, Width	W
American National	8N	**T**		Wire Wound	WW
8 Pitch		Tabulate	TAB	Wood	WD
American Standard	NTP	Tangent	TAN	Wrought Iron	WI
Taper Pipe		Tapping	TAP		
American Standard	NPSC	Technical Manual	TM	**Y**	
Straight Pipe		Teeth	T	Yield Point (PSI)	YP
American Standard	NPTF	Television	TV	Yield Strength (PSI)	YS
Taper (Dryseal)		Temper	TEM		

Unified National Coarse and Unified National Fine Thread Series and Tap and Clearance Drills

Size	Threads Per Inch	Major Dia.	Pitch Dia.	Tap Drill (75% Max. Thread)	Decimal Equivalent	Clearance Drill	Decimal Equivalent
2	56	.0860	.0744	50	.0700	42	.0935
	64	.0860	.0759	50	.0700	42	.0935
3	48	.099	.0855	47	.0785	36	.1065
	56	.099	.0874	45	.0820	36	.1065
4	40	.112	.0958	43	.0890	31	.1200
	48	.112	.0985	42	.0935	31	.1200
6	32	.138	.1177	36	.1065	26	.1470
	40	.138	.1218	33	.1130	26	.1470
8	32	.164	.1437	29	.1360	17	.1730
	36	.164	.1460	29	.1360	17	.1730
10	24	.190	.1629	25	.1495	8	.1990
	32	.190	.1697	21	.1590	8	.1990
12	24	.216	.1889	16	.1770	1	.2280
	28	.216	.1928	14	.1820	2	.2210
1/4	20	.250	.2175	7	.2010	G	.2610
	28	.250	.2268	3	.2130	G	.2610
5/16	18	.3125	.2764	F	.2570	21/64	.3281
	24	.3125	.2854	I	.2720	21/64	.3281
3/8	16	.3750	.3344	5/16	.3125	25/64	.3906
	24	.3750	.3479	Q	.3320	25/64	.3906
7/16	14	.4375	.3911	U	.3680	15/32	.4687
	20	.4375	.4050	25/64	.3906	29/64	.4531
1/2	13	.5000	.4500	27/64	.4219	17/32	.5312
	20	.5000	.4675	29/64	.4531	33/64	.5156
9/16	12	.5625	.5084	31/64	.4844	19/32	.5937
	18	.5625	.5264	33/64	.5156	37/64	.5781
5/8	11	.6250	.5660	17/32	.5312	21/32	.6562
	18	.6250	.5889	37/64	.5781	41/64	.6406
3/4	10	.7500	.6850	21/32	.6562	25/32	.7812
	16	.7500	.7094	11/16	.6875	49/64	.7656
7/8	9	.8750	.8028	49/64	.7656	29/32	.9062
	14	.8750	.8286	13/16	.8125	57/64	.8906
1	8	1.0000	.9188	7/8	.8750	1-1/32	1.0312
	14	1.0000	.9536	15/16	.9375	1-1/64	1.0156
1-1/8	7	1.1250	1.0322	63/64	.9844	1-5/32	1.1562
	12	1.1250	1.0709	1-3/64	1.0469	1-5/32	1.1562
1-1/4	7	1.2500	1.1572	1-7/64	1.1094	1-9/32	1.2812
	12	1.2500	1.1959	1-11/64	1.1719	1-9/32	1.2812
1-1/2	6	1.5000	1.3917	1-11/32	1.3437	1-17/32	1.5312
	12	1.5000	1.4459	1-27/64	1.4219	1-17/32	1.5312

Screw Thread Elements for Unified and National Thread Form

Threads per Inch (n)	Pitch (p) $p = \frac{1}{n}$	Single Height — Subtract from basic major diameter to get basic pitch diameter	Double Height — Subtract from basic major diameter to get basic minor diameter	83 1/3% Double Height — Subtract from basic major diameter to get minor diameter of ring gage	Basic Width of Crest and Root Flat $\frac{p}{8}$	Constant for Best Size Wire Also Single Height of 60° V-Thread	Diameter of Best Size Wire
3	.333333	.216506	.43301	.36084	.0417	.28868	.19245
3 1/4	.307692	.199852	.39970	.33309	.0385	.26647	.17765
3 1/2	.285714	.185577	.37115	.30929	.0357	.24744	.16496
4	.250000	.162379	.32476	.27063	.0312	.21651	.14434
4 1/2	.222222	.144337	.28867	.24056	.0278	.19245	.12830
5	.200000	.129903	.25981	.21650	.0250	.17321	.11547
5 1/2	.181818	.118093	.23619	.19682	.0227	.15746	.10497
6	.166666	.108253	.21651	.18042	.0208	.14434	.09623
7	.142857	.092788	.18558	.15465	.0179	.12372	.08248
8	.125000	.081189	.16238	.13531	.0156	.10825	.07217
9	.111111	.072168	.14434	.12028	.0139	.09623	.06415
10	.100000	.064952	.12990	.10825	.0125	.08660	.05774
11	.090909	.059046	.11809	.09841	.0114	.07873	.05249
11 1/2	.086956	.056480	.11296	.09413	.0109	.07531	.05020
12	.083333	.054127	.10826	.09021	.0104	.07217	.04811
13	.076923	.049963	.09993	.08327	.0096	.06662	.04441
14	.071428	.046394	.09279	.07732	.0089	.06186	.04124
16	.062500	.040595	.08119	.06766	.0078	.05413	.03608
18	.055555	.036086	.07217	.06014	.0069	.04811	.03208
20	.050000	.032475	.06495	.05412	.0062	.04330	.02887
22	.045454	.029523	.05905	.04920	.0057	.03936	.02624
24	.041666	.027063	.05413	.04510	.0052	.03608	.02406
27	.037037	.024056	.04811	.04009	.0046	.03208	.02138
28	.035714	.023197	.04639	.03866	.0045	.03093	.02062
30	.033333	.021651	.04330	.03608	.0042	.02887	.01925
32	.031250	.020297	.04059	.03383	.0039	.02706	.01804
36	.027777	.018042	.03608	.03007	.0035	.02406	.01604
40	.025000	.016237	.03247	.02706	.0031	.02165	.01443
44	.022727	.014761	.02952	.02460	.0028	.01968	.01312
48	.020833	.013531	.02706	.02255	.0026	.01804	.01203
50	.020000	.012990	.02598	.02165	.0025	.01732	.01155
56	.017857	.011598	.02320	.01933	.0022	.01546	.01031
60	.016666	.010825	.02165	.01804	.0021	.01443	.00962
64	.015625	.010148	.02030	.01691	.0020	.01353	.00902
72	.013888	.009021	.01804	.01503	.0017	.01203	.00802
80	.012500	.008118	.01624	.01353	.0016	.01083	.00722
90	.011111	.007217	.01443	.01202	.0014	.00962	.00642
96	.010417	.006766	.01353	.01127	.0013	.00902	.00601
100	.010000	.006495	.01299	.01082	.0012	.00866	.00577
120	.008333	.005413	.01083	.00902	.0010	.00722	.00481

Note: Using the Best Size Wires, measurement over three wires minus Constant for Best Size Wire equals Pitch Diameter.

Machine Screw and Cap Screw Heads

		SIZE	A	B	C	D
Fillister Head		#8	.260	.141	.042	.060
		#10	.302	.164	.048	.072
		1/4	3/8	.205	.064	.087
		5/16	7/16	.242	.077	.102
		3/8	9/16	.300	.086	.125
		1/2	3/4	.394	.102	.168
		5/8	7/8	.500	.128	.215
		3/4	1	.590	.144	.258
		1	1 5/16	.774	.182	.352
Flat Head		#8	.320	.092	.043	.037
		#10	.372	.107	.048	.044
		1/4	1/2	.146	.064	.063
		5/16	5/8	.183	.072	.078
		3/8	3/4	.220	.081	.095
		1/2	7/8	.220	.102	.090
		5/8	1 1/8	.293	.128	.125
		3/4	1 3/8	.366	.144	.153
Round Head		#8	.297	.113	.044	.067
		#10	.346	.130	.048	.073
		1/4	7/16	.1831	.064	.107
		5/16	9/16	.236	.072	.150
		3/8	5/8	.262	.081	.160
		1/2	13/16	.340	.102	.200
		5/8	1	.422	.128	.255
		3/4	1 1/4	.526	.144	.320
Hexagon Head		1/4	.494	.170	7/16	
		5/16	.564	.215	1/2	
		3/8	.635	.246	9/16	
		1/2	.846	.333	3/4	
		5/8	1.058	.411	15/16	
		3/4	1.270	.490	1 1/8	
		7/8	1.482	.566	1 5/16	
		1	1.693	.640	1 1/2	
Socket Head		#8	.265	.164	1/8	
		#10	5/16	.190	5/32	
		1/4	3/8	1/4	3/16	
		5/16	7/16	5/16	7/32	
		3/8	9/16	3/8	5/16	
		7/16	5/8	7/16	5/16	
		1/2	3/4	1/2	3/8	
		5/8	7/8	5/8	1/2	
		3/4	1	3/4	9/16	
		7/8	1 1/8	7/8	9/16	
		1	1 5/16	1	5/8	

Twist Drill Data

Metric Drill Sizes (mm)[1]		Decimal Equivalent in Inches (Ref)	Metric Drill Sizes (mm)[1]		Decimal Equivalent in Inches (Ref)
Preferred	Available		Preferred	Available	
	.40	.0157	1.70		.0669
	.42	.0165		1.75	.0689
	.45	.0177	1.80		.0709
	.48	.0189		1.85	.0728
.50		.0197	1.90		.0748
	.52	.0205		1.95	.0768
.55		.0217	2.00		.0787
	.58	.0228		2.05	.0807
.60		.0236	2.10		.0827
	.62	.0244		2.15	.0846
.65		.0256	2.20		.0866
	.68	.0268		2.30	.0906
.70		.0276	2.40		.0945
	.72	.0283	2.50		.0984
.75		.0295	2.60		.1024
	.78	.0307		2.70	.1063
.80		.0315	2.80		.1102
	.82	.0323		2.90	.1142
.85		.0335	3.00		.1181
	.88	.0346		3.10	.1220
.90		.0354	3.20		.1260
	.92	.0362		3.30	.1299
.95		.0374	3.40		.1339
	.98	.0386		3.50	.1378
1.00		.0394	3.60		.1417
	1.03	.0406		3.70	.1457
1.05		.0413	3.80		.1496
	1.08	.0425		3.90	.1535
1.10		.0433	4.00		.1575
	1.15	.0453		4.10	.1614
1.20		.0472	4.20		.1654
1.25		.0492		4.40	.1732
1.30		.0512	4.50		.1772
	1.35	.0531		4.60	.1811
1.40		.0551	4.80		.1890
	1.45	.0571	5.00		.1969
1.50		.0591		5.20	.2047
	1.55	.0610	5.30		.2087
1.60		.0630		5.40	.2126
	1.65	.0650	5.60		.2205
				5.80	.2283

[1] Metric drill sizes listed in the "Preferred" column are based on the R'40 series of preferred numbers shown in the ISO Standard R497. Those listed in the "Available" column are based on the R80 series from the same document.

Twist Drill Data (continued)

Metric Drill Sizes (mm)[1]		Decimal Equivalent in Inches (Ref)	Metric Drill Sizes (mm)[1]		Decimal Equivalent in Inches (Ref)
Preferred	Available		Preferred	Available	
6.00		.2362		19.50	.7677
	6.20	.2441	20.00		.7874
6.30		.2480		20.50	.8071
	6.50	.2559	21.00		.8268
6.70		.2638		21.50	.8465
	6.80[2]	.2677	22.00		.8661
	6.90	.2717		23.00	.9055
7.10		.2795	24.00		.9449
	7.30	.2874	25.00		.9843
7.50		.2953	26.00		1.0236
	7.80	.3071		27.00	1.0630
8.00		.3150	28.00		1.1024
	8.20	.3228		29.00	1.1417
8.50		.3346	30.00		1.1811
	8.80	.3465		31.00	1.2205
9.00		.3543	32.00		1.2598
	9.20	.3622		33.00	1.2992
9.50		.3740	34.00		1.3386
	9.80	.3858		35.00	1.3780
10.00		.3937	36.00		1.4173
	10.30	.4055		37.00	1.4567
10.50		.4134	38.00		1.4961
	10.80	.4252		39.00	1.5354
11.00		.4331	40.00		1.5748
	11.50	.4528		41.00	1.6142
12.00		.4724	42.00		1.6535
12.50		.4921		43.50	1.7126
13.00		.5118	45.00		1.7717
	13.50	.5315		46.50	1.8307
14.00		.5512	48.00		1.8898
	14.50	.5709	50.00		1.9685
15.00		.5906		51.50	2.0276
	15.50	.6102	53.00		2.0866
16.00		.6299		54.00	2.1260
	16.50	.6496	56.00		2.2047
17.00		.6693		58.00	2.2835
	17.50	.6890	60.00		2.3622
18.00		.7087			
	18.50	.7283			
19.00		.7480			

[1] Metric drill sizes listed in the "Preferred" column are based on the R'40 series of preferred numbers shown in the ISO Standard R497. Those listed in the "Available" column are based on the R80 series from the same document.
[2] Recommended only for use as a tap drill size.

Wood Screw Table

Length	Gauge Steel Screw	Gauge Brass Screw	Gauge No.	Decimal	Approx. Fract.	Drill Size A	B	C
1/4	0 to 4	0 to 4	0	.060	1/16	1/16		
3/8	0 to 8	0 to 6	1	.073	5/64	3/32		
1/2	1 to 10	1 to 8	2	.086	5/64	3/32	1/16	3/16
5/8	2 to 12	2 to 10	3	.099	3/32	1/8	1/16	1/4
3/4	2 to 14	2 to 12	4	.112	7/64	1/8	1/16	1/4
7/8	3 to 14	4 to 12	5	.125	1/8	1/8	3/32	1/4
1	3 to 16	4 to 14	6	.138	9/64	5/32	3/32	5/16
1 1/4	4 to 18	6 to 14	7	.151	5/32	5/32	1/8	5/16
1 1/2	4 to 20	6 to 14	8	.164	5/32	3/16	1/8	3/8
1 3/4	6 to 20	8 to 14	9	.177	11/64	3/16	1/8	3/8
2	6 to 20	8 to 18	10	.190	3/16	3/16	1/8	3/8
2 1/4	6 to 20	10 to 18	11	.203	13/64	7/32	5/32	7/16
2 1/2	8 to 20	10 to 18	12	.216	7/32	7/32	5/32	7/16
2 3/4	8 to 20	8 to 20	14	.242	15/64	1/4	3/16	1/2
3	8 to 24	12 to 18	16	.268	17/64	9/32	7/32	9/16
3 1/2	10 to 24	12 to 18	18	.294	19/64	5/16	1/4	5/8
4	12 to 24	12 to 24	20	.320	21/64	11/32	9/32	11/16
4 1/2	14 to 24	14 to 24	24	.372	3/8	3/8	5/16	3/4
5	14 to 24	14 to 24						

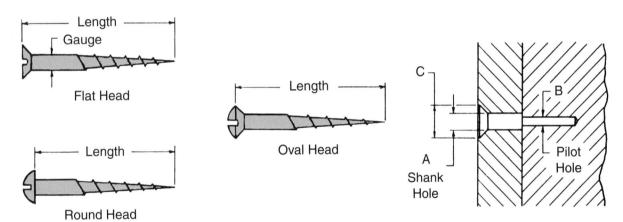

Length
Gauge
Flat Head

Length
Round Head

Length
Oval Head

C
A
Shank Hole
B
Pilot Hole

Screws also available with Phillips heads.

Preferred Metric Sizes for Engineers

SIZES 1 mm to 10 mm			SIZES 10 mm to 100 mm			SIZES 100 mm to 1000 mm		
CHOICE 1st	2nd	3rd	CHOICE 1st	2nd	3rd	CHOICE 1st	2nd	3rd
1			10			100		
								105
	1.1			11		110		
								115
1.2			12			120		
								125
		1.3			13		130	
								135
	1.4			14		140		
								145
		1.5			15		150	
								155
1.6			16			160		
								165
		1.7			17		170	
								175
	1.8			18		180		
								185
		1.9			19		190	
								195
2			20			200		
		2.1			21		210	
	2.2			22		220		
					23		230	
		2.4			24		240	
2.5			25			250		
		2.6			26		260	
								270
	2.8			28		280		
								290
3			30			300		
		3.2		32			320	
					34			340
	3.5			35		350		
					36			360
		3.8		38			380	
4			40			400		
		4.2		42			420	
					44			440
	4.5			45		450		
					46			460
		4.8		48			480	
5			50			500		
		5.2		52			520	
					54			540
	5.5			55		550		
					56			560
		5.8		58			580	
6			60			600		
					62		620	
								640
		6.5		65			650	
								660
					68		680	
	7			70		700		
					72		720	
								740
		7.5		75			750	
								760
					78		780	
8			80			800		
					82			820
		8.5		85			850	
					88			880
	9			90		900		
					92			920
		9.5		95			950	
					98			980
10			100			1000		

Inch-Metric Thread Comparison

Inch Series			Metric			
Size	Dia. (In.)	TPI	Size	Dia. (In.)	Pitch (mm)	TPI (Approx)
			M1.4	.055	.3 .2	85 127
#0	.060	80				
			M1.6	.063	.35 .2	74 127
#1	.073	64 72				
			M2	.079	.4 .25	64 101
#2	.086	56 64				
			M2.5	.098	.45 .35	56 74
#3	.099	48 56				
#4	.112	40 48				
			M3	.118	.5 .35	51 74
#5	.125	40 44				
#6	.138	32 40				
			M4	.157	.7 .5	36 51
#8	.164	32 36				
#10	.190	24 32				
			M5	.196	.8 .5	32 51
			M6	.236	1.0 .75	25 34
1/4	.250	20 28				
5/16	.312	18 24				
			M8	.315	1.25 1.0	20 25
3/8	.375	16 24				
			M10	.393	1.5 1.25	17 20
7/16	.437	14 20				
			M12	.472	1.75 1.25	14.5 20
1/2	.500	13 20				
			M14	.551	2 1.5	12.5 17
5/8	.625	11 18				
			M16	.630	2 1.5	12.5 17
			M18	.709	2.5 1.5	10 17
3/4	.750	10 16				
			M20	.787	2.5 1.5	10 17
			M22	.866	2.5 1.5	10 17
7/8	.875	9 14				
			M24	.945	3 2	8.5 12.5
1"	1.000	8 12				
			M27	1.063	3 2	8.5 12.5

Number and Letter Size Drills Conversion Chart

Drill No. or Letter	Inch	mm
	.001	0.0254
	.002	0.0508
	.003	0.0762
	.004	0.1016
	.005	0.1270
	.006	0.1524
	.007	0.1778
	.008	0.2032
	.009	0.2286
	.010	0.2540
	.011	0.2794
	.012	0.3048
	.013	0.3302
80 .0135	.014	0.3556
79 .0145	.015	0.3810
1/64	.0156	0.3969
78	.016	0.4064
	.017	0.4318
77	.018	0.4572
	.019	0.4826
76	.020	0.5080
75	.021	0.5334
	.022	0.5588
74 .0225	.023	0.5842
73	.024	0.6096
72	.025	0.6350
71	.026	0.6604
	.027	0.6858
70	.028	0.7112
	.029	0.7366
69 .0292	.030	0.7620
68	.031	0.7874
1/32	.0312	0.7937
67	.032	0.8128
66	.033	0.8382
	.034	0.8636
65	.035	0.8890
64	.036	0.9144
63	.037	0.9398
62	.038	0.9652
61	.039	0.9906
	.0394	1.0000
60	.040	1.0160
59	.041	1.0414
58	.042	1.0668
57	.043	1.0922
	.044	1.1176
	.045	1.1430
56 .0465	.046	1.1684
3/64	.0469	1.1906
	.047	1.1938
	.048	1.2192
	.049	1.2446
	.050	1.2700
55	.051	1.2954
	.052	1.3208
	.053	1.3462
	.054	1.3716
54	.055	1.3970
	.056	1.4224
	.057	1.4478
	.058	1.4732
	.059	1.4986
53 .0595	.060	1.5240
	.061	1.5494
	.062	1.5748
1/16	.0625	1.5875
52 .0635	.063	1.6002
	.064	1.6256
	.065	1.6510
	.066	1.6764
51	.067	1.7018
	.068	1.7272
	.069	1.7526
50	.070	1.7780
	.071	1.8034
	.072	1.8288
49	.073	1.8542
	.074	1.8796
	.075	1.9050
48	.076	1.9304
	.077	1.9558
47 .0785	.078	1.9812
5/64	.0781	1.9844
	.0787	2.0000
	.079	2.0066
	.080	2.0320
46	.081	2.0574
45	.082	2.0828
	.083	2.1082
	.084	2.1336
	.085	2.1590
44	.086	2.1844
	.087	2.2098
	.088	2.2352
43	.089	2.2606
	.090	2.2860
	.091	2.3114
	.092	2.3368
42 .0935	.093	2.3622
3/32	.0937	2.3812
	.094	2.3876
	.095	2.4130
41	.096	2.4384
	.097	2.4638
40	.098	2.892
39 .0995	.099	2.5146
	.100	2.5400
	.101	2.5654
38 .1015	.102	2.5908
	.103	2.6162
37	.104	2.6416
	.105	2.6670
36 .1065	.106	2.6924
	.107	2.7178
	.108	2.7432
	.109	2.7686
7/64	.1094	2.7781
35	.110	2.7490
34	.111	2.8194
	.112	2.8448
33	.113	2.8702
	.114	2.8956
	.115	2.9210
32	.116	2.9464
	.117	2.9718
	.118	2.9972
	.1181	3.0000
	.119	3.0226
	.120	3.0480
31	.121	3.0734
	.122	3.0988
	.123	3.1242
	.124	3.1496
1/8	.125	3.1750
	.126	3.2004
	.127	3.2258
	.128	3.2512
30 .1285	.129	3.2766
	.130	3.3020
	.131	3.3274
	.132	3.3528
	.133	3.3782
	.134	3.4036
	.135	3.4290
29	.136	3.4544
	.137	3.4798
	.138	3.5052
	.139	3.5306
28 .1405	.140	3.5560
9/64	.1406	3.5519
	.141	3.5814
	.142	3.6068
	.143	3.6322
27	.144	3.6576
	.145	3.6830
	.146	3.7084
26	.147	3.7338
	.148	3.7592
25 .1495	.149	3.7846
	.150	3.8100
	.151	3.8354
24	.152	3.8608
	.153	3.8162
23	.154	3.9116
	.155	3.9370
	.156	3.9624
5/32	.1562	3.9687
22	.157	3.9878
	.1575	4.0000
	.158	4.0132
	.159	4.0386
21	.160	4.0640
	.161	4.0894
20	.162	4.1148
	.163	4.1402
	.164	4.1656
	.165	4.1910
19	.166	4.2164
	.167	4.2418
	.168	4.2672
	.169	4.2926
18 .1635	.170	4.3180
	.171	4.3434
11/64	.1719	4.3656
	.172	4.3688
17	.173	4.3942
	.174	4.4196
	.175	4.4450
	.176	4.4704
16	.177	4.4958
	.178	4.5212
	.179	4.5466
15	.180	4.5720
	.181	4.5974
14	.182	4.6228
	.183	4.6482
	.184	4.6736
13	.185	4.6990
	.186	4.7244
	.187	4.7498
3/16	.1875	4.7625
	.188	4.7752
12	.189	4.8006
	.190	4.8260
11	.191	4.8514
	.192	4.8768
	.193	4.9022
10 .1935	.194	4.9278
	.195	4.9530
9	.196	4.9784
	.1969	5.0000
	.197	5.0038
	.198	5.0292
8	.199	5.0546
	.200	5.0800
7	.201	5.1054
	.202	5.1308
	.203	5.1562
13/64	.2031	5.1594
6	.204	5.1816
5 .2055	.205	5.2070
	.206	5.2324
	.207	5.2578
	.208	5.2832
4	.209	5.3086
	.210	5.3340
	.211	5.3594
	.212	5.3848
3	.213	5.4102
	.214	5.4356
	.215	5.4610
	.216	5.4864
	.217	5.5118
	.218	5.5372
7/32	.2187	5.5562
	.219	5.5626
	.220	5.5880
2	.221	5.6134
	.222	5.6388
	.223	5.6642
	.224	5.6896
	.225	5.7150
	.226	5.7404
	.227	5.7658
1	.228	5.7912
	.229	5.8166
	.230	5.8410
	.231	5.8674
	.232	5.8928
	.233	5.9182
A	.234	5.9436
15/64	.2344	5.9531
	.235	5.9690
	.236	5.9944
	.2362	6.0000
	.237	6.0198
B	.238	6.0452
	.239	6.0706
	.240	6.0960
	.241	6.1214
C	.242	6.1468
	.243	6.1722
	.244	6.1976
	.245	6.2230
D	.246	6.2484
	.247	6.2738
	.248	6.2992
	.249	6.3246
E 1/4	.250	6.3500
	.251	6.3754
	.252	6.4008
	.253	6.4262
	.254	6.4516
	.255	6.4770
	.256	6.5024
F	.257	6.5278
	.258	6.5532
	.259	6.5786
	.260	6.6040
G	.261	6.6294
	.262	6.6548
	.263	6.6802
	.264	6.7056
	.265	6.7310
17/64	.2656	6.7469
H	.266	6.7564
	.267	6.7818
	.268	6.8072
	.269	6.8326
	.270	6.8580
	.271	6.8834
I	.272	6.9088
	.273	6.9342
	.274	6.9596
	.275	6.9850
	.2756	7.0000
	.276	7.0104
J	.277	7.0358
	.278	7.0612
	.279	7.0866
	.280	7.1120
K	.281	7.1374
9/32	.2812	7.1437
	.282	7.1628
	.283	7.1882
	.284	7.2136
	.285	7.2390
	.286	7.2644
	.287	7.2898
	.288	7.3152
	.289	7.3406
L	.290	7.3660
	.291	7.3914
	.292	7.4168
	.293	7.4422
	.294	7.4676
M	.295	7.4930
	.296	7.5184
19/64	.2969	7.5406
	.297	7.5438
	.298	7.5692
	.299	7.5946
	.300	7.6200
	.301	7.6454
N	.302	7.6708
	.303	7.6962
	.304	7.7216
	.305	7.7470
	.306	7.7724
	.307	7.7978
	.308	7.8232
	.309	7.8486
	.310	7.8740
	.311	7.8994
	.312	7.9248
5/16	.3125	7.9375
	.313	7.9502
	.314	7.9756
	.3150	8.0000
	.315	8.0010
O	.316	8.0264
	.317	8.0518
	.318	8.0772
	.319	8.1026
	.320	8.1280
	.321	8.1534
	.322	8.1788
P	.323	8.2042
	.324	8.2296
	.325	8.2550
	.326	8.2804
	.327	8.3058
	.328	8.3312
21/64	.3281	8.3344
	.329	8.3566
	.330	8.3820
	.331	8.4074
Q	.332	8.4328
	.333	8.4582
	.334	8.4836
	.335	8.5090
	.336	8.5344
	.337	8.5598
	.338	8.5852
R	.339	8.6106
	.340	8.6360
	.341	8.6614
	.342	8.6868
	.343	8.7122
11/32	.3437	8.7312
	.344	8.7376
	.345	8.7630
	.346	8.7884
	.347	8.8138
S	.348	8.8392
	.349	8.8646
	.350	8.8900
	.351	8.9154
	.352	8.9408
	.353	8.9662
	.354	8.9916
	.3543	9.0000
	.355	9.0170
	.356	9.0424
	.357	9.0678
T	.358	9.0932
	.359	9.1186
23/64	.3594	9.1281
	.360	9.1440
	.361	9.1694
	.362	9.1948
	.363	9.2202
	.364	9.2456
	.365	9.2710
	.366	9.2964
	.367	9.3218
U	.368	9.3472
	.369	9.3726
	.370	9.3980
	.371	9.4234
	.372	9.4488
	.373	9.4742
	.374	9.4996
3/8	.375	9.5250
	.376	9.5504
V	.377	9.5758
	.378	9.6012
	.379	9.6266
	.380	9.6520
	.381	9.6774
	.382	9.7028
	.383	9.7282
	.384	9.7536
	.385	9.7790
W	.386	9.8044
	.387	9.8298
	.388	9.8552
	.389	9.8806
	.390	9.9060
25/64	.3906	9.9219
	.391	9.9314
	.392	9.9568
	.393	9.9822
	.3937	10.0000
	.394	10.0076
	.395	10.0330
	.396	10.0584
X	.397	10.0838
	.398	10.1092
	.399	10.1346
	.400	10.1600
	.401	10.1854
	.402	10.2108
	.403	10.2362
Y	.404	10.2616
	.405	10.2870
	.406	10.3124
13/32	.4062	10.3187
	.407	10.3378
	.408	10.3632
	.409	10.3886
	.410	10.4140
	.411	10.4394
	.412	10.4648
Z	.413	10.4902
	.414	10.5156
	.415	10.5410
	.416	10.5664
	.417	10.5918
	.418	10.6172
	.419	10.6426
	.420	10.6680
	.421	10.6934
27/64	.4219	10.7156
	.422	10.7188
	.423	10.7442
	.424	10.7696
	.425	10.7950
	.426	10.8204
	.427	10.8458
	.428	10.8712
	.429	10.8966
	.430	10.9220
	.431	10.9474
	.432	10.9728
	.433	10.9982
	.4331	11.0000
	.434	11.0236
	.435	11.0490
	.436	11.0744
	.437	11.0998
7/16	.4375	11.1125
	.438	11.1252
	.439	11.1506
	.440	11.1760
	.441	11.2014
	.442	11.2268
	.443	11.2522
	.444	11.2776
	.445	11.3030
	.446	11.3284
	.447	11.3538
	.448	11.3792
	.449	11.4046
	.450	11.4300
	.451	11.4554
	.452	11.4808
	.453	11.5062
29/64	.4531	11.5094
	.454	11.5316
	.455	11.5570
	.456	11.5824
	.457	11.6078
	.458	11.6332
	.459	11.6586
	.460	11.6840
	.461	11.7094
	.462	11.7348
	.463	11.7602
	.464	11.7856
	.465	11.8110
	.466	11.8364
	.467	11.8618
	.468	11.8872
15/32	.4687	11.9062
	.469	11.9126
	.470	11.9380
	.471	11.9634
	.472	11.9888
	.4724	12.0000
	.473	12.0142
	.474	12.0396
	.475	12.0650
	.476	12.0904
	.477	12.1158
	.478	12.1412
	.479	12.1666
	.480	12.1920
	.481	12.2174
	.482	12.2428
	.483	12.2682
	.484	12.2936
31/64	.4844	12.3031
	.485	12.3190
	.486	12.3444
	.487	12.3698
	.488	12.3952
	.489	12.4206
	.490	12.4460
	.491	12.4714
	.492	12.4968
	.493	12.5222
	.494	12.5476
	.495	12.5730
	.496	12.5984
	.497	12.6238
	.498	12.6492
	.499	12.6746
1/2	.500	12.7000

Glossary

A

Absolute coordinates: In a CAD system, coordinates located in relation to the Cartesian coordinate system origin (0,0,0).

Acute angle: An angle less than 90°.

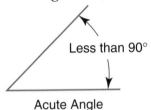

Acute Angle

Aligned dimensioning: A method of dimensioning in which dimensions are placed parallel to the dimension line and read from the bottom and right side of the drawing.

Alloy: A mixture of two or more metals fused or melted together to form a new metal.

Alphabet of Lines: A collection of the different lines used in drafting, with classifications for line weight (thickness) and linetype. See also *Line conventions*.

Alphanumeric: Pertaining to a series of characters containing both letters and numbers.

Angle: The figure formed by two lines coming together to a point.

Annealing: The process of heating metal to a given temperature and cooling it slowly to remove stresses and induce softness.

ANSI: American National Standards Institute. A nongovernmental organization that proposes, modifies, approves, and publishes drafting and manufacturing standards for voluntary use in the United States.

Arc: Portion of a circle.

Arc

Array: In a CAD system, an orientation of copied objects in a rectangular or polar pattern.

Artificial intelligence (AI): Computer techniques that mimic certain functions typically associated with human intelligence. Also refers to a computer or machine capable of improving its operation as a result of repeated experience.

Asphalt roofing: A roofing material made by saturating felt with asphalt.

Assembly: A unit fitted together from manufactured parts.

Assembly drawing: A type of working drawing that contains views showing where and how the various parts of an object fit into the assembled product.

Attributes: In CAD drafting, text strings of information about related symbols, such as product numbers, sizes, or materials.

Auxiliary view: A view showing the true length and true width of an angular surface, projected in a perpendicular direction from an edge view of the surface.

Axis: The center line of a view or of a geometric figure. Plural: *axes*.

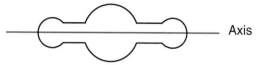

Axis

B

Beam: A horizontal structural support member. Examples include joists, rafters, purlins, and girders.

Beam compass: Compass used to draw large circles and arcs.

Bearings: Angular measurements on a map used to represent the direction of boundary lines in relation to due north and south.

Bevel: A surface formed or trimmed so as to not be perpendicular to adjoining surfaces.

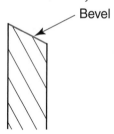

Bevel

Bisect: To divide into two parts of equal size or length.

Bit: The smallest unit of information for a computer. It is represented by a zero (0) or a one (1) by the absence (0) or presence (1) of an electric current.

Blowhole: A hole produced in a casting when gases are entrapped during the pouring operation.

Blueprint: A reproduction of a drawing that has a blue background with white lines. Also, a general term used to describe any reproduced drawing.

Border lines: The heaviest lines used in drafting, serving as a "frame" for a drawing and establishing a space between the drawing and the edge of the paper.

Border Line (very thick)

Bore: To enlarge a hole to an exact size.

Brazing: Joining metals by the fusion of nonferrous alloys that have melting temperatures above 800°F but lower than the metals being joined.

Broach: A multi-tooth cutting tool in which succeeding teeth are greater in size, allowing the removal of internal or external material.

Building codes: Laws that provide for the health, safety, and general welfare of the people in a community.

Burnishing tool: A tool used to transfer rub-on (dry transfer) materials to a drawing.

Bushing: A bearing for a revolving shaft. Also, a hardened steel tube used on jigs to guide drills and reamers.

Byte: A group of eight bits treated as a unit and often used to represent one alphanumeric character.

C

Cabinet oblique: An oblique drawing in which the depth axis lines are drawn at one-half scale.

CAD: Computer-aided drafting and design.

CAD software: Computer applications designed to automate manual drafting functions.

Cartographer: A professional mapmaker.

Case hardening: A process of surface hardening iron base alloys so that the surface layer or case is made substantially harder than the interior or core of the material.

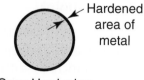

Hardened area of metal

Case Hardening

Casting: An object made by pouring molten metal into a mold.

Cavalier oblique: An oblique drawing in which the depth axis lines are drawn at full scale (full size).

Centerlines: Thin lines made up of long and short dashes with spaces in between, used to indicate centers of symmetrical objects.

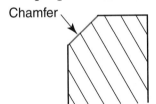
Centerline (thin)

Central processing unit (CPU): The primary component of a computer, where operations are performed and data is processed.

Chain dimensioning: Placing several dimensions in a straight line along an object to describe successive features.

Chamfer: An angled cut made to remove the "corner" of two perpendicular surfaces.

Chamfer

Chip: A small piece of material, usually silicon, in which tiny amounts of other elements (with desired electronic properties) are deposited to form an integrated circuit (IC).

Circumference: The perimeter of a circle.

Circumscribe: To draw one geometric figure around another figure.

Clearance: The distance by which one part clears another part.

Clockwise: From left to right in a circular motion. The direction clock hands move.

Clockwise

Color boards: Tools interior designers use to describe the interior decoration of the structure.

Compass: A drafting instrument used to draw circles and arcs.

Computer-aided design/computer-aided manufacturing (CAD/CAM): A type of manufacturing in which machining data is generated from CAD drawings and used by computer numerical control (CNC) machines.

Computer numerical control (CNC): A system in which a program is used to precisely position tools and/or the workpiece and to carry out the sequence of operations needed to produce a part.

Concave surface: A curved depression in the surface of an object.

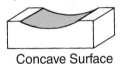
Concave Surface

Concentric: Having a common center.

Concentric Circles

Conical: Having a shape with a circular base and sides converging to a single point.

Conical

Construction lines: Very light lines used as guides for positioning objects on drawings.

Construction and Guidelines (very thin)

Contour: The outline of an object.

Contour lines: Irregular lines on a plot plan spaced at intervals to show differences in elevation. Each contour line shows all points where the ground has a single elevation.

Conventional: Not original; customary, or traditional.

Convex surface: A rounded surface on an object.

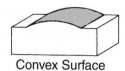

Convex Surface

Coordinates: The positions or locations of points on the X, Y, and Z planes. In a CAD system, the points represent units of real measurement from a fixed point.

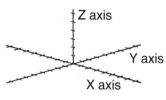

Coordinate System

Core: A body of sand or other material that is formed to a desired shape and placed in a mold to produce a cavity or opening in a casting.

Counterbore: A deep recess at the end of a smaller hole used to provide a bearing surface for the head of a bolt or nut.

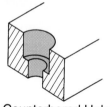

Counterbored Hole

Counterclockwise: From right to left in a circular motion.

Counterclockwise

Countersink: A chamfered recess at the end of a smaller hole used to receive the head of a fastener.

Countersunk Hole

Cutting-plane lines: Heavy, dashed lines used to show sectional views. Arrows are extended from the endpoints to illustrate the viewing direction.

Cutting-Plane Lines (thick)

Cylinder: A geometric figure with a uniform circular cross-section through its entire length.

Cylinder

D

Datum: An exact point, axis, plane, or surface from which features of a part are located.

Design: A plan for the simple and direct solution to a technical problem.

Detail drawing: A type of working drawing that includes one or more views of a product, with dimensions and other pertinent information required to make the part.

Detailed representation: A screw thread representation in which the threads are drawn to look like the actual threads.

Diagonal: A line connecting the opposite corners of a figure.

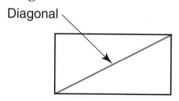

Diagonal

Diameter: The distance from one side of a circle to the other, running directly through the circle's center.

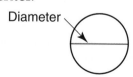

Diameter

Diazo process: A reproduction method for making direct positive prints consisting of dark lines on a white background.

Die: A tool used to cut external threads. Also, a tool used to shape materials.

Die casting: A method of casting metal under pressure by injecting it into the metal dies of a die casting machine.

Digitizing tablet: A CAD input device on which a puck is maneuvered to select commands and position the on-screen cursor.

Dimension lines: Thin lines normally drawn between two extension lines, with arrows or ticks at the ends and a dimension at the center.

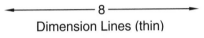
Dimension Lines (thin)

Dimensions: Lettering or text on a drawing defining object sizes and locations.

Dividers: A drafting instrument used to divide and transfer measurements.

Draft: The clearance on a pattern or mold that allows easy withdrawal of the pattern from the mold.

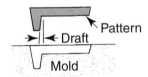

Drafter: A designer who uses manual or CAD methods to make working drawings and detail drawings.

Drafting film: Translucent drafting paper made from acetate, mylar, or polyester, used for work requiring great print stability.

Drafting machine: A device that combines the functions of the T-square and triangles, used to draw straight and inclined lines.

Drafting media: Materials used for creating drawings, such as paper, tracing vellum, and drafting film.

Drawing board: A smooth, flat surface on which drafters create drawings. A vinyl cover is commonly used to protect the surface.

Drawing ink: A dense, black, waterproof ink used for inking drawings.

Drilling: Cutting round holes by use of a cutting tool called a drill.

Drill rod: An accurately ground and polished tool steel rod.

Drive fit: Using force or pressure to fit two pieces together.

Dry cleaning pad: A small mesh pouch filled with very fine eraser particles. It is used to distribute the particles on a drawing surface in order to remove excess graphite.

Dry transfer lettering: A lettering method in which letters or symbols on a preprinted sheet are transferred to drawing media by rubbing the image with a burnishing tool over the media.

Dusting brush: A drafting tool used to remove unwanted debris from a drawing.

E

Eccentric: Not on a common center.

Eccentric Circles

Elevations: Architectural drawings used to represent the front, rear, and side views of a house.

Ellipse: A closed curve in the form of a symmetrical oval.

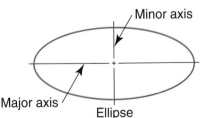
Ellipse

Engineering working drawings: Drawings used to manufacture or construct objects.

Equidistant: Equal in distance from a given point.

Equilateral: Term referring to a figure having equal length sides.

Erasing shield: A drafting instrument used to remove small errors without erasing a large section of the drawing.

Ergonomics: The science of adapting the working environment to fit the needs of different people.

Expansion fit: The reverse of shrink fit. The piece to be fitted is placed in liquid nitrogen or dry ice until it shrinks enough to fit into the mating piece. Interference develops between the fitted pieces as the cooled piece expands to normal size.

Exploded assembly drawing: A series of pictorial drawings that show how the parts of a disassembled object fit together.

Extension lines: Light lines used to project dimension lines to specific points on an object.

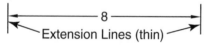
Extension Lines (thin)

F

Fastener: A device used to hold two or more parts together.

Feature control frame: A rectangular compartment that contains a divided series of symbols identifying geometric tolerance.

Ferrous metal: A metal that contains iron as its major ingredient.

Fillet: An arc representing an inside rounded corner. See also *Round.*

Fillet

First-angle projection: A method of orthographic projection in which views of an object are projected to the sides of an imaginary glass box and away from the viewer.

Fixture: A device for holding metal while it is being machined.

Flash: A thin fin of metal formed at the parting line of a forging or casting where a small portion of metal is forced out between the edges of the die.

Flask: A frame of wood or metal for a casting mold consisting of a cope (the top portion) and a drag (the bottom portion), used to hold the sand that forms the mold.

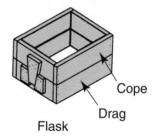
Cope
Drag
Flask

Floor plan: An architectural drawing that shows the size and shape of a building, along with the interior arrangement of rooms.

Force fit: The interference between two mating parts sufficient to require force to press the pieces together. The joined pieces are considered permanently assembled.

Forge: To form material using heat and pressure.

Free fit: Used when tolerances are liberal. Clearance is sufficient to permit a shaft to turn freely without binding or overheating when properly lubricated.

French curve: A drafting tool used to draw irregular curved lines.

Frustum: A figure formed by removing the upper portion of a cone or pyramid, leaving a top parallel to its base.

Frustum

G

Gate: An opening in a casting mold that guides the molten metal into the cavity that forms the mold. See also *Sprue.*

Gears: Toothed wheels that transmit rotary motion without slippage.

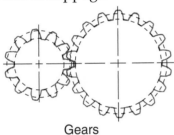

Gears

General oblique: An oblique drawing in which the scale of the depth axis lines varies from one-half to full scale.

Geometric characteristic symbols: Symbols used in GD&T to specify and explain form and positional tolerances.

Geometric dimensioning and tolerancing (GD&T): A standard system devised to control interpretation of the form, profile, orientation, location, and runout of features on drawings.

Grid: In a CAD system, a network of uniformly spaced points used to determine distances.

Grinding: An operation that removes material by rotating an abrasive wheel against the workpiece.

Guidelines: Very light lines used as guides for lettering a drawing.

H

Hard copy: Any printed or plotted output.

Hard drive: The primary storage device of a computer.

Hardening: The heating and quenching of certain iron-base alloys for the purpose of producing a hardness superior to that of the untreated metal.

Hardware: The components that make up a computer system.

Heat treatment: The careful application of a combination of heating and cooling cycles to a metal or alloy to bring about certain desirable conditions such as hardness and toughness.

Helix: The basic shape of a screw thread, formed by a point curve that wraps around a cylinder in a spiral.

Hems: Folds that strengthen the lips of sheet metal objects.

Hexagon: A six-sided figure with each side forming a 60° angle.

Hexagon

Hidden lines: Thin, dashed lines used to identify features that cannot be seen in a given view.

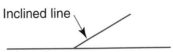

Hidden Line (thin)

Horizon line: A line in a perspective drawing where receding lines converge to one or more vanishing points.

I

ID: Abbreviation for *inside diameter.*

Inclined: Making an angle with another line or plane.

Inclined line

Industrial designer: An engineer responsible for simplifying and improving the operation and appearance of industrial products.

Inkjet printer: A computer output device that forms images by depositing droplets of ink onto the sheet.

Inscribe: To draw one geometric figure within another figure.

Inscribed Star in Pentagon

Inspection: The measuring and checking of finished parts to determine whether they have been made to specifications.

Integrated circuit (IC): An electronic device made up of multiple components such as transistors and resistors, often manufactured for use on a circuit board.

Interior designer: A space-planning specialist responsible for the physical design and decoration of interior spaces of buildings.

Investment casting: A process that involves making a wax, plastic, or a frozen mercury pattern, surrounding it with a wet refractory material, melting or burning the pattern out after the investment material has dried and set, and finally pouring molten metal into the cavity.

Isometric drawing: A pictorial drawing in which two horizontal axes at 30° to horizontal and a vertical axis are used to show an object's width, length, and depth.

Isometric Drawing

J

Jig: A device that holds the work in position and guides the cutting tool.

K

Key: A small piece of metal partially fitted into a shaft and partially into a hub to prevent rotation of a gear, wheel, or pulley on the shaft. The slot in the hub is the *keyway.* The slot in the shaft is the *keyseat.*

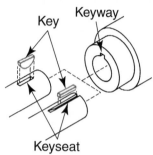

Key Assembly

Keyboard: A computer hardware device used for inputting text and other operations.

L

Lathe: A machine tool that performs cutting operations by rotating a workpiece against the edge of a cutting tool.

Layers: In CAD drafting, user-defined object settings that can be displayed or "turned off" to distinguish the different types of content in a drawing.

Lay out: To locate and scribe points for machining and forming operations.

Leader: An angular dimension line used to point out special characteristics of objects.

Lead holder: A type of drafting pencil, used with different grades of 2 mm lead.

Lettering: Text on a drawing used to show dimensions and other important information needed to describe objects.

Line conventions: Symbols that furnish a means of representing or describing some part of an object. They are expressed by a combination of line weight and appearance. See also specific types of lines—*Construction lines, Border lines, Dimension lines, Extension lines, Hidden lines, Centerlines, Cutting-plane lines, Section lines,* and *Phantom lines.*

Linetype: In CAD drafting, a user-defined object setting used to describe a line definition in the Alphabet of Lines.

Location dimensions: Dimensions that indicate where particular object details lie along or within an object.

M

Machine tool: A power-driven machine that holds a workpiece and cutting tool and brings them together so that material is drilled, cut, shaved, or ground.

Major diameter: The largest diameter of a thread measured perpendicular to the axis.

Manual drafting: Drafting that is performed without the aid of a computer. Also called *board drafting.*

Map: A graphic representation of a portion of the earth's surface.

Mechanical drawing: A drawing made with the aid of instruments.

Mechanical pencil: A type of drafting pencil, classified by lead diameter.

Mesh: To engage gears to a working contact.

Milling: Removing metal with a rotating cutter by use of a milling machine.

Minor diameter: The smallest diameter on a screw thread measured across the root of the thread and perpendicular to the axis. Also known as the *root diameter.*

Mockup: A full-size, three-dimensional copy of a product.

Model: A reduced scale replica of a proposed, planned, or existing product.

Mold: A cavity or opening into which molten metal is poured to make a casting.

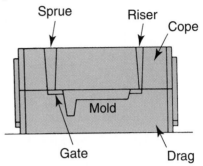

Parts of a Mold

Monitor: The main display device of a computer. Different types include the cathode ray tube and liquid crystal display.

Mouse: A computer input device with a trackball that allows the user to move the on-screen cursor quickly and easily.

Multiview drawing: A drawing that requires more than one two-dimensional view in order to provide an accurate shape and size description of the object being produced.

N

Nonisometric lines: Lines that form the inclined edges of inclined surfaces on isometric drawings.

O

Object lines: Thick lines drawn to indicate the visible edges and intersections of an object. Also called *visible lines.*

Object Line (thick)

Object snap: In a CAD system, a function that allows the cursor to be aligned, or snapped, to specific locations on an object.

Oblique drawing: A pictorial drawing in which the front view of an object is parallel to the projection plane and shown in its true size and shape.

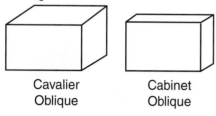

Cavalier
Oblique

Cabinet
Oblique

Oblique Drawings

Obtuse angle: An angle greater than 90°.

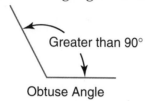

Greater than 90°

Obtuse Angle

Octagon: An eight-sided geometric figure with each side forming a 45° angle.

Octagon

OD: Abbreviation for *outside diameter.*

Orthogonal mode: In a CAD system, a drawing mode used to draw straight lines by confining the cursor to horizontal and vertical movement.

Orthographic projection: A method of showing a three-dimensional object in two dimensions by displaying various views.

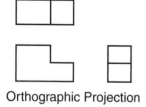

Orthographic Projection

Outline sectioning: A method for drawing sectional views in which section lines are only drawn near the boundary of the sectioned area and the interior portion is left clear.

Overall dimensions: Dimensions that provide the overall size of an object.

P

Parallel line development: A pattern development method in which lines are projected at right angles to each other, used for prisms and cylinders.

Parametric modeling: In CAD drafting, a type of 3D-based drawing in which changes to object parameters during the modeling process affect the entire model.

Pattern: A full-size drawing of the various outside surfaces of an object stretched out on a flat plane. Also known as a *stretchout.*

Pencil pointer: A drafting tool (such as a sandpaper pad) used to sharpen, or point, the lead of a pencil.

Pentagon: A five-sided geometric figure with each side forming a 72° angle.

Pentagon

Perimeter: The boundary of a geometric figure.

Permanent mold: A mold ordinarily made of metal, used for the repeated production of similar castings.

Perpendicular: A line at right angles to a given line.

Perspective drawing: A pictorial drawing in which lines are projected to one or more vanishing points to show the depth of an object as it would appear when viewed from a certain position. A *parallel (one-point) perspective* has lines that converge to a single vanishing point. An *angular (two-point) perspective* has lines that converge to two vanishing points.

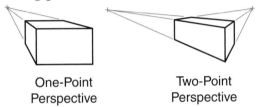

One-Point   Two-Point
Perspective   Perspective

Perspective Drawings

Phantom lines: Thin lines made up of long and short dashes, used to indicate alternate positions for moving parts, repeated details, or motion paths.

——— —— —— —— —— ———
Phantom Line (thin)

Pictorial drawing: A single-view drawing showing an object in three dimensions as it appears to the human eye.

Pitch: A screw thread designation measuring the distance from a point on one thread to a corresponding point on the next thread.

Pixels: In computer drawing, tiny shapes of data making up a raster image. Also called *picture elements.*

Plan: A drawing showing the top view of something relatively large, such as a building or plot of land. Specific plan drawings include site plans, foundation plans, structural plans, and floor plans.

Plat plan: A drawing that shows property and boundary lines in a given area.

Plot plan: The drawing of a lot on which a house or building is to be constructed. Also called a *site plan.*

Plotter: A large-format output device used to print CAD drawings. Classified as *inkjet* or *pen.*

Polar coordinates: In a CAD system, coordinates located at a given distance and angle from Cartesian world coordinate system origin (0,0,0) or from the last coordinate specified.

Primary centerline: A thin line used to indicate the center of a round object in a primary (true-shape) view.

Primary view: In a multiview drawing, a view in which an object feature appears in its true shape and size.

Primitive objects: In a CAD program, simple geometric shapes that can be used to develop solid models or surface models.

Principal planes: In orthographic projection, the frontal, profile, and horizontal planes used to project views of an object.

Principal views: The six basic views (front, top, right side, left side, rear, and bottom) used to develop three-dimensional objects in orthographic projection.

Prints: Reproduced copies of original drawings. Also called *blueprints.*

Profile: The outline of an object.

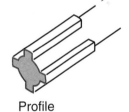

Profile

Project: To extend from.

Prototype: A full-size, operating model of an item to be produced.

Protractor: A drafting tool with degree graduations, used to measure and lay out angles.

Puck: An input device used with a digitizing tablet to input commands and maneuver the on-screen cursor.

Q

Quadrant: One-fourth of a plane figure, such as a circle or ellipse. Quadrants are separated by the figure's axes.

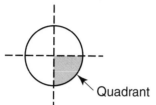

Quadrant

R

Rack: A flat strip of metal with teeth designed to mesh with teeth on a gear. Used to change rotary motion to a reciprocating motion.

Radial line development: A pattern development method in which lines are projected out from a single point, used for cones and pyramids.

Radius: The distance from any point on a circle to the circle's center. Plural: *radii*.

Radius

Random access memory (RAM): Temporary storage where data is placed and retrieved by a computer.

Raster objects: In computer drawing, objects made up of pixels. Also known as *bitmap graphics.*

Ream: To finish a drilled hole to an exact size.

Rectangle: A geometric figure with opposite sides equal in length and each corner forming a 90° angle.

Rectangle

Regular polygon: A geometric shape having all sides equal in length and all interior and exterior angles equal.

Relative coordinates: In a CAD system, coordinates located in relation to the last point specified or the Cartesian coordinate system origin (0,0,0).

Rendering: In CAD drafting, a highly realistic representation of a model with lighting, shadows, and other visual effects applied.

Resolution: A term used to describe the visual quality of a raster image, determined by the number of pixels making up the image.

Right angle: A 90° angle. The angle is formed by lines that are perpendicular to one another.

90°

Right Angle

Riser: An opening in a mold that permits gases to escape (when molten metal is poured into the mold). Also, the vertical surface of a step in a flight of stairs.

Rough layout: A rough pencil plan that arranges lines and symbols so that they have a pleasing relation to one another.

Round: An arc representing an outside rounded corner. See also *Fillet.*

S

Sand casting: A metal forming method in which objects are made by pouring molten metal into sand molds.

Scale: A measuring device used to convert full-size dimensions to the drawing scale. Different types of scales include the architect's scale, engineer's scale, mechanical drafter's scale, and metric scale. The term *scale* also refers to the size to which a drawing is made.

Scale clip: A device fastened to a triangular scale, used to identify the scale currently in use.

Scanner: A computer hardware device used to convert a hard copy image into digital form.

Schedule: In architectural drawings, a table listing required materials and items. Common schedules include door schedules, window schedules, and lighting schedules.

Schematic diagram: A drawing with symbols and single lines to show electrical connections and functions of a specific circuit.

Schematic representation: A screw thread representation in which schematic symbols are used to represent the threads.

Screw-thread series: Standard specification groupings used to classify different types of screw threads.

Seams: In sheet metal products, joints formed between sections.

Secondary centerline: A thin line used to indicate the center of a round object in a secondary (not true-shape) view.

Section lines: Thin lines used when drawing inside features of an object exposed by a cutting plane. Lines are drawn using patterns corresponding to different materials.

Section Lines (thin)

Sectional view: A secondary drawing showing the interior structure of an object as if it were cut by an imaginary cutting plane.

Segment: Any part of a divided line.

Simplified representation: A screw thread representation that uses regular object and hidden lines to show details.

Size dimensions: Dimensions that specify the size of particular details within an object.

Sketch: To draw without the aid of drafting instruments.

Snap: In a CAD system, a function that allows the user to align or "snap" the cursor to specific increments in an invisible grid.

Solid modeling: In CAD drafting, a type of 3D-based drawing used to create *solids* (objects that represent the entire mass of an object).

Spline: A series of grooves, cut lengthwise, around a shaft or hole.

Spotface: A recess at the end of a smaller hole used to provide a bearing surface for the head of a bolt or nut.

Spotfaced Hole

Sprue: The opening in a mold that leads to the gate, which in turn leads to the cavity into which molten metal is poured.

Square: To machine or cut at right angles. Also, a geometric figure with four equal length sides and four right (90°) angles.

Stylus: A hand-held input device used with a digitizing tablet to input commands and maneuver the on-screen cursor.

Surface modeling: In CAD drafting, a type of 3D-based drawing used to create *surface models* (objects that have an outer "skin" to represent exterior surfaces).

Surveyor: A collector of data and measurements establishing land features on a map, such as boundary and property lines.

Symbol library: In CAD drafting, a collection of related drawing symbols.

Symbols: In CAD drafting, saved or predrawn objects designed for multiple use in drawing projects.

Symmetrical: Having the same size, shape, and relative position on opposite sides of a dividing line or plane.

Symmetry centerline: A thin line used to indicate the center of a symmetrical object.

T

Tangent: A term used to describe a line, arc, or circle that comes into contact with an arc or circle at a single point.

Tap: A tool used to cut internal threads.

Taper: A piece that increases or decreases in size at a uniform rate to assume a wedge or conical shape.

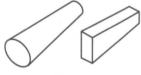

Tapers

Technical illustrator: A designer who prepares pictorial matter for engineering, marketing, or educational purposes.

Technical pen: Drafting instrument used to ink drawings, available in different line widths.

Template: In manual drafting, a plastic sheet with openings of different sizes and shapes that can be traced accurately. In CAD drafting, a saved set of configurations used to start a drawing file.

Text: Lettering in a CAD program.

Text styles: In CAD drafting, lettering styles used to generate text with text commands.

Third-angle projection: A method of orthographic projection in which views of an object are projected to the sides of an imaginary glass box and toward the viewer.

Thread: The act of cutting a screw thread.

Tolerance: An allowable variance from the original dimension.

Tracing: A drawing made on translucent paper, normally used as an original for making copies.

Tracing paper: Translucent drafting paper used for making preliminary plans or sketches.

Train: A series of meshed gears.

Tread: The horizontal surface of a step in a flight of stairs.

Triangle: A three-sided geometric figure. Also, a drafting instrument used to draw vertical and inclined lines.

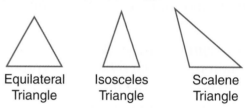

Equilateral   Isosceles   Scalene
Triangle   Triangle   Triangle

True face: In orthographic projection, an object surface drawn in its true shape and size within a view.

Truncate: To cut off a geometric solid at an angle to its base.

Truncated Prism

T-square: A drafting instrument consisting of a head and a blade, used to lay out and draw horizontal lines.

U

Unidirectional dimensioning: A method of dimensioning in which dimensions are placed horizontally on the drawing sheet and read from the bottom of the drawing.

Unified National Coarse (UNC): Thread series used to specify standards for coarse screw threads.

Unified National Fine (UNF): Thread series used to specify standards for fine screw threads.

V

Vanishing point: The point to which lines converge in a perspective drawing.

Vector objects: In computer drawing, objects made up of lines and arcs, defined with point coordinates in space.

Vellum: Treated, moisture-resistant drafting paper used for making pencil and ink drawings.

W

Weld symbol: A standard drawing symbol used to describe a specific type of weld.

Welding: An industrial process for joining metal pieces by heating them to a high temperature, causing them to melt and fuse.

Welding symbol: A drawing symbol consisting of basic and supplementary weld symbols, used to provide specific information about the required weld. See also *Weld symbol.*

Wiring diagram: A drawing used to show the distribution of electricity or the general physical arrangement of the various components that make up an electronic circuit. Also known as a *connection diagram.*

Working drawing: A drawing that gives the craftworker the necessary information to make and assemble a product.

World coordinate system: In a CAD program, a system for locating points using Cartesian coordinates on the XYZ axes in relation to the 0,0,0 origin.

X

Xerography: A print-making process that uses an electrostatic charge to duplicate an original. Also known as *electrostatic reproduction.*

Index